# IT'S A
# DOG'S LIFE

HARGREAVES

'I have a Rex . . . Is there anyone present who knows a Rex?'

# IT'S A DOG'S LIFE

## A Canine Cartoon Collection

Edited by
Mark Bryant

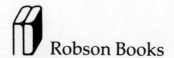

Robson Books

First published in Great Britain in 1991 by Robson Books Ltd,
Bolsover House, 5–6 Clipstone Street, London W1P 7EB



British Library Cataloguing in Publication Data

It's a dog's life : a canine cartoon collection.
I. Bryant, Mark
741.5942

ISBN 0 86051 752 7



Printed in Great Britain by
Butler and Tanner Ltd, Frome and London

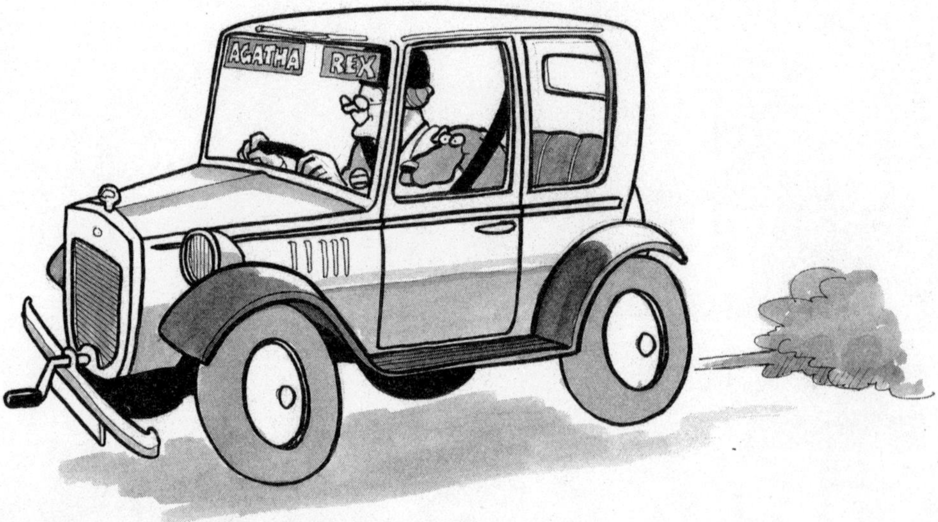
AGATHA
REX
— CLIVE COLLINS —

# PREFACE

All the cartoons in this book were originally donated to the National Canine Defence League either individually or as entries for the regular NCDL Dog Cartoonist of the Year awards and have been assembled here for the first time in book form to mark the centenary of the founding of the NCDL in 1891.

Thanks are due to all the cartoonists whose generosity has made this book possible and to the editors of the various newspapers and magazines in which some of the cartoons first appeared. Thanks also to Intervet and, more recently, Spillers Bonio, whose sponsorship over the years has made the NCDL Dog Cartoonist of the Year awards such a great success. The selection has been made from over 400 cartoons of consistently high quality, many being drawn specially and in full colour, and 81 artists are represented here from all corners of the British Isles.

Special thanks also go to all who have helped in the preparation of this book, in particular Clarissa Baldwin and Catherine Barton-Smith of the National Canine Defence League and Jeremy Robson and Louise Dixon of Robson Books.

M.B.

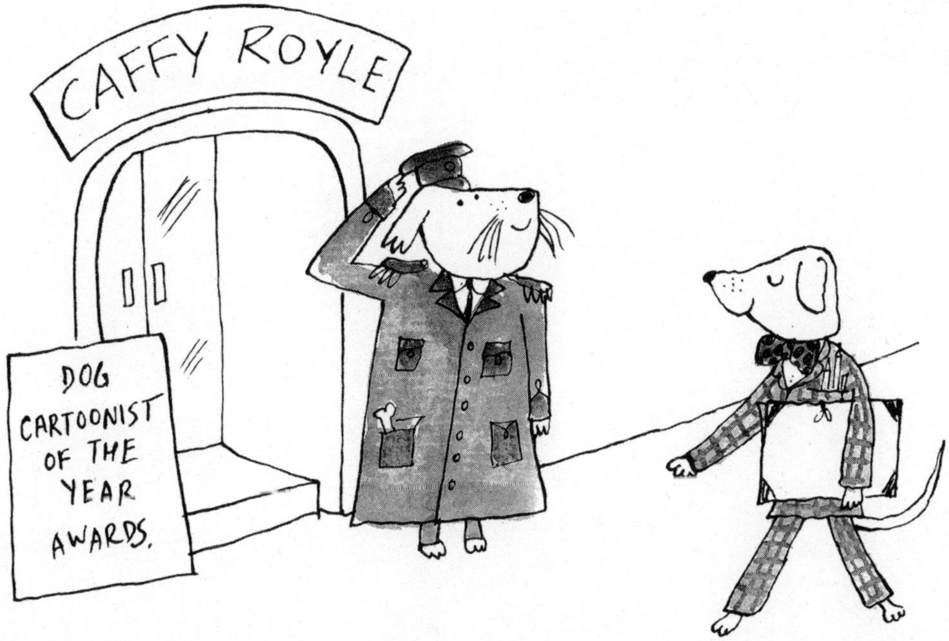

CAFFY ROYLE
DOG CARTOONIST OF THE YEAR AWARDS.

# ACKNOWLEDGEMENTS

For their kind permission to use the cartoons in this book, the National Canine Defence League and the publishers would like to thank the following:

Animals Magazine

Birmingham Evening Mail

Christian Science Monitor

Daily Mail

Daily Mirror

Punch

# ARGUS

WHEN wise Ulysses, from his native coast
Long kept by wars, and long by tempests toss'd,
Arrived at last, poor, old, disguised, alone,
To all his friends and even his queen unknown;
Changed as he was with age, and toils, and cares,
Furrow'd his reverend face, and white his hairs,
In his own palace forced to ask his bread,
Scorn'd by those slaves his former bounty fed,
Forgot of all his own domestic crew;
The faithful dog alone his rightful master knew!
Unfed, unhoused, neglected, on the clay,
Like an old servant, now cashier'd, he lay;
Touch'd with resentment of ungrateful man,
And longing to behold his ancient lord again.
Him when he saw he rose and crawl'd to meet
('Twas all he could), and fawn'd, and kiss'd his feet,
Seized with dumb joy – then falling by his side,
Own'd his returning lord, look'd up, and died!

Alexander Pope

● Another work by Pope, 'Bounce', written c.1736, was the first poem in
praise of his own dog ever written by a major British author.

● In 1933 the National Canine Defence League inaugurated its Argus Medal,
designed by sculptor Frank Bowcher and awarded in recognition of long and
distinguished service to dogs. The Medal was not easily won – only six were
awarded between its inception and its replacement in 1978 by the Phyllis
Mayer Argus Award, which to date has also had six winners.

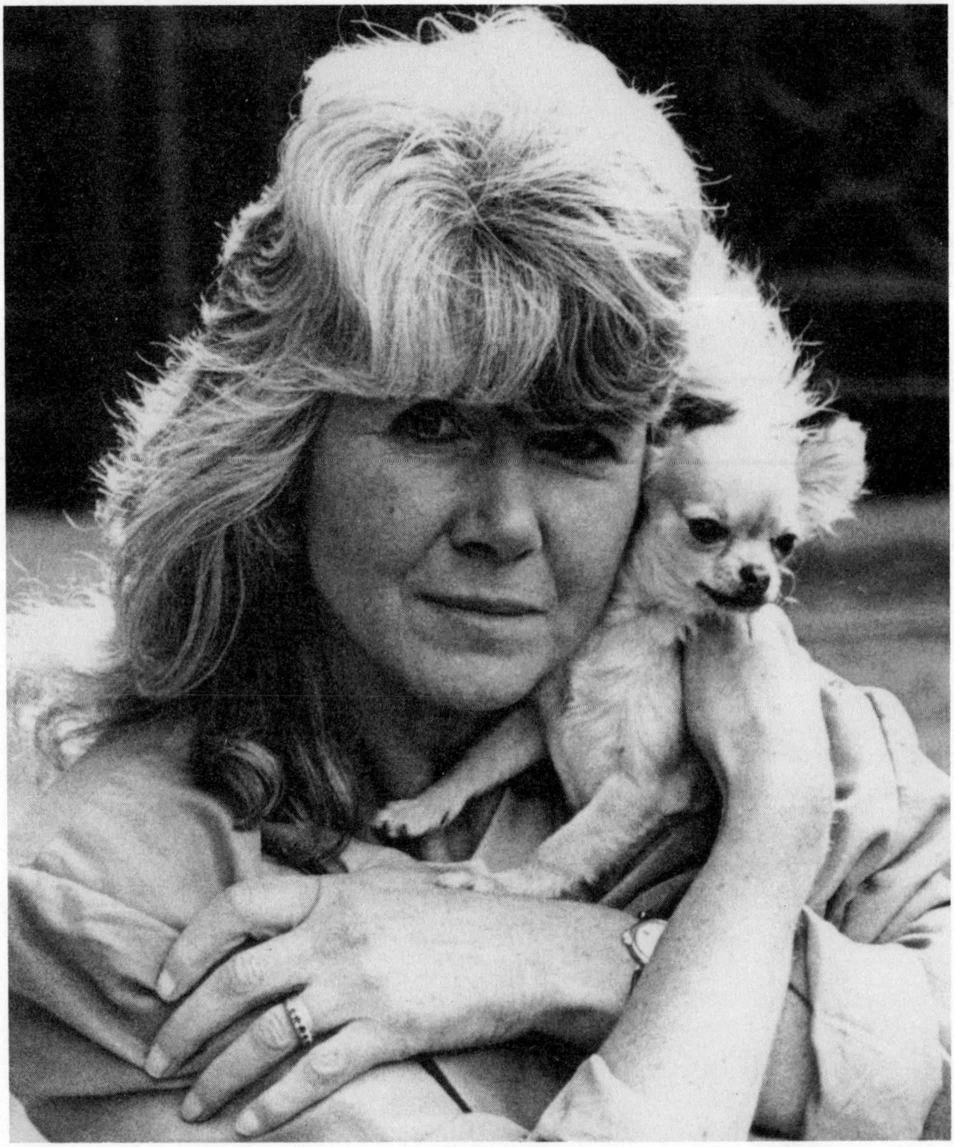

Photo by courtesy of Marc Henrie

# FOREWORD

It seems ironic that the most compulsively readable things in our house are always to be found in the sheets of newspaper which lie under the cats' and dogs' bowls in the kitchen. Yesterday I discovered a fascinating article on André Previn's resignation from the Royal Philharmonic which was almost entirely obscured by chicken fat and smears of salmon-flavoured Whiskas. Today it was a milk-soaked cartoon from the *Independent on Sunday* dated October 1990. In this drawing, Mrs Thatcher, portrayed as a plump and somewhat elderly mongrel, gazed up in a slightly bewildered fashion at a young man who was holding a piece of paper on which was written 'Education', 'NHS' and 'Europe'. The caption underneath said: 'You can't teach an old dog new tricks.' A joke, which could have been bitchy (pardon the pun), had been made funny, charming and infinitely more telling because a dog had been introduced.

In the same way, the marvellous cartoons gathered together in this very funny but often moving book, get across far more effectively than any prose or verbal tubthumping the message of the National Canine Defence League: that the dog is a wonderful, loving, intelligent creature, capable of bringing intense happiness and protection to the human race and should in return be treated with love and kindness.

As a lifelong dog freak and a proud member of the League for nearly ten years, I was thrilled to be asked to write this paw-word. I am convinced that this book will raise a giggle from anyone who picks it up, regardless of whether they love dogs or not.

Owning a dog is a hugely rewarding experience. It is incredible how quickly – despite the occasional chewed-up slipper or pot-hole dug in the lawn – a puppy, or an older dog, becomes an essential adored member of the family, taking on all too human characteristics.

Writing this foreword on Easter Sunday, I remember the first Easter we moved to the country in 1983, when our dog Barbara was seen cantering home across the fields with a ginger moustache. On closer inspection it was discovered that she had 'taken-away' our neighbours' lunchtime roast chicken from the table outside their house. An incident which caused great embarrassment at the time has now gone into cherished family folklore. In the same way, many of the situations portrayed by cartoons in this book will remind readers of their own dogs.

The NCDL Dog Cartoonist of the Year competition, for which most of these cartoons were submitted, is just one of the many events the League runs every year to raise money and increase public awareness of its work. In addition to funding the charity's rescue centres across the country, which save and rehome stray and abandoned dogs, the NCDL campaigns tirelessly to teach people to look after their dogs properly. Sadly, however, all too often the League's work is heartbreaking – man's inhumanity to dog never fails to horrify us – so it is wonderful to look at the lighter side of things in this book.

As a writer, one of my worst burdens is the letters that pour in asking me to write something free for charity, or to read a manuscript or an article for some writer who wants advice on how to get it published. It is the same with every cartoonist I know. Most people wouldn't dream of asking a lawyer or an accountant for free advice, but the poor creative artist is regularly expected to produce rabbits out of a hat at the drop of another hat. It is therefore with particular warmth that I thank all the cartoonists who have donated drawings and allowed us to reprint them free of charge. We are very grateful for their support.

All royalties from the sale of this book go to the NCDL to help it continue and expand its work, so in buying a copy you are not only guaranteeing yourself a lot of laughs, but also bringing happiness to dogs who need it and supporting a very worthwhile charity.

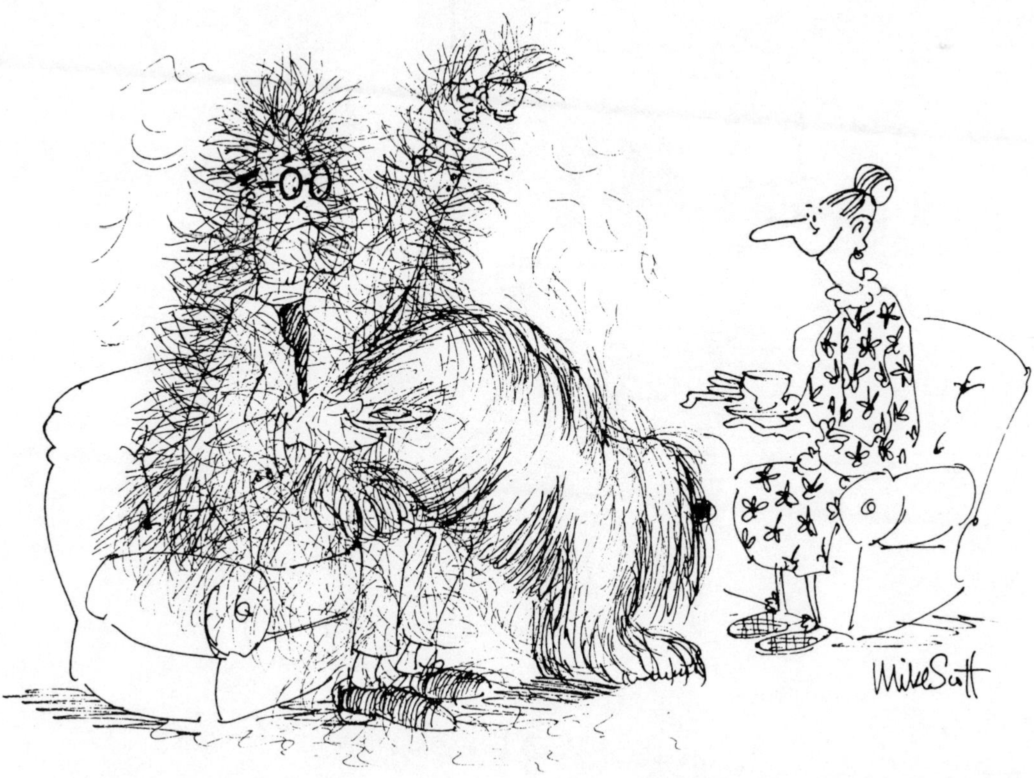
MikeScott

'There now – she was no trouble on your lap, was she, Vicar?'

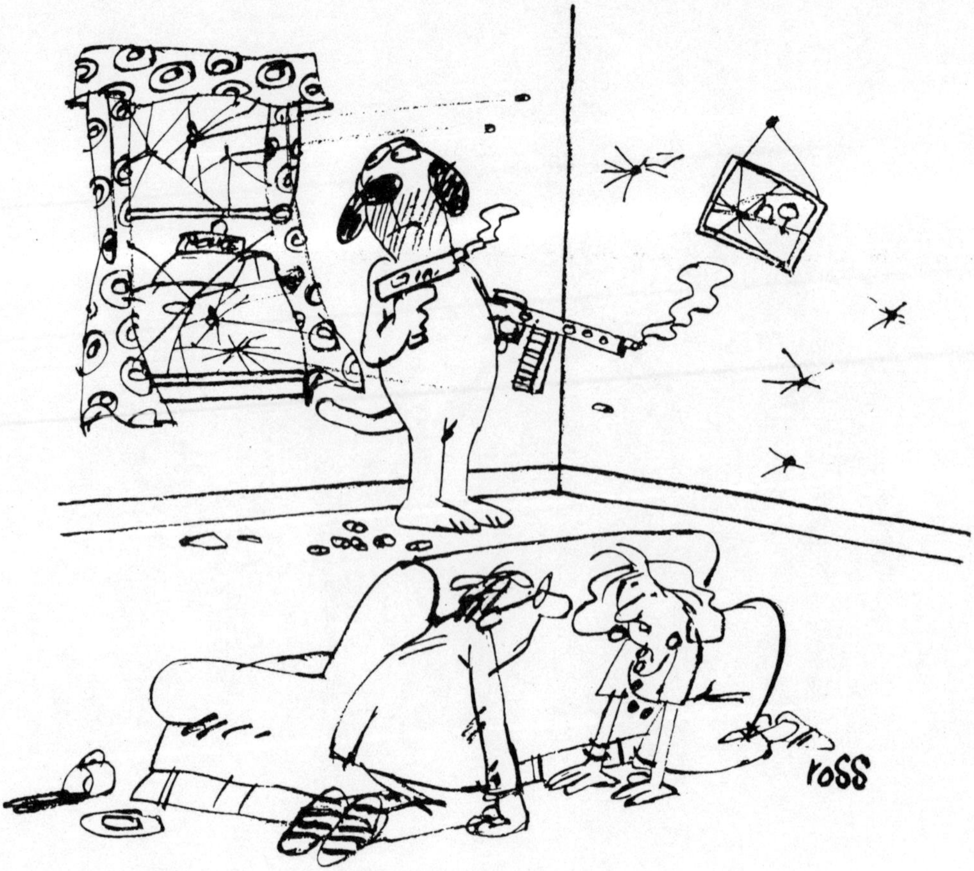

ROSS


'I wish we'd gone for an ordinary gundog like everyone else!'

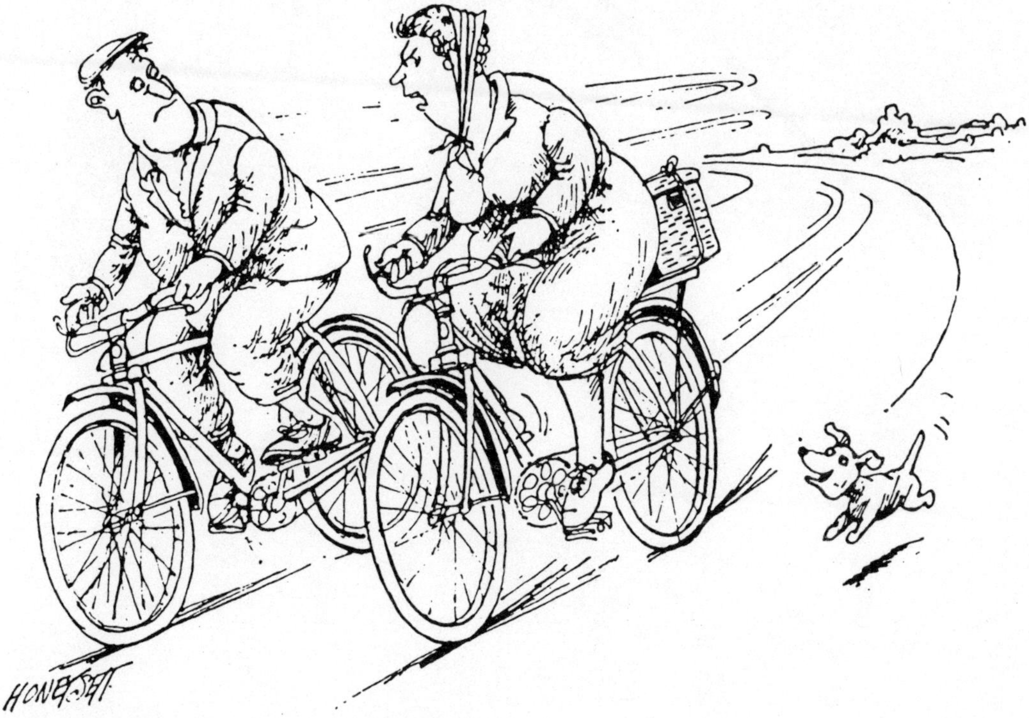
HONEYSETT

'So much for dumping him on the motorway.'

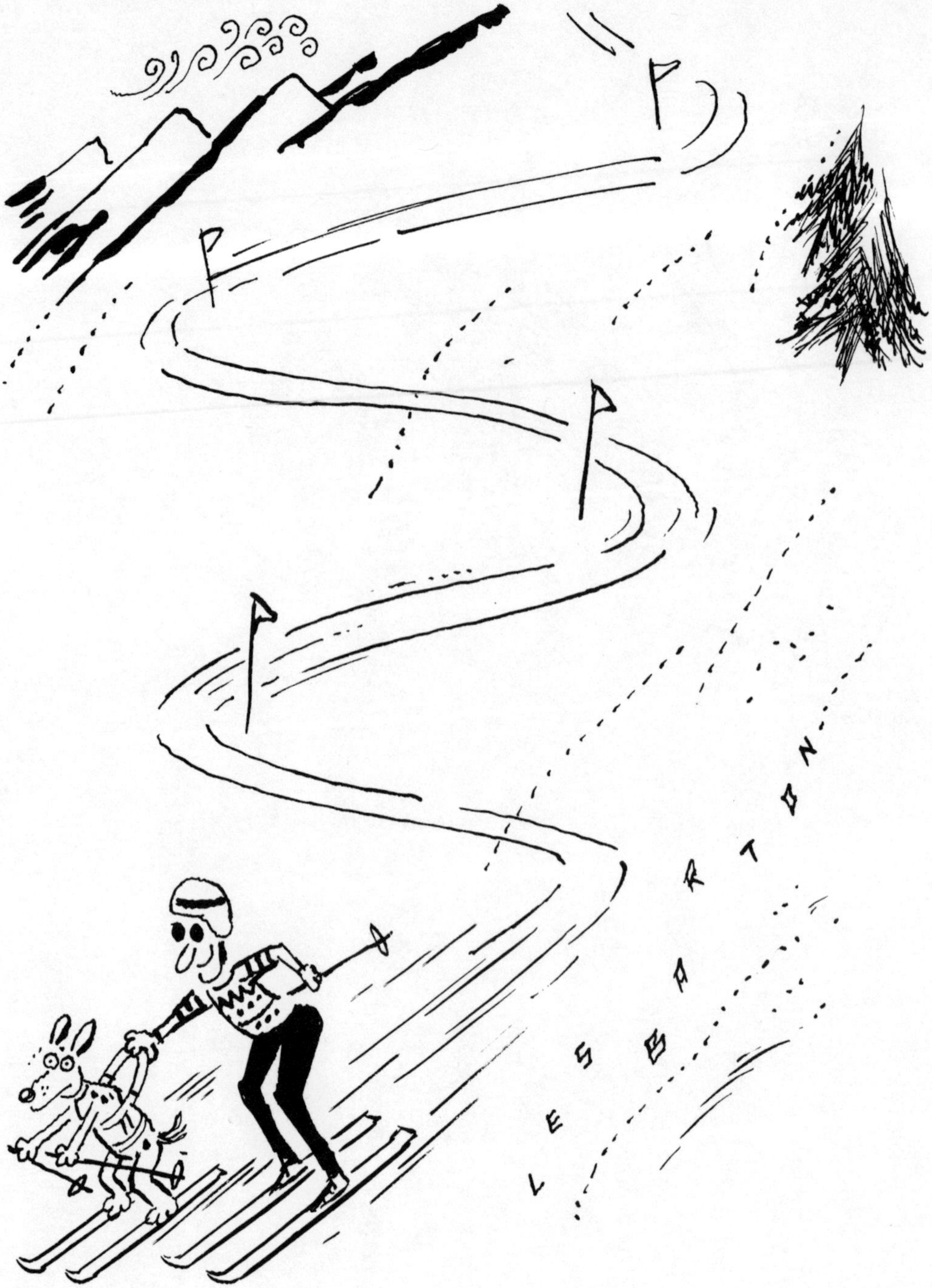
LES BARTON

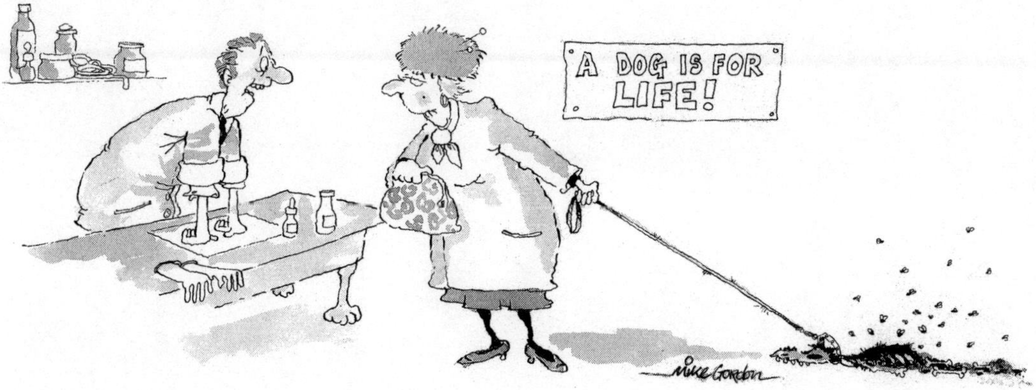
A DOG IS FOR
LIFE!
Mike Gordon

'No, no, Mrs Fogarty, not *your* life!'

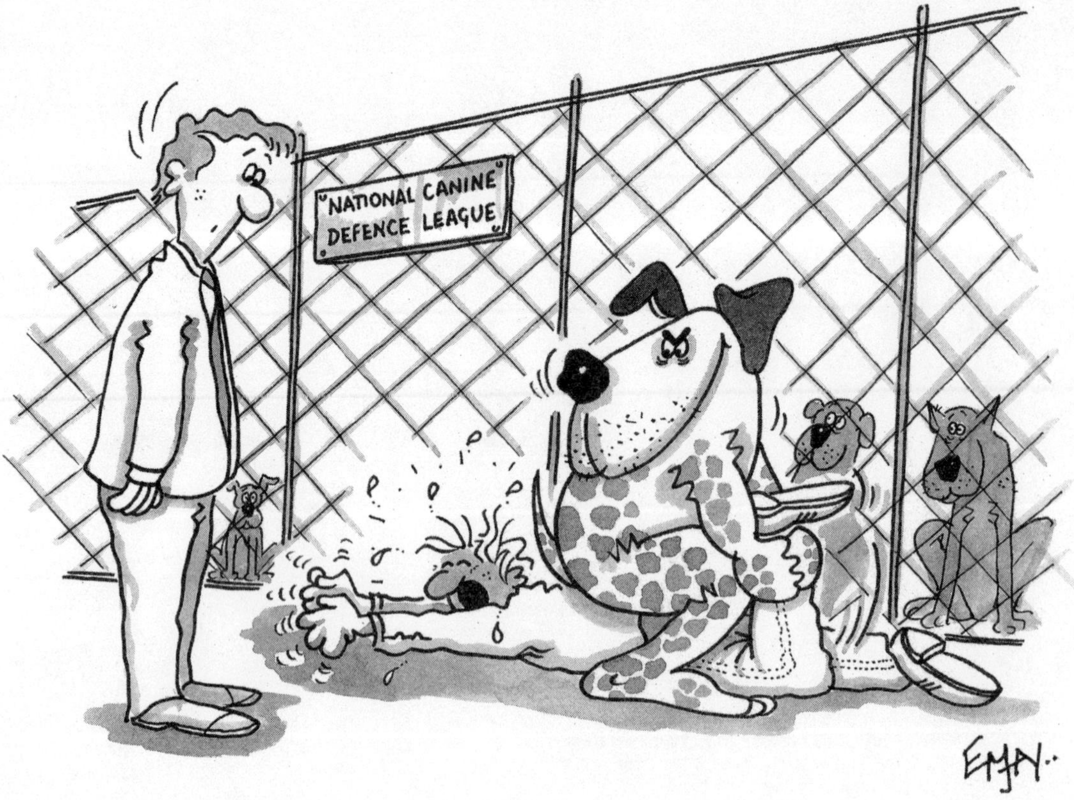
NATIONAL CANINE
DEFENCE LEAGUE

'I'll take this one!'

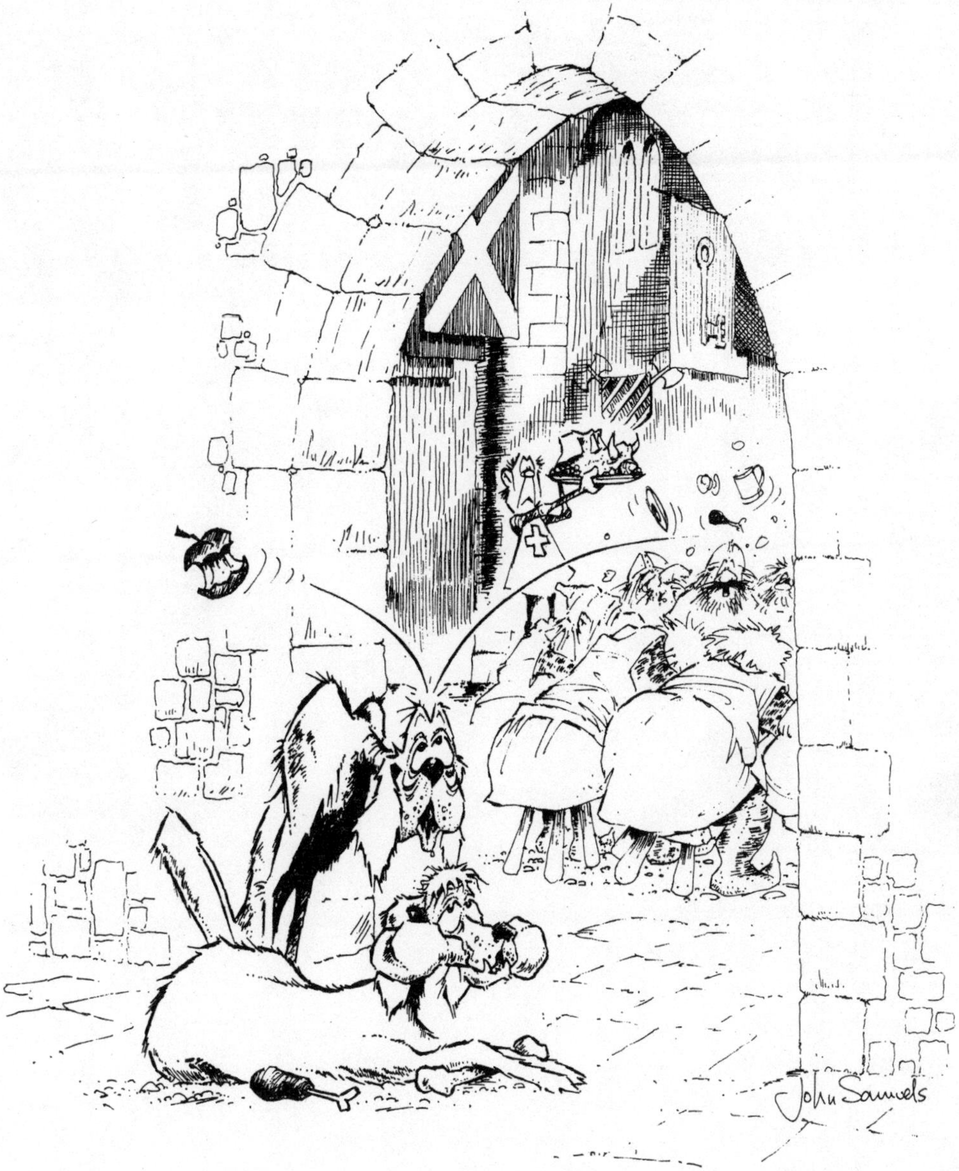
John Samuels

'A kingdom full of meat-eating knights and I get the only vegetarian.'

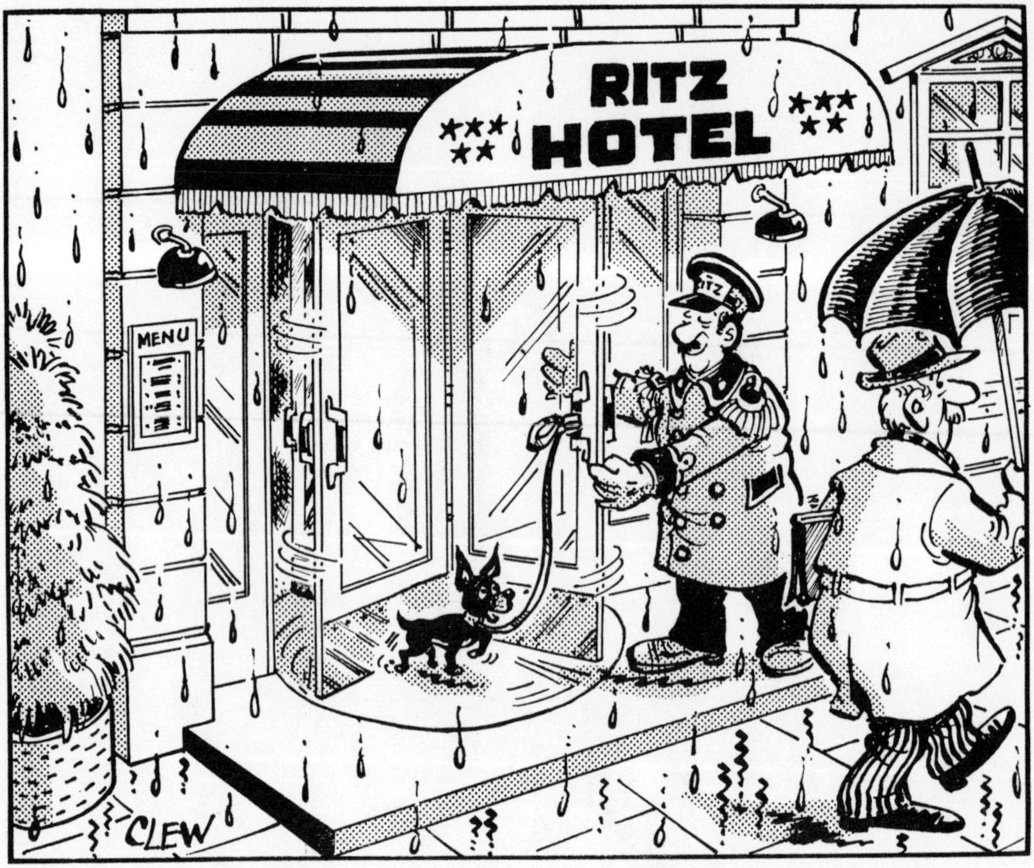
RITZ
HOTEL
MENU
RITZ
CLEW

'Ah well, back to the drawing-board.'

DIZZY
·TONI GOFFE©


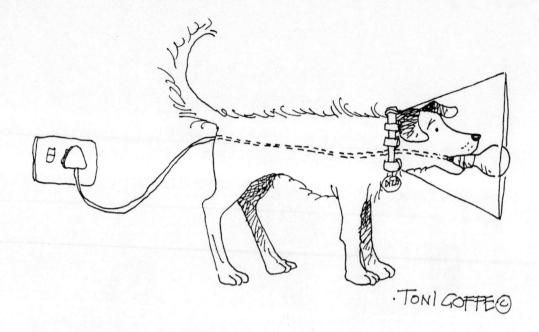

Fun things you can do with your dog when he has to wear a protective collar.

·TONI·GOFFE©

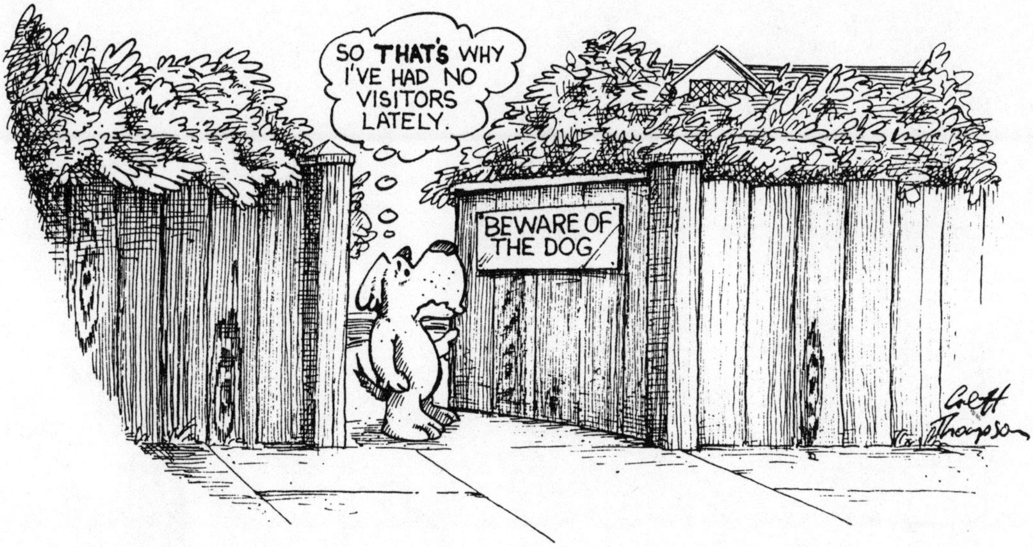
SO THAT'S WHY I'VE HAD NO VISITORS LATELY.
BEWARE OF THE DOG
Colett Thompson

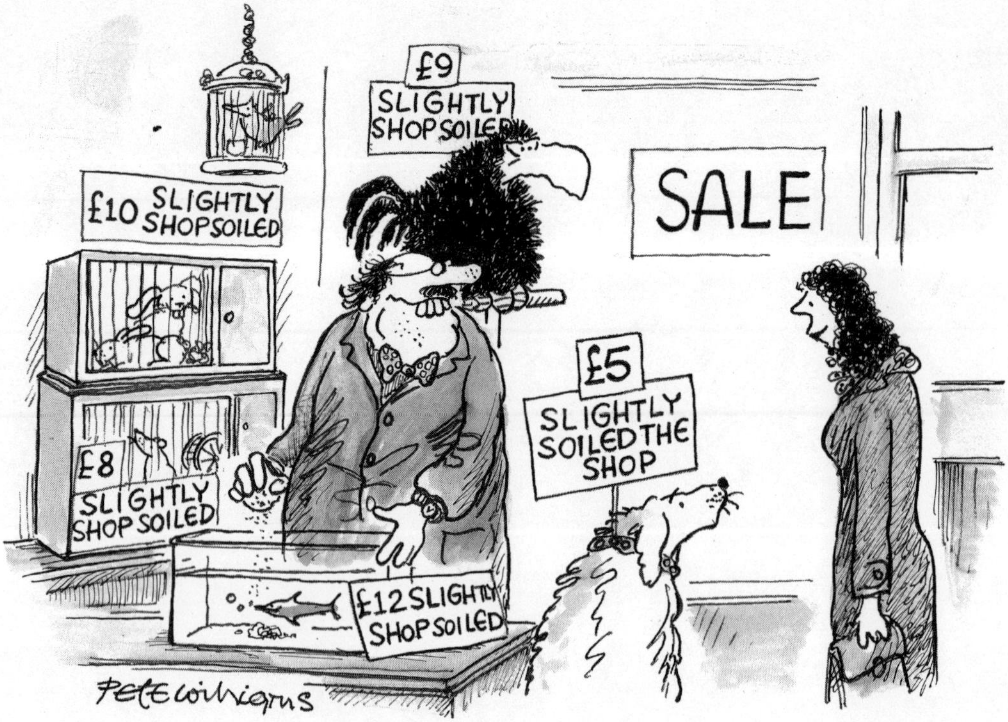
£9
SLIGHTLY
SHOP SOILED
£10 SLIGHTLY SHOPSOILED
SALE
£5
SLIGHTLY SOILED THE SHOP
£8
SLIGHTLY SHOP SOILED
£12 SLIGHTLY SHOPSOILED
PETE WILLIAMS

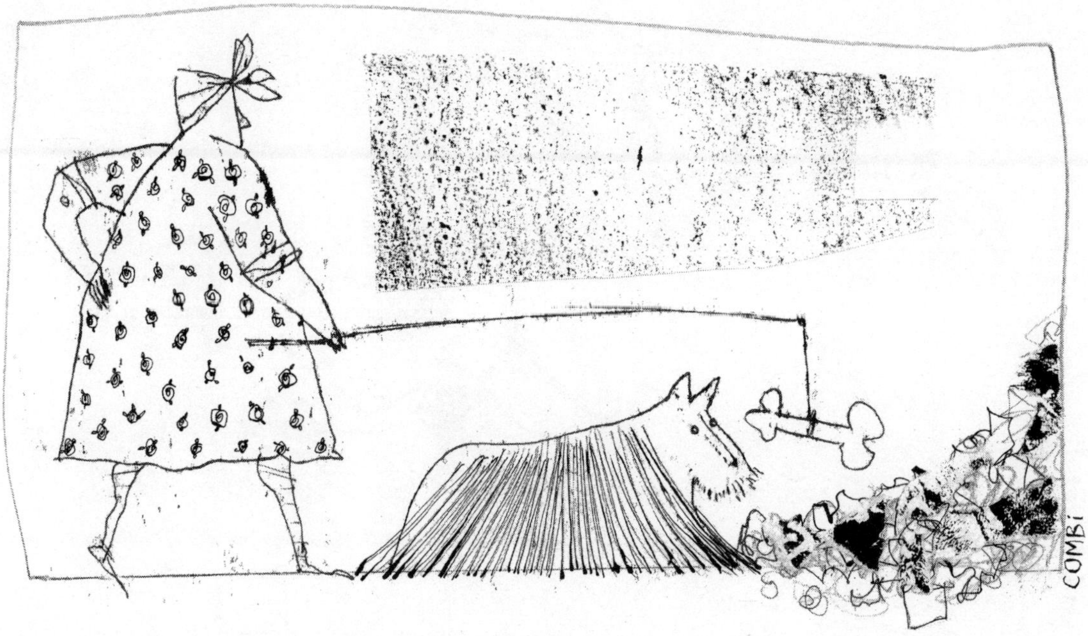
COMBI

HARGREAVES.

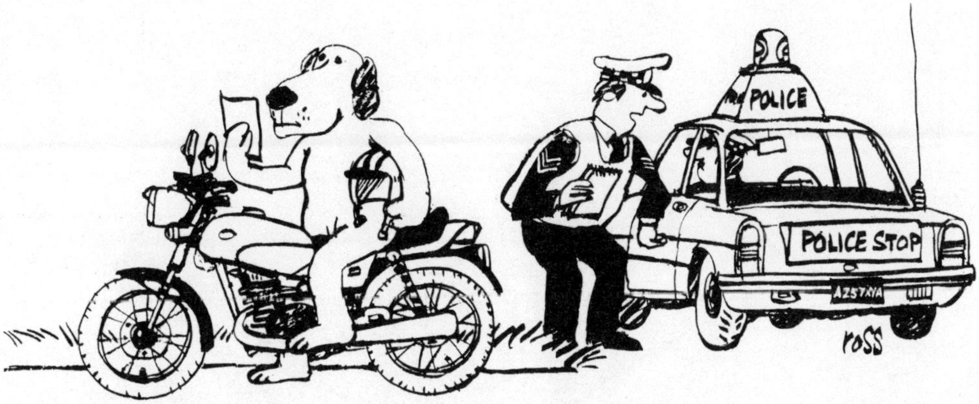
POLICE
POLICE STOP
ross

'The only thing I could get him for was he didn't have a dog licence!'

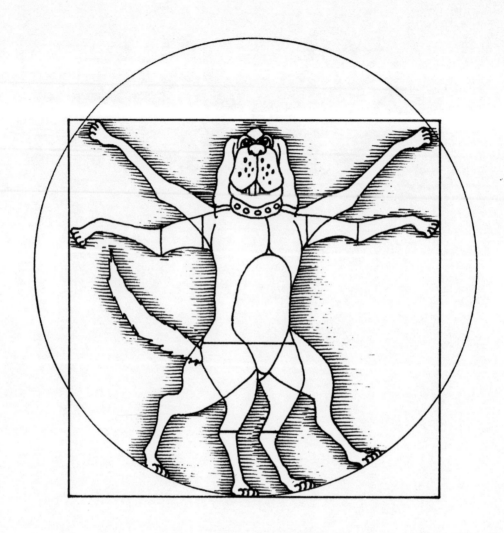

Man's Best Friend

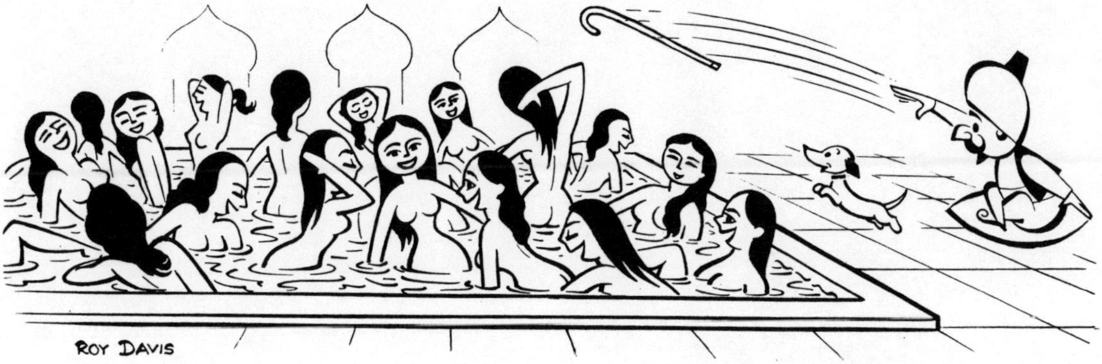
ROY DAVIS

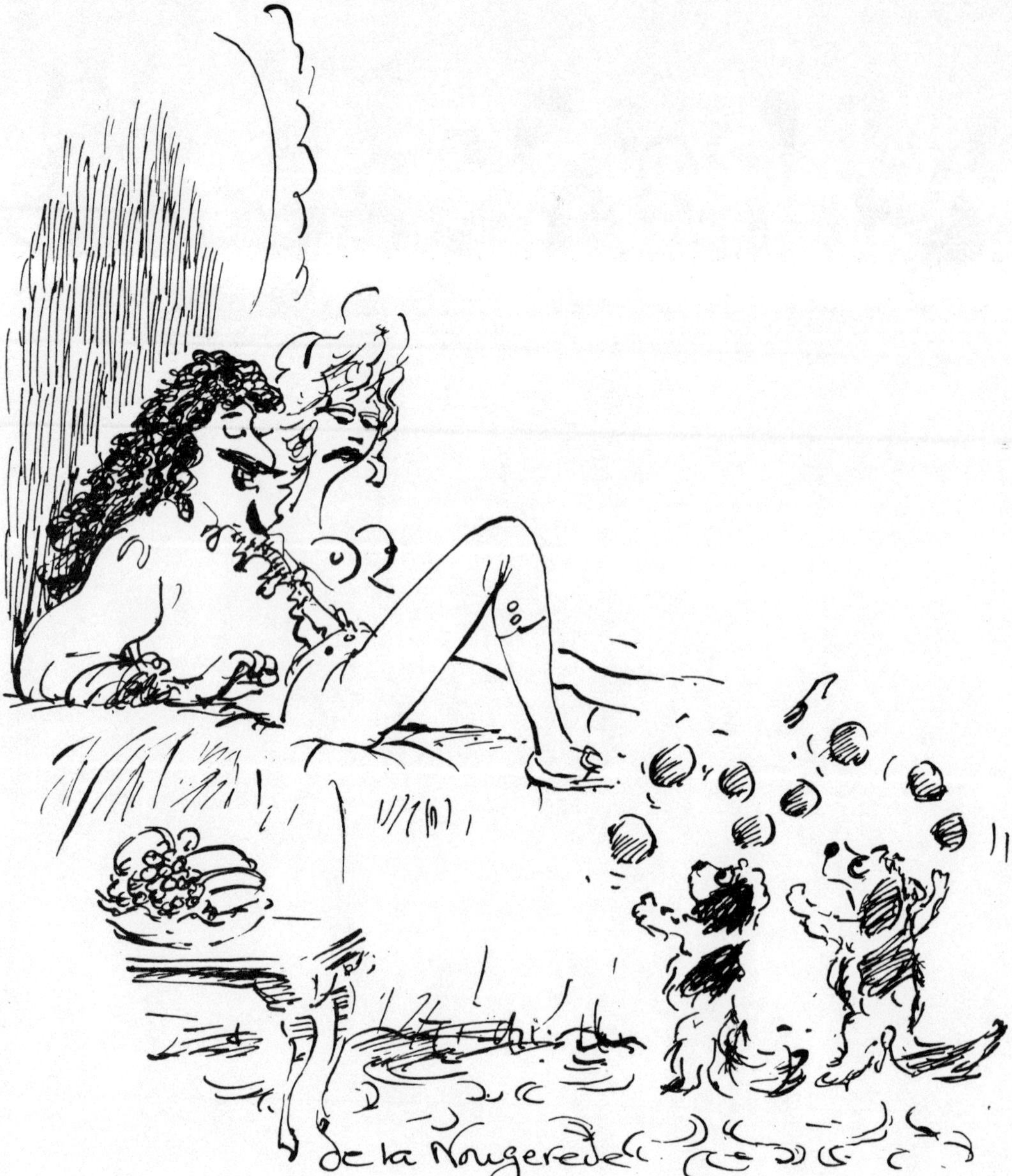
de la Nougerede

'How sweet! They're jealous and think it is oranges that attract me to you, Nell!'

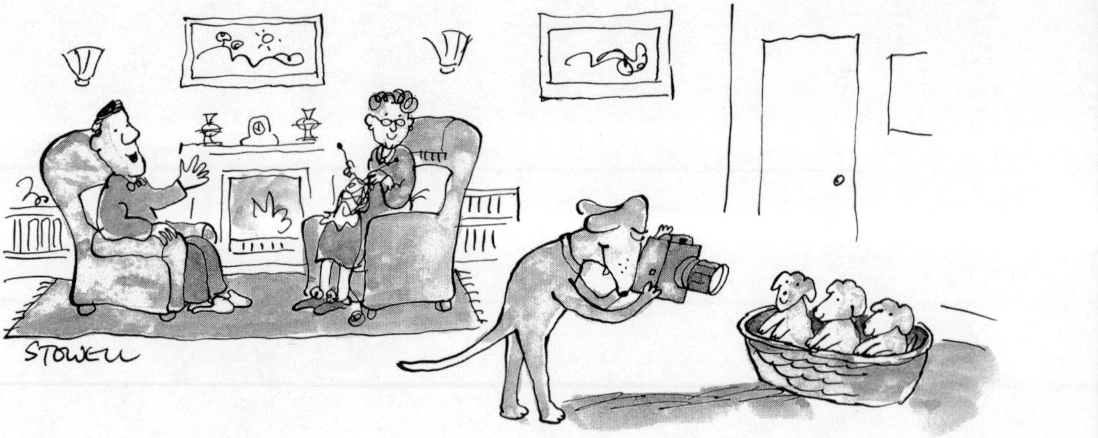
STOWELL

'See! I told you that these modern cameras are dead easy to use!'

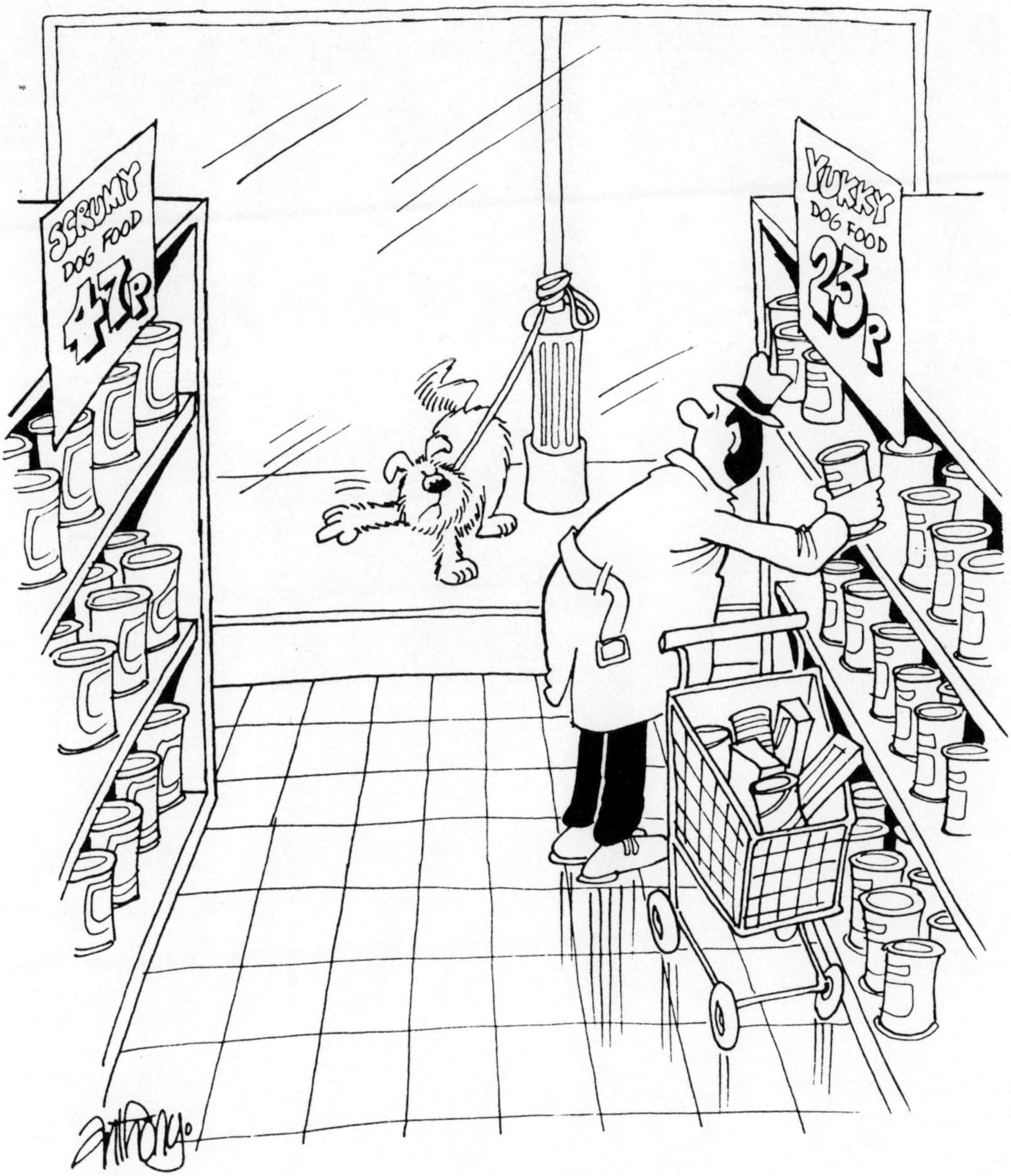
SCRUMY
DOG FOOD
47p
YUKKY
DOG FOOD
23p

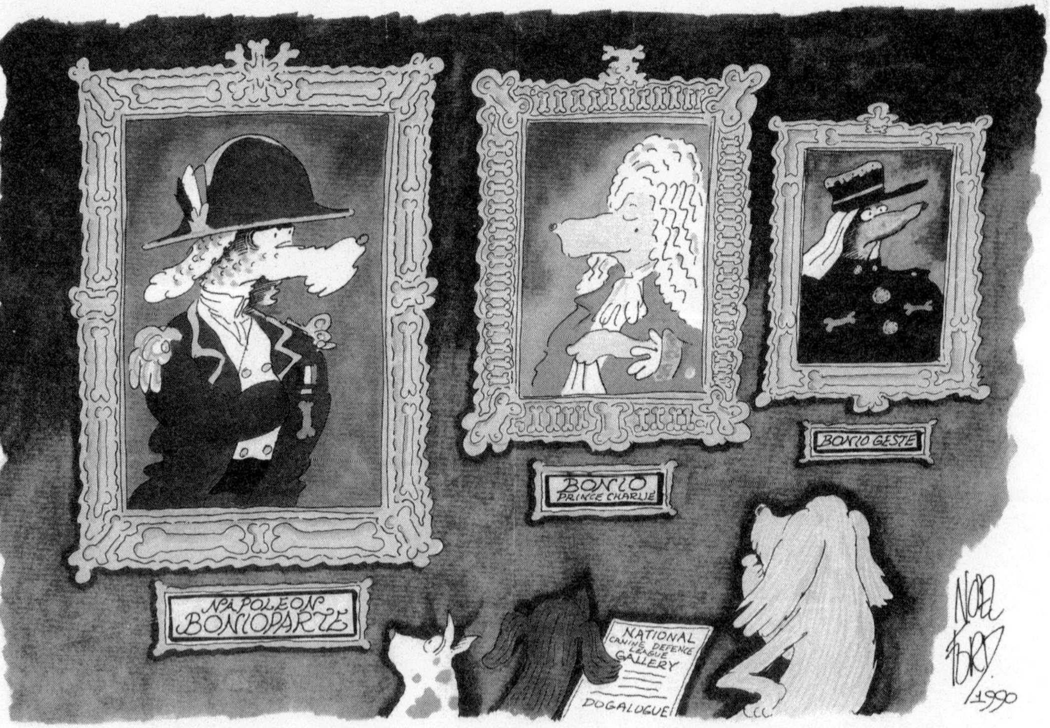

NAPOLEON BONIOPARTE
BONIO PRINCE CHARLIE
BONIO GESTE
NATIONAL CANINE DEFENCE LEAGUE GALLERY
DOGALOGUE
NOEL FORD 1990

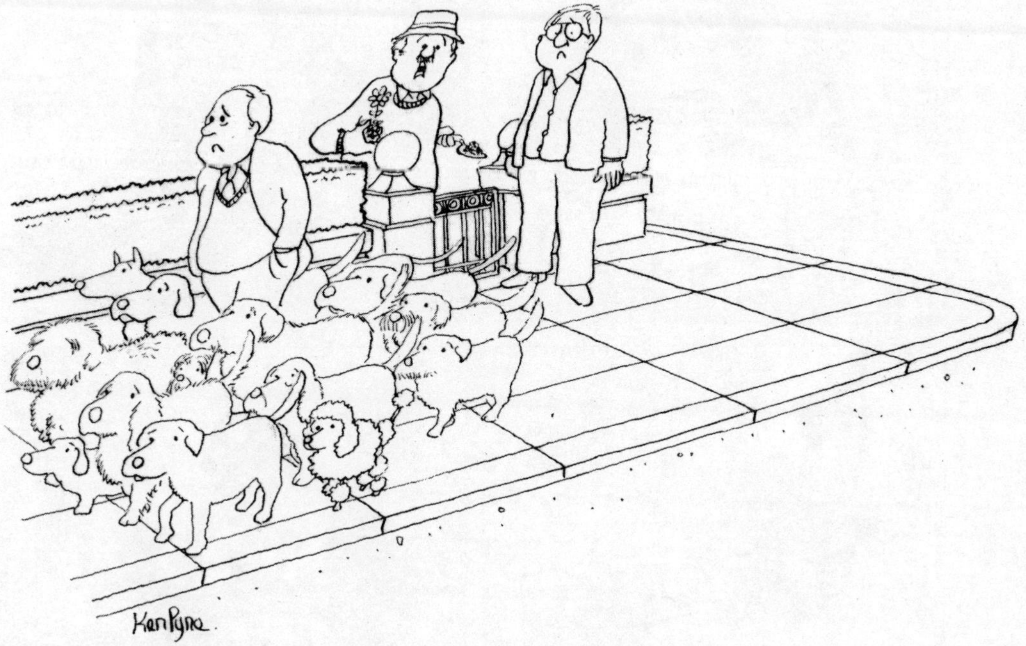
Ken Pyne

'It's his sad eyes and forlorn expression they fall for.'

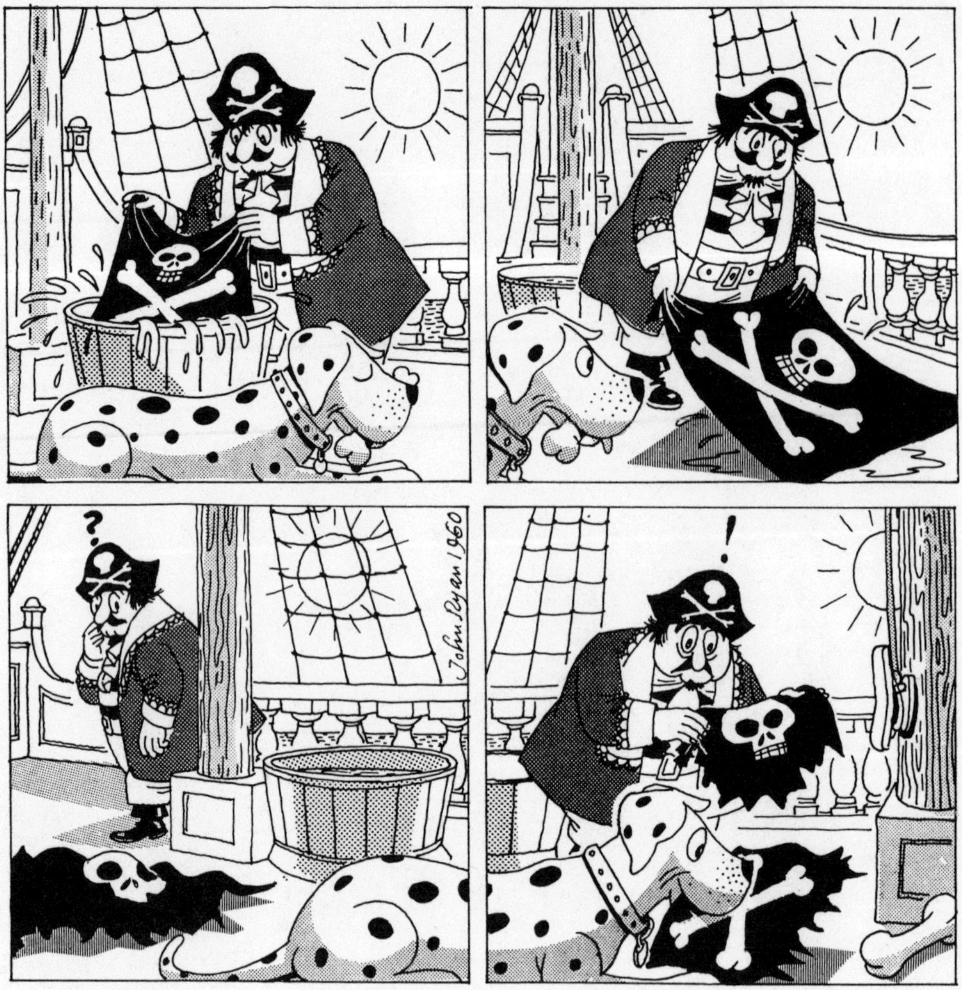
John Ryan 1960

'There goes that cartoonist chap with his dog.'

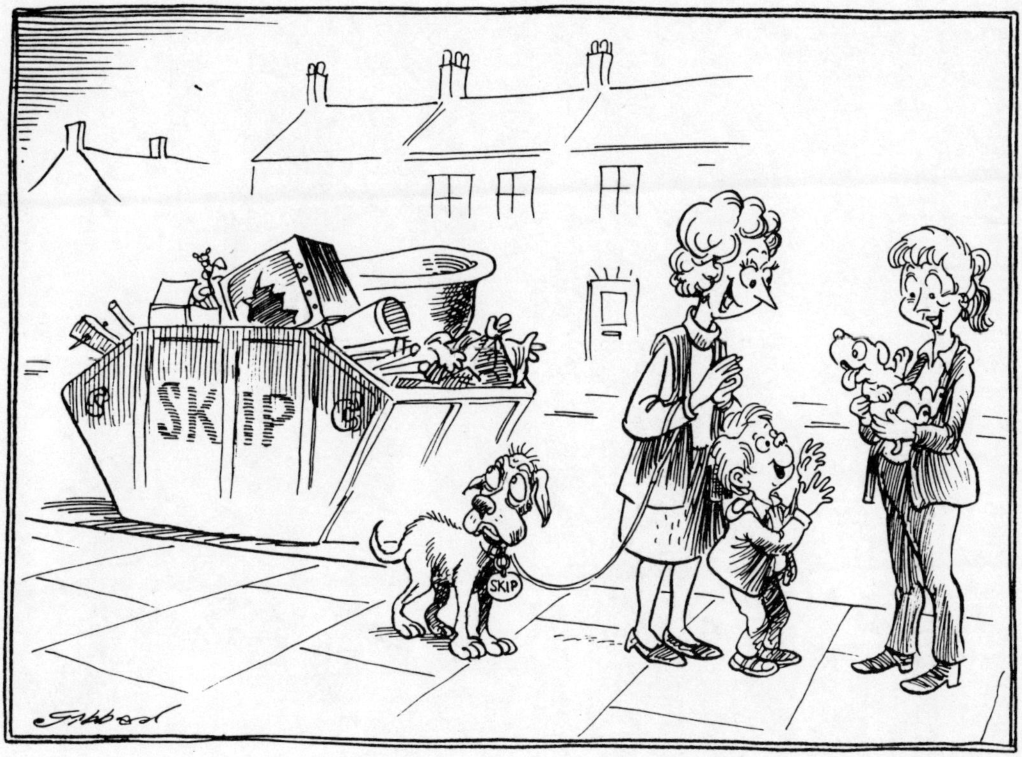
SKIP
SKIP

BEWARE OF THE GOD!
POST
DICK HOWETT

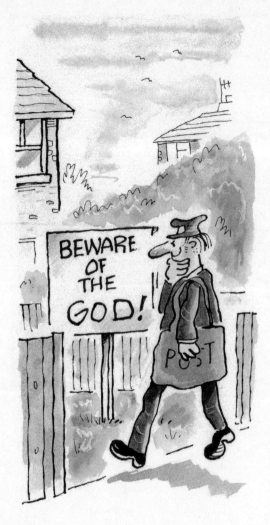

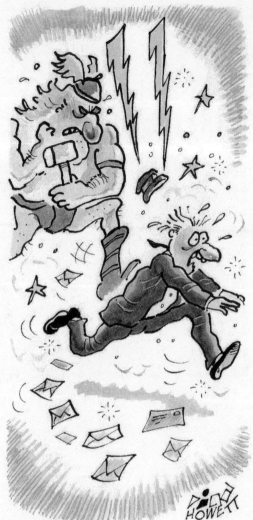

'I still say it would be kinder to have him put down.'

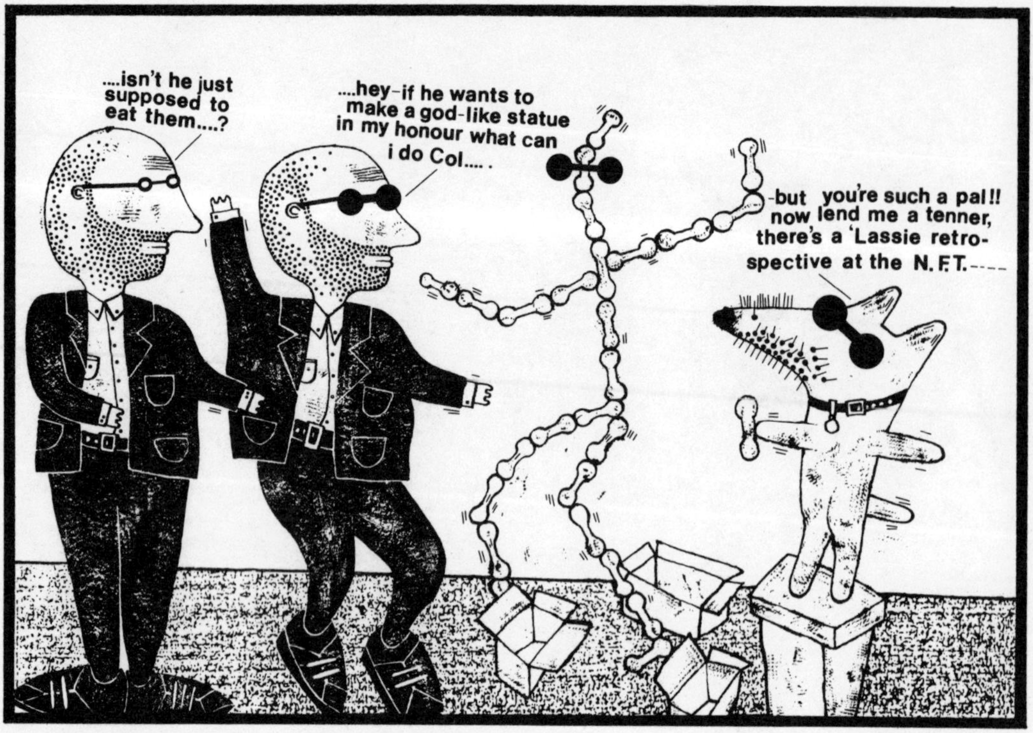
....isn't he just supposed to eat them....?
....hey-if he wants to make a god-like statue in my honour what can i do Col.... .
-but you're such a pal!! now lend me a tenner, there's a 'Lassie retro-spective at the N.F.T.----

'He's really taken to going for walkies!'

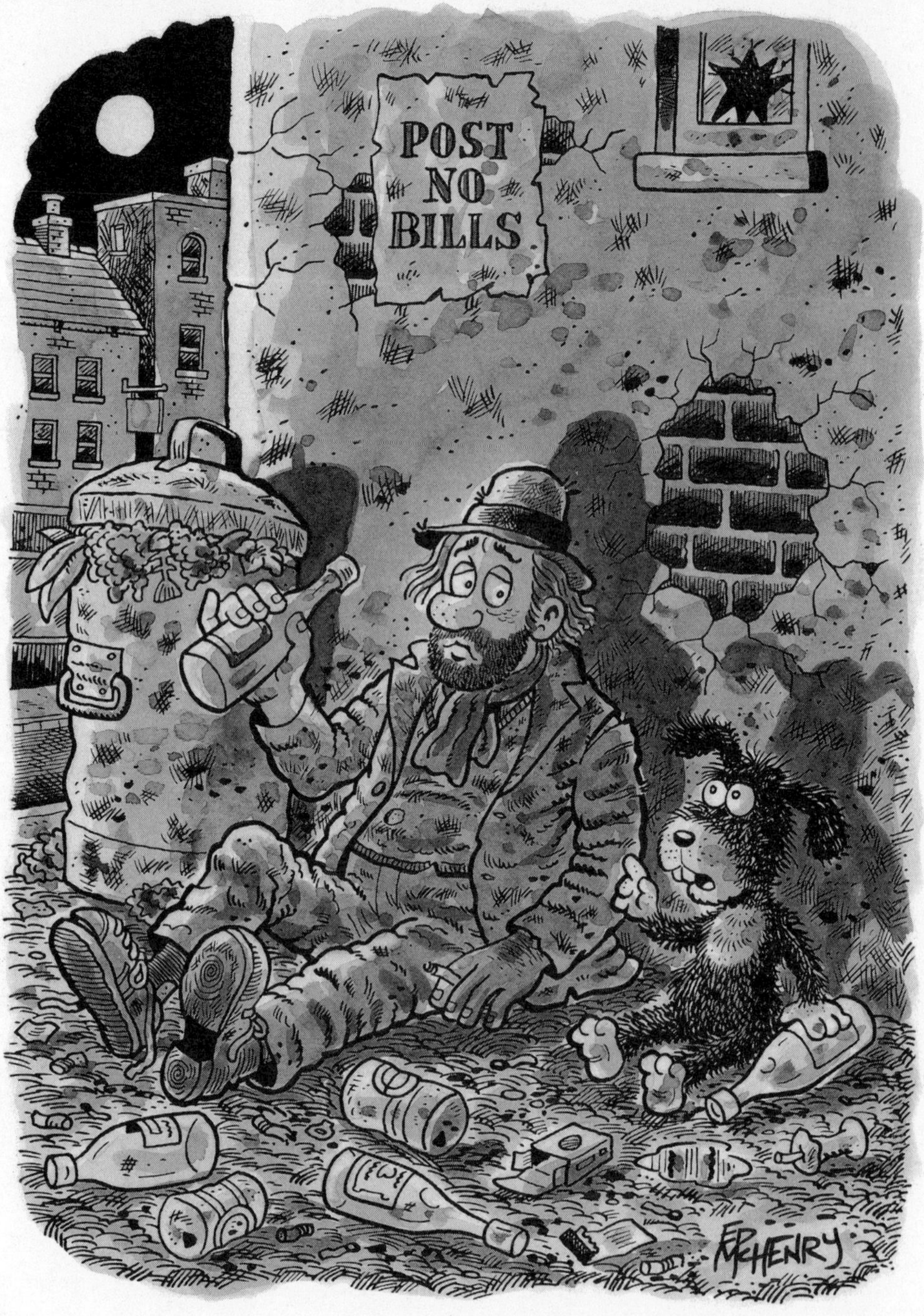
POST
NO
BILLS
McHENRY

'We've been fools, Charlie, we should have gone into show business!'

'You expect too much of that dog!'

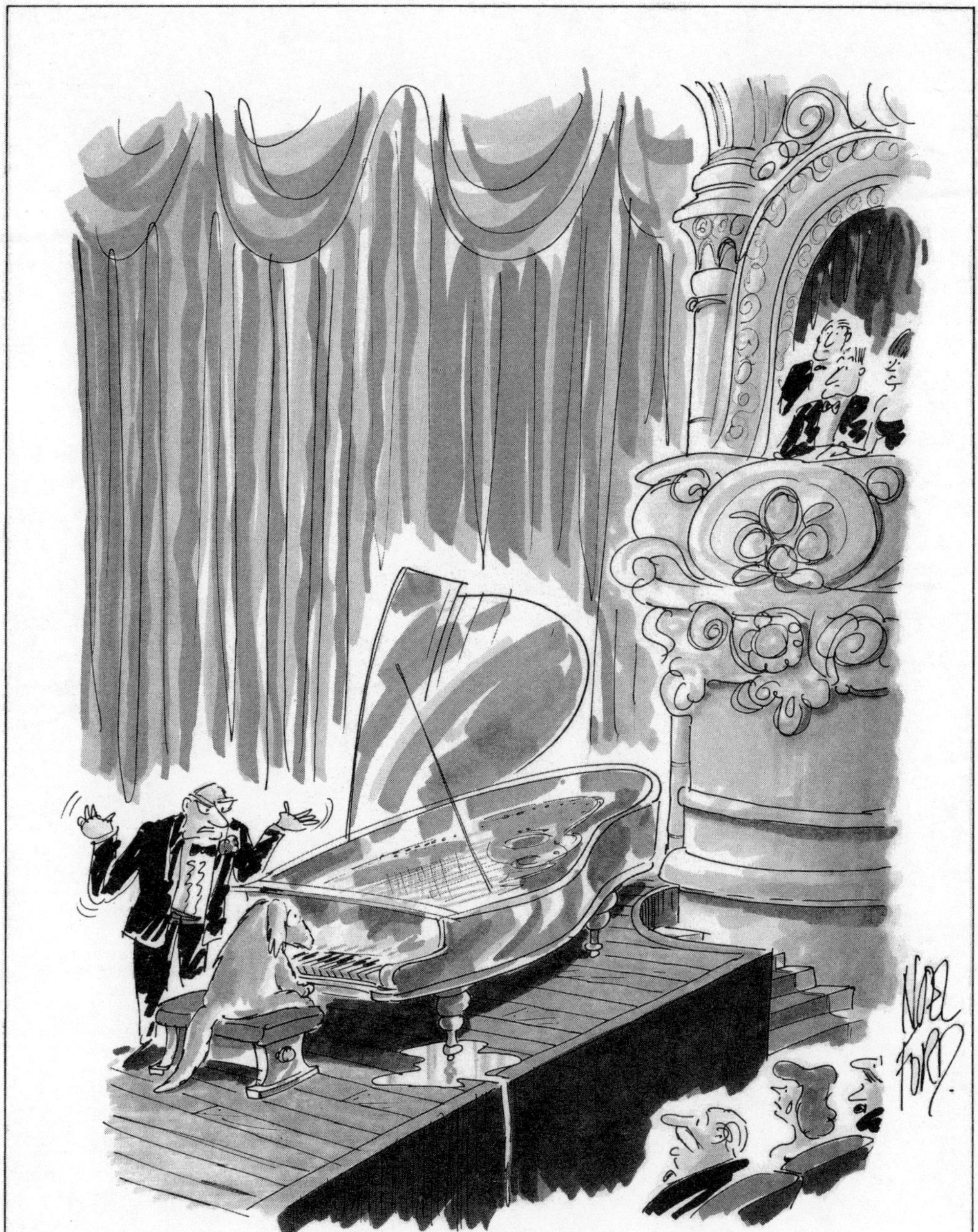

'It was going so well – then you have to go and disgrace yourself between the third and fourth movements!'

'What's the whistle to make him turn?'

ACTUALLY, I USED TO BE **MAN'S BEST FRIEND** UNTIL YOU MUSCLED IN.
ROVER
ROVER
S. Navarro

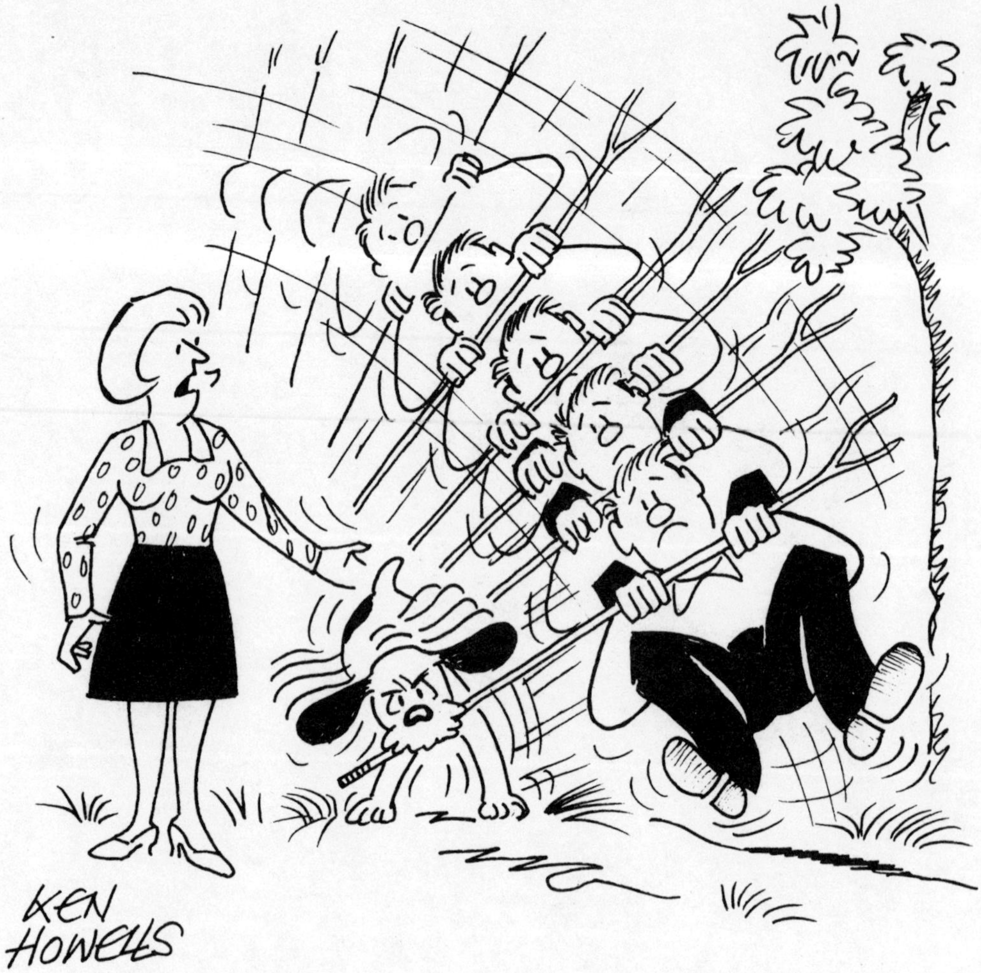
KEN HOWELLS

'For goodness' sake, Harold, let him have the stick!'

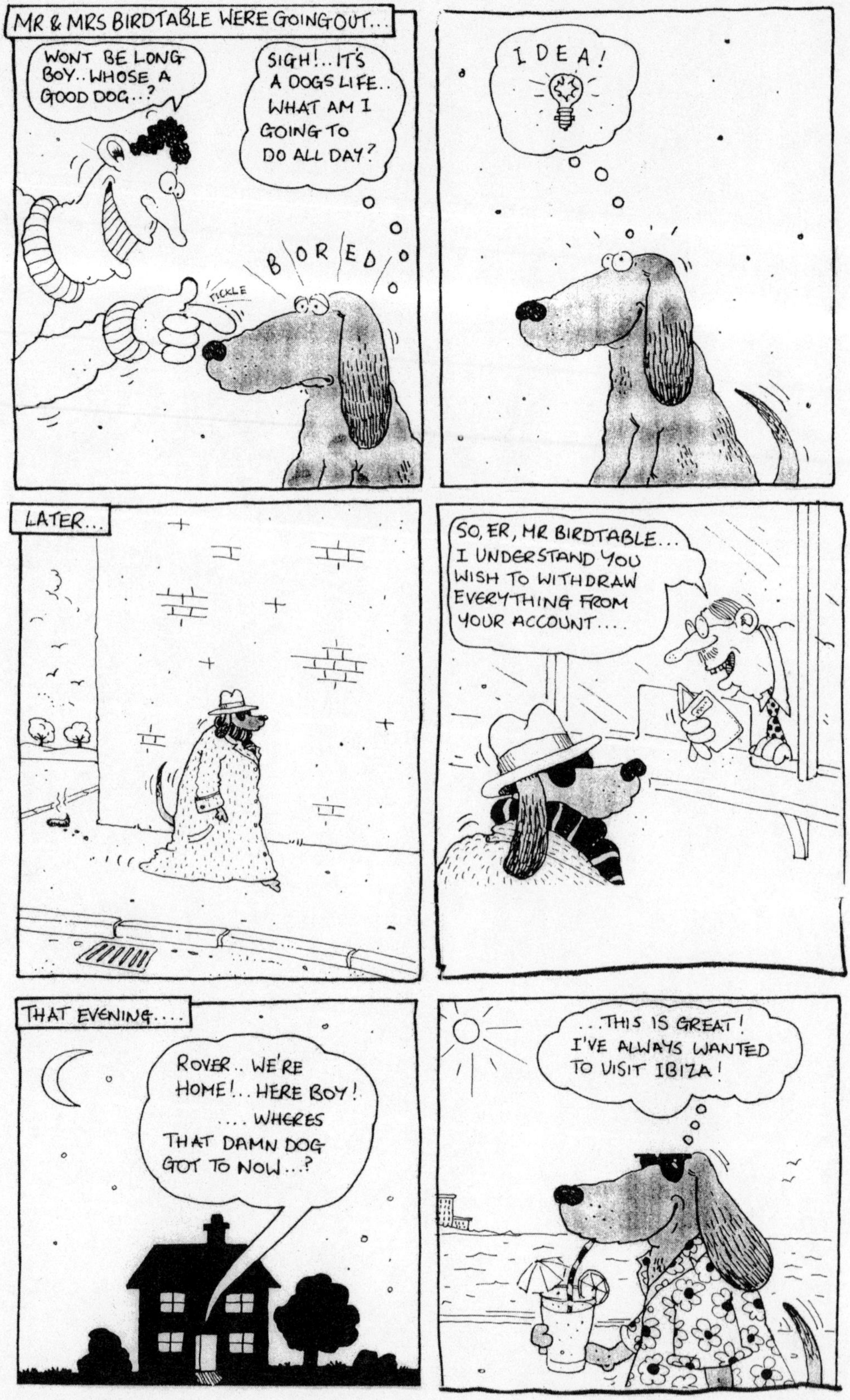
MR & MRS BIRDTABLE WERE GOINGOUT...
WONT BE LONG BOY.. WHOSE A GOOD DOG..?
SIGH!... IT'S A DOGS LIFE.. WHAT AM I GOING TO DO ALL DAY?
TICKLE
BORED
IDEA!
LATER...
SO, ER, MR BIRDTABLE... I UNDERSTAND YOU WISH TO WITHDRAW EVERYTHING FROM YOUR ACCOUNT....
THAT EVENING....
ROVER.. WE'RE HOME!.. HERE BOY! .... WHERES THAT DAMN DOG GOT TO NOW...?
...THIS IS GREAT! I'VE ALWAYS WANTED TO VISIT IBIZA!

'Warning . . . warning . . . Laddie is hunkering down in a restricted area.
Warning . . . warning . . .'

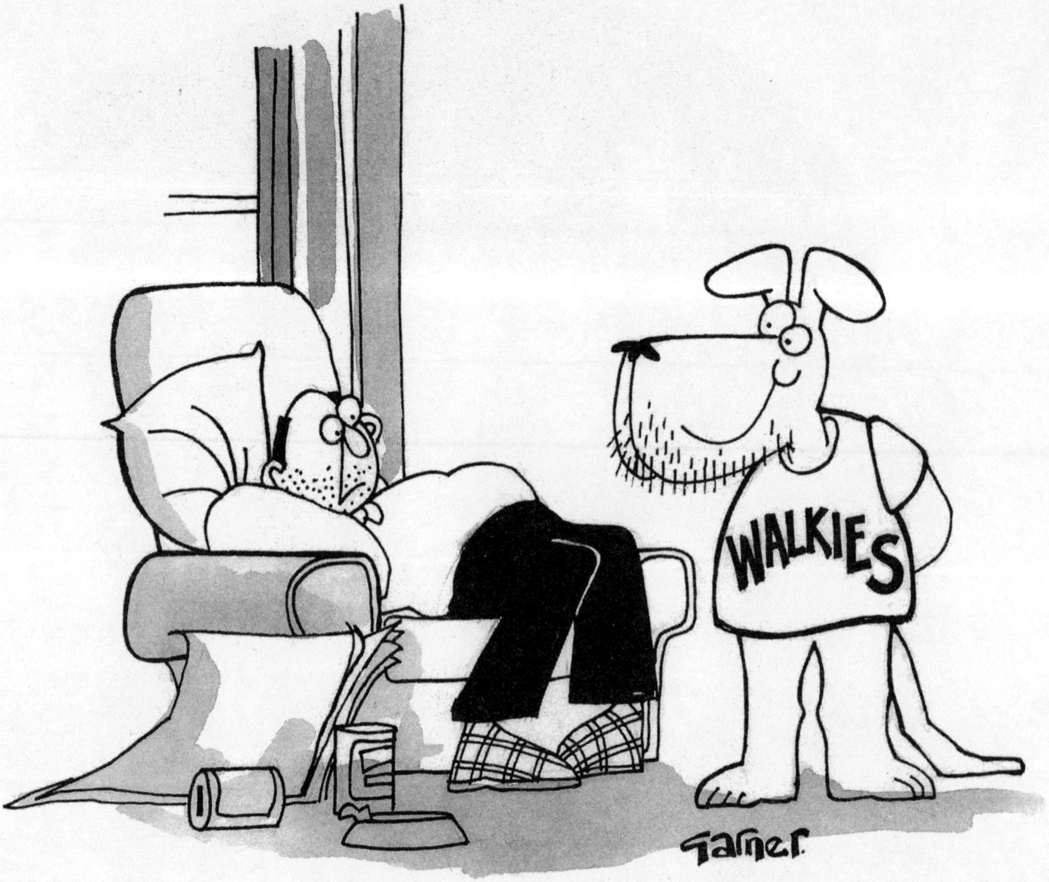
WALKIES
Garner

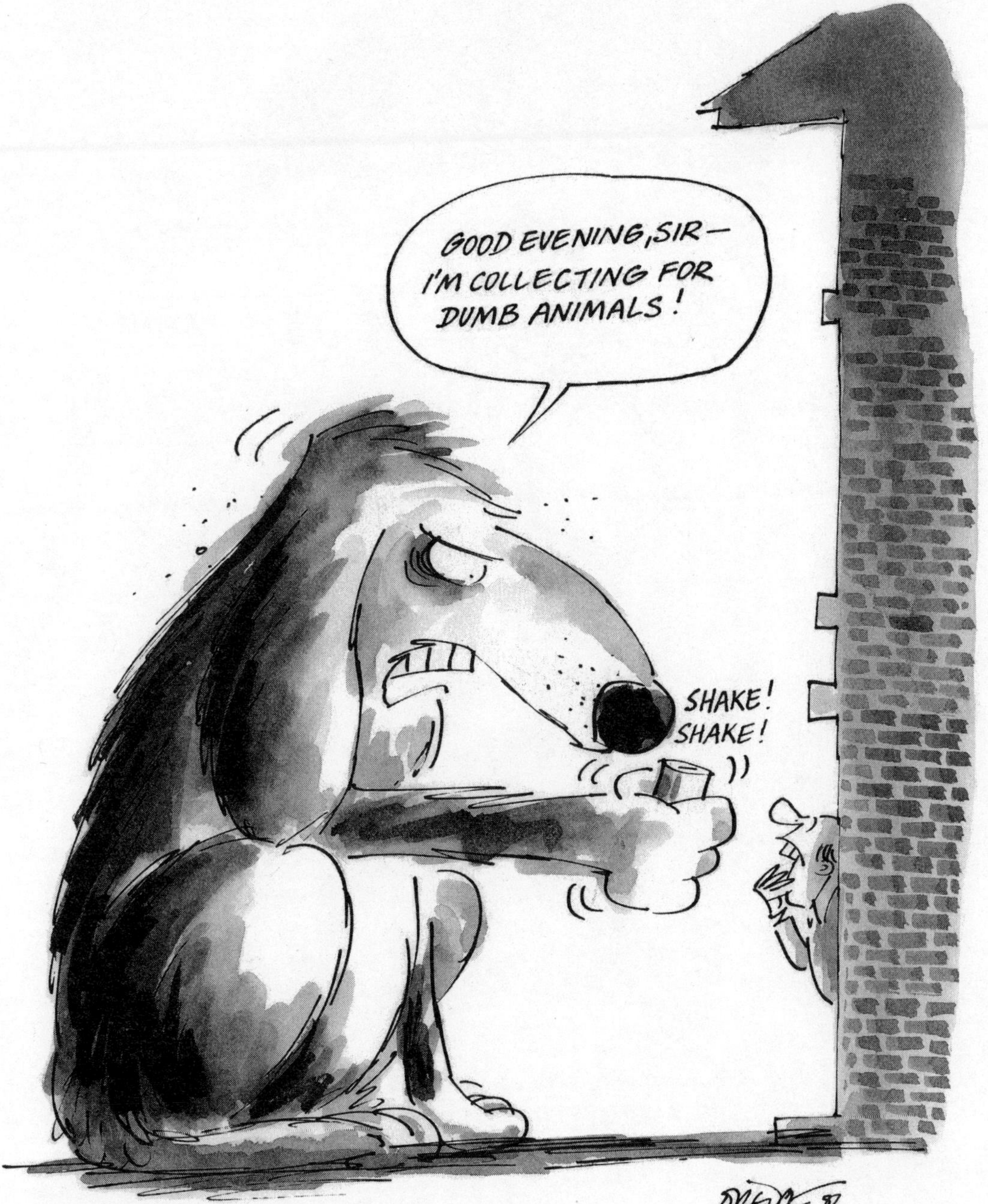
GOOD EVENING, SIR— I'M COLLECTING FOR DUMB ANIMALS!
SHAKE! SHAKE!

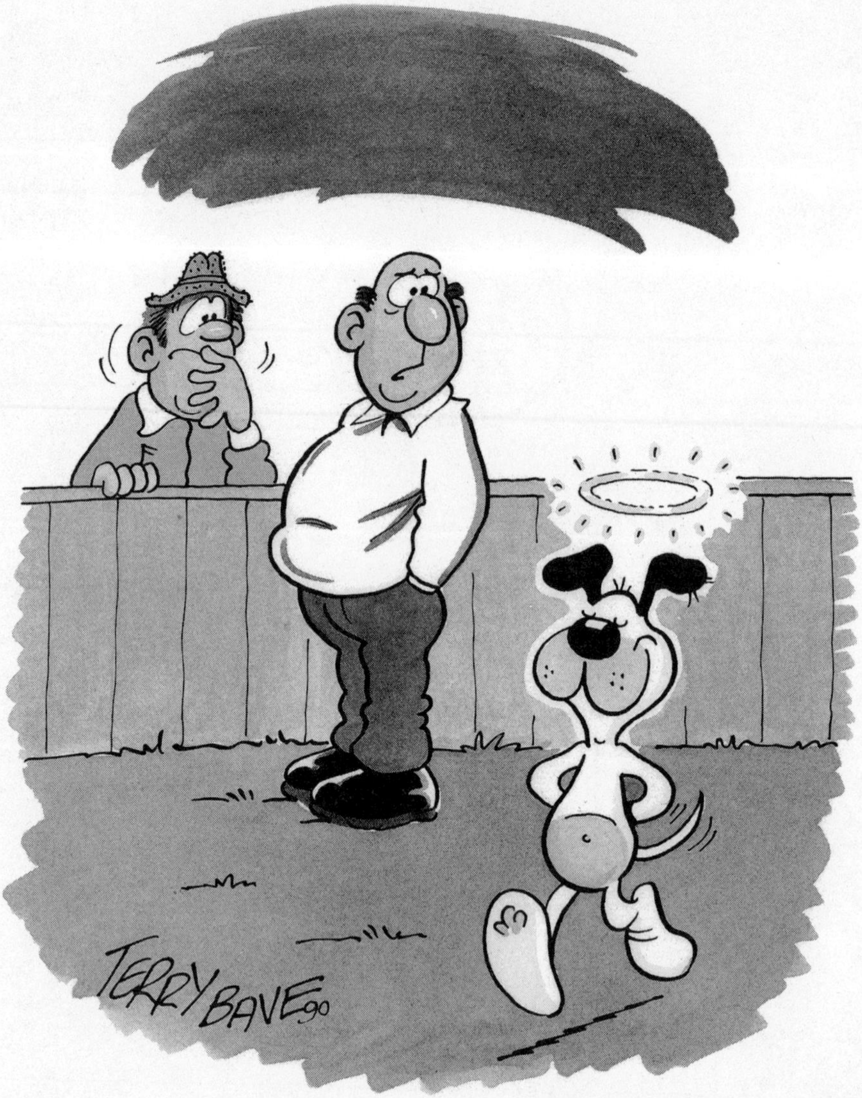
TERRY BAVE 90

'I've cured him of chasing sheep, now he just runs around creating dozens of mystery cornfield circles!'

Chipper
THAT SCOTTIE HAD THE CHEEK TO TELL ME HE HAD A CLOSE SHAVE THIS MORNING...
BELL
I BET HE DOESN'T EVEN KNOW WHAT A RAZOR LOOKS LIKE!
HAVE YOU HAD ANY CLOSE SHAVES LATELY?
NO...
BUT I HAD A NARROW SQUEAK LAST NIGHT
6699

'When you said there was a sitting tenant, I thought . . .'

'I think he wants to go out.'

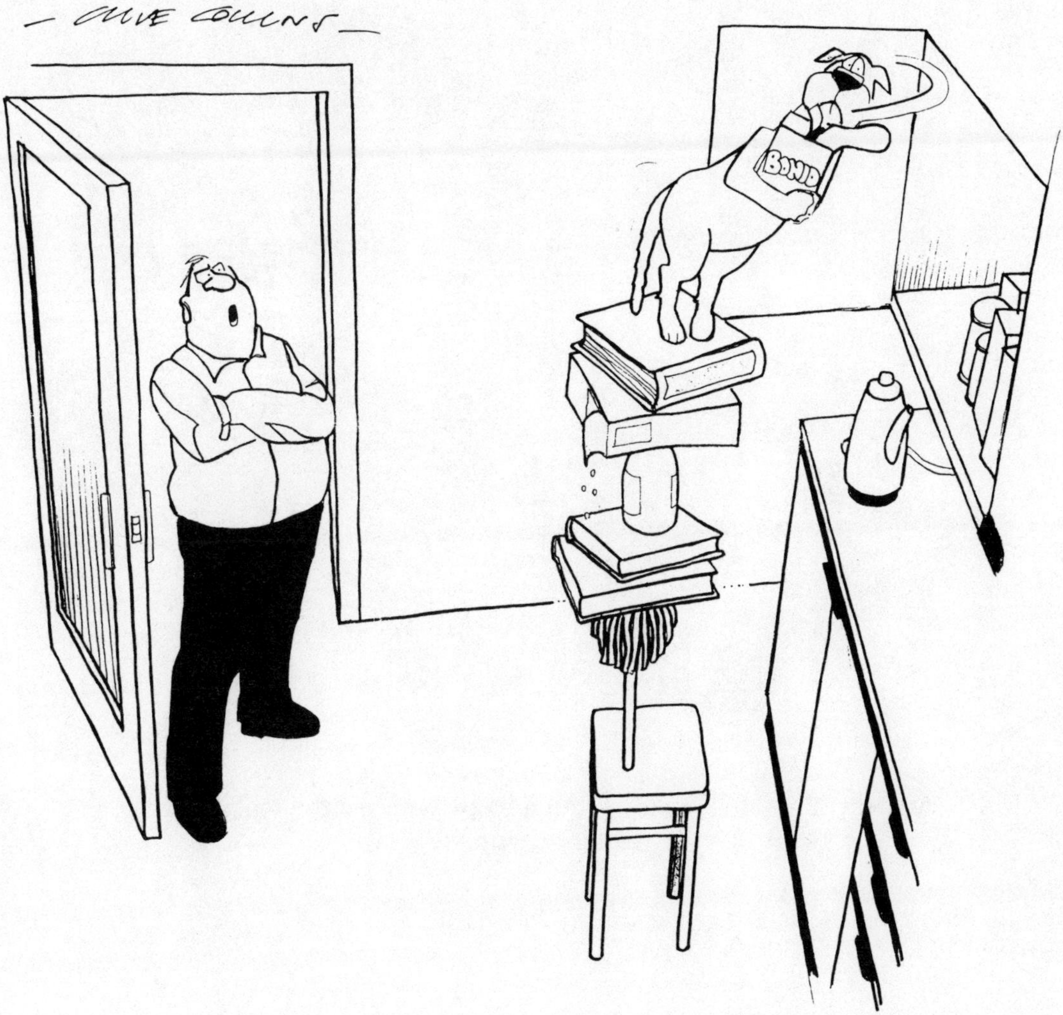
CLIVE COLLINS
BONIO

'Well! Excuse *me*!'

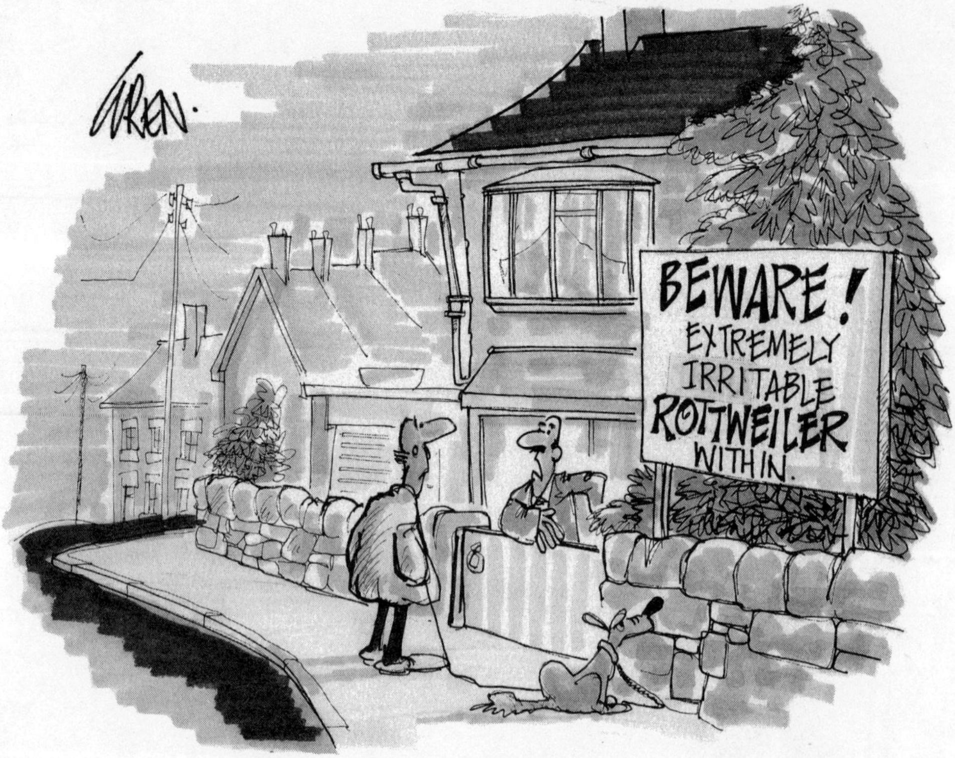
BEWARE!
EXTREMELY
IRRITABLE
ROTTWEILER
WITHIN.

'Actually it's a little poodle – but it helps keep out the replacement window people!'

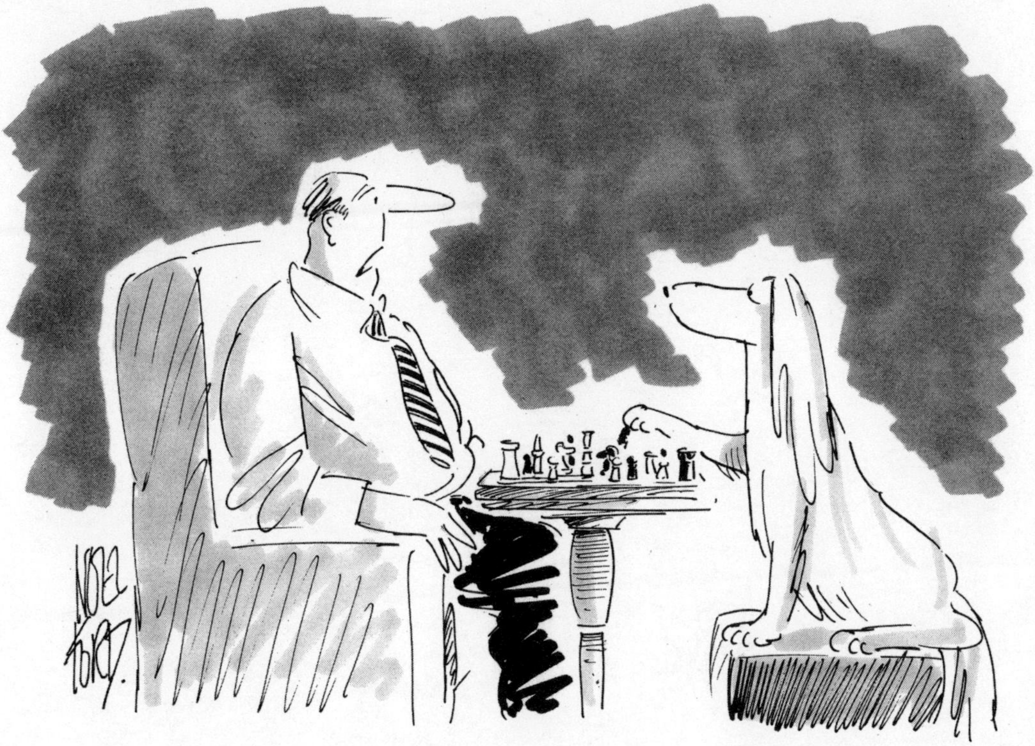
NOEL FORD.

'You carry loyalty *too* far, Goldy – you shouldn't let me win *every* time.'

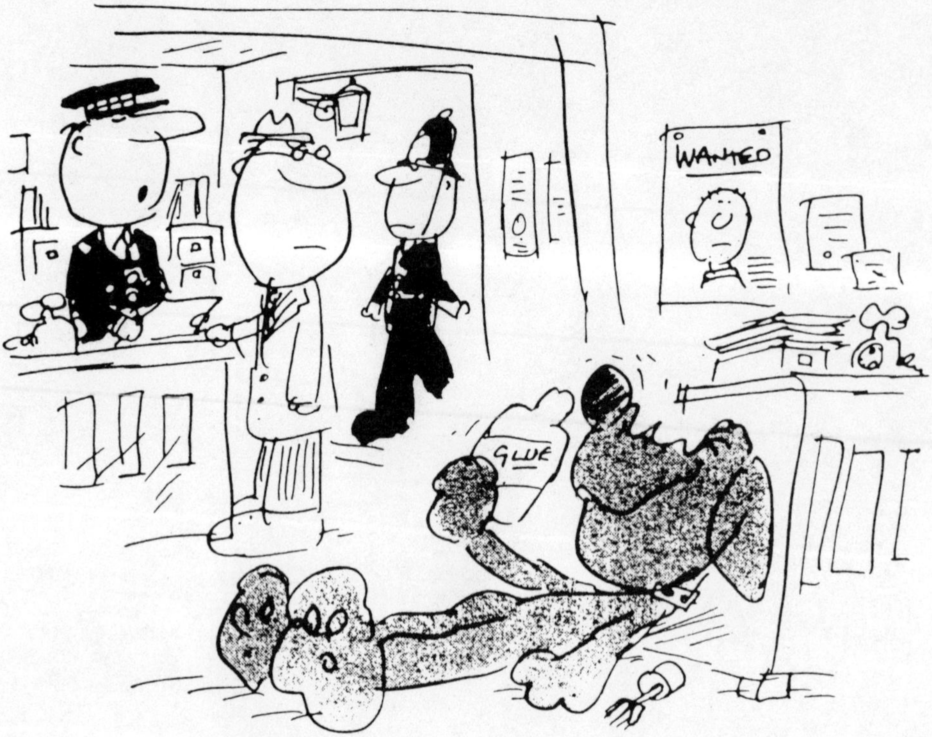
WANTED
GLUE

'As sniffer dogs go he's been a great disappointment.'

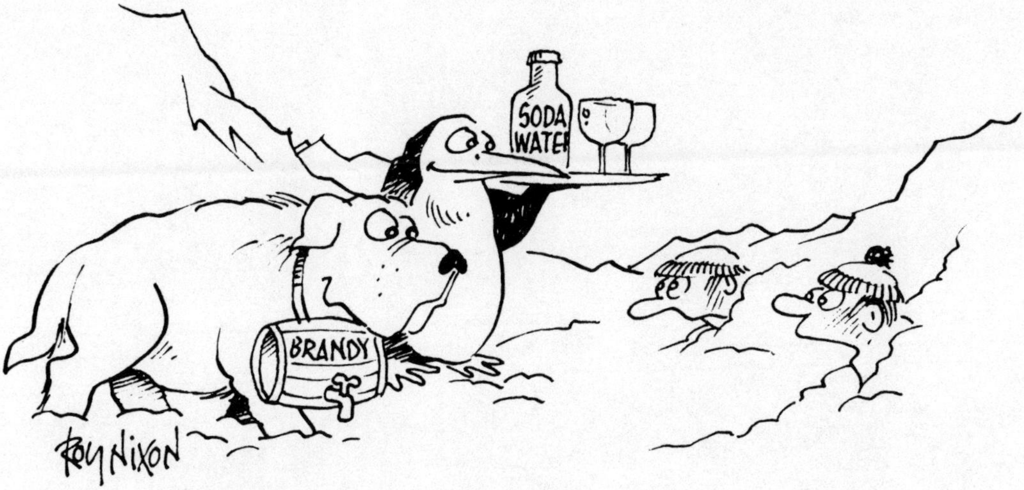
SODA WATER
BRANDY
ROY NIXON

'They really look after you here.'

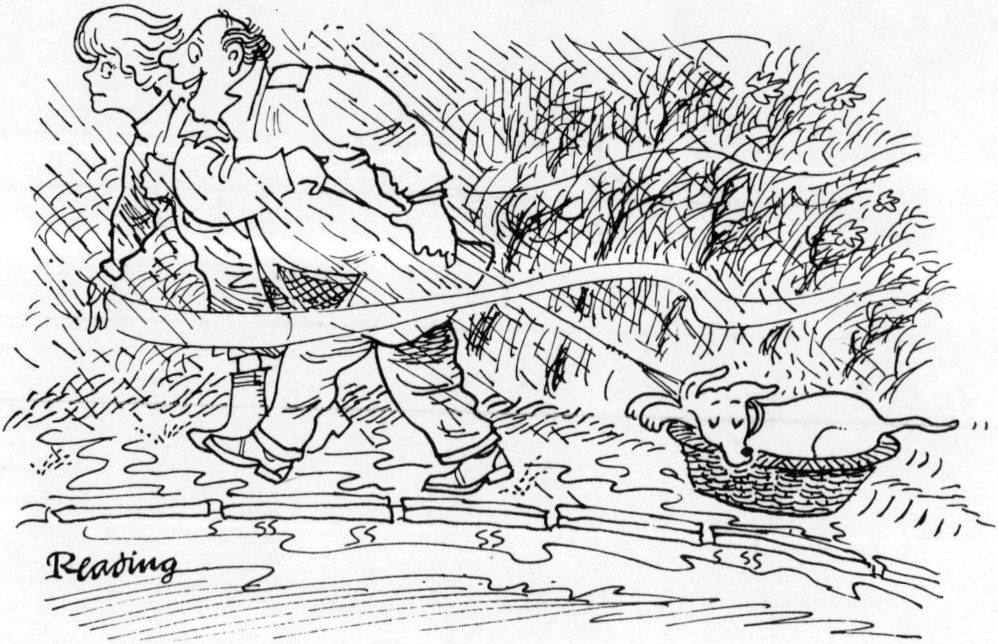
Reading

'He's only *pretending* he doesn't want to come.'

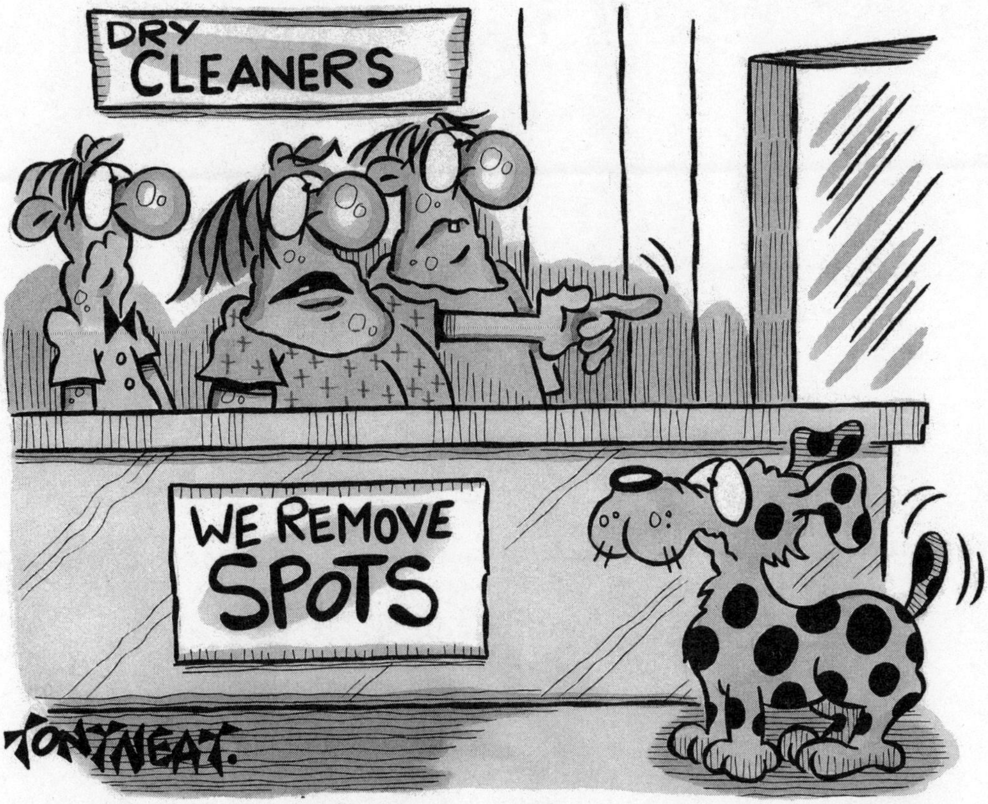
DRY CLEANERS
WE REMOVE SPOTS
TONY NEAT.

'Get out, Spot!'

'Of course it's taking him a long time. Nobody likes to be stared at.'

**LUKE**
BY CHAS.

IF A CAT HAS NINE LIVES

WHY DOES HE WASTE EIGHT OF THEM

STILL BEING A CAT?

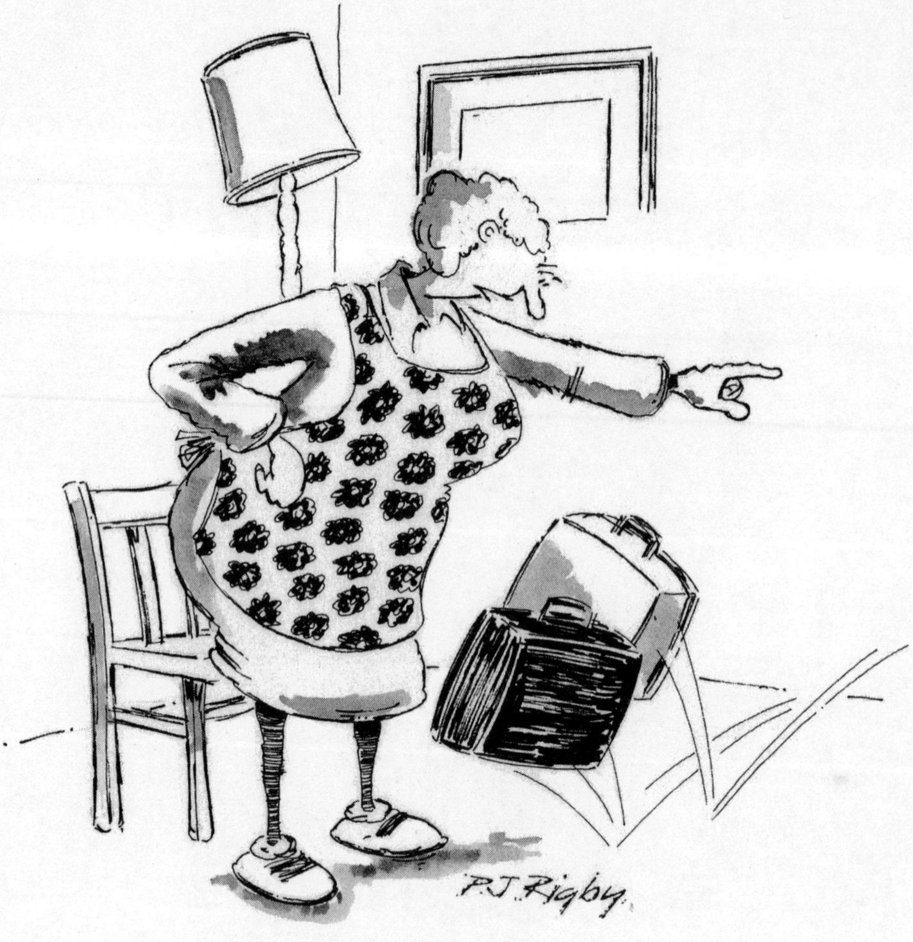
P.J. Rigby

'I'm warning you. Either that dog goes or I g. . . !'

WE'VE GOT LOTS OF PAINTINGS BY FAMOUS ARTISTS AT THE PALACE
I THINK THIS ONE IS MY FAVOURITE...
ANDY WARHOL'S 'CORGI'

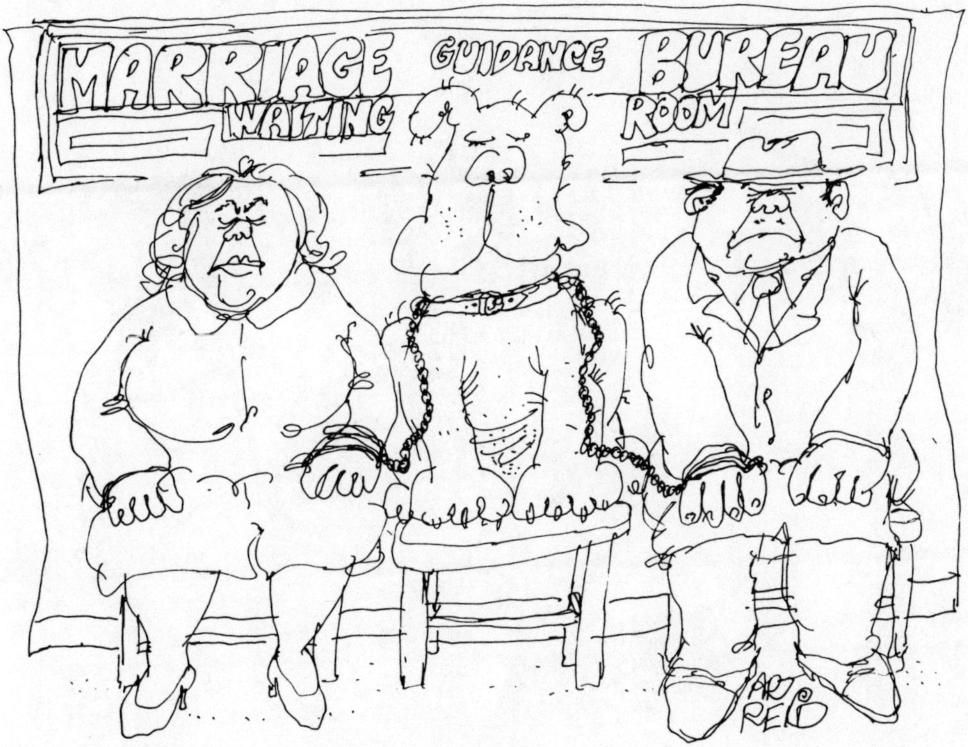
MARRIAGE GUIDANCE BUREAU
WAITING ROOM
ART REID

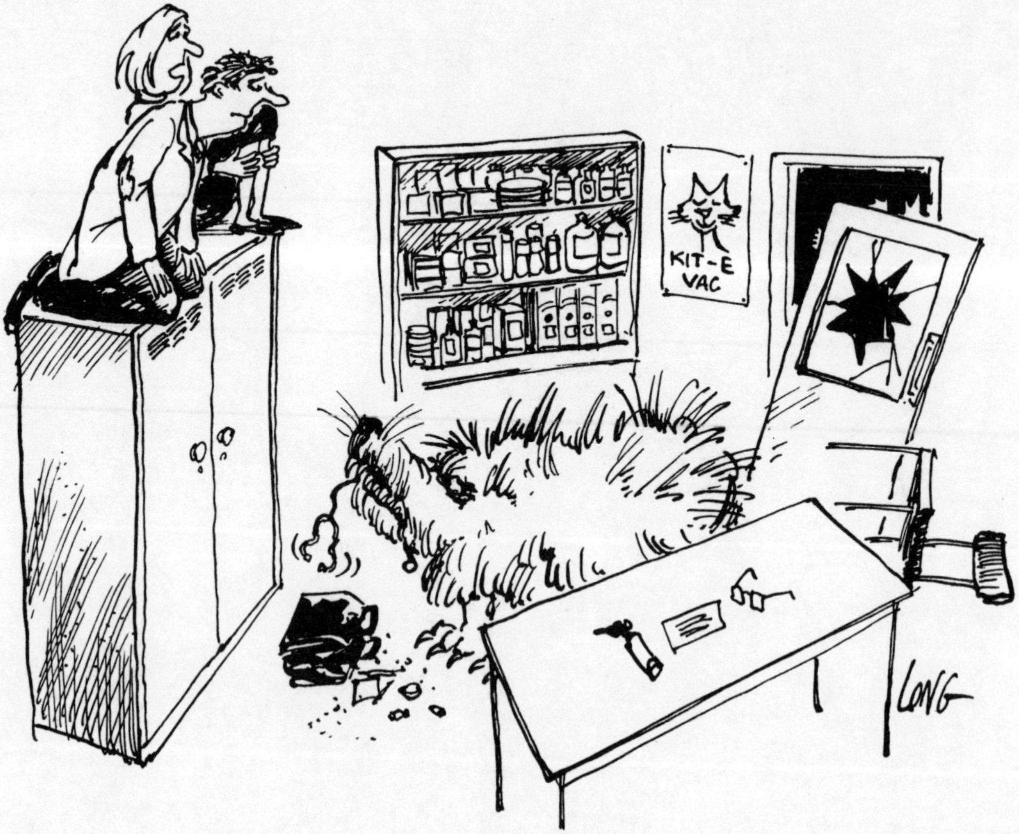
KIT-E
VAC
LONG

'He looked so appealing when we first saw him in the pet shop!'

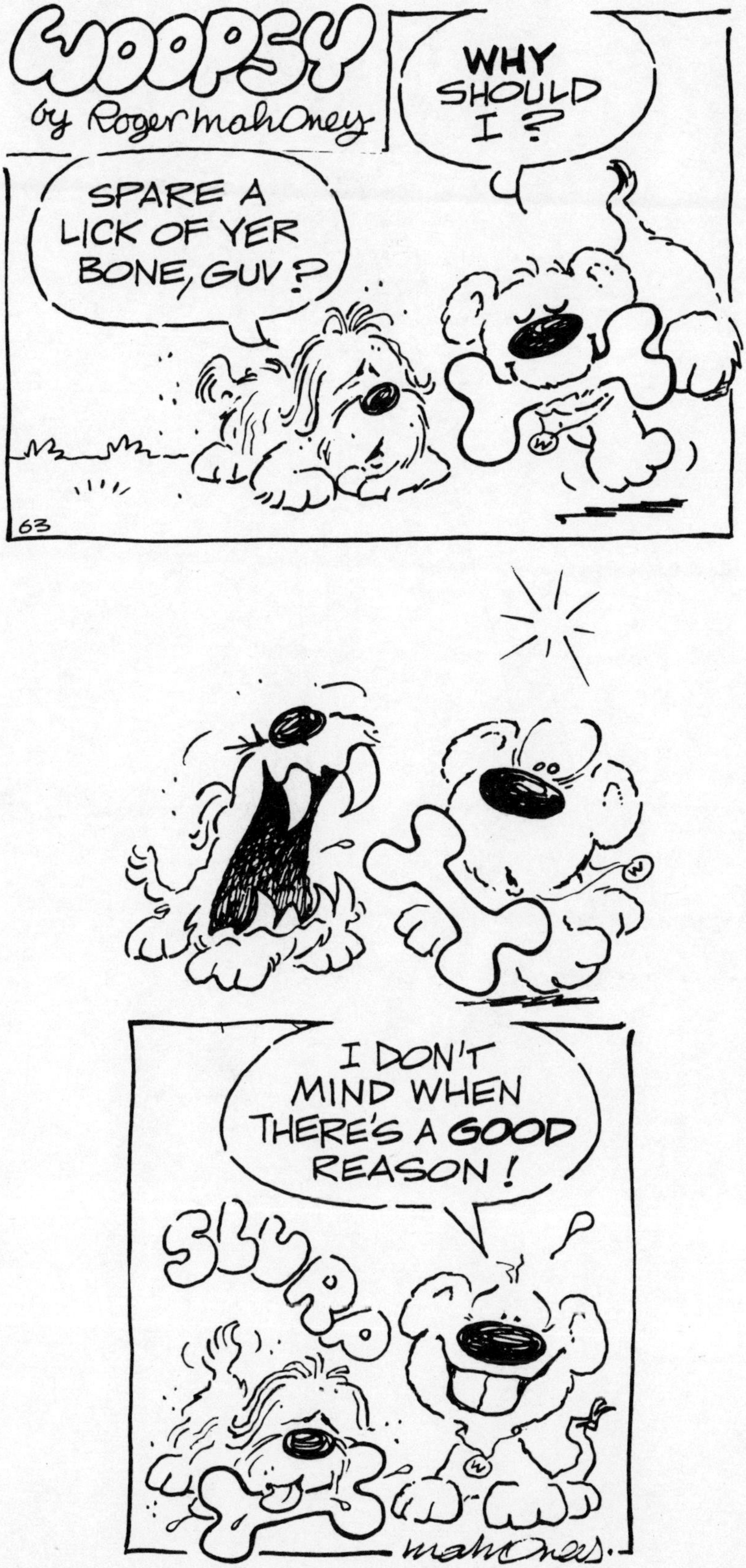
WOOPSY
by Roger mahoney
WHY SHOULD I?
SPARE A LICK OF YER BONE, GUV?
63
I DON'T MIND WHEN THERE'S A GOOD REASON!
SLURP
mahoney

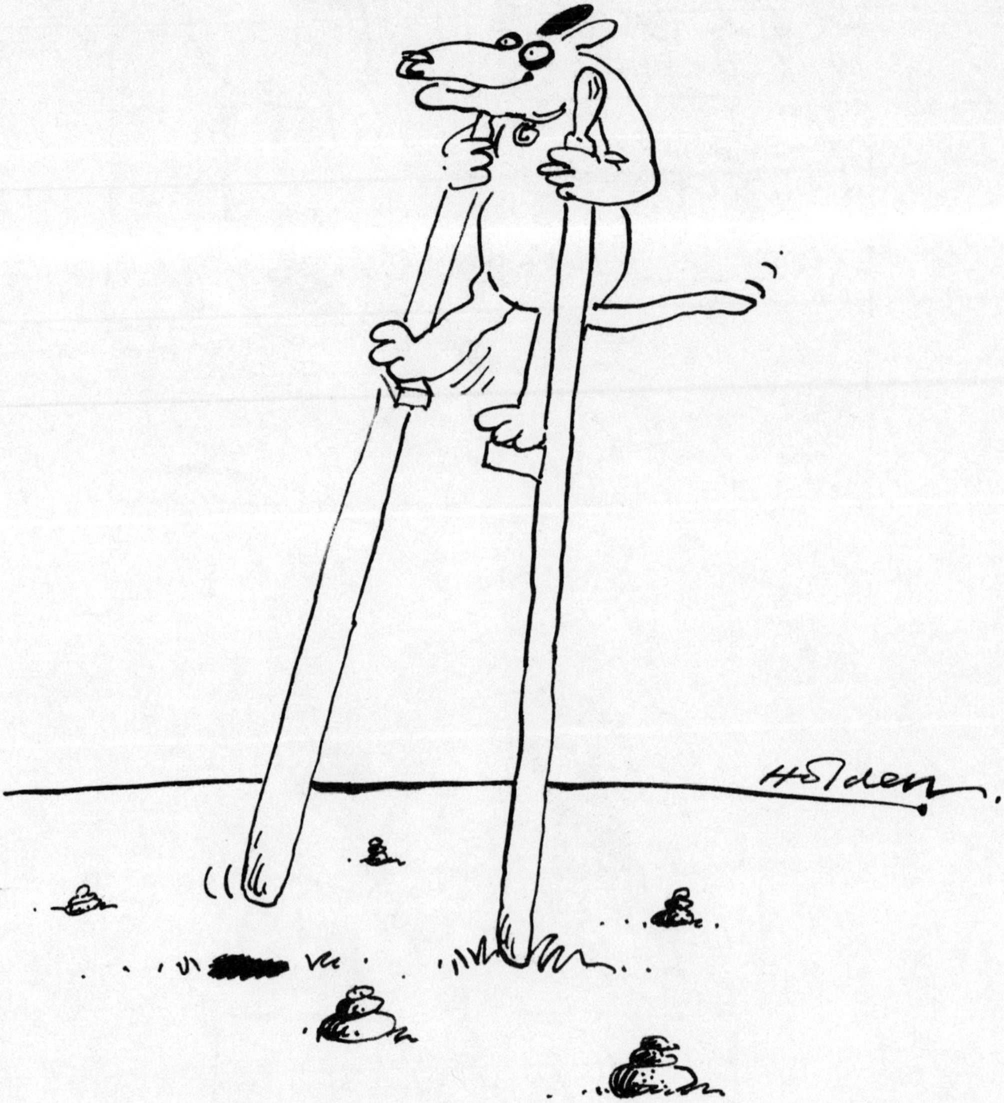
Holden

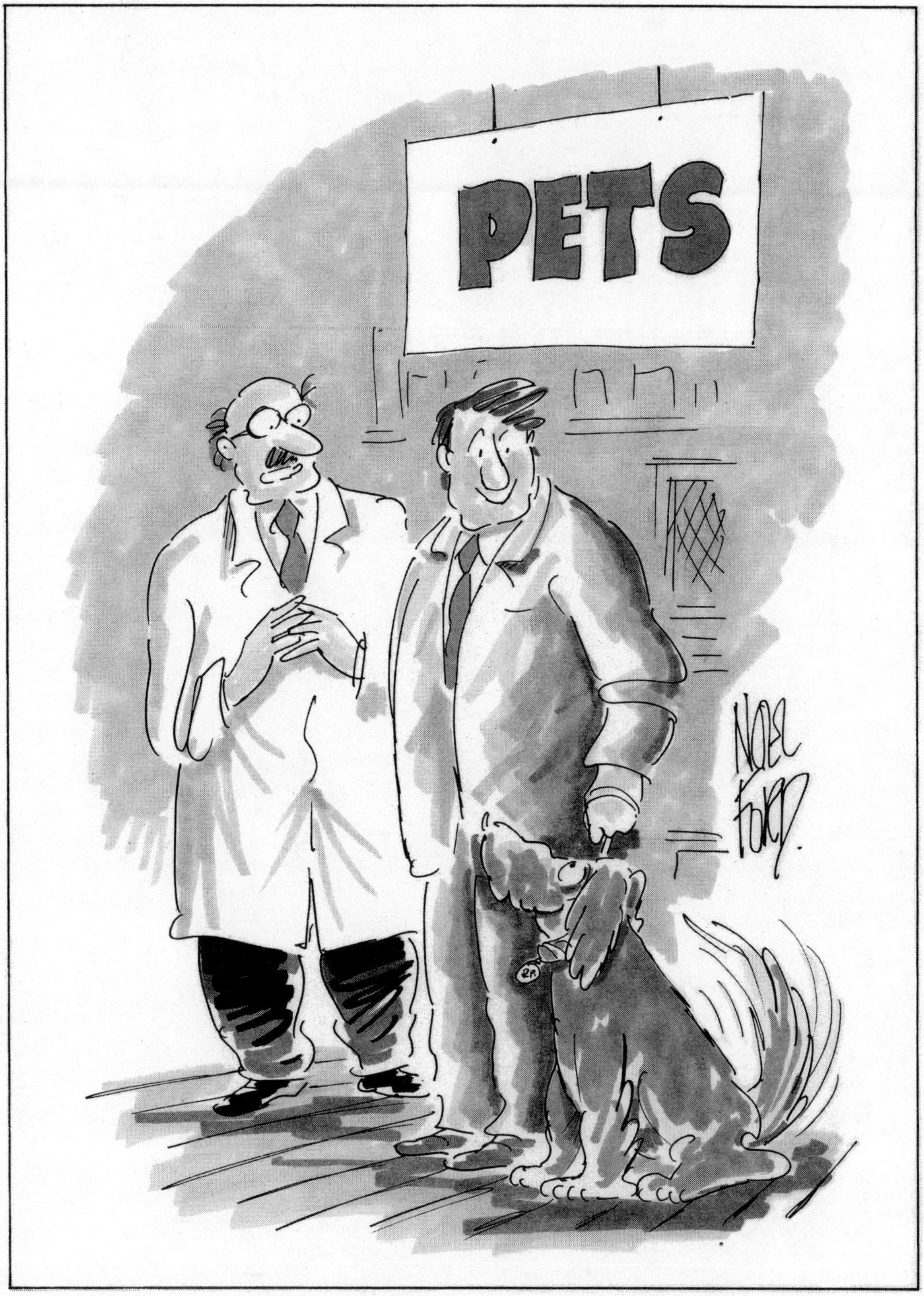
PETS
NOEL FORD

'I now pronounce you man and dog.'

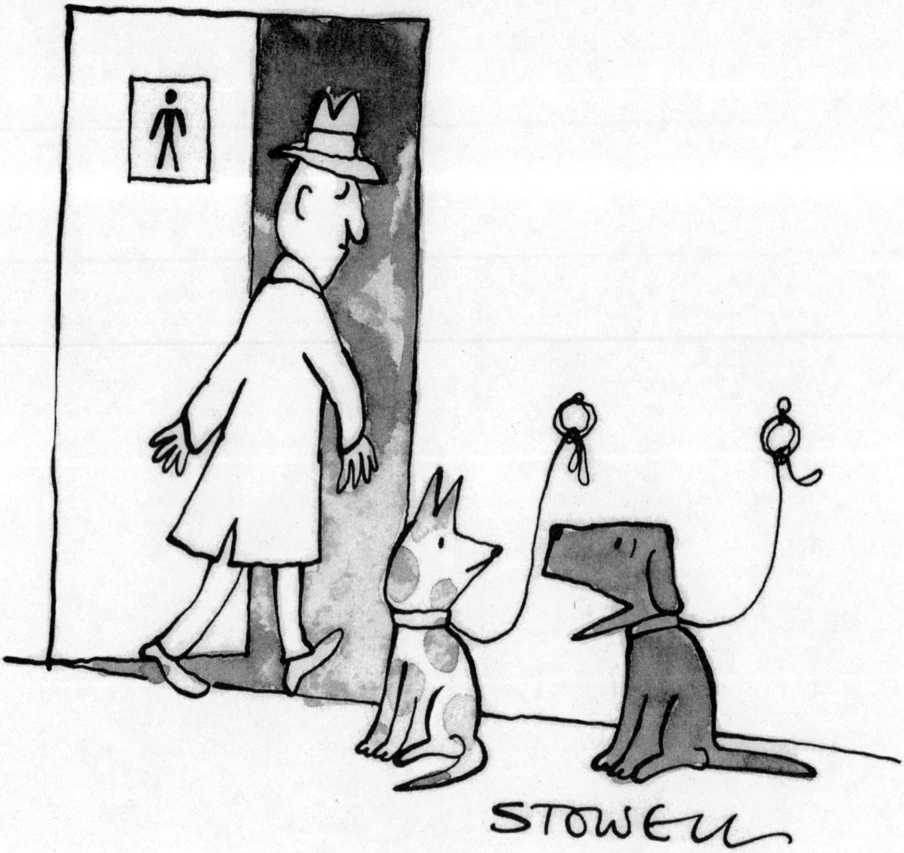
STOWELL

'I'm told that they go in there to mark their territory.'

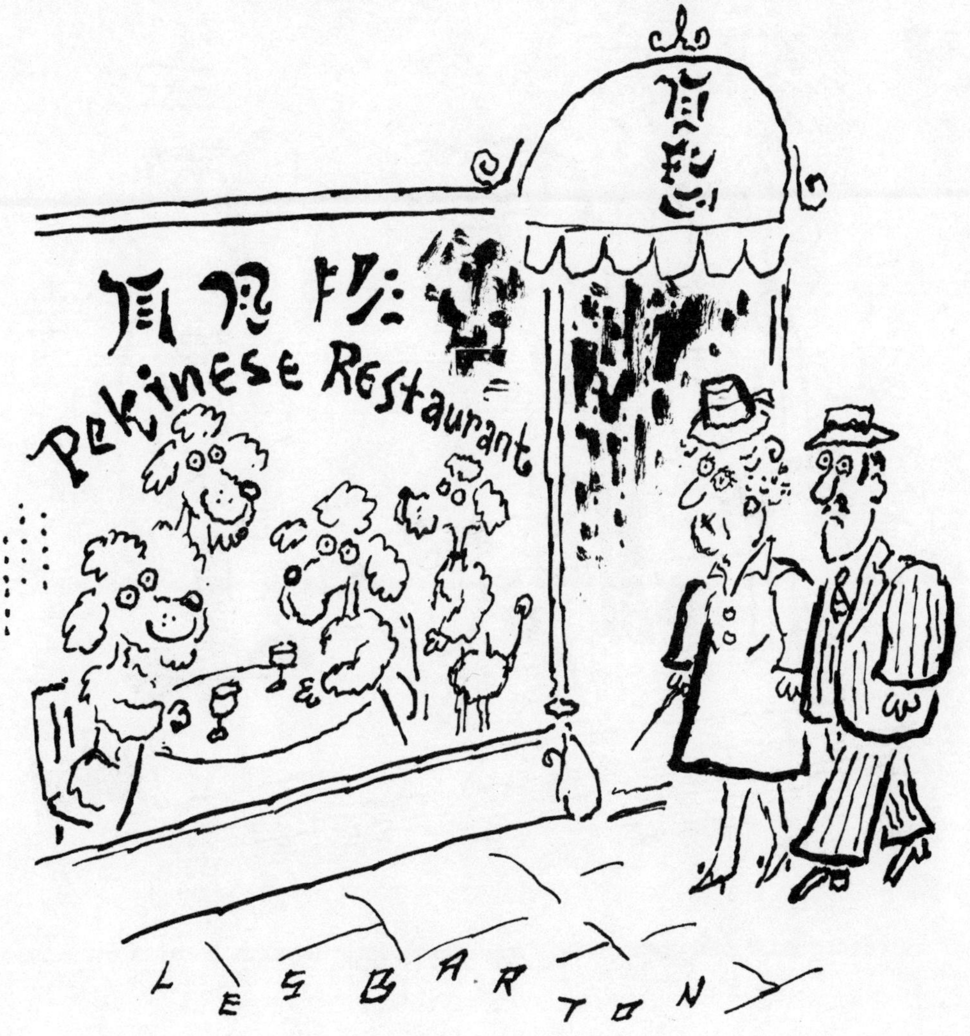
Pekinese Restaurant
LES BARTON

'He's just like one of the family really.'

POOCHY PET PILLS TO MAKE YOUR DOG LIVELY WITH ZIP AND BOUNDLESS ENERGY
WE MUST GET SOME FOR FRED
No, thank you!
7-29
Who wants to be lively with zip and boundless energy?
© Associated Newspapers Group p.l.c., 1987 Dist. North America Syndicate, Inc. All rights reserved.

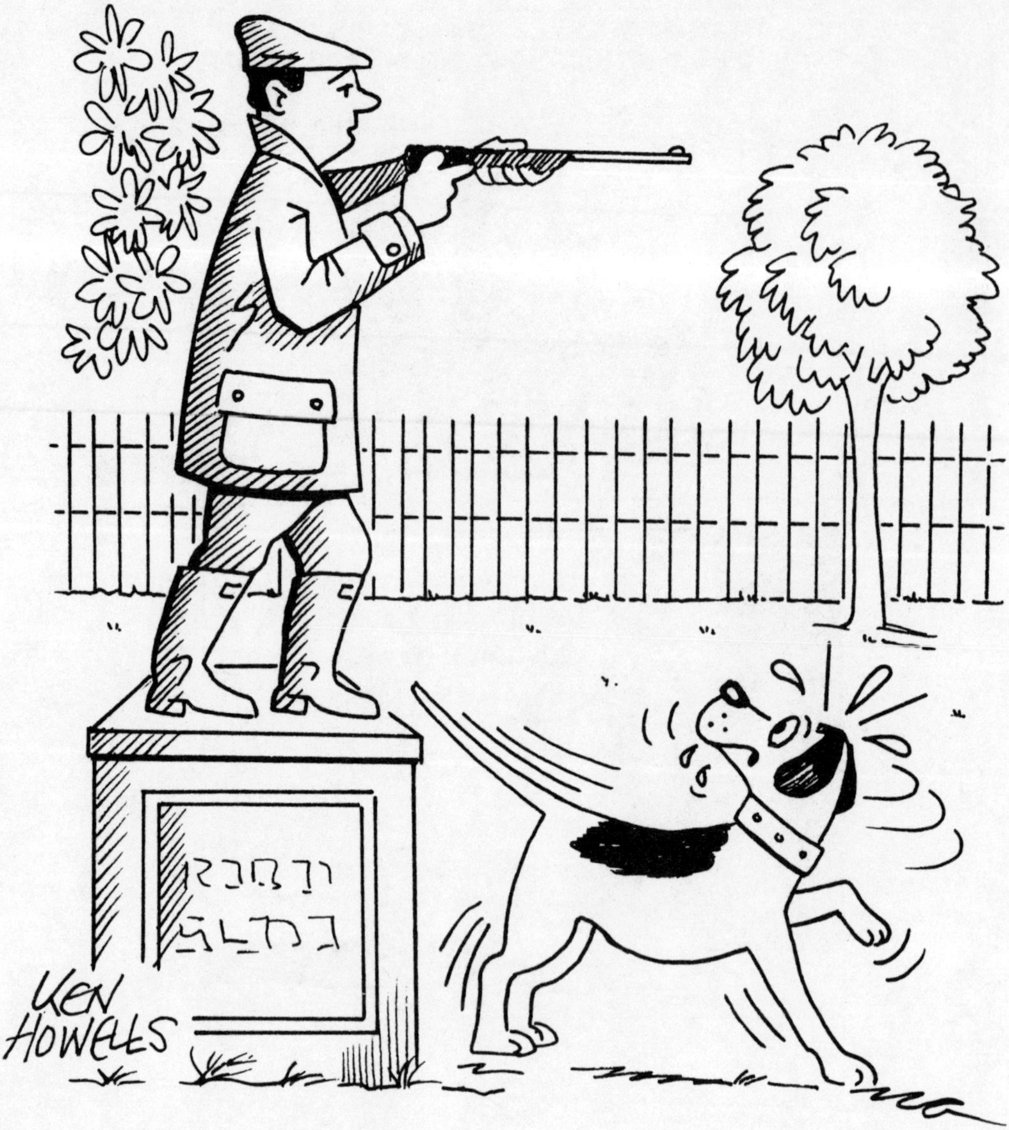
KEN HOWELLS

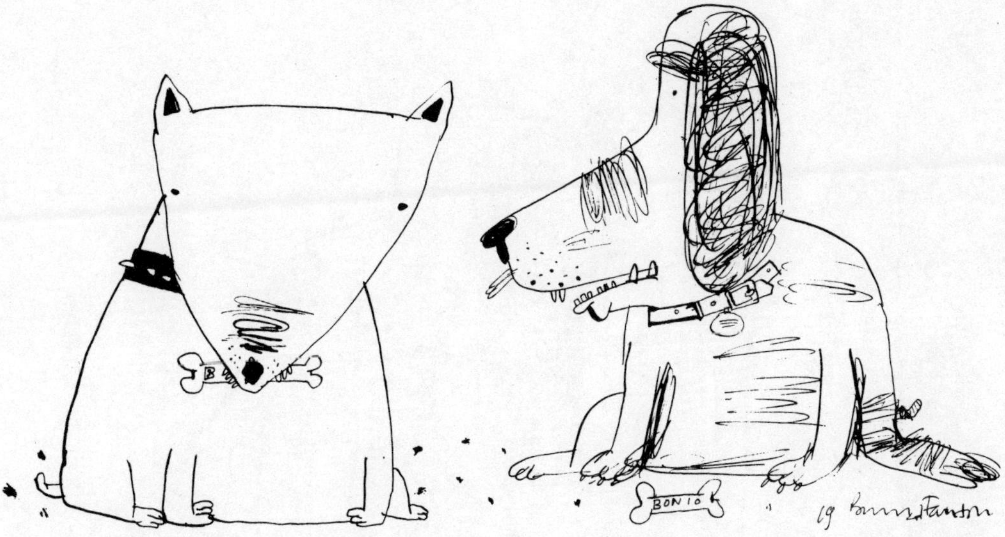
BONIO

'No wonder he gives you half of his beefburger to eat first. Remember BSE?'

Identity Parade

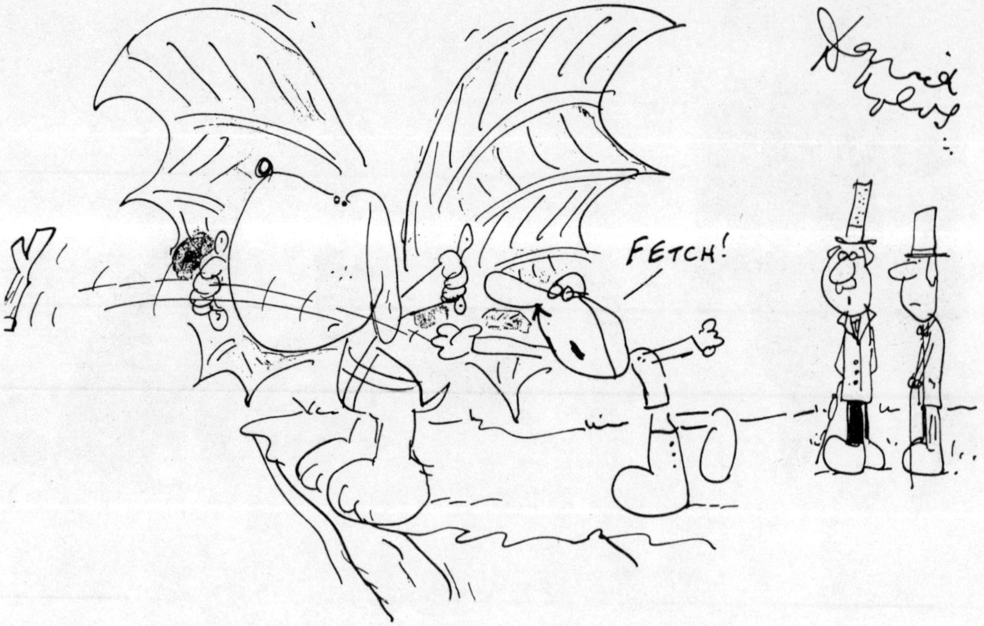
FETCH!

'You'd think he'd test it himself.'

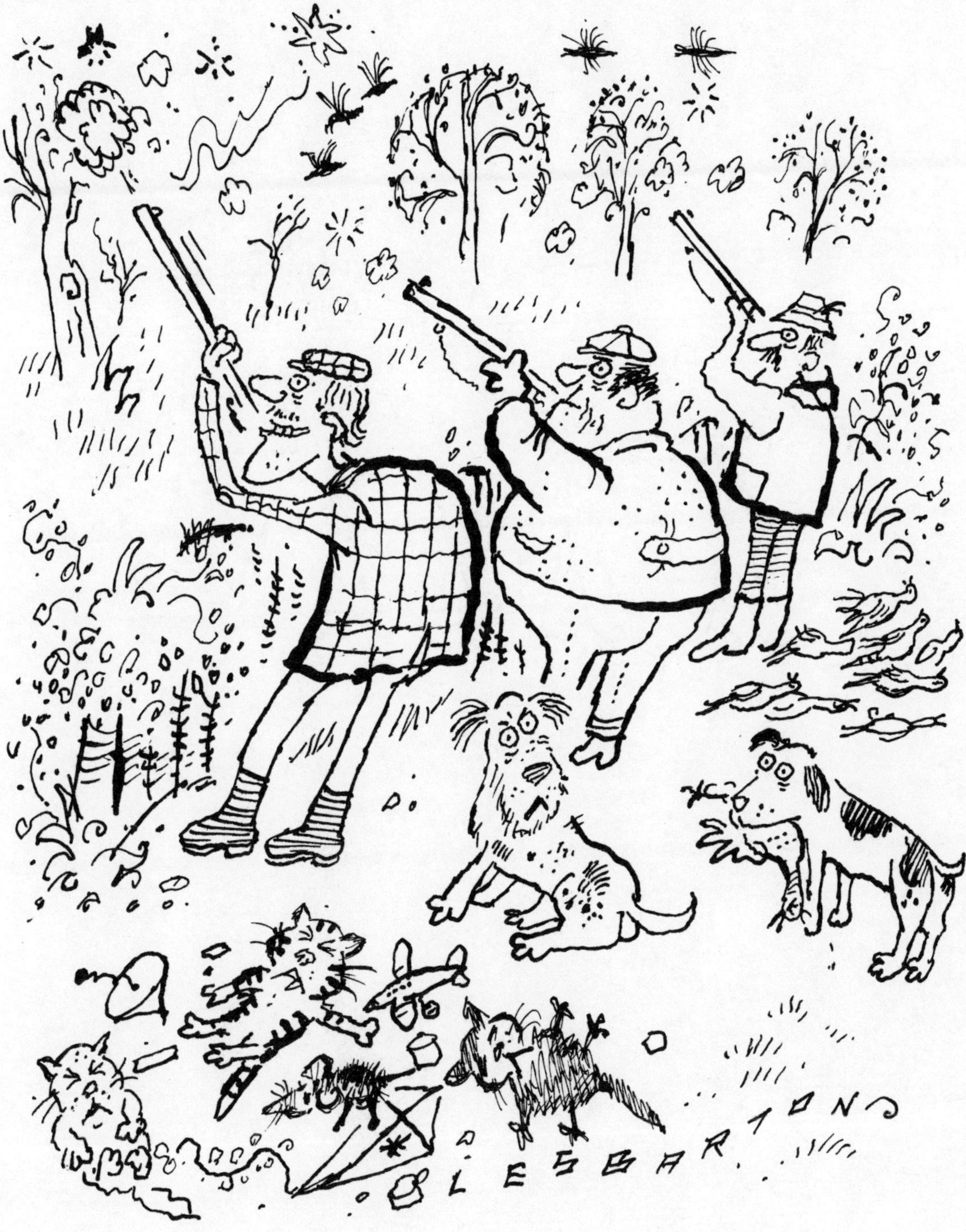
LES GIBARD 1980

'Look, I never make mistakes but I take orders from someone who does!'

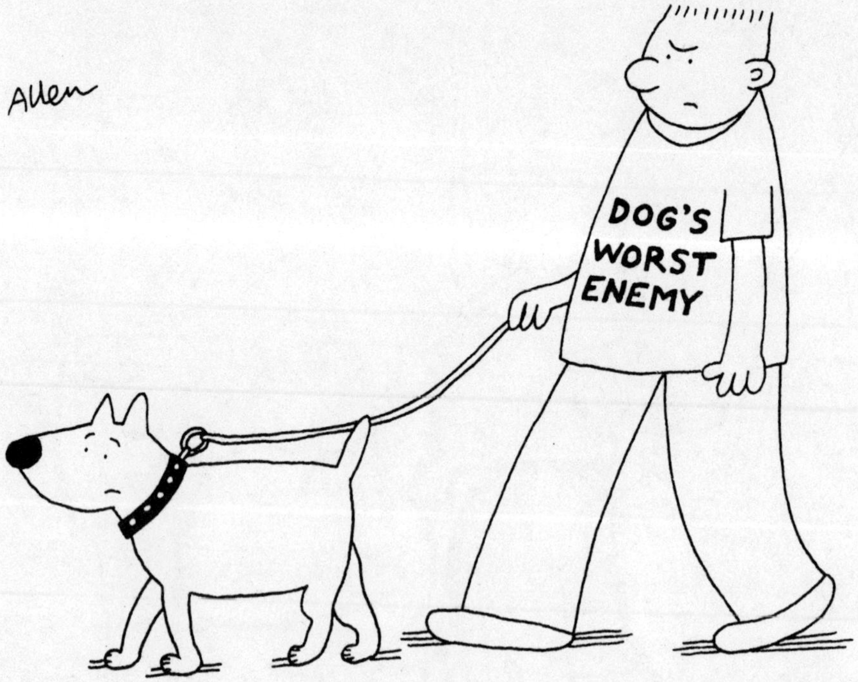
Allen
DOG'S
WORST
ENEMY

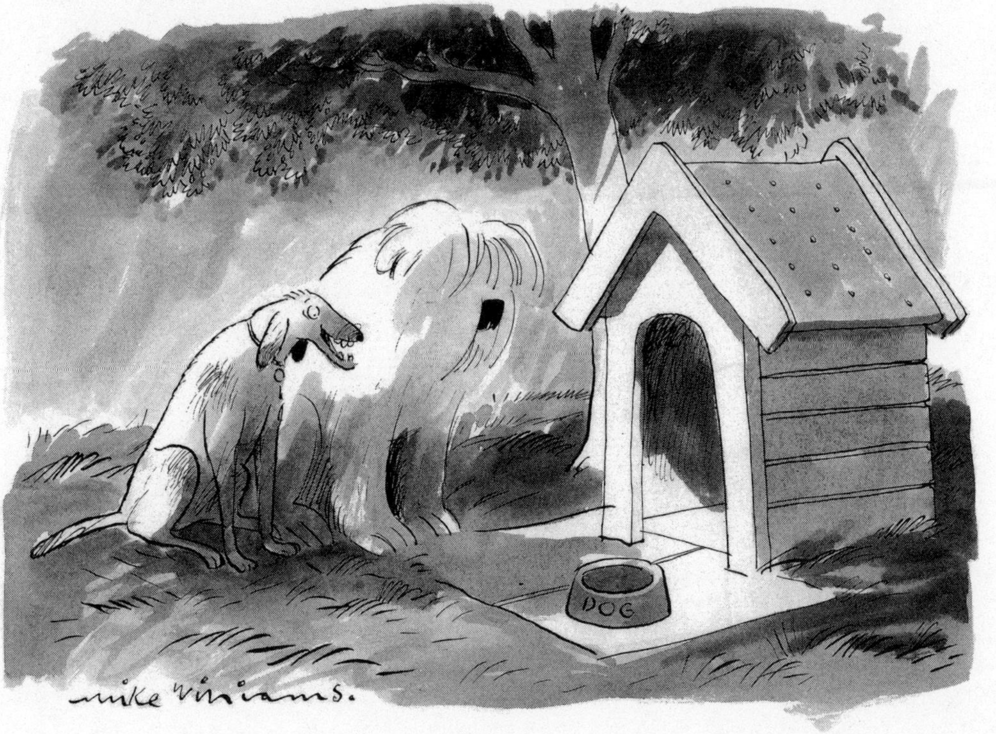
DOG
mike williams.

'Mmm . . . sounds really nice . . . eggshell or gloss?'

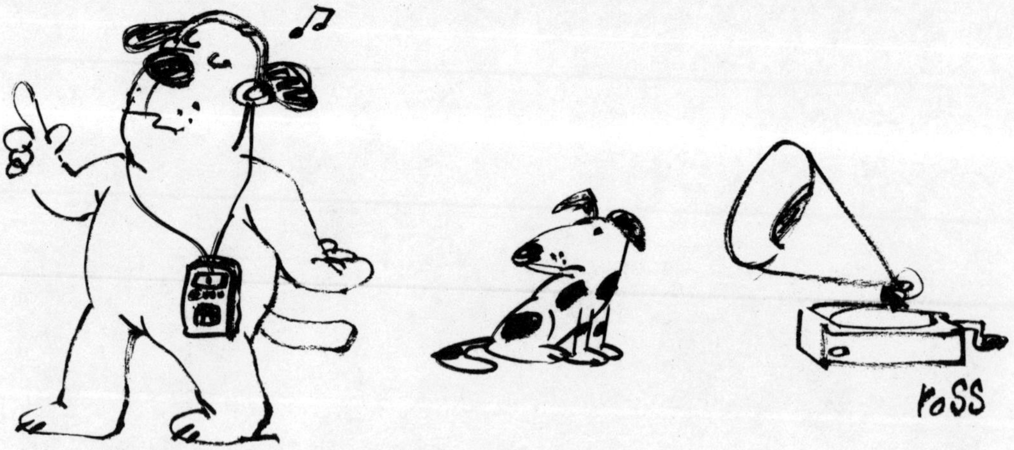
ROSS

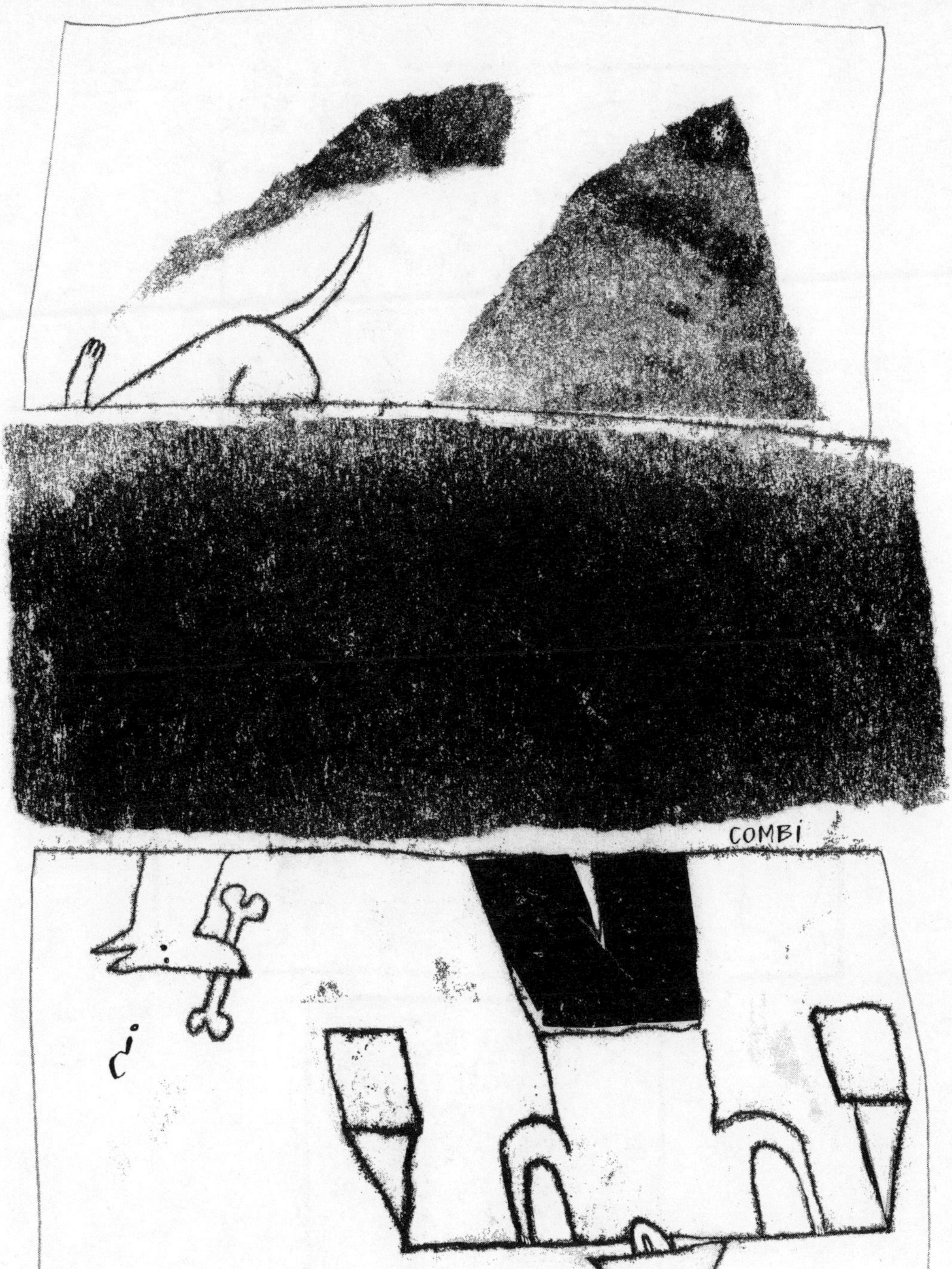
COMBI

YOU ARE ACTING IN A VERY PECULIAR MANNER
IN FACT I THINK YOU'RE A VERY SICK DOG
Maurice Dodd
I THINK THIS CALLS FOR THE OLE THERMOMETER
DON'T WORRY -I'LL SORT IT OUT IN THE END
NOT IN MY END YOU WON'T
W19

'No, no . . . I meant fetch *my* slippers!'

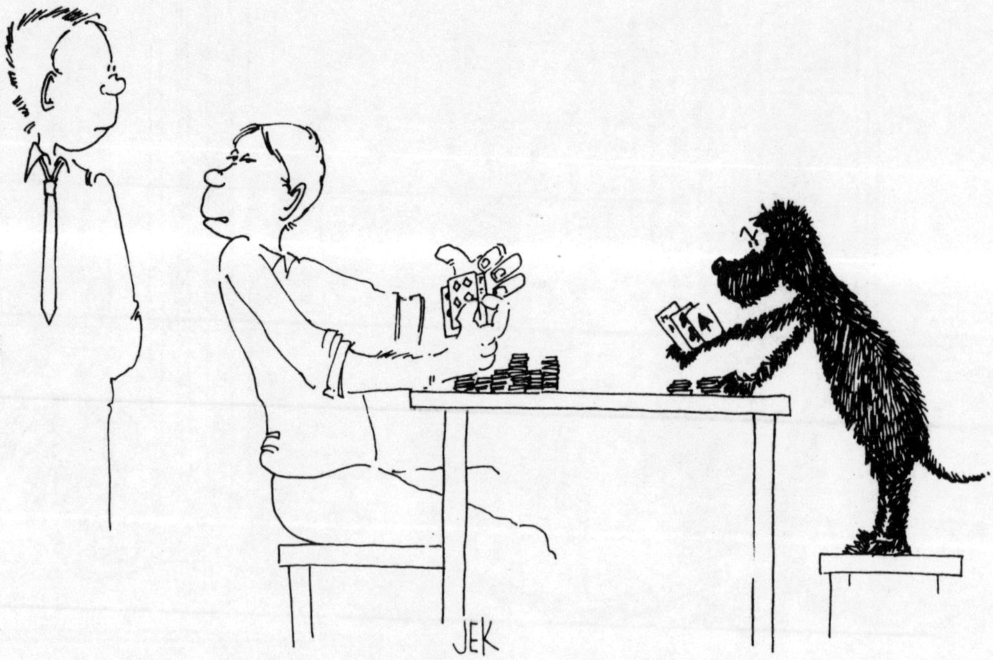
JEK

'He's not that clever. Every time he gets a good hand he wags his tail . . .'

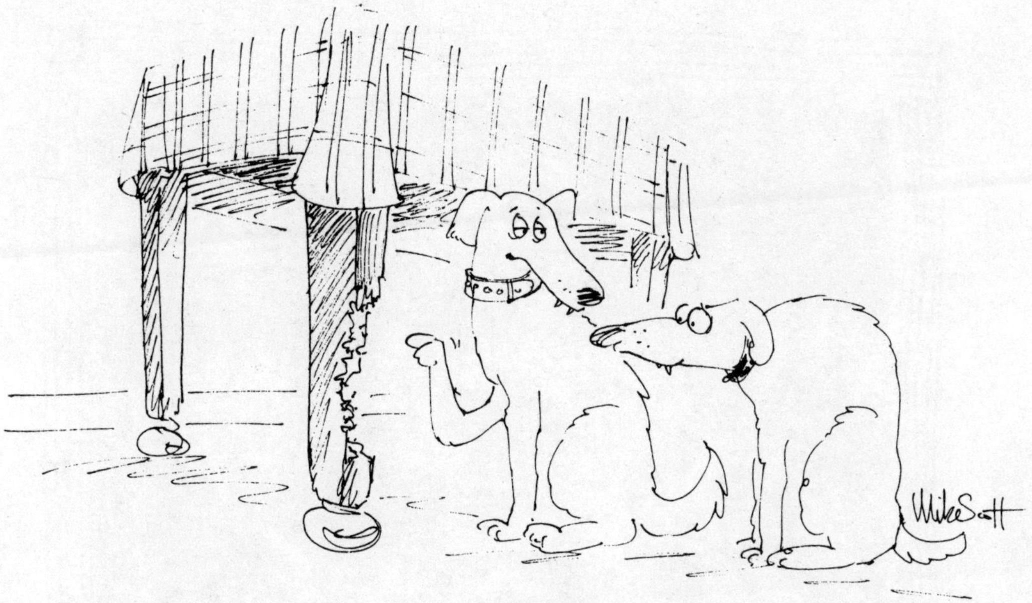
MikeScott

'This is some of my earlier work . . .'

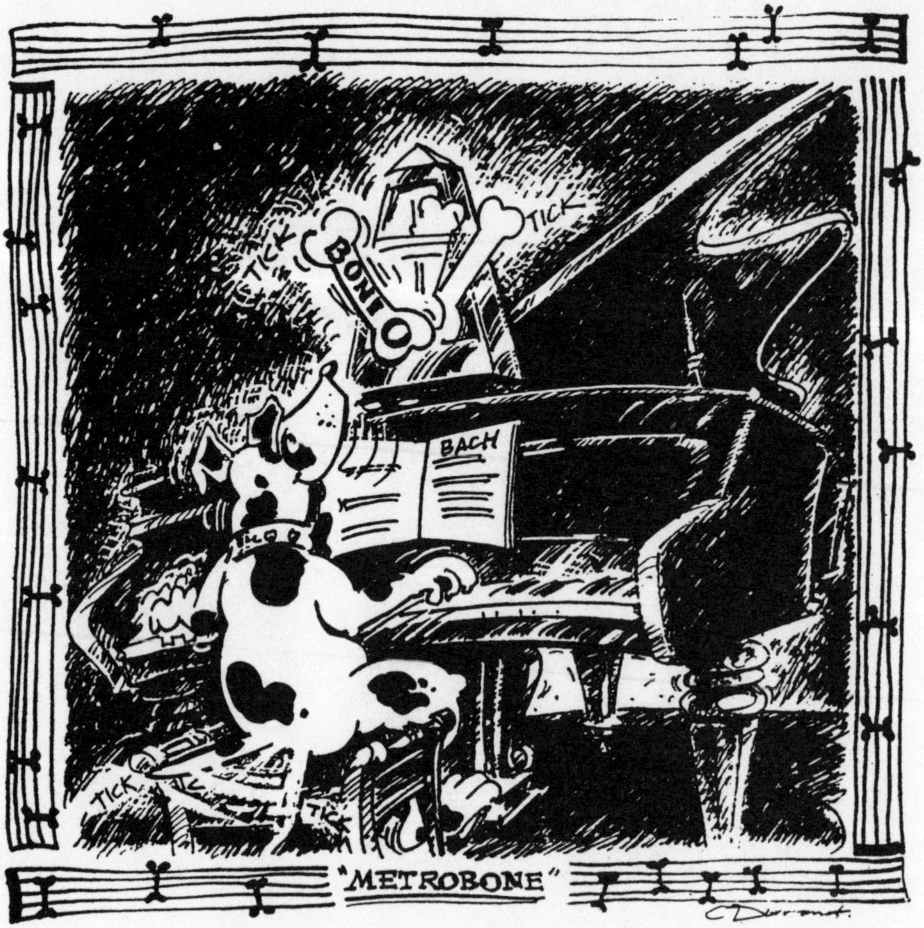
TICK
BONIO
TICK
BACH
TICK
TICK
"METROBONE"
C Durrant

WAKE UP BARNEY...
...HOME!
ROY DAVIS

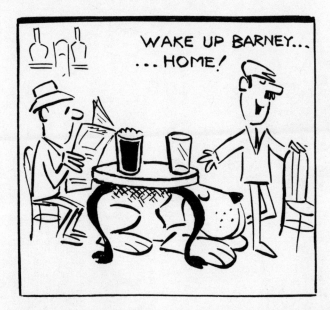

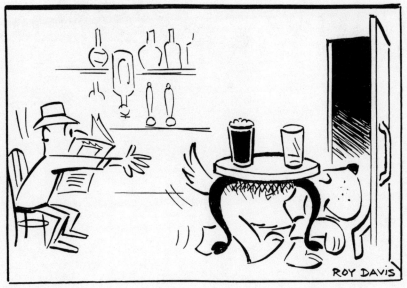

86

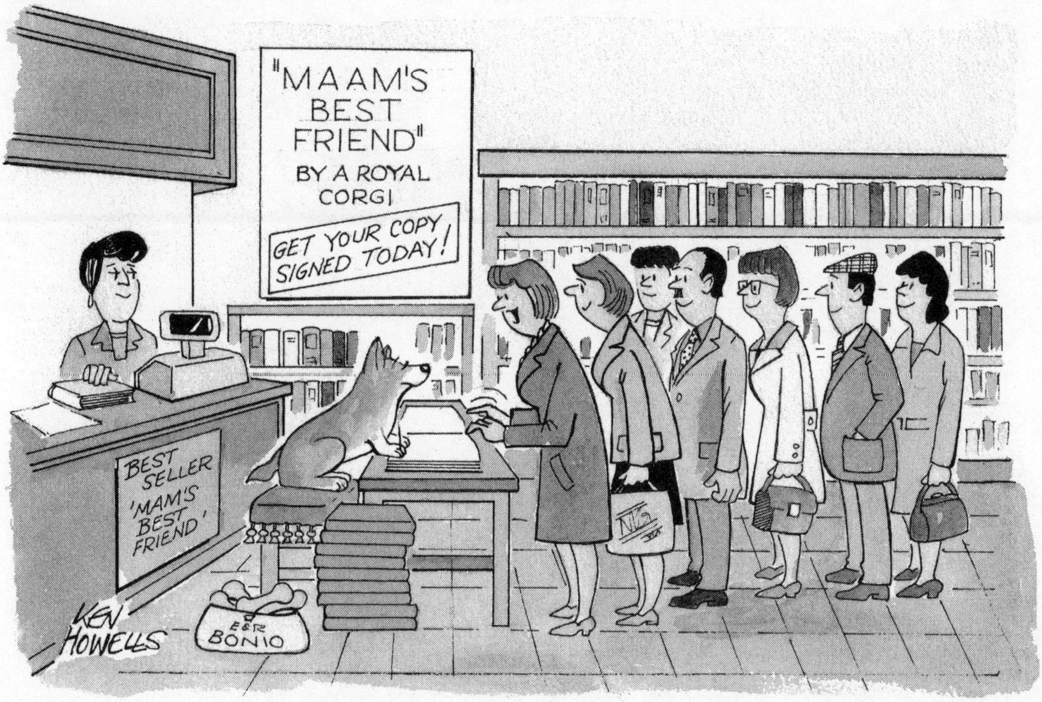
"MAAM'S BEST FRIEND"
BY A ROYAL CORGI
GET YOUR COPY SIGNED TODAY!
BEST SELLER 'MAM'S BEST FRIEND'
KEN HOWELLS
E&R
BONIO

'Would you sign it ''To Fido'' please?'

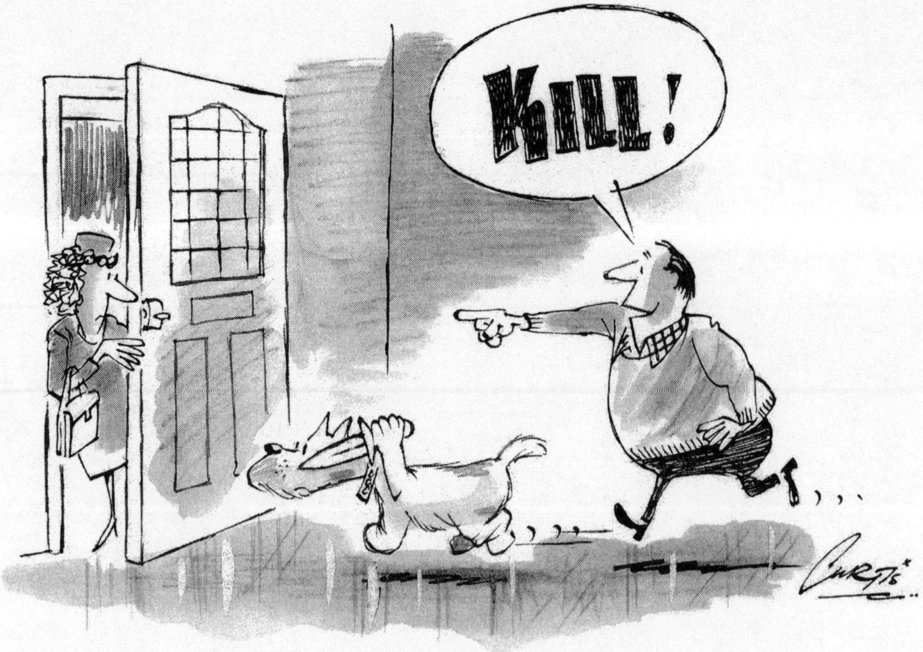
KILL!

Sophie
I HATE ALL THIS...
...MODERN TECHNOLOGY
WHATEVER HAPPENED...
...TO THAT NICE LITTLE STICK?
GASP
PANT
John Samuels

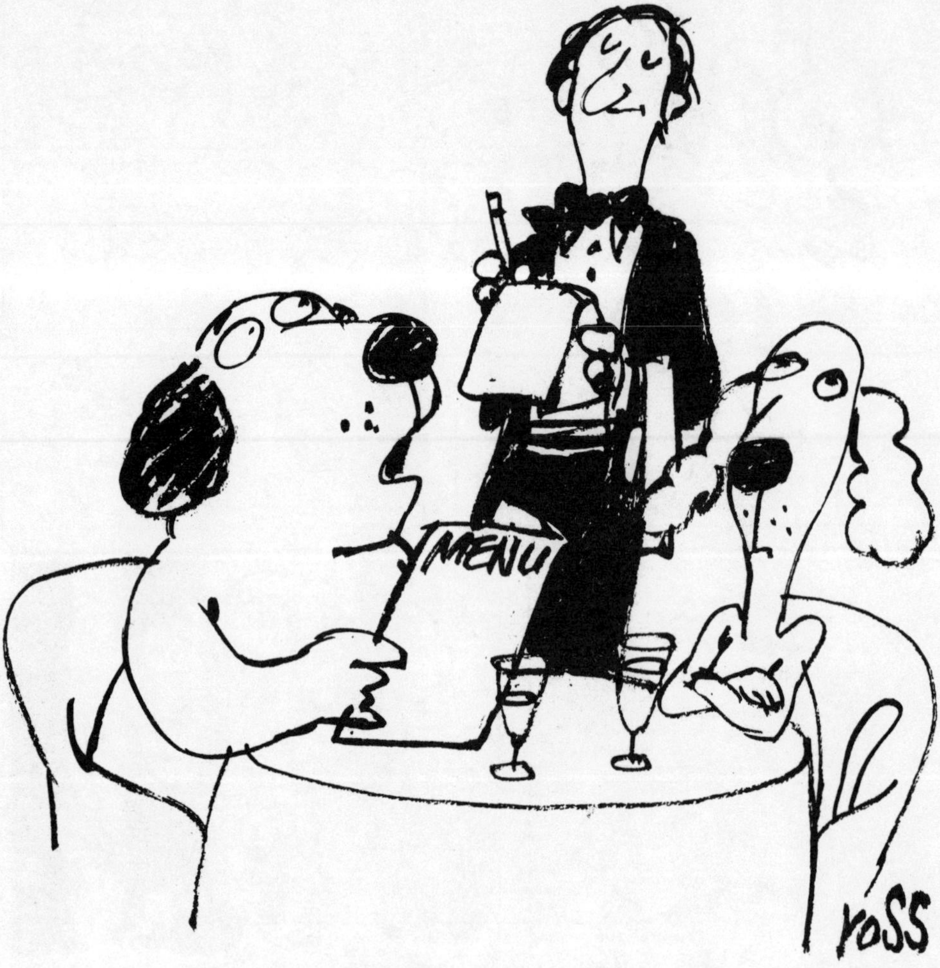
MENU
YOSS

'Two doggie-bags to eat in, please!'

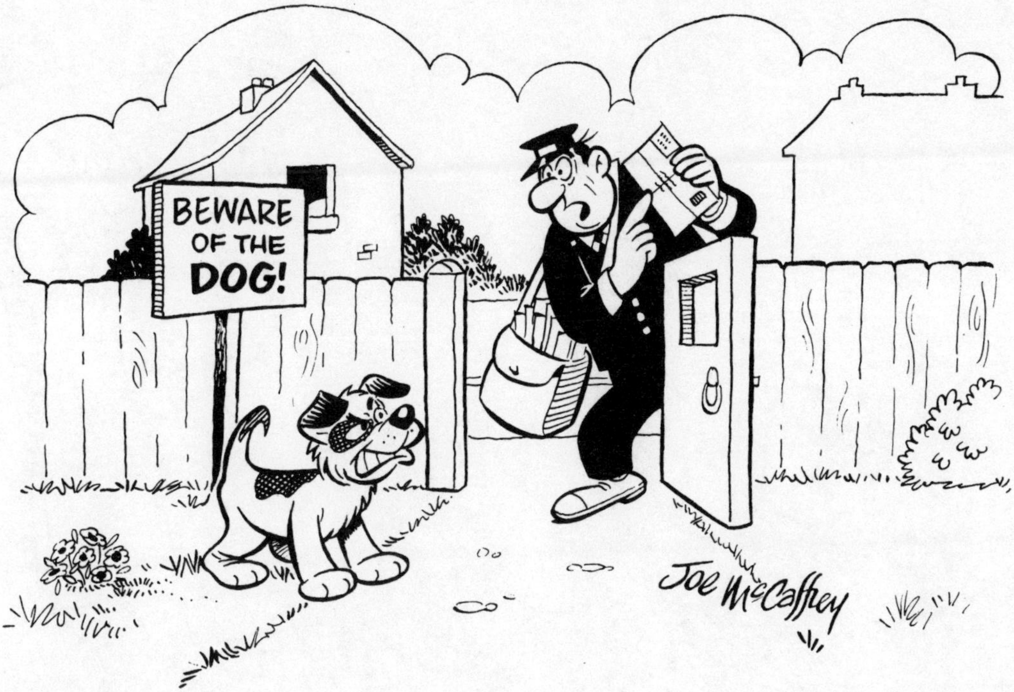
BEWARE
OF THE
DOG!
JOE McCAFFREY

'Recorded delivery – honest!'

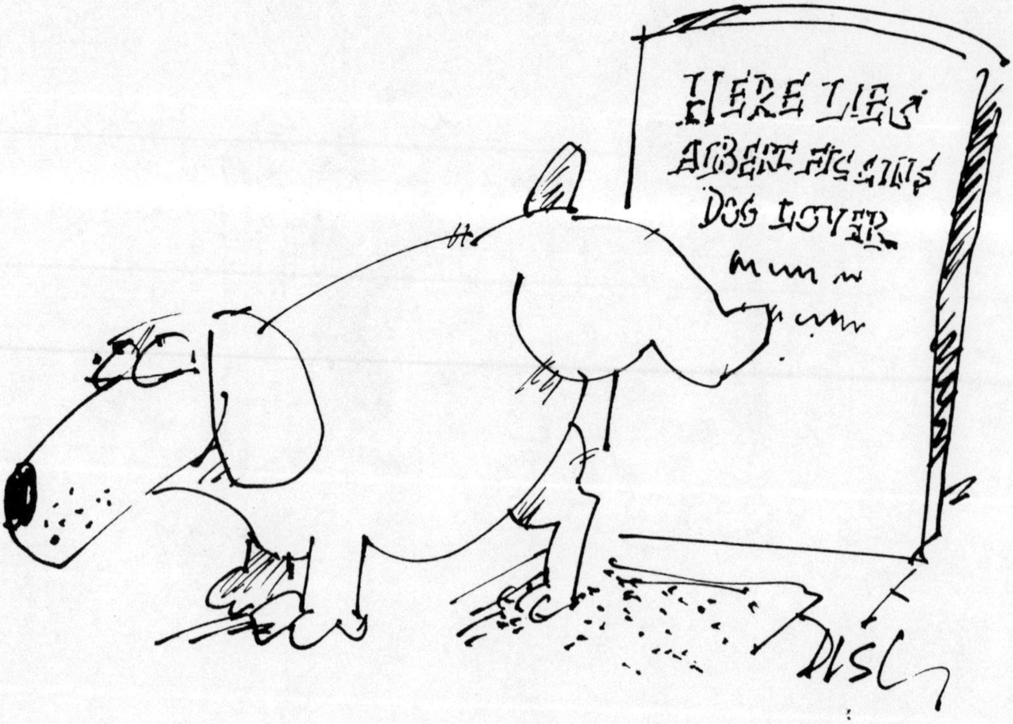
HERE LIES
ALBERT FIGGINS
DOG LOVER

'There goes another abandoned Christmas pet.'

FETCH MY SLIPPERS, BOY
FETCH 'EM YOURSELF
YOU KNOW DARLING, I THINK THE OLD BOY'S GOING DEAF. MAYBE I SHOULD TAKE HIM TO THE VET'S
IT ALWAYS WORKS . . .

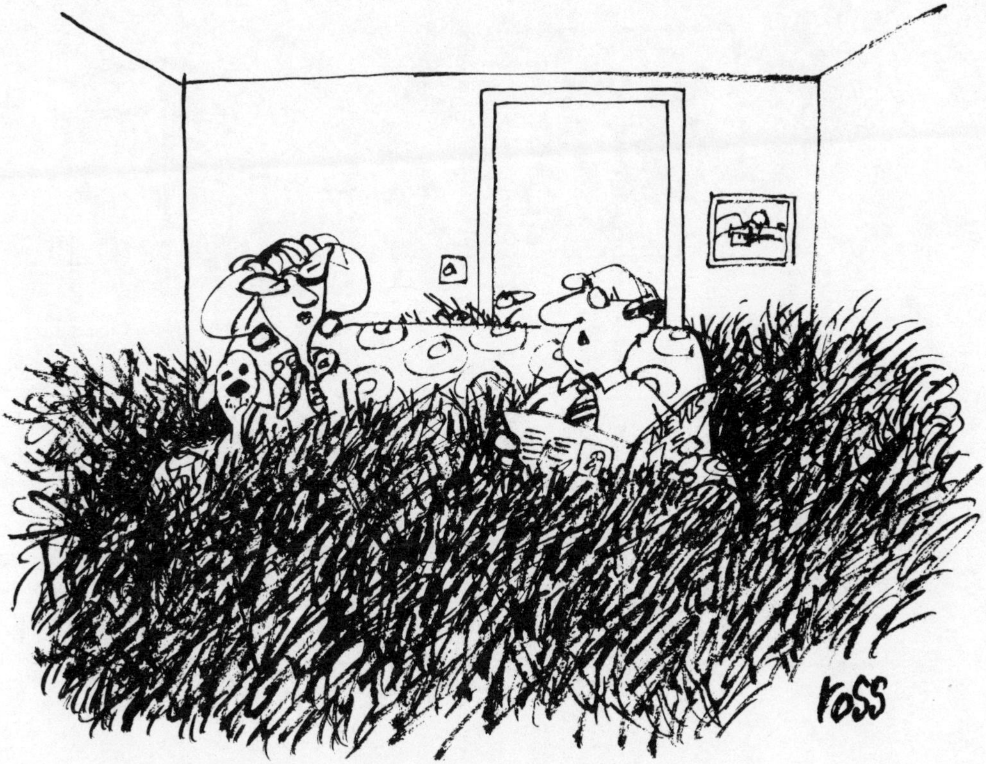
ross

'Surely she's finished moulting now!'

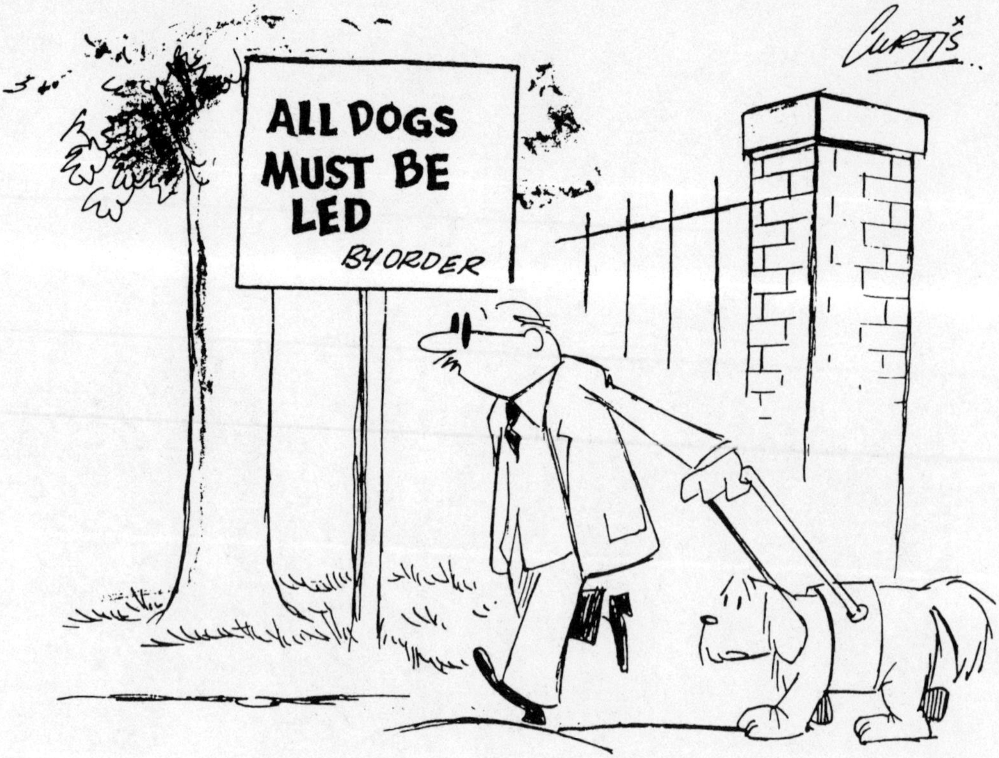
ALL DOGS
MUST BE
LED
BY ORDER
CURTIS

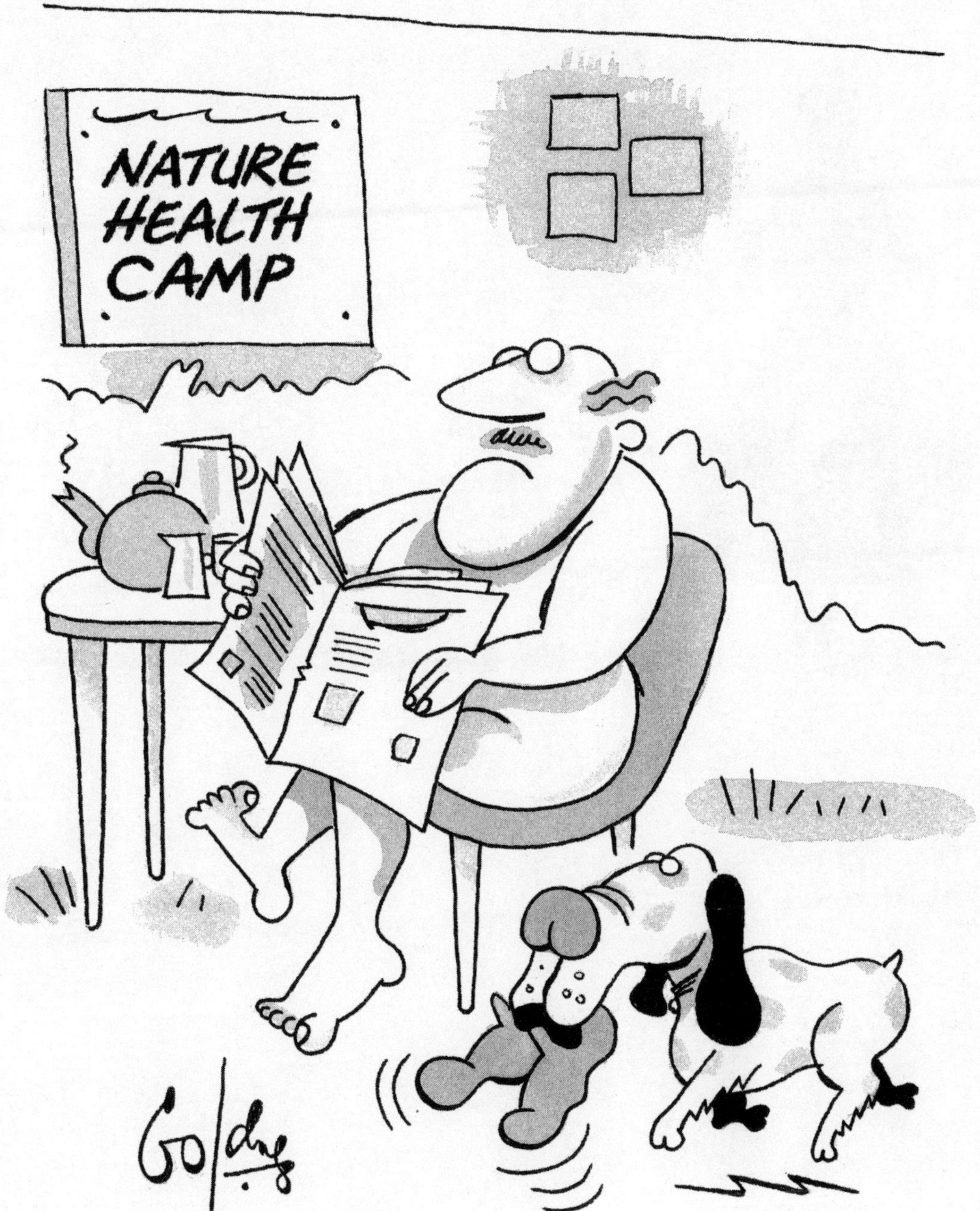
NATURE
HEALTH
CAMP

COMBi

98

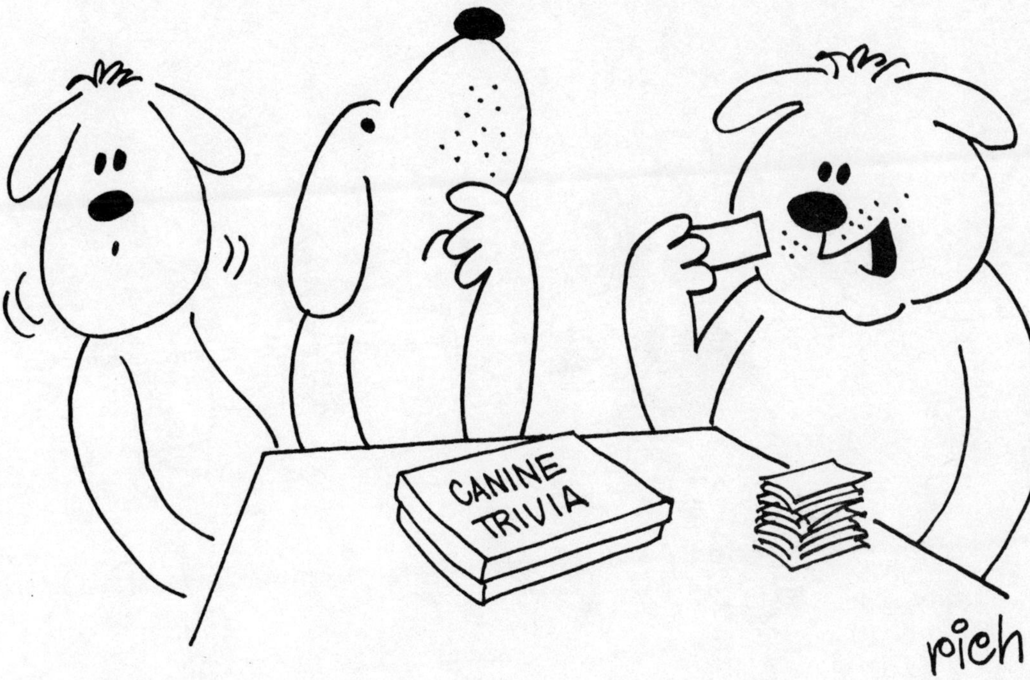
CANINE
TRIVIA
rich

'Films . . . who played the part of Lassie?'

'Brother Dominic, don't you ever tire of gimmicks?'

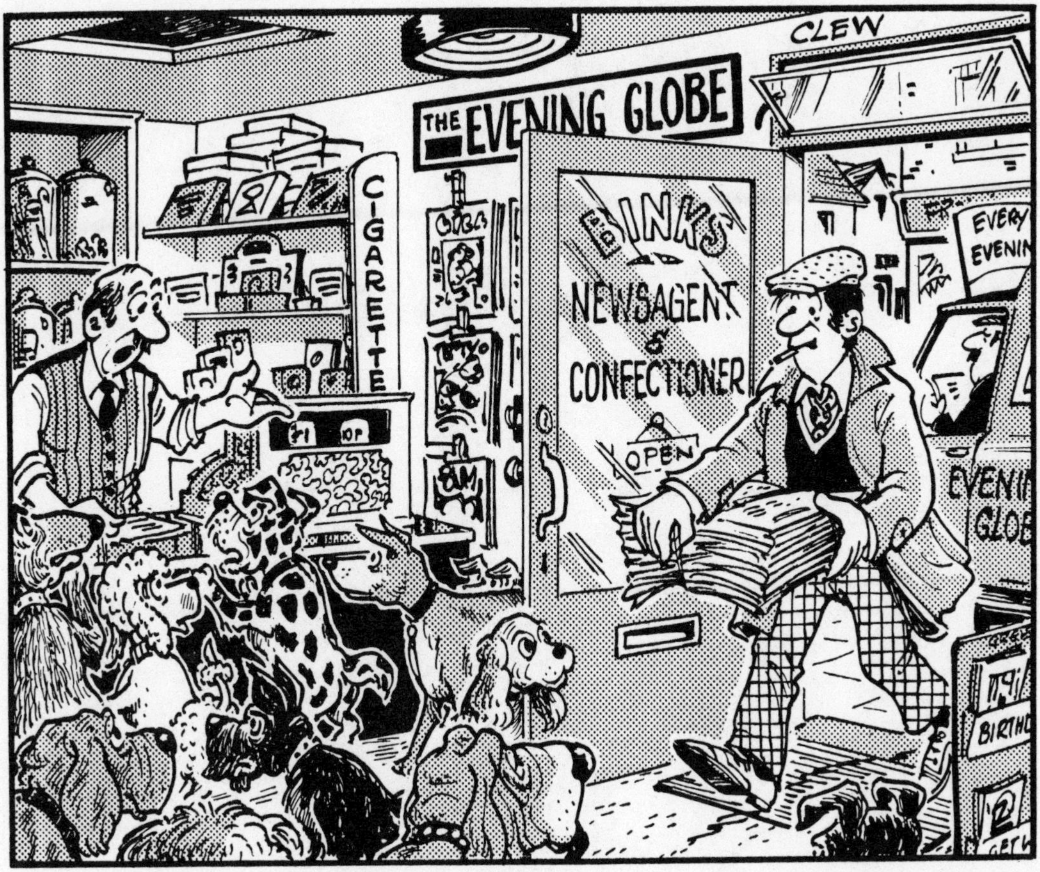
CLEW
THE EVENING GLOBE
BINKS
NEWSAGENT & CONFECTIONER
OPEN

'Thank goodness you're here – the customers are getting restless!'

WE'VE HAD A FEW TOO MANY THIS EVENING...
I LOST COUNT OF HOW MANY PINTS OF BITTER HE HAD...
...BUT I DRANK AT LEAST FOUR ASHTRAYS FULL!
© Dave Follows

'I said slippers, not kippers.'

'Six hours sitting in this and we have to be rescued by a bloody dog trained on
British licensing hours!'

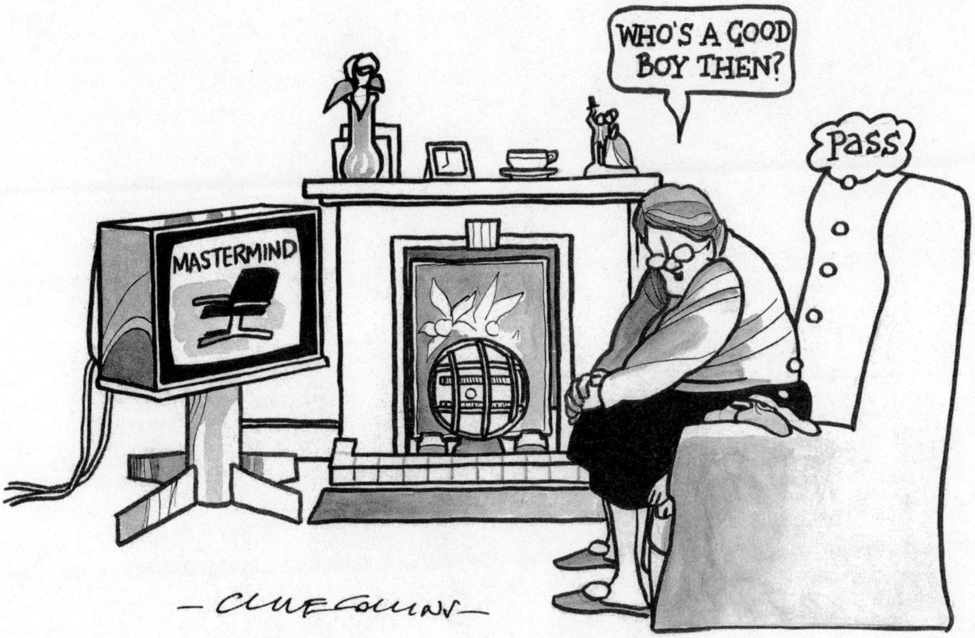
WHO'S A GOOD BOY THEN?
Pass
MASTERMIND

'Sorry, she's part lurcher . . .'

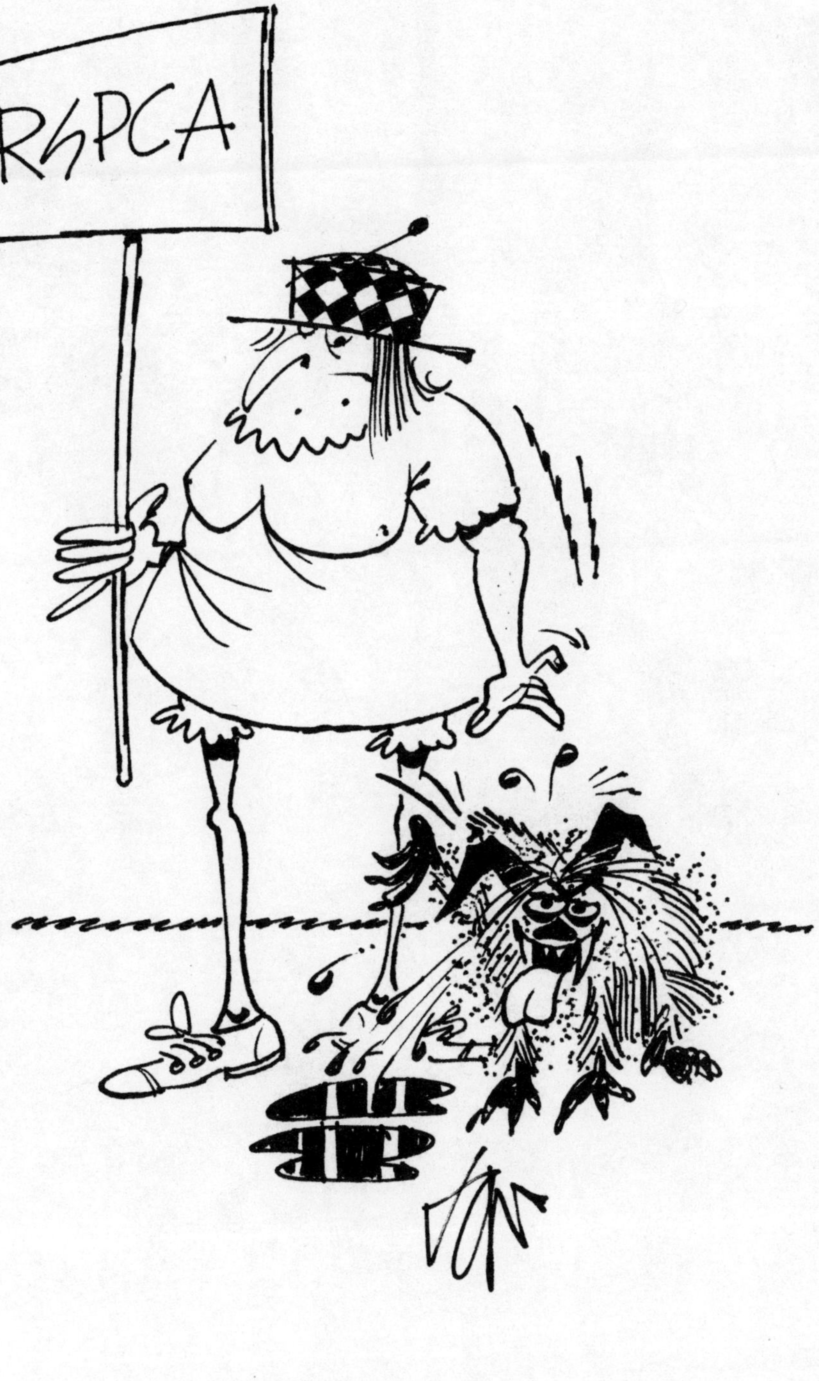
RSPCA

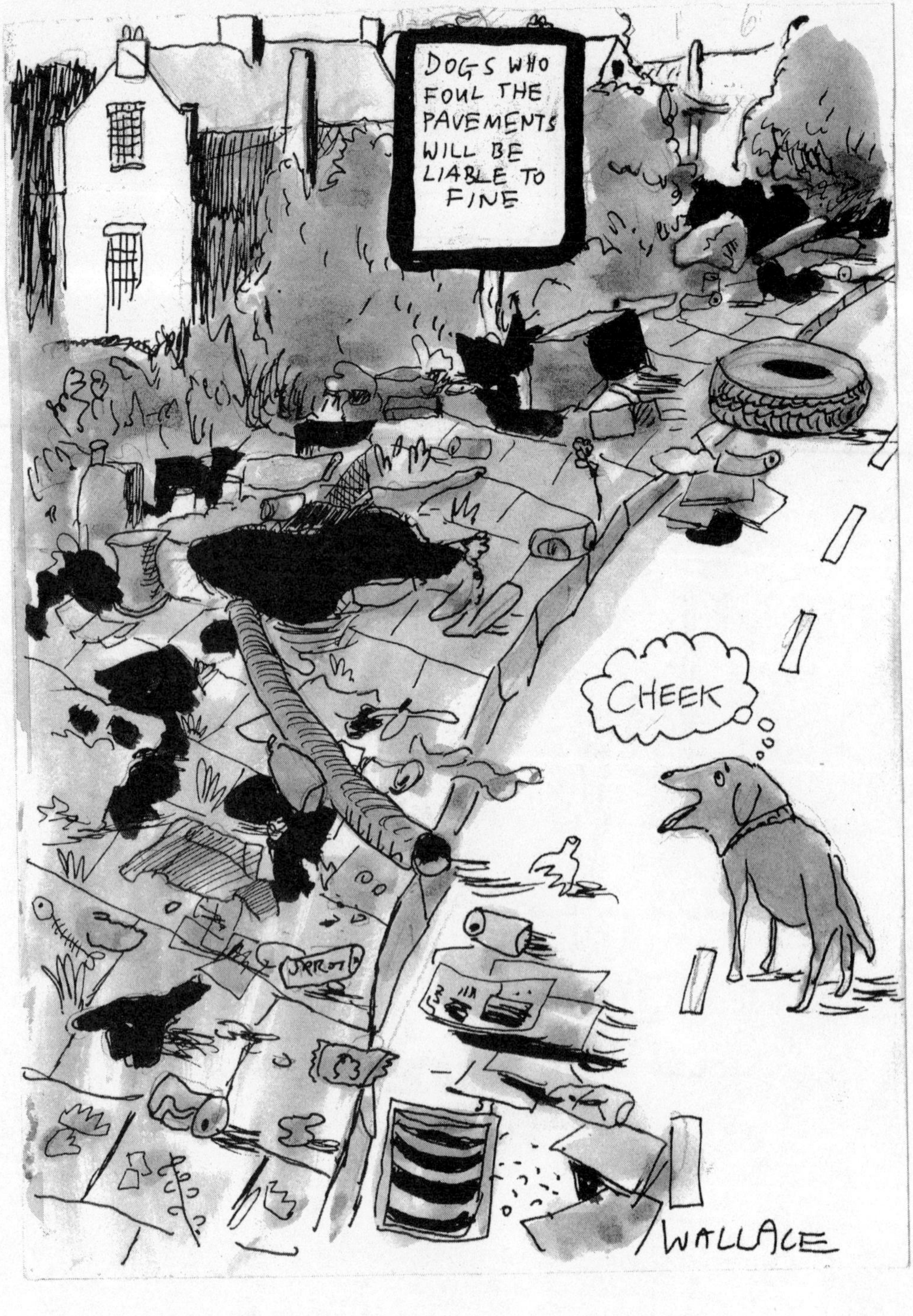
DOGS WHO FOUL THE PAVEMENTS WILL BE LIABLE TO FINE
CHEEK
WALLACE

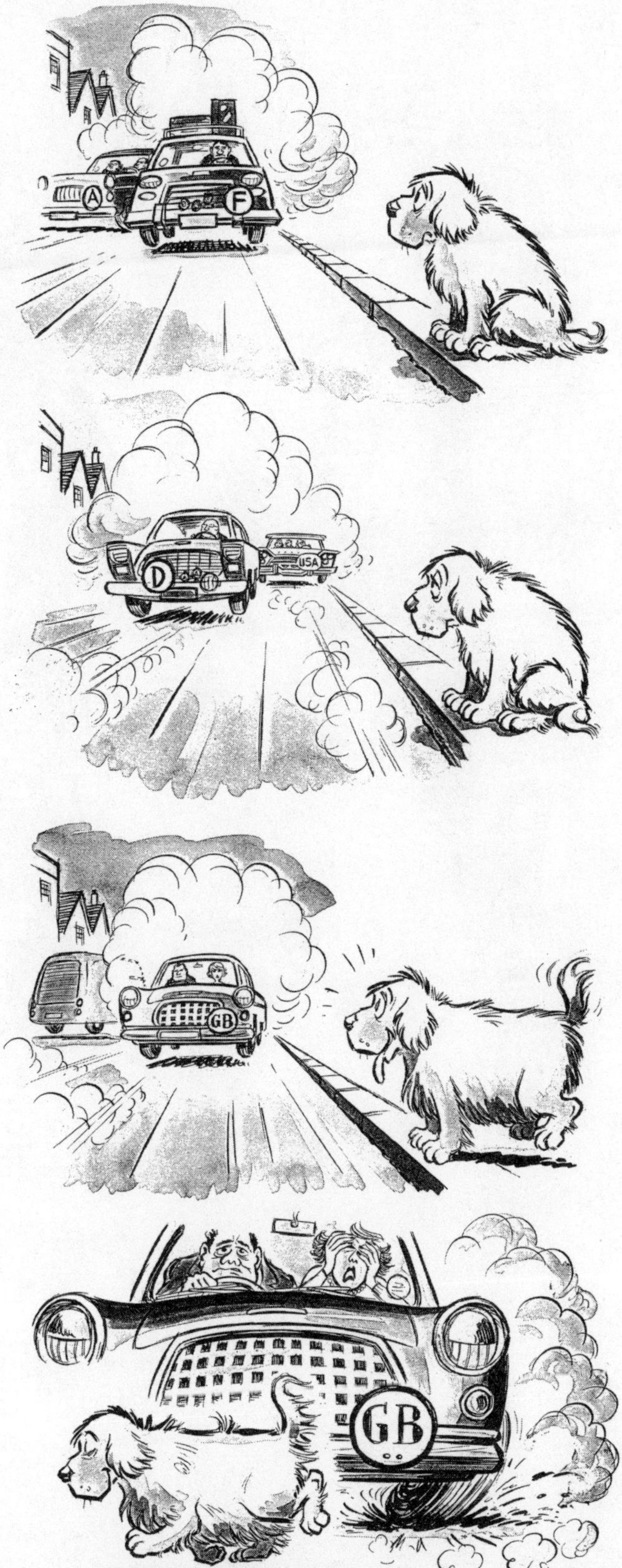
A
F
D
USA
GB
GB

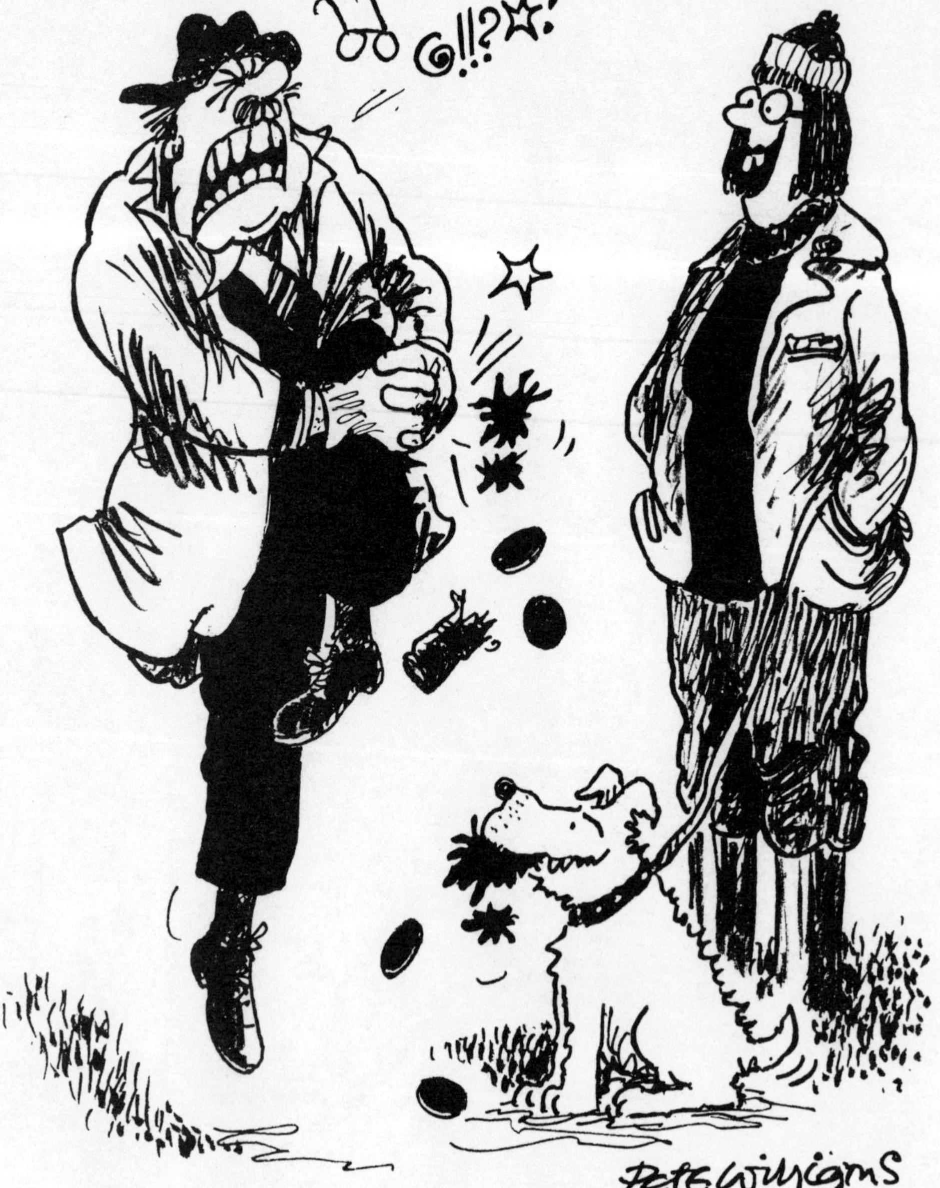
PETE WILLIAMS

'That was rather silly – he *hates* chocolate biscuits!'

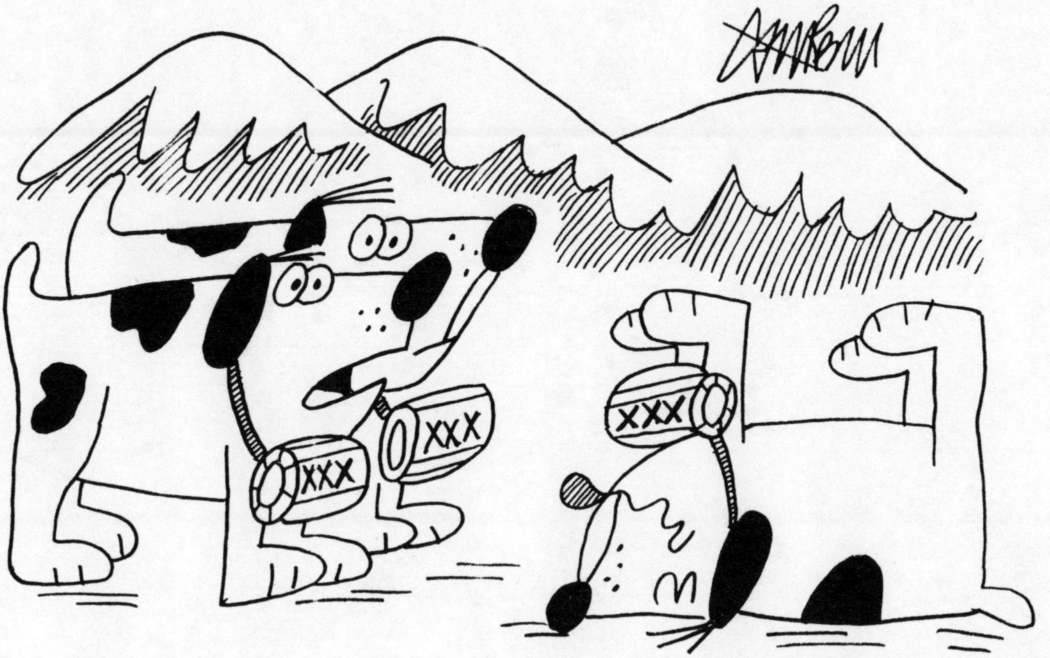
XXX
XXX
XXX
XXX

'Of course, drink ruined him as a rescue dog.'

'Hello, another flash bugger with satellite TV!'

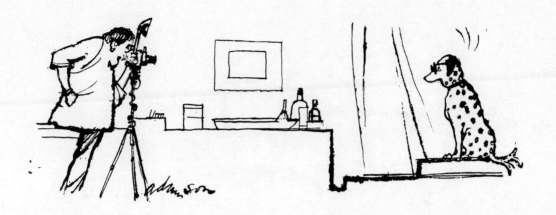

'All right, wear them if they prevent red-eye.'

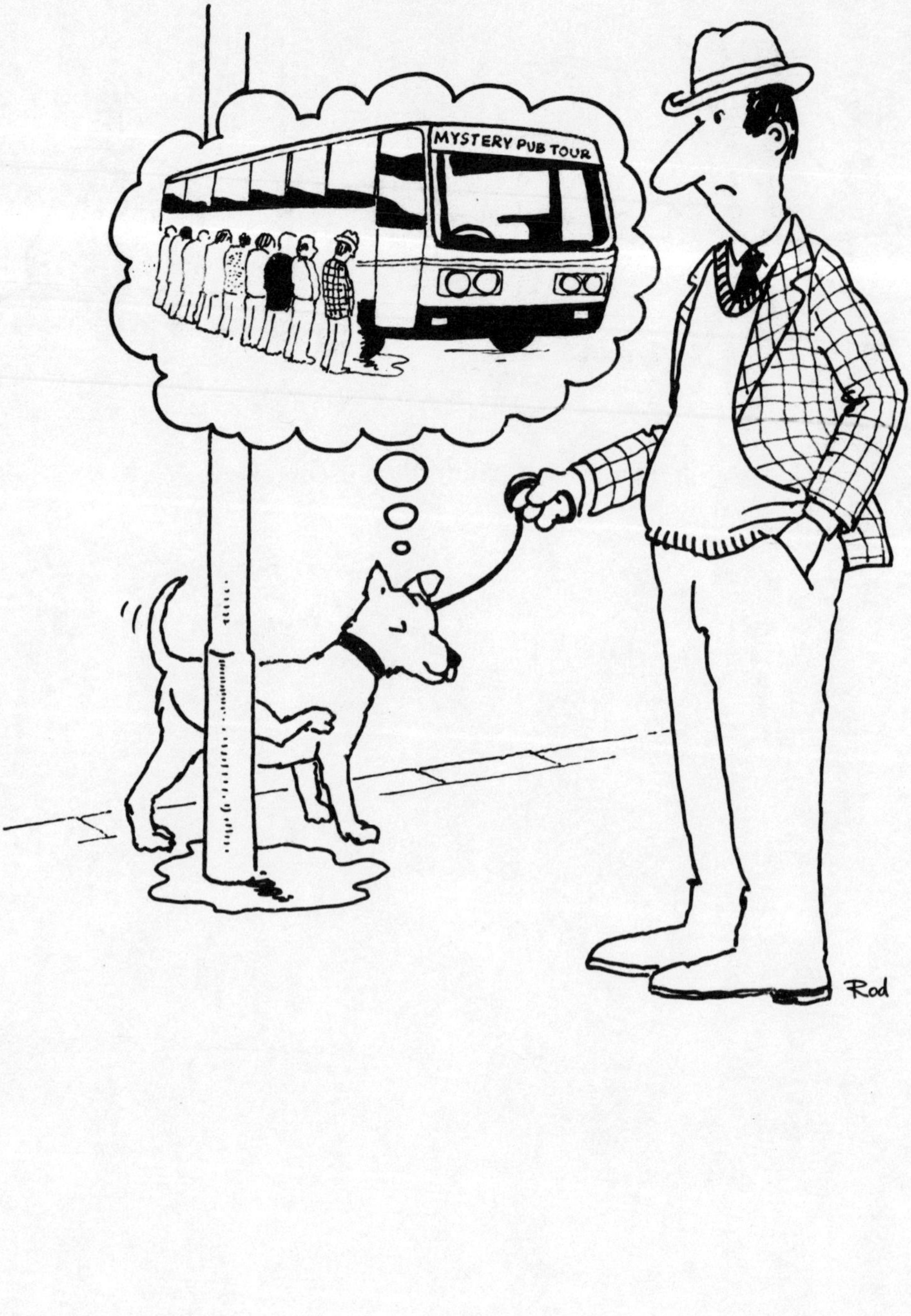
MYSTERY PUB TOUR
Rod

YOU'RE GOING TO THROW THE BALL, AND FRED'S GOING TO CATCH IT IN HIS MOUTH, ISN'T HE ?
Not THAT old trick!
MY SPANIEL CAN DO THIS TRICK
ANY dog can catch a ball in his mouth
But I bet his spaniel can't do THIS!
2-19
GRAHAM

'Gee, for a bunch of social outcasts, they certainly cope amazingly well.'

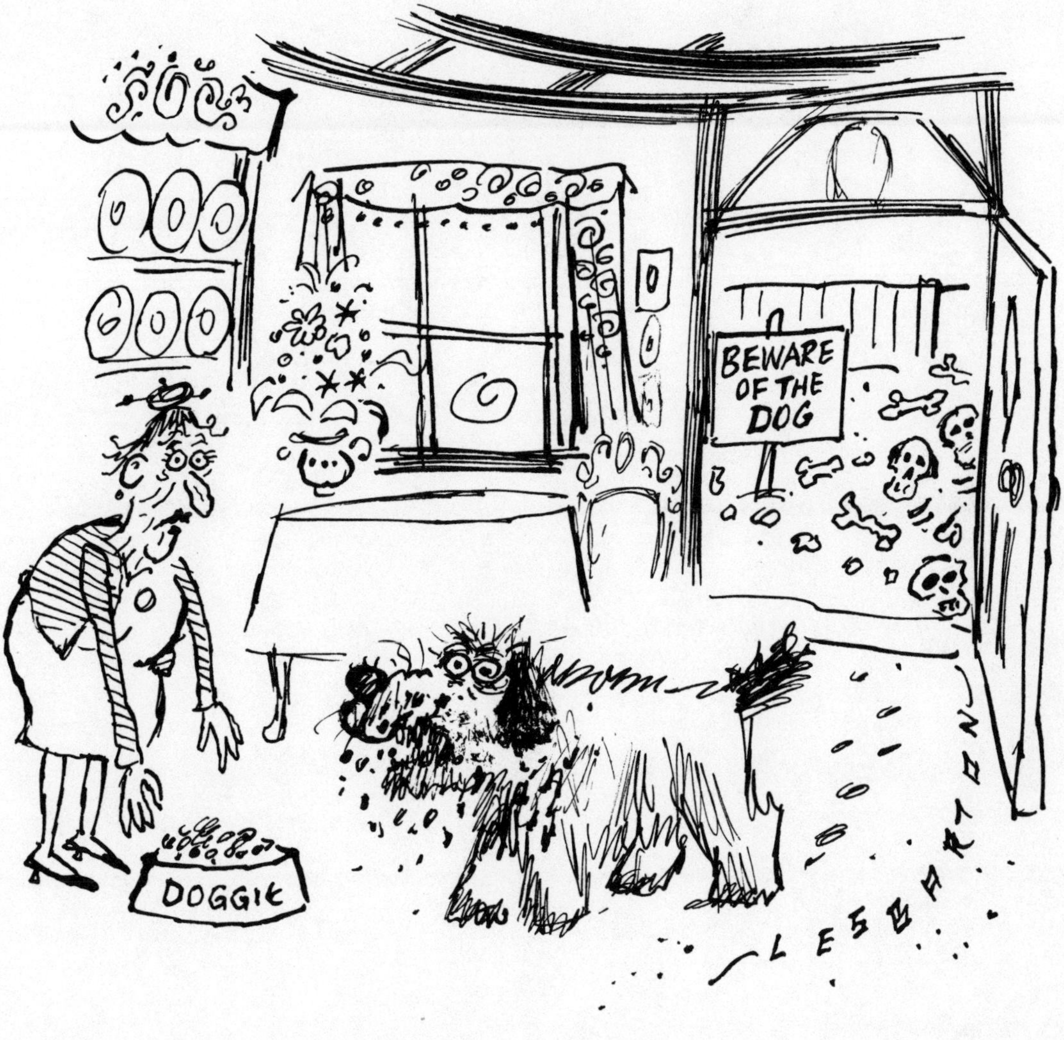
BEWARE
OF THE
DOG
DOGGIE
LEE BARTON

'Sorry I'm late, pressure of work!'

'You're right, the red-and-black ones *are* poisonous . . .'

Chipper
THIS IS RIDICULOUS! MY LUNCH IS GETTING SOAKING WET
PUT THE LUNCH INSIDE YOUR KENNEL YOU IDIOT
CHOMP, SLURP. CHOMP!
WHY DIDN'T I THINK OF THAT?
HE'S THE IDIOT, THIS IS EVEN WORSE. NOW I'M GETTING SOAKING WET!
BELL
6903

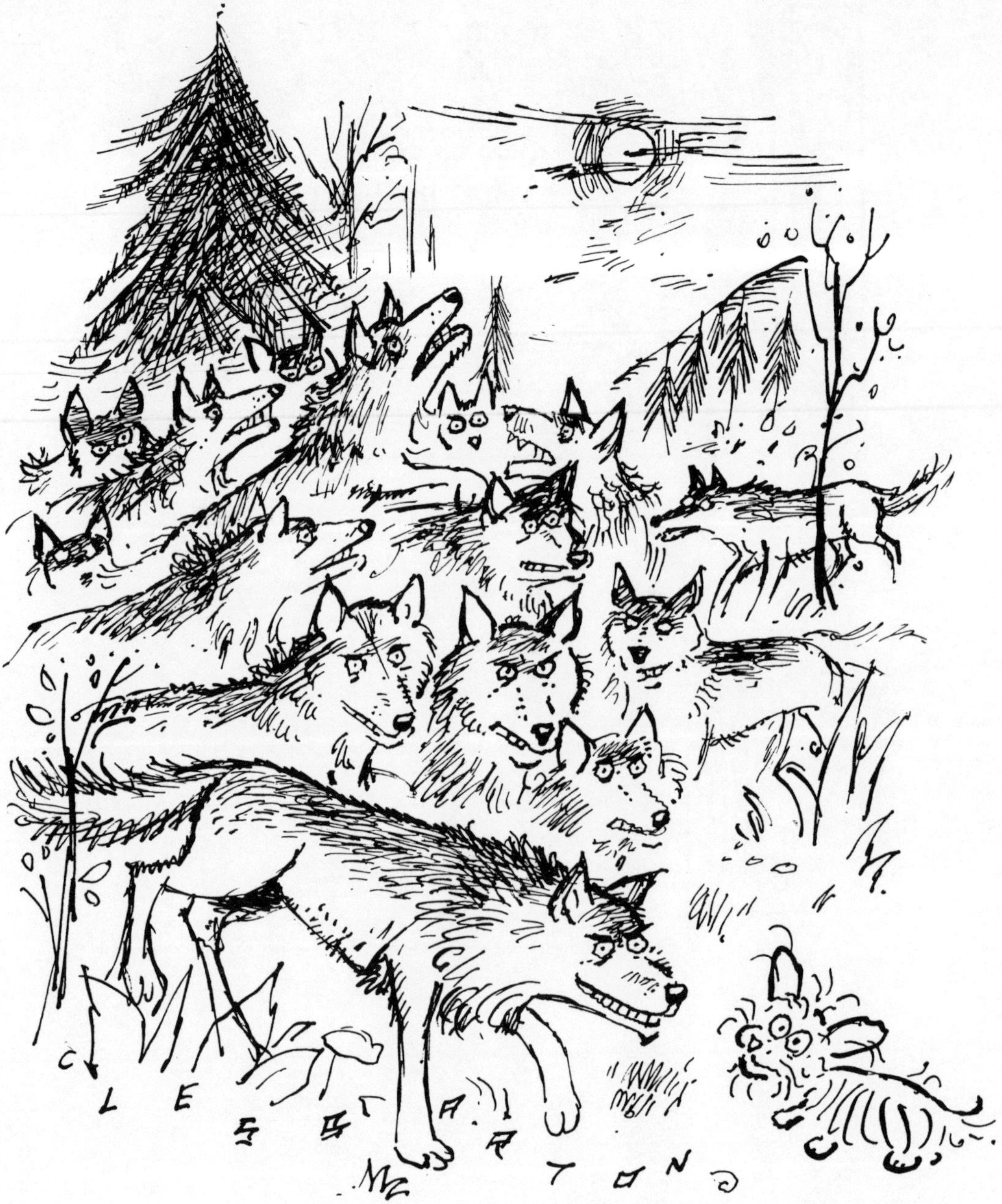

'I hope you can join us. We need a joker to complete the pack!'

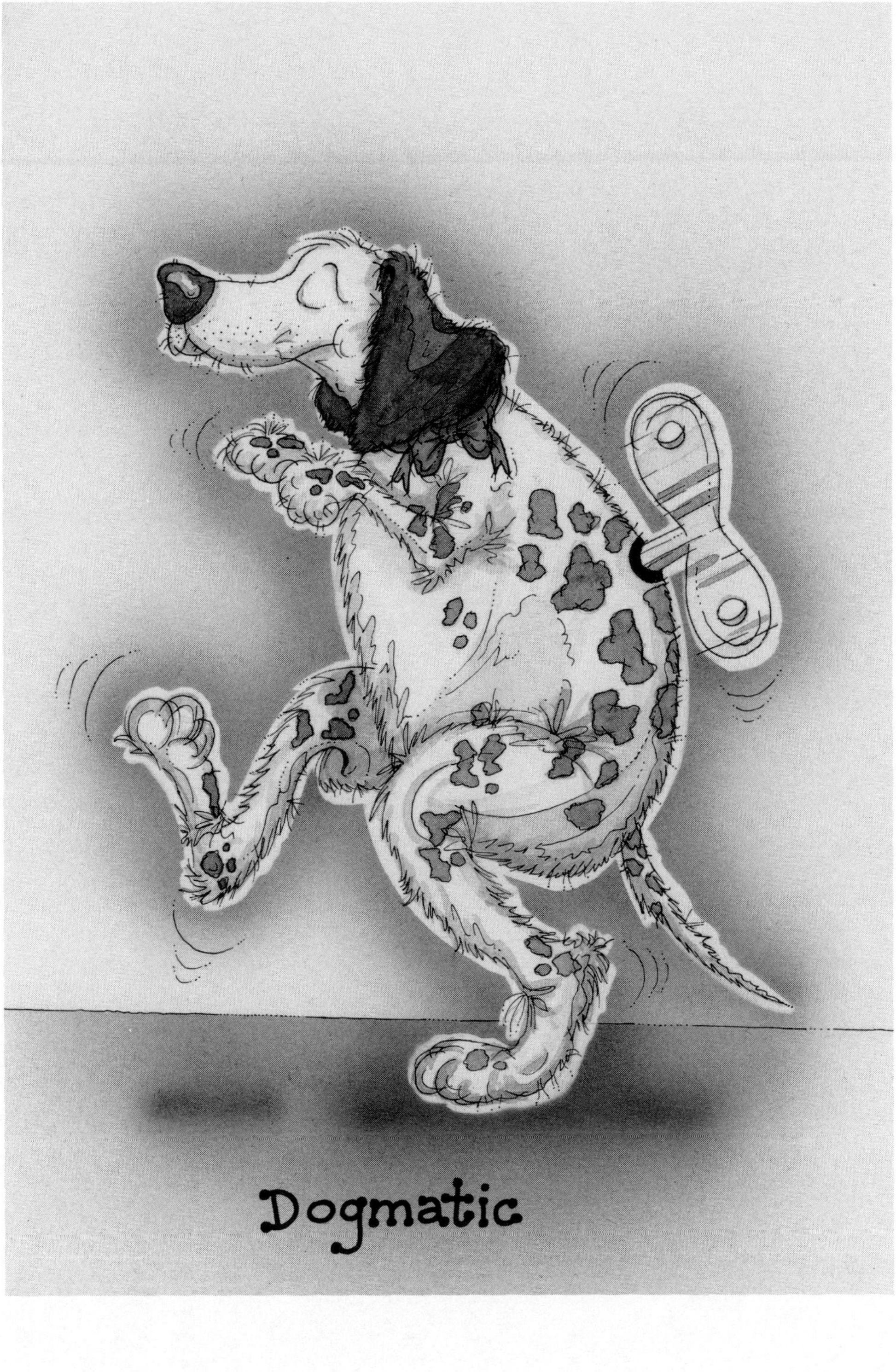
Dogmatic

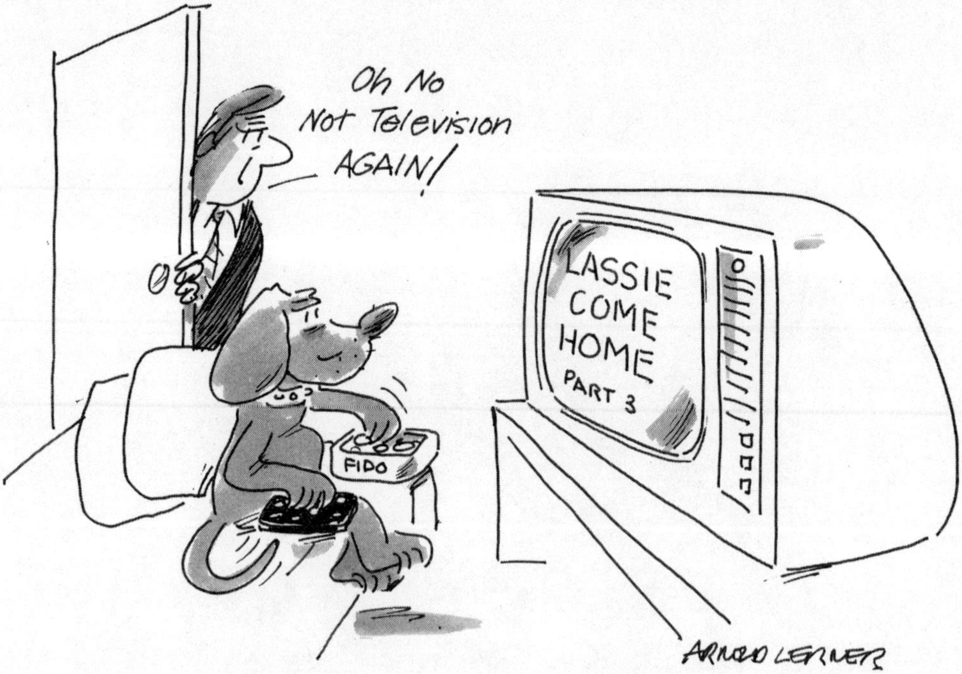
Oh No
Not Television
AGAIN!
LASSIE
COME
HOME
PART 3
FIDO
ARNOLD LERNER

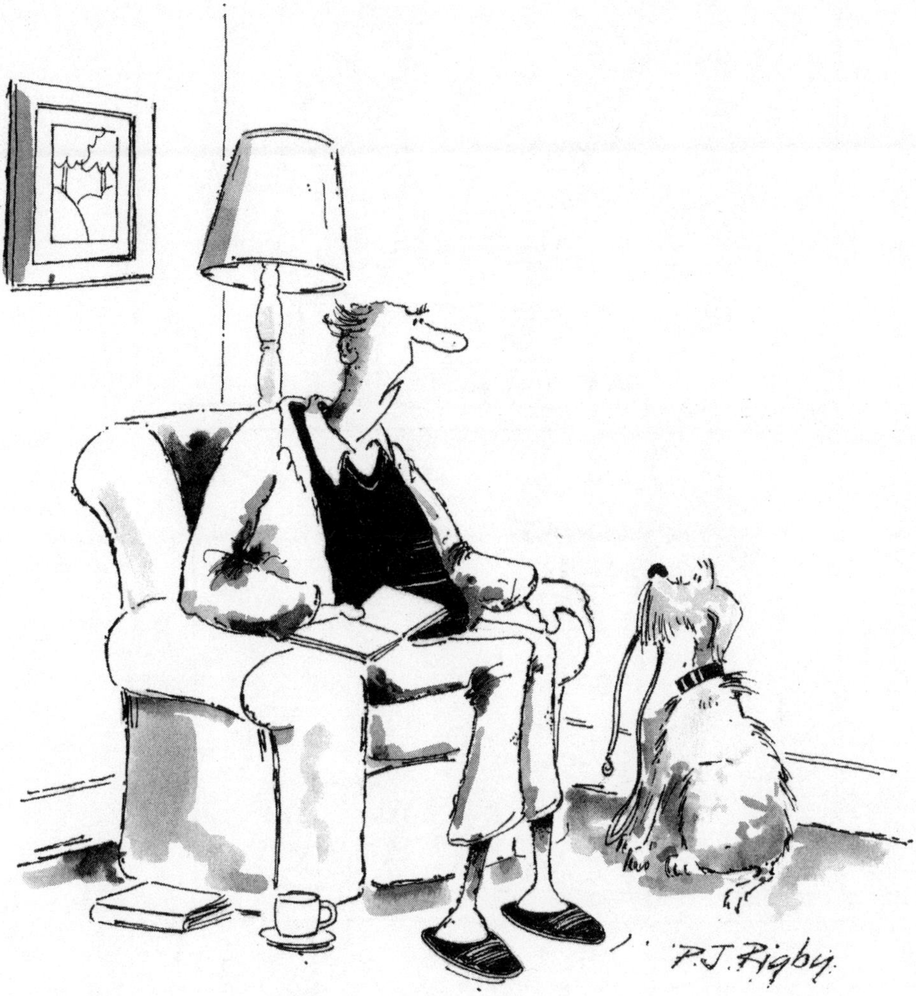
P.J. Rigby

'Oh, all right. There's no need for that "A dog is for life – not just for Christmas" look of yours.'

HE YOURS?
YEP
LOOKS ALMOST CANINE!
?
HARF
HARF
HARF
HARF
HARF

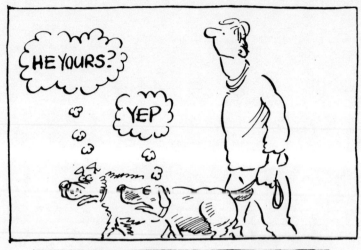

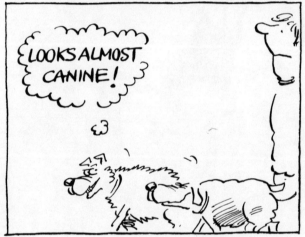

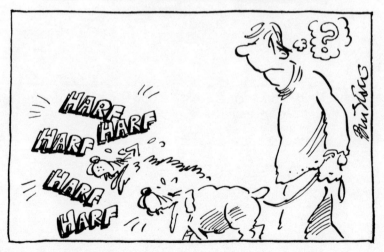

'I don't know why she can't just go into heat like any other bitch!'

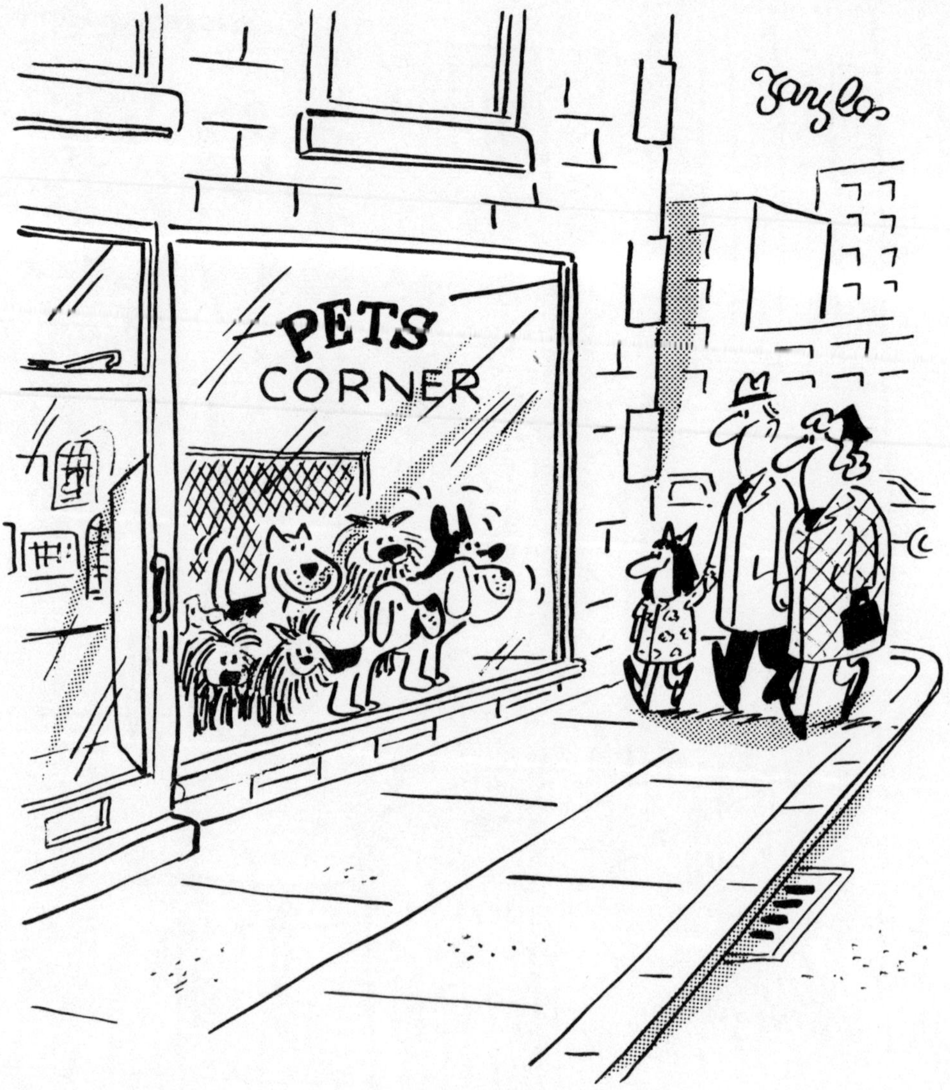
PETS
CORNER

'OK everybody, smiles all round. This is their seventh time around the block this morning!'

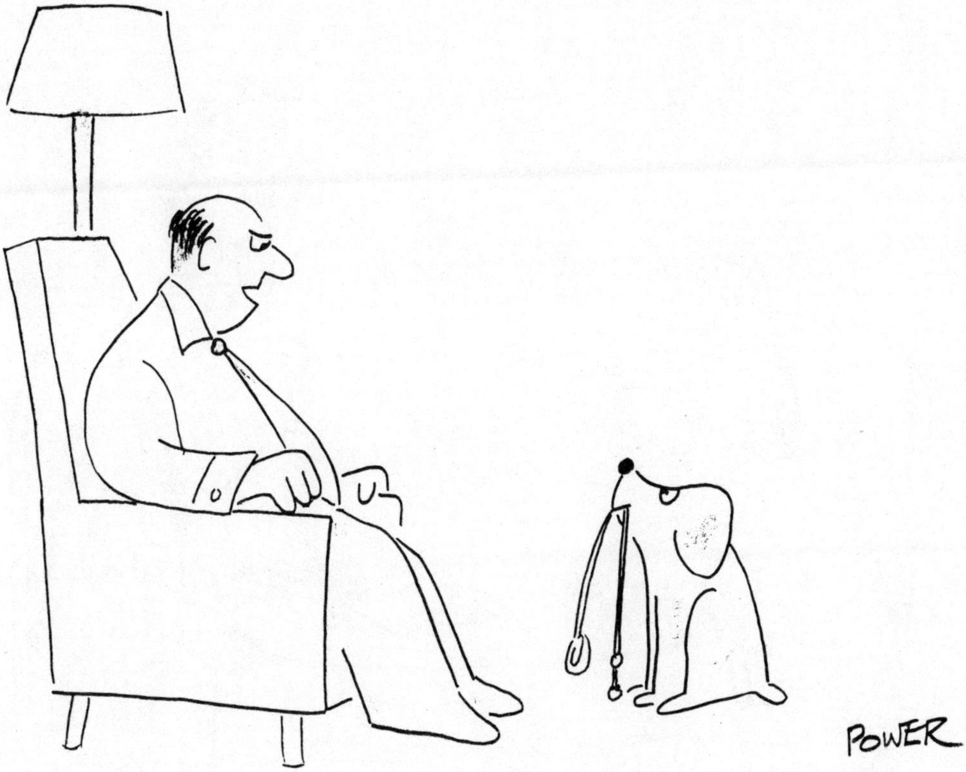
POWER

'*I'll* decide when we go walkies!'

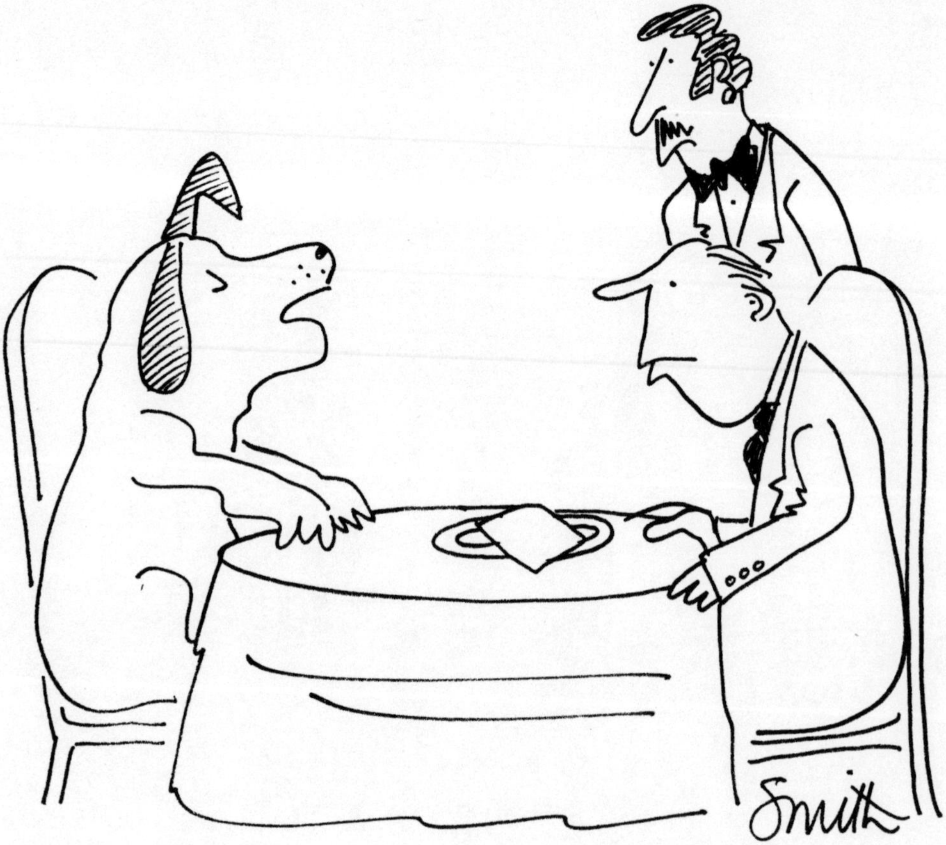
Smith

'*You* said I was your best friend. *I* didn't. *You* pay the bill.'

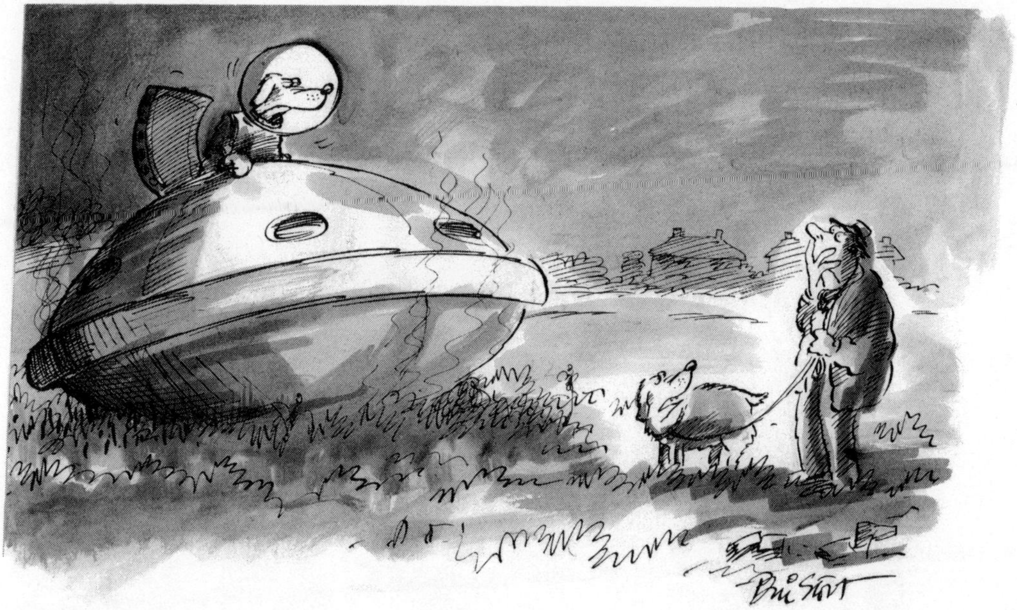
Bri Starr

'Oh no! Don't tell me I ate all the chocolate drops!'

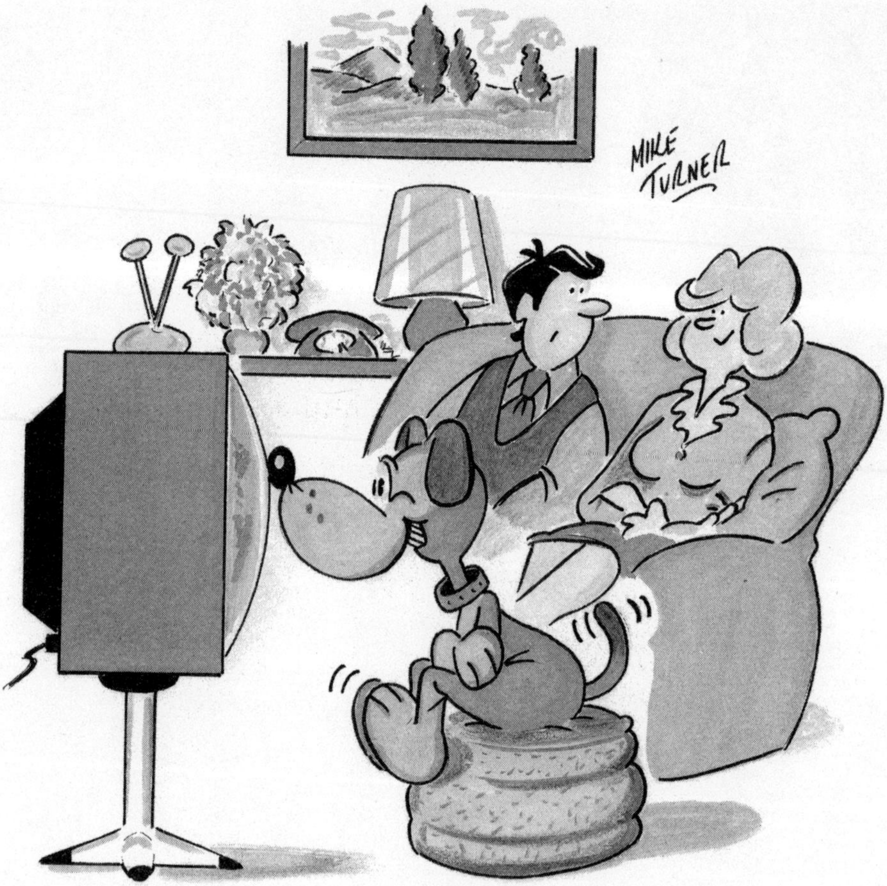
MIKE TURNER

'Call him a watchdog! The place could be ransacked when *One Man and His Dog* is on the telly!'

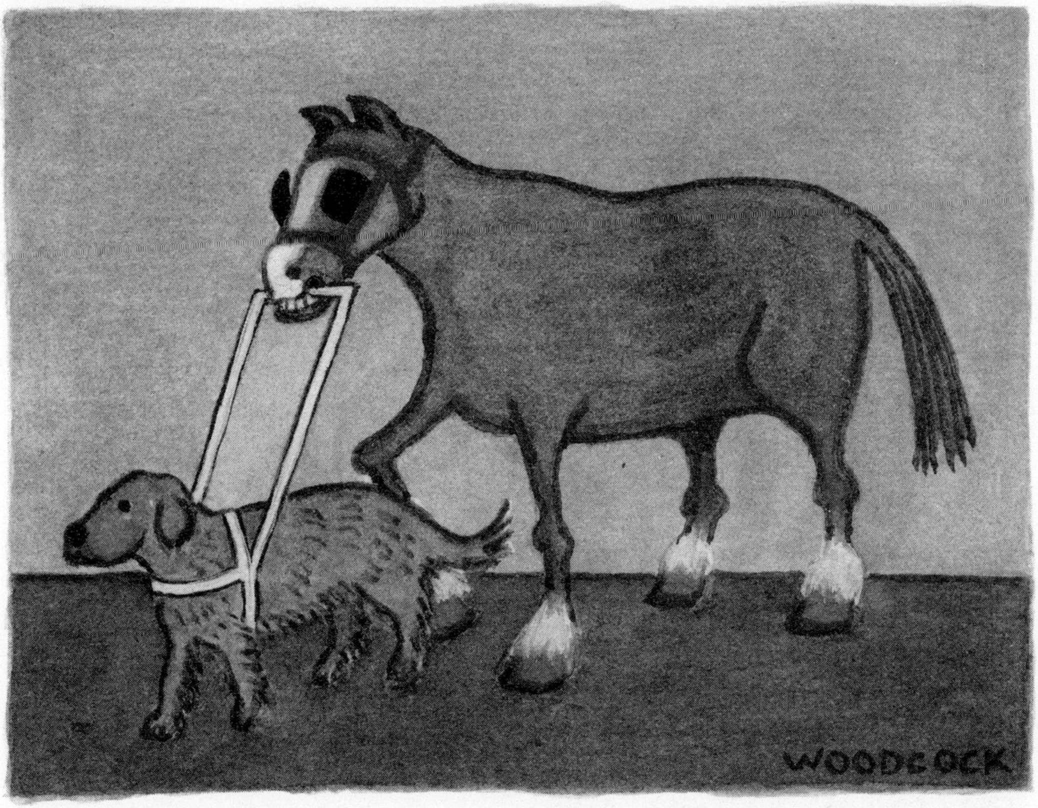
WOODCOCK

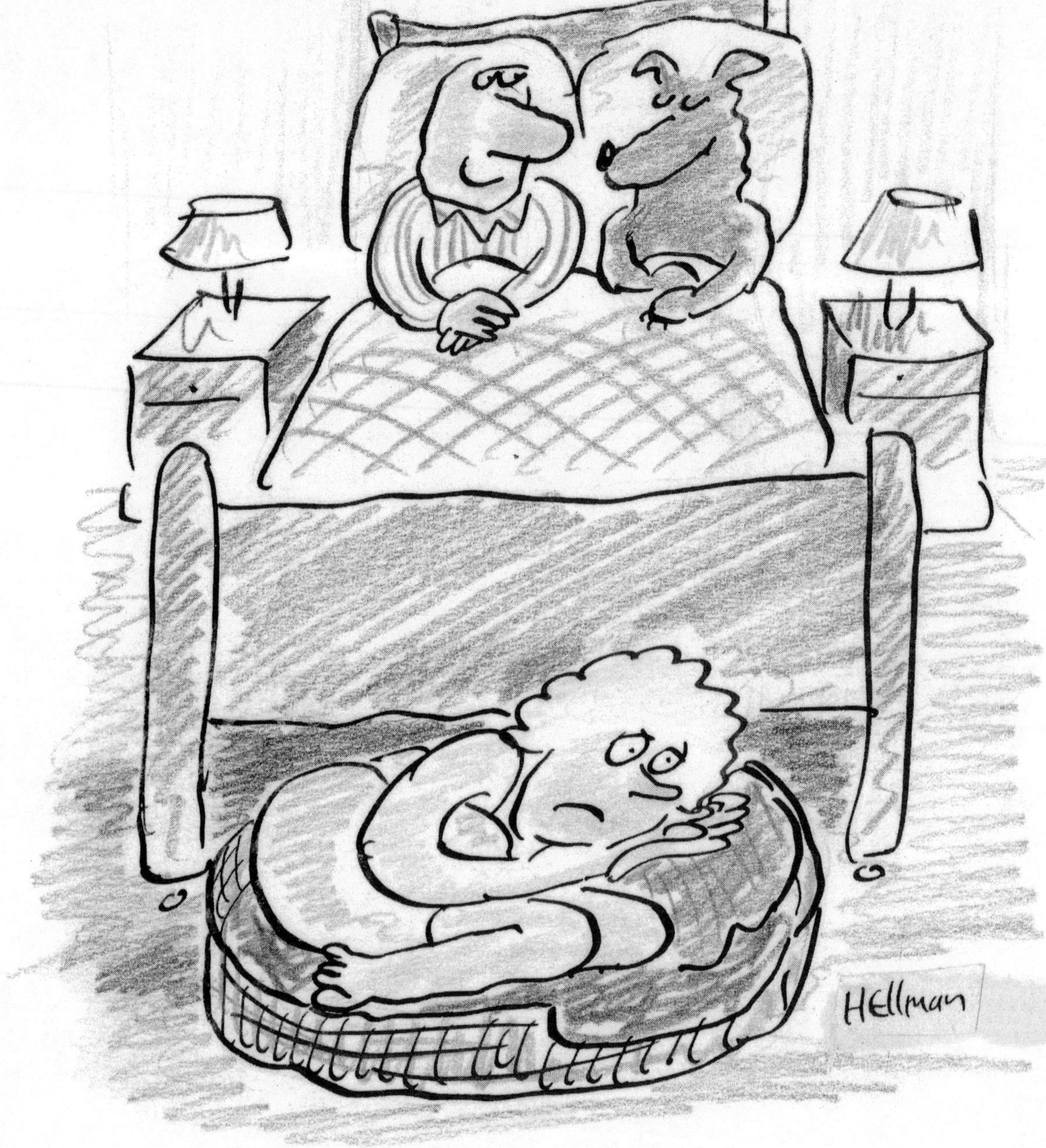
HELLMAN

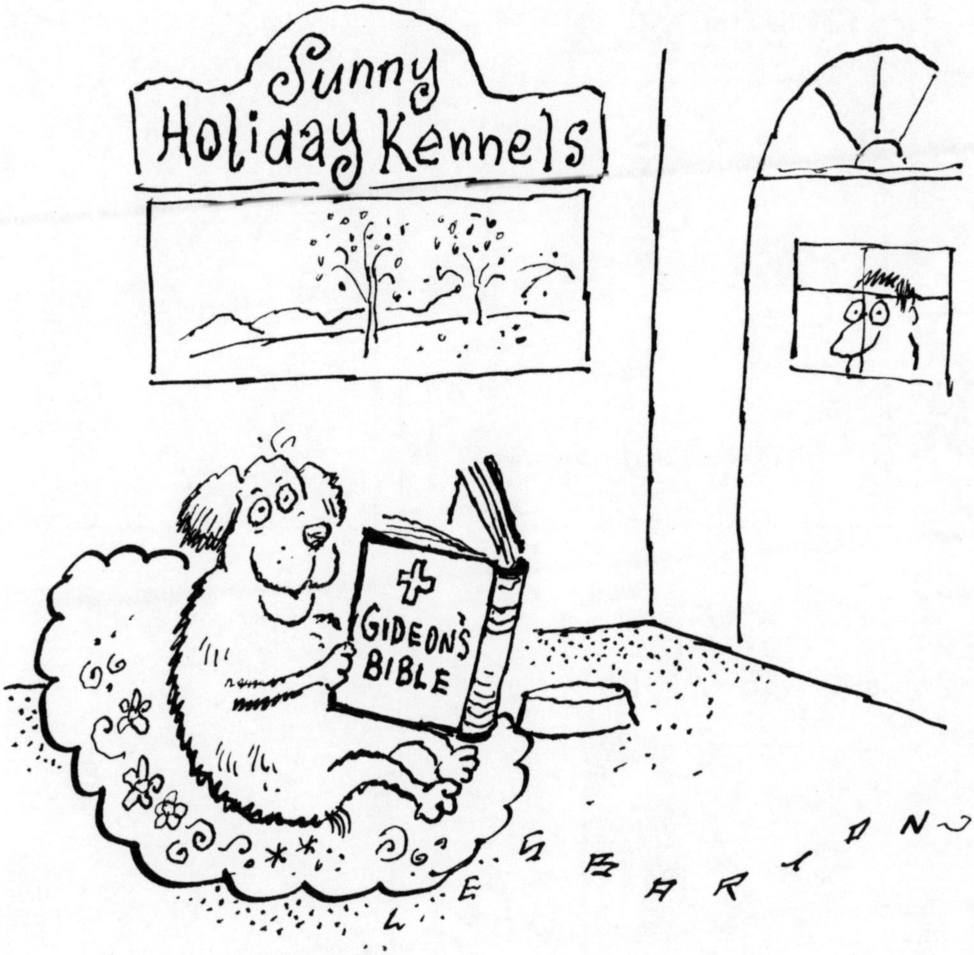
Sunny Holiday Kennels
GIDEON'S BIBLE
LES BARTON

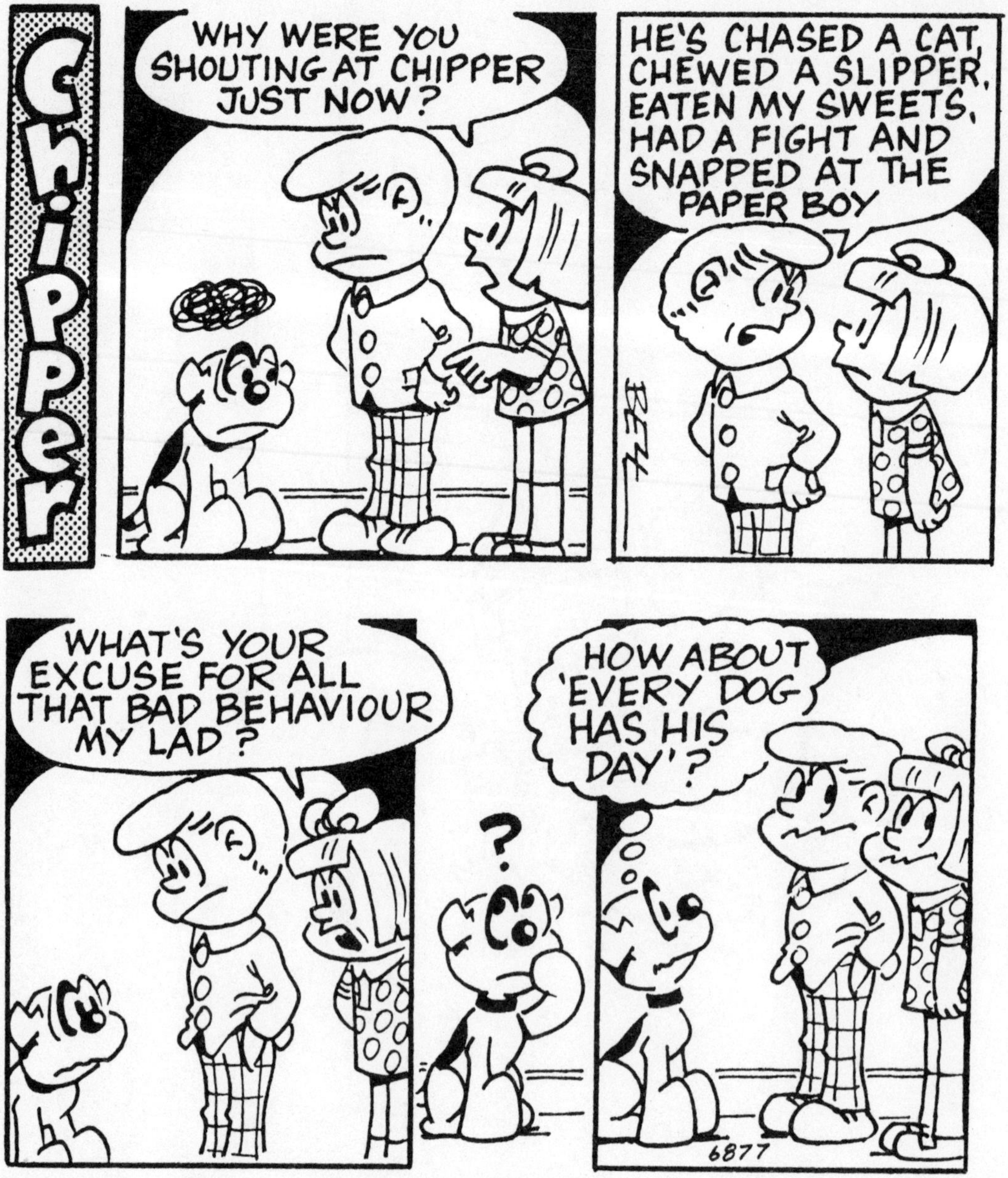
Chipper
WHY WERE YOU SHOUTING AT CHIPPER JUST NOW?
HE'S CHASED A CAT, CHEWED A SLIPPER, EATEN MY SWEETS, HAD A FIGHT AND SNAPPED AT THE PAPER BOY
WHAT'S YOUR EXCUSE FOR ALL THAT BAD BEHAVIOUR MY LAD?
?
HOW ABOUT 'EVERY DOG HAS HIS DAY'?
6877

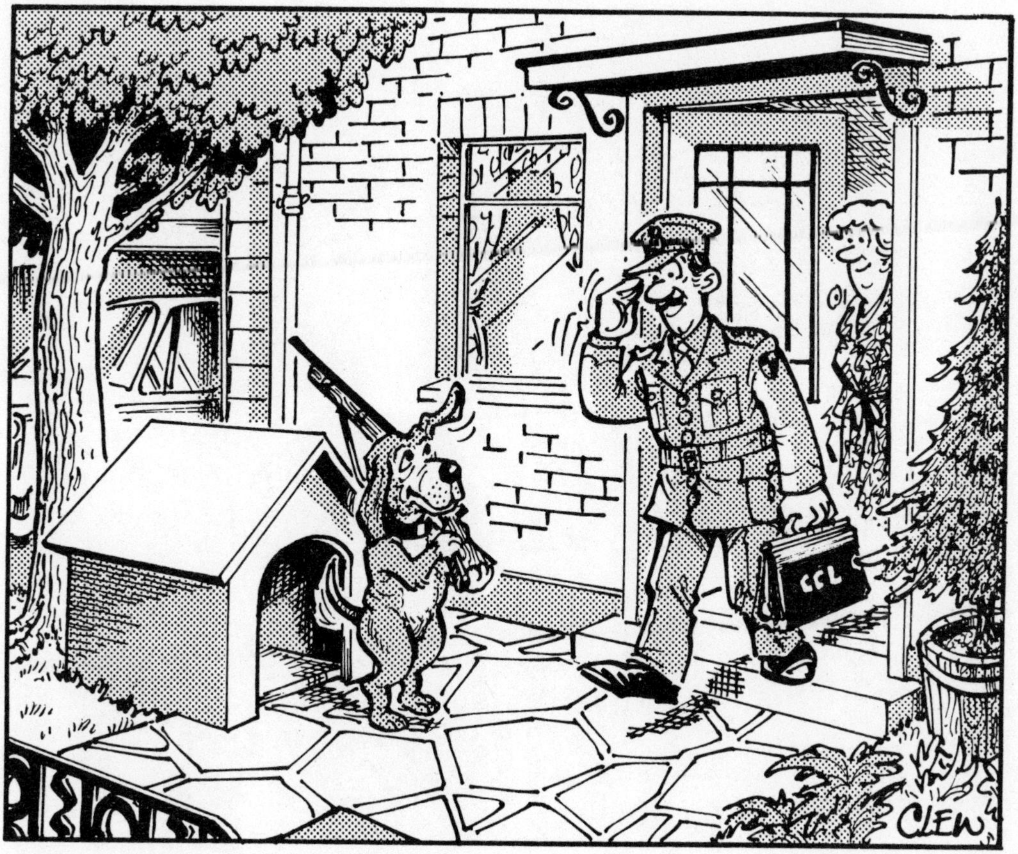
CCL
CLEW

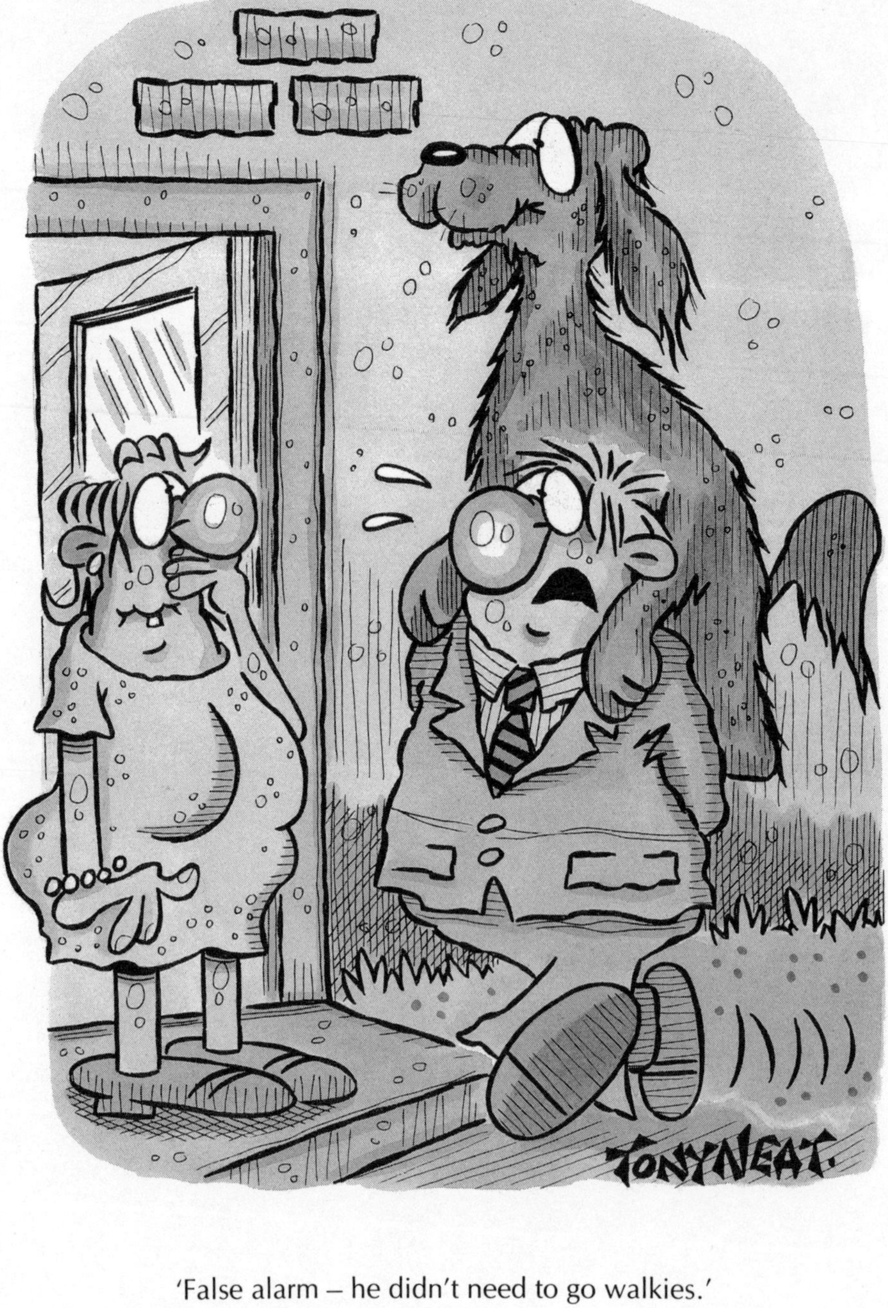
TONY NEAT.

'False alarm – he didn't need to go walkies.'

HAYSEEDS
by HARGREAVES
2994
WOOF! WOOF!
Harry Hargreaves,
YOU'RE BARKING UP THE WRONG TREE!
I SAID I'D MEET YOU AT THAT ONE!
HARGREAVES

'I bet Barbara Woodhouse would be really proud of us.'

'Mush! Pass it on . . .'

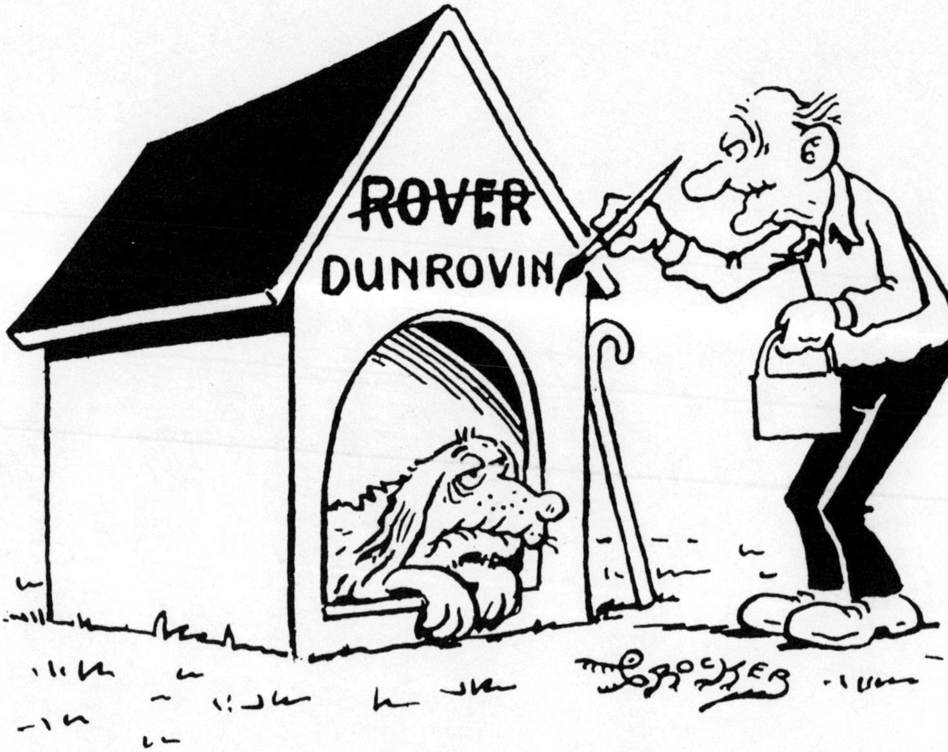
ROVER
DUNROVIN
BROCKER

# INDEX OF CARTOONS

# CONTRIBUTING CARTOONISTS

## GEORGE ADAMSON

A US citizen but a British subject, George Adamson was a Catalina flying-boat navigator for Coastal Command in the war years and an official war artist when his duties allowed. He became a Fellow of the Royal Society of Painter-Etchers and Engravers in 1987 and has exhibited at the Royal Academy. There are also collections of his work in the British Museum, V&A, New York Public Library and elsewhere. A humorist and regular contributor to *Punch*, he has also illustrated a number of books, including the first five volumes of *Private Eye*'s 'Dear Bill' series and a collection of P. G. Wodehouse short stories for the Folio Society.

## KEN ALLEN

Born in Newcastle-upon-Tyne in 1961, Ken Allen lives and works in Liverpool. Until recently, he drew a daily pocket cartoon for the *Liverpool Daily Post*, but now contributes mainly to *Punch*, *Private Eye*, the *Spectator* and books like this. A keen DIY man, he recently made a table.

## 'ANTHONY' – Anthony Hutchings

Went to art college to study commercial art, but decided it wasn't for him and turned to cartooning so he could 'enjoy' earning a living. Married with two children and two cats ('Sorry, no dogs. I go and get my own paper each morning') he is now a full-time cartoonist working for children's comics, *Mayfair*, greetings cards companies etc. Cartoonists' Club of Great Britain Joke Cartoonist of the Year Award winner 1987 and 1989.

## SALLY ARTZ

Born in London in 1935, Sally Artz sold her first cartoon in 1955 and has since contributed to a wide variety of publications, including *Reader's Digest* and *Penthouse* (USA), plus long-running features in the *Daily Mirror* and the *People*. She has also worked in book illustration, advertising and cartoon animation, is married with three children and now lives in Bath.

## MIKE ATKINSON

Mike Atkinson is 49 years old and 'slightly nervous about the impending half century'. He is married to Linda and they have three children. A full-time cartoonist drawing daily, weekly, bi-weekly and bi-quarterly (twice a year) strips for newspapers and magazines, he also produces ideas and designs for greetings cards. His other interests include beer, steam trains, ice-hockey, collecting original cartoons and fighting with Ben (his three-year-old).

## LES BARTON

Having had no formal training as an artist, Les Barton became a cartoonist – which qualified him as a retouching artist for photographs of cars, cans and cattle. He then worked in advertising and comics (*Billy Bunter*, *I Spy* and *Harry's Haunted House*) and now draws mainly for *Punch* and *Private Eye* when not designing humorous greetings cards. He is also Treasurer of the Cartoonists' Club of Great Britain.

## TERRY BAVE

A member of the Cartoonists' Club of Great Britain since the 1960s, Terry Bave has been drawing cartoons since early childhood. For the past 25 years he and his wife and partner, Sheila, have been specializing in children's comic strips for the 7–11 age group.

## JOHN BELL

A former engineer and sergeant in the RASC Army Fire Service, John Bell began cartooning part-time for the *Doncaster Gazette* after the war. He then worked full-time as sports cartoonist and caricaturist on the *Yorkshire Evening News*, later moving to the *Birmingham Post* and *Evening Mail* where he remained for 23 years before retiring three years ago. He has recently been catching up on his painting, working in watercolours, oils and acrylics.

## RUPERT BESLEY

Born in Norfolk in 1950 and now living on the Isle of Wight, Rupert Besley taught for several years before moving into full-time cartoon work – book illustrations, postcards, anything legal considered.

## 'CHAS' – Charles Sinclair

Chas Sinclair left school at 14 and began work in the aircraft industry before leaving to draw editorial cartoons for the *TV Post*. After a period working as a designer for a linen manufacturer he was made redundant in 1967 and has been a freelance cartoonist ever since, contributing to the *Mail on Sunday*, *Shoot!* etc.

## 'CLEW' – Clifford C. Lewis

'Clew' has been drawing cartoons since 1948, selling his first to *London Opinion* in 1949 for six guineas. He gave up his day job as an architect to become a full-time freelance cartoonist in 1953 and during the past 38 years has sold around 25,000 drawings to hundreds of British and foreign publications.

## CLIVE COLLINS

Clive Collins was born in 1942 and went to Kingston Art School, following which he worked in insurance, as a film extra, ran a film studio and repped for a small artwork studio before becoming political cartoonist for the *Sunday People*. He is now deputy political cartoonist on the *Daily Mirror* and regularly draws cartoons for *Punch* and *Playboy*. He was selected as Cartoonist of the Year by the Cartoonists' Club of Great Britain in 1984, 1985 and 1987, is currently its Chairman, and has won numerous international awards for his work.

## DAVE COLTON

Dave Colton is 33 and lives in Crewe with Julie and Yasmin. He draws cartoons for comics and magazines in the UK and Europe and also spends some time teaching. His interests are travelling, thinking and sleeping.

## LINDA COMBI

Linda Combi is an American freelance illustrator, now resident in the UK. Specializing in humorous art she is a member of Yorkshire County Cricket Club and is currently working on a book of cricket cartoons from an American woman's point of view entitled *A Broad on the Boundary*.

## JIM CROCKER

Born in 1928, Jim Crocker has had numerous occupations including botanical lab assistant, radio mechanic, army gunner, medical orderly, sailor in the Merchant Navy, salesman in India, goldminer in South Africa, copper miner in Zambia, coalminer in England, quarrying etc. He has been cartooning and drawing for children's comics since 1965 and lists his hobby as herpetology. Married with two children, he and his wife have just celebrated their 40th anniversary.

## MANNY CURTIS

Manny Curtis has had work published in most major publications at home and overseas and is presently involved in corporate cartooning. A past Hon. Secretary of the Cartoonists' Club of Great Britain he has also been Chairman of the Society of Strip Illustration.

## ROY DAVIS

A wallpaper designer with A. Sanderson's Studio from 1938 until he joined the RAF in 1940, Roy Davis worked as a storyman in animated cartoons from 1946 until 1950 when he became a freelance cartoonist. His work has appeared in *The Tatler*, *Punch*, *Tit-Bits* etc and he has also been an artist/scriptwriter for various comic magazines. He has never owned a dog.

## ALAN DE LA NOUGEREDE

Born in Nowgong, India, Alan de la Nougerede was a professional accountant in the City and the provinces before becoming a full-time artist/cartoonist. His first cartoon for *Punch* appeared in 1970 and he is now widely published in the UK and USA. He has produced strip cartoons for the *Daily Express*, *Evening News* and *Post* and was editorial cartoonist of the *People* 1986–8. His watercolours have been exhibited in Ebury St and Bayswater Rd, London. He is married with one daughter.

## 'DISH' – Neil Dishington

Born: a long time ago. Art school, teaching, illustrations, cartoonist, mending the fence, bringing up children etc. Now over 50 but, like Tomi Ungerer, believes that all he has done is 'merely an apprenticeship for what is to follow'.

## MAURICE DODD

Ex-RAF and ex-SAS (TA), Maurice Dodd says that in his long struggle to the peak of penury as an artist and writer he has passed through the roles of apprentice fitter and car salesman, grinder operator, spray-painter, baker's roundsman, school caretaker, locomotive fireman, postman, aircraftman, paratrooper, painter (apart from other exhibitions his work was also hung when for the first and only time he submitted to the Royal Academy) as well as enjoying an award-winning career in advertising – but does not consider it all constitutes a required course for becoming a cartoonist.

## PETE DREDGE

Born in Nottingham in 1952, Pete Dredge has been a professional cartoonist since 1976 and is a regular contributor to *Punch*, *Private Eye*, *Spectator*, *Radio Times* and *Daily Express*. He was voted Joke Cartoonist of the Year 1986 and Provincial Press Cartoonist of the Year 1987 by the Cartoonists' Club of Great Britain.

## CLIVE DURRANT

Clive Durrant has a design studio in Chelsea called Red Pencil. He was brought up by wolves from the age of three and supports the National Canine Defence League via cartoons as a way of repaying that debt to those four-legged foster parents.

## STAN EALES

Stan Eales is four years old (approximately 29 in human terms). He is of antipodean pedigree and is of the long-haired, tail-less, shaggy-faced variety. He doggedly submits scratchings (usually dog-eared ones) to *Punch*, *Private Eye* and *Green Magazine*. He was abandoned in a wild metropolis at birth and brought up by surrogate parents – hence his tendency to behave uncannily like a human being. His wife is still despairingly attempting to house-train him.

## BARRY FANTONI

A novelist, broadcaster, cartoonist and jazz musician, Barry Fantoni was born in 1940 and studied at Camberwell School of Arts and Crafts. He has been on the editorial staff of *Private Eye* since 1963, was diary cartoonist at *The Times* 1983–90 and has drawn cartoons for the *Listener*. He has also been art critic of *The Times* and a TV and film actor. His recreations are road-running and animal welfare.

## NOEL FORD

The current NCDL/Bonio Dog Cartoonist of the Year Supreme Champion, Noel Ford is a regular contributor to *Punch* and many other magazines. He is also the author of *Golf Widows*, *Cricket Widows* and *Business Widows* as well as a number of children's books such as *Nuts*, *Limeroons* and *The Lost Wag*. He lives with his wife, Margaret, their daughter, Sara, and two demented golden retrievers, Tuppence and Penny, in a small Leicestershire village which has a Warwickshire postal address and a Staffordshire telephone exchange (which perhaps explains why he sometimes seems a little confused). Tuppence and Penny are a source of great inspiration and are probably the only two dogs in existence who have had to be taught to swim by their owners!

## STEVE GARNER

Steve Garner became a full-time freelance cartoonist in 1979 at the age of 21. Since then his work has been published in *Punch*, *Daily Mirror* etc and his sporting cartoons have appeared on table mats and in his first book, *The Golden Age of Village Cricket*. He enjoys the life of a freelancer which enables him to watch repeats of *Stingray* during school holidays and carry on illicit affairs with the local postmistress.

## LES GIBBARD

Les Gibbard was born in New Zealand and became a newspaper reporter at the age of 16. Upon arrival in England he began to specialize in cartooning, initially as arts caricaturist for the *Sunday Telegraph*. He has also worked as an animator for Richard Williams' studio and produced a series of political cartoons for Granada TV and sequences for Channel 4's *A Week in Politics*. He has been political cartoonist of the *Guardian* since 1969 and is married with two Irish wolfhounds, a black labrador and nine cats.

## TONI GOFFE

Born in Southampton, Toni Goffe studied painting and illustration at Southampton College of Art before moving to London where, whilst continuing his studies, he supported himself playing double bass in various jazz bands. During the next 10 years he wrote and illustrated over 200 children's books, including the popular 'XYZ' series and 'Toby's Animal Rescue Service' based on the fanciful adventures of his son Tobin. Moving back to Hampshire he then started the Pendulum Gallery in Selborne, followed by three years in America, running the John Stobart Gallery in Boston and exhibiting his work in one-man shows along the east coast. Now back in Hampshire again he has recently started his own publishing company, the Pendulum Gallery Press, which has produced 15 books of his cartoons. Toni Goffe has also exhibited widely in the UK and Europe, particularly Germany.

## 'GOLDY' – Martin Goldring

Martin Goldring (1925–90) was born in the East End of London and began to draw at an early age. Demobbed from the RAF in 1947 he studied at St Martin's School of Art and spent several years as a silkscreen printer and display designer, all the while producing cartoons freelance in his spare time. He later joined IPC Magazines and subsequently left to become a full-time freelance cartoonist, working for the national and trade press.

## MIKE GORDON

Born: Lancashire, too many years ago. Education painful. Sidetracked into plumbing until 1983. Now in sunny Sussex, spends each Christmas mildly confused, drawing cartoons for Easter and Valentine cards and the rest of the year illustrating books, making faces like hairy dogs and bank managers so that he can draw them exactly right.

## ALEX GRAHAM

A Scot from Dumfries, Alex Graham was educated at Dumfries Academy and Glasgow School of Art and has been a full-time cartoonist since 1945. He is perhaps best known for the 'Fred Basset' strip in the *Daily Mail* which, since it began in 1963, has been syndicated worldwide and been made into 20 TV shorts. His work has also appeared in all the leading British magazines as well as the *New Yorker*. He is married with a grown-up son and daughter and lives in Sussex beside a lake, where he plays golf and bridge and enjoys gardening. He has a Basset hound and a Yorkshire terrier.

## 'GREN' – Grenfell Jones MBE

Grenfell Jones, better known as 'Gren', was born in Hengoed and has produced a daily cartoon for the *South Wales Echo* for over 20 years. Best known for his creation of the village of Aberflyarff, his work has also won him numerous awards, including being Provincial Cartoonist of the Year four times. He has also produced 24 books and illustrated many others – including Max Boyce's bestseller *I Was There* – and his golf, cricket and rugby calendars have won him international acclaim. Honoured by the Variety Club of Great Britain for his charity work, Gren was awarded an MBE in 1990. His latest book, *How To Be a Welshman*, includes an array of such fellow-countrymen as Leonardo dai Vinci (painter of Mona Pugh), Casanova Llewellyn and Isambard Kingdom Pugh, the man who grew rugby posts. Gren is also a founder member of the Campaign for Real Chips and lives in Cardiff though he insists it's really a holiday home, his heart is still in Hengoed.

## HARRY HARGREAVES

Born in Manchester, Harry Hargreaves studied engineering before serving with RAF Signals in the Far East during the Second World War. Since then he has been a film animator (Disney-trained) and an internationally syndicated freelance cartoonist and illustrator working in television, advertising etc. His interests include dogs, birds, cricket, anthropology, conservation, the countryside, the Wildfowl Trust and the Army Air Corps. He is married with two daughters and lives in Somerset.

## LOUIS HELLMAN

Born in London in 1936, Louis Hellman studied architecture at universities in London and Paris (BArch 1962) and now works as an architect/designer/illustrator. He has been cartoonist for the *Architects Journal* since 1967 and his work has also appeared in the *Architectural Review, Building Design, Observer, Sunday Times, New Statesman* etc. He produced an animated cartoon film for BBC2 in 1974 and there was an exhibition of his work at the Architectural Association in 1979. Louis Hellman has published three books (including *Architecture for Beginners*, 1986) and has lectured widely in the UK, USA, Australia and Singapore.

## CAROLINE HOLDEN

Born in Leicester in 1954, Caroline Holden studied graphics at Loughborough College of Art & Design before coming to London to work as a freelance designer/illustrator. She has illustrated books since 1978, notably Sue Townsend's 'Adrian Mole' series and titles by Michael Palin and Mike Rosen among others as well as her own *Securi-Skunk* and *Danger, God Working Overhead*. She has also had work published in *Private Eye, Law Gazette* etc and has exhibited at the Cartoon Gallery, London.

## MARTIN HONEYSETT

Born in 1943, Martin Honeysett left Croydon School of Art after one year to take to the road. He then spent six years abroad in various jobs – as a lumberjack and trucker in Canada – before returning to England in 1969. He began cartooning on his return whilst working as a bus-driver for London Transport and is now a full-time cartoonist, appearing mostly in *Private Eye* and *Punch*.

## KEN HOWELLS

Born in Carmarthen (Dyfed), South Wales, 'at an early age', Ken Howells started drawing cartoons in the army and later for a South Wales newspaper. For some time he worked as an art teacher at HM Borstal but now cartoons for trade journals, a greetings card company and various advertising agencies. He also lectures on communication and human behaviour.

## DICKY HOWETT

A published cartoonist since 1962, Dicky Howett's directly commissioned work appears worldwide. He is also a featured writer for several national magazines and is a regular broadcaster for BBC radio.

## IAN JACKSON

Born in 1964, Ian Jackson studied at Jacob Kramer College of Art in Leeds and has been designing greetings cards since 1982 and cartooning regularly for *Punch* since 1984. He also occasionally draws cartoons for *Playboy*. When he is not doing any of the above he stuffs animals.

## 'JAN' – Graham Foster

Graham Foster joined the Royal Navy as an apprentice in 1950 and transferred to the Fleet Air Arm as an aircraft engineer in 1952, leaving in 1975 to work in civil aviation but signing on again in 1980 for a further 10 years. Most of his cartoon work is syndicated abroad. He owns a border collie 'a lively, intelligent dog', who destroys his garden.

## 'JEK' – John Edward Knight

John Knight studied graphic design before joining the Royal Navy in 1968. His work has been published in many magazines and newspapers as well as on T-shirts and greetings cards etc. He lives in Cornwall with his wife and three black labradors.

## ARNOLD LERNER

Born in 1923, Arnold Lerner studied at St Martins School of Art and worked as an art director in advertising before becoming art and cartoon editor for various publications in groups such as Associated Newspapers and IPC. In 1987 he turned freelance, specializing in caricature, and has had work published in the *Daily Mail*, *Listener*, *Motor*, *Autocar* etc. A member of the Cartoonists' Club of Great Britain and the Federation of European Cartoonists' Organizations, he has won a number of international awards for his cartoon and photographic work and hopes to have a combined exhibition of photography and art in the near future. He also teaches cartoon art at St Albans College. Arnold Lerner is married with two children and lives in Hampstead.

## JOE McCAFFREY

Joe McCaffrey spent his early years at sea and came ashore to take up comics, drawing 'Jack Pott' and 'Mustapha Million' amongst others. He then drifted into animation, working on *Count Duckula* and *The BFG*, and has just completed work on Spielberg's *American Tale II*.

## ROGER MAHONEY

Trained as an interior designer at the Portsmouth College of Art, Roger Mahoney later became a professional musician. He has written story-scripts for the *Daily Mirror*'s famous 'Jane' series, drawn a caricature strip based on BBC TV's *Last of the Summer Wine* for the *Daily Star* and currently illustrates 'Millie' for the *Mirror* as well as writing and drawing cartoons for overseas syndication and producing pocket cartoons for various magazines and newspapers. He lives in a converted 1900s isolation hospital situated in six acres of Sussex woodland and uses the old mortuary as his studio. 'I've ghosted for many famous cartoonists since moving in,' he says. 'Whatever I come up with down here seems funny – except after midnight!'

## MIKE MOSEDALE

Mike Mosedale studied at Farnham and Exeter art colleges and after a brief spell at sea became a professional cartoonist drawing for anything from T-shirts to television, though most of his work is for newspapers and magazines. 'I enjoy this existence and so does my dog.'

## DAVID MYERS

A freelance cartoonist for 37 years, David Myers went to Sir John Cass and St Martins art colleges on an army grant after service with the Royal Fusiliers. While still at St Martins he stood in for Osbert Lancaster at the *Daily Express* and since that time he has been lead cartoonist on the *Evening News*, pocket cartoonist on the Melbourne *Argus*, drawn 20,000 cartoons for *Punch* and other magazines and papers, designed 500 greetings cards and invented a toy. He also devised and wrote the BBC TV children's series *Sebastian the Incredible Drawing Dog* which has been repeated three times (with a new series in the pipeline) and published in book form. David Myers has been voted Social and Political Cartoonist of the Year by the Cartoonists' Club of Great Britain.

## SERGIO NAVARRO

Sergio Navarro, who comes from Culiacan in the north of Mexico, is equally well known for his drawing, murals and cartoons. Since arriving in London nine years ago he has taught visual arts and graphics, produced cartoons and illustrations for a variety of books and magazines – including *Punch* – created three murals and designed publicity material for the tenth anniversary of the Nicaraguan Revolution. His work has been exhibited at a number of galleries in London and Mexico.

## TONY NEAT

Born in Lambeth, London, in 1937, Tony Neat spent many years in New York as a telegraphist and later as a copy-editor for Hearst Special News SVC. He has been a professional cartoonist for 30 years and also owns the Cartoonist Hotel in Margate, Kent which he runs with his wife Jarmila. They have two sons, Steven and Michael, who live in New York.

## ROY NIXON

Roy Nixon was born in London in 1933 but has lived in Chelmsford since 1961. A self-taught artist, he has worked freelance since 1956 (full-time from 1970) for such magazines as *Punch*, *Private Eye* etc as well as various national newspapers and overseas publications. He is married with two sons and a daughter.

## ROD PAGE

Art school and agency trained, Rod Page was an artist for the *Nottingham Evening Post* for 12 years and also drew 'The Adventures of Annabel Bear' (now deceased), a children's cartoon strip which appeared in several provincial newspapers. At present he is involved with an Apple Mac in an agency in Winchester. His ambition is to stop doing cartoons for a pint . . .

## MIKE PAYNE

An award-winning cartoonist/illustrator, Mike Payne has had his work published in newspapers, magazines and on textiles and is particularly renowned for his colour greetings cards which are sold worldwide. He is also Art Director of Carte Blanche Greetings Ltd, drawing under the name of 'Miranda' and is currently working on a new concept for television with Richard Digance.

## JOHN POWER

John Power lives in the Somerset village of Norton Fitzwarren, spending much of his time sitting in an armchair thinking up ideas, most of which are aimed at American markets such as the *New Yorker*, *Playboy* and the *Saturday Evening Post*. He also writes material for American comic strips.

## KEN PYNE

Started off as a layout artist on *Scrap* and *Waste Reclamation and Disposal Weekly* before turning freelance, since when he's been taken up by *The Times*, *Private Eye*, *Punch*, *Observer*, *Independent*, *Independent Magazine* and others. He has also had five books of his own cartoons published.

## BRYAN READING

Bryan Reading was roughed out in 1935 and after too many years in advertising became a full-time inker in 1978. The colours may have faded a bit, but the general outline remains. He works for all the usual cartoon markets.

## ARTHUR REID

An international freelance cartoonist, illustrator and sculptor, ARThur (sic) Reid was educated at Aberdeen College of Commerce, Gray's School of Art and Aberdeen College of Education. His work has appeared in *Punch*, *Private Eye*, *Playboy* and *Penthouse* and has been exhibited worldwide, earning him numerous medals and awards including being the first-ever British prizewinner of the World Cartoon Exhibition in Belgium in 1980. He is also the organizer of the Edinburgh International Cartoon Festival and is employed as a part-time art specialist by Grampian Regional Council. He lives and sometimes works in Scotland and lists his hobbies as beer and collecting 'first edition' rejection slips.

## JOHN RYAN

Born in 1921, John Ryan spent his early life in Turkey, Morocco and 'abroad' generally. He was educated at Ampleforth College and after spending the war in Burma taught art at Harrow School, contributing 'Captain Pugwash', 'Harris Tweed' and 'Lettice Leefe' to *Eagle* and *Girl*. Since then he has produced about 35 books on Pugwash and others, as well as innumerable BBC TV films, and has been the cartoonist on the *Catholic Herald* since 1964. Happily married, with children and grandchildren, he lives in Rye, Sussex, surrounded by the ghosts of smugglers.

## JOHN SAMUELS

Born in Edmonton, North London, in 1945, John Samuels now lives in Hampshire with his wife and two teenage daughters (moving soon to the West Country). With no formal training in art he works as a mechanical engineer in the aerospace industry and cartooning is a hobby. Animal subjects predominate in his work, a parrot called Jasper being a particular favourite.

## MIKE SCOTT

Mike Scott's cartoons have appeared in various newspapers and magazines including *Punch*, *Private Eye*, *Reader's Digest* and IPC comics.

## SAM SMITH

Sam Smith works for a variety of newspapers and magazines and quite likes dogs.

## BILL STOTT

Bill Stott was born in Preston in 1944 and studied painting and lithography at Harris College in his home town. His greatest influence has been Bill Tidy, and he carries a kidney donor card. He has also recently given up smoking and yearns to write an autobiography as cool as Clive Collins'.

## GORDON STOWELL

Gordon Stowell has worked as a freelance designer, illustrator and cartoonist for over 30 years. Much of his work has been for children's books, some of which he has written himself. Cartooning is his first love and he has drawn for a number of national magazines and publishers.

## DENNIS TAYLOR

A graduate of Salford School of Art, Dennis Taylor's cartoons are now published worldwide and in 1981 he was nominated for the Joke Cartoonist of the Year award by the Cartoonists' Club of Great Britain.

## KATE TAYLOR

An artist who enjoys working both in colour and black-and-white, Kate Taylor is a freelance illustrator working for many different magazines and publishing companies.

## BILL THACKER

C. F. 'Bill' Thacker, now semi-retired and living in Wales, has been a freelance cartoonist for the last 35 years. Most of his work has appeared in aviation, motoring, handyman and industrial magazines.

## GEOFF THOMPSON

Geoff Thompson is 37 and is married with three children. He works and sleeps in the bedroom of his thatched cottage near Yeovil. A redundancy casualty of the Westland affair, he took to professional cartooning in the autumn of 1986. His drawings have appeared in *Mail on Sunday*, *Private Eye*, *Punch*, *Spectator* and *UK Press Gazette* amongst others.

## MIKE TURNER

Mike Turner is 47 and has been cartooning since 1976. His work has appeared in many publications including *Reader's Digest*, *Private Eye*, *Spectator* and *Punch*. He was Hon. Secretary of the Cartoonists' Club of Great Britain for five years and lists his hobby as decoding British Rail timetables. He lives in Colchester.

## JOHN WALLACE

A graduate in Theology from St Catharine's College, Cambridge, John Wallace, who is 24, has worked as a political cartoonist on the *Daily Gleaner* in Kingston, Jamaica and is currently working on a children's picture book.

## MIKE WILLIAMS

Born in 1940 in the spa city of Liverpool-on-Sea, Mike Williams trained as a commercial artist and illustrator and worked in advertising for about ten years. He started cartooning in the late 1960s and now draws for *Punch*, *Private Eye* and the *Spectator*. His books include *The Very, Very Last Book Ever*, *You Can't Still Be Hungry* and *Oh No! Not the '23*. Married with two daughters, five cats and an overdraft, he nearly did National Service and once got his foot run over by a pop star's car.

## PETE WILLIAMS

Pete Williams has drawn for many publications including *Punch*, *Private Eye*, the Express and Mirror Groups etc and has won a number of awards, at home and away. He claims to know the whereabouts of Lord Lucan, Kenny Dalglish etc . . . and is the creator of such unforgettable doggybilia as 'Heel, Rover!', 'Down, Toby!' and 'You fetch the bloody stick! You're the dog . . .'

*Note:* Biographical details of other contributors have been omitted at their own request (*Ed.*).

*Patron:* Her Majesty The Queen
*President:* Her Grace Lavinia Duchess of Norfolk, KG, CBE

The National Canine Defence League (NCDL) was founded at the first all-breed Cruft's Dog Show in 1891 to promote the welfare of dogs. Today it is Britain's largest canine-rescue charity with a network of rescue centres across the country.

The NCDL's policy is that *no healthy dog in its care is ever destroyed*. It aims to find caring new owners to give the dogs a second chance, and those that are not rehomed become permanent residents of the kennels, living out the remainder of their lives in the NCDL's care.

Rescue and rehabilitation are the main areas of the NCDL's work, but it also endeavours to educate dog-owners, encouraging responsibility towards their pets. The NCDL also actively campaigns on both a local and national level on dog-related subjects, ensuring that the welfare of dogs is not forgotten. And it is always available to offer advice and assistance to people with regard to their pets.

The NCDL is only able to continue this work because of the generosity of the public. As a registered charity without state aid, it relies entirely upon voluntary contributions and subscriptions and, sadly, every year brings more work caring for abandoned, mistreated and forgotten dogs. In an ideal world there would be no need for the NCDL — but this world is far from ideal and there is always more that could be done. Please support us.

Registered Charity No 227523    **A DOG IS FOR LIFE**    Dependent Entirely on Voluntary Contributions

---

For more information about the NCDL, or any of the activities listed overleaf, please contact:

National Canine Defence League,
1 Pratt Mews,
London NW1 0AD
Tel: 071-388 0137

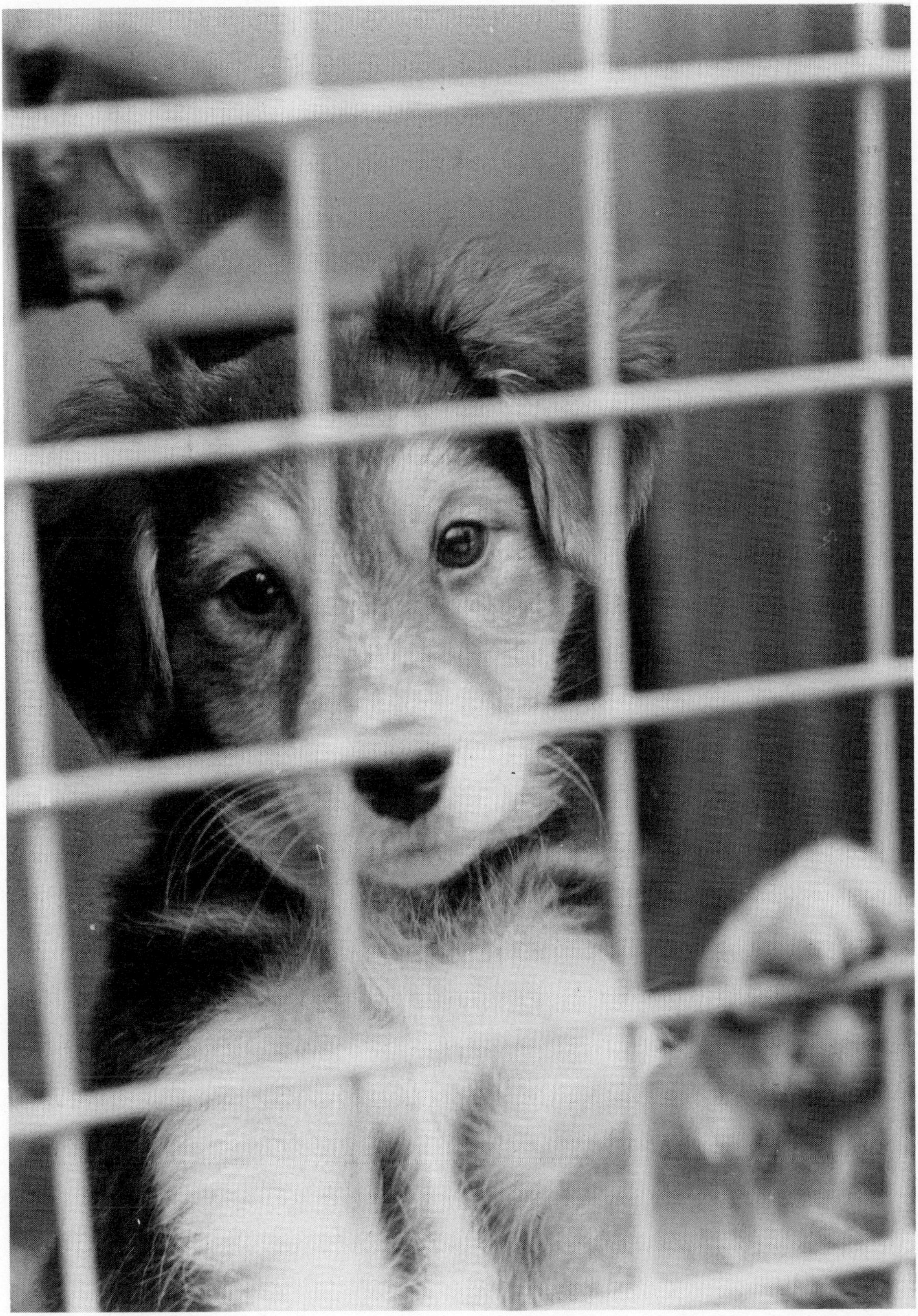

Photo by courtesy of *Coventry Evening Telegraph*

# SOME OF THE NCDL'S ACTIVITIES

- ## Shelters

The NCDL maintains rescue centres at Ballymena, Bridgend, Dumfries, Evesham, Farringdon, Ilfracombe, Kenilworth, Leeds, Newbury, Shoreham, Shrewsbury, Snetterton and Whitby.

- ## Sponsored Dog Scheme

The 'Sponsored Dog Scheme' helps to support the NCDL's long-stay residents. Members of the public are able to adopt a dog at one of the kennels and are updated on his or her progress – an ideal scheme for dog-lovers who are unable to keep a dog in their own homes.

- ## Campaigning

The NCDL is actively involved in formulating legislation affecting dogs in society.

- ## Lucky Dog Club

This is the charity's identification and registration scheme. A 'Lucky Dog Disc' is free to new members or for a small charge to non-members.

- ## Canine Care Card

The NCDL's 'Canine Care Card' is designed to ensure that a dog is cared for in the event of its owner's hospitalization or death. The card gives details needed for alternative arrangements to be made.

- ## Pet Cemeteries

The NCDL runs three pet cemeteries (Bushey, Evesham and Ilfracombe) where NCDL members are able to choose a final resting-place for their pets in peaceful and well-maintained surroundings.

# crazy for

# COOKIES BROWNIES & BARS

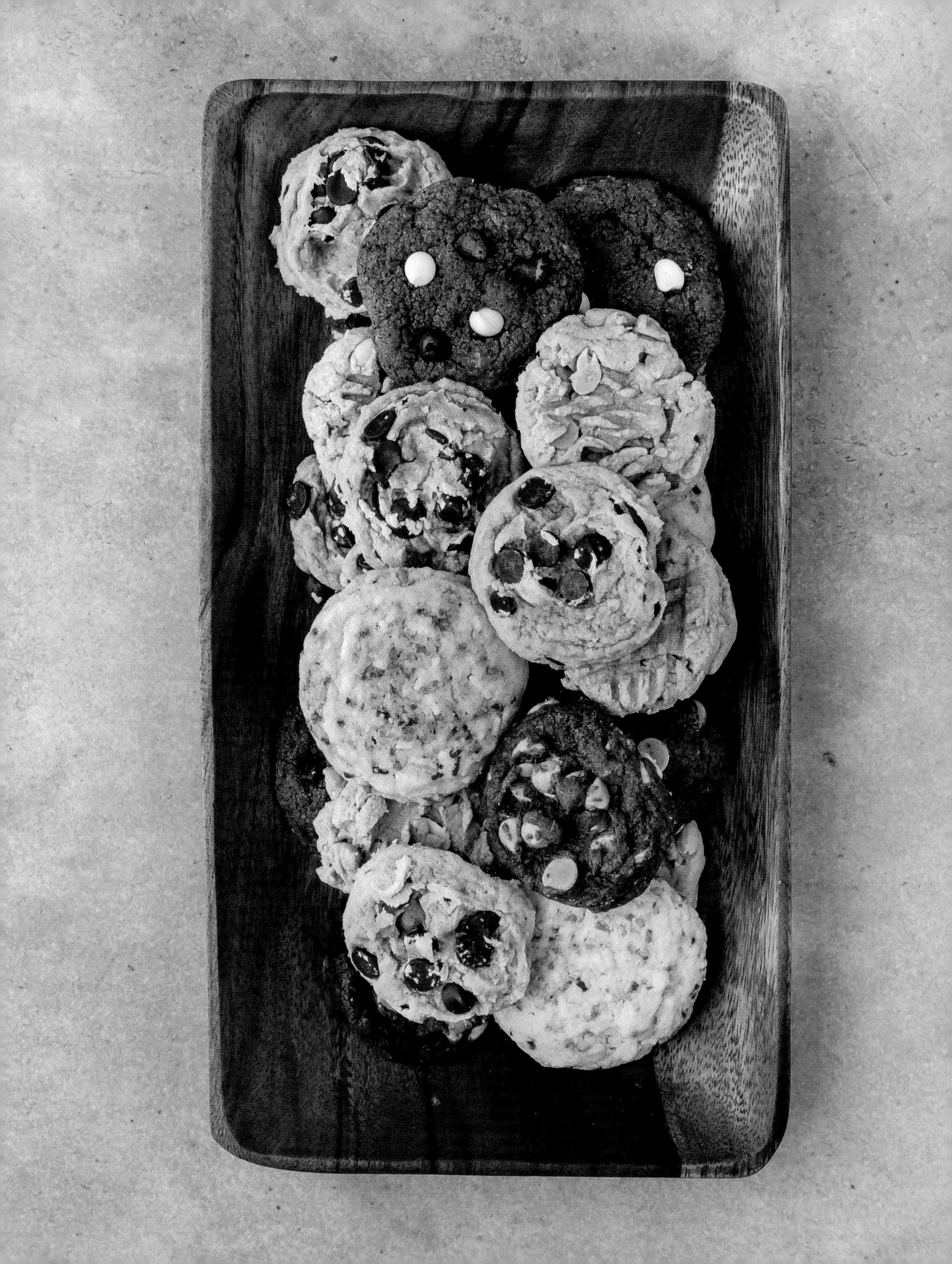

# crazy for

# COOKIES BROWNIES & BARS

Super-Fast, Made-from-Scratch
Sweets, Treats, and Desserts

## Dorothy Kern

HARVARD
COMMON
PRESS

First Published in 2022 by The Harvard Common Press, an imprint of The Quarto Group, 100 Cummings Center, Suite 265-D, Beverly, MA 01915, USA.
T (978) 282-9590 F (978) 283-2742 QuartoKnows.com

The Harvard Common Press titles are also available at discount for retail, wholesale, promotional, and bulk purchase. For details, contact the Special Sales Manager by email at specialsales@quarto.com or by mail at The Quarto Group, Attn: Special Sales Manager, 100 Cummings Center, Suite 265-D, Beverly, MA 01915, USA.

26 25 24 23 22     1 2 3 4 5

ISBN: 978-0-7603-7281-4

Digital edition published in 2022
eISBN: 978-0-7603-7282-1

Library of Congress Cataloging-in-Publication Data

Kern, Dorothy, author.
Crazy for cookies, brownies, and bars : super-fast,
  made-from-scratch sweets, treats, and desserts / Dorothy Kern.
ISBN 9780760372814 (hardcover) | ISBN 9780760372821 (ebook)
1.  Cookies. 2. Brownies (Cooking) 3. Bars (Desserts) 4. Cookbooks.
LCC TX772 .K47 2022  (print) | LCC TX772  (ebook) | DDC
  641.86/54--dc23

LCCN 2021029152 (print) | LCCN 2021029153 (ebook)

Design: Tanya Jacobson, jcbsn.co
Page Layout: Tanya Jacobson, jcbsn.co
Photography: Dorothy Kern, except pages 8, 18, 50, 102, 122, 196, 202, 205 by Beth Baugher

Printed in China

# Dedication

**For my PARENTS,** who gave me my love of food.

**For MEL and JORDAN,** who always believe I can do anything.

**And for my BLOG READERS,** without whom this book would not be possible. Thank you for being Crazy for Crust (and cookies!) with me since 2010.

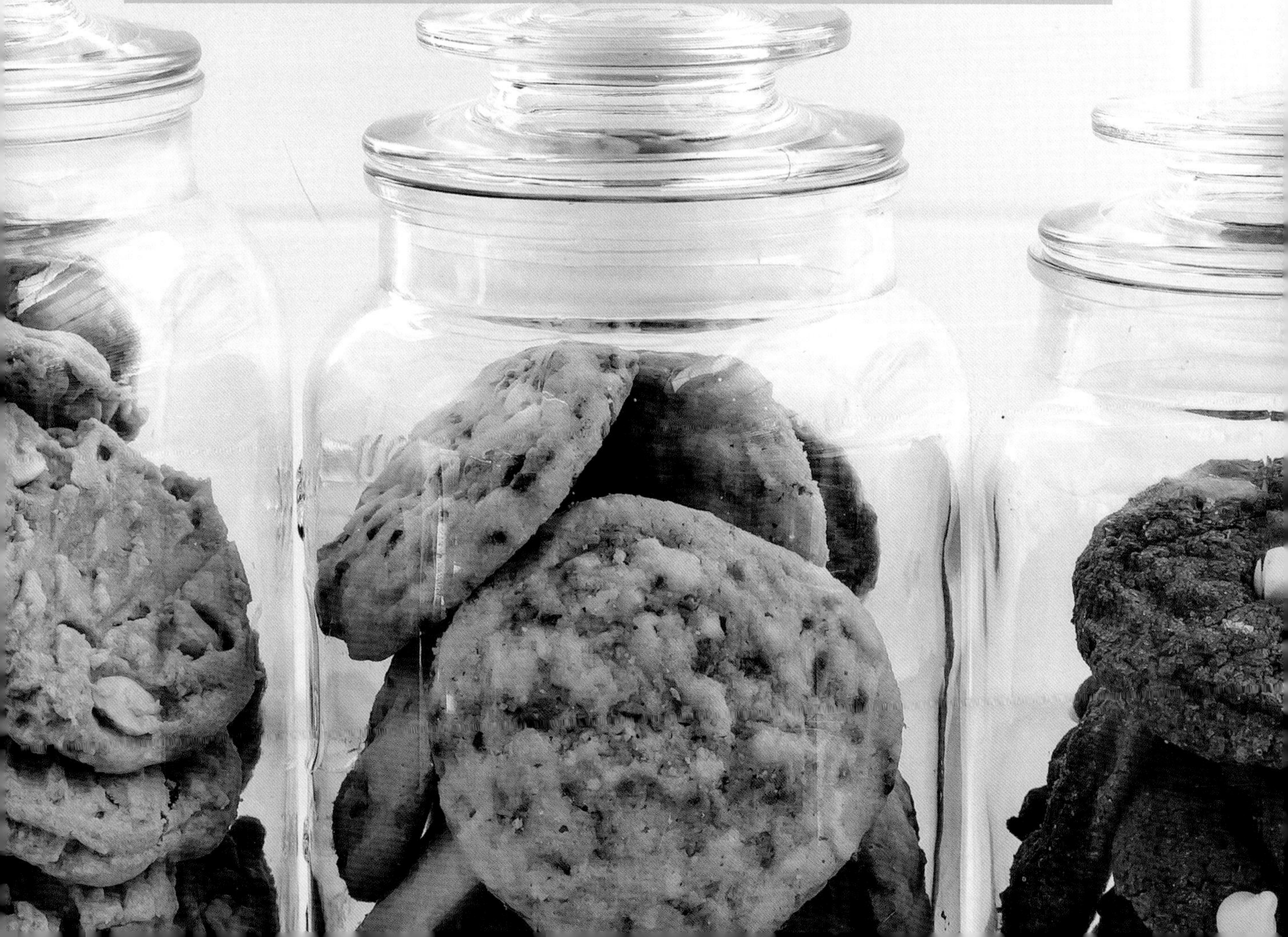

# Introduction:

# Chapter 1

## Cookie Jar Favorites     19

# Chapter 2

## Brownies     51

# Chapter 3

## Blondies and Bars     75

# Chapter 4

## Cookie Cakes, Skillet Bakes, and Cups—Oh My!     103

# Chapter 5

## Crazy Cookies

# Chapter 6

## Stuffed and Sandwiched

# Chapter 7

## No Oven, No Problem: No-Bake Cookies and Bars

# Chapter 8

## For Man's Best Friend: Dog Cookies for Your BFF

# Introduction
## Let's Get
## Crazy About Cookies

Growing up, my parents had a photo collage of preschooler me baking "Mr. Cookie Man" with my aunt. In the photos I'm laughing, smiling wide with my tooth-gapped grin, as I roll the dough and decorate the cookie man with raisins for eyes and jacket buttons. In a way, that photo montage was a foreshadowing of my future: I still feel that child-like joy when I make a new cookie recipe.

Since making Mr. Cookie Man when I was four years old, I've made hundreds of cookies and bars. As a preteen I was gifted a kids' baking book (a trusty old spiral board book that came with measuring spoons), and I turned perfecting the chocolate chip cookie recipe into a sport. Fast-forward to the present and my Seriously the *Best* Chocolate Chip Cookies recipe has been seen over a million times and is loved by so many people. Cookies and bars are some of the most popular recipes on my website and, honestly, I'm not at all surprised.

Cookies are probably my favorite things to bake because they're so easy. There's not a lot of skill or guesswork needed when you're making cookies: Just mix, drop, and bake! That's the kind of cookies I love: easy, fast, no frills. Just delicious.

I'm pretty sure that cookie bars and blondies were born because someone didn't want to scoop cookie dough. Same goes for cookie cakes: Sometimes you don't want to spend hours decorating a cake only for it to be lopsided. And as for brownies, well, let me just put it this way: I'm pretty sure I have *chocoholic* stamped on my medical chart.

This book is filled with eighty-five recipes, some of which are a little crazy, but all of them are super simple. From Seriously the *Best* Chocolate Chip Cookies to the Fudgiest Brownies Ever, I'm showing you how to level up some of the best basic recipes. Go on a journey with me through the land of cookies, brownies, and bars while I teach you how to make decorated cookie cakes, frosted brownies, blondies, stuffed and filled cookies, and so many more (even my labradoodle Abby had a paw in some of the recipes in this book).

My hope is that in this book you will find a new favorite (or favorites) that will be made and handed down in your family for years and that someday, somewhere, there will be a photo of a little boy or girl making one of my cookie recipes and inspiring another generation of crazy cookie lovers.

XO,
Dorothy

# Know Your Key Ingredients

Cookies are fun and easy, which makes them the perfect place to start if you're a baking novice, and they're a tasty way to get in the kitchen for regular bakers. Cookie recipes aren't finicky or intricate and can be very forgiving, but there are still a few things we should talk about before you start your journey into cookie wonderland. First up: ingredients. Using good ingredients—and paying attention to what the recipe is calling for—means everything for a successful outcome.

**Baking Soda and Baking Powder:** These are different ingredients and do very different things to your recipe. Many of the cookie recipes in this book use baking soda but you'll notice a few calling for baking powder. Make sure that yours is not expired (if you don't bake very often, you may need to check the expiration date).

**Butter:** The recipes in this book were tested with unsalted butter. If you wish to substitute salted butter, reduce the amount of salt in the recipe by ¼ teaspoon per ½ cup (113 g) of butter. A lot of the recipes call for softened butter, which means that the butter is soft to the touch. A good rule of thumb is to leave the butter out on the counter for an hour or two before beginning the recipe.

**Chocolate:** Be sure to pay attention to what kind of chocolate the recipe requires. Chocolate chips are obvious and come in different flavors (semi-sweet, milk, dark, white, and so on). For the most part, you can substitute any kind of chocolate chip if they are being used as mix-ins for cookies or bars. Baking chocolate, often referred to as unsweetened chocolate or semi-sweet chocolate, comes in bar form in the baking aisle of the grocery store. Be sure to use the kind that is called for in the recipe, as the sweetness of the final product can be affected by interchanging the kinds of baking chocolate.

**Cocoa:** The recipes in this book were tested using unsweetened cocoa powder, just the basic kind you get at the grocery store. Unless otherwise specified, use a regular cocoa powder (such as Hershey's brand). A few recipes call for Special Dark Cocoa, which is also a Hershey's product, but you can substitute regular unsweetened if you cannot find the Special Dark. A few also call for Dutch process cocoa, which shouldn't be substituted unless specified. However, you can substitute regular unsweetened cocoa or Hershey's Special Dark for the Dutch process.

**Eggs:** Any recipe calling for eggs was tested with large eggs. Eggs are important for structure in cookies, and any substitution of other-size eggs can alter the recipe.

**Flour:** All of the recipes in this book use all-purpose flour. Substituting different kinds of flour in these recipes can probably be done but will alter the texture and outcome of the recipe. To measure your flour, spoon the flour into your measuring cup, then level with the flat side of a knife, if not using a scale.

**Milk and Heavy Whipping Cream:** The recipes using milk have been tested using whole milk, unless otherwise noted. Sometimes you can use whole or nonfat interchangeably; when that is the case, it will be noted. When it comes to heavy whipping cream, make sure to buy the one labeled heavy, not plain, whipping cream. They act differently depending on the recipe, so be sure and double-check.

**Nonstick Cooking Spray:** This is my savior when it comes to bar cookies. I always grease my pans with nonstick cooking spray (such as Pam). Occasionally, as is the case with cookie cups, I like to use nonstick *baking* spray (the kind with flour in it). You can also just grease your pans with butter or shortening, but the spray is so much easier.

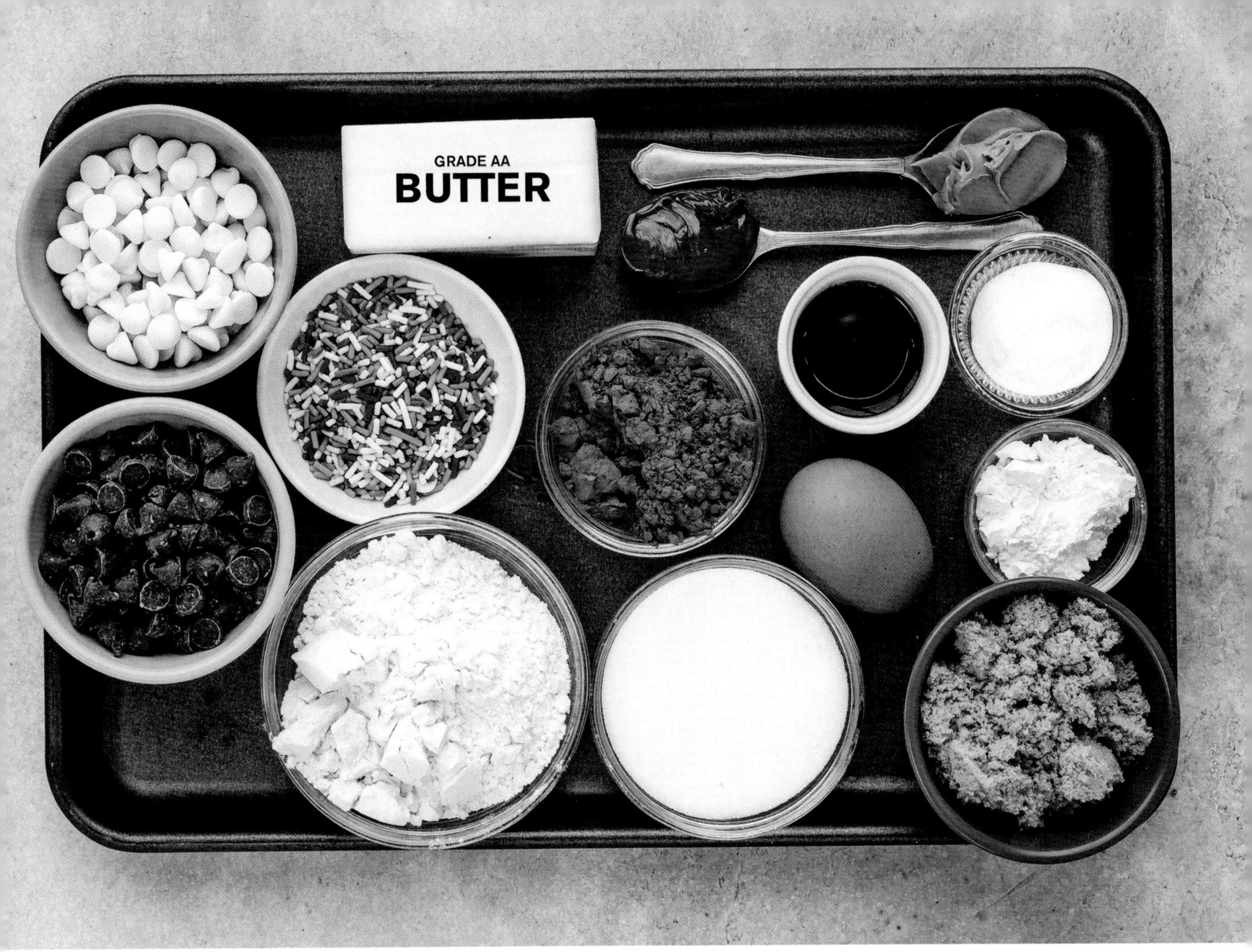
GRADE AA
BUTTER

**Oil:** All recipes tested for this book calling for oil used vegetable oil. You can substitute canola oil instead.

**Peanut Butter:** We are huge peanut butter lovers and the recipes in this book reflect that. All recipes in this book were tested with regular store-bought peanut butter. Homemade peanut butter or peanut butter that requires stirring aren't suitable for the recipes in this book. You can use any kind of Skippy or Jif (or similar brands), including Skippy or Jif Naturals, for my recipes.

**Sprinkles:** Several of the recipes in this book call for sprinkles, so I wanted to discuss my favorite kind for baking. If you're just using sprinkles as a decoration, as in the Sugar Cookie Bites (see page 188), then you can use any kind of sprinkles you like. However, if you're adding them to something that will be baked, like the Sprinkle Cookies on page 38, then I recommend using the standard, small, rod-shaped "rainbow" sprinkles you get in the grocery store. They hold their shape better in the oven, unlike nonpareils (the small round balls). If at all possible, use a regular sprinkle brand from the grocery store and don't use dollar store or discount sprinkles, as those tend to melt in the oven.

**Frosting Tips**

- The mixer matters: Using a hand mixer will take longer for the frosting to come together than if you're using a stand mixer. Hand mixer users: Feel free to add the milk before the mixture becomes smooth; once the powdered sugar is incorporated but the mixture is still crumbly, you can add the milk to aid in smoothing it out.
- Milk matters: The kind of milk, and the fat content in it, can alter the amount you need for a spreadable frosting. You can make this frosting with any kind of milk (dairy or nondairy), or even with heavy whipping cream or half-and-half, but the less fat in the milk, the less you will need. That's why I always recommend starting with 1 tablespoon milk to thin and adding more as needed.
- Softened butter matters: How soft your butter is when you start your frosting will also affect the consistency. Colder butter takes more time to mix with the powdered sugar, making it seem drier. Sometimes, if your butter is extra soft, you won't need very much milk at all because the butter mixes with the powdered sugar more easily.
- Freezing and storing frosting: Store unused frosting in an airtight container in the refrigerator for up to 4 days. You can also freeze frosting in an airtight container for up to 3 months. To thaw frozen frosting, allow it to sit at room temperature until thawed. You may need to mix in a bit of milk or heavy whipping cream to thin the thawed frosting enough for spreadable consistency.

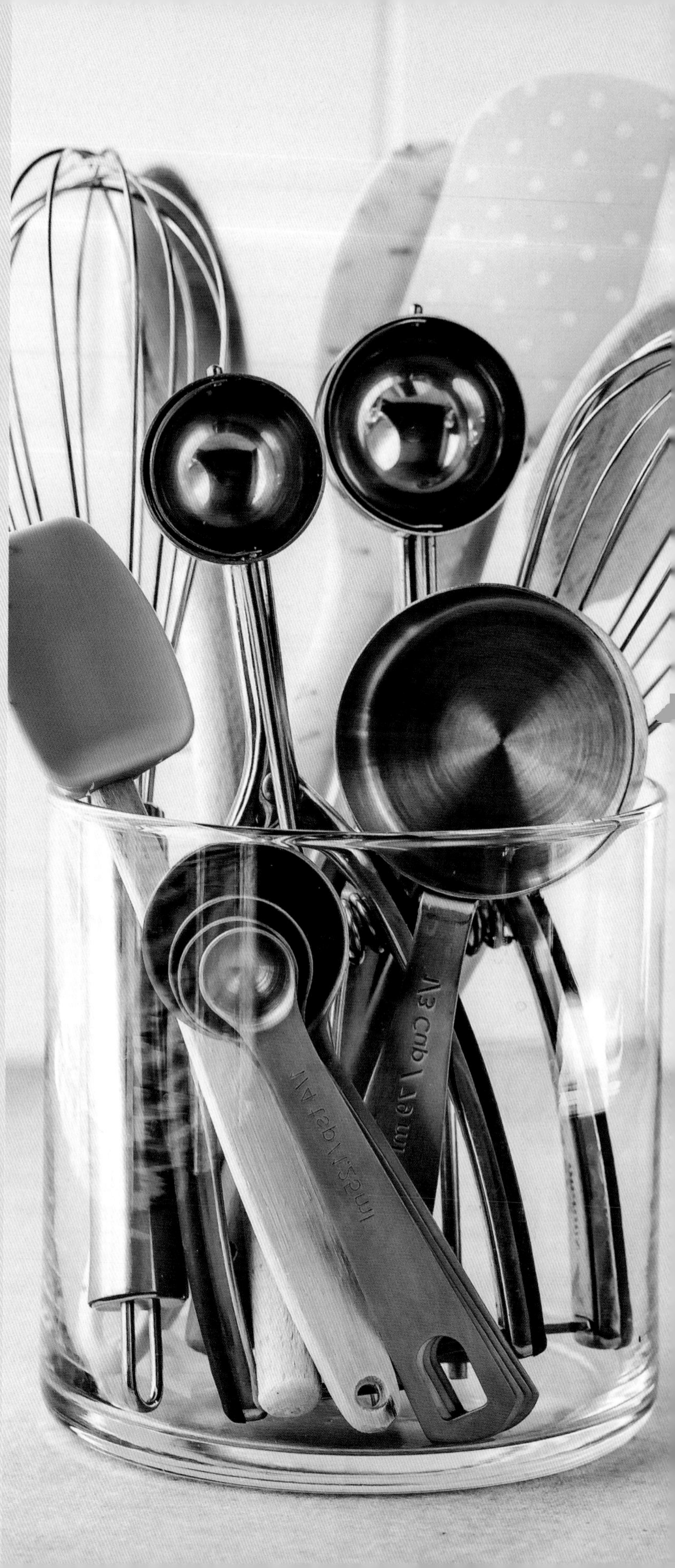

**Sugar:** Granulated sugar (white sugar) and brown sugar are used plentifully in this book. Unless otherwise called for, the recipes use light brown sugar, but dark brown can be substituted. If not using a scale, granulated sugar should be scooped into your measuring cup while brown sugar is packed. Confectioners' sugar, also called powdered sugar, should be spooned and leveled like flour.

**Vanilla Extract:** Be sure to buy only pure vanilla extract, not imitation. Imitation extracts can be cloying and have an unpleasant result. No need to buy name-brand extract; store brand or whatever is on sale is fine, but just be sure to buy pure.

# Tools for Successful Baking

I find that less is more, especially when it comes to baking tools and equipment. While it's nice to have all the fancy gadgets and tools, you don't necessarily need them all. The following are the ones I think are the most important for the recipes in this book.

**Baking Pans:** You'll need the following varieties: 9 × 13–inch (23 × 33 cm), 9 × 9–inch (23 × 23 cm), 8 × 8–inch (20 × 20 cm), 8-inch (20 cm) rounds, 9-inch (23 cm) rounds, muffin pans (see below), and cookie sheets (see below). Those are all pretty standard pans to have in your cabinet, but in a pinch you can use a 9 × 9–inch (23 × 23 cm) pan in recipes that call for 8 × 8–inch (20 × 20 cm) ones.

**Cookie Scoops:** These are, by far, my favorite kitchen item. I use them for everything, not just measuring out cookies. I recommend three sizes: 1 tablespoon, 2 tablespoons, and ¼ cup. If you

want, you can also get a ½ or ¾ tablespoon too, for smaller, bite-sized cookies. These are inexpensive and totally worth the cost. I use them for cookies, to portion muffin or cupcake batter into pans, and even to measure out things like 1 or 2 tablespoons of peanut butter.

**Cookie Sheets:** You'll need these to bake cookies! I prefer large sheets (either 11 × 15–inch [28 × 38 cm] or half sheet–sized), so if you're buying new, go big. I also recommend having at least four cookie sheets. That way you don't have to wait for them to cool in between baking. My most-used pans, cookie sheets are great for so many things in the kitchen.

**Foil:** I like to bake all bar cookies and brownies using foil-lined pans. It's just what I've always done. Using foil makes for easy cleanup and easy removal from the pan. If you don't like using foil, you can instead use parchment paper.

**Food Processor:** Another of my must-haves is a food processor. I use it all the time to crush cookies for crust or to make pie dough, among other things. I recommend buying a large one (one that can hold at least 9 cups [2.1L]) so that you don't have to work in batches.

**Kitchen Scale:** My favorite way to measure out dry ingredients is using a kitchen scale. While using measuring cups is the standard way to do things in the United States, weighing dry ingredients is so much more precise. If I measure out flour using a measuring cup, I'm going to get a different weight each time, but if I stick to one measurement for 1 cup (124 g) of all-purpose flour, then it will always be exact. If you're looking for a kitchen scale, get one that is digital and has different units (ounces, grams, and so on). It will completely change your life!

**Measuring Cups and Measuring Spoons:** If you don't have a scale, you can use regular dry measuring cups. Be sure to get dry measuring cups for dry ingredients and choose ones that have straight sides and squared-off edges for easy leveling. Wet ingredients should be measured in liquid measuring cups (the kind with pourable edges). And don't forget measuring spoons—you'll need those for extracts and things like baking soda and salt. I like to have a few different sets of each to make life easier in the kitchen.

**Microplane Zester:** This tool really gets a workout in my kitchen! If you do anything with citrus zest, a microplane is so good to have. You can also use the small side of a box grater to zest, but the microplane is created with the user in mind: easy to control and easy to clean all the zest off the back, unlike how difficult it is with a traditional grater.

**Mixers:** My preferred method for mixing is using an electric stand mixer (such as KitchenAid). They are my favorite for their ease of use, quick mixing, and versatility; plus they last practically forever. (I realized that one of mine will be twenty years old this year!) Now, I know that stand mixers take up a lot of space and are quite expensive, so a hand mixer is a good option. I recommend going more name brand (such as Cuisinart). You'll need at least one kind of mixer to make most of the recipes in this book.

**Mixing Bowls:** If you're not using a stand mixer that comes with a bowl, you'll need some large mixing bowls. It's good to have a variety of sizes, but make sure some are extra large for making things like buttercream that can make a mess in a too-small bowl. Plastic, glass, or porcelain doesn't matter, but it's good to have some that are microwave safe.

**Muffin Pans:** If you're making cookie cups, you will need a muffin pan. The recipes in this book call for both a standard muffin pan and a mini muffin pan. I recommend having two of each for ease, especially the mini muffin pans. Those come in different sizes (from twelve cavities to twenty-four cavities and even bigger); I recommend getting the twenty-four-cavity size. Mini muffin cup recipes usually have a high yield so it's nice to have more. Make sure to get nonstick.

**Parchment Paper (and/or Silicone Baking Mats):** I never bake straight on a cookie sheet. Using parchment or a silicone baking mat (such as Silpat) will be a game changer for you if you don't already use them. You don't have to grease the pans and cleanup is super easy. Cookies bake more evenly on these as well. Some cookies bake differently on parchment than they do on silicone, but regardless of which you use, you'll get a better outcome than baking straight on a greased cookie sheet.

**Pastry Bags and Tips:** A few of the recipes in this book require frosting cookies. You are more than welcome to just frost using a knife or offset spatula, but I love using a piping bag fitted with a decorative tip. My favorite tip is the Wilton 1M followed by the Ateco 849. I also use disposable piping bags, which makes cleanup a breeze.

**Rolling Pin:** Always good to have in any kitchen, rolling pins do double duty rolling out dough and as a blunt instrument to crush cookies. Choose a standard size without engravings. I prefer the kind without handles (also known as a French rolling pin).

**Spatulas, Whisks, and Wooden Spoons:** Heat-safe spatulas will be your best friends! I have several that I use every day. I prefer a spatula to a wooden spoon for stirring because I can use it to scrape out the bowl as well as stir. I also love having a variety of sizes of whisks: larger ones for bigger mixing and small ones for dry ingredients.

**Thermometer:** It's very important to have an instant-read thermometer or a candy thermometer when baking certain things. If you're making candy or no-bake cookies, precise temperature matters, and only a thermometer will tell you what you need to know. While I do have both types of thermometer, I recommend the instant-read version because it can be used for both baking and cooking, giving you more bang for your buck.

# Storing and Freezing Tips

If you are a normal person making a batch of cookies, you won't need to worry much about storing and freezing, because you and your family will eat what you make. I, however, am not a normal person: I bake for a living and have so many desserts coming out of my kitchen on a weekly basis there is no way we could eat them all, so I am a pro at storing and freezing pretty much anything.

Another reason I love freezing cookies: getting ahead for the holidays. There is nothing I hate more than being rushed and stressed two days before Christmas because I have all the things to bake for all the people. I've perfected the freezing

process for my favorite holiday cookies so they can go from the oven to the freezer, where I can get a month or so of breathing room before it's time to package them all up as gifts.

These tips are a guide to the basics, and you should refer to each recipe for any specifics.

## Storing Cookies

Almost all baked goods should be stored in airtight containers. My favorite containers are gallon-sized resealable bags. They're easy and inexpensive, and they don't take up a ton of room. Refer to specific recipes to see if they should be refrigerated or not.

Cookies and bars with frostings need to be stored loosely covered. For these, I prefer using plastic containers (like Tupperware) or a deep plate or container I can cover with plastic wrap.

Most cookies will last three to four days before going stale. If you're not going to be able to finish them in that time period, I suggest freezing.

## Freezing Cookies

**Paper Towels (My Freezing Secret):** This tip will change your life! Whenever I'm stacking cookies for freezing, I lay down a layer of cookies and then top them with a paper towel (the choose-a-size towels are the best for this). Then I continue stacking, layering each layer between a new paper towel, and freeze the cookies in a container.

The paper towel hack happens after you take the cookies out of the freezer to thaw: The paper towel absorbs the moisture when the cookies thaw, leaving you with perfectly dry and freshly thawed cookies!

The only cookies I don't use the paper towel with are sticky or frosted cookies, because the paper towel would stick.

**Freezing Regular Cookies and Bars:** By "regular" I mean without frosting or sticky tops, just basic cookies that you could stack on a platter. These are by far the easiest to freeze. You can freeze them in layers in gallon-sized bags or reusable containers, usually for up to two or three months (although I have had things even longer than that).

**Freezing Frosted Cookies and Bars:** If you want to make frosted cookies or bars ahead of time, I suggest freezing the cookies (or brownies/bars) unfrosted as already directed. Then, freeze your frosting in an airtight container of its own (see Frosting Tips, page 12). To freeze already frosted cookies, place them in a single layer on a cookie sheet lined with wax or parchment paper. Freeze until solid, and then stack them in gallon-sized bags between layers of parchment or wax paper. Be sure to place them in a single layer when thawing.

**Thawing Cookies:** If you've done the paper towel hack, you can thaw regular cookies and bars right in the gallon-sized bag on the counter. For thawing frosted or sticky cookies and bars, place them in a single layer when thawing so you don't wreck the tops.

# The Seven Rules for Successful Cookie Baking

1. **Read the recipe before you begin.**

   This seems obvious, but it's such a necessary step, one even I forget to do now and again. Read the entire recipe before you bake, which will make sure you have the proper ingredients and tools and time to make your cookies. Some recipes need to be chilled while others don't; reading this information beforehand can ensure you're not up until all hours getting those bake sale cookies ready for the next day's class period.

2. **Assemble all your ingredients and tools before you begin.**

   There is nothing worse than starting a recipe only to find out that the vanilla extract you knew you had is no longer in the pantry. While you're reading the recipe, make sure you have all the ingredients and that they aren't expired. (Spoiler alert: Baking soda and baking powder do expire, and so do spices. If you don't bake very often, it's a good idea to check the dates!) Same goes for tools: Does the recipe call for a 9 × 13–inch (23 × 33 cm) pan, but you only have a 9 × 9–inch? Sometimes substitution of pans and ingredients work, but sometimes it will affect the outcome of the recipe. Save yourself the hassle and check the pantry before you bake!

### 3. Did you soften your butter?

While many of my cookie recipes start with melted butter, several use softened butter. Starting a recipe with softened butter when it calls for it is important to get the butter/sugar mixture just right. I recommend leaving the butter out for at least an hour before you start, or just until a finger pressed into the top leaves a finger indent. (But don't worry, I forget all the time too. In a pinch, microwave your butter on 50 percent power for ten seconds. Flip and heat in five-second increments, until softened to the touch.)

And, while we're on the topic of room temperature ingredients, I don't normally stress about room temperature eggs. If you remember to take them out, great. But it's not going to make or break the outcome—usually—unless the recipe specifies it.

### 4. Do you know how to measure ingredients?

I have several posts about this on my site, and it's a topic that can be lengthy, but I'll just give you the important basics. Use dry measuring cups for dry ingredients (such as flour and sugar). Use a wet measuring cup for liquids, and be sure to use measuring spoons too. If you have one, a kitchen scale is invaluable and will ensure you are measuring correctly.

To measure flour, spoon the flour into the measuring cup and then level it off with the back of a knife. Do *not* pack flour! Same goes for granulated and confectioners' (powdered) sugar. Brown sugar is the only thing that should be packed into the measuring cup.

### 5. Don't skip the chill time.

I know, it's tempting to just bake the cookies, but if a recipe calls for chilling the dough, then it's a necessary evil. Don't skip it!

### 6. Do you know your oven?

Originally, this list had only six items on it . . . until my oven died in the middle of writing this book. When I got my new oven, I realized something I'd already known: how important it is that you know and cater to your oven. Have an oven thermometer so you can test the interior temperature (sometimes those digital readouts can be off). All ovens bake differently, so get to know yours. For example, my old oven baked the back faster than the front, so I was constantly needing to rotate my pans during baking, releasing heat and causing odd baking times. My new oven bakes more evenly, so I can just leave the pans alone the entire time. All the nuances between ovens will affect baking times, which is why I always give a range in my recipes.

### 7. Know how to double a recipe!

Most of the recipes in this book call for somewhere between twenty and thirty cookies. That's because rarely do people need dozens and dozens of cookies, unless it's the holidays. A simple batch can last a family a few days as a special treat, but what if you want to make more? Easy: Double the recipe. Almost every recipe in this book can be doubled by simply multiplying all the ingredients by two. When it comes to pans, you'll just need more cookie sheets or a second 9 × 13–inch (23 × 33 cm) pan. The baking time, as long as you're not using a different pan size, will stay the same. If you want to double a recipe in a 9 × 9–inch pan, you can use two pans or use a 9 × 13–inch, but then your bake time will be longer, as the result will be thicker than shown in the photos.

*Now that we've talked about all that, are you ready? Let's get in the kitchen and bake some cookies!*

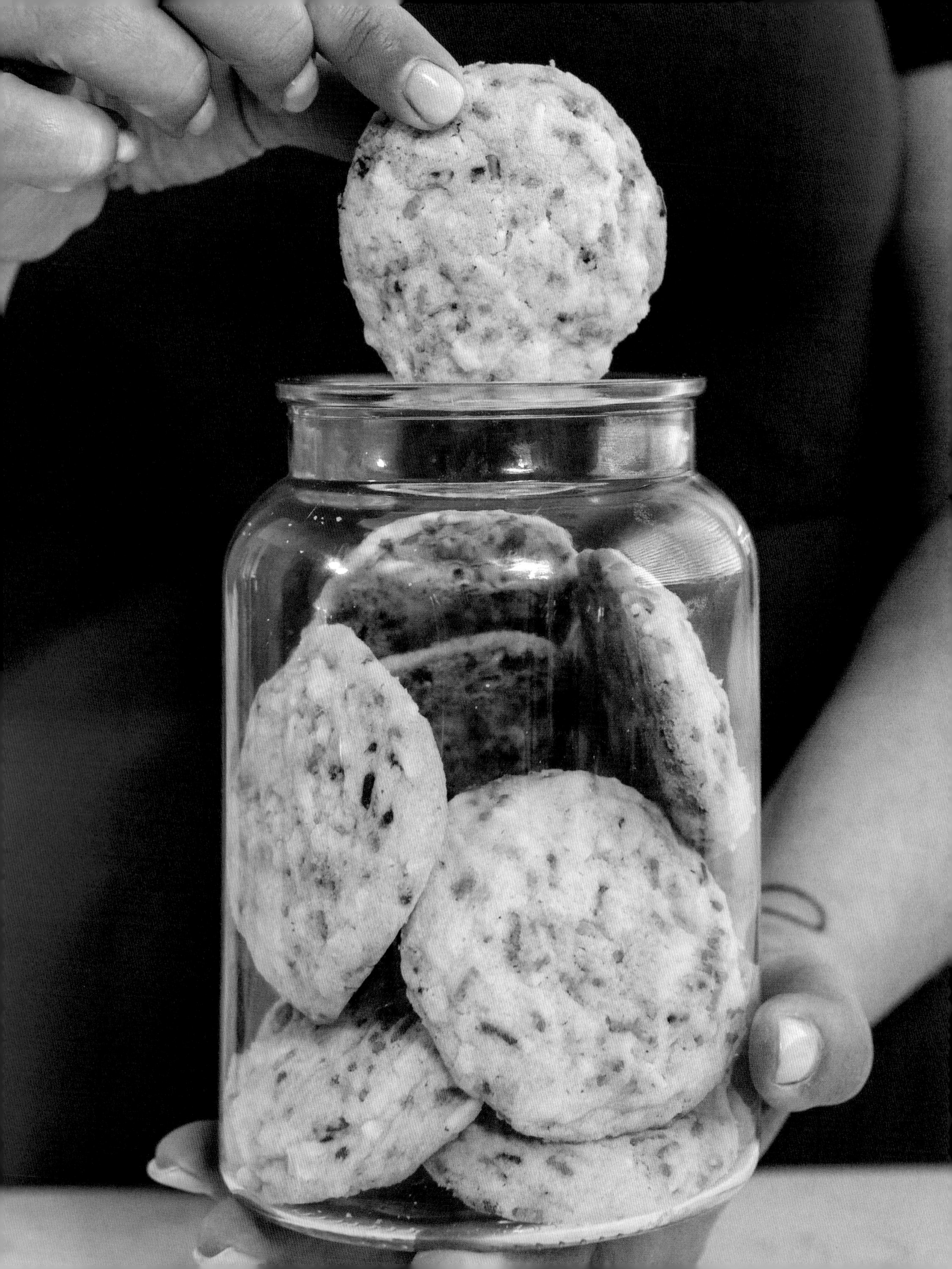

# Cookie Jar Favorites

# CHAPTER 1

These are the classics, the cookies you always gravitate to for comfort or to remember your childhood. From Chocolate Chip to Peanut Butter to my Nana's Sugar Cookies, this chapter is for the child in you, the kid who loved baking with grandma, and the adult who just wants something familiar and delicious.

A few more cookie baking tips:

• **Want to make your cookies look picture-perfect? Here's how:** My friend Karen taught me how to get that gooey and extra pretty look on top of my cookies: Add some extra chocolate chips (or other toppings) when they are done baking. As soon as your cookie sheets come out of the oven, press a few chocolate chips (or whatever the filling of the cookie is) into the tops of the hot just-baked cookies. Let them cool before stacking—and you'll always have gorgeous cookies!

• **Don't overbake your cookies!** Underbaked cookies are soft and chewy and stay gooey for days. Always err on the side of underbaked.

• **Don't crowd the pan:** I usually get about ten to twelve cookies on my large baking sheets. Don't crowd your pan with more cookies or they will bake unevenly.

• **Parchment paper versus silicone:** As noted in the Tools section (see page 13), cookies will bake differently sometimes on parchment paper than they do on silicone baking mats. The silicone often helps them stay puffier while parchment paper can make them flatter. The difference isn't usually hugely significant, but if you want puffier cookies, use silicone (and don't crowd them).

• **Cookie size:** Almost any normal cookie in this chapter or the Crazy Cookies chapter (see page 123) can be made using a 1- or 2-tablespoon cookie scoop. If I call for one or the other, it's because I like the look of them that size, but feel free to interchange them. Just remember smaller cookies bake faster than larger ones!

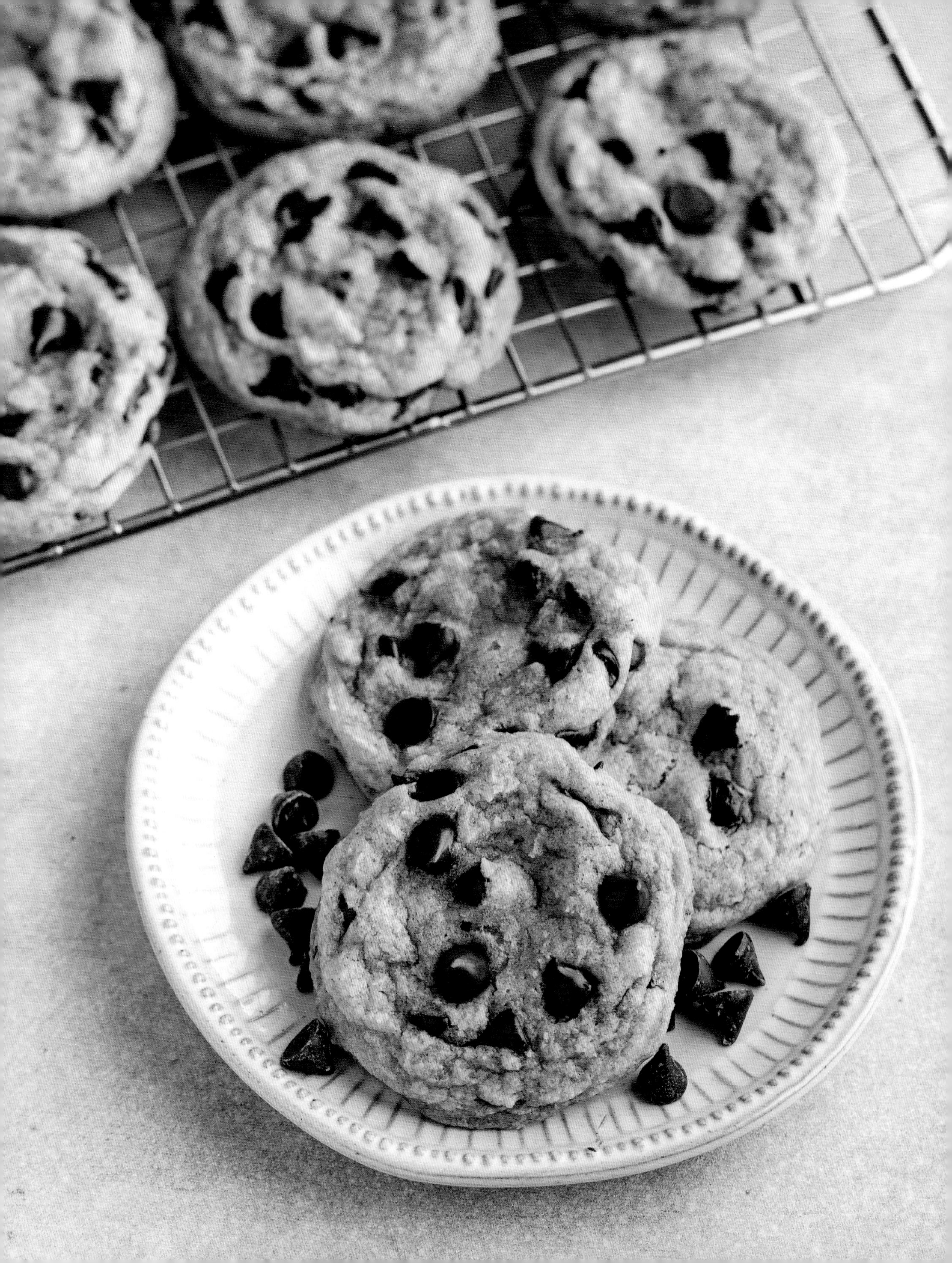

# Seriously the *Best* Chocolate Chip Cookies

To me, chocolate chip cookies are the ultimate comfort food. If I'm craving a cookie, it's not going to be just any chocolate chip cookie—it's going to be *this* one. It's been made thousands of times by my readers and is loved by so many. The cookie dough comes together easily because it starts with melted butter. This recipe is perfect as a cookie, but it can easily be made into bars, cookie cups, or even pie. When you're craving the perfect chocolate chip cookie, this is the one you need. They're worth the wait for the chill time, I promise!

## INSTRUCTIONS

1 Place the melted butter in a large bowl and add both sugars. Stir with a wooden spoon or spatula or mix with an electric mixer until smooth. Mix in the eggs and vanilla extract.

2 Mix in the baking soda and salt, then slowly mix in the flour and combine just until the batter is smooth and comes together. Be sure to scrape the sides of the bowl during mixing. Slowly stir in the chocolate chips.

3 Line a cookie sheet with a silicone baking mat or parchment paper. Scoop balls of cookie dough (each about 2 tablespoons) onto the cookie sheet. Spacing doesn't matter because you will be chilling the dough. Cover the cookie sheet with plastic wrap and chill it in the refrigerator for at least 1 hour.

4 Preheat the oven to 350°F (177°C). Line a second cookie sheet with parchment paper or a silicone baking mat.

5 Remove the chilled cookie dough balls from the refrigerator and space them 2 inches (5 cm) apart on the cookie sheets. Bake for 11 to 13 minutes or just until they lose their glossy sheen. Cool slightly before removing from cookie sheets.

6 Store in an airtight container for up to 3 days or freeze for up to a month.

- 1 cup (226 g) unsalted butter, melted
- ⅔ cup (133 g) granulated sugar
- 1 cup (200 g) packed brown sugar
- 2 large eggs
- 1 teaspoon vanilla extract
- 1 teaspoon baking soda
- 1 teaspoon salt
- 3 cups (372 g) all-purpose flour
- 3 cups (510 g) chocolate chips (semi-sweet or milk)

**Yield:** 38 cookies
**Prep time:** 25 minutes
**Chill time:** 1 hour
**Bake time:** 12 minutes

## Tip:

Try using white chocolate chips or a combination of milk, semi-sweet, and white chocolate chips instead of all one flavor. You can even use flavored chips, chopped candy, or your favorite nuts. Just keep the measurement of add-ins to 3 cups.

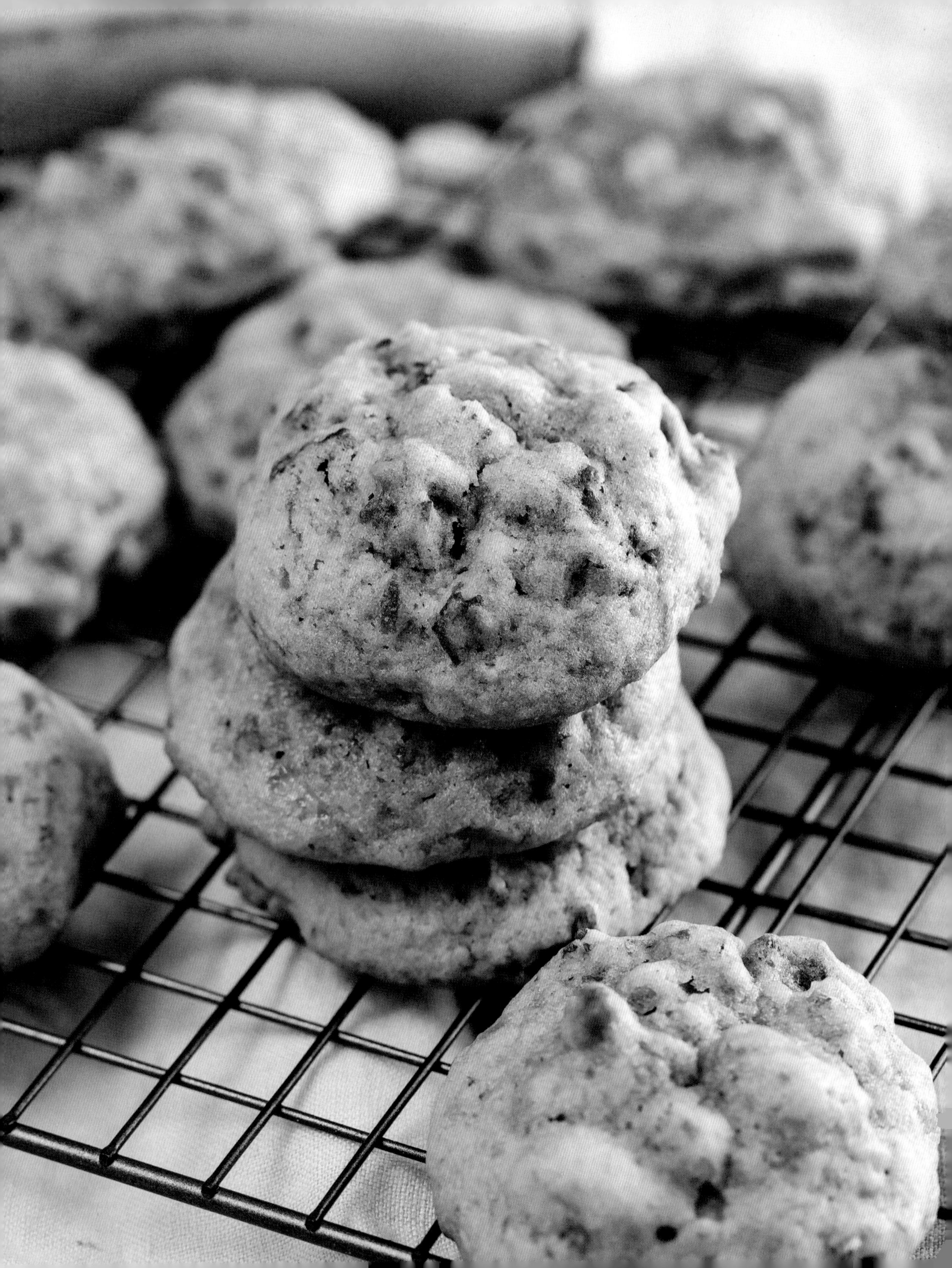

# Banana Nut Cookies

One of my fondest memories from growing up is waking up Saturday mornings to the smells of my mom baking something special for breakfast. On busy days she'd make biscuits I'd slather with butter, on lazier days she'd bake blueberry muffins, but my favorite days were the ones when she'd make banana bread. Her banana bread is legendary: soft and moist with so much banana flavor and the perfect crack right down the center. I decided to bring a little of those weekend mornings to this book with Banana Nut Cookies, dedicated to my mom. These delightful cookies are a cross between cookie and cake with a chewy outside and a soft inside. The banana flavor is perfectly balanced, and the chopped nuts add a delicious crunch. It might not be Saturday morning, but I'll eat one anyway.

## INSTRUCTIONS

1 Preheat the oven to 350°F (177°C). Line 2 cookie sheets with parchment paper or silicone baking mats.

2 Cream the butter and both sugars with an electric mixer (use a paddle attachment if using a stand mixer).

3 Mix in banana, egg yolk, vanilla extract, salt, and baking soda. Add the flour and mix until smooth. Stir in chopped pecans.

4 Scoop balls of cookie dough (each about 2 tablespoons) onto the prepared cookie sheets, spacing 2 inches (5 cm) apart. Bake for 13 to 16 minutes, or until the tops have lost their glossy sheen and the edges are golden.

5 Cool for 5 minutes on the cookie sheets before removing. Store in an airtight container for up to 3 days or freeze for up to 2 months.

- ½ cup (113 g) unsalted butter, softened
- ½ cup (100 g) packed brown sugar
- ¼ cup (50 g) granulated sugar
- 1 medium overripe banana (approximately 116 g), mashed
- 1 large egg yolk
- 1 teaspoon vanilla extract
- ½ teaspoon salt
- ½ teaspoon baking soda
- 1¾ cups (217 g) all-purpose flour
- 1¼ cups (139 g) chopped pecans

**Yield:** 22 cookies
**Prep time:** 20 minutes
**Bake time:** 15 minutes

## Tip:

We also love adding 1 cup (176 g) mini chocolate chips to the batter in place of the nuts. The chocolate and banana flavor are so good together!

# Toffee Chippers

*I* used to love grocery shopping with my mom because she'd usually let me get one or two things that weren't on her list. One of my favorites: Entenmann's English Toffee Cookies. That white box with the blue scroll—just walking by the box now brings so many memories to my mind. This cookie is an ode to those little bites— and homemade too, so you never have to wait to go shopping to have your fill. Sometimes I use Heath Bits O' Brickle toffee bits and sometimes I use the milk chocolate; it just depends on my mood. Both taste amazing in these little bites of heaven!

## INSTRUCTIONS

1   Line cookie sheets with parchment paper or silicone baking mats.

2   Cream the butter and both sugars with a hand or a stand mixer until light and fluffy. Mix in the egg and vanilla extract until smooth.

3   Mix in the baking soda and salt, then slowly mix in the flour. Stir in the toffee bits.

4   Scoop balls of cookie dough (each about 1 tablespoon) and place about 2 inches (5 cm) apart on the prepared cookie sheets. Chill the cookies for 30 minutes.

5   Preheat the oven to 350°F (177°C). Bake the cookies for 10 to 13 minutes or until they are lightly golden around the edges and no longer glossy on top.

6   Cool the cookies for 5 minutes before removing them from the cookie sheets. Store in an airtight container for up to 3 days or freeze for up to a month.

- ½ cup (113 g) unsalted butter, softened
- ⅓ cup (67 g) granulated sugar
- ½ cup (100 g) brown sugar, packed
- 1 large egg
- 1 teaspoon vanilla extract
- ½ teaspoon baking soda
- ½ teaspoon salt
- 1½ cups (186 g) all-purpose flour
- 1½ cups (236 g) toffee bits

**Yield:** 36 cookies
**Prep time:** 20 minutes
**Chill time:** 30 minutes
**Bake time:** 12 minutes

## Tip:

Feeling like chocolate? Use ¾ cup (118 g) toffee bits and ¾ cup (126 g) mini chocolate chips!

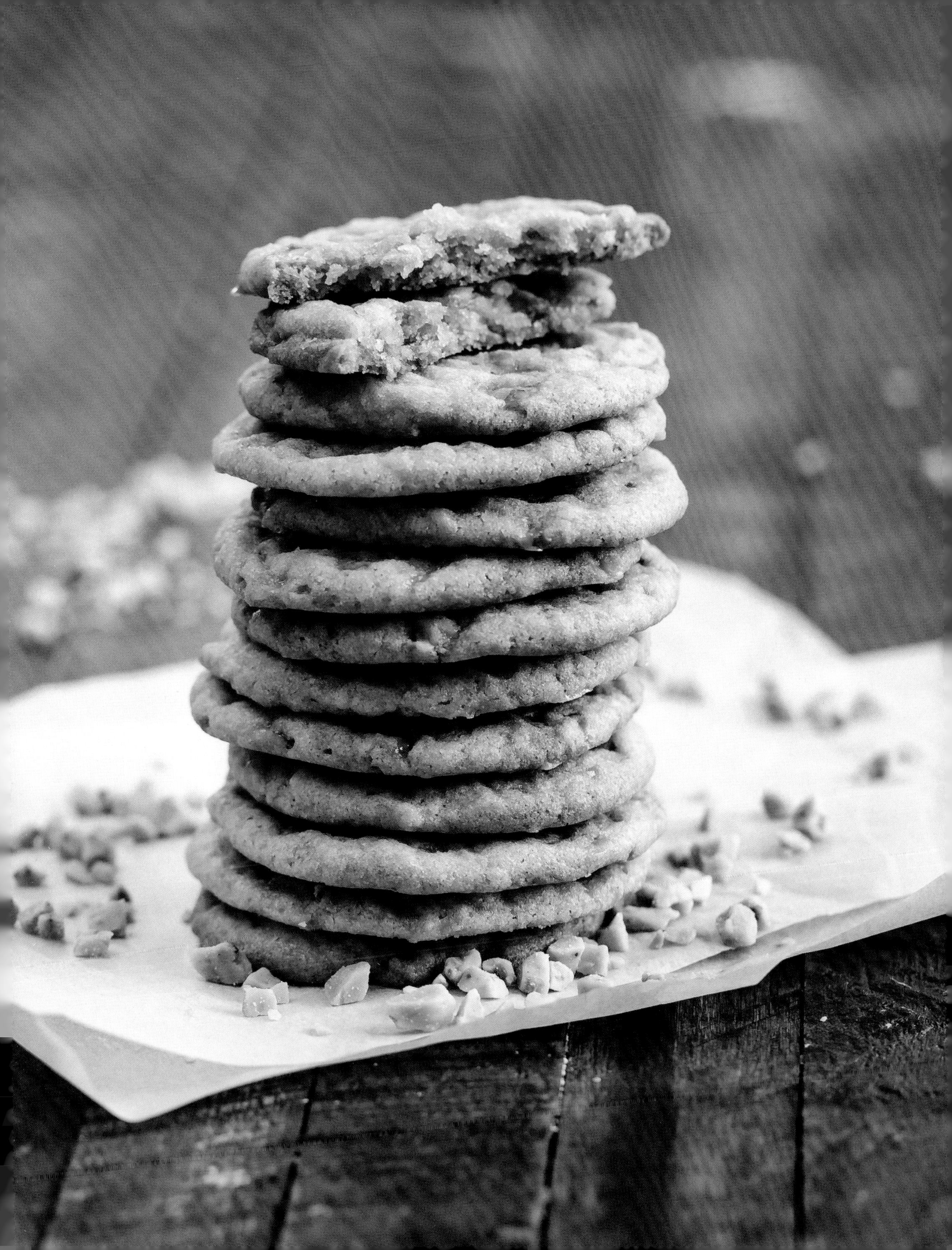

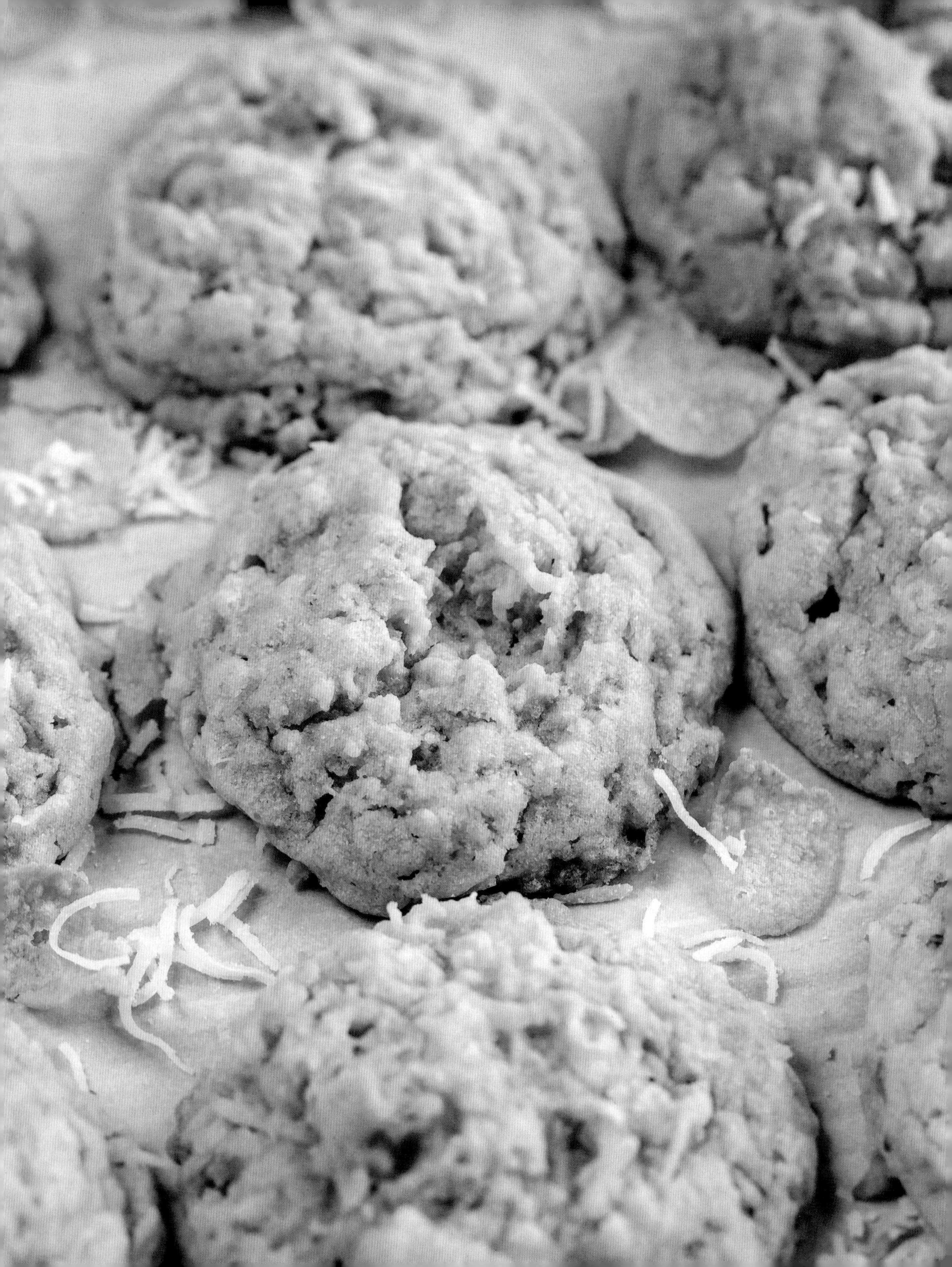

# Coconut Cornflake Cookies

*A* few years back, while visiting my parents, I spent a few hours going through my mom's recipe box, making copies of all the recipes I wanted to make. These Coconut Cornflake Cookies are one of those recipes, one that intrigued me because it has both butter *and* oil. I'm glad I was curious, because the texture of these cookies is a completely new breed. It's not quite a chocolate chip cookie texture, not quite shortbread, but a combination of the two. Chewy, rich, buttery, and slightly sandy, the cookies themselves are the perfect blank canvas. In this version I went with coconut and cornflakes, but I've also used other cereals and added chocolate. Watch out, though—you can't eat just one of these. They're more addicting than they seem!

## INSTRUCTIONS

1  Cream the butter and both sugars in a large bowl with an electric mixer until fluffy and smooth. Mix in the vegetable oil (mixture may be chunky).

2  Add the egg, baking soda, salt, and vanilla extract and mix until combined; then slowly mix in the flour until smooth. Mix in the coconut and cornflakes.

3  Scoop balls of cookie dough (each about 2 tablespoons) and place on a cookie sheet covered with parchment paper or a silicone baking mat. Chill for 30 minutes.

4  Preheat the oven to 350°F (177°C). Line 2 cookie sheets with parchment paper or silicone baking mats. Place cookie dough balls 2 inches (5 cm) apart on the prepared cookie sheets. Bake for 13 to 16 minutes or until lightly golden around the edges and no longer glossy on top.

5  Cool the cookies slightly before removing them from the cookie sheets. Store in an airtight container for up to 4 days or freeze for up to 2 months.

- ½ cup (113 g) unsalted butter, softened
- ½ cup (100 g) granulated sugar
- ½ cup (100 g) packed brown sugar
- ½ cup (120 ml) vegetable oil
- 1 large egg
- ½ teaspoon baking soda
- ½ teaspoon salt
- 1 teaspoon vanilla
- 2¼ cups (273 g) all-purpose flour
- 1½ cups (180 g) sweetened shredded coconut
- 2 cups (50 g) cornflakes, lightly crushed

**Yield:** 25 cookies
**Prep time:** 20 minutes
**Chill time:** 30 minutes
**Bake time:** 15 minutes

## Tip:

Want even more coconut flavor? Add ½ teaspoon coconut extract with the vanilla extract in step 2. These are also fantastic made with 1 cup (170 g) chocolate chips and Frosted Flakes in place of cornflakes!

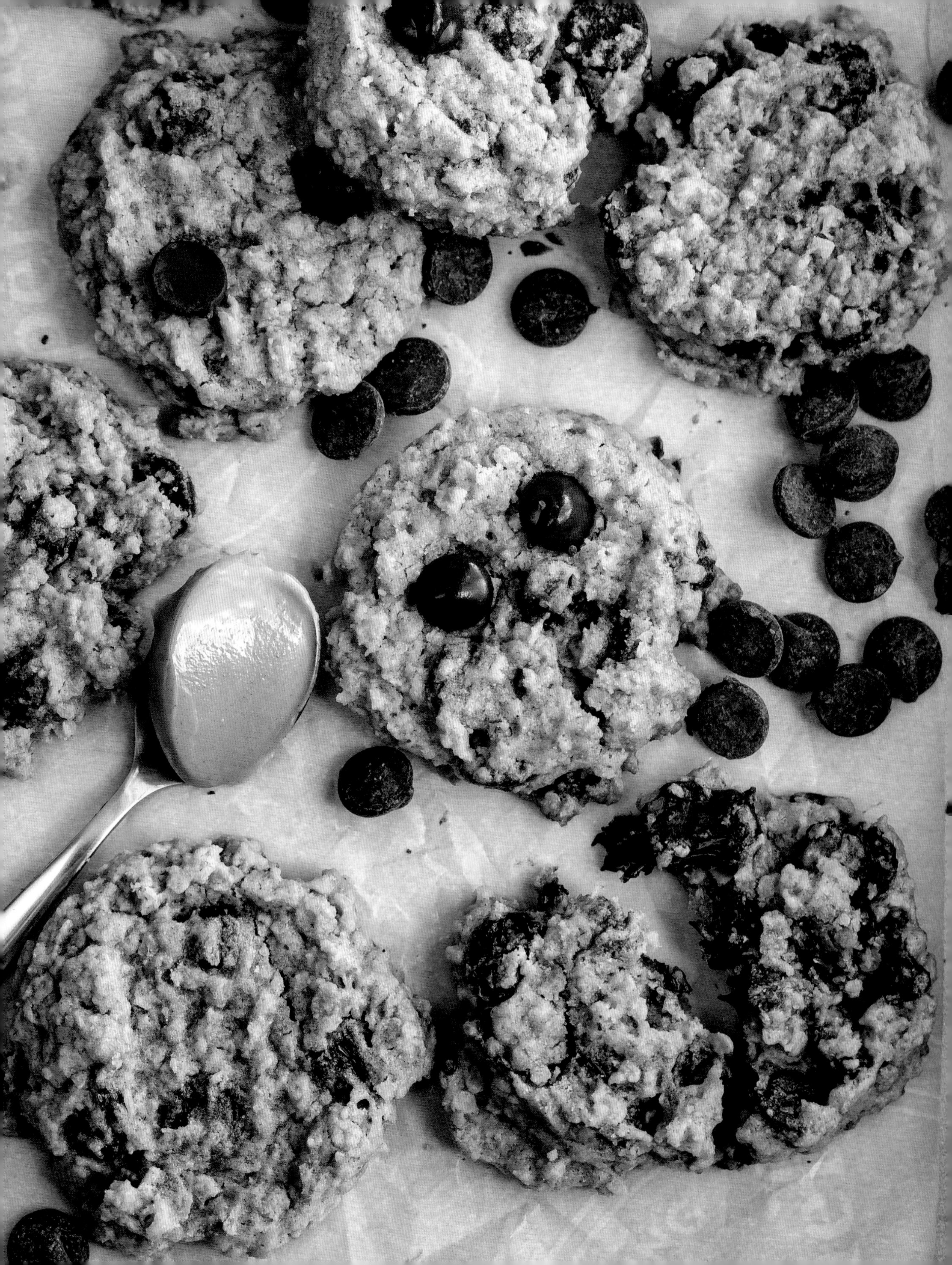

# Peanut Butter Oatmeal Chocolate Chip Cookies

**M**any of the recipes I come up with for my blog are done purely for search reasons: I see that people search for certain recipes, so I create my own and hope that it will show up on Google. This was one of those recipes I created purely for that reason, not expecting much. I mean, of course it was going to be delicious—peanut butter + oatmeal cookies—but the response I got from my audience was truly shocking. To date it's still one of my more popular recipes, so I wanted to share a new version of it here. This one, dare I say, is even better: It has chocolate chips. And everything is better with chocolate!

## INSTRUCTIONS

1 Preheat the oven to 350°F (177°C). Line 2 cookie sheets with parchment paper or silicone baking mats.

2 Mix the butter and peanut butter in a large bowl with an electric mixer until smooth. Add both sugars and cream until fluffy.

3 Add the egg, milk, vanilla extract, baking soda, cinnamon, and salt and mix until smooth. Mix in the oats; then mix in the flour. Stir in the chocolate chips.

4 Scoop balls of cookie dough (each about 2 tablespoons) 2 inches (5 cm) apart onto prepared cookie sheets. Use a fork to press them down with crisscross marks, like you would with regular peanut butter cookies. If the fork sticks to the cookie dough, dip the fork in some granulated sugar.

5 Bake for 11 to 14 minutes or until they just lose their glossy sheen. Cool for at least 5 minutes before removing them from the cookie sheets.

6 Store in an airtight container for up to 3 days or freeze for up to 3 months. The recipe can easily be doubled.

- ½ cup (113 g) unsalted butter, softened
- ½ cup (134 g) creamy peanut butter
- ½ cup (100 g) packed brown sugar
- ⅓ cup (67 g) granulated sugar
- 1 large egg
- 1 tablespoon (15 ml) milk
- 1 teaspoon vanilla extract
- ½ teaspoon baking soda
- 1 teaspoon cinnamon
- ¼ teaspoon salt
- 1½ cups (128 g) quick-cooking oats
- ¾ cup (93 g) all-purpose flour
- 1 cup (170 g) chocolate chips

**Yield:** 30 brownies
**Prep time:** 20 minutes
**Bake time:** 12 minutes

# Nana's Drop Sugar Cookies

From age eight to eleven I stayed with my Nana after school and during summers while my parents worked. She would cook three-course meals for me at lunch and bake me cookies every day. I loved her sugar cookies—I looked forward to them every day! They were soft and chewy and rolled in granulated sugar before baking so they had that crunchy exterior—I can still taste them. Years after she passed away, I mentioned that to my mom and she laughed and spilled my Nana's deep dark secret: Her amazing sugar cookies were actually cookie dough from the grocery store. We had a good laugh that afternoon! This cookie is a tribute to my Nana: They're softer than hers and I serve them plain and with frosting, but every time I take a bite, I think back to those days spent with her. Hopefully they can create some fun memories with your family too.

## MAKE THE COOKIES

1  Preheat the oven to 350°F (177°C). Line 2 cookie sheets with parchment paper or silicone baking mats.

2  Cream the butter and sugar in the bowl of a stand mixer fitted with the paddle attachment (or a large bowl if using a hand mixer). Cream until the mixture is fluffy, about 1 to 2 minutes.

3  Add the egg, egg yolk, and vanilla extract and mix until smooth; then mix in the baking soda, cream of tartar, and salt. Add the flour and mix until a cookie dough forms.

4  Scoop balls of cookie dough (each about 2 tablespoons) 2 inches (5 cm) apart on the cookie sheets. Bake for 11 to 15 minutes, or until the tops are just no longer glossy and the edges are slightly golden. Cool on the cookie sheets before frosting.

## MAKE THE FROSTING (SEE FROSTING TIPS, PAGE 12)

1  Mix the butter in a large bowl with a hand mixer until smooth, then slowly mix in the powdered sugar a little bit at a time. The mixture will be very crumbly. Add the vanilla extract and mix; then add the salt and milk. Beat until smooth and creamy.

2  Tint with the food coloring, if desired.

3  Frost the cookies as desired, decorating with sprinkles.

4  Store in an airtight container in a single layer for up to 3 days or freeze unfrosted cookies for up to a month. You can also freeze prepared frosting.

### For the Cookies

- ¾ cup (170 g) unsalted butter, softened
- ¾ cup (150 g) granulated sugar
- 1 large egg
- 1 large egg yolk
- 1 teaspoon vanilla extract
- ½ teaspoon baking soda
- ½ teaspoon cream of tartar
- ½ teaspoon salt
- 2 cups (248 g) all-purpose flour

### For the Frosting

- 4 tablespoons (47 g) unsalted butter, softened
- 1⅓ cups (151 g) powdered sugar
- 1 teaspoon vanilla extract
- ⅛ teaspoon salt
- 1 tablespoon (15 ml) milk
- Food coloring and sprinkles, optional

**Yield:** 17 cookies
**Prep time:** 25 minutes
**Bake time:** 12 minutes

## Tip:

Skip the frosting and roll the cookie dough balls in granulated sugar before baking. These are good with or *without* frosting!

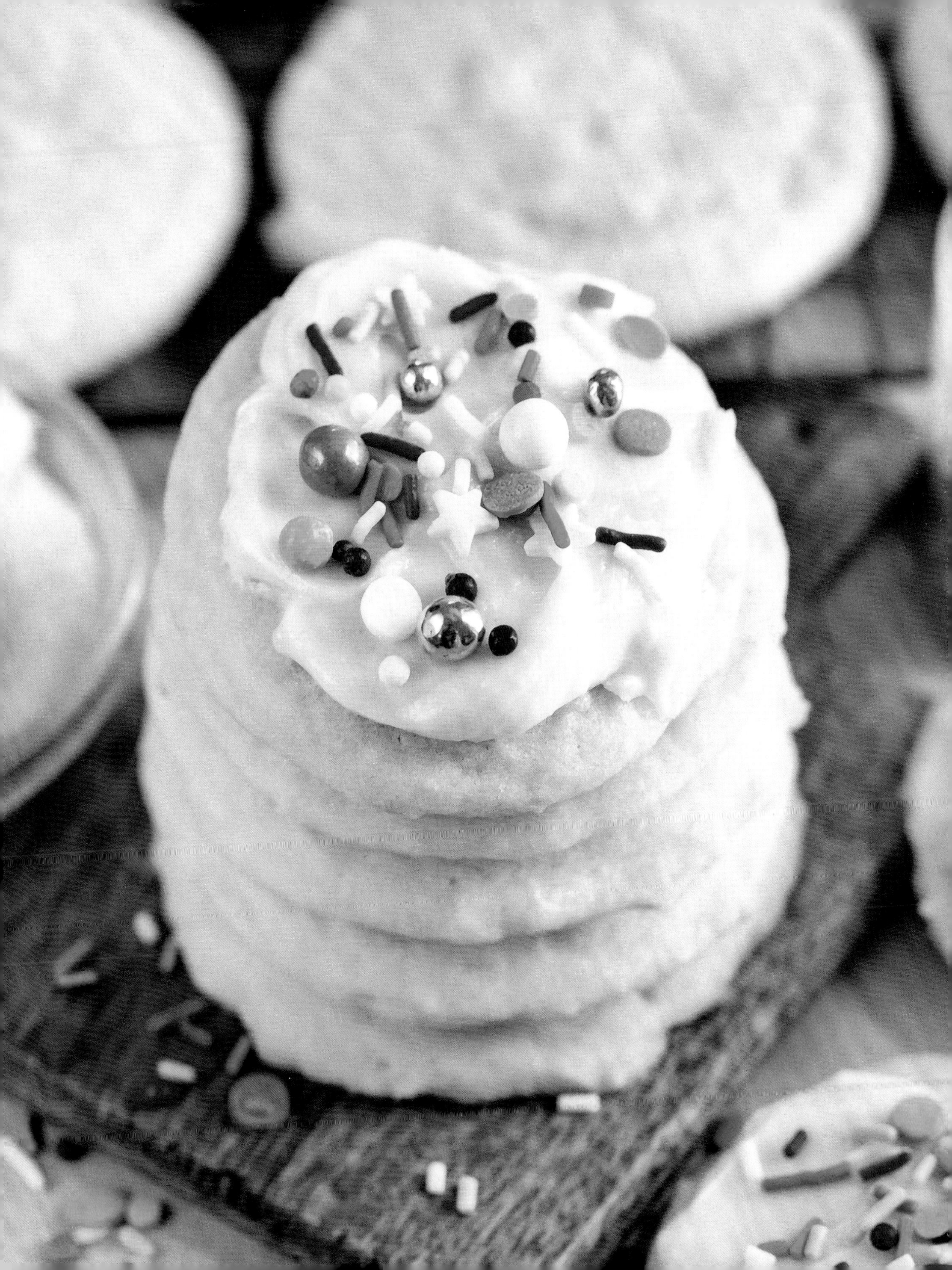

# Trail Mix Oatmeal Cookies

I started out making these cookies years ago as a way to use up trail mix no one wanted to eat. See, my daughter always begged me to buy it (I guess it was a popular schoolyard snack), but then she'd eat just the chocolate out of it. For months I'd clean out her lunchbox and find baggies of trail mix leftovers: nuts and raisins. I guess I should be thankful she never thought to hide her selectiveness by just throwing away the rest! Her pickiness is now your gain: Trail Mix Oatmeal Cookies. Crunchy nuts, soft raisins, and, yes, the chocolate, all in one cookie. I love the flavors with the chewy oatmeal—it makes me think I'm hiking when I'm really indoors binging *Real Housewives*.

## INSTRUCTIONS

1  In a medium bowl, whisk together the flour, cinnamon, salt, and baking soda. Set aside.

2  Cream the butter and sugar in the bowl of a stand mixer fitted with the paddle attachment. (You can also use a large bowl and a hand mixer.) Cream until smooth, about 1 to 2 minutes. Mix in eggs and vanilla extract; beat until smooth.

3  Gradually mix in the dry ingredients until smooth, being careful not to overmix. Add the oats and mix, and then stir in the trail mix.

4  Scoop balls of cookie dough (each about 2 tablespoons) and place on a cookie sheet lined with parchment or wax paper. Cover with plastic wrap and chill for at least 1 hour.

5  When ready to bake, preheat the oven to 350°F (177°C). Line 2 cookie sheets with parchment paper or silicone baking mats and place the cookie dough balls 2 inches (5 cm) apart.

6  Bake for 10 to 12 minutes, until the bottoms are slightly golden. Cool on the cookie sheets for 10 minutes, then remove to a rack to cool completely.

7  Store cookies in an airtight container for up to 4 days. They can also be frozen in an airtight container or resealable bag for up to 2 months.

- 1½ cups (186 g) all-purpose flour
- 1 teaspoon ground cinnamon
- 1 teaspoon salt
- 1 teaspoon baking soda
- 1 cup (226 g) unsalted butter, softened
- 1½ cups (300 g) packed brown sugar
- 2 large eggs
- 1 teaspoon vanilla extract
- 3¼ cups (276 g) quick-cooking oats
- 1½ cups (212 g) trail mix (any kind)

**Yield:** 36 cookies
**Prep time:** 15 minutes
**Chill time:** 1 hour
**Bake time:** 12 minutes

## Tip:

Make cookie bars by pressing the dough into a 9 × 13–inch (23 × 33 cm) pan lined with foil and sprayed with nonstick cooking spray. Bake for 20 to 25 minutes for bar cookies!

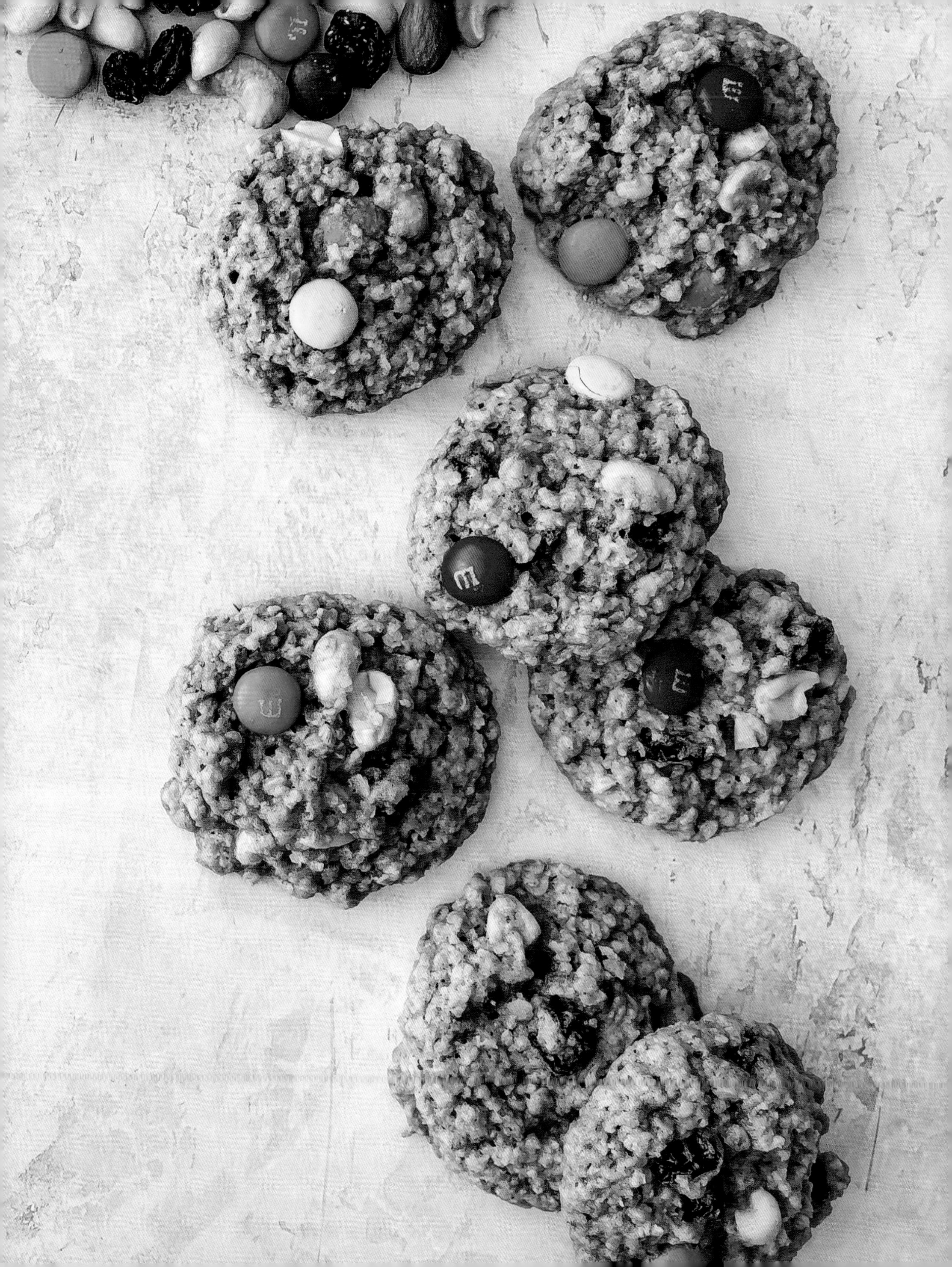

# Mel's Peanut Butter Lovers' Cookies

People often find it funny when I tell them my husband rarely eats my desserts. Even on holidays he might just have one bite of pie or one cookie—if anything at all! However, there are two desserts he cannot resist, and peanut butter cookies are one of them. I know with 100 percent certainty that if I make peanut butter cookies he is bound to eat at least one, which is the reason I created this recipe. This is a not-so-basic peanut butter cookie with added chopped peanuts and peanut butter chips for triple the peanut flavor. He ate two of these cookies: a record!

## INSTRUCTIONS

1  Preheat the oven to 350°F (177°C). Line 2 cookie sheets with silicone baking mats or parchment paper.

2  Mix the butter and peanut butter in a large bowl with a hand mixer (or the bowl of a stand mixer fitted with the paddle attachment) until smooth. Add both sugars and cream until fluffy.

3  Add the vanilla extract, egg, milk, baking soda, and salt and mix until smooth. Then add the flour and mix just until a cookie dough forms. Mix in chopped peanuts and peanut butter chips.

4  Scoop cookie dough balls (each about 2 tablespoons) onto the prepared cookie sheets, spacing the cookies 2 inches (5 cm) apart. Use a fork to press the cookies, adding the crisscross pattern.

5  Bake for 10 to 12 minutes, rotating pans halfway through baking, until they just lose their glossy sheen and the bottoms are slightly golden.

6  Cool the cookies on the cookie sheets before removing and baking additional cookies.

7  Store in an airtight container for up to 3 days or freeze for up to a month.

- ½ cup (113 g) unsalted butter, softened
- ¾ cup (200 g) creamy peanut butter
- ¾ cup (150 g) packed brown sugar
- ¼ cup (50 g) granulated sugar
- 1 teaspoon vanilla extract
- 1 large egg
- 1 tablespoon (15 ml) milk (any kind)
- ½ teaspoon baking soda
- ¼ teaspoon salt
- 1¾ cups (217 g) all-purpose flour
- ¾ cup (108 g) coarsely chopped honey roasted peanuts (or your favorite peanuts)
- 1 cup (165 g) peanut butter chips

**Yield:** 26 cookies
**Prep time:** 20 minutes
**Bake time:** 12 minutes

## Tip:

Substitute chocolate chips for the peanut butter chips and you'll have a cookie that tastes like a crunchy peanut butter cup!

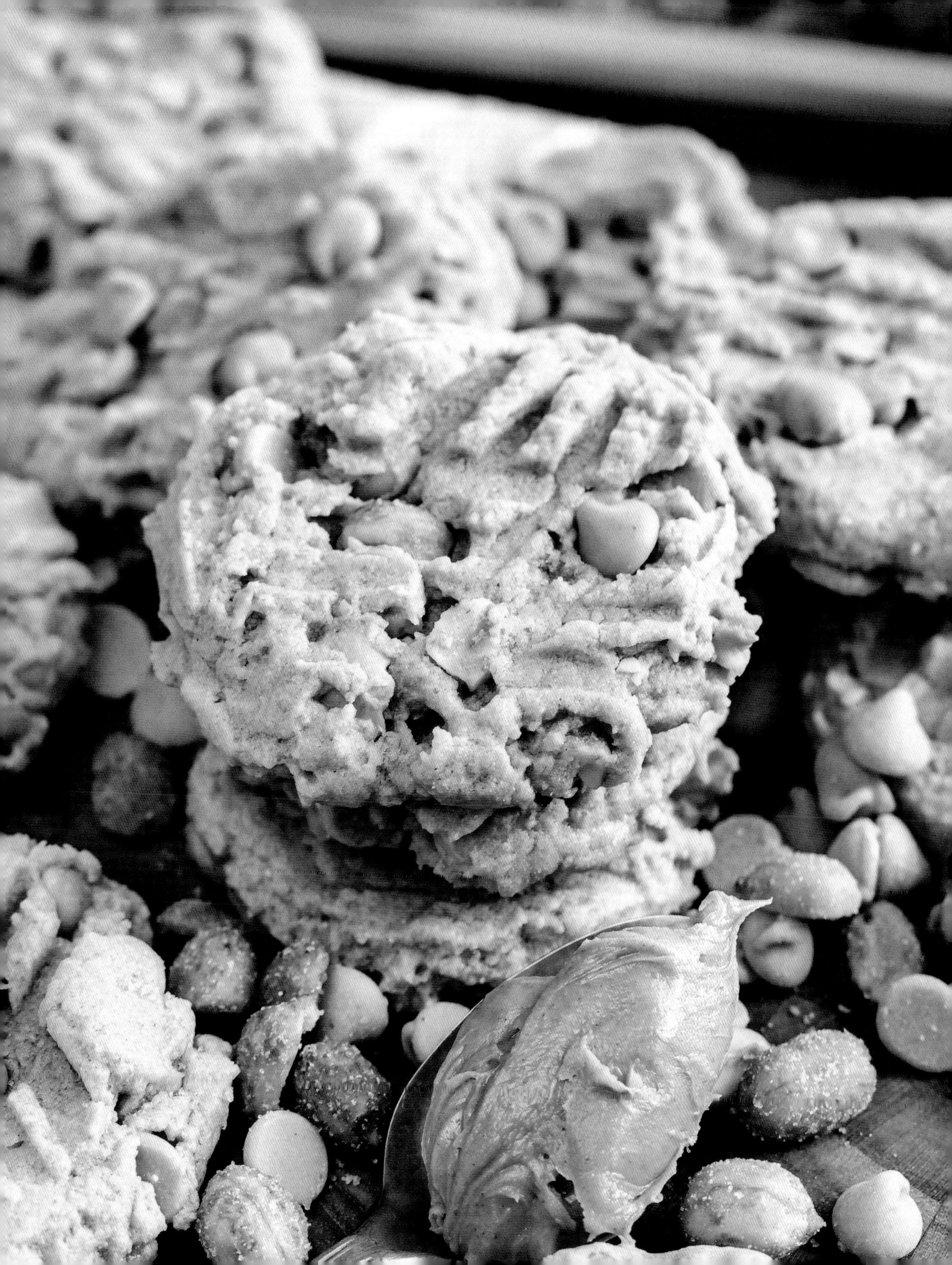

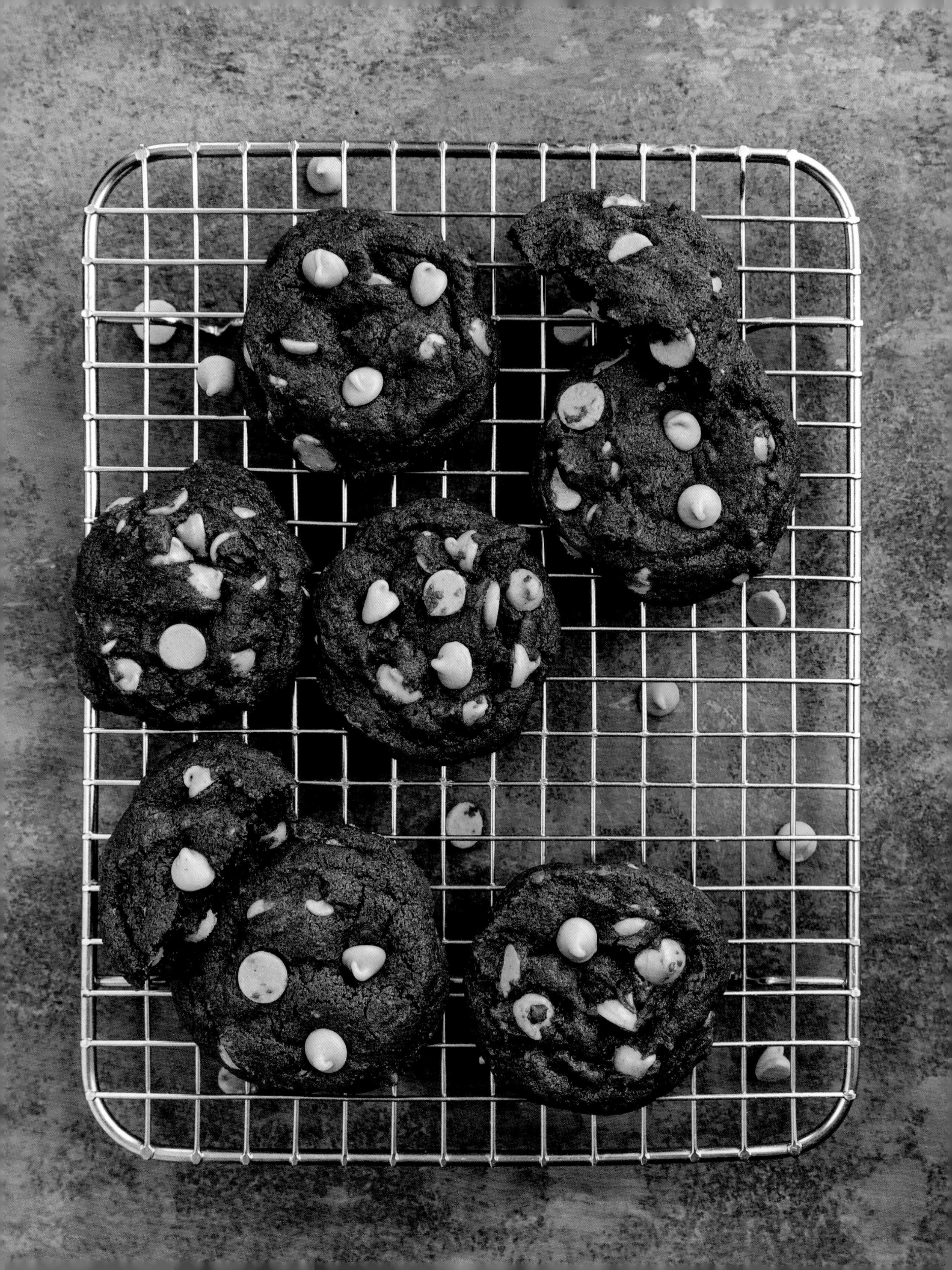

# Peanut Butter Chip Chocolate Cookies

*J* am obsessed with trying new bakeries whenever I travel. I've been known to drive an hour out of the way just to try a popular Instagram spot, so when we were in New York City a few years ago I knew I was going to try Levain Bakery. I'd seen them on social media for years: ginormous cookies with gooey insides in just a few simple flavors. We ended up at their flagship store one day—going out of our way, of course—and they did not disappoint. My favorite was the chocolate cookie with peanut butter chips: a giant softball-sized cookie that could easily have served four.

This cookie recipe is an ode to that amazing cookie, but smaller and more manageable. In everyday life I rarely make ginormous cookies because then I'll just eat three huge cookies instead of three normal-sized ones. (I've never known willpower—what's that like?) I used my favorite chocolate cookie base and added a hefty dose of peanut butter chips. If you can't find these in the baking aisle, you can definitely find them on Amazon and it's worth the order, I promise. A little piece of NYC, right in your kitchen.

- ½ cup (113 g) unsalted butter, melted
- ⅓ cup (67 g) granulated sugar
- ½ cup (100 g) packed brown sugar
- 1 large egg
- 1 teaspoon vanilla extract
- ½ teaspoon salt
- ½ teaspoon baking soda
- ¼ cup (20 g) unsweetened cocoa powder
- 1⅓ cups (165 g) all-purpose flour
- 1½ cups (248 g) peanut butter chips

**Yield:** 22 cookies
**Prep time:** 15 minutes
**Chill time:** 1 hour
**Bake time:** 11 minutes

## INSTRUCTIONS

1 Stir together the butter and both sugars until smooth and combined. You can do this with a spoon or use a mixer.

2 Stir in the egg, vanilla extract, salt, baking soda, and cocoa; then add the flour and stir carefully until combined and smooth. Stir in the peanut butter chips.

3 Scoop balls of cookie dough (each about 2 tablespoons) and place on a parchment-lined cookie sheet. Spacing doesn't matter; we are chilling the dough. Chill the dough for 1 to 2 hours.

4 Preheat oven to 350°F (177°C). Line 2 cookie sheets with parchment paper or silicone baking mats. Place cookies 2 inches (5 cm) apart on the cookie sheets and bake for about 10 to 12 minutes, or until they are no longer glossy.

5 Cool slightly on the cookie sheets before removing. Store in an airtight container for up to 3 days or freeze for up to a month.

*Tip:*
You can chill the dough up to 24 hours before baking—just be sure to cover them so they don't dry out. If they have chilled longer than 4 hours, lightly press with the palm of your hand to slightly flatten the cookies before baking.

# Sprinkle Cookies

**U**ntil 2004 I thought of pink as a silly color. Really, I'd never have been caught dead wearing pink, carrying pink, or doing anything using the color. Pink was childish! But then pink came back in fashion big time (remember monogrammed pink sweaters?) and, all of a sudden, I was obsessed. I remember seeing a pink raincoat in an Old Navy and having to have it. Mind you, we lived in Arizona at the time, but I wore it everywhere the second it dipped below 70°F (21°C).

I call the pink period my awakening to all things glittery, sparkly, and *sprinkled*. And so began my love affair with putting sprinkles in every baked good, especially cookies. These are one of my favorite cookies: a soft and chewy sugar cookie filled with sprinkles! Be sure to use sprinkles for these—they hold up better than nonpareils—and you can use any color, but rainbow is the best, obviously.

- ¾ cup (170 g) unsalted butter, softened
- ¾ cup (150 g) granulated sugar
- 1 large egg
- 1 egg yolk
- 1 teaspoon vanilla extract
- ½ teaspoon baking soda
- ½ teaspoon cream of tartar
- ½ teaspoon salt
- 2 cups (248 g) all-purpose flour
- 1 cup (194 g) sprinkles, any colors

**Yield:** 22 cookies
**Prep time:** 15 minutes
**Bake time:** 10 minutes

## INSTRUCTIONS

1  Preheat the oven to 350°F (177°C). Line 2 cookie sheets with parchment paper or silicone baking mats. These cookies spread more on parchment paper than on silicone.

2  Cream the butter and sugar with a stand mixer fitted with the paddle attachment (or you may use a hand mixer). Once the mixture is creamed and fluffy, mix in the egg, egg yolk, and vanilla extract until smooth; then mix in the baking soda, cream of tartar, and salt. Slowly mix in the flour until the mixture is just combined. Stir in the sprinkles.

3  Scoop balls of cookie dough (each about 2 tablespoons) and place them 2 inches (5 cm) apart on the prepared cookie sheets. Bake for 9 to 11 minutes, or until the bottoms just start to turn golden brown. (These taste better if you err on the side of under- rather than overdone.) Cool for at least 5 minutes on the cookie sheets before removing.

4  Store in an airtight container for up to 3 days or freeze for up to 3 months. You can easily double the recipe for more cookies.

## Tip:

Can't find cream of tartar? Add 1 teaspoon fresh lemon juice instead!

**Parchment Paper Versus Silicone Baking Mats (Silpat)**

While both work in a similar manner (as nonstick surfaces, they bake cookies more evenly and help with easy cleanup), there can be baking differences between the two. Most of the time the differences aren't noticeable (as with chocolate chip cookies). However, occasionally with more tender cookies (like sugar or sprinkle cookies) the differences are more obvious. Cookies baked on parchment paper will often be flatter than those baked on silicone: The silicone helps to grip the cookies, leaving them a bit puffier. So, if you're baking on parchment paper and your cookies fall flatter, that could be why.

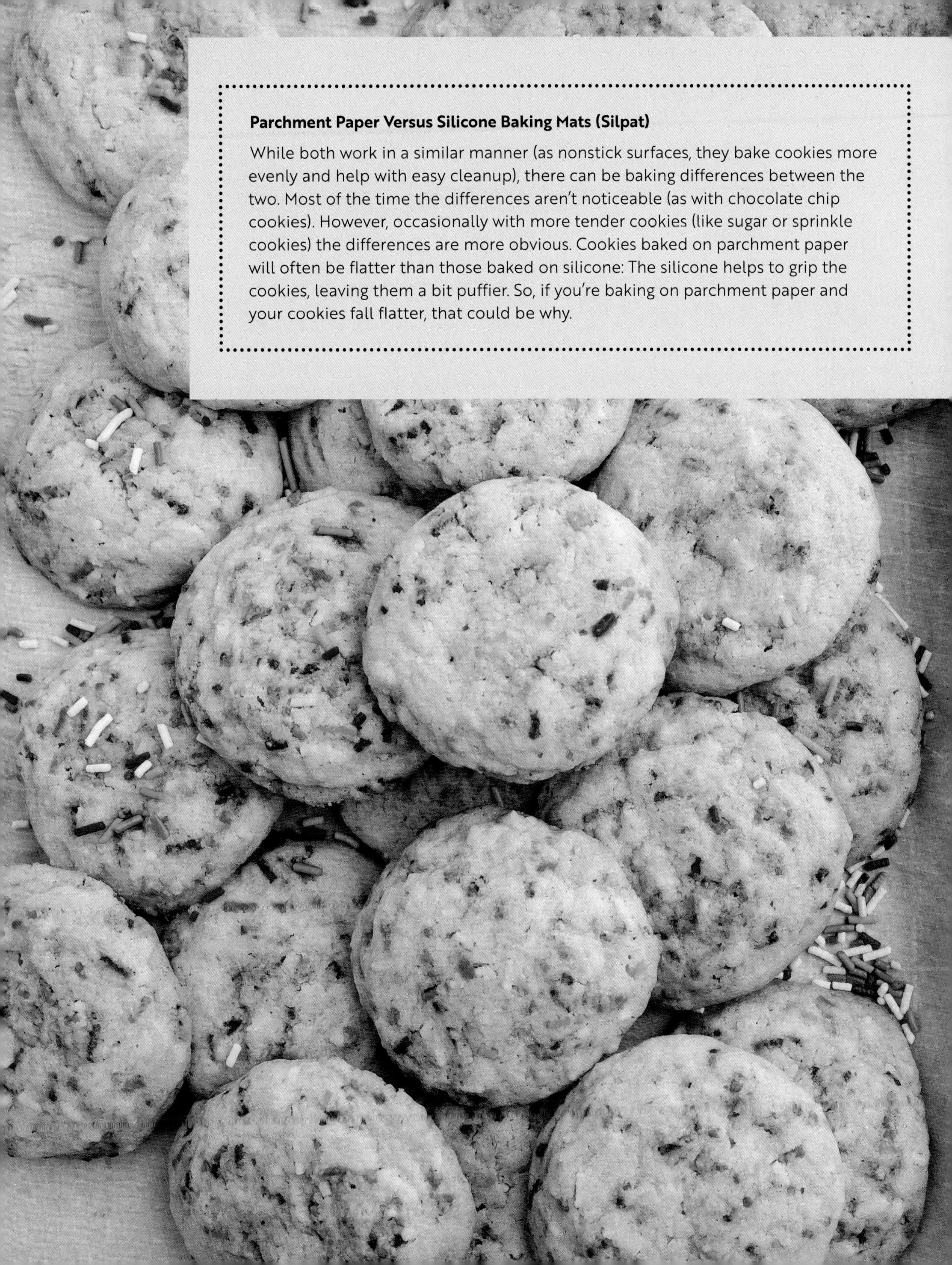

# The Great Pumpkin Cookie Recipe

When I set out to create the perfect pumpkin cookie recipe that was chewy and soft but not cakey, I didn't realize how many batches of pumpkin cookies I'd have to make. Pumpkin is a finicky ingredient because it's wet and practically flavorless by itself, so it takes quite a bit of finessing to get the recipe just right. I used my old standby—melted butter—to give these a caramelized taste with all the delicious brown sugar. These are soft and pillowy and are (dare I say) even better than pumpkin pie. It's The Great Pumpkin Cookie Recipe because you can do almost anything to it: add any flavors, mix-ins, or frostings, or even make it as bars or a cookie cake. I'm showing you four different ways to dress this cookie . . . pumpkin cookies are in fashion any time of year!

## INSTRUCTIONS

1  Whisk the flour, baking soda, salt, nutmeg, cinnamon, ginger, and allspice in a medium bowl. Set aside.

2  Place melted butter, pumpkin puree, brown sugar, and granulated sugar in a large bowl. You can mix this with an electric mixer or stir by hand with a wooden spoon. Mix until combined. Add the egg yolk and vanilla extract, stir to combined, and then mix in the dry ingredients.

3  At this point, add your mix-ins (if using) or skip them to make frosted cookies.

4  Scoop balls of cookie dough (each about 2 tablespoons) and place them on the cookie sheet. You can place them right next to each other for this chilling step. Cover the cookie sheet with plastic wrap and chill for at least 1 hour.

5  Preheat the oven to 350°F (177°C). Place the cookies 2 inches (5 cm) apart onto two lined cookie sheets and bake for 12 to 15 minutes, until the tops are no longer glossy and the bottoms just start to turn brown. Let them cool completely before removing. Store in an airtight container for up to 3 days or freeze for up to a month. This recipe can easily be doubled.

## FOR THE FROSTING

1  Mix the cream cheese and butter in a large bowl with an electric mixer until smooth. Slowly mix in the powdered sugar; then mix in the vanilla extract and cinnamon and beat until smooth and creamy. Frost cookies as desired.

2  Store frosted cookies in a single layer in an airtight container in the refrigerator for up to 3 days.

- 1¾ cups (217 g) all-purpose flour
- ½ teaspoon baking soda
- ½ teaspoon salt
- ½ teaspoon ground nutmeg
- 1 teaspoon ground cinnamon
- ¼ teaspoon ground ginger
- ¼ teaspoon ground allspice
- ½ cup (113 g) unsalted butter, melted
- ⅓ cup (82 g) pumpkin puree
- ¾ cup (150 g) packed brown sugar
- ¼ cup (50 g) granulated sugar
- 1 large egg yolk
- 1 teaspoon vanilla extract
- 1½ cups mix-ins (see Variations) or leave them plain for frosted cookies

### Cinnamon Cream Cheese Frosting

- 4 ounces (112 g) cream cheese, softened
- ¼ cup (57 g) unsalted butter, softened
- 1½ cups (170 g) powdered sugar
- ½ teaspoon vanilla extract
- 1 teaspoon cinnamon

**Yield:** 20 to 24 cookies, depending on mix-ins
**Prep time:** 25 minutes
**Chill time:** 1 hour
**Bake time:** 13 minutes

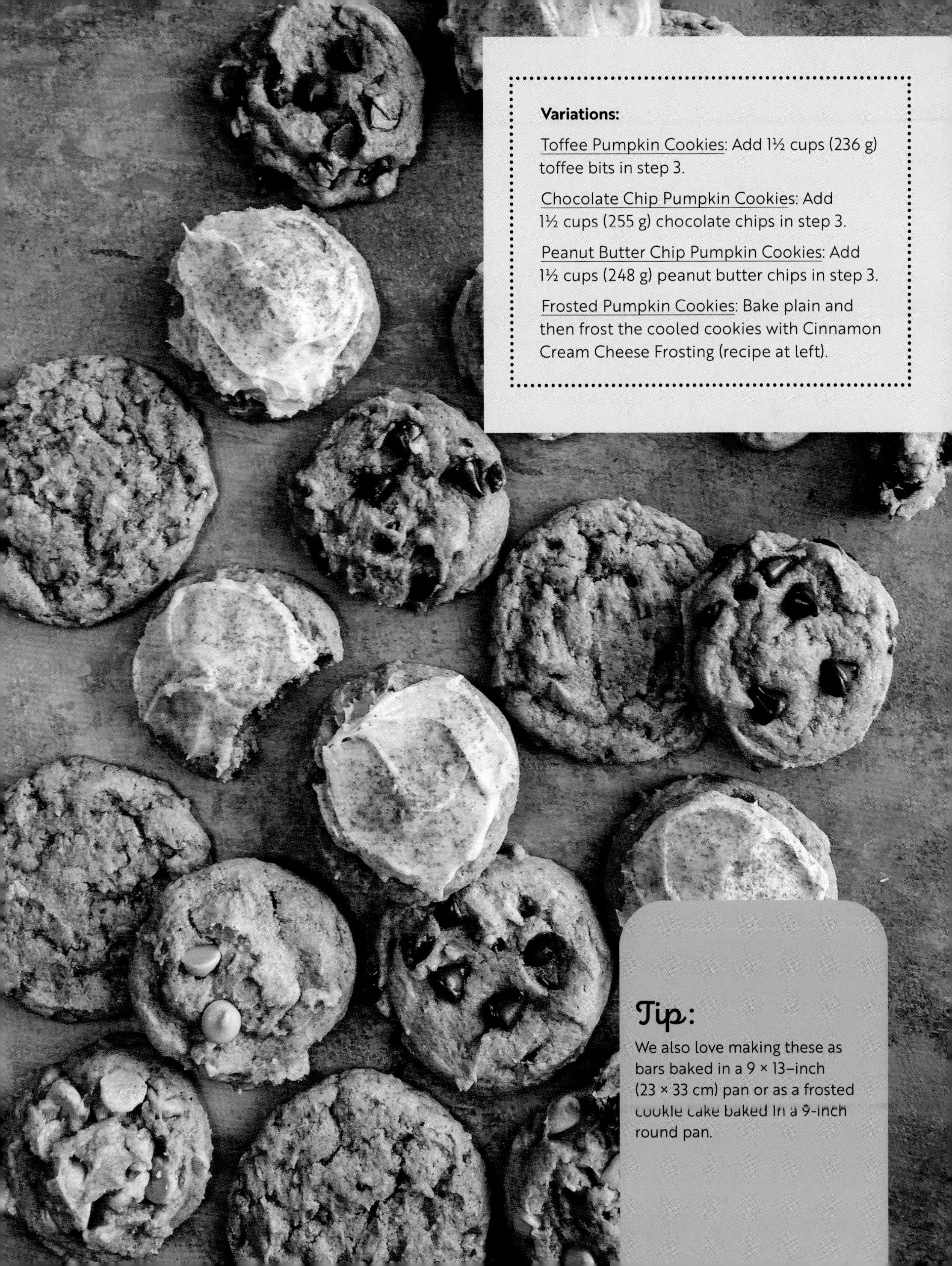

**Variations:**

Toffee Pumpkin Cookies: Add 1½ cups (236 g) toffee bits in step 3.

Chocolate Chip Pumpkin Cookies: Add 1½ cups (255 g) chocolate chips in step 3.

Peanut Butter Chip Pumpkin Cookies: Add 1½ cups (248 g) peanut butter chips in step 3.

Frosted Pumpkin Cookies: Bake plain and then frost the cooled cookies with Cinnamon Cream Cheese Frosting (recipe at left).

## Tip:

We also love making these as bars baked in a 9 × 13–inch (23 × 33 cm) pan or as a frosted cookie cake baked in a 9-inch round pan.

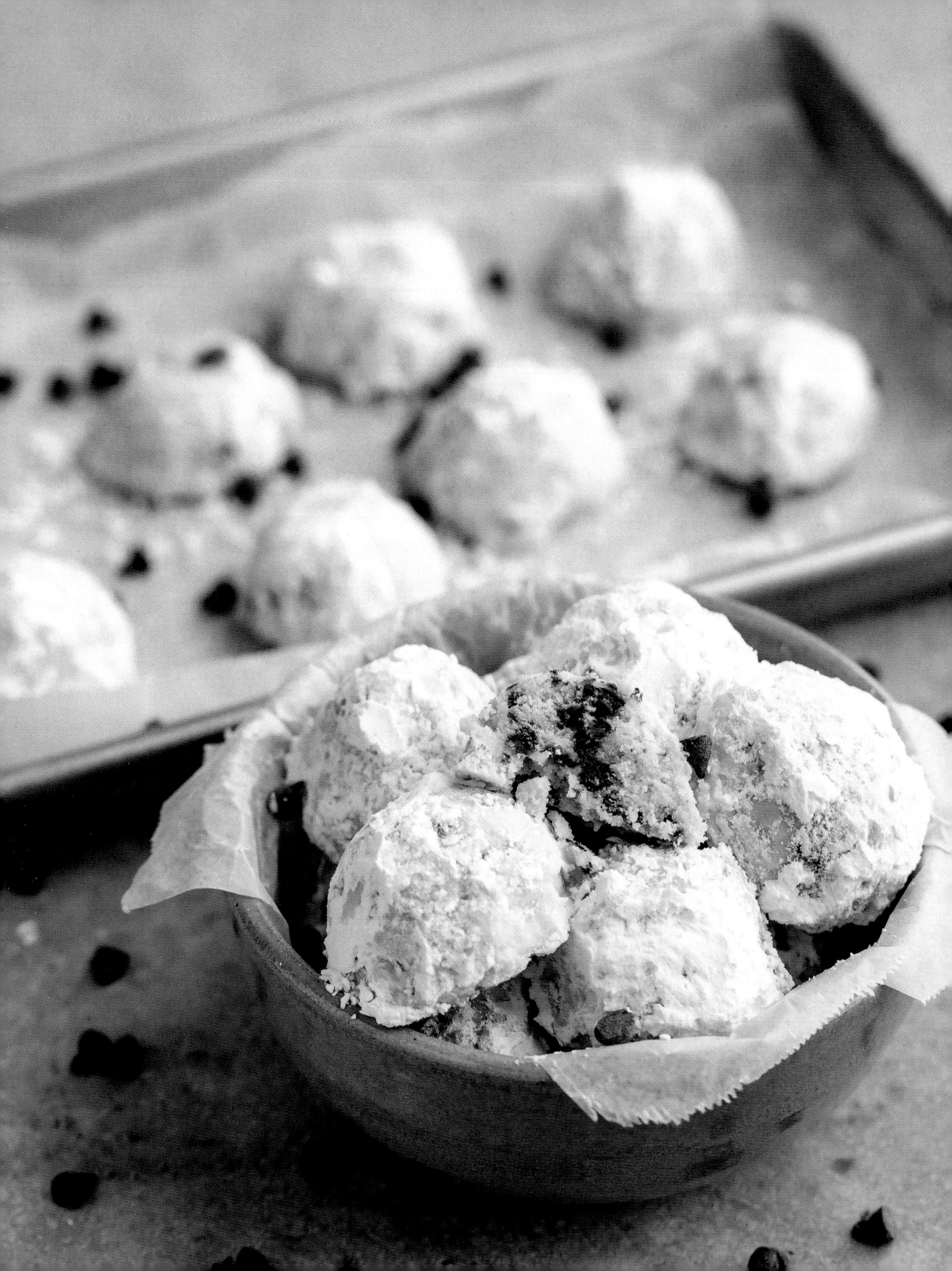

# Chocolate Chip Snowball Cookies

Some of my earliest Christmas memories involve eating my mom's Russian Tea Cakes. She got the recipe from a neighbor when I was just a baby, and she's been making them multiple times a year ever since. She loves using chopped pecans and making them in teeny tiny bite sizes, and she always has a stash in her freezer for Snowball Emergencies (that is, when I visit and request them!). This chocolate chip version is her recipe without the nuts. We love pecans, but I love chocolate even more. Using chocolate chips makes them allergy friendly—and who doesn't love more chocolate?

- 1 cup (226 g) unsalted butter, softened
- ½ cup (57 g) powdered sugar
- 1 teaspoon vanilla extract
- 2¼ cups (273 g) all-purpose flour
- ½ teaspoon salt
- 1 cup (180 g) mini chocolate chips
- Additional powdered sugar, for rolling

**Yield:** 48 cookies
**Prep time:** 15 minutes
**Bake time:** 10 minutes

## INSTRUCTIONS

1   Preheat the oven to 375°F (191°C). Line 2 cookie sheets with parchment paper or silicone baking mats.

2   Mix the butter, ½ cup (57 g) powdered sugar, and vanilla extract until smooth in a large bowl using a hand mixer or stand mixer (fitted with the paddle attachment). Add the flour and salt, and mix until a cookie dough forms. This dough is thick and takes a long time to form into a traditional cookie dough. It goes fastest with a stand mixer and will take a bit longer using a hand mixer.

3   Once the dough has come together, mix in the chocolate chips.

4   Scoop balls of cookie dough (each about 1 tablespoon) and place on the prepared cookie sheets. Bake for 8 to 11 minutes or until the bottoms are just slightly golden. Remove from the oven and cool until you can touch them. Place additional powdered sugar in a small bowl and roll each cookie in the powdered sugar to coat.

5   Store in an airtight container for up to 4 days or freeze for up to a month. The recipe can easily be doubled.

*Tip:*
You can use any mix-ins you like in these cookies. Traditionally you would use 1 cup chopped pecans, walnuts, or almonds, but I love using the chocolate chips to make them nut-free. You can also use mini M&M's!

# Almond Joy Macaroons

$\mathcal{N}$either my daughter nor I thought we liked macaroons until we tried a Matterhorn Macaroon at Disneyland. She'd even proclaimed coconut "the worst food ever" prior to the first taste of those cookies. Those macaroons are soft on the inside and almost fudgy, piled high into the shape of the Matterhorn. Maybe it's the fact you're eating them in Disneyland, but they taste so good, we get at least one every trip.

The center of these macaroons reminds me of the ones they're modeled after: soft and chewy with a gooey, almost-fudgy-like center. I tried almost every single macaroon recipe I could find on the internet before settling on this one—and we love the added crunch of the almonds and, of course, the chocolate dip. You can skip the chocolate (or use white chocolate instead) but really, don't. They're so good with it!

- 4 cups (273 g) shredded sweetened coconut
- ⅔ cup (83 g) all-purpose flour
- ¼ teaspoon salt
- 1 cup (86 g) sliced almonds, chopped
- 1 (14-ounce or 396 g) can sweetened condensed milk
- 1 teaspoon vanilla extract
- ¾ cup (132 g) chocolate melts or almond bark

**Yield:** 32 cookies
**Prep time:** 45 minutes
**Bake time:** 18 minutes

## INSTRUCTIONS

1   Preheat the oven to 350°F (177°C). Line 2 cookie sheets with parchment paper or silicone baking mats.

2   Add the coconut, flour, salt, and almonds to a large bowl. Add the sweetened condensed milk and vanilla extract. Stir to combine.

3   Scoop balls of the mixture (each about 1 tablespoon) and roll the balls between your palms to push them together and make sure that no pieces of coconut are sticking out (they'll burn if so). The mixture is sticky, so I recommend wetting your hands before doing this. Place the balls on the prepared cookie sheets. They won't spread, so you don't need to space them out; however, a packed cookie sheet will take longer to bake.

4   Bake for about 15 to 20 minutes, or until the tops are golden. Cool for at least 10 minutes before moving to a rack to cool completely before dipping.

5   To decorate, place the chocolate melts in a microwave-safe bowl. Heat on 50 percent power in 30-second increments, stirring between each, until melted and smooth.

6   Dip the bottom of each cookie in the melted chocolate and set it on a cookie sheet lined with parchment or wax paper. Drizzle any leftover chocolate over the tips of the cookies, if desired. Chill to set.

7   Store in an airtight container for up to 4 days.

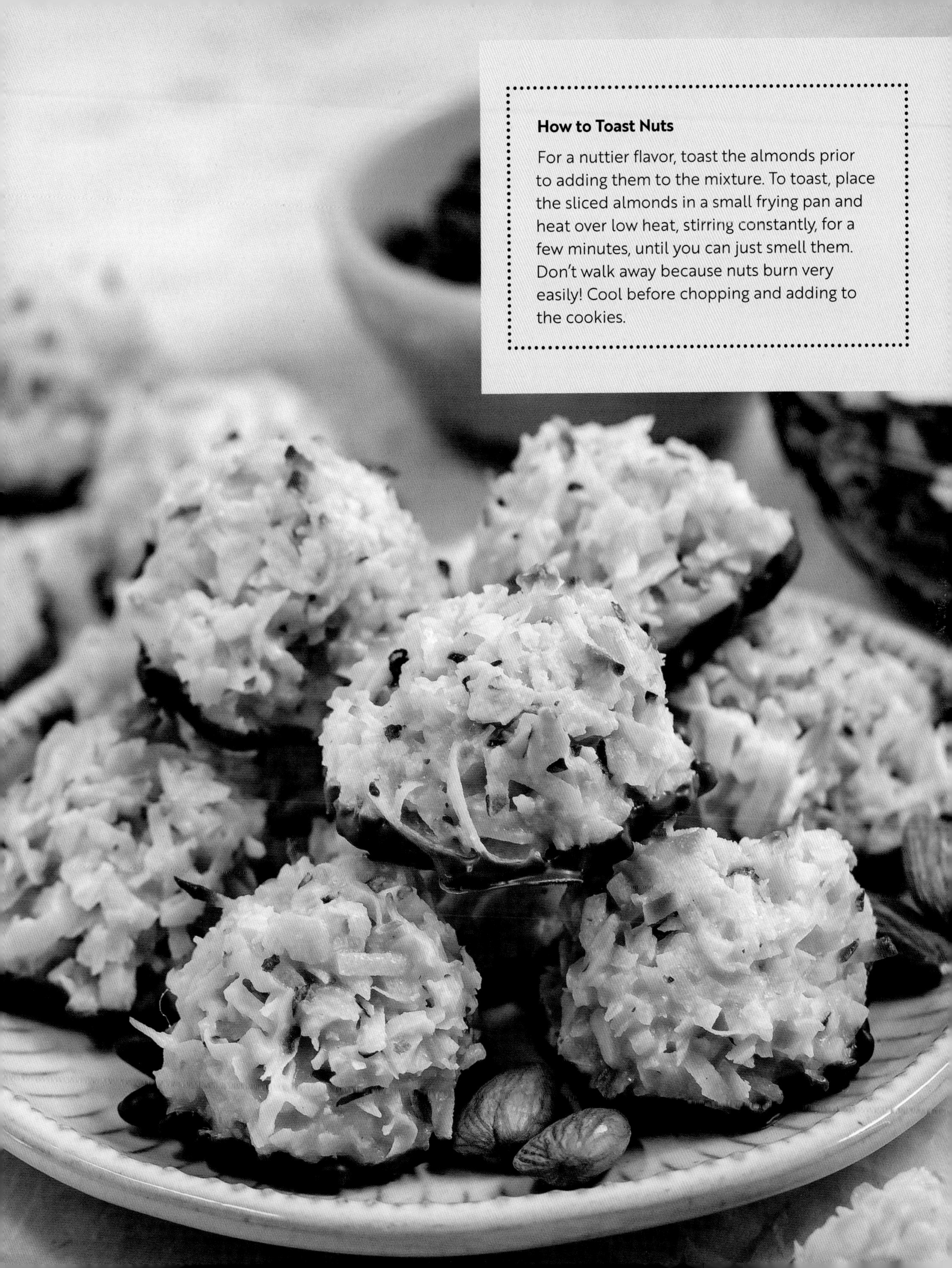

**How to Toast Nuts**

For a nuttier flavor, toast the almonds prior to adding them to the mixture. To toast, place the sliced almonds in a small frying pan and heat over low heat, stirring constantly, for a few minutes, until you can just smell them. Don't walk away because nuts burn very easily! Cool before chopping and adding to the cookies.

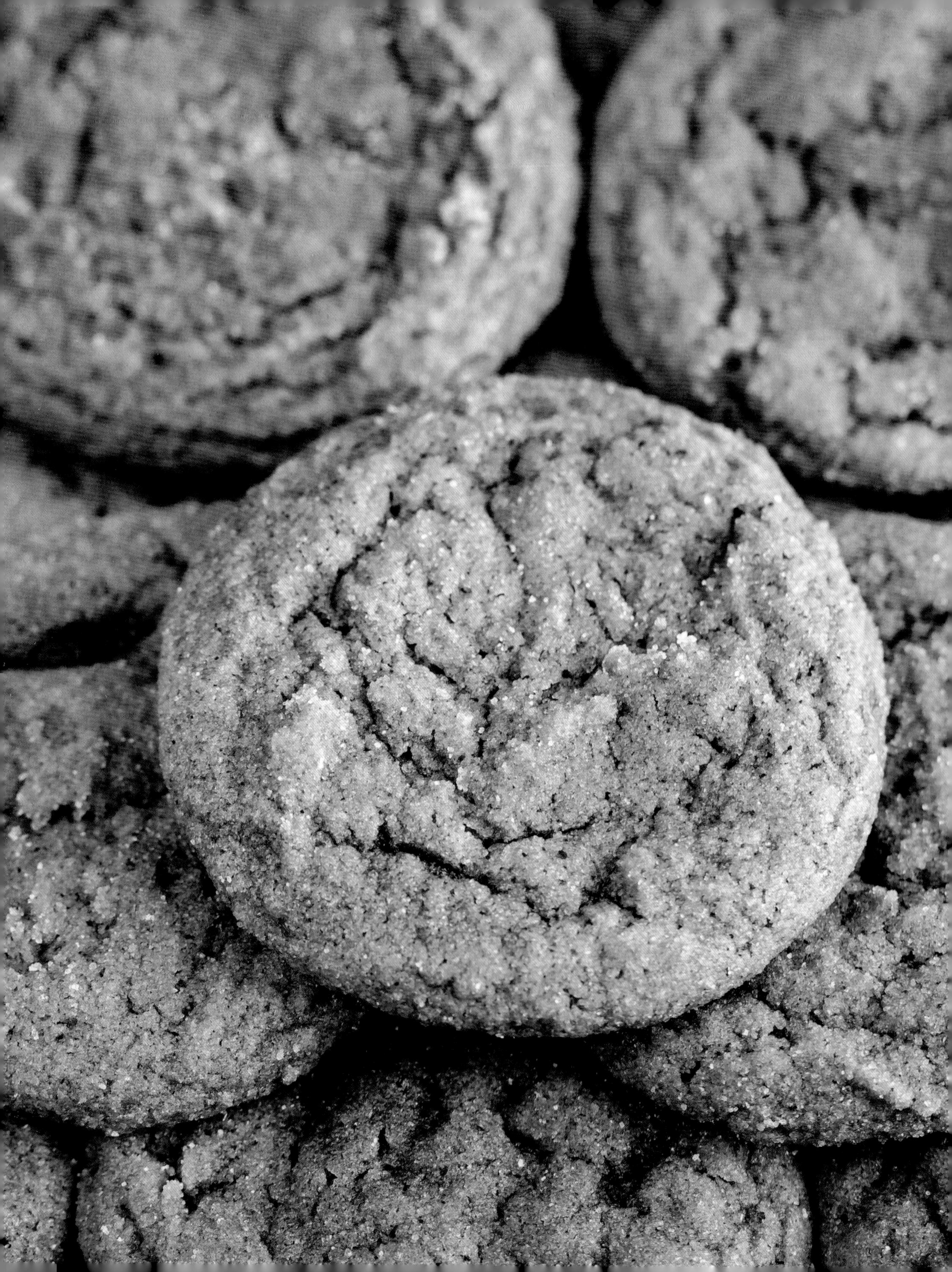

# Molasses Cookies

One of my earliest childhood memories is eating gingerbread cookies with my dad. He and I both love gingerbread, and they were our favorite cookies to make each year. As an adult I have come to love molasses cookies almost more than gingerbread: The soft and chewy cookie is wonderfully flavored from the molasses and warm spices, but you don't have to worry about rolling or frosting them. These are made with only brown sugar in the dough, which keeps them super soft for days. You can also bake these in a 9 × 13–inch (23 × 33 cm) pan and make a cookie cake out of them, frosted with the simple frosting from Nana's Drop Sugar Cookies (see page 30).

## INSTRUCTIONS

1. Cream the butter and brown sugar in a large bowl with a hand mixer (or a stand mixer fitted with the paddle attachment). Add in the molasses and egg and mix until smooth.

2. Mix in baking soda, cinnamon, ginger, nutmeg, cloves, and salt. Slowly mix in the flour until the cookie dough is smooth.

3. Place parchment paper or a silicone baking mat on a cookie sheet. Scoop balls of cookie dough (each about 2 tablespoons) and place them on the cookie sheet. Don't worry about spacing because you're chilling the dough.

4. Chill the cookie dough for at least 2 hours.

5. Preheat oven to 350°F (177°C). Line 2 cookie sheets with parchment paper or silicone baking mats.

6. Place granulated sugar in a small bowl.

7. Remove the chilled cookies from the refrigerator. Roll each into a uniform ball between your palms and then roll them in the granulated sugar to coat. Place 2 inches (5 cm) apart on the prepared cookie sheets.

8. Bake the cookies for about 11 to 15 minutes, or until they lose their glossy sheen. Cookies will be a bit puffy while baking but should settle flat as they cool.

9. Store in an airtight container for up to 3 days or freeze for up to a month.

- ½ cup (113 g) unsalted butter, softened
- ¾ cup (150 g) packed brown sugar
- ⅓ cup (79 ml) unsulphured molasses
- 1 large egg
- 1 teaspoon baking soda
- 1½ teaspoons ground cinnamon
- 1 teaspoon ground ginger
- ½ teaspoon ground nutmeg
- ½ teaspoon ground cloves
- ½ teaspoon salt
- 2 cups (248 g) all-purpose flour
- ¼ cup (50 g) granulated sugar, for rolling

**Yield:** 22 cookies
**Prep time:** 20 minutes
**Chill time:** 2 hours
**Bake time:** 12 minutes

## Tip:

Add 1 cup (170 g) white chocolate chips to the batter in step 2, or press holiday-colored M&M's onto the top before baking in step 7.

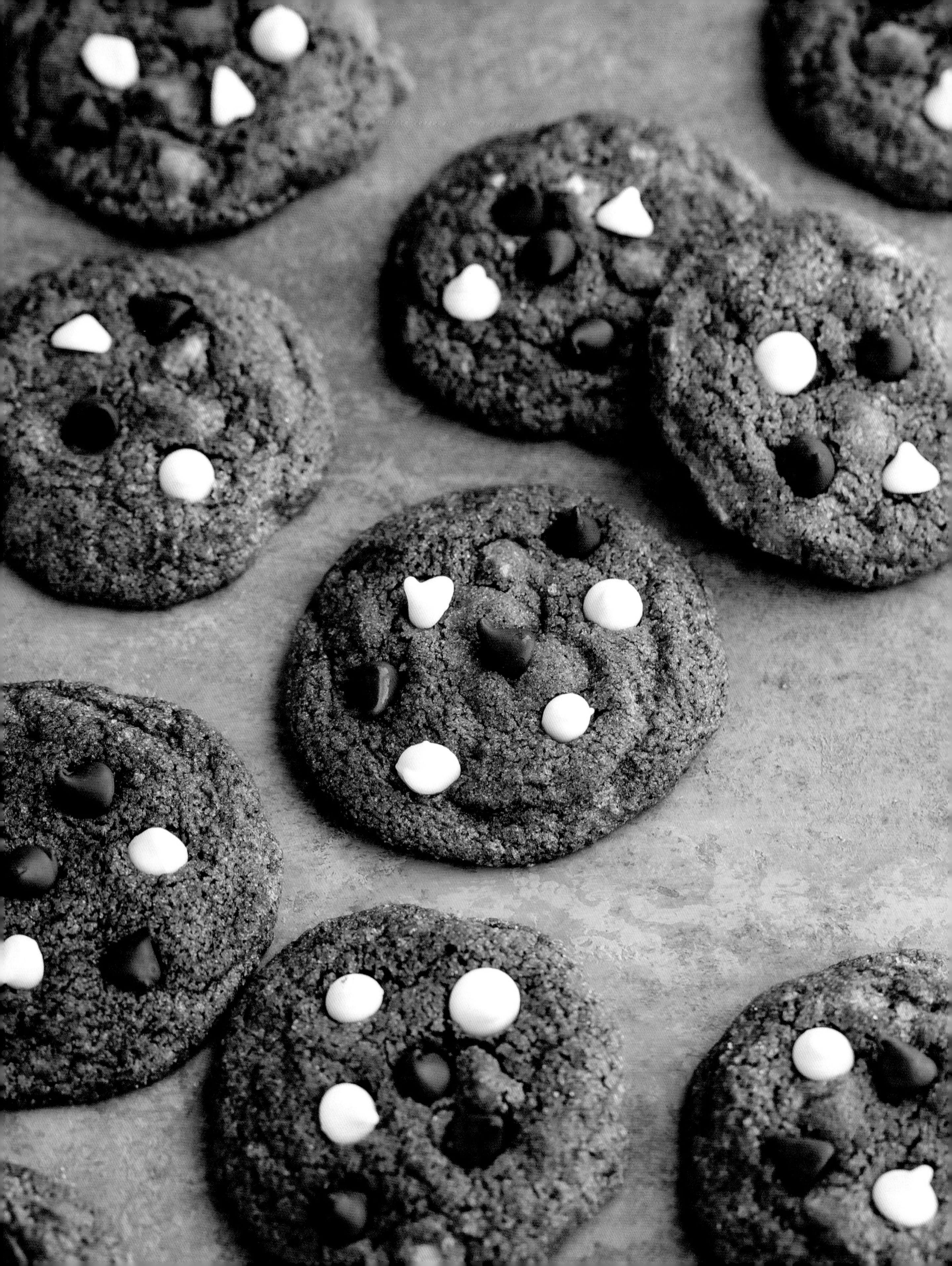

# Tuxedo Cookies

**W**hen I was in middle school, I decided I wanted a tuxedo. My parents had found a secondhand one somewhere, if I remember correctly, and I decided to get it to wear for fancy occasions. I never remember actually wearing it (I think I thought the idea of it was more fun than the actual execution), although I seem to remember owning a hot pink cummerbund at one point. Anyway, I may never have worn an actual tuxedo, but you know what's better? Tuxedo Cookies! These cookies are actually chocolate sugar cookies that are soft and rich, filled with semi-sweet and white chocolate chips. I don't know why the dark/light combination gives me tuxedo vibes, but it totally does. These are a new twist on a chocolate cookie that I think will go over way better than twelve-year-old me in a tuxedo.

- 1¼ cups (155 g) all-purpose flour
- ⅓ cup (27 g) unsweetened cocoa powder
- ½ teaspoon salt
- ½ teaspoon baking soda
- ½ teaspoon cream of tartar
- ½ cup (113 g) unsalted butter, softened
- ½ cup (100 g) packed brown sugar
- ¼ cup (50 g) granulated sugar
- 1 large egg
- 1 teaspoon vanilla extract
- ½ cup (85 g) white chocolate chips
- ½ cup (85 g) chocolate chips
- ⅓ cup (67 g) granulated sugar, for rolling

**Yield:** 23 cookies
**Prep time:** 25 minutes
**Bake time:** 13 minutes

## INSTRUCTIONS

1  Preheat the oven to 350°F (177°C). Line cookie sheets with silicone baking mats or parchment paper. These cookies bake differently depending on if you bake them on parchment paper or a silicone baking mat. For puffier cookies, use the silicone mat.

2  Whisk the flour, cocoa powder, salt, baking soda, and cream of tartar in a medium bowl. Set aside.

3  Cream the butter with both sugars in a large bowl with an electric mixer until light and fluffy, about 2 minutes. Mix in the egg and vanilla extract, and then mix the dry ingredients into the wet ingredients. Mix until a cookie dough forms, being sure to scrape the sides of the bowl. Stir in the chocolate and white chocolate chips.

4  Place remaining ⅓ cup granulated sugar in a small bowl. Scoop balls of cookie dough (each about 2 tablespoons) and drop them in the bowl of sugar. Roll to coat. The dough is sticky, so it's best to scoop it right into the sugar to reduce the transfer to your hands.

5  Place the cookies 3 inches (8 cm) apart on the prepared cookie sheets. Do not crowd the cookies as they do spread. Bake for 11 to 14 minutes or until they lose their glossy sheen. Cool completely before removing from cookie sheets.

6  Store in an airtight container for up to 3 days. Can be frozen for up to 2 months.

*Tip:*

Like a frosted cookie? Omit the chips and frost these with the chocolate frosting from the Birthday Cake Sandwich Cookies on page 175.

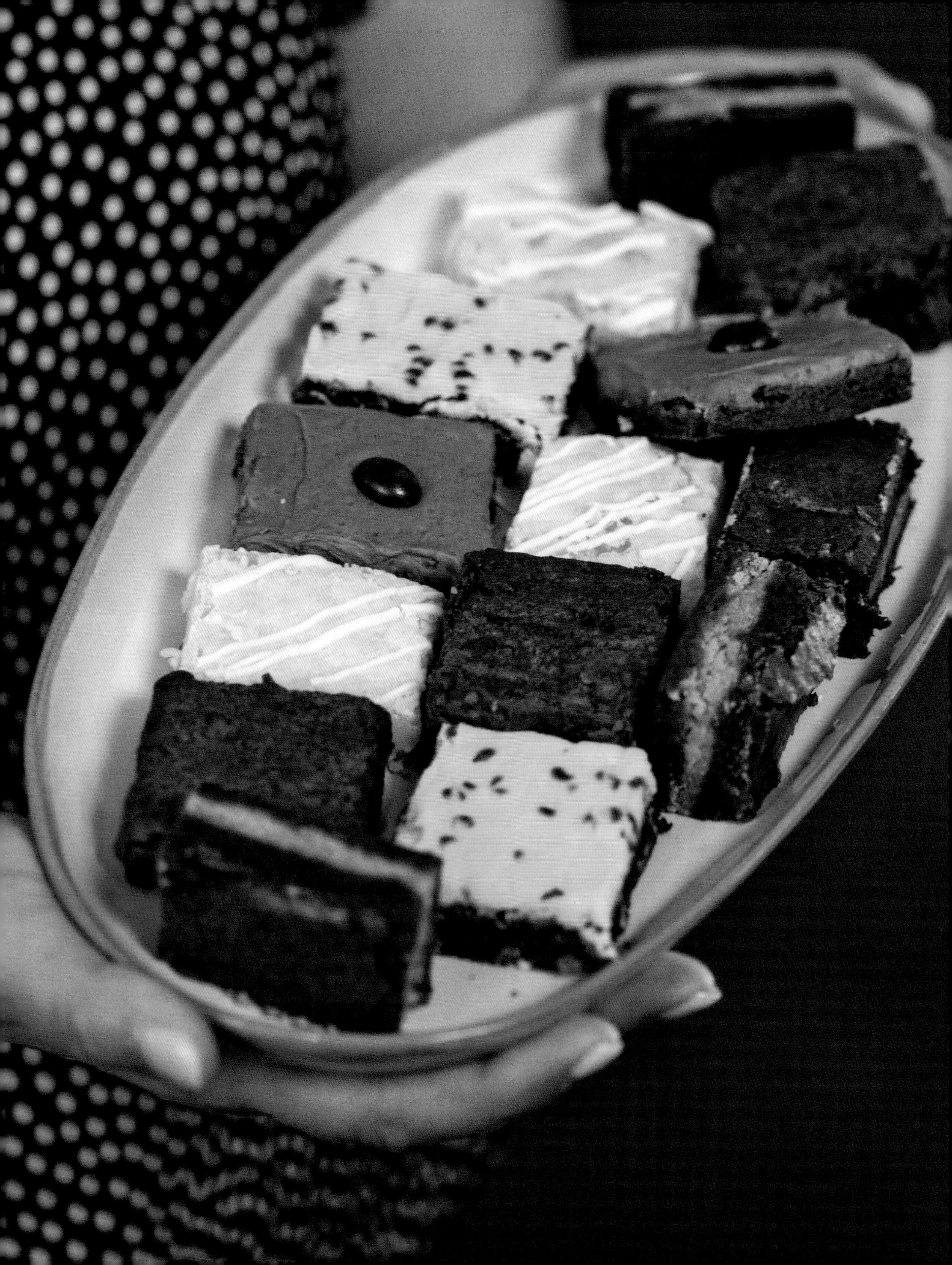

# Brownies

I f I'm craving chocolate, then I'm craving a brownie. I remember making box brownies with my mom and eating them straight from the pan, a tradition I've continued with my daughter, except we make brownies from scratch. I consider myself a brownie expert: fudgy versus cakey, cocoa versus melted chocolate, butter versus oil. This chapter has a little bit of everything: Some are simple and comforting, and others are more extreme and grown-up. If you're an intense chocolate lover like I am, then you are going to love this chapter!

A few tips for making the *best* brownies:

- **The key to fudgy brownies is to make sure not to overbake them.** They are done as soon as the top loses its glossy sheen. I give a range of times for baking to the perfect sweet spot of under- and overdone, but if you like brownies more done, you may need to add a few minutes here or there.

- **Do you have to use foil or parchment to line your pan?** No, but it makes cleanup and slicing a total breeze. From a food photography standpoint, removing the whole slab of brownies or blondies from a pan is a requirement, but you don't have to (unless the recipe requires it, as in the Bacon and Caramel Brownies on page 64).

- **Want perfect cuts of brownie?** We've all cut brownies and had half the pan come off on the knife, but I'm going to share a not-so-secret tip my Instagram followers taught me: Use a plastic knife. Just one of those disposable plastic knives cuts right through without all the mess!

# Fudgiest Brownies Ever

I grew up in a city called Burlingame, a small suburb of San Francisco, and one of the more popular things about the town is that it often smells of chocolate. Yes, you read that right—occasionally you'll just smell chocolate when driving through. That's because Guittard Chocolate Company makes their chocolate right off the freeway in the north end of town. Even still, twenty years after leaving, when I depart the freeway toward my parents' house and cross Rollins Road, smelling the scent makes me feel at home. It also causes an intense urge for brownies because the scent of melted chocolate is almost exactly that of nice, warm, gooey brownies. Maybe that's why brownies are one of my absolute favorite desserts, and this recipe is my favorite. It produces the best chocolatey and fudgiest brownies ever, and it's a great blank canvas because you can add almost anything to this recipe, like nuts or candy. However, if you're like me and want a pure rich and fudgy brownie with nothing else, this is the one you should try.

## INSTRUCTIONS

1   Preheat the oven to 350°F (177°C). Line a 9 × 13–inch (23 × 33 cm) pan with foil and spray with nonstick cooking spray.

2   Place the baking chocolate and butter in a large microwave-safe bowl. Heat on high power in 30-second increments, stirring between each, until mixture is melted and smooth, about 2 to 2½ minutes depending on your microwave.

3   Stir the sugar and cocoa into the butter mixture, then stir in the eggs until the mixture is combined. Mix in the vanilla extract and salt, and then slowly mix in the flour until smooth.

4   Pour the mixture immediately into the prepared pan and spread evenly. Bake for 22 to 25 minutes or until the top is no longer glossy and a toothpick inserted 2 inches (5 cm) from the edge comes out clean.

5   Store in an airtight container for up to 3 days or freeze the brownies for up to a month.

- 4 ounces (114 g) unsweetened baking chocolate, broken into pieces
- 1 cup (226 g) unsalted butter
- 2 cups (400 g) granulated sugar
- ¼ cup (20 g) unsweetened cocoa powder
- 4 large eggs
- 1 teaspoon vanilla extract
- ½ teaspoon salt
- 1⅓ cups (165 g) all-purpose flour

**Yield:** 20 brownies
**Prep time:** 15 minutes
**Bake time:** 23 minutes

## Tip:

Think brownies are boring without nuts? Add 1 cup chopped nuts (any kind, weight varies) to the batter after you mix in the flour in step 3.

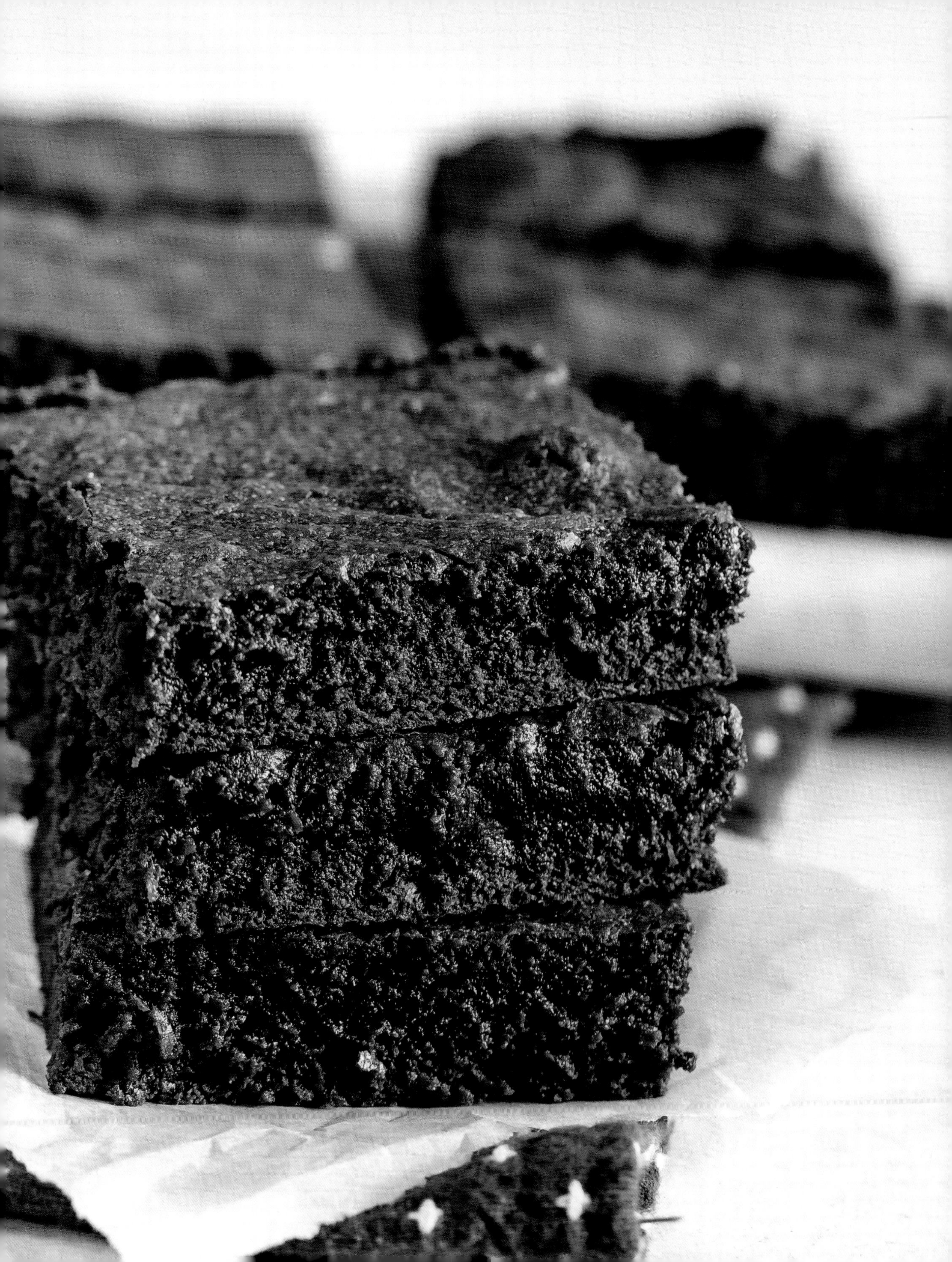

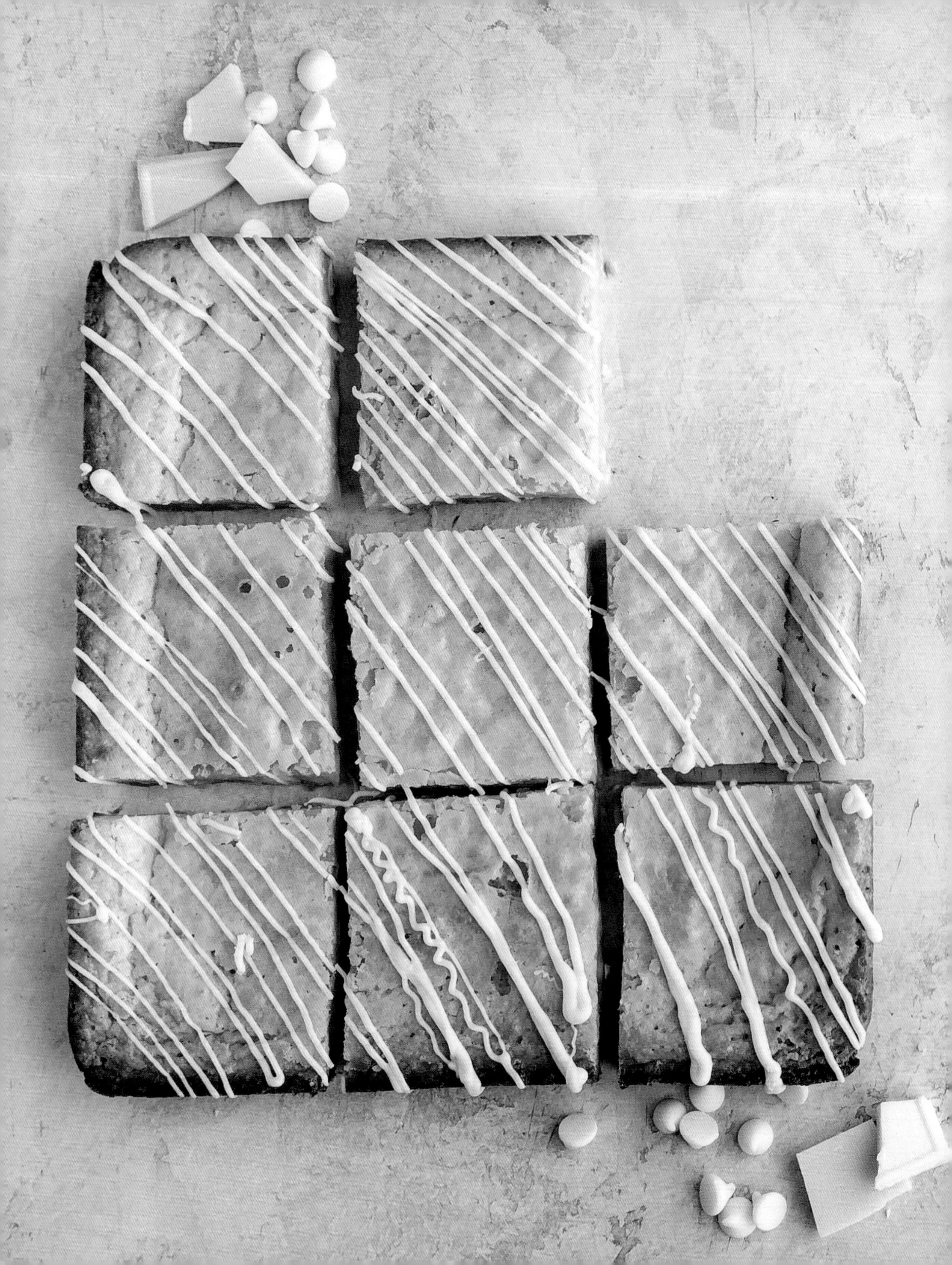

# Vanilla Lovers' White Chocolate Brownies

When you're a food blogger, you make lots of recipes—lots and lots and lots! Early on in my career I attempted to make brownies with white chocolate and they failed miserably. If I remember correctly, I tried twice that time and then gave up. Fast-forward a couple of years and a few hundred recipes and I tried again—and failed. The funny part: I'd forgotten I'd even tried it at all the first time! I call it "blogger brain": when you forget you've made something or put something on the site and make it again and then realize—*oops!* Third time's the charm for this recipe: I've finally perfected the white chocolate brownie!

White chocolate is sweeter than regular chocolate, and it is way more finicky too—it burns easily and doesn't melt as well. That's why it's not just as easy as plugging in white chocolate for unsweetened in any old brownie recipe: You need to adjust other things like butter and sugar so that they'll bake properly and turn out just right. For all of you white chocolate lovers, these are for you—and I'm betting they'll convert a few chocolate purists out there too.

- 6 ounces (170 g) premium white chocolate, broken into pieces
- ½ cup (113 g) unsalted butter
- 1 cup (200 g) granulated sugar
- 2 large eggs
- 1 teaspoon vanilla extract
- 1 cup (124 g) all-purpose flour
- 1 cup (170 g) white chocolate chips
- Additional premium white chocolate or white chocolate chips, for drizzle

**Yield:** 12 brownies
**Prep time:** 25 minutes
**Bake time:** 22 minutes

## INSTRUCTIONS

1   Preheat the oven to 350°F (177°C). Line a 9 × 9–inch (23 × 23 cm) pan with parchment paper. Do not use foil; the brownies will get too brown around the edges.

2   Place the white chocolate and butter in a large microwave-safe bowl. Heat on 50 percent power in 30-second increments, stirring between each, until melted and smooth. This will take approximately 3 minutes depending on your microwave. You can also melt them together on the stovetop using a small saucepan over low heat.

3   Stir the sugar into the melted butter and chocolate mixture. Stir in the eggs and vanilla extract, then slowly stir in the flour. Stir in the chocolate chips and spread in the prepared pan.

4   Bake for 20 to 25 minutes or until the top is lightly golden and puffed. Cool completely before removing from the pan and decorating.

5   To decorate the tops, place 2 ounces (57 g) premium baking white chocolate (or ¼ cup [43 g] white chocolate chips with 1 teaspoon vegetable oil) in a small microwave-safe bowl and heat on 50 percent power in 30-second increments, stirring between each, until melted and smooth. Place melted white chocolate in a sandwich bag, cut off a tiny edge of the tip, and drizzle over the cooled bars. Let set before slicing.

6   Store in an airtight container for up to 3 days or freeze for up to 2 months.

## Tip:

I cannot wait to turn these into Lemon Brownies by adding ½ teaspoon lemon extract and the zest of a lemon. Go ahead and try it—I know they'll be amazing!

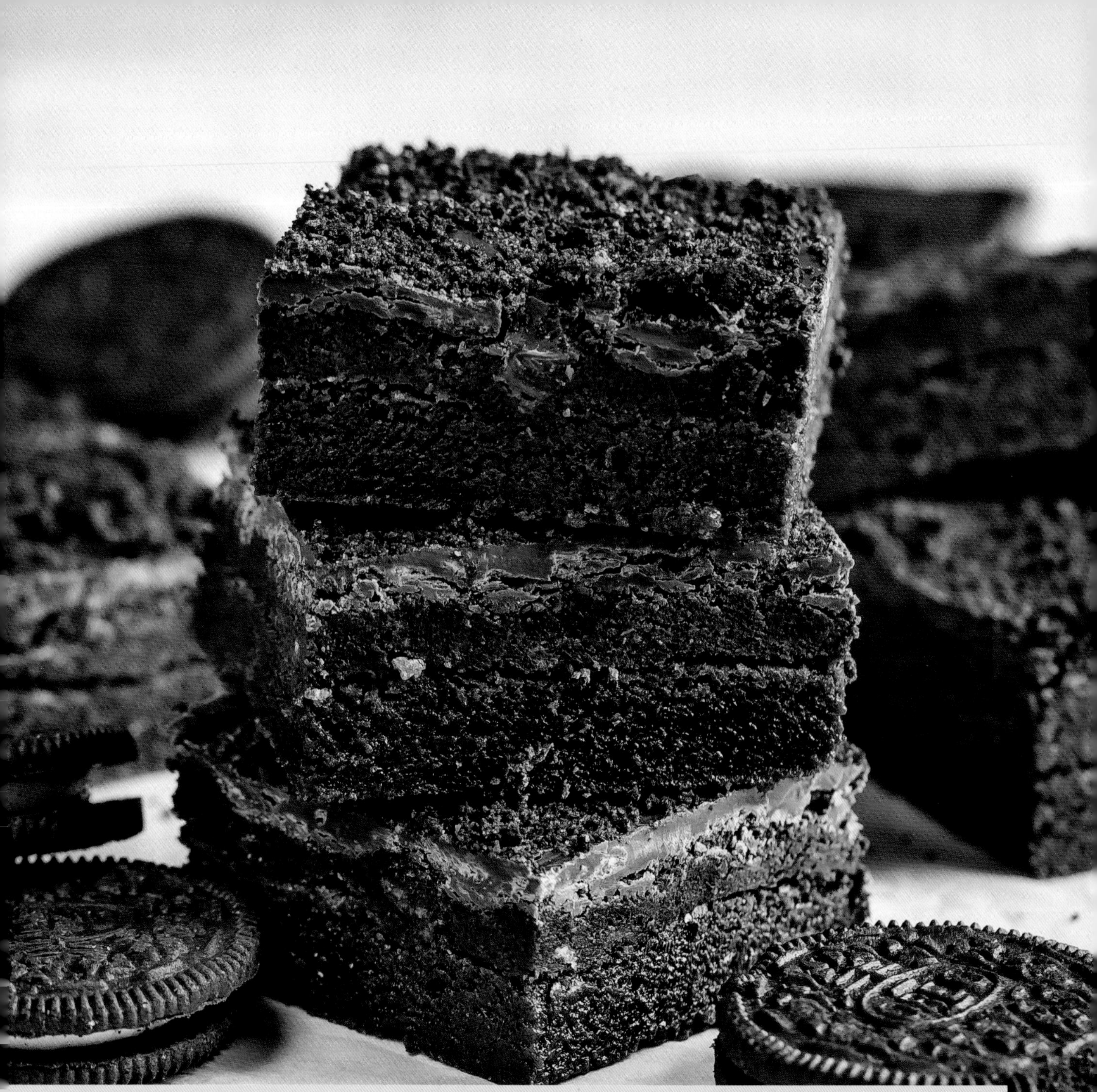

**There's More Than One Way to Crush an Oreo!**

My favorite way to crush Oreos to use in recipes like Oreo Truffle Brownies or Cookies 'n' Cream Mud Bars (see page 190) is using a food processor. It's the best way to get a fine crumb. If you don't have a food processor, here's what to do: Roughly chop the Oreos on a cutting board, then place them in a large, gallon-sized bag. Seal all but 1 inch (2.5 cm) of the bag and roll with a rolling pin until you get a fine crumb. And no, no matter what method you use, you do not have to remove the cream from inside the cookie!

# Oreo Truffle Brownies

*I*f these brownies were a person, we'd call them "Extra": trying too hard, over the top, maybe a little dramatic. Back in the early days of my career I was an expert at making Extra Recipes. *What can I stuff in a cookie? How can I turn my favorite pie into a cake? How much is too much candy to stuff in a blondie?* Those were the days of blogging when no one worried about search engines and we created things that would WOW people on social media. That's how I got the idea for these brownies: Oreo truffles were all the rage and I figured I'm not going to make Oreo truffles—too boring. I'm going to put Oreo truffles *on brownies!* And what a result: a rich fudgy brownie topped with a thick Oreo-like soft mixture and then topped with more chocolate. If that's not Extra, I don't even know what is!

### INSTRUCTIONS

1   Preheat the oven to 350°F (177°C). Line a 9 × 9–inch (23 × 23 cm) pan with foil and spray with nonstick cooking spray.

2   Place the oil in a large bowl. Stir in the sugar and cocoa powder until smooth using a wooden spoon.

3   Add the eggs, vanilla extract, and salt. Stir to combine, then slowly mix in the flour. The batter will be thick. Spread the batter into the prepared pan.

4   Bake for 21 to 25 minutes or until the brownies just lose that glossy sheen around the edges and a toothpick inserted 1 inch (2.5 cm) from the edge comes out clean. Cool completely before topping.

5   Finely crush Oreo cookies in a food processor. Remove 2 tablespoons (13 g) crumbs for the topping; set aside. Add the cream cheese to the food processor and pulse until the mixture is combined and smooth, scraping down the sides of the machine as needed. Spread over the brownies and press to compact.

6   Place the chocolate chips and oil in a microwave-safe bowl and heat on high in 30-second increments, stirring between each, until melted and smooth. Spread evenly over the Oreo truffle mixture using an offset spatula. Sprinkle with the reserved Oreo cookie crumbs. Chill to set before slicing into bars.

7   Store in an airtight container in the refrigerator for up to 4 days. Can be frozen for up to 2 months.

## For the Brownies
- ⅔ cup (160 ml) vegetable oil
- 1⅓ cups (267 g) granulated sugar
- ⅔ cup (54 g) unsweetened cocoa powder
- 2 large eggs
- 1 teaspoon vanilla extract
- ½ teaspoon salt
- ½ cup (62 g) all-purpose flour

## For the Topping
- 25 Oreo cookies (286 g)
- 4 ounces (112 g) cream cheese
- 1 cup (170 g) chocolate chips
- 1 tablespoon (15 ml) vegetable oil

**Yield:** 16 brownies
**Prep time:** 30 minutes
**Bake time:** 23 minutes

## Tip:
Make new versions by using *any* flavor Oreo or even any sandwich cookie. Hint: These are fantastic with Nutter Butters!

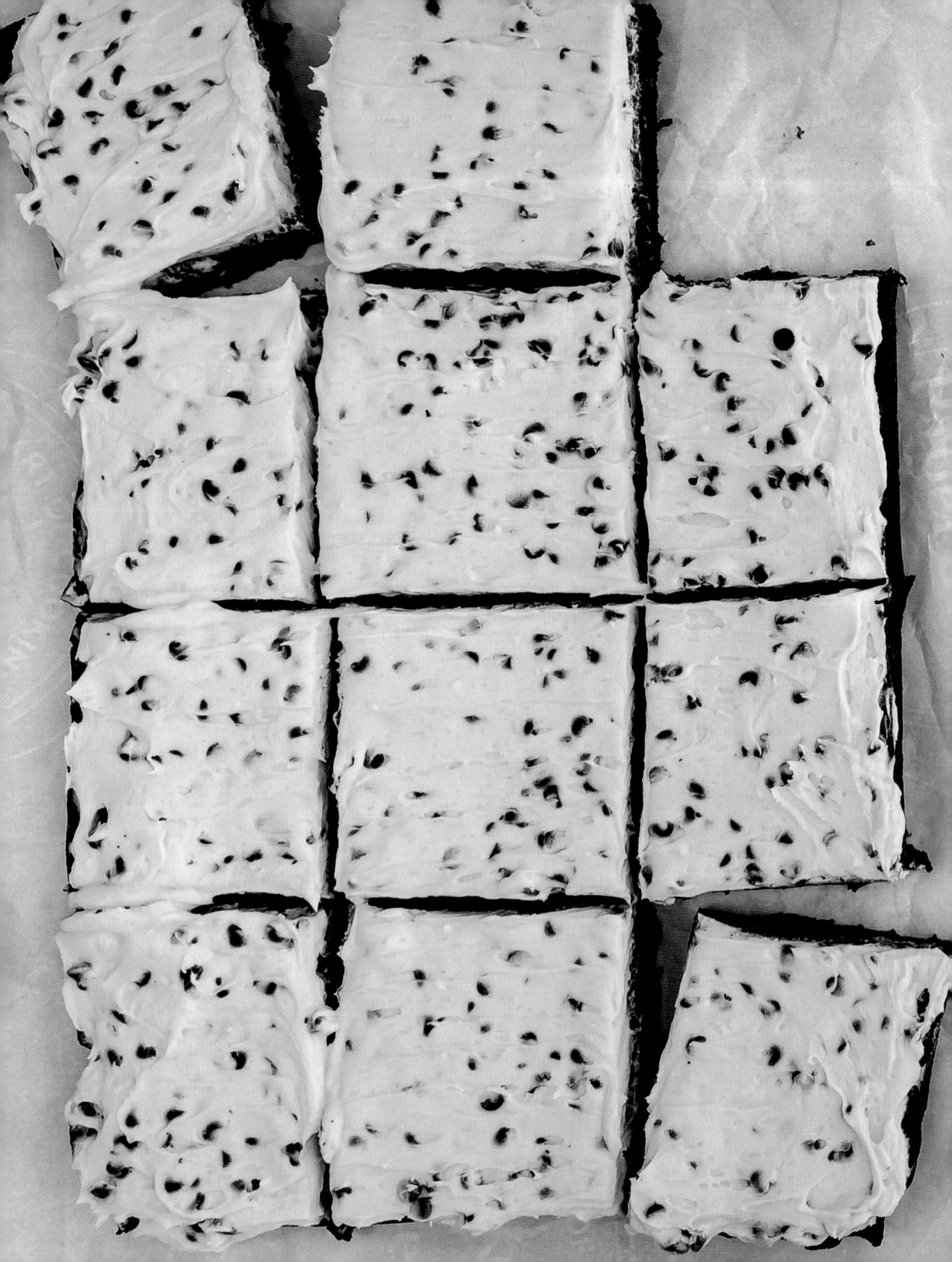

# Mint Chip Brownies

This recipe is dedicated to my daughter, Jordan. She discovered the chocolate and mint combination when she was about eight and was obsessed with it. Once we learned that her birthday, February 19, was actually National Chocolate Mint Day, she loved it even more. For several years I'd make her chocolate mint desserts every birthday: cake rolls and cupcakes, cookie sandwiches and popcorn treats . . . everything you can imagine as chocolate mint, I made. A few years ago, she shifted away from her favorite combination in lieu of cookie cakes for birthday treats. But when she tasted these brownies for me, her love of chocolate mint came rushing back. She told me she'd forgotten how much she loved the combination, and this recipe became one of her favorites in this book.

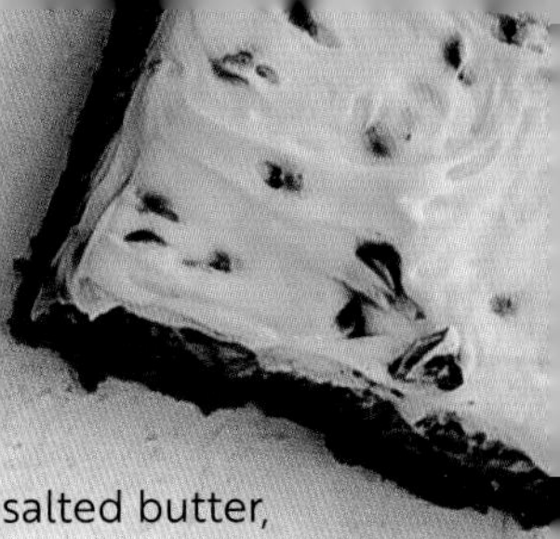

**For the Brownies**

- ¾ cup (170 g) unsalted butter, melted
- 1¾ cups (350 g) granulated sugar
- ¾ cup (60 g) unsweetened cocoa powder
- 3 large eggs
- 1 teaspoon vanilla extract
- ½ teaspoon salt
- ¾ cup (93 g) all-purpose flour
- 1 cup (176 g) mini chocolate chips

**For the Frosting**

- ¾ cup (170 g) unsalted butter, softened
- 3 cups (342 g) powdered sugar
- ¼ teaspoon salt
- 1 to 2 tablespoons (15 to 30 ml) milk
- ¼ teaspoon peppermint extract
- ⅛ teaspoon green food coloring
- ½ cup (88 g) mini chocolate chips

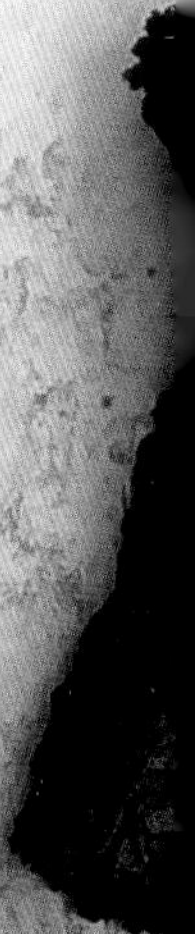

**Yield:** 20 brownies
**Prep time:** 30 minutes
**Bake time:** 23 minutes

### MAKE THE BROWNIES

1 Preheat the oven to 350°F (177°C). Line a 9 × 13–inch (23 × 33 cm) pan with foil and spray with nonstick cooking spray.

2 Place the melted butter in a large bowl. Stir in the sugar and cocoa powder until smooth using a wooden spoon.

3 Add eggs, vanilla extract, and salt. Stir to combine, then slowly mix in the flour. The batter will be thick. Stir in the chocolate chips.

4 Spread the batter into the prepared pan and top with more chocolate chips, if desired.

5 Bake for 18 to 23 minutes or until the brownies just lose that glossy sheen around the edges and a toothpick inserted 1 inch (2.5 cm) from the edge comes out clean. Cool before frosting.

### MAKE THE FROSTING

1 Beat the butter with an electric mixer until smooth. Slowly mix in the powdered sugar, 1 cup (113 g) at a time, until smooth, then mix in the salt. Add 1 tablespoon (15 ml) of milk and mix until incorporated, adding more milk as needed for spreadable consistency.

2 Mix in the peppermint extract and food coloring. Taste the frosting and add more peppermint extract as desired (it's a very strong extract and different tastes may want more). Mix in the chocolate chips.

3 Spread the frosting over the cooled brownies. Slice to serve. Store loosely covered for up to 3 days. You can freeze the brownies and frosting separately or freeze the frosted brownies for up to 2 months.

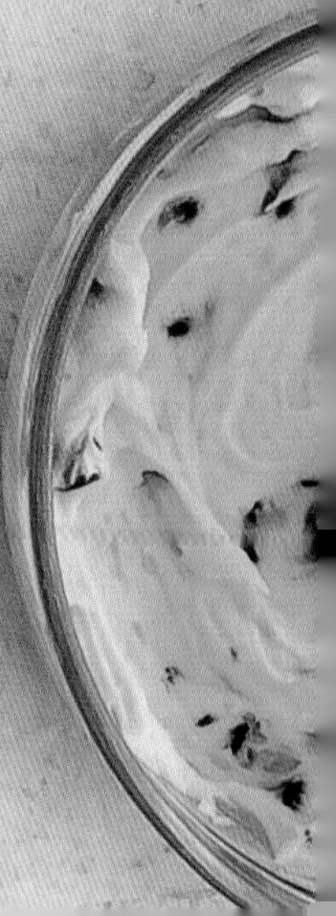

# Peanut Butter Stuffed Brownies

*I*f there was ever one brownie I'd want for the rest of my life, it would be this one: a rich chocolate brownie filled with peanut butter. It's like a peanut butter cup married a brownie and had a baby (my favorite kind of baby, I might add). These are rich and sweet and a little bit salty and everything a brownie should be. It can be a little messy to get the peanut butter mixture flattened and into the center of the brownies, but it's 100 million percent worth every handwashing.

## INSTRUCTIONS

1   Preheat the oven to 350°F (177°C). Line a 9 × 9–inch (23 × 23 cm) pan with foil and spray with nonstick cooking spray.

2   Place the baking chocolate and butter in a large microwave-safe bowl. Heat on high power for 2 to 3 minutes, stirring every 30 seconds, until chocolate is smooth. Stir in the sugar. Add the eggs, vanilla extract, and cocoa and stir well. Add the flour and stir carefully. Spread half of the batter in the prepared pan.

3   Place the peanut butter in a medium microwave-safe bowl. Heat for 45 seconds, or until it's smooth and liquid. Whisk in the powdered sugar, vanilla extract, and milk. Switch to a wooden spoon or spatula and stir until combined. The mixture will be thick.

4   Carefully spread the peanut butter mixture over the brownie batter in the pan, leaving a small edge around the pan. If it's easier, lay a piece of plastic wrap on your counter and turn out the peanut butter mixture onto it. Press it into a flat square about 8 × 8 inches (20 × 20 cm) and then carefully transfer it to the top of the brownie batter in the pan. Top with the remaining brownie batter, evenly spreading it in the pan so that it reaches the edges.

5   Bake about 30 to 40 minutes, until the center seems set. Let cool before cutting. These brownies, baked this way, will be super gooey inside. If you like your brownies more done and less gooey, bake them longer.

6   Store in an airtight container in the refrigerator for up to 4 days. Can be frozen for up to 2 months.

## For the Brownies

- 4 ounces (114 g) semi-sweet baking chocolate, broken into pieces
- ¾ cup (170 g) unsalted butter
- 1¾ cups (350 g) granulated sugar
- 3 large eggs
- 1 teaspoon vanilla extract
- 2 tablespoons (10 g) unsweetened cocoa
- 1 cup (124 g) all-purpose flour

## For the Peanut Butter Filling

- ¾ cup (200 g) creamy peanut butter
- 1 cup (113 g) powdered sugar
- 1 teaspoon vanilla extract
- 2 tablespoons (30 ml) milk

**Yield:** 16 brownies
**Prep time:** 30 minutes
**Bake time:** 35 minutes

## Tip:

If the peanut butter sticks to your hands, spray them with nonstick cooking spray or lightly wet them with water.

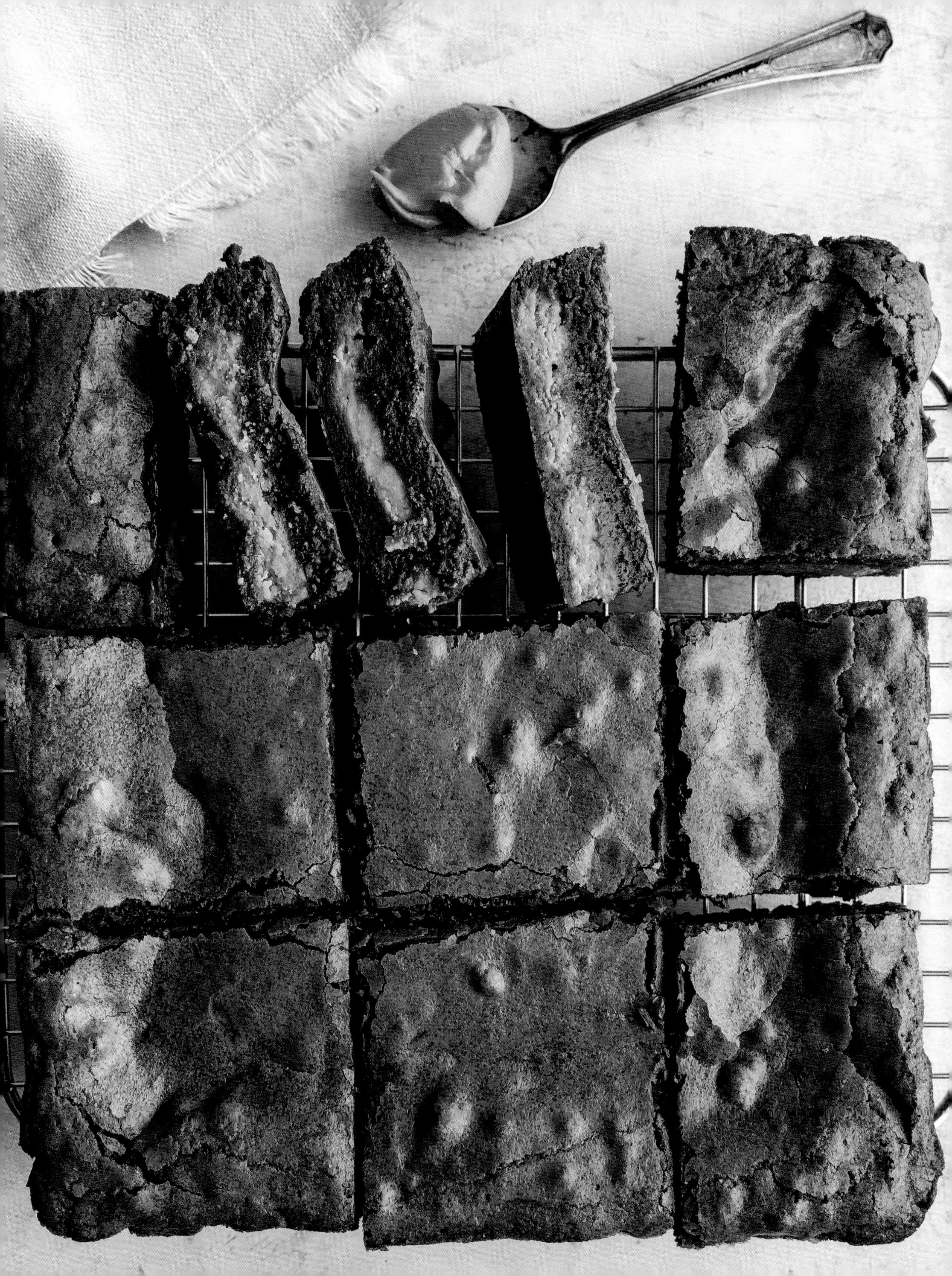

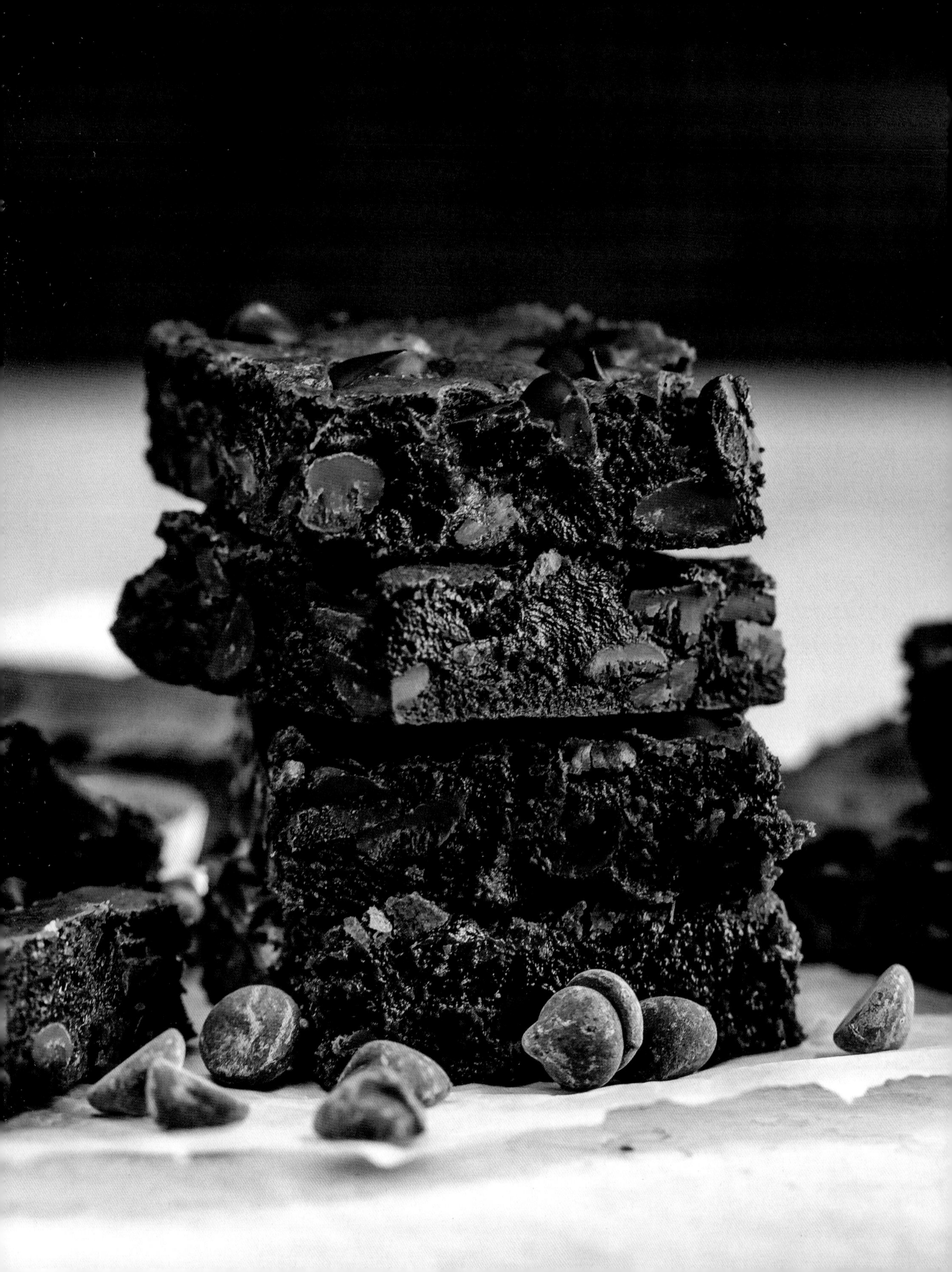

# Death by Chocolate Brownies

**W**hen you are hoping to satisfy a chocolate craving, look no further: *This* is the brownie recipe you want. It's a dangerous recipe because it's so easy and fast—brownies in your belly in under forty minutes. These are extra rich, thanks to a combination of butter and oil, and the bit of espresso powder enriches the chocolate flavor. Whenever my daughter asks for brownies, these are the ones I throw together—but be warned, you'll want a glass of milk to go with them!

## INSTRUCTIONS

1   Preheat the oven to 350°F (177°C). Line a 9 × 9–inch (23 × 23 cm) pan with foil and spray with nonstick cooking spray.

2   Place the melted butter and oil in a large bowl. Stir in the sugar and cocoa powder until smooth using a wooden spoon.

3   Add the eggs, vanilla extract, espresso powder, and salt, stir to combine, and then slowly mix in the flour. The batter will be thick. Stir in the chocolate chips.

4   Spread the batter into the prepared pan and top with more chocolate chips, if desired.

5   Bake for 21 to 25 minutes or until the brownies just lose that glossy sheen around the edges and a toothpick inserted 1 inch (2.5 cm) from the edge comes out clean. Cool before cutting.

6   Store in an airtight container for up to 4 days or freeze for up to a month.

- ½ cup (113 g) unsalted butter, melted
- 2 tablespoons (30 ml) vegetable oil
- 1⅓ cups (267 g) granulated sugar
- ⅔ cup (54 g) unsweetened cocoa powder
- 2 large eggs
- 1 teaspoon vanilla extract
- 1 teaspoon instant espresso powder
- ½ teaspoon salt
- ½ cup (62 g) all-purpose flour
- 1 cup (170 g) semi-sweet or milk chocolate chips, plus more for topping

**Yield:** 16 brownies
**Prep time:** 10 minutes
**Bake time:** 23 minutes

*Tip:*
Feel free to add ½ cup (50 g) chopped walnuts or pecans in addition to the chocolate chips.

# Bacon and Caramel Brownies

The idea for this recipe came from my friend Brandy. One day we were chatting, and she ended our session by telling me if I hadn't already sprinkled bacon on brownies, then I was doing life wrong. That very day I was trying to think of more brownie recipes for this book, so I looked at it as fate. I knew they would be delicious because I've had chocolate-covered bacon before (seriously life changing). To make these even more fun, I added caramel on top! The chocolate brownies with the gooey caramel and the salt from the bacon . . . these are pure heaven. If you have never tasted bacon as a sweet treat, you really are missing out—and this is the recipe you should try first.

## MAKE THE BROWNIES

1 Preheat the oven to 350°F (177°C). Line a 9 × 13–inch (23 × 33 cm) pan with foil and spray with nonstick cooking spray (or use parchment paper).

2 Place the baking chocolate and butter in a large microwave-safe bowl. Heat on high power for 2 to 3 minutes, stirring every 30 seconds, until the mixture is smooth.

3 Stir the sugar into the melted chocolate mixture. Add the eggs, vanilla extract, cocoa powder, and salt and stir well. Add the flour and stir carefully.

4 Spread the batter in the prepared pan. Bake for 20 to 25 minutes or until a toothpick comes out clean 2 inches (5 cm) from the side of the pan. Cool completely before topping with the caramel.

## MAKE THE CARAMEL (SEE PHOTOS ON OPPOSITE PAGE)

1 Gather all your ingredients and read the directions before starting.

2 Place the sugar in a medium heavy-bottomed (2- to 3-quart) saucepan. Do not use a shallow pan because it will boil up when you add the cream later.

3 Place the pan over medium heat. Cook, stirring often, being careful not to spread the sugar up the sides of the pan too much. The sugar will form clumps and then melt into a light amber liquid. Keep stirring until all of the clumps have dissolved. This will take about 7 to 12 minutes, depending on your pot and the heat of your stove. Do not walk away from the stove while you're making the caramel.

4 As soon as the lumps are dissolved, add the butter and stir until it's melted. Add half of the heavy whipping cream, stir, then add the rest. It will bubble up as you add it to the mixture. Remove from the heat and then stir in the vanilla extract and salt. Stir until smooth.

### For the Brownies

- 4 ounces (114 g) unsweetened baking chocolate, coarsely chopped
- ¾ cup (170 g) unsalted butter
- 1¾ cups (350 g) granulated sugar
- 3 large eggs
- 1 teaspoon vanilla extract
- 2 tablespoons (10 g) unsweetened cocoa powder
- ½ teaspoon salt
- 1 cup (124 g) all-purpose flour

### For the Caramel

- 1 cup (200 g) granulated sugar
- 5 tablespoons (71 g) unsalted butter, sliced into tablespoons
- ⅔ cup (157 ml) heavy whipping cream (no substitutions)
- 1 teaspoon vanilla extract
- ¼ teaspoon salt
- 5 slices bacon, cooked crisp and crumbled

**Yield:** 24 brownies
**Prep time:** 45 minutes
**Bake time:** 23 minutes

## Tip:

Don't like bacon? Skip it and sprinkle the top of the caramel with sea salt for Salted Caramel Brownies!

5   Cool the caramel for 10 minutes, then pour over the top of the brownies.

6   Sprinkle immediately with crumbled crispy bacon pieces. Let cool until the caramel is room temperature and has semi-set. Slice and serve.

7   Store in a single layer in an airtight container for up to 3 days. I don't recommend freezing brownies once they've been topped with the caramel, but the brownies alone can freeze for up to 2 months. Caramel will last 1 week in a jar with a tight-fitting lid in the refrigerator. To reheat it, heat in the microwave in 30-second increments, stirring between each, until warmed to the desired consistency.

**Caramel-Making Tips**

1   As you heat the sugar, it will start to clump. Be sure to stir often, but be careful not to get sugar on the sides of the pot or it might burn (or cause crystallization in your final caramel).

2   After clumping, the sugar melts into an amber-colored liquid. Keep stirring often, waiting for the last of the melting to occur.

3   The mixture will bubble up quite a bit once the butter and heavy whipping cream are added.

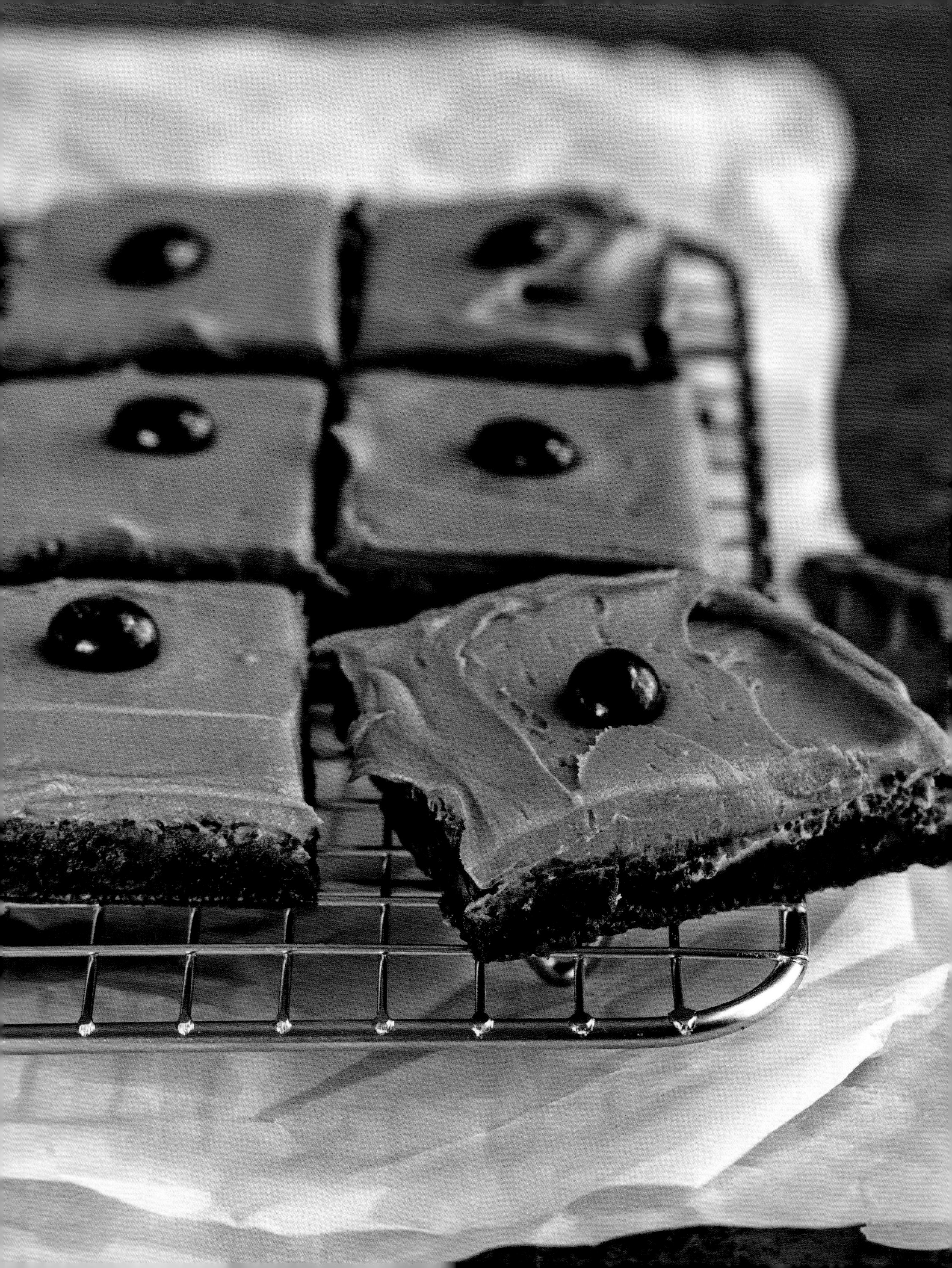

# Mocha Brownies

The summer I was sixteen my parents and I took a two-week road trip in our RV. This was our normal summer vacation MO: drive north or south for a week, turn around and come back. The difference was that now I was a teenager and wanted nothing to do with the entire thing. That year, we drove north from San Francisco to our turnaround point, Seattle. My uncle lived there, and we'd stay with his family for a few days before heading home. My savior that trip was my cousin Diana—she was a year or two older than me and took pity on me. We spent the entire day touring downtown Seattle, visiting every single Starbucks we came upon. This was back when Starbucks was just becoming popular, and I'd never been before. She told me I'd like the Mochas, so I got one at every stop, starting my years-long mocha obsession. These rich chocolatey brownies have a mocha frosting that is coffee forward with a hint of chocolate. Eaten together, they are the food version of my favorite café drink!

## MAKE THE BROWNIES

1 Preheat the oven to 350°F (177°C). Line a 9 × 13–inch (23 × 33 cm) baking pan with foil and spray with nonstick cooking spray.

2 Place the baking chocolates and butter in a large microwave-safe bowl. Heat on high power in 30-second increments, stirring between each, until melted and smooth (about 2 minutes).

3 Stir the sugar and cocoa into the chocolate mixture. Then stir in the eggs, vanilla extract, and salt. Slowly stir in the flour until smooth.

4 Pour the mixture into the prepared pan and bake for 20 to 25 minutes or until a toothpick inserted 1 inch (2.5 cm) from the edge comes out clean. Cool completely before topping.

## MAKE THE FROSTING

1 Add the instant coffee to the hot water and stir to dissolve. Let cool for 5 minutes.

2 Beat the butter until smooth in a large mixing bowl with an electric mixer. Add the cocoa and powdered sugar, 1 cup (113 g) at a time, and mix until crumbly. Mix in the vanilla extract, salt, and cooled coffee. Mix until smooth. If the frosting is not spreadable, add 1 teaspoon milk or heavy cream and continue mixing, adding more milk in 1-teaspoon increments until the desired consistency. You shouldn't need more than 3 to 4 teaspoons, if any.

3 Frost the cooled brownies. Slice and serve. Store loosely covered in the refrigerator for up to 3 days

### For the Brownies

- 4 ounces (114 g) unsweetened baking chocolate
- ¾ cup (170 g) unsalted butter
- 1¾ cups (350 g) granulated sugar
- 2 tablespoons (10 g) Dutch process cocoa powder
- 3 large eggs
- 1 teaspoon vanilla extract
- ½ teaspoon salt
- 1 cup (124 g) all-purpose flour

### For the Frosting

- 1 teaspoon instant coffee or instant espresso powder
- 1 tablespoon hot water
- ½ cup (113 g) unsalted butter, softened
- 1 tablespoon (5 g) Dutch process cocoa powder
- 3 cups (339 g) powdered sugar
- 1 teaspoon vanilla extract
- ¼ teaspoon salt
- Milk or heavy whipping cream, as needed for consistency

**Yield:** 24 brownies
**Prep time:** 45 minutes
**Bake time:** 23 minutes

## Tip:

The amount of milk (if any) needed in this recipe really depends on how soft your butter is when you start and how warm your coffee mixture still is when it's mixed in. See Frosting Tips on page 12.

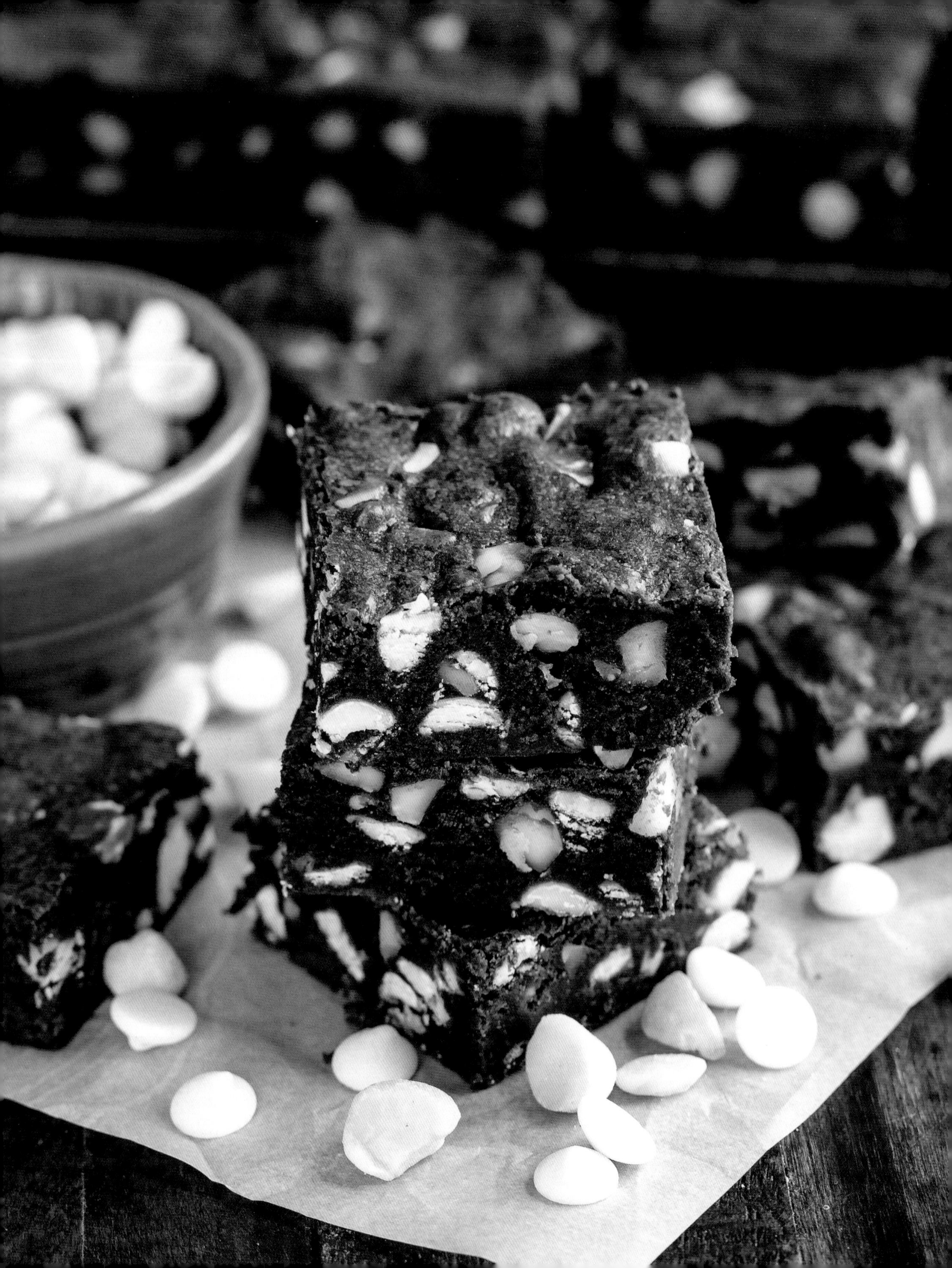

# Macadamia Nut Brownies

*J* can't think about macadamia nuts without thinking about Hawaii. It doesn't matter where I am, or what the context is. I could be at home or across the country as far away from the islands as could be, and if I see macadamia nuts, I'll be instantly transported to one of my favorite places: Maui. Whenever we visit, I do lots of shopping, and the charges for macadamia nuts and desserts that contain them (cookies, brownies, candy, you name it) exceeds my food budget for a week. Whenever I get home from Hawaii, I savor every single macadamia thing I've brought back with me until I'm extra sad once they're all gone. This brownie recipe is my ode to one of the favorites I had on a trip years ago: a rich chocolate brownie filled with my favorite nut and white chocolate chips for good measure. If you love chocolate-covered macadamia nuts as much as I do, you're going to love these brownies! Take a bite, close your eyes, and pretend you're sunning on Ka'anapali Beach.

## INSTRUCTIONS

1 Preheat the oven to 350°F (177°C). Line a 9 × 13–inch (23 × 33 cm) pan with foil and spray with nonstick cooking spray.

2 Place the baking chocolate and butter in a large microwave-safe bowl. Heat on high power in 30-second increments, stirring between each, until the mixture is melted and smooth, about 2 to 2½ minutes, depending on your microwave.

3 Stir the sugar and cocoa into the butter mixture, then stir in the eggs until the mixture is combined. Mix in the vanilla extract and salt, and then slowly mix in the flour until smooth. Stir in the white chocolate chips and macadamia nuts.

4 Pour the mixture immediately into the prepared pan and spread evenly. Bake for 28 to 35 minutes or until the top is no longer glossy and a toothpick inserted 2 inches (5 cm) from the edge comes out clean.

5 Store in an airtight container for up to 3 days or freeze brownies for up to a month.

- 4 ounces (114 g) unsweetened baking chocolate, broken into pieces
- 1 cup (226 g) unsalted butter
- 2 cups (400 g) granulated sugar
- ¼ cup (20 g) unsweetened cocoa powder
- 4 large eggs
- 1 teaspoon vanilla extract
- ½ teaspoon salt
- 1⅓ cups (165 g) all-purpose flour
- 1½ cups (255 g) white chocolate chips
- 1 cup (124 g) chopped macadamia nuts

**Yield:** 20 brownies
**Prep time:** 25 minutes
**Bake time:** 30 minutes

## Tip:

Can't find macadamia nuts? These are also fantastic with walnuts or almonds!

# Nutella Brownies

For our second wedding anniversary, Mel and I went to Paris. He'd had business in London the week prior, so I flew over and met him and we spent four glorious days in the City of Light. I know that I had Nutella before that trip—I must have—but I have no Nutella memory before the crêpes we ate on Rue Cler. It's like my love of chocolate hazelnut spread was bloomed during that trip and it stuck with me forever after. In the twenty years since, I've bought so many jars of Nutella to make crêpes or brownies and ended up just eating it straight from the jar with a spoon. To me, Nutella tastes like a melted brownie smells and I can never get enough! It's why, when I buy it, I know it has to immediately go *in* something or it'll never make it. If you're like me, you should grab a jar and make these brownies ASAP: They're full of Nutella and have it swirled on top. They might just look like plain old chocolate brownies, but they sure don't taste like them!

- 4 ounces (114 g) unsweetened baking chocolate
- ¾ cup (170 g) unsalted butter
- 1¼ cups (250 g) granulated sugar
- 3 large eggs
- 1 teaspoon vanilla extract
- ½ teaspoon salt
- 1 cup (336 g) Nutella, divided
- 1 cup (124 g) all-purpose flour
- 1 cup (170 g) chocolate chips

**Yield:** 12 brownies
**Prep time:** 20 minutes
**Bake time:** 30 minutes

## INSTRUCTIONS

1  Preheat the oven to 350°F (177°C). Line a 9 × 9–inch (23 × 23 cm) pan with foil or parchment paper and spray with nonstick cooking spray.

2  Place the baking chocolate and butter in a large microwave-safe bowl. Heat in 30-second increments, stirring between each, until melted and smooth (about 2 minutes, depending on your microwave).

3  Stir the sugar into the chocolate mixture, then stir in the eggs until well mixed. Stir in ½ cup (168 g) Nutella, and then add the vanilla extract and salt and stir until smooth. Carefully stir in the flour, then stir in the chocolate chips.

4  Pour the batter into the pan. Scoop tablespoons of the remaining Nutella and drop them on top of the batter. Use a knife to swirl it around the top of the brownies.

5  Bake for about 26 to 32 minutes, or until a toothpick inserted 1 inch (2.5 cm) from the side of the pan comes out with just a few crumbs.

6  Cool before slicing into bars. Store in an airtight container for up to 3 days or freeze for up to 2 months.

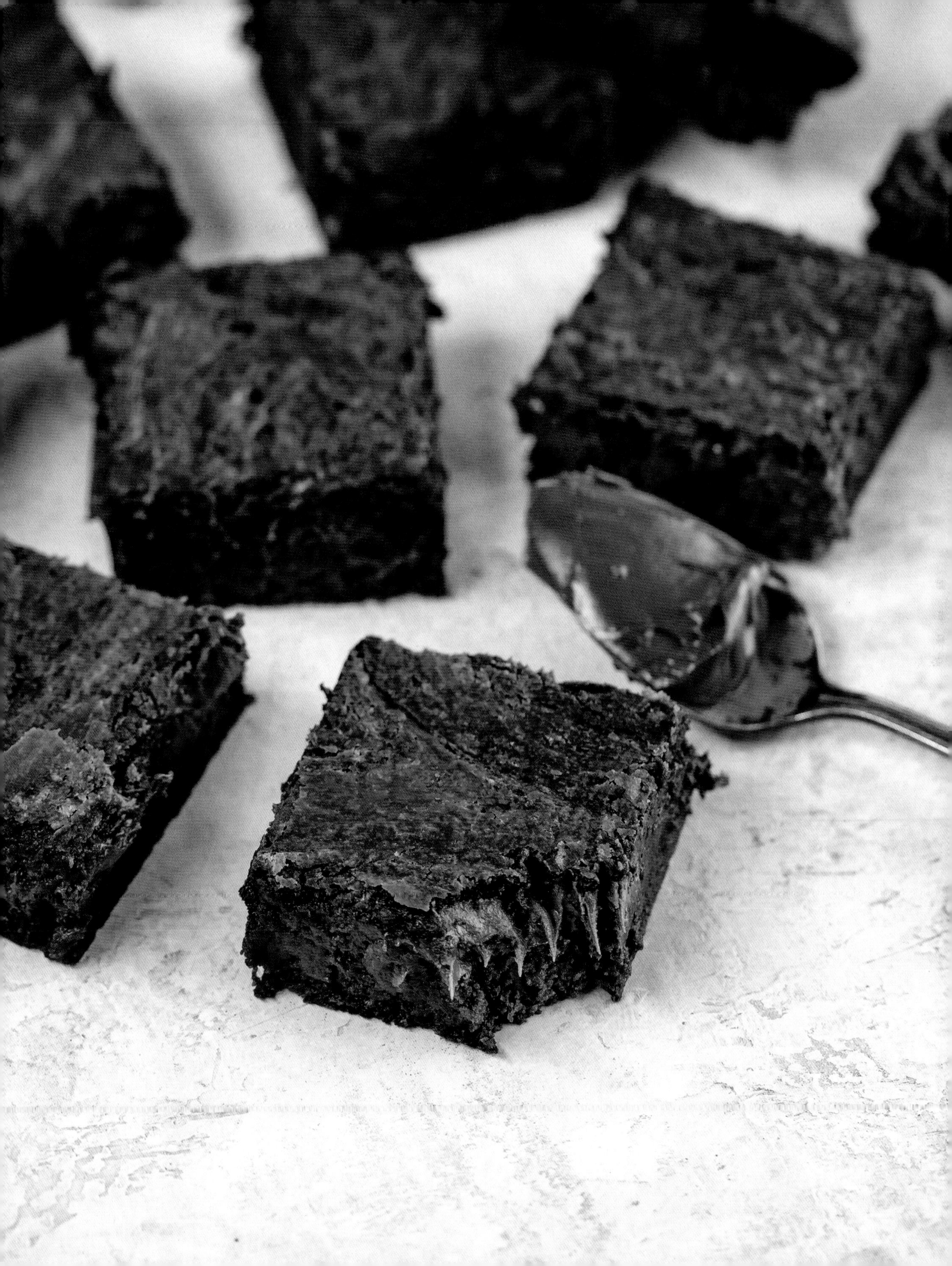

# Zucchini Brownies

*J* am an utterly hopeless gardener. I always have good intentions, but I can't even keep a plant sitting next to my kitchen sink alive (true story). My husband is much better with all things outdoors, thank goodness, and for several years we planted gardens. I always wanted to have zucchini on hand all summer long and after three years of trying (and moving to a house that had bees nearby), we finally got actual zucchini from our plants. That summer we had so much zucchini! Anyone who has ever had a garden knows that you can check for squash one day and literally check again the next day and you have a baseball bat–sized one you missed just the day before. We got back from a trip (after having someone check the plant for a week) and had so many huge zucchinis we couldn't even hold them all at once. That's when I first started making these brownies, and I've been making them multiple times a year ever since.

These brownies aren't fudgy and thick like my other brownie recipes; plain they're more cakey than dense. They taste good, of course, but where they really shine is with the frosting. The gooey poured chocolate frosting turns these into the most rich and chocolatey tasting brownies you'll ever try. And if you worry about your kids eating brownies with green things in them, don't: My daughter is the pickiest of all eaters, but these are one of her favorites.

## MAKE THE BROWNIES

1  Preheat the oven to 350°F (177°C). Line a 9 × 13–inch baking pan with foil and spray with nonstick cooking spray. Set aside.

2  In a medium bowl, whisk together the flour, cocoa powder, baking soda, and salt. Set aside.

3  Using an electric mixer, mix together the oil, sugar, and vanilla extract until well combined. Add the dry ingredients and mix until sandy. (At this point the mixture will be sandy and dry.)

4  Fold in the zucchini. Let the mixture sit for a few minutes so the batter can absorb the moisture from the zucchini. Then, if your mixture is still very powdery, add up to 5 tablespoons (75 ml) water (start with 1 tablespoon [15 ml] and work up from there, stirring well after each addition). The batter will be very thick but shouldn't be powdery. The dough is thick, like cookie dough. Be sure not to add too much water. Spread in the prepared pan.

5  Bake for 25 to 30 minutes until the brownies spring back when gently touched.

## For the Brownies

- 2 cups (248 g) all-purpose flour
- ½ cup (40 g) unsweetened cocoa powder
- 1½ teaspoons baking soda
- 1 teaspoon salt
- ½ cup (118 ml) vegetable oil
- 1½ cups (300 g) granulated sugar
- 1 teaspoon vanilla extract
- 2 cups (254 g) shredded zucchini
- 3 to 5 tablespoons (45 to 75 ml) water

## For the Frosting

- 3 tablespoons (15 g) unsweetened cocoa powder
- Pinch of salt
- 2 cups (226 g) powdered sugar
- ¼ cup (57 g) unsalted butter, melted
- ¼ cup (59 ml) milk
- 1 teaspoon vanilla extract

**Yield:** 20 brownies
**Prep time:** 30 minutes
**Bake time:** 28 minutes

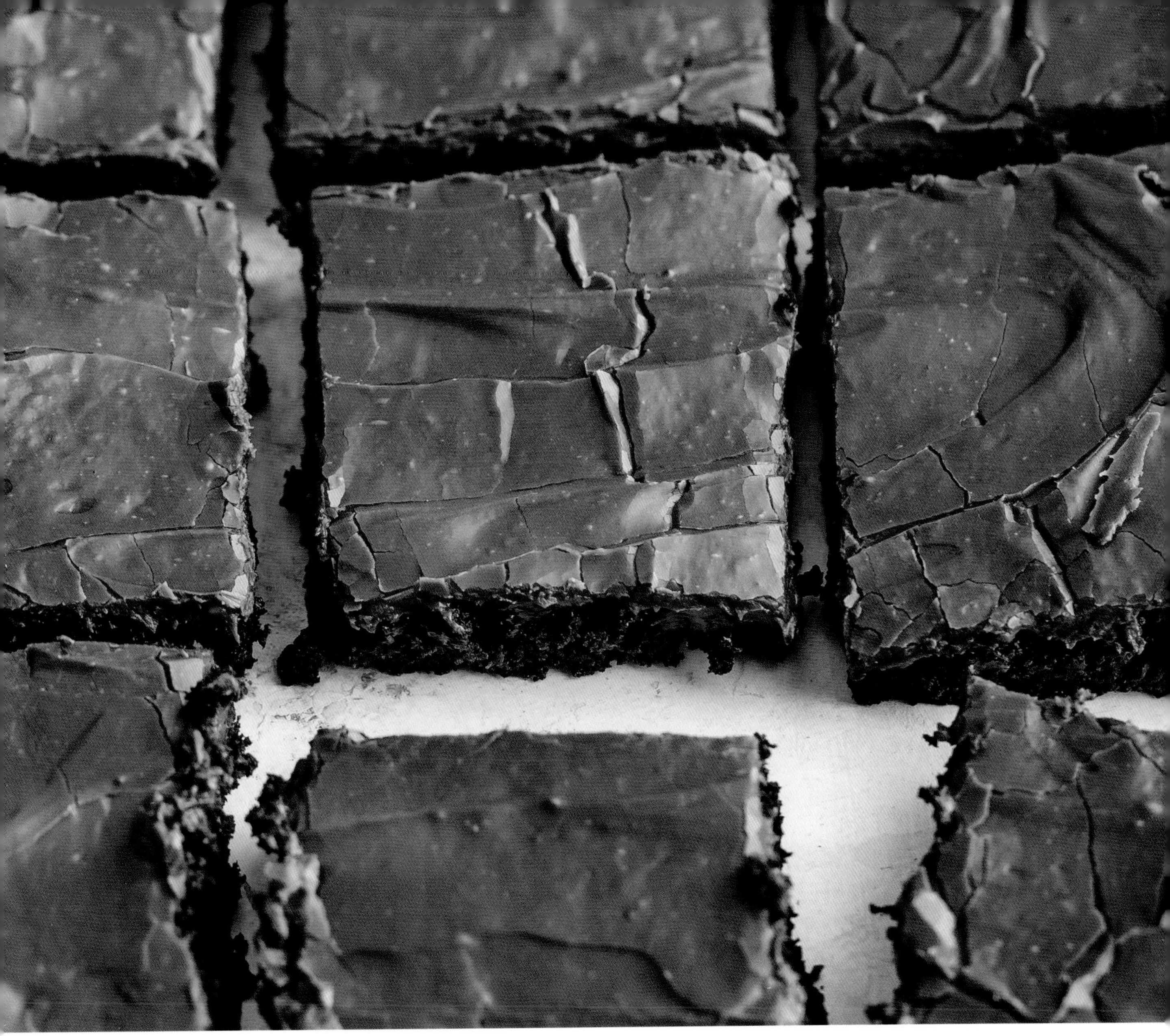

**MAKE THE FROSTING**

1 Whisk the cocoa powder, salt, and powdered sugar into hot melted butter. Whisk in the milk and vanilla. Spread over the cooled brownies. The frosting thickens as it cools but will not be hard set.

2 These brownies are best stored in an airtight container and eaten within 2 days. Chill them to make them last an extra day. You can also freeze them in a single layer in an airtight container for up to 2 months.

**Tip:**

I normally add at least 3 tablespoons (45 ml) of water in step 4. This recipe takes a little patience, but it's worth it!

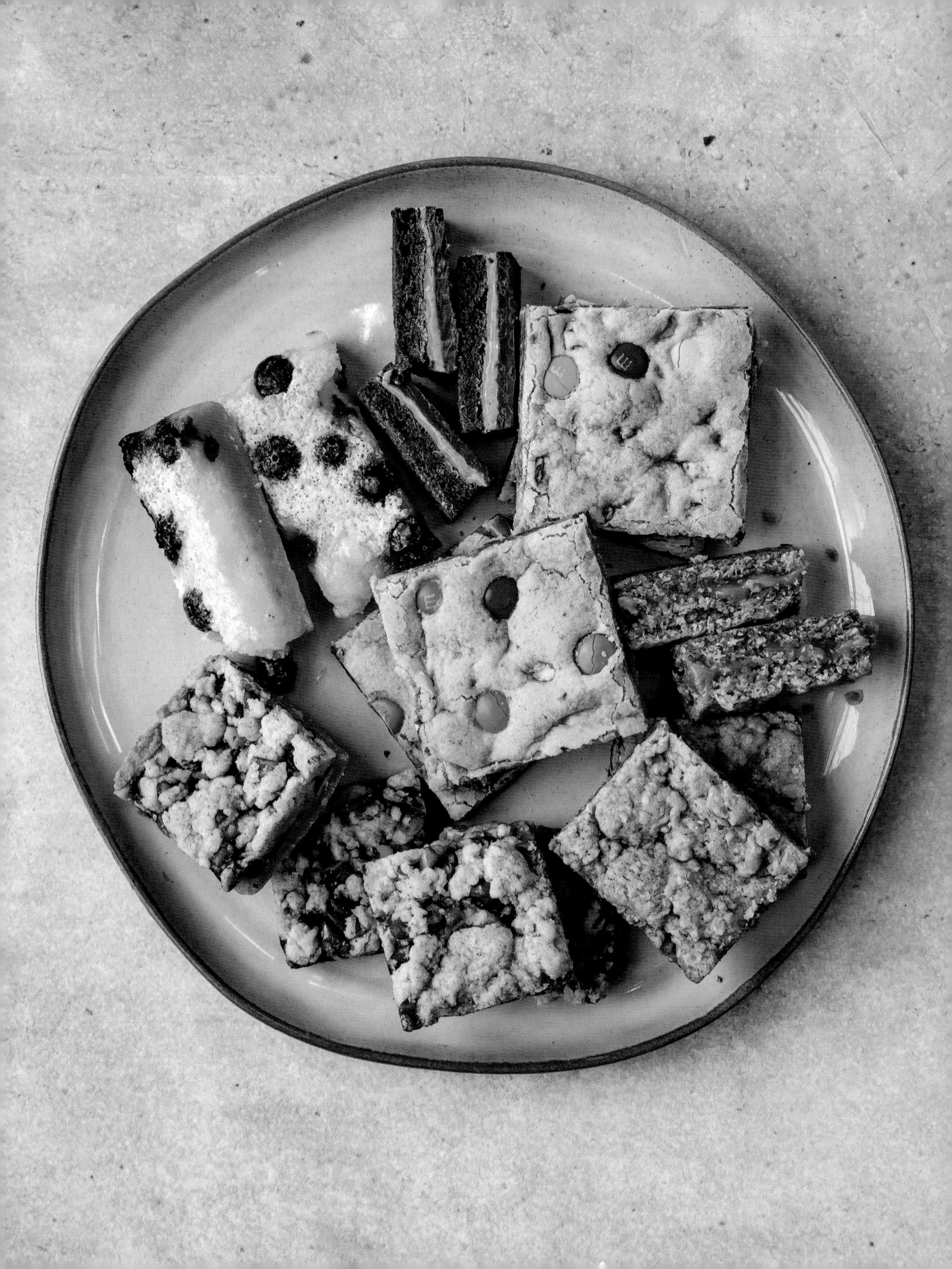

# Blondies and Bars

**A**s much as I adore chocolate, I equally love vanilla. (If I'm being 100 percent honest, there isn't a dessert I won't say no to.) When you don't feel like chocolate, you make blondies. And when you don't feel like scooping cookies, you make bars. Bars are some of my favorite things to make because I'm all about not having to wash silicone baking mats – give me a 9 × 13–inch (23 × 33 cm) pan and some foil and I'm good to go!

This chapter could have had a hundred recipes in it, and it was hard for me to narrow it down to just a few of my absolute favorite go-to ones. I tried to provide a range of options, from blondies to bars, fruit to candy, peanut butter to . . . not peanut butter. From my Bake Sale Blondies with variations on page 80 to an update of an old classic, Blueberry Lemon Bars, on page 99, you're sure to find a flavor (or several) that I hope become a cherished favorite.

Some blondie and bar tips:

- **Sticky dough:** Many of these recipes require pressing dough into the pan because blondies and bars often have the texture of cookie dough; they don't pour and spread as nicely as brownies. I find spreading with a spatula to be difficult if you've lined your pan with foil, so I like to get my hands into the pan. To avoid the dough sticking to your hands, grease them with butter or non-stick cooking spray.

- **Foil:** Again, I like to line my pans with foil or parchment paper for easy removal. Be sure to spray it with nonstick cooking spray so your bars don't stick. And it's best to remove them from the pan once they've cooled, so they don't break.

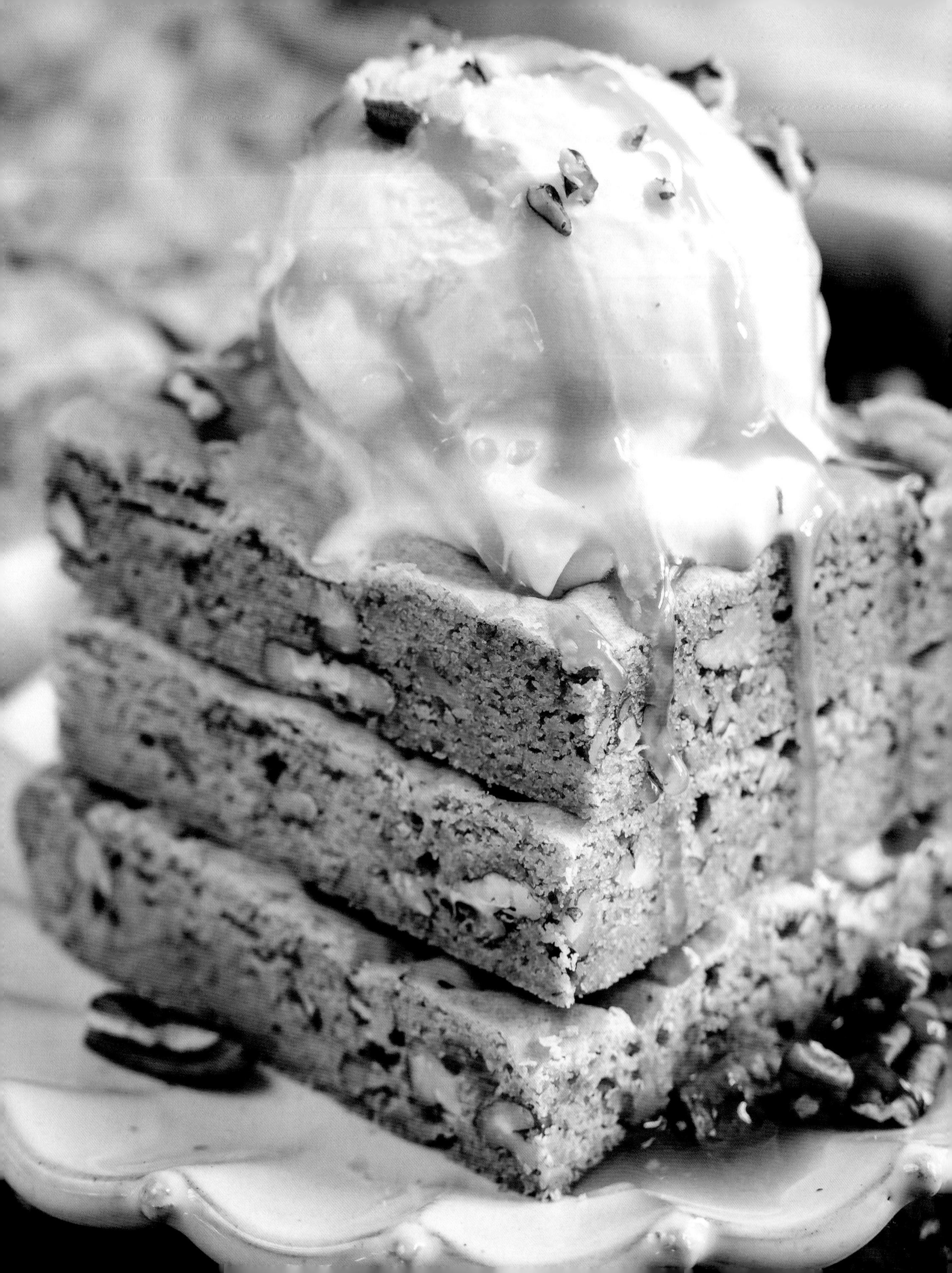

# Brown Butter Pecan Blondies

Sometimes you feel like chocolate and other times . . . you make blondies. I am a total chocoholic, but sometimes I just crave, well, *not* chocolate. That's when I reach for this blondie recipe. It's a super versatile recipe that is always perfectly soft and chewy, thanks to all that brown sugar! This is one of my absolute favorite ways to make them: with brown butter and toasted pecans. Brown butter requires one extra step but is so worth it because it adds such a depth of flavor. And the toasted pecans . . . I can't ever get enough. I love these plain, but topping them with ice cream and caramel is heaven.

- 2 cups (205 g) pecan halves
- ½ cup (113 g) unsalted butter
- 1¾ cups (350 g) packed brown sugar
- 2 large eggs
- 1 teaspoon vanilla extract
- 1 teaspoon baking powder
- ½ teaspoon salt
- 2 cups (248 g) all-purpose flour

**Yield:** 24 bars
**Prep time:** 15 minutes
**Bake time:** 20 minutes

## INSTRUCTIONS

1   Preheat the oven to 350°F (177°C). Line a 9 × 13–inch (23 × 33 cm) pan with foil and spray with nonstick cooking spray.

2   Place the pecan halves in a medium-sized skillet and toast over medium-low heat, stirring often, until fragrant, just a few minutes. Don't walk away from the stove—nuts burn very easily. Remove from the pan to cool, then coarsely chop them.

3   Wipe out the skillet you used for the pecans and add the butter to the pan. Place over medium heat and melt the butter, then cook it until it turns slightly golden, about 5 minutes. The butter will foam and then little brown flecks will form at the bottom of the skillet, and the foam will turn golden brown. Stir often and watch it carefully; it can go from browned to burned fast. Place brown butter in a large bowl (be sure to scrape all those little brown bits out of the bottom of the skillet).

4   Add the brown sugar to the butter and stir with a wooden spoon (or use a hand mixer to combine). Stir in the eggs and vanilla extract, and then add the baking powder and salt, stirring or mixing until smooth. Stir in the flour until smooth, and then add the chopped pecans.

5   Press the dough into the prepared pan and bake for 18 to 21 minutes, or just until the top starts to look solid and lightly golden. Err on the side of underbaked for gooey blondies!

6   Cool before removing from the pan and slicing into bars. Store in an airtight container for up to 3 days or freeze for up to a month.

## Tip:

Reduce the pecans to 1 cup (103 g) and add 1 cup (170 g) white or semi-sweet chocolate chips for a delicious blondie twist!

# Cinnamon Blondies

Who doesn't love cinnamon rolls? Those glorious gooey rolls can be my undoing; never leave me alone with a pan—ever. I took the flavors of my favorite breakfast indulgence and turned them into a new version of a blondie, and the result is amazing: a soft and spicy cookie bar topped with a cream cheese frosting. These are sure to be a hit with anyone who loves cinnamon!

## MAKE THE BLONDIES

1  Preheat the oven to 350°F (177°C). Line a 9 × 13–inch (23 × 33 cm) baking dish with foil and spray with nonstick cooking spray.

2  Cream the butter and brown sugar in the bowl of an electric mixer fitted with a paddle attachment. Add the eggs and vanilla extract and beat until combined. Add the cinnamon, baking powder, salt, and flour, and mix.

3  Press into the prepared pan (the dough is sticky, so spray your hands with cooking spray to avoid it sticking to your hands).

4  Bake for 18 to 22 minutes. (Be careful not to overcook: The center will still be jiggly when you take these out of the oven, and they will finish cooking and firming up as they cool.) Cool completely before frosting.

## MAKE THE FROSTING

1  Cream the butter and cream cheese with a hand mixer until smooth. Slowly mix in the powdered sugar and vanilla extract. Add 1 teaspoon heavy whipping cream or milk and mix until smooth, adding more as needed for desired consistency.

2  Frost the cooled bars, then cut into squares.

3  Store in an airtight container in the refrigerator for up to 3 days or freeze in a single layer for up to 1 month.

### For the Blondies

- ½ cup (113 g) unsalted butter, softened
- 2 cups (400 g) packed brown sugar
- 2 large eggs
- 1 teaspoon vanilla extract
- 1½ teaspoons cinnamon
- 1 teaspoon baking powder
- ½ teaspoon salt
- 2 cups (248 g) all-purpose flour

### For the Frosting

- 2 tablespoons (28 g) unsalted butter, softened
- 4 ounces (112 g) cream cheese, softened
- 2 cups (226 g) powdered sugar
- 1 teaspoon vanilla extract
- 1 to 2 teaspoons heavy whipping cream or milk

**Yield:** 12 brownies
**Prep time:** 20 minutes
**Bake time:** 30 minutes

## Tip:

Skip the frosting and add 1½ cups (255 g) white chocolate chips to the blondie batter!

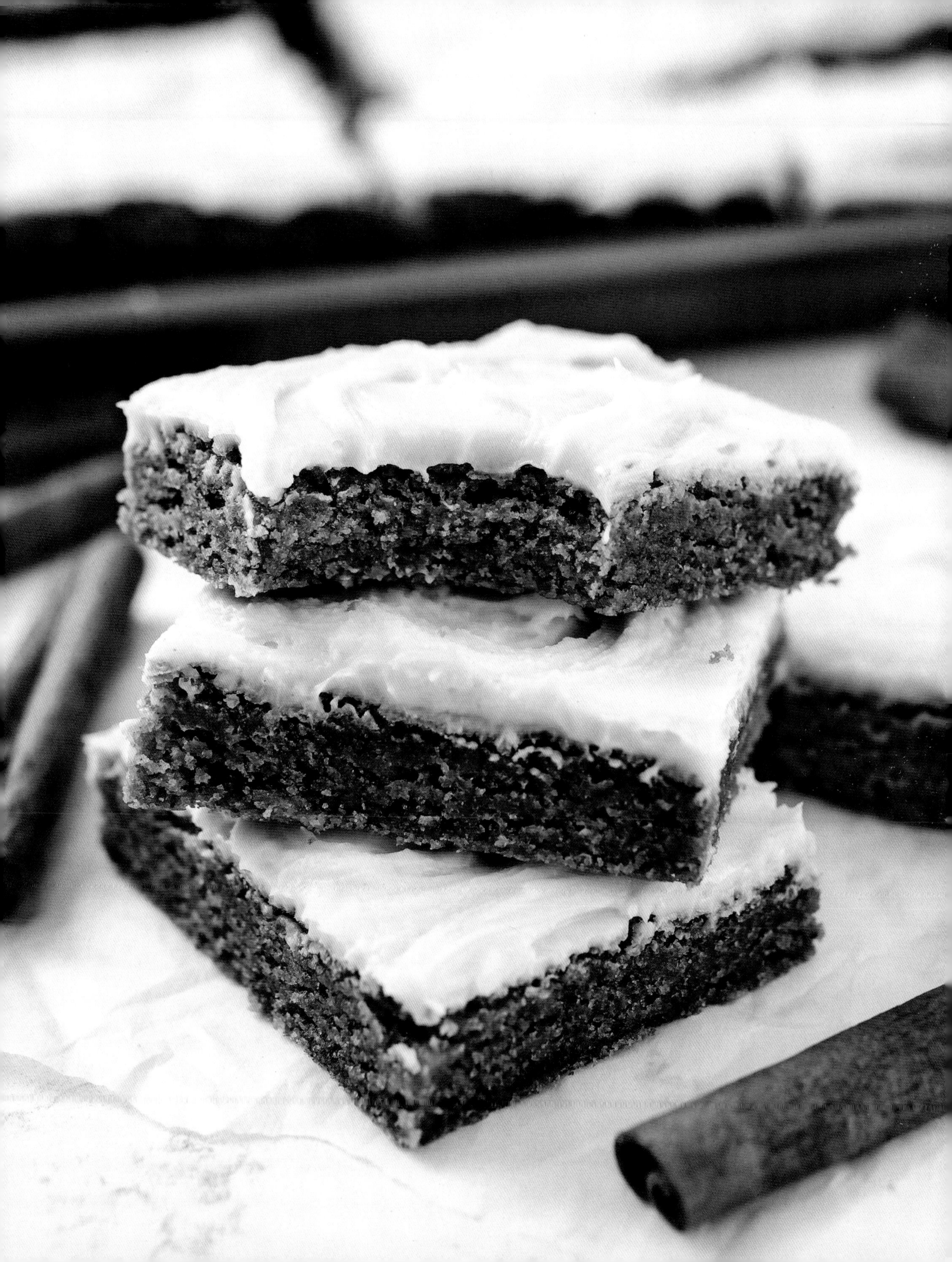

# Bake Sale Blondies

I first found this recipe at a school carnival bake sale when my daughter was in kindergarten. Always being one to support a bake sale, I was perusing the table when I realized my neighbor was the salesperson. She, of course, recommended her contribution: a toffee blondie. I'm never one to say no to toffee (or really, sugar in general) so gave her my $1 and took a bite. Holy heaven—it shocked me how good they were. Blondies kind of have a bad rap: They're not a cookie bar, but they certainly aren't brownies, and often they are bland or plain or dry. These were, dare I say, fudgy? Of course, I asked my neighbor for the recipe. The secret to their fudginess is a whopping 2 full cups (400 g) of brown sugar. Yes, you read that right: 2 cups of packed brown sugar to just ½ cup butter. It's indulgent and a little bit insane, but once you taste them, you'll understand.

I've included a few different versions of these blondies for you: the original Toffee Blondies but also other ideas for how to switch them up. The sky is the limit for these; add anything you like. Sometimes I'll just clean out my baking cabinet to make them, using a mix of ten different things. They're good loaded or they're good plain, and they're never boring!

- ½ cup (113 g) unsalted butter, softened
- 2 cups (400 g) packed brown sugar
- 2 large eggs
- 1 teaspoon vanilla extract
- ½ teaspoon salt
- 1 teaspoon baking powder
- 2 cups (248 g) all-purpose flour
- 2 cups mix-ins (see ideas opposite)

**Yield:** 24 bars
**Prep time:** 20 minutes
**Bake time:** 25 minutes

## INSTRUCTIONS

1 Preheat the oven to 350°F (177°C). Line a 9 × 13–inch (23 × 33 cm) pan with foil and spray well with nonstick cooking spray.

2 Mix the butter and brown sugar with a stand or a hand mixer until crumbly. Mix in the eggs and vanilla extract until smooth. Mix in the salt, baking powder, and flour. Stir in the desired mix-ins.

3 Spread in the prepared pan. The mixture is wet, so it's best to spray your hands with nonstick cooking spray and then smooth the dough with your hands to get an even layer.

4 Bake for 23 to 28 minutes, until they start to turn golden. Err on the side of underbaked with these; they'll finish baking as they cool, and you don't want them overbaked. The center will still be a bit jiggly when you take them from the oven.

5 Cool before slicing into bars. Store in an airtight container for up to 5 days or freeze for up to 2 months.

**Tip:**

It's really important not to overbake these. I always err on the side of underdone to get that rich and fudgy texture. Take them out of the oven when they're still a little jiggly, and they'll set as they cool.

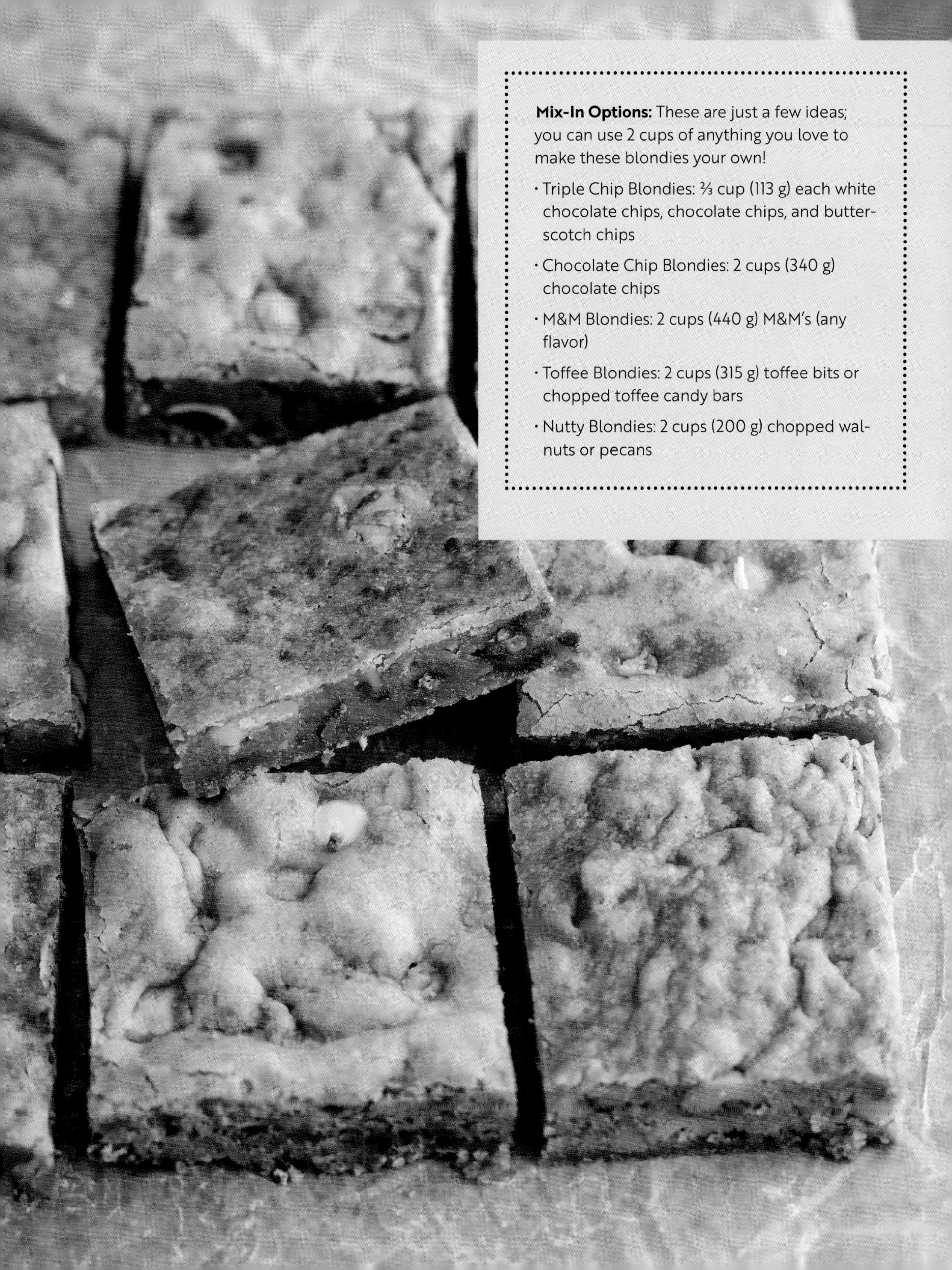

**Mix-In Options:** These are just a few ideas; you can use 2 cups of anything you love to make these blondies your own!

- Triple Chip Blondies: ⅔ cup (113 g) each white chocolate chips, chocolate chips, and butter-scotch chips
- Chocolate Chip Blondies: 2 cups (340 g) chocolate chips
- M&M Blondies: 2 cups (440 g) M&M's (any flavor)
- Toffee Blondies: 2 cups (315 g) toffee bits or chopped toffee candy bars
- Nutty Blondies: 2 cups (200 g) chopped wal-nuts or pecans

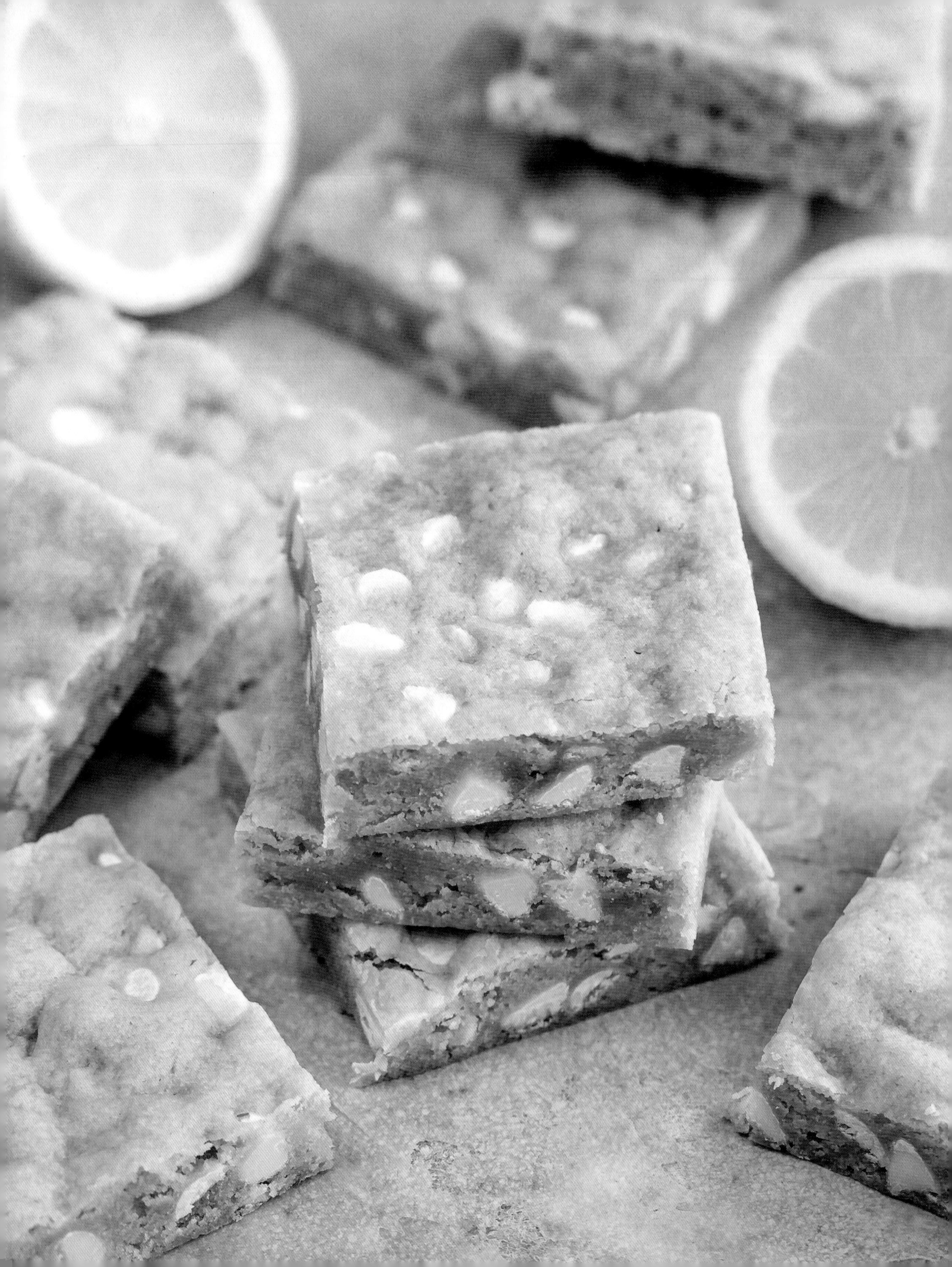

# White Chocolate Lemonies

Until my daughter was a Daisy Scout, I would tell everyone who asked that I couldn't stand lemon desserts. I'd avoid them like the plague at any party, I would never even think about adding lemon to cookies or eating lemon curd, and I'd skip lemon juice or zest whenever a recipe called for it. Then came our first Girl Scout Cookie sale: I was volunteering at the meeting where the girls all got to taste the cookies (you have to know all about the product you're selling, after all). When they got to the Lemonades, my daughter Jordan turned up her nose, so I gave them a try and it was love at first bite. Or maybe *infatuation* would be a better word, because I went home that day and made a pie inspired by the cookies. Then I bought more cookies and ate them. And I started making all the lemon desserts I could think of for the blog.

I know I'm not alone in my love of lemon desserts, so I had to put Lemonies in this book. These are a lemon blondie, soft and rich and never dry, with a good amount of lemon flavor from zest, juice, and extract. Lemon baking tip: The zest is where most of the flavor comes from, not the juice, so it's always important to add it when baking. Because I wanted even more lemon flavor, I added extract and I highly recommend it. Be sure to buy pure lemon extract (not artificial) and these bars will become your new favorite. Of course, white chocolate just pairs so well that I had to add the chips to the batter, but if you're a purist, you can skip them. And if you think you don't like lemon desserts, learn from me. I wasted thirty years of my life not eating them, and I kick myself for all I missed out on!

- ½ cup (113 g) unsalted butter, softened
- 1 cup (200 g) packed brown sugar
- ½ cup (100 g) granulated sugar
- 2 large eggs
- 1 teaspoon vanilla extract
- 1 tablespoon (15 ml) lemon juice
- ½ teaspoon lemon extract
- 2 tablespoons lemon zest
- 1 teaspoon baking powder
- ½ teaspoon salt
- 2 cups (248 g) all-purpose flour
- 1½ cups (255 g) white chocolate chips

**Yield:** 24 bars
**Prep time:** 20 minutes
**Bake time:** 20 minutes

## INSTRUCTIONS

1   Preheat the oven to 350°F (177°C). Line a 9 × 13–inch (23 × 33 cm) pan with foil or parchment paper and spray with nonstick cooking spray.

2   Cream the butter, brown sugar, and granulated sugar in a large bowl using an electric mixer. Add the eggs, vanilla extract, lemon juice, and lemon extract and beat until combined. Add the lemon zest, baking powder, salt, and flour, and mix. Stir in the white chocolate chips.

3   Press into the prepared pan (the dough is sticky, so spray your hands with nonstick cooking spray to avoid it sticking to your hands).

4   Bake for 18 to 23 minutes or until the bars just lose their glossy sheen and are light golden around the edges. Be careful not to overcook: The center should still be jiggly when you take these out of the oven. They will finish cooking and firming up as they cool.

5   Store in an airtight container in the refrigerator for up to 3 days or freeze in a single layer for up to a month.

## Tip:

Want even more lemon flavor? Make a simple glaze with ½ cup (57 g) powdered sugar and 1 to 2 tablespoons (15 to 30 ml) lemon juice. Drizzle over the Lemonies and prepare to pucker!

# Triple Decker Cookie Bars

Several years ago, there was a popular cookie-Oreo-brownie combination that went viral on social media. It had a brownie base and a chocolate chip cookie top with Oreos stuffed in the middle, and a less-than-desirable name. I didn't create those brownies, but I've made them several times and they are beyond fantastic. This cookie bar is my homage to those brownies completely in cookie form: a chocolate cookie base and chocolate chip cookie top stuffed with Oreos. Crunchy and chewy, these are soft and rich and, like their inspiration, should be served with a big glass of milk.

## MAKE THE CHOCOLATE COOKIE LAYER

1 Preheat the oven to 350°F (177°C). Line a 9 × 13–inch (23 × 33 cm) pan with foil and spray with nonstick cooking spray.

2 Place ⅓ cup (57 g) chocolate chips in a microwave-safe bowl. Heat on 50 percent power in 30-second increments, stirring between each, until melted and smooth. Set aside to cool while mixing cookie dough.

3 Cream the butter and both sugars in the bowl of a stand mixer fitted with the paddle attachment (or a large bowl using a hand mixer) until fluffy, 1 to 2 minutes. Mix in the vanilla extract, egg, baking soda, and salt.

4 Add the melted chocolate to the mixture along with the cocoa powder, and mix until smooth. Then slowly mix in the flour until dough forms.

5 Press the dough into a thin layer in the prepared pan. Place Oreos in even rows on top of the cookie dough.

## MAKE THE CHOCOLATE CHIP LAYER

1 Stir the melted butter and both sugars with a wooden spoon until combined. Mix in the egg and vanilla extract until smooth.

2 Stir in the baking soda and salt, then slowly mix in the flour. Stir in the chocolate chips.

3 Press the chocolate chip cookie dough evenly over the top of the Oreos in the pan, making sure to completely cover the bottom layer.

4 Bake for 25 to 30 minutes or until the cookie bars are lightly golden and no longer glossy. Cool completely before slicing.

5 Store in an airtight container for up to 3 days or freeze for up to 2 months.

### For the Chocolate Cookie Layer

- 1⅓ cups (227 g) semi-sweet chocolate chips, divided
- ½ cup (113 g) unsalted butter, softened
- ¾ cup (150 g) packed brown sugar
- ¼ cup (50 g) granulated sugar
- 1 teaspoon vanilla extract
- 1 large egg
- ½ teaspoon baking soda
- ¼ teaspoon salt
- 1 tablespoon (5 g) unsweetened cocoa powder
- 1¼ cups (155 g) all-purpose flour
- 24 Oreos (or similar-sized cookie)

### For the Chocolate Chip Cookie Layer

- ½ cup (113 g) unsalted butter, melted
- ⅓ cup (67 g) granulated sugar
- ½ cup (100 g) brown sugar, packed
- 1 large egg
- 1 teaspoon vanilla extract
- ½ teaspoon baking soda
- ½ teaspoon salt
- 1½ cups (186 g) all-purpose flour
- 1½ cups (255 g) semi-sweet chocolate chips

**Yield:** 24 bars
**Prep time:** 45 minutes
**Bake time:** 28 minutes

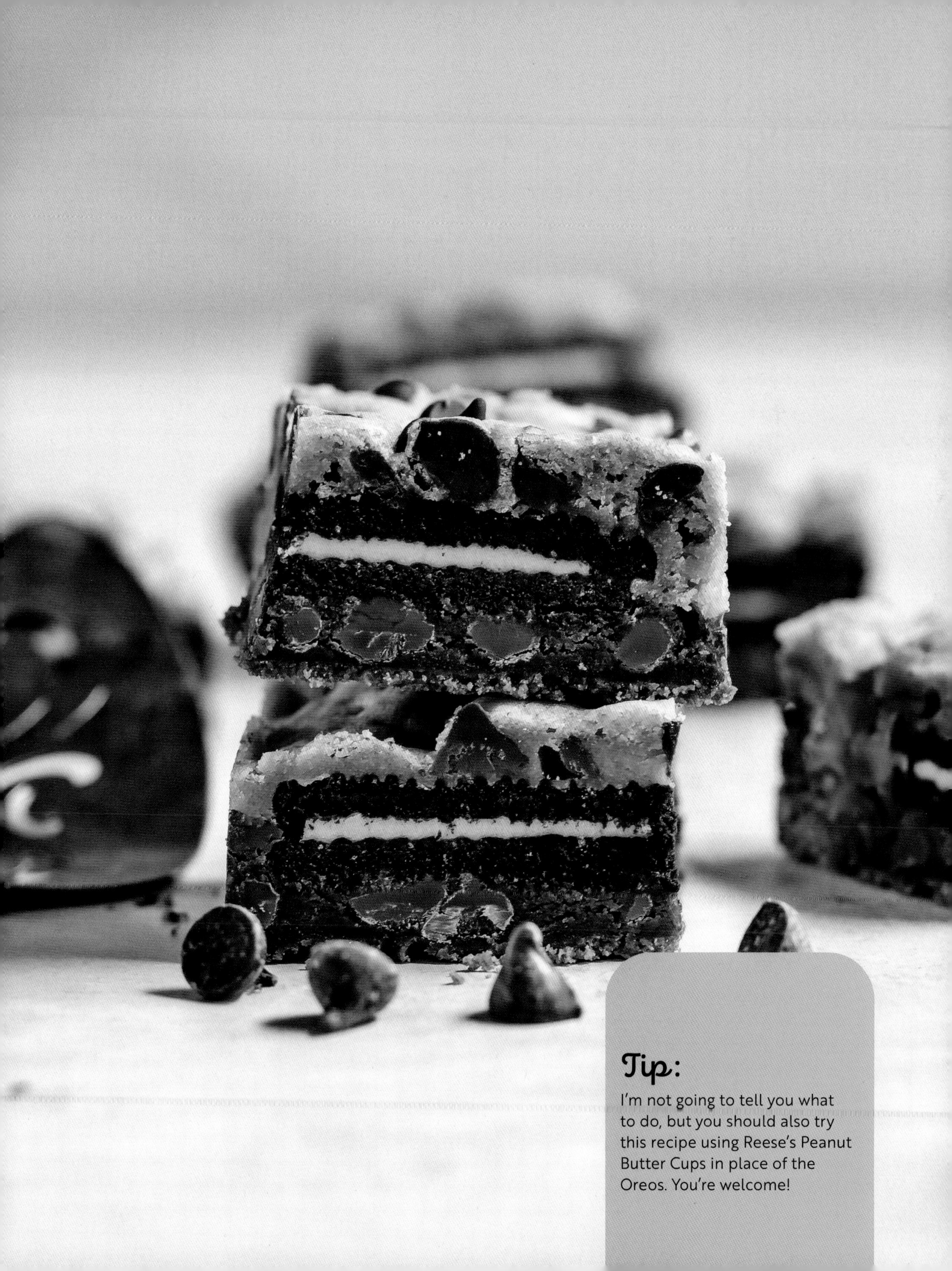

## Tip:

I'm not going to tell you what to do, but you should also try this recipe using Reese's Peanut Butter Cups in place of the Oreos. You're welcome!

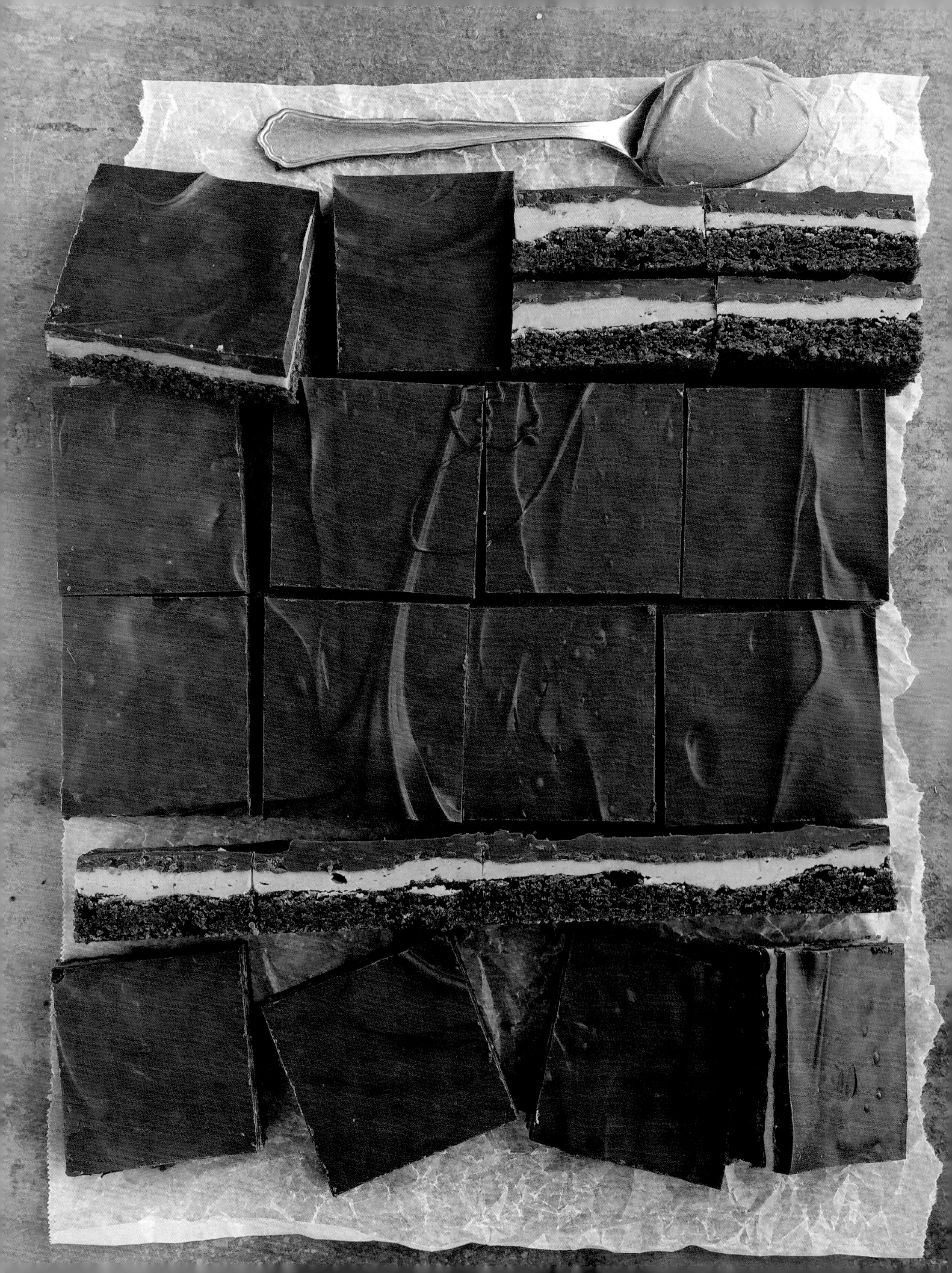

# Peanut Butter Patty Bars

*A*re you *#TeamPeanutButterPatty* or *#TeamTagalong*? Those are the two names for the most underrated (and one of the best) Girl Scout Cookies: a shortbread cookie topped with peanut butter and then the whole thing is coated in chocolate. For me, the Peanut Butter Patties are second only to Thin Mints, but my husband would disagree. He doesn't care what we call them, but he is 100 percent *#TeamPeanutButterPatty* all the way. These bars are inspired by those cookies, except instead of a shortbread crust I did it one better and made a chocolate cookie crust. I'm sorry, but you can never, ever go wrong with more chocolate!

## INSTRUCTIONS

1  Preheat the oven to 350°F (177°C). Line a 9 × 13–inch (23 × 33 cm) pan with foil (for easy removal) and spray with nonstick cooking spray.

2  In a medium bowl, whisk together the cocoa powder, baking soda, salt, and flour. Set aside.

3  In the bowl of an electric mixer fitted with the paddle attachment, cream the butter and both sugars. Mix in the egg and 1 teaspoon vanilla extract and mix until smooth. Add the dry ingredients and mix until combined.

4  Spread the cookie dough in the prepared pan. Bake for about 17 to 20 minutes until it's no longer shiny. Cool completely before continuing.

5  Place 1 cup (276 g) peanut butter in a microwave-safe bowl and heat for 45 seconds on high power (or just until it's runny). Whisk in the powdered sugar and vanilla extract, then spread the mixture evenly over the bars. (Alternately you can use a hand mixer to mix the powdered sugar and vanilla into room-temperature peanut butter.)

6  Place the chocolate chips and 3 tablespoons (50 g) peanut butter in a medium microwave-safe bowl. Heat on high heat in the microwave in 30-second increments, stirring between each, until melted and smooth (about 1½ to 2 minutes). Spread over the peanut butter layer. Chill to set.

7  Store in an airtight container for up to 5 days or freeze for up to 1 month. You can freeze these, but note that the chocolate on top will bloom when defrosted (it will be cloudy and spotty instead of smooth).

### For the Bars
- ⅓ cup (27 g) unsweetened cocoa powder
- ½ teaspoon baking soda
- ¼ teaspoon salt
- 1¼ cups (155 g) all-purpose flour
- ½ cup (113 g) butter, softened
- ⅔ cup (134 g) packed brown sugar
- ¼ cup (50 g) granulated sugar
- 1 large egg
- 1 teaspoon vanilla extract

### For the Peanut Butter Filling
- 1 cup (268 g) creamy peanut butter
- ½ cup (57 g) powdered sugar
- 1 teaspoon vanilla extract

### For the Coating
- 2 cups (340 g) semi-sweet or milk chocolate chips
- 3 tablespoons (50 g) creamy peanut butter

**Yield:** 24 bars
**Prep time:** 35 minutes
**Bake time:** 18 minutes

## *Tip:*
The bars slice prettiest at room temperature, when the chocolate is not rock hard straight from the refrigerator.

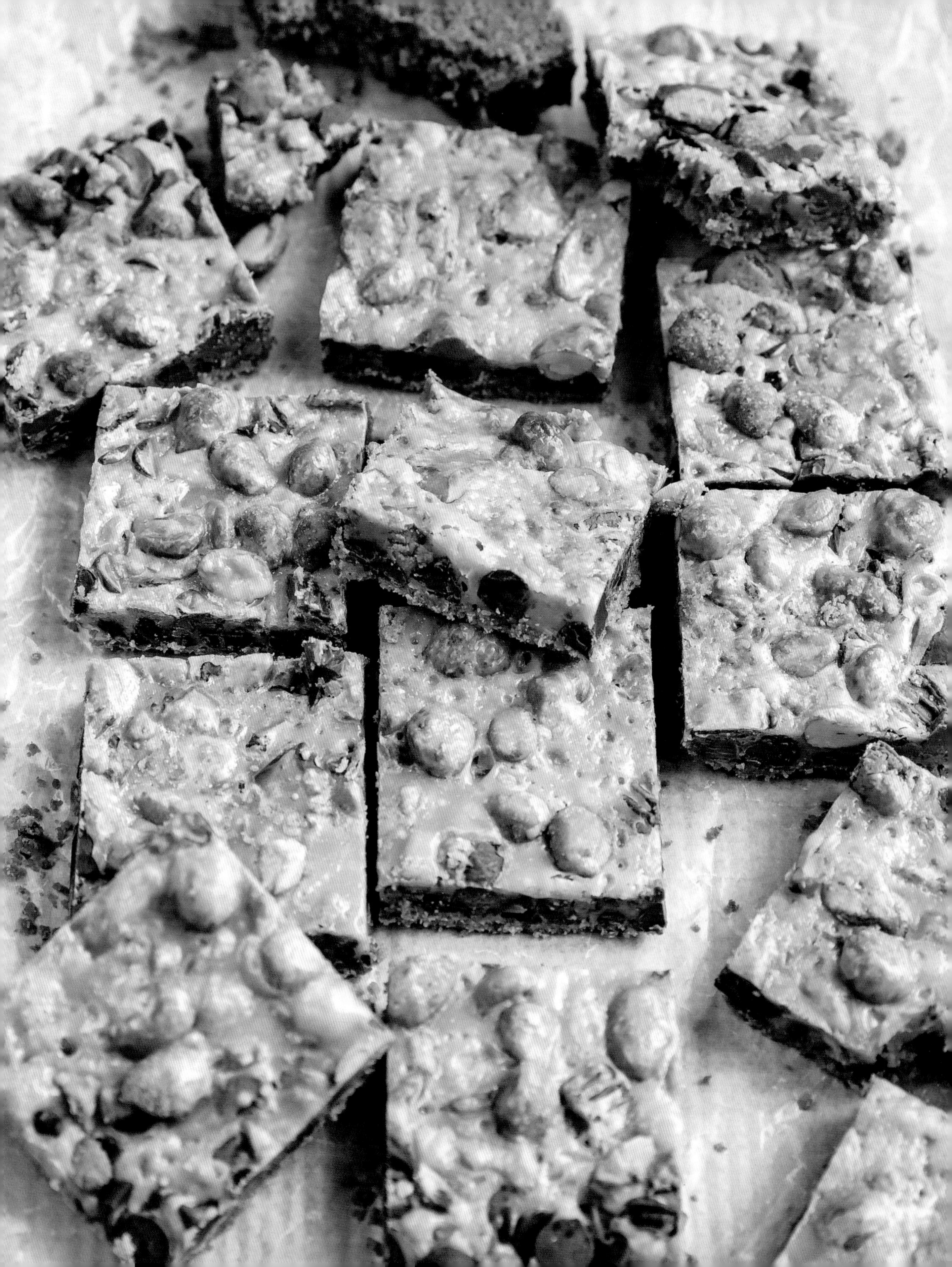

# Peanut Butter Magic Bars

The first time my mom made the original magic bar recipe was when I was young, and I remember actually thinking magic had occurred in the oven. How did all those separate ingredients turn into a cohesive bar without any mixing unless it was the stuff of unicorns? As an adult, I realized that all the chocolate and candy melt, while still holding their shape, and the sweetened condensed milk is the glue. This peanut butter version has a graham cracker crust and is filled with all things peanut: peanuts, peanut butter, and peanut butter cups. If you are a peanut butter lover like we are, these are going to feel like you found the pot of gold and a unicorn all at once.

## INSTRUCTIONS

1. Preheat the oven to 350°F (177°C). Line a 9 × 13–inch (23 × 33 cm) pan with foil and spray with nonstick cooking spray.

2. Make the crust by stirring together the graham cracker crumbs and melted butter with a fork. Press into the bottom of the prepared pan.

3. Sprinkle the chocolate chips evenly over the top of the crust, followed by the chopped peanut butter cups and peanuts.

4. Place the sweetened condensed milk and peanut butter in a medium-sized bowl and whisk until combined. Pour evenly over the toppings in the pan.

5. Bake for 27 to 31 minutes or until the edges are golden. Cool completely before slicing.

6. Store in an airtight container for up to 3 days or freeze in a single layer for up to 2 months.

### For the Crust

- 1½ cups (160 g) graham cracker crumbs
- 7 tablespoons (99 g) unsalted butter, melted

### For the Toppings

- 2 cups (340 g) semi-sweet or milk chocolate chips
- Heaping 1 cup (171 g) chopped peanut butter cups (about 20 miniatures)
- ½ cup (67 g) salted peanuts
- 1 (14 ounce or 396 g) can sweetened condensed milk
- ¼ cup (67 g) creamy peanut butter

**Yield:** 24 bars
**Prep time:** 25 minutes
**Bake time:** 28 minutes

## Tip:

I love changing up the flavors in these bars. You can substitute M&M's, peanut butter chips, dark chocolate—anything you like!

**Substitution**

Want to use a jarred caramel (or the caramel on page 64)? You can! Omit the caramel squares and heavy whipping cream and instead use a 12- to 14-ounce (340 to 396 g) jar of caramel. Stir the flour into the caramel and spread over the bottom layer as directed in step 4.

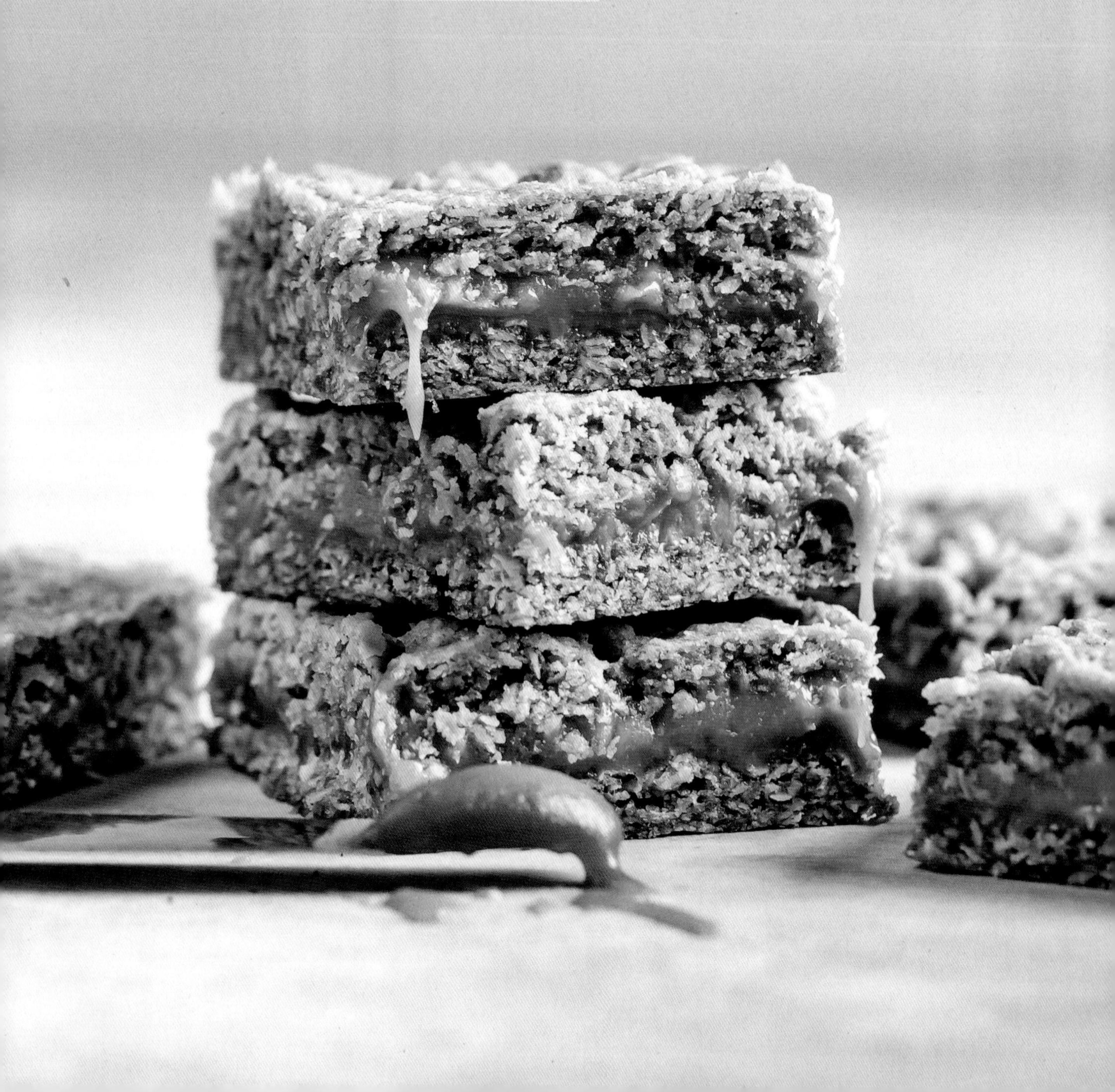

# Caramel Oatmeal Cookie Bars

*I*t's funny how I look at my life before and after I started blogging. In my pre-blogging life, stuffing caramel into the middle of cookie bars would be something mind-blowing. In my blogging life, it's just like, *meh, okay, caramel, what else you got?* I think that's why I love these bars so much: because they don't have *so much* going on. A simple oatmeal cookie bar filled with caramel. No chocolate, no candy, no nuts, no peanut butter . . . but you don't miss any of those things. Because of how simple they are, you really get the feel and taste of the oats and cookie and caramel. Sometimes, simple is actually better, which is something I constantly need to remind myself when I'm creating recipes for the blog, or just living life. Simple and content, like these cookie bars.

## INSTRUCTIONS

1   Preheat the oven to 350°F (177°C). Line a 9 × 13–inch (23 × 33 cm) pan with foil and spray with nonstick cooking spray.

2   In a medium bowl, whisk the cinnamon, baking soda, salt, and 1¾ cups (217 g) flour. Set aside.

3   Cream the butter and both sugars in the bowl of a stand mixer fitted with the paddle attachment. (You can also use a large bowl and a hand mixer.) Cream until smooth, about 1 to 2 minutes. Mix in the eggs and vanilla extract, and beat until smooth. Gradually mix in the dry ingredients until smooth, being careful not to overmix, then mix in the oats. Press two-thirds of the batter in the prepared pan in a thin layer. (The batter is sticky, so spray your hands with cooking spray.) Bake for 10 minutes.

4   While the bottom layer is baking, place the caramels and cream in a small saucepan. Heat, stirring often, until melted and smooth. Whisk in 1 tablespoon (8 g) flour until smooth. After the 10-minute bake, pour the caramel mixture over the hot cookie dough in the pan, leaving a small border around all the edges.

5   Break off pieces of the remaining dough and flatten between your hands (the dough will be sticky). Place on top of the caramel. Continue until the entire pan is covered, pressing the edges to seal them together. A little of the caramel may peek through, which is okay.

6   Bake for an additional 24 to 28 minutes, or until the bars are light golden around the edges and on top. Cool completely before slicing.

7   Store in an airtight container for up to 3 days. Can be frozen for up to 2 months.

- 2 teaspoons ground cinnamon
- 1 teaspoon baking soda
- 1 teaspoon salt
- 1¾ cups (217 g) all-purpose flour
- 1 cup (226 g) unsalted butter, softened
- 1 cup (200 g) packed brown sugar
- ½ cup (100 g) granulated sugar
- 2 large eggs
- 1 teaspoon vanilla extract
- 3¼ cups (276 g) quick cooking oats
- 11-ounce bag (317 g) caramel squares, unwrapped
- ⅓ cup (79 ml) heavy whipping cream
- 1 tablespoon (8 g) flour

**Yield:** 24 bars
**Prep time:** 30 minutes
**Bake time:** 36 minutes

## Tip:

I know I went on and on about keeping things simple, but it would be wrong of me not to mention how good these are with 1 cup (170 g) of chocolate chips sprinkled over the caramel in step 4.

# Margarita Bars

*I* love a good tart margarita on the rocks with an extra salty rim. However, as much as I love it, tequila does not love me! I could tell you too many stories about why it doesn't love me, but I'm guessing we all get the point (ha)! No worries if you're in the same boat—or even if you're not—these Margarita Bars taste like the traditional cocktail but have none of the adverse side effects. There's a small bit of tequila in the recipe, which can be omitted if preferred, but the alcohol cooks out. If you're feeling a little salty, sprinkle some over the top of the powdered sugar. Cheers!

## INSTRUCTIONS

1   Preheat the oven to 350°F (177°C). Line a 9 × 9–inch (23 × 23 cm) square pan with foil or parchment paper and spray with nonstick cooking spray.

2   Mix crumbs, ¼ cup (50 g) sugar, and melted butter with a fork in a large bowl. Press into the bottom of the prepared pan. Be sure to compact it very well. Any little holes in the crust will cause the filling to leak through. Bake for 10 minutes.

3   While the crust is baking, prepare the filling. Whisk the eggs with 2 cups (400 g) of sugar. Whisk in juices, zest, and tequila, and then whisk in the flour until no lumps remain.

4   Pour the lime mixture slowly and carefully over the hot crust. Continue baking for 25 to 30 minutes, or until the top starts to brown and is no longer jiggly. Cool bars completely before cutting. It's easiest to cut cold bars, so I suggest chilling them before cutting. Dust the tops with powdered sugar. Store in the refrigerator for up to 3 days.

### For the Crust

· 1½ cups (160 g) graham cracker crumbs
· ¼ cup (50 g) granulated sugar
· 7 tablespoons (99 g) unsalted butter, melted

### For the Filling

· 2 cups (400 g) granulated sugar
· 4 large eggs
· ⅓ cup (80 ml) lime juice (fresh or bottled)
· 1 tablespoon (15 ml) fresh orange juice
· Zest of one lime
· 1 tablespoon (15 ml) tequila
· ¼ cup (31 g) all-purpose flour
· Powdered sugar for dusting

**Yield:** 12 bars
**Prep time:** 25 minutes
**Bake time:** 40 minutes

## Tips:

You can omit the tequila if you wish. Use an extra tablespoon (15 ml) of orange or lime juice in its place.

If you are crushing your own graham crackers for the crust, you'll need about 9 full graham crackers (18 squares) to make the 1½ cups (160 g) crumbs.

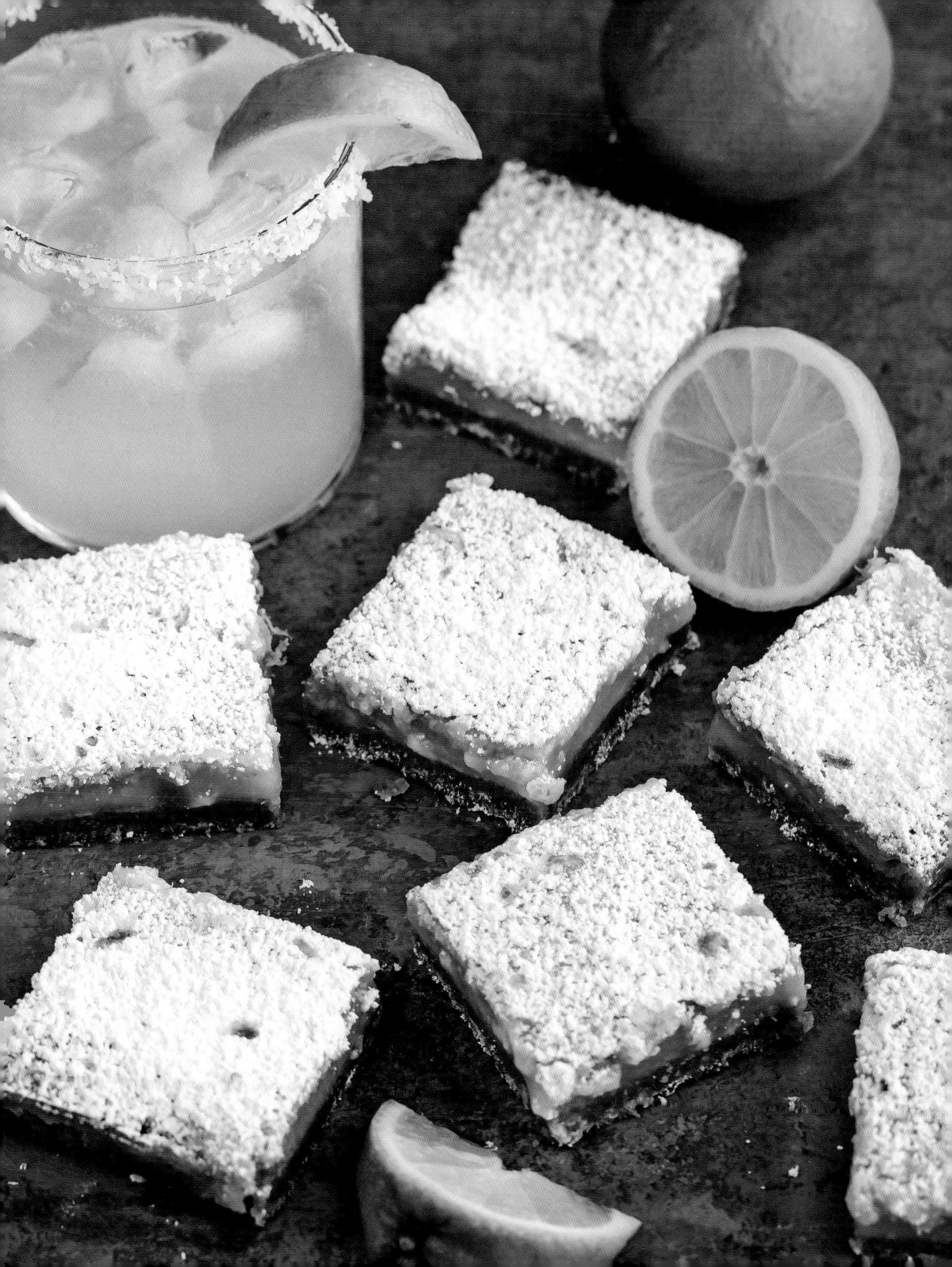

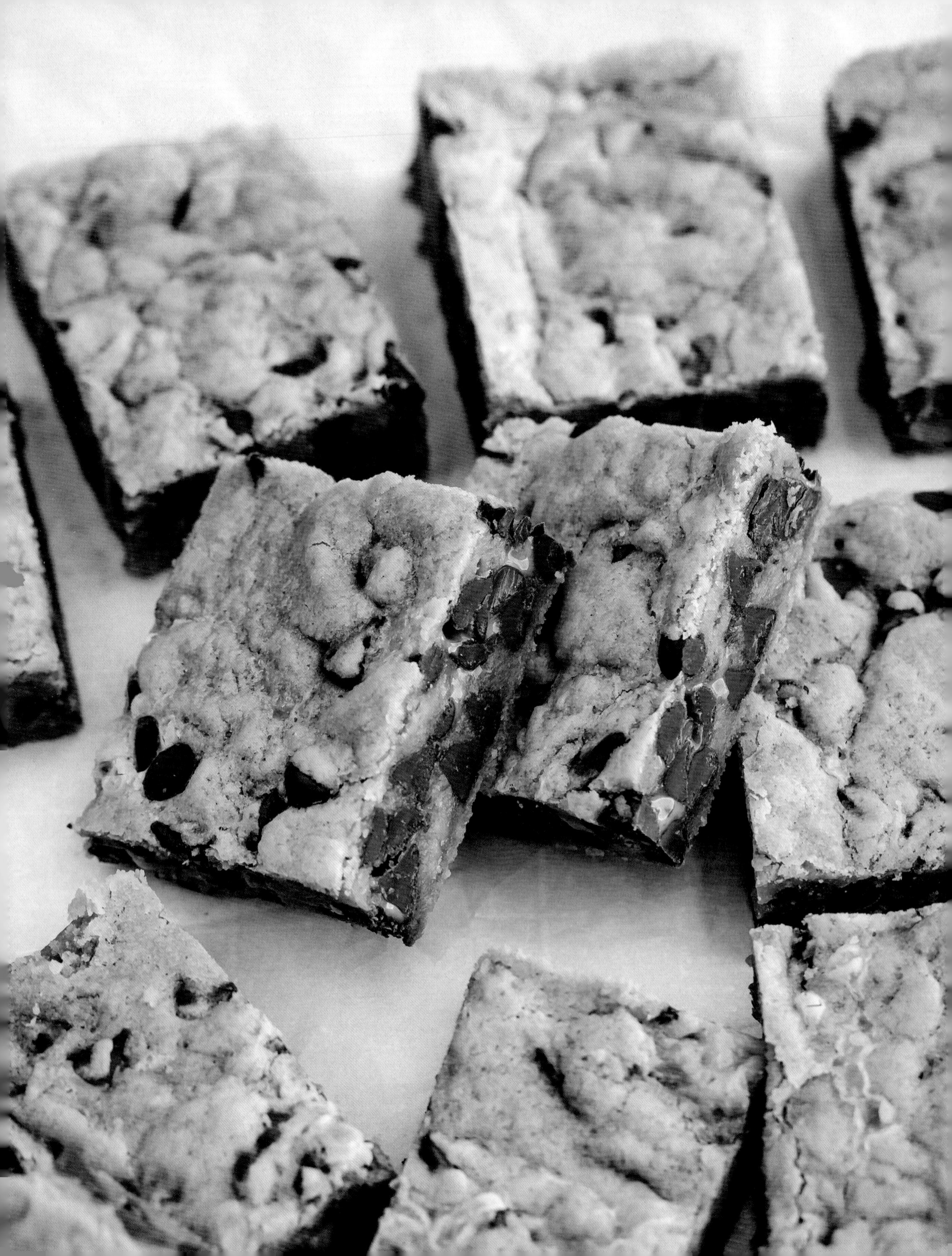

# Chocolate Chip Cookie Gooey Bars

Once I have perfected a recipe on the blog, I rarely make it again. I see every baking opportunity as a chance to make something new and check another box off my list of to-make. There are only a handful of recipes I make over and over again, and this is one of them. I remember once I made them to take on a blogging retreat with a bunch of women I didn't really know. My blog was a lot smaller than theirs, and I felt anxious about being in the presence of these really popular food bloggers. I pulled these bars out after dinner one evening and one of the women—the one with the most popular site, a renowned food enthusiast—closed her eyes and sighed after the first bite . . . and then she took a second bar. It was the highest praise I'd ever been given, and these bars have continued to make appearances at blog retreats—and holidays—ever since.

This is a basic chocolate chip cookie bar that's leveled up 120 notches by filling them with sweetened condensed milk and more chocolate. Warm from the pan, they're gooey to the extreme; cooled and cut, they're rich and almost fudgy. These bars are complete perfection!

- 3 cups (372 g) all-purpose flour
- 1 teaspoon baking soda
- ½ teaspoon salt
- 1 cup (226 g) unsalted butter, melted
- ¾ cup (150 g) granulated sugar
- 1 cup (200 g) light brown sugar
- 2 large eggs
- 1 teaspoon vanilla extract
- 3 cups (510 g) semi-sweet chocolate chips, divided
- 1 (14 ounce or 396 g) can sweetened condensed milk

**Yield:** 24 bars
**Prep time:** 25 minutes
**Bake time:** 30 minutes

## INSTRUCTIONS

1. Preheat the oven to 350°F (177°C). Line a 9 × 13–inch (23 × 33 cm) baking pan with foil and spray with nonstick cooking spray for easy removal.

2. Whisk the flour, baking soda, and salt in a medium bowl. Stir and set aside.

3. Add the melted butter and both sugars to a large bowl. Stir using a wooden spoon (or use a mixer) until smooth.

4. Add the eggs, one at a time, mixing completely. Stir in the vanilla extract. Add the flour mixture to the wet ingredients and mix until combined. Stir in 2 cups (340 g) chocolate chips.

5. Press half the cookie dough in the prepared pan. Pour the sweetened condensed milk over the top of the pressed cookie dough (be careful to leave about a ¼-inch (6 mm) edge around the pan so the milk doesn't touch the foil), then sprinkle the remaining chocolate chips over the top. Break up the remaining cookie dough and place on top of the milk. Press with your hands to flatten. It will mostly but not completely cover the bottom layer.

6. Bake for 28 to 34 minutes until the tops of the bars start to get a light golden brown. Cool completely before slicing into bars. These stay very gooey until they cool, so for easy cutting, remove use the foil or chill before slicing.

7. Store in an airtight container for up to 3 days or freeze for up to 2 months.

## Tip:

Another favorite version of this same recipe fills the center with 2 cups (278 g) of chopped peanut butter cups in place of the third cup (170 g) of chocolate chips. You should try that recipe too; you won't be sorry.

# Chocolate Chip Shortbread Bars

We look forward to lots of things when we go to Maui, but there are three absolutes: One, I'll get boatloads of macadamia nuts (see page 69); two, we'll get pizza from Lahaina Pizza Company; and three, we'll buy more Honolulu Cookies than is probably deemed socially acceptable. Our favorite Honolulu Cookie Company cookie is their mini chocolate chip shortbread. They're crunchy and bite-sized with tons of mini chocolate chips. This shortbread bar is modeled after those cookies: simple and rich with loads of mini chips! You can bake these one of two ways: soft-baked or crunchy. I can't pick which way I like more, but rest assured, they're both amazing.

## INSTRUCTIONS

1 Preheat the oven to 350°F (177°C). Line a 9 × 13–inch (23 × 33 cm) pan with foil and spray with nonstick cooking spray.

2 Cream the butter and sugar in a large bowl with an electric mixer. Mix in the vanilla extract, salt, and cornstarch. Slowly mix in the flour until combined, then stir in the chocolate chips.

3 Press the dough into a thin layer in the prepared pan. Bake for 25 to 30 minutes for soft-baked texture or up to 35 minutes for crunchy shortbread.

4 Cool completely before slicing into bars. Store in an airtight container for up to 4 days or freeze for up to 3 months.

- 1 cup (226 g) unsalted butter, softened
- ⅔ cup (134 g) granulated sugar
- 1 teaspoon vanilla extract
- ½ teaspoon salt
- 1 tablespoon (8 g) cornstarch
- 2 cups (248 g) all-purpose flour
- 1½ cups (245 g) mini chocolate chips

**Yield:** 24 bars
**Prep time:** 20 minutes
**Bake time:** 30 minutes

## Tip:

I think of this recipe as a blank slate and can't wait to add all the things. Try toasting 1½ cups (165 g) of chopped pecans in place of the chocolate chips—simple but *so* good!

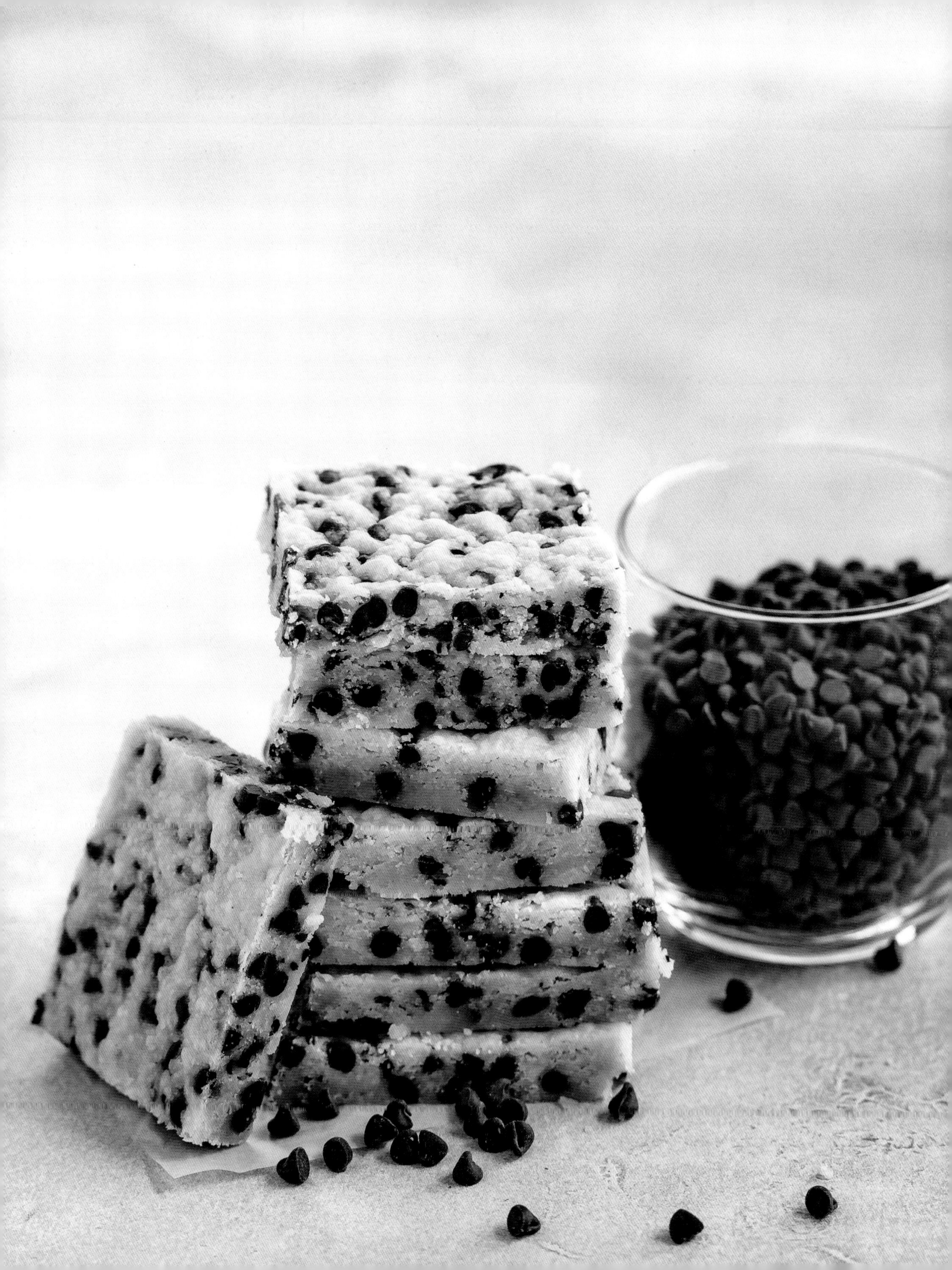

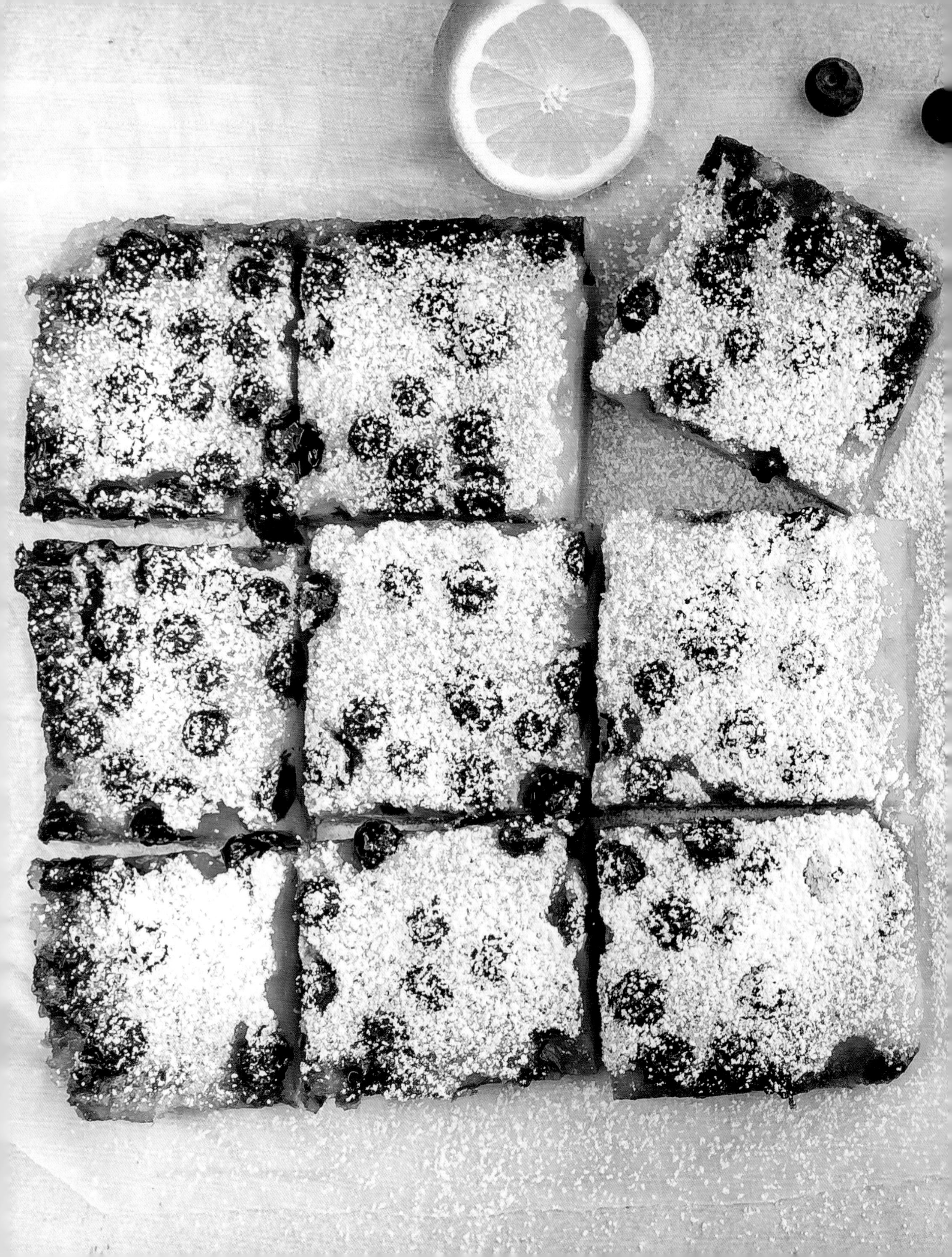

# Blueberry Lemon Bars

My husband and I moved around a bit after we first got married and didn't live by family until our daughter was two when we moved to a suburb of Sacramento, near his sister. I remember after our move going to visit his sister as she was cooking for a dinner party; her menu included a batch of lemon bars. I wasn't a fan of lemon desserts at the time, but I loved the concept: a shortbread crust with a gooey lemon curd–like filling. I remember her saying they were her favorite. In the years since, I've made lemon bars so many times and each time I'm testing them, I know she'll take them off my hands—because now that I love lemon desserts, I have to get them out of my house ASAP because I usually take a fork to the pan before I can cut them into bars. I cannot make a new lemon bar version without thinking of Katie, and I'm pretty sure she'd love these as much as the traditional: a rich lemony bar filled with blueberries and that trademark shortbread crust. These are pure heaven for us lemon lovers!

## INSTRUCTIONS

1 Preheat the oven to 350°F (177°C). Line a 9 × 9–inch (23 × 23 cm) pan with foil and spray with nonstick cooking spray. You can also use parchment paper instead.

2 Make the crust by creaming the butter with a hand or a stand mixer (fitted with the paddle attachment) until smooth. Add the powdered sugar, flour, and salt and mix slowly until the mixture is crumbly but sticks together when you press it between your fingers. Press the crust into the bottom of the prepared pan. Bake for about 25 to 28 minutes, or until it just starts to get a light golden brown around the edges and looks white on the top (instead of opaque).

3 While the crust is baking, whisk the eggs until beaten. Whisk in the sugar, lemon zest, lemon juice, and salt.

4 Sprinkle the blueberries on the hot crust, then pour the lemon mixture carefully over the blueberries. If the blueberries bunch up too much, use your fingers to gently spread them out.

5 Continue to bake for 25 to 30 minutes, or until the mixture is no longer liquid in the center and it is lightly golden brown around the edges.

6 Cool completely before removing from the pan. Remove the foil, then dust with powdered sugar. Slice and serve, dusting with more powdered sugar as desired.

7 Store in an airtight container in the refrigerator for up to 4 days. Can be frozen for up to 2 months.

## For the Crust

- 1 cup (226 g) unsalted butter, softened
- ½ cup (57 g) powdered sugar
- 2 cups (248 g) all-purpose flour
- ¼ teaspoon salt

## For the Filling

- 4 large eggs
- 1½ cups (300 g) granulated sugar
- 1 tablespoon (6 g) lemon zest
- ½ cup (120 ml) fresh lemon juice
- Pinch of salt
- 1 cup (135 g) fresh blueberries
- Powdered sugar for topping

**Yield:** 9 bars
**Prep time:** 30 minutes
**Bake time:** 54 minutes

## Tip:

If using frozen berries, make sure they are completely thawed, drained, and patted dry before adding to the hot crust. We also love making this with the tiny wild blueberries, if you can find them.

# Apple Shortbread Bars

One day back in 2010, my husband and I were chatting about my apple pie recipe. He rarely eats anything I bake, with the exception of carrot cake, anything peanut butter, and that apple pie with its signature crumble topping. He joked we should start a pie bakery and just serve crust with crumble, because that's the best part. The joke was on him though because that simple conversation turned into my blog, Crazy for Crust. I literally wouldn't be writing this book if it wasn't for apple pie, so I knew it would for sure make an appearance in these pages.

These bars are a riff on that original pie: They have a shortbread crust that doubles as a crumble topping, and instead of filling them with apple pie filling, I went with apple butter. Apple butter is one of those underrated ingredients that gets an out-of-date stigma, when it's really such a delicious addition to anything all year long (we love it on toast). You can buy apple butter where you find jams and jellies, but if you can't find it, you can use my recipe. It makes enough for the bars and a little extra to serve with some scones.

- 1 cup (226 g) unsalted butter, softened
- ¾ cup (150 g) granulated sugar
- 1 teaspoon cinnamon
- 2 cups (248 g) all-purpose flour
- ¾ cup (235 g) apple butter (recipe on next page)
- ½ cup (55 g) chopped pecans

**Yield:** 12 bars
**Prep time:** 30 minutes
**Bake time:** 32 minutes

## INSTRUCTIONS

1   Preheat the oven to 350°F (177°C). Line a 9 × 9–inch (23 × 23 cm) pan with foil and spray with nonstick cooking spray.

2   Cream the butter and sugar in a large bowl with an electric mixer until smooth, and then mix in the cinnamon. Slowly mix in the flour (mixture will be crumbly).

3   Press two-thirds of the mixture in the bottom of the prepared pan.

4   Spread the apple butter over the bottom layer, leaving a small border around the edge of the pan.

5   Mix the pecans with the remaining dough. Sprinkle on top of apple butter, starting with the edges and then filling in the center, making sure the topping goes all the way to the edges of the pan.

6   Bake for 30 to 35 minutes or until the top is a light golden brown. Cool before cutting into bars.

7   Store in an airtight container in the refrigerator for up to 3 days or freeze for up to 2 months.

## Tip:

Don't have apple butter? Use your favorite flavor jam instead or make homemade apple butter. We love this with pie filling too—use your favorite recipe or grab a can at the store.

### Apple Butter

This recipe makes more than you need for the Apple Shortbread Bars. Use extra on toast or freeze it for later.

· 3 pounds (1.4 kg) apples (Fuji, Gala, Honey Crisp, Red Delicious, or similar)

· ½ cup (100 g) granulated sugar

· ½ cup (100 g) packed brown sugar

· 1 tablespoon (7 g) cinnamon

· 1 teaspoon vanilla extract

· ¼ teaspoon salt

1  Slice and core the apples. You can peel them if you want, but I don't. Cut them into small chunks (smaller pieces cook faster).

2  Place the apples in the bottom of a 7-quart (6.6 L) slow cooker. Top with both sugars and cinnamon, and then toss to combine.

3  Cover and cook on high for 3 to 5 hours, stirring after 2 hours. Cook until the apples look translucent (about 4 hours in my slow cooker).

4  Use a hand blender to blend the apples and their liquid into a smooth sauce. If you don't have a hand blender, you can do this in a regular blender, but work in batches, being careful not to overfill the blender with hot apples. Leave the lid cracked when you run it so it doesn't explode.

5  Once your apples are blended, place them back in the slow cooker (if you've removed them to blend). Continue cooking on high with the lid cracked for 30 minutes to an hour, or until the mixture reduces to your desired thickness.

6  Stir in the vanilla extract and salt, and then cool and place in jars or freezer containers. The butter will last for up to 2 weeks in the refrigerator or in the freezer for up to 2 months.

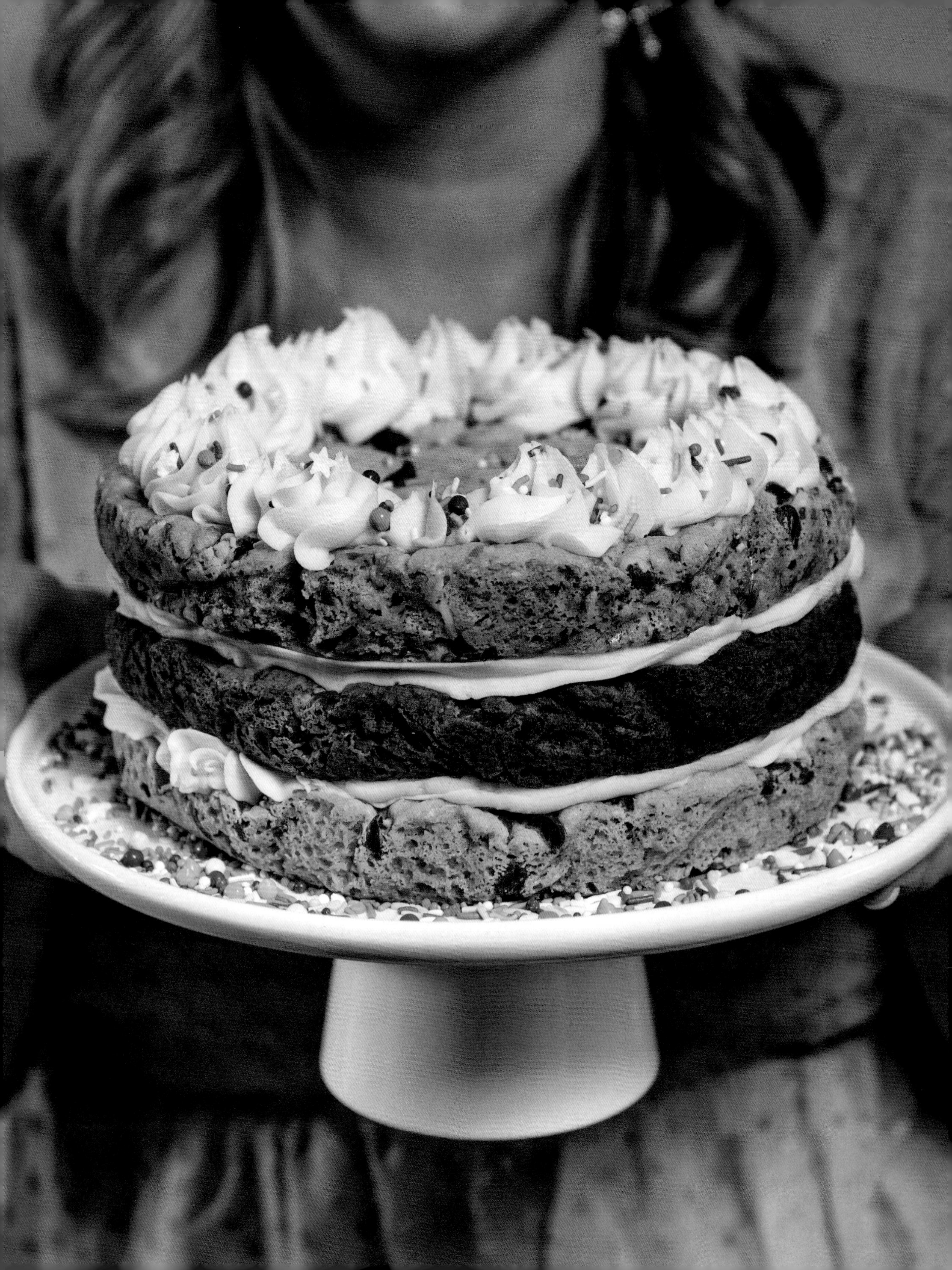

# Cookie Cakes, Skillet Bakes, and Cups— Oh My!

These cookies are perfect for parties and entertaining. From the three-layer cookie cake for a dessert table centerpiece to a range of cookie cups to serve alongside, this is one of my favorite ways to make cookies. Cookie cakes are perfect when you want something a little classier than just a blondie, and cookie cups are fun bite-sized treats that look more difficult than they actually are. And skillets? Those are perfect for Friday night movie night!

Before you get started on the recipes in this chapter, consider the following tips:

• When making cookie cakes, I like to line my pans with foil or parchment paper. It makes them so easy to remove and decorate, but it's not needed if you want to serve them in the pan.

• When it comes to frosting, most of the time you can change up the flavor of frosting to suit your likes. And make sure to read the Frosting Tips on page 12.

• I like to form my indentations in my cookie cups after baking, while the cookies are hot. You can use a wooden spoon handle, but my favorite way to do this is to use the back of a ¼ teaspoon (see Thumbprint Tips, page 168).

# Birthday Cookie Cake

*I* loved getting cookies at the mall when I was a kid. I lost my first tooth while eating a ginormous chocolate chip cookie when I was only five; I remember it was cold and I was wearing a jacket inside because we were sitting next to the ice rink. I can still taste the flavor and textures of that cookie, if you can believe it. When I was older, there was a Mrs. Fields shop at the mall, and I'd go get a giant M&M cookie (my favorite) and stare longingly at the cookie cakes. I thought they were so cool—a cake that was actually a cookie was just so different back in the late 1980s. Fast-forward to today and I make cookie cakes all the time—and they're better than the ones you get at the mall, I promise. This is my favorite chocolate chip cookie baked into a 9-inch (23 cm) round pan with sprinkles, two kinds of chocolate chips, and a chocolate frosting you'll absolutely love.

## MAKE THE COOKIE CAKE

1  Preheat the oven to 350°F (177°C). Line a 9-inch (23 cm) round cake pan with foil and spray with nonstick cooking spray.

2  Place the melted butter in a large bowl (or bowl of a stand mixer fitted with the paddle attachment). Add both sugars and mix on low speed until the mixture is smooth. Add the egg and vanilla extract and mix on medium speed until combined.

3  Mix in the salt and baking soda, then slowly mix in the flour just until the batter is smooth and comes together. Be sure to scrape the sides of the bowl during mixing. Slowly mix in the chocolate chips, white chocolate chips, and sprinkles.

4  Press the batter into the prepared pan. Bake for 21 to 25 minutes or until the cookie is just slightly golden brown on top and a toothpick inserted in the center comes out clean. Let cool before frosting.

## MAKE THE FROSTING (SEE FROSTING TIPS, PAGE 12)

1  Add the butter to a large bowl and beat until smooth with a hand mixer. Add powdered sugar, cocoa powder, and salt and mix until crumbly; then mix in the vanilla extract.

2  Add 1 tablespoon (15 ml) milk or heavy cream and mix until smooth, adding more cream as needed for piping consistency.

3  To assemble the cookie cake, place the frosting in a piping bag fitted with a large star tip and pipe swirls around the edges. Add more sprinkles and serve.

4  Store in an airtight container for up to 3 days or freeze unfrosted cake for up to a month.

### For the Cookie Cake

- ½ cup (113 g) unsalted butter, melted
- ⅓ cup (67 g) granulated sugar
- ½ cup (100 g) packed brown sugar
- 1 large egg
- 1 teaspoon vanilla extract
- ½ teaspoon salt
- ½ teaspoon baking soda
- 1½ cups (186 g) all-purpose flour
- ½ cup (85 g) chocolate chips
- ½ cup (85 g) white chocolate chips
- ½ cup (97 g) sprinkles

### For the Frosting

- 4 tablespoons (57 g) unsalted butter, softened
- 1 cup (113 g) powdered sugar
- 2 tablespoons (10 g) unsweetened cocoa powder
- ¼ teaspoon salt
- ½ teaspoon vanilla extract
- 1 to 2 tablespoons (15 to 30 ml) heavy whipping cream or milk

**Yield:** 1 9-inch (23 cm) cake
**Prep time:** 45 minutes
**Bake time:** 23 minutes

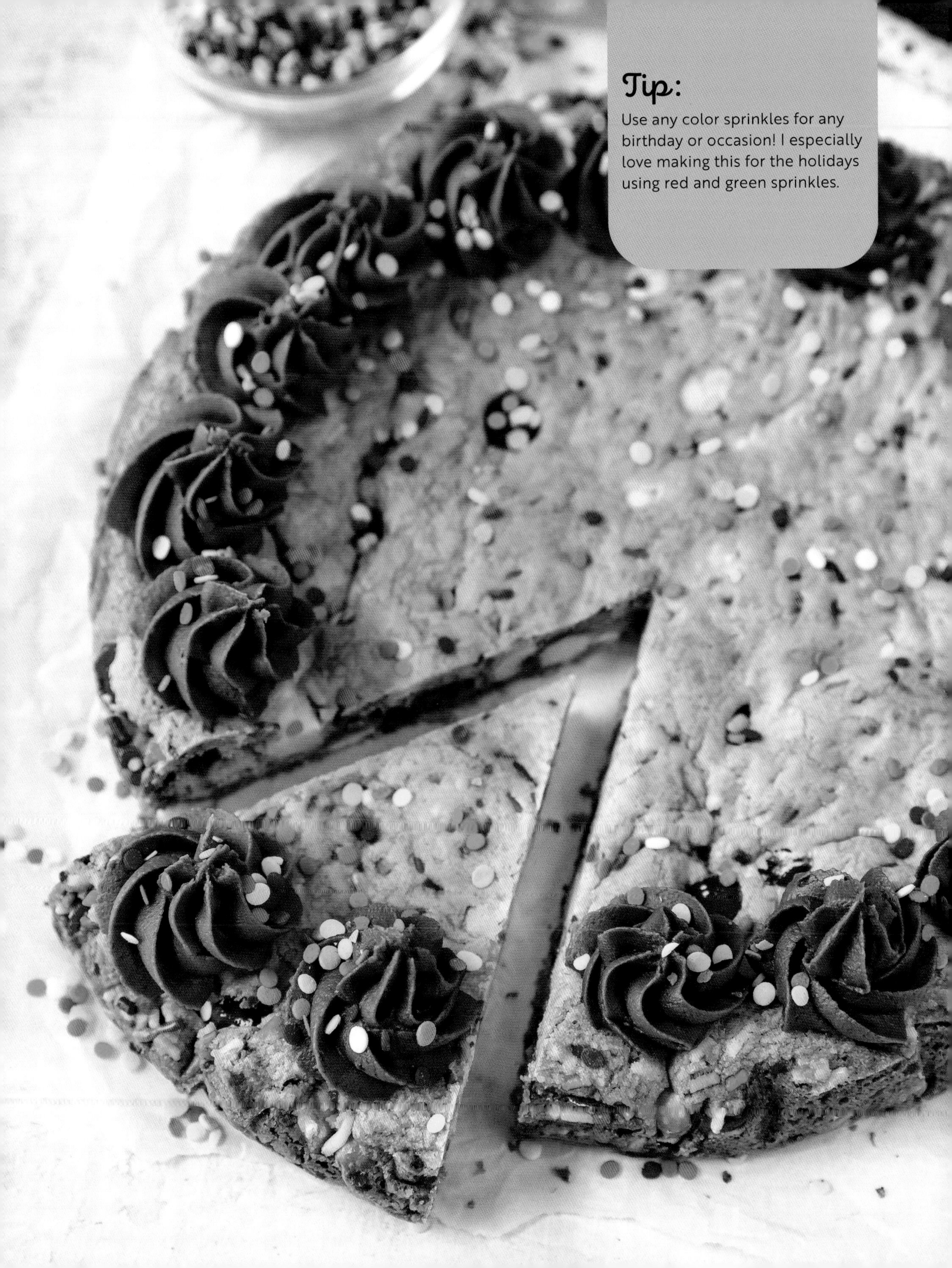

## Tip:

Use any color sprinkles for any birthday or occasion! I especially love making this for the holidays using red and green sprinkles.

# Three-Layer Cookie Cake

*T*his is an *epic* cake for a cookie lover. A few summers ago, my husband and I renewed our wedding vows and instead of having cake at the reception I made a version of this. If someone you know doesn't love cake but you want to make them a special treat, *this* is the one to make. I used one large cookie base to make three different flavors for the three layers and added frosting and sprinkles for good measure. I think if I had to choose only one birthday cake to have for the rest of my life, this would be it.

### MAKE THE COOKIE CAKE

1. Preheat the oven to 350°F (177°C). Line three 8-inch (20 cm) round cake pans with foil and spray with nonstick cooking spray.

2. Make the base cookie dough by stirring together the melted butter with brown and granulated sugars in a large bowl. You can do this with a spatula or wooden spoon or an electric mixer. Stir in the eggs, vanilla extract, baking soda, and salt; then slowly stir in the flour until combined.

3. Divide the dough into three equal portions. Stir 1 cup chocolate chips into one portion; press into one of the prepared pans. Stir ¾ cup (128 g) chocolate chips and the sprinkles into the second portion; press in the prepared pan.

4. Place ¼ cup (42 g) chocolate chips in a small microwave-safe bowl. Heat on 50 percent power in 30-second increments, stirring between each, until the chocolate is melted and smooth (about 2 to 3 minutes total). Stir the melted chocolate into the third portion of cookie dough. Add remaining 1 cup (170 g) chocolate chips and stir, and then press into the third prepared pan.

5. Bake all three pans for 28 to 34 minutes or until lightly golden and no longer glossy on the top. Cool completely before frosting.

   Note: If you only have two 8-inch (20 cm) pans, you can bake the first two and then cool for 10 minutes in pan; then remove to add the remaining cookie dough to bake.

### MAKE THE FROSTING (SEE FROSTING TIPS, PAGE 12)

1. Cream the butter in a very large bowl with an electric mixer. Mix in the powdered sugar, 1 cup (113 g) at a time, until smooth. Mix in the vanilla extract and salt. Add 1 tablespoon (15 ml) heavy whipping cream and mix until smooth and fluffy, adding more cream as needed for desired consistency. (Amount of cream will vary based on other factors; see Frosting Tips, page 12.)

## For the Cookie Cake

- 1 cup (226 g) unsalted butter, melted
- 1 cup (200 g) packed brown sugar
- ⅔ cup (134 g) granulated sugar
- 2 large eggs
- 1 teaspoon vanilla extract
- 1 teaspoon baking soda
- ½ teaspoon salt
- 3 cups (372 g) all-purpose flour
- 3 cups (510 g) chocolate chips, divided
- ⅓ cup (65 g) rainbow sprinkles

## For the Frosting

- 1 cup (226 g) unsalted butter, softened
- 4 cups (452 g) powdered sugar
- ½ teaspoon salt
- 1 teaspoon vanilla extract
- 1 to 3 tablespoons (15 to 45 ml) heavy whipping cream

**Yield:** 16 servings
**Prep time:** 1 hour 15 minutes
**Bake time:** 30 minutes

## *Tip:*

You don't have to stick with just chocolate chips—replace them with chopped peanut butter cups, M&M's, or your favorite candy or Oreos instead.

**ASSEMBLE THE CAKE**

1 Place one layer on the cake plate and frost, making sure the frosting goes to the edges. Top with the second layer and repeat. Place third layer on top.

2 Frost the top of the cake as desired or place remaining frosting in a pastry bag fitted with an open star tip. Frost around the edges and dust with sprinkles.

3 Store loosely covered for up to 3 days.

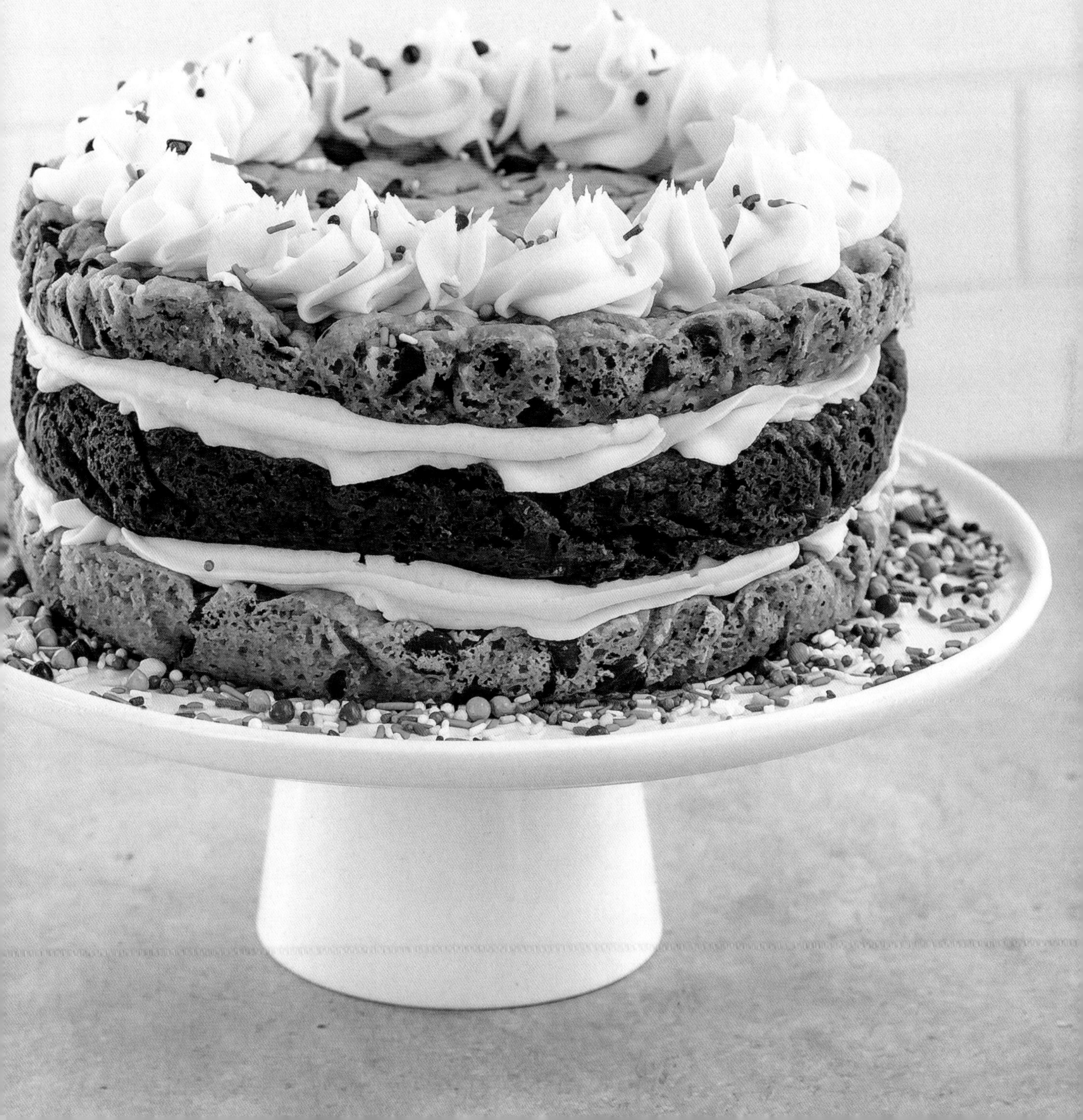

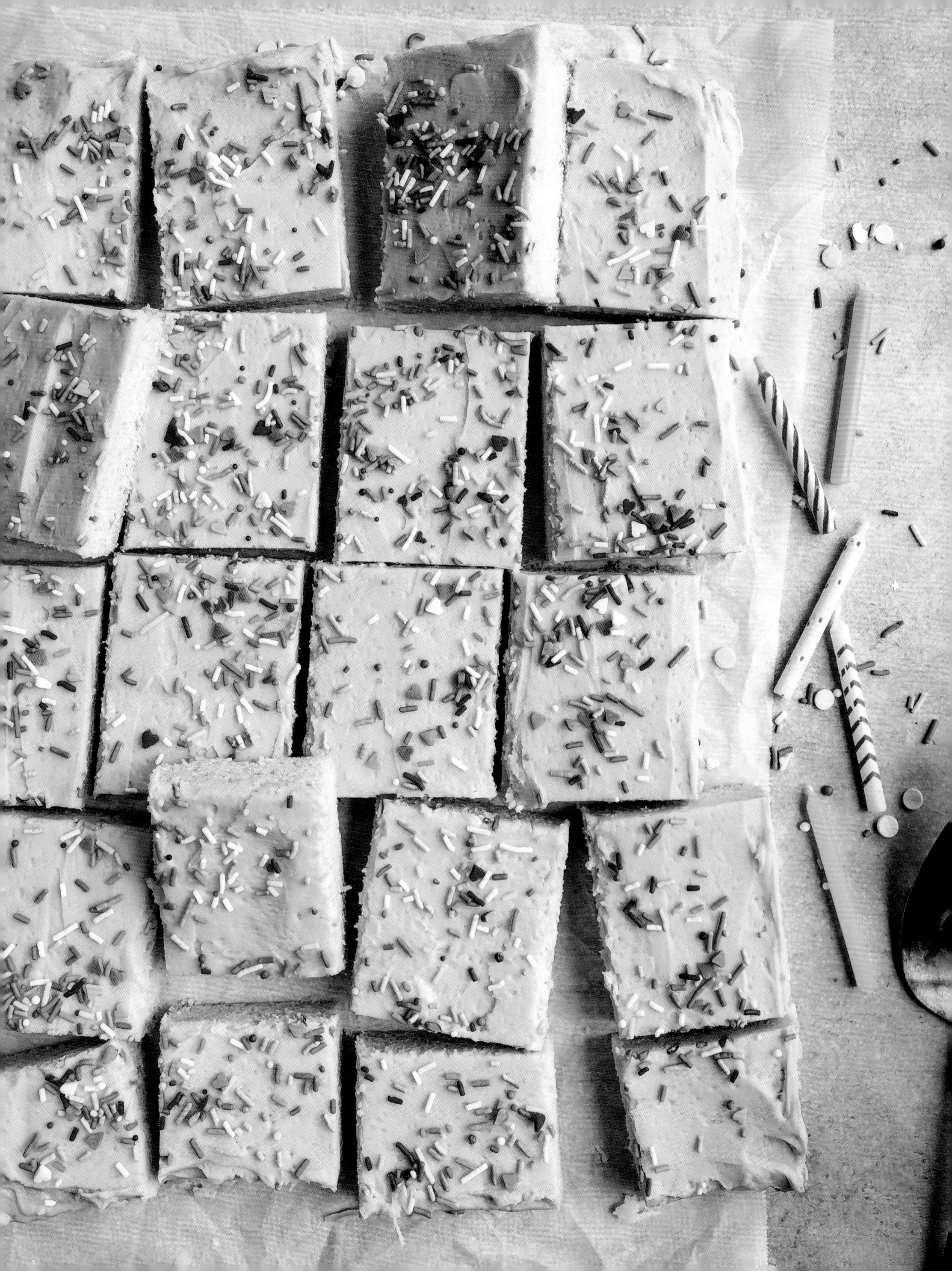

# Sugar Cookie Cake

I get asked all the time what my favorite kind of cookie is, and it's usually a struggle for me to name just one. However, whenever I make this recipe, I am reminded that no, my favorite cookies are sugar cookies. I would give up chocolate, brownies, pie, and bread if I could eat sugar cookie cakes for the rest of my life (and if calories didn't count, of course). You can underbake these to make them soft and almost falling apart, or you can bake them for a couple of extra minutes for a sturdier soft but also crunchy cookie. The almond extract is what sets these apart: That almond flavor is intoxicating to me. Add to that a fluffy buttercream? I'm dead. If I make this cookie cake, everyone better know that they're getting one slice and the rest is mine.

## MAKE THE COOKIE CAKE

1 Preheat the oven to 350°F (177°C). Line a 9 × 13–inch (23 × 33 cm) pan with foil and spray with nonstick cooking spray.

2 Cream the butter and sugar in the bowl of a stand mixer fitted with the paddle attachment. Beat in the egg and both extracts. Mix in the baking soda, cream of tartar, and salt. Slowly mix in the flour.

3 Press the dough into the prepared pan.

4 Bake for 14 to 19 minutes. The sides will just be getting golden, and the center will look a little underdone. Cool completely before frosting.

## MAKE THE FROSTING (SEE FROSTING TIPS, PAGE 12)

1 Beat the butter until creamy with an electric mixer in a large bowl. Mix in the salt.

2 Slowly add in the powdered sugar until the mixture is crumbly. (It will be very crumbly if using a hand mixer, smoother if using a stand mixer.) Add vanilla extract and 1 tablespoon (15 ml) milk or cream. Mix until the frosting comes together and becomes smooth, adding additional teaspoons of milk as needed for consistency.

3 Tint the frosting with food coloring, if desired.

4 Remove the cooled cookie cake from the pan. Carefully remove the foil and place on a serving platter. (You can also leave it in the pan if you prefer.) Frost the top and sides of the cookie cake, then sprinkle with sprinkles and decorate as desired.

5 Store loosely covered for up to 3 days or freeze for up to a month. You can freeze the frosted cake or freeze the cake and frosting separately

### For the Cookie Cake

- ¾ cup (170 g) unsalted butter, softened
- ¾ cup (150 g) granulated sugar
- 1 large egg
- 1 teaspoon vanilla extract
- ½ teaspoon almond extract
- ½ teaspoon baking soda
- ½ teaspoon cream of tartar
- ½ teaspoon salt
- 2 cups (248 g) all-purpose flour

### For the Frosting

- 1 cup (226 g) unsalted butter, softened
- ¼ teaspoon salt
- 4 cups (452 g) powdered sugar
- 1 teaspoon vanilla extract
- 1 to 3 tablespoons (15 to 45 ml) milk or heavy whipping cream
- Sprinkles and/or food coloring for decorating

**Yield:** 1 9 × 13–inch (23 × 33 cm) cake or 24 bars
**Prep time:** 1 hour
**Bake time:** 16 minutes

## Tip:

Make this into a Christmas Sugar Cookie Cake by adding red and green sprinkles to the batter (or even M&M's).

# Fruit Tart Cookie Cups

Being a baking blogger comes with certain responsibilities, one being that I am always assigned to bring dessert or create dessert tables for parties. A few years ago, I did a full table for a friend's fortieth birthday with these little cookie cups front and center. The guest of honor loves fruity desserts, and she had an array of them, but these little ones were our favorite. With a sugar cookie base filled with a creamy cheesecake-like filling, they are topped with berries (or your favorite fruit) and then brushed with a lime glaze. The crunchy cookie with the creamy filling and sweet fruit with tart glaze is, quite simply, perfection.

## MAKE THE COOKIE CUPS

1   Preheat the oven to 350°F (177°C). Spray mini muffin pans with non-stick baking spray or grease well with butter or shortening.

2   Cream the butter and sugar in a large bowl with a hand or a stand mixer. Mix in the egg, vanilla extract, baking soda, cream of tartar, and salt, and mix until smooth. Slowly mix in the flour until a cookie dough forms.

3   Scoop about 1 tablespoon of dough into each mini muffin cavity. Bake for 10 to 12 minutes, or until the edges are golden brown and the center is no longer glossy.

4   Immediately after removing from the oven, use the handle of a wooden spoon or the rounded part of a ¼ teaspoon to create a shell, pressing the center of the cookie down. Cool the cookie shells completely before removing from the pan.

5   When ready to remove the shells from the pan, run a butter knife carefully around the edges to loosen and use it to pop the cookies out of the pan.

## MAKE THE GLAZE

1   Whisk the lime juice, sugar, and cornstarch in a small saucepan over medium-low heat, stirring often, until the sugar dissolves and the mixture starts to thicken. Remove from the heat and place in a bowl to cool for at least 15 minutes before using.

### For the Cookies

- ½ cup (113 g) unsalted butter, softened
- ½ cup (100 g) granulated sugar
- 1 large egg
- 1 teaspoon vanilla extract
- ½ teaspoon baking soda
- ½ teaspoon cream of tartar
- ¼ teaspoon salt
- 1⅓ cups (165 g) all-purpose flour

### For the Glaze

- 3 ounces (89 ml) lime juice (from about 3 limes)
- 2 tablespoons (24 g) granulated sugar
- 1 teaspoon cornstarch

### For the Filling

- 6 ounces (168 g) cream cheese, softened
- ⅓ cup (67 g) granulated sugar
- ½ teaspoon vanilla extract
- 6 to 8 ounces (170 to 227 g) blueberries, raspberries, or strawberries (or a combination)

**Yield:** 23 cookie cups (24 if you put just under 1 tablespoon of dough in each cup)
**Prep time:** 40 minutes
**Bake time:** 11 minutes

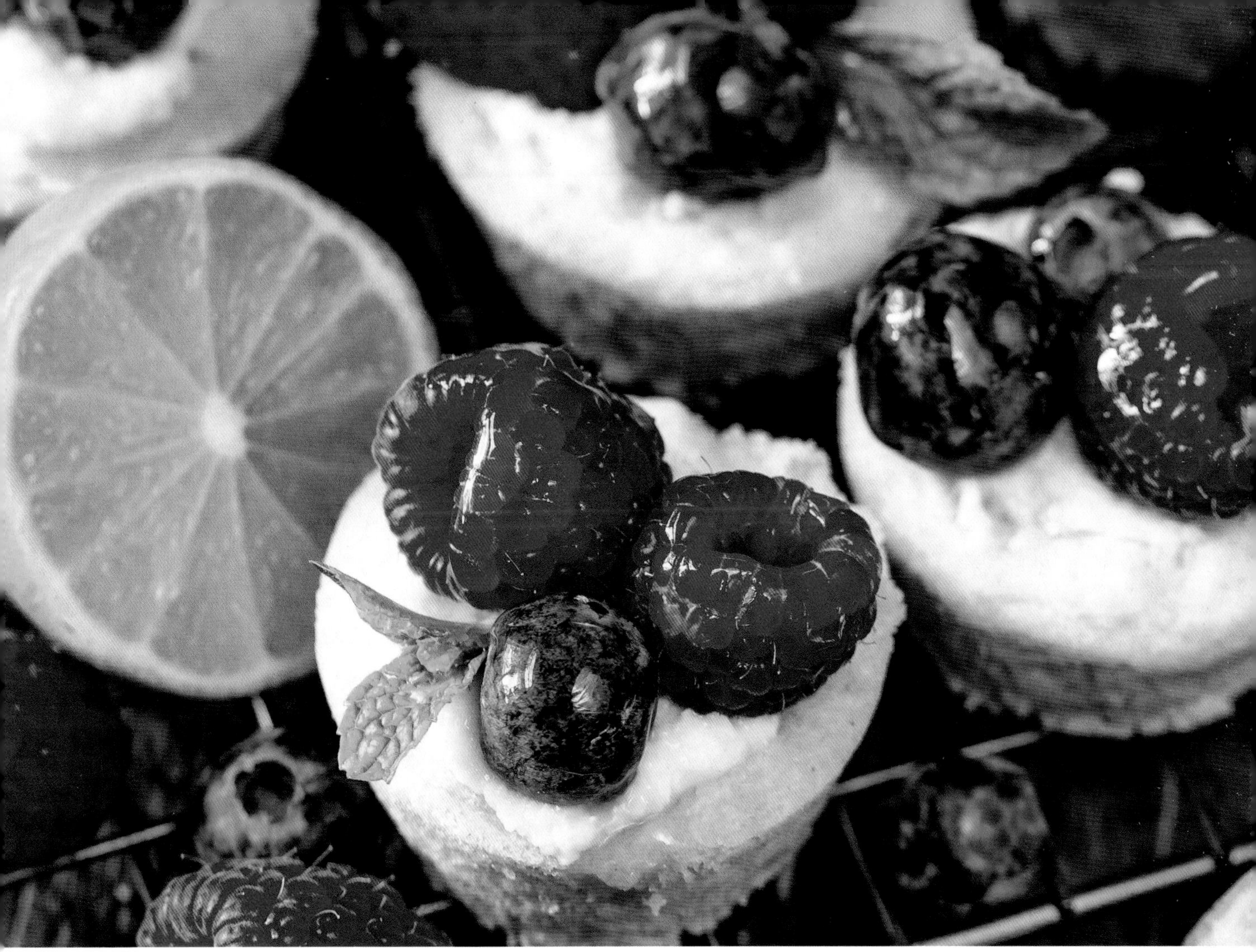

**MAKE THE FILLING AND ASSEMBLE THE TARTS**

1. Add the cream cheese, sugar, and vanilla extract to a large bowl. Beat using a hand or a stand mixer until creamy and smooth.
2. Add a small bit of the filling to each cookie tart shell.
3. Top each tart with berries as desired. Using a pastry brush, lightly brush the fruit with the lime glaze. You will have some glaze left over.
4. Serve within a few hours after glazing. Store loosely covered in the refrigerator. Plain cookie cups will last in an airtight container for up to 3 days or frozen for up to 2 months, but once the fruit tarts are assembled, you should enjoy them within 2 days.

## Tips:

You can prepare the cookies, filling, and glaze up to 24 hours ahead. Wait to assemble until ready to serve.

Skip making the lime glaze and instead use ¼ cup (80 g) apricot or seedless raspberry jam thinned with 2 tablespoons (30 ml) water to brush over the fruit.

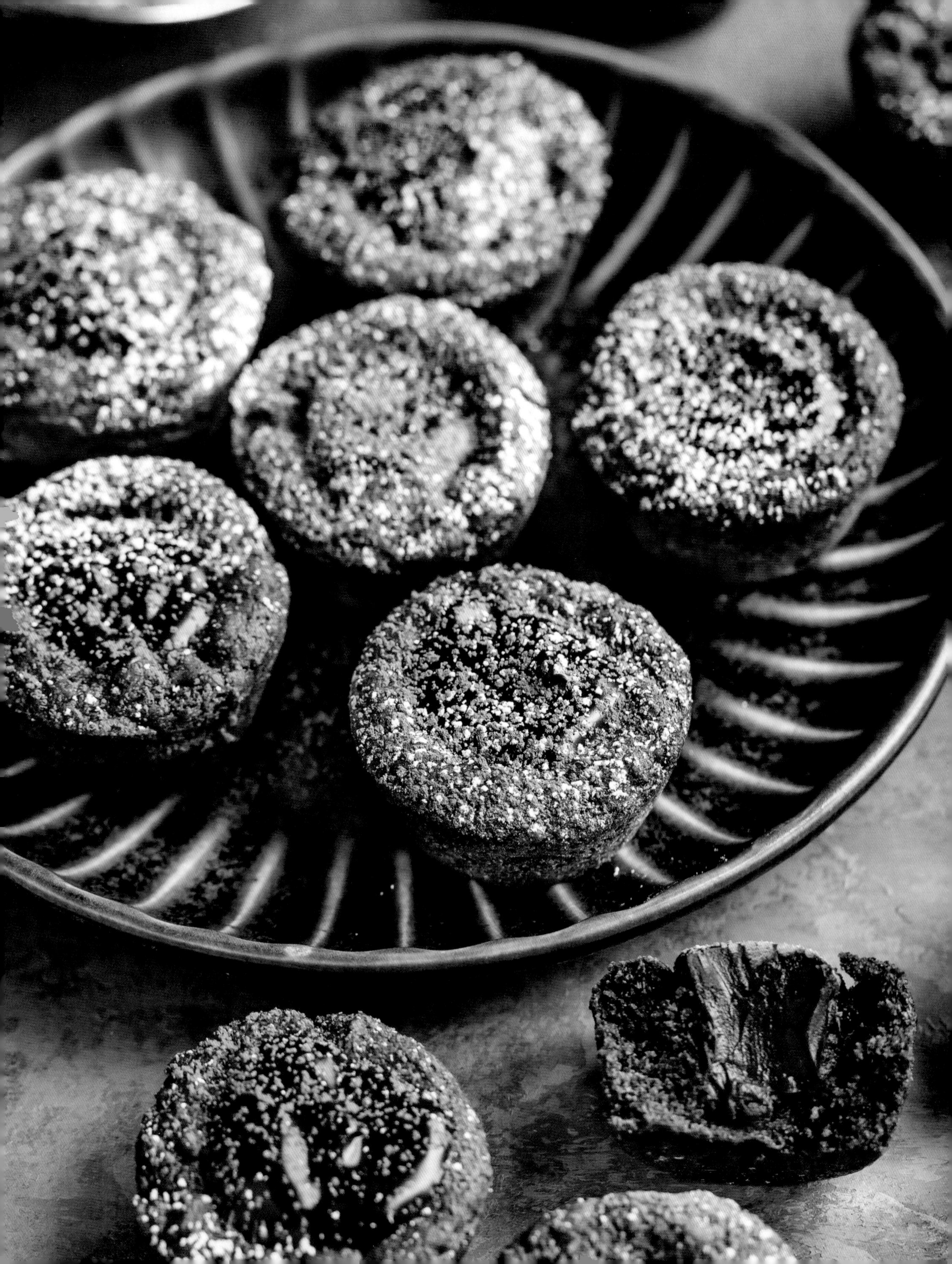

# Chocolate Lovers' Cookie Cups

Before my daughter started kindergarten, I was in a local chapter of the MOMS Club. We had weekly playdates and monthly Mom's Nights Out and it was a godsend for me, because we'd moved to our current city when my daughter Jordan was only two and I knew no one. The Mom's Nights were always themed, and one was all about chocolate: The host had someone teach us how to make truffles and dip chocolate. This was before I was a blogger, and this one class opened up a world to me (and also helped me create my tutorial about how to dip truffles without crying, a popular YouTube video). I made countless truffles back in those days, and, to be honest, I like truffles, but I like them more when they're combined with cookies. This is my favorite chocolate cookie, baked in a mini muffin pan, and then filled with chocolate ganache (the stuff you use to make truffles). This cookie cup is chocolate-intense—only true chocolate lovers need apply.

## INSTRUCTIONS

1  Preheat the oven to 350°F (177°C). Spray a mini muffin pan with non-stick baking spray (or grease and flour it).

2  Stir together the butter and both sugars until smooth and combined. You can do this by hand or use a mixer.

3  Stir in the egg, vanilla extract, salt, baking soda, and cocoa. Then add the flour and stir carefully until combined and smooth.

4  Scoop 1 tablespoon of dough into each mini muffin cavity. Press lightly to flatten. Bake for 11 to 13 minutes or until cookies just lose their glossy sheen. Remove from the oven and immediately use the back of a wooden spoon or ¼ teaspoon to press an indent into the cookies to create a shell to hold the ganache (see Thumbprint Tips, page 168). Cool completely before adding the ganache.

5  To create the ganache, place the chocolate chips and heavy whipping cream in a microwave-safe bowl. Heat on high power for 1 minute, then whisk, heating an additional 30 seconds or as needed to create a smooth chocolate ganache.

6  Fill each cookie cup cavity with chocolate ganache. Let cool to set the ganache, and then remove from the muffin pan.

7  Dust with cocoa or powdered sugar before serving.

8  Store in an airtight container for up to 3 days. Can be frozen for up to 2 months.

- ½ cup (113 g) unsalted butter, melted
- ⅓ cup (67 g) granulated sugar
- ½ cup (100 g) packed brown sugar
- 1 large egg
- 1 teaspoon vanilla extract
- ½ teaspoon salt
- ½ teaspoon baking soda
- ¼ cup (20 g) unsweetened cocoa powder
- 1⅓ cups (165 g) all-purpose flour
- ½ cup (85 g) bittersweet or semi-sweet chocolate chips
- ½ cup (118 ml) heavy whipping cream
- Powdered sugar and/or additional cocoa powder, for dusting

**Yield:** 24 cookie cups
**Prep time:** 40 minutes
**Bake time:** 12 minutes

## Tip:

Another way to dress these up even further: Sprinkle with sea salt instead of a dusting of powdered sugar!

# Piñata Cookie Cups

$\mathcal{I}$ think it was for my tenth birthday when my mom and I made a piñata for my party. We blew up the balloon as big as it would go, then covered it with papier-mâché. Once it was dry, I painted it like the outdoors, with grass and sky and flowers. I don't remember the actual hitting of the piñata or what was inside, but I vividly remember making it with her. It's the memory that always pops into my mind when I hear the word *piñata*, and I thought about it often when creating this recipe. I've seen piñata cakes and cupcakes all over the internet and knew I had to turn the idea into a cookie. These are simple cookie cups baked in a mini muffin pan, which you press cavities into once they're baked. Then you fill them with your favorite sprinkles and frost them with a chocolate buttercream. They look like cute little cookie cups and offer a nice surprise when you bite into them. Plus, it was a way for me to get sprinkles into another recipe in this book!

## INSTRUCTIONS

1   Preheat the oven to 350°F (177°C). Spray a 24-cavity mini muffin pan with nonstick cooking or nonstick baking spray.

2   Stir the butter and brown sugar in a large bowl. Stir in the egg and vanilla extract.

3   Add the baking soda and salt, and stir until smooth. Then slowly mix in the flour.

4   Scoop 1 tablespoon of dough into each cavity of the mini muffin pan. Press lightly to flatten.

5   Bake for 10 to 12 minutes or until no longer glossy and the edges are light golden. While the cookies are hot, use the back of a ¼ teaspoon or the handle of a wooden spoon to create an indent in the center (see Thumbprint Tips, page 168). Cool completely in the pan before removing.

6   While cookies are cooling, make the frosting (see Frosting Tips, page 12): Beat butter with an electric mixer in a large bowl until smooth. Slowly mix in powdered sugar and cocoa until crumbly, then mix in vanilla extract and salt. Add 1 tablespoon heavy whipping cream and beat until smooth, adding more cream as needed for consistency.

### For the Cookie Cups

- ½ cup (113 g) unsalted butter, melted
- ¾ cup (150 g) packed brown sugar
- 1 large egg
- 1 teaspoon vanilla extract
- ½ teaspoon baking soda
- ¼ teaspoon salt
- 1½ cups (186 g) all-purpose flour

### For the Frosting

- ½ cup (113 g) unsalted butter, softened
- 1¾ cups (198 g) powdered sugar
- ¼ cup (20 g) cocoa powder
- 1 teaspoon vanilla extract
- ¼ teaspoon salt
- 1 to 2 tablespoons (15 to 30 ml) heavy whipping cream
- Sprinkles

**Yield:** 22 cups
**Prep time:** 45 minutes
**Bake time:** 11 minutes

## Tip:

Use the vanilla frosting from the Three-Layer Cookie Cake (page 106) instead of chocolate frosting or use the chocolate cookie base from the Chocolate Lovers' Cookie Cups (page 113) to mix it up!

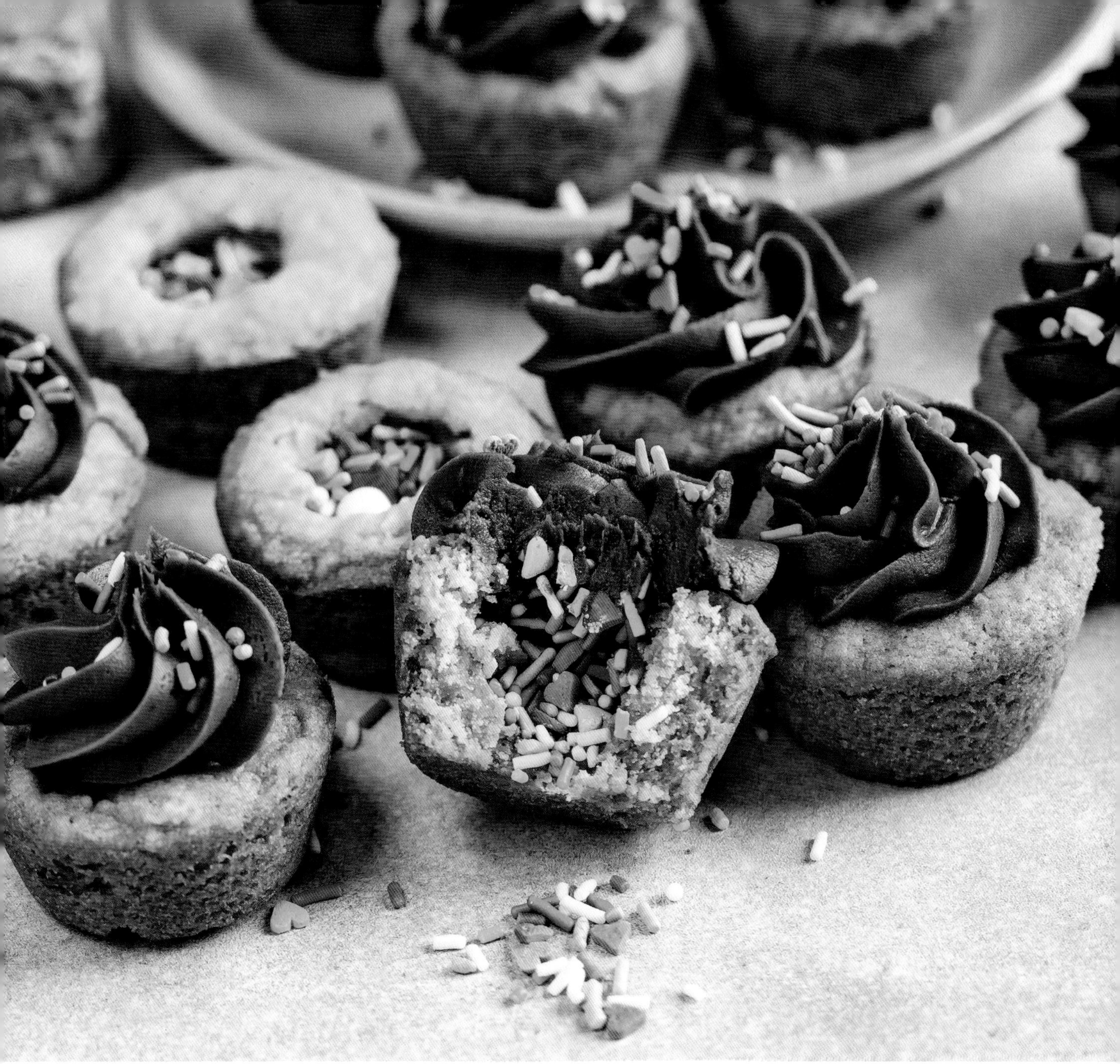

7 To assemble the cookie cups, remove the cooled cups from the pan. Fill the cavity of each cup with sprinkles. Frost the top as desired. (To frost as shown: Fill a piping bag with a large star tip and pipe swirls of frosting on top.) Decorate with more sprinkles.

8 You can make the cookie cups up to 2 days ahead, store in an airtight container, or freeze unfrosted for up to 3 months. Frosting can be made ahead and stored in an airtight container for up to 2 days. Let it come to room temperature before frosting. Store frosted cookie cups loosely covered.

# Strawberry Shortcake Cups

When I was a kid, my mom would buy those shortcake cups you can find in the produce aisles, along with fresh berries and a can of whipped cream, and serve shortcake for dessert. I still remember my dad eating his strawberry shortcake and loving it so much he'd have a second serving. In fact, he loved strawberry shortcake so much that it was always the flavor of birthday cake we'd get him from the grocery store: white cake with fresh strawberries and whipped cream frosting. Normally fruit didn't belong in dessert—unless it was Dad's birthday! These cups are my version of those childhood summer evenings: a sugar cookie cup baked in a muffin pan, then filled with chopped fresh berries and my favorite homemade whipped cream.

## MAKE THE COOKIE CUPS

1  Preheat the oven to 350°F (177°C). Spray muffin pans with nonstick baking spray or grease well with butter or shortening.

2  Cream the butter and granulated sugar in a large bowl with a hand or a stand mixer. Mix in the egg, vanilla extract, baking soda, cream of tartar, and salt, and mix until smooth. Slowly mix in the flour until a cookie dough forms.

3  Scoop about 2 tablespoons of dough into each muffin cavity. Bake for 14 to 15 minutes, or until the edges are golden brown and the center is no longer glossy.

4  Immediately after removing from the oven, use a wooden spoon handle or the rounded part of a teaspoon to create a shell, pressing the center of the cookie down. Cool the cookie shells completely before removing from the pan. When ready to remove from the pan, run a butter knife carefully around the edges to loosen and use it to pop the cookie cups out of the pan.

## MAKE THE FILLING

1  Beat the cold heavy whipping cream with powdered sugar and vanilla at high speed until stiff peaks form.

2  To assemble the shortcake cups, fill each cookie cavity with diced strawberries. Top with whipped cream. Serve immediately.

3  You can make the cookie cups up to 2 days ahead of time (store in an airtight container) or freeze for up to 2 months. Don't make whipped cream or prepare the strawberries until the day of serving.

### For the Cookie Cups

- ½ cup (113 g) unsalted butter, softened
- ½ cup (100 g) granulated sugar
- 1 large egg
- 1 teaspoon vanilla extract
- ¼ teaspoon baking soda
- ½ teaspoon cream of tartar
- ¼ teaspoon salt
- 1⅓ cups (165 g) all-purpose flour

### For the Filling

- 6½ ounces (181 g) fresh strawberries, diced small
- 1 teaspoon granulated sugar

### For the Topping

- ½ cup (118 ml) cold heavy whipping cream
- 1 tablespoon (7 g) powdered sugar
- ½ teaspoon vanilla

**Yield:** 12 cookie cups
**Prep time:** 35 minutes
**Bake time:** 14 minutes

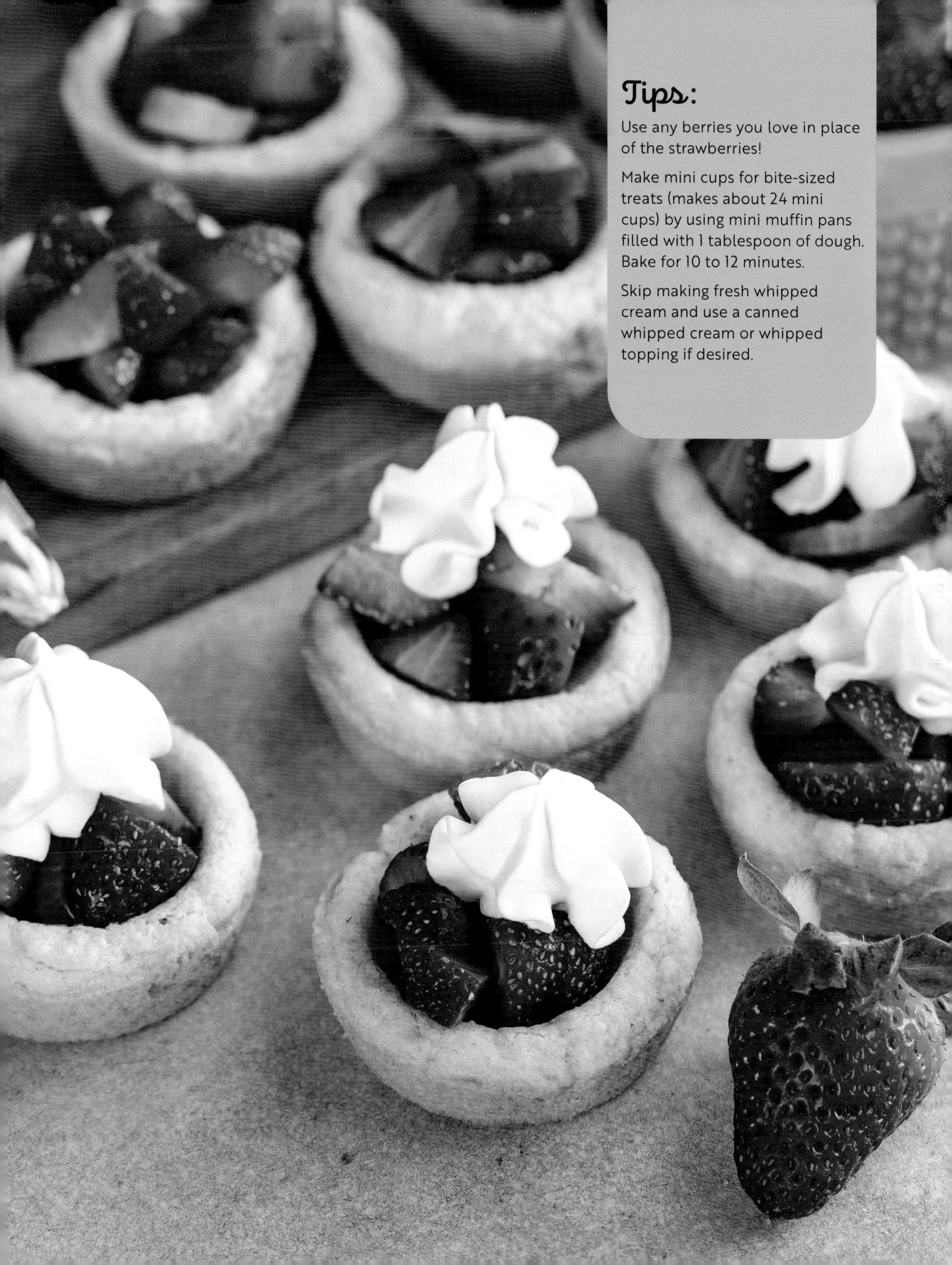

## Tips:

Use any berries you love in place of the strawberries!

Make mini cups for bite-sized treats (makes about 24 mini cups) by using mini muffin pans filled with 1 tablespoon of dough. Bake for 10 to 12 minutes.

Skip making fresh whipped cream and use a canned whipped cream or whipped topping if desired.

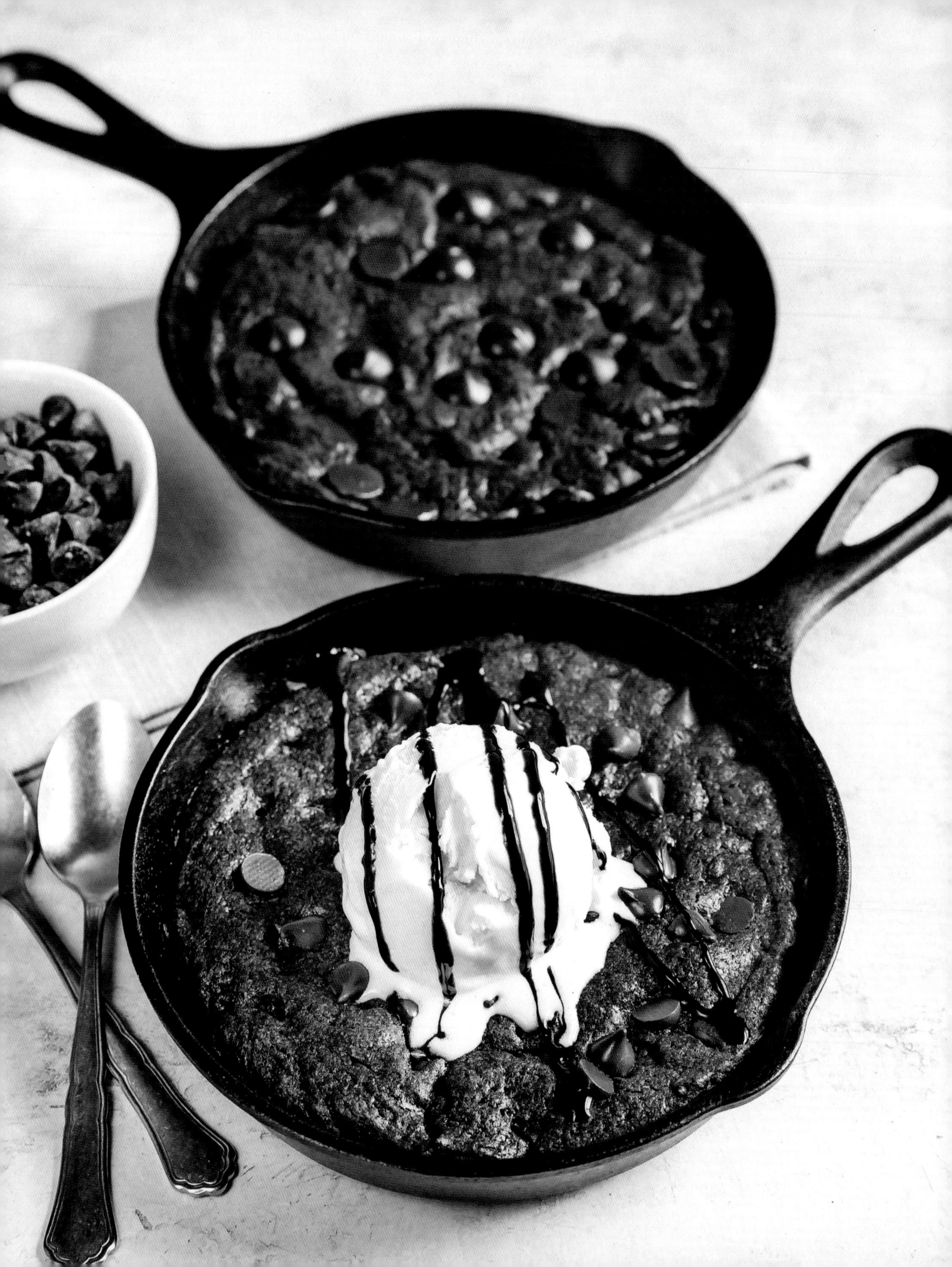

# Skillet Brownie for Two

I love small-batch dessert recipes because I can eat the entire thing and it's socially acceptable—ha! Breaking down a dessert into smaller portions can be tricky because of things like eggs and fractions, but don't worry: Math Teacher Dorothy is here to do all the hard work for you. This Skillet Brownie is designed as two servings and is baked in a small skillet, cake pan, or even a bread pan. It's perfect when you want a little chocolate treat but don't want any leftovers—and if you want to eat the entire thing, I won't judge you.

## INSTRUCTIONS

1   Preheat the oven to 350°F (177°C). Spray a 6-inch (15 cm) cast-iron skillet with nonstick cooking spray. You can also use a 5- or 6-inch (13 or 15 cm) round cake pan or an 8 × 4–inch (20 × 10 cm) loaf pan.

2   Stir together the flour, sugar, cocoa powder, and salt in a medium bowl. Add the oil and egg and stir until thick and moist. Stir in the chocolate chips. Spread in the prepared pan, and sprinkle with more chocolate chips if desired.

3   Bake for 17 to 22 minutes until the top just loses its glossy sheen. For more done brownies, wait until a toothpick comes out with just a few crumbs when inserted 1 inch (2.5 cm) from the edge of the pan.

4   Cool and then slice and serve, or eat straight from the pan.

- 5 tablespoons (42 g) all-purpose flour
- 6 tablespoons (79 g) granulated sugar
- 3 tablespoons (15 g) unsweetened cocoa powder
- ⅛ teaspoon salt
- 3 tablespoons (45 ml) vegetable oil
- 1 large egg
- ⅓ cup (57 g) chocolate chips, plus more to sprinkle on top

**Yield:** 2 servings
**Prep time:** 10 minutes
**Bake time:** 20 minutes

## Tip:

Omit the chocolate chips and add nuts or chopped candy to your liking. We also love making these for parties: Set up a brownie bar with skillets filled with batter and people can add their favorite toppings. It's a fun activity, especially for a birthday party!

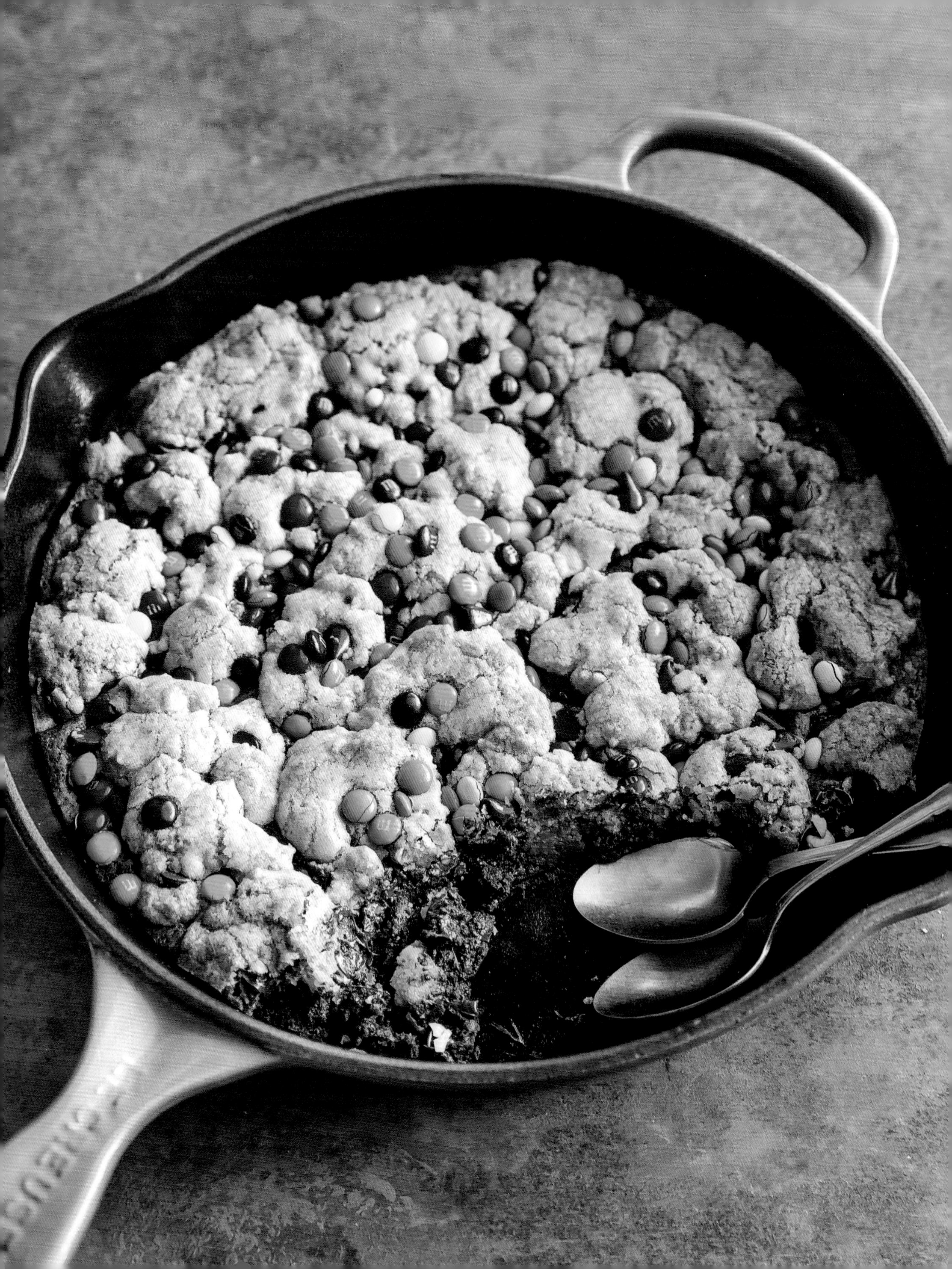

# Brookie Skillet

*J*'m going to tell you right now: This recipe is trouble. Good, heavenly trouble, but trouble nonetheless. It's going to make you want another bite . . . and then another and another. Like I've said before, I cannot choose a favorite dessert, but cookies and brownies are pretty high on the list, so whenever I can make them both in the same recipe? *Perfection!* The brownie layer in these stays gooey, even with prebaking, so don't expect to slice them. These are scoop-and-plate brookies, made only better when served with a generous scoop of your favorite ice cream.

## MAKE THE BROWNIE LAYER

1   Preheat the oven to 350°F (177°C). Grease a 10-inch (25 cm) skillet. You can also use a 9-inch (23 cm) or 10-inch (25 cm) round cake pan.

2   Place the melted butter in a large bowl. Stir in the sugar and cocoa powder until smooth, using a wooden spoon. Add the eggs, vanilla extract, and salt; stir to combine, then slowly mix in the flour. The batter will be thick.

3   Spread the batter into the prepared pan. Bake for 8 minutes while you prepare the cookie dough.

## MAKE COOKIE LAYER

1   Stir together the melted butter with both sugars in a large bowl. Stir in the egg yolk, vanilla extract, baking soda, and salt. Slowly stir in the flour. Stir in the chocolate chips.

2   Scoop tablespoons of dough and flatten between your fingers, then drop evenly over the brownie layer in the pan. It's okay if some of the brownie shows through. Sprinkle with M&M's, if using.

3   Bake for an additional 23 to 28 minutes or until the cookie is golden on top. The brownie will stay super fudgy. This is best served on a plate with a fork . . . and ice cream!

### For the Brownie Layer

- 10 tablespoons (140 g) unsalted butter, melted
- 1⅓ cups (267 g) granulated sugar
- ⅔ cup (54 g) unsweetened cocoa powder
- 2 large eggs
- 1 teaspoon vanilla extract
- ½ teaspoon salt
- ½ cup (62 g) all-purpose flour

### For the Cookie Layer

- 4 tablespoons (57 g) unsalted butter, melted
- ¼ cup (50 g) packed brown sugar
- 3 tablespoons (35 g) granulated sugar
- 1 large egg yolk
- ½ teaspoon vanilla extract
- ¼ teaspoon baking soda
- ¼ teaspoon salt
- ⅔ cup (83 g) all-purpose flour
- ½ cup (85 g) semi-sweet chocolate chips
- ¼ cup (55 g) mini M&M's for topping (optional)

**Yield:** 12 servings
**Prep time:** 40 minutes
**Bake time:** 33 minutes

## Tip:

The M&M's add color but are optional. Add nuts or other chopped candy to your liking. Don't have a skillet? Use a round cake pan!

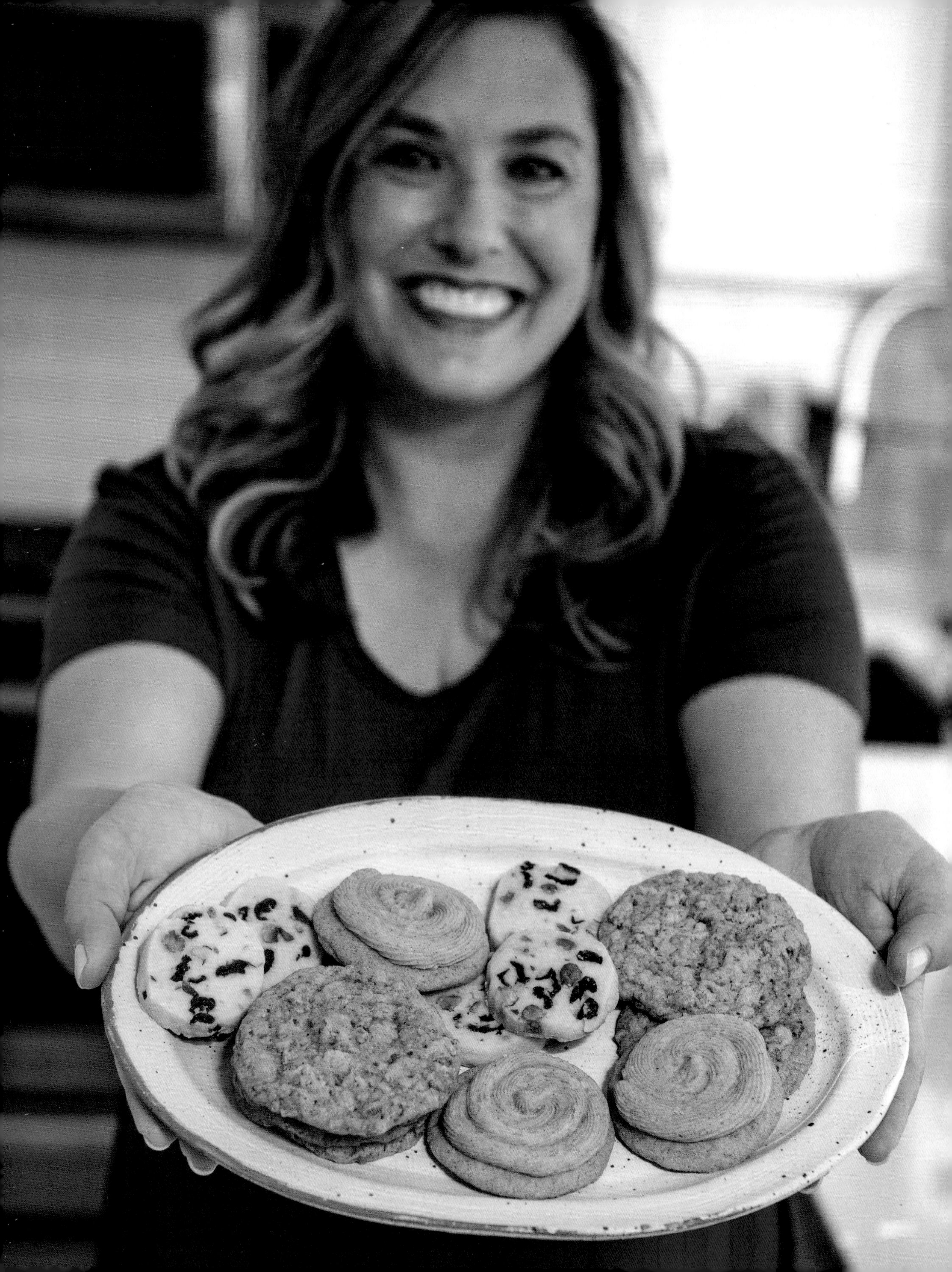

# Crazy Cookies

These cookies are a little bit crazy and a lot of fun: I took my favorite flavors and turned them up a notch. These cookies span the spectrum, from chocolate to cereal to frosted and so much more. There really is a little bit for everyone in this chapter—and those Churro Cookies (see page 150) are the reigning favorite cookie among all the testers and tasters combined. These cookies are meant to stretch your imagination and get your creative juices flowing. Once you realize that yes, you can put Fruity Pebbles in cookies, which means you can put other cereals in too, then my job will be done. No, that's not true: There are always more cookie recipes!

To get the most out of your cookies, take a minute to review all the cookie baking tips at the beginning of the Cookie Jar Favorites chapter on page 19.

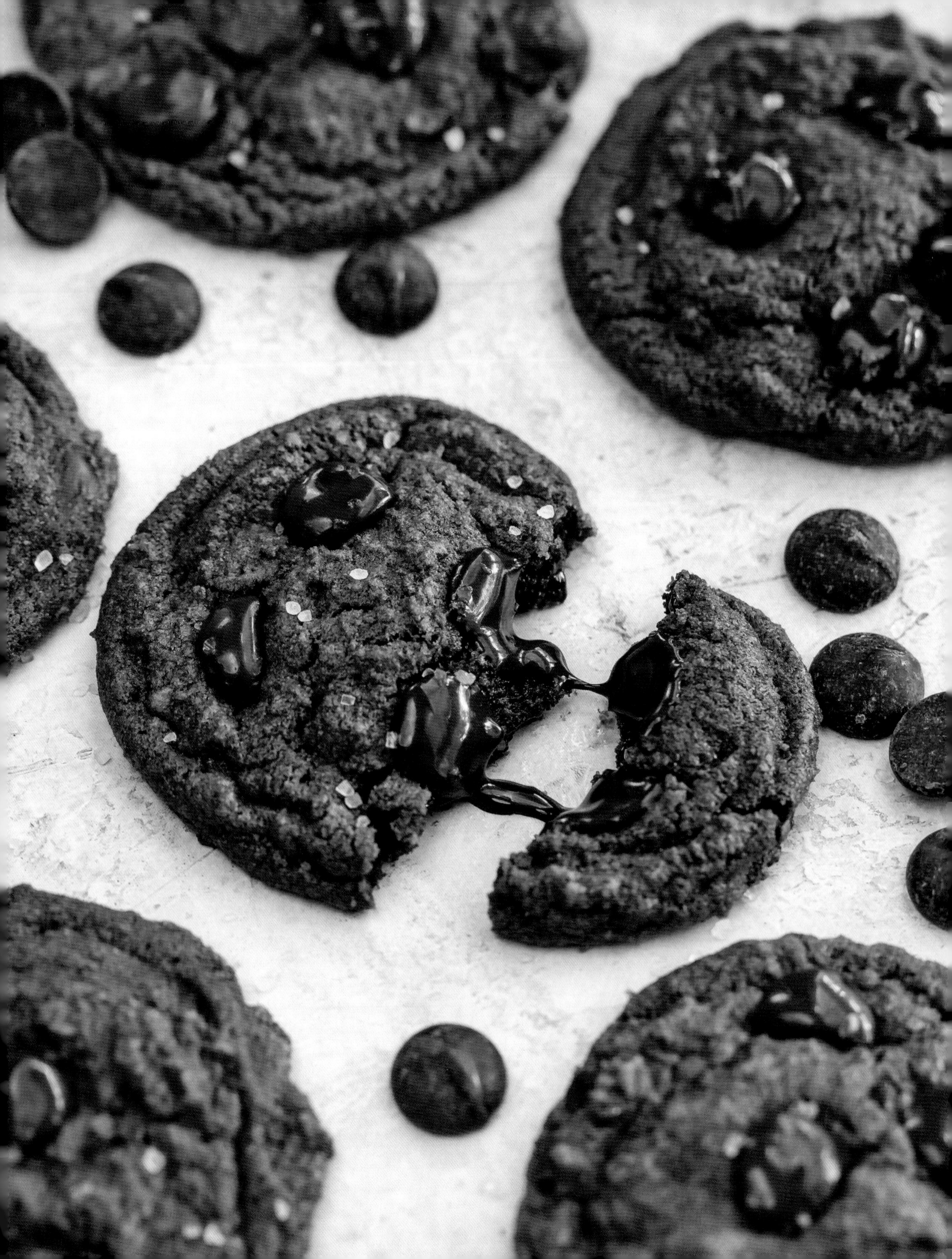

# Dark Chocolate Espresso Cookies

𝒰ntil I started blogging and teaching myself about ingredients and baking, I didn't know that people often added coffee to chocolate recipes to enhance chocolate flavor. Sometimes the added coffee was meant not to be tasted but instead to bring out the richness of the chocolate—and all my life I'd been omitting it because I didn't like coffee (until I started working full time and then it became my savior). The espresso powder in these cookies does double duty: It accentuates the chocolate *and* adds a kick of coffee flavor to the recipe. I know it's often hard to find instant espresso powder, so if you can't find it, you can substitute a dark instant coffee (like Starbucks Via). But if you can find instant espresso powder, use that—it adds so much flavor to the cookies.

- 1⅔ cups (262 g) bittersweet chocolate chips, divided (plus more for topping)
- ½ cup (113 g) unsalted butter, softened
- ¾ cup (150 g) packed brown sugar
- ¼ cup (50 g) granulated sugar
- 1 teaspoon vanilla extract
- 1 large egg
- ½ teaspoon baking soda
- 1¼ teaspoon salt
- 1 tablespoon instant espresso powder
- 1 tablespoon (5 g) unsweetened cocoa powder
- 1¼ cups (155 g) all-purpose flour
- Sea salt, for sprinkling (optional)

**Yield:** 21 cookies
**Prep time:** 20 minutes
**Chill time:** 1 hour
**Bake time:** 12 minutes

## INSTRUCTIONS

1  Place ⅓ cup (57 g) bittersweet chocolate chips in a microwave-safe bowl. Heat on 50 percent power in 30-second increments, stirring between each, until melted and smooth. Set aside to cool while mixing the cookie dough.

2  Cream the butter and both sugars in the bowl of a stand mixer fitted with the paddle attachment (or a large bowl using a hand mixer) until fluffy, 1 to 2 minutes. Mix in the vanilla extract, egg, baking soda, and salt.

3  Add the melted chocolate to the mixture along with the instant espresso powder and cocoa powder and mix until smooth. Slowly mix in the flour until a dough forms. Stir in the remaining 1⅓ cups (205 g) chocolate chips.

4  Scoop balls of cookie dough (each about 2 tablespoons) onto a cookie sheet lined with parchment paper. Chill for at least 1 hour.

5  Preheat the oven to 350°F (177°C). Line a second cookie sheet with parchment paper. Space cookies 2 inches (5 cm) apart on baking sheets, using a third cookie sheet if needed. Bake for 11 to 13 minutes or until the cookies just lose their glossy sheen. The cookies will still be soft at this point, but they will set as they cool.

6  As soon as the cookies come out of the oven, press a few chocolate chips on top of each hot cookie. Sprinkle with sea salt, if desired.

7  Cool on the cookie sheets, and then store in an airtight container for up to 3 days or freeze for up to 2 months.

## Tip:

You can also use Dutch process cocoa or Hershey's Special Dark unsweetened cocoa in this recipe for an extra-dark punch of flavor.

# Orange Dream Cookies

When I was little, my dad would take me to get orange soda and Cheetos and we'd go watch the planes take off at the Half Moon Bay airport. I barely remember the planes, but what I remember is stopping at the convenience store and getting my orange soda and my chips. These cookies remind me of those days: lots of orange flavor and bright orange color, like that soda. The orange flavor in these cookies comes from fresh orange juice, orange zest, and orange extract. The zest and extract are both important because orange juice doesn't have tons of flavor, so adding the zest and the extract pumps it up a bit. With the white chocolate chips, they might remind me of those orange soda days, but the flavor is reminiscent of a frozen creamsicle treat.

## INSTRUCTIONS

1  Preheat the oven to 350°F (177°C). Line 2 cookie sheets with parchment paper or silicone baking mats.

2  Cream the butter and both sugars with an electric mixer (use a paddle attachment if using a stand mixer).

3  Mix in the egg, orange zest, orange juice, orange extract, baking soda, and salt. Add the flour and mix until smooth.

4  Add the food coloring, if desired, and stir until combined. Then stir in the white chocolate chips.

5  Scoop balls of cookie dough (each about 2 tablespoons) onto the prepared cookie sheets, spacing 2 inches (5 cm) apart. Bake for 12 to 15 minutes, or until the tops have lost their glossy sheen.

6  Cool for 5 minutes on cookie sheets before removing. Store in an airtight container for up to 3 days or freeze for up to 2 months.

- ½ cup (113 g) unsalted butter, softened
- ½ cup (100 g) granulated sugar
- ⅓ cup (67 g) packed brown sugar
- 1 large egg
- 1 tablespoon (6 g) orange zest
- 1 tablespoon (15 ml) fresh orange juice
- 1 teaspoon (15 ml) orange extract
- 1 teaspoon baking soda
- ¼ teaspoon salt
- 1¾ cups (217 g) all-purpose flour
- 3 to 4 drops orange food coloring (optional)
- 1½ cups (255 g) white chocolate chips

**Yield:** 22 cookies
**Prep time:** 20 minutes
**Bake time:** 14 minutes

## Tip:
Skip the white chocolate chips and frost these with the vanilla frosting from my Nana's Drop Sugar Cookies (see page 30).

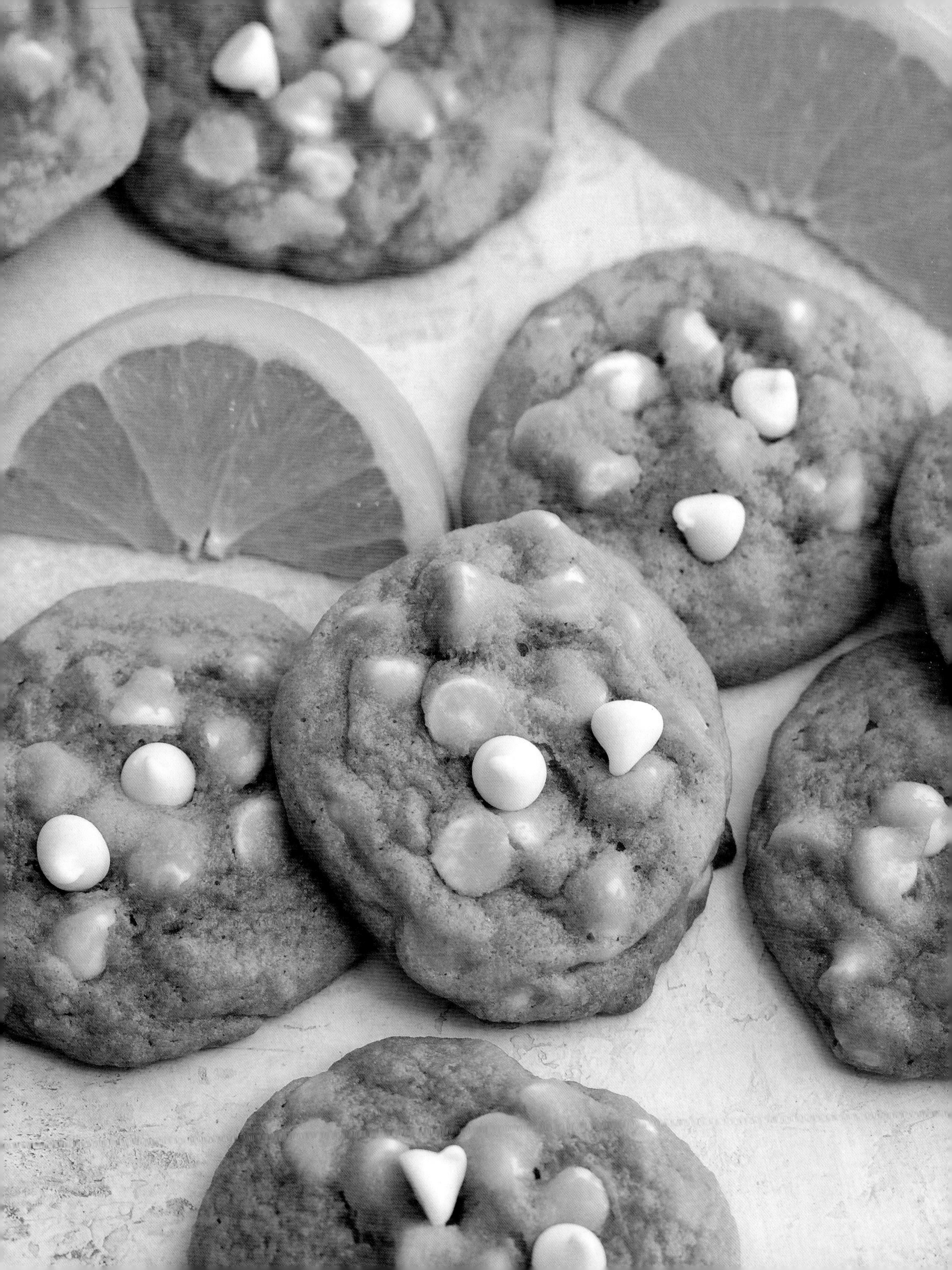

# Chocolate Peanut Butter Potato Chip Cookies

The first time I saw chocolate-covered potato chips, I balked at the idea. I actually saw them at one of those discount stores that sells all varieties of things and has a food aisle where you question why the food is discounted . . . possibly that's why I thought the whole idea of them strange. And then dessert recipes with potato chips started showing up all over the internet. Dipped potato chips, potato chips in cookies, potato chip crumbs as a dusting on brownies . . . I figured all those recipes couldn't be wrong, right? So, I tried dipping some potato chips in melted chocolate, and—*oh my goodness*—they were amazing. The salty/sweet combination was outstanding! Since then, I have loved putting potato chips (and pretzels) in everything, especially when the recipe has chocolate. This recipe is a mishmash of several of my favorite things: peanut butter cookies, chocolate, and salty potato chips. These might not look the prettiest or most refined, but they definitely score 100 on the taste meter.

- 2 ounces (57 g) semi-sweet baking chocolate
- ½ cup (113 g) unsalted butter, softened
- ½ cup (134 g) creamy peanut butter
- ¾ cup (150 g) packed brown sugar
- ¼ cup (50 g) granulated sugar
- 1 large egg
- 1 teaspoon vanilla extract
- 1 tablespoon (15 ml) milk
- ½ teaspoon baking soda
- 2 tablespoons (10 g) unsweetened cocoa powder
- ¼ teaspoon salt
- 1¾ cups (217 g) all-purpose flour
- 1 cup (170 g) chocolate chips
- 1¼ cups (54 g) lightly crushed kettle chip potato chips

**Yield:** 26 cookies
**Prep time:** 20 minutes
**Bake time:** 13 minutes

## INSTRUCTIONS

1. Preheat the oven to 350°F (177°C). Line 2 cookie sheets with silicone baking mats or parchment paper.

2. Place the baking chocolate in a microwave-safe bowl and heat on 50 percent power in 30-second increments, stirring between each, until melted and smooth (approximately 2 to 3 minutes, depending on your microwave). Set aside to cool slightly while you start the cookie dough.

3. Place the butter and peanut butter in a large bowl. Using a hand or a stand mixer, mix until combined, and then add both sugars. Cream until smooth. Mix in the egg, vanilla extract, melted chocolate, and milk, and mix on medium speed until combined.

4. Mix in the baking soda, cocoa powder, and salt, and then slowly mix in the flour just until the batter is smooth and comes together. Be sure to scrape the sides of the bowl during mixing.

5. Mix in the chocolate chips and potato chips.

6. Scoop balls of cookie dough (each about 2 tablespoons) and place 2 inches (5 cm) apart on the prepared cookie sheets. Using a fork, create a crisscross pattern on the cookies to slightly flatten. (Tip: If the dough starts sticking to the fork, dip it in a bit of granulated sugar.) You can also press them with the palm of your hand to flatten.

7. Bake for 11 to 14 minutes, or until the edges are just golden brown and the tops are no longer glossy. Cool on the cookie sheets at least 10 minutes before removing.

8. Store in an airtight container for up to 3 days. Can be frozen for up to 2 months.

## Tip:

Try using coarsely chopped pretzels instead of potato chips—both options are fantastic in this cookie.

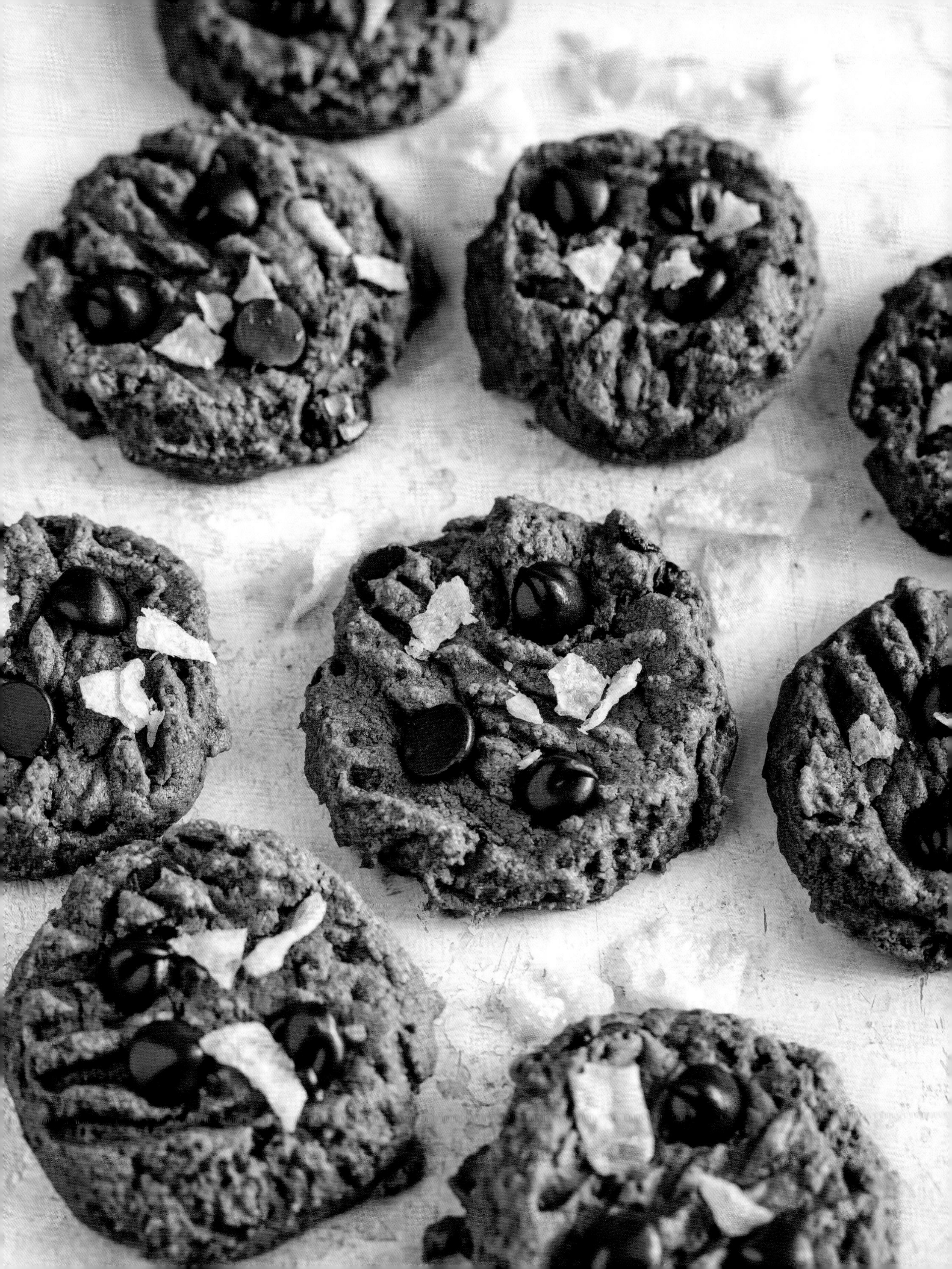

# Ice Cream Cookies

*I* do not like the cold. Not. At. All. This is probably because my fingers turn purple as soon as the temps drop below 70°F (21°C) and, for most of winter, I cannot feel my feet. I've been skiing once, and it was in the middle of a storm. Bad idea: The second I walked out those doors onto the mountain, I immediately lost all feeling in all of my extremities, my nose, and my ears. Because of this I'm not a huge ice cream fan. I mean, I like ice cream and I won't say no to a cone on vacation or a fro-yo from our favorite place, but I prefer cookies. But what if you want ice cream *and* cookies? Then you should make these cookies: There is ice cream *in* them! Yep, ice cream is mixed into the batter, so your final cookie has a hint of the flavor you used. You can use any regular ice cream in this recipe, so choose your favorite flavor. Even better: Change up your mix-ins to fit the flavor of your ice cream. Check out all my variations below and then get creative and make your own flavors—no gloves needed!

## INSTRUCTIONS

1 Let your ice cream sit out on the counter for about 30 minutes before making the cookie dough, or, in a pinch, you can heat the carton for about 30 seconds in the microwave. You want the ice cream to be soft-serve texture instead of hard from the freezer.

2 Melt the butter in a microwave-safe bowl. Add both sugars and mix with an electric mixer on low speed until combined. Add the ice cream and mix until smooth.

3 Add the egg and vanilla extract, mix for just a few seconds, and then add the baking soda and salt. Mix until smooth, and then slowly mix in the flour. Mix just until the dough comes together, then stir in the chocolate chips, nuts, and sprinkles.

4 Scoop balls of cookie dough (each about 2 tablespoons) onto a cookie sheet covered with parchment paper. You're going to chill the dough balls, so there is no need to space them out. Cover with plastic wrap and chill for at least 30 minutes.

5 Preheat the oven to 350°F (177°C). Place the cookies 2 inches (5 cm) apart on cookie sheets covered with parchment paper or silicone baking mats. (If you've chilled them longer than 4 hours, you might want to press them down slightly with the palm of your hand; otherwise they won't flatten.) Bake for about 11 to 14 minutes, or until they start to get light golden around the edges and are no longer glossy. Cool for at least 5 minutes on cookie sheets before moving to a rack to cool completely.

6 Cookies can be stored in an airtight container for up to 4 days or frozen for up to 2 months.

- ½ cup (90 g) ice cream (use your favorite flavor)
- ½ cup (113 g) unsalted butter, melted
- ⅓ cup (67 g) granulated sugar
- ½ cup (100 g) packed brown sugar
- 1 large egg
- 1 teaspoon pure vanilla extract
- ½ teaspoon baking soda
- ¼ teaspoon salt
- 2 cups (248 g) all-purpose flour
- 1 cup (170 g) chocolate chips
- ½ cup (65 g) chopped nuts, any kind
- ½ cup (97 g) rainbow sprinkles

**Yield:** 27 cookies
**Prep time:** 20 minutes
**Chill time:** 30 minutes
**Bake time:** 13 minutes

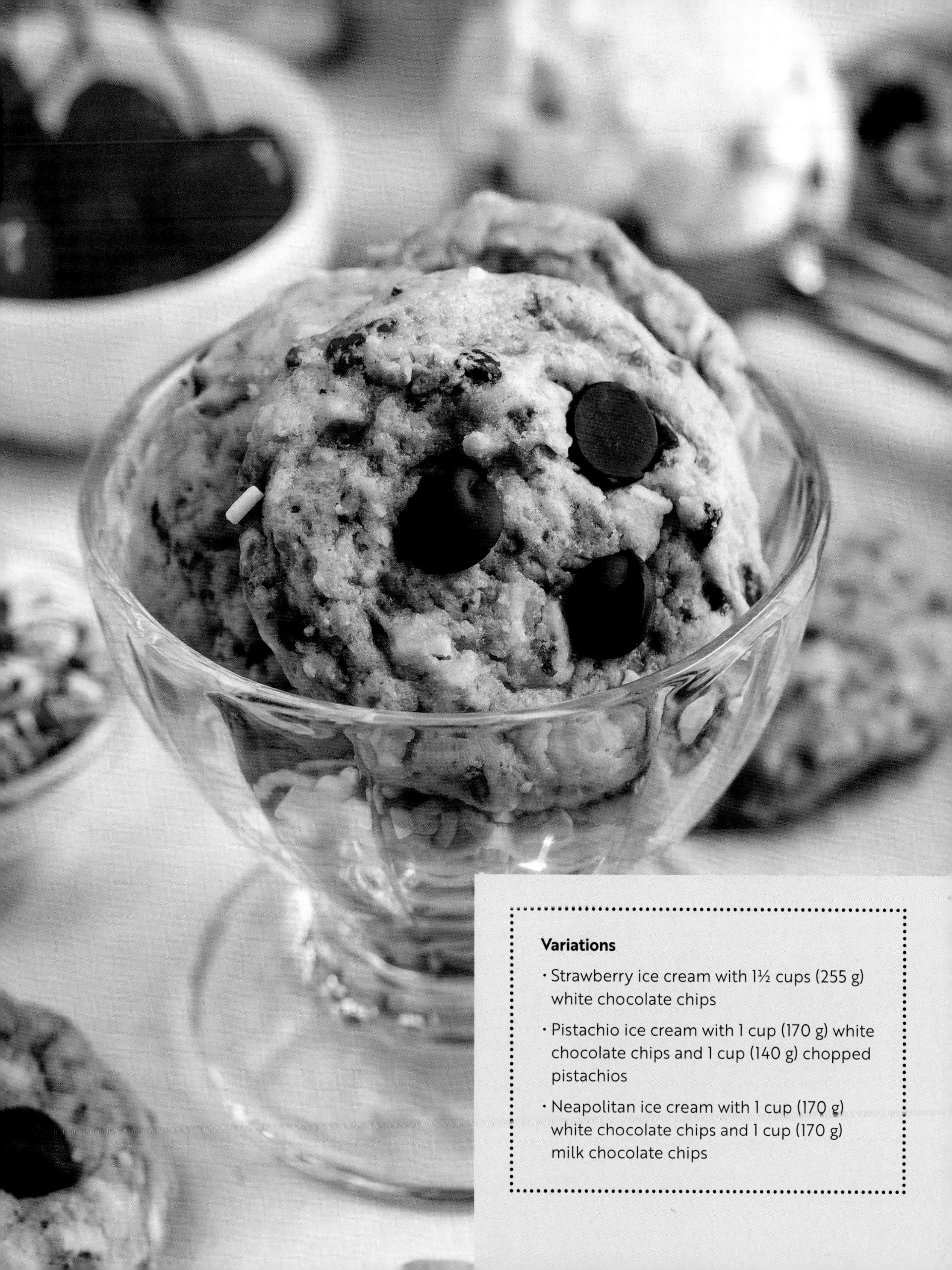

**Variations**

- Strawberry ice cream with 1½ cups (255 g) white chocolate chips
- Pistachio ice cream with 1 cup (170 g) white chocolate chips and 1 cup (140 g) chopped pistachios
- Neapolitan ice cream with 1 cup (170 g) white chocolate chips and 1 cup (170 g) milk chocolate chips

# Mochadoodles

𝓘'm sorry, but I cannot say the name of this cookie—or even "snickerdoodles" in general—because the "doodle" reminds me of my labradoodle, Abby. I'm obsessed with all things doodle—their fluffy faces and stuffed animal bodies—and the cookie version too. It doesn't help that these mocha-flavored snickerdoodles are the same color as Abby's spots! Now that you'll only think of dogs when you see snickerdoodles (you're welcome), let's talk about these: They're a chocolate and coffee-flavored snickerdoodle that is super soft and pillowy. We really love these cookies and you will too, especially if you love mocha flavor. And don't worry—cinnamon pairs really well with both chocolate and coffee!

## INSTRUCTIONS

1   Preheat the oven to 350°F (177°C). Line 2 cookie sheets with parchment paper.

2   Cream the butter and ¾ cup (150 g) granulated sugar using a stand or a hand mixer until fluffy. Mix in the egg and vanilla extract, then mix in the baking soda, cream of tartar, cocoa powder, espresso powder, and salt. Slowly mix in the flour until the dough is combined.

3   Place the ¼ cup (50 g) granulated sugar and cinnamon in a small bowl. Scoop cookie balls (each about 2 tablespoons) and roll them in the cinnamon sugar mixture. Place them 2 inches (5 cm) apart on the cookie sheets.

4   Bake for 10 to 13 minutes or until they are cracked on the tops and just lose their glossy sheen. Err on the side of underbaked for the best results.

5   Store in an airtight container for up to 3 days or freeze for up to 1 month.

## For the Cookies

- ½ cup (113 g) unsalted butter, softened
- ¾ cup (150 g) granulated sugar
- 1 large egg
- 1 teaspoon vanilla extract
- ½ teaspoon baking soda
- 1½ teaspoons cream of tartar
- ¼ cup (20 g) unsweetened cocoa powder
- 2 teaspoons instant espresso powder
- ½ teaspoon salt
- 1½ cups (186 g) all-purpose flour

## For the Coating

- ¼ cup (50 g) granulated sugar
- 1 teaspoon ground cinnamon

**Yield:** 23 cookies
**Prep time:** 25 minutes
**Bake time:** 12 minutes

## 𝒯ip:

Add 1 cup (170 g) of chocolate chips (in step 2) for an extra chocolatey flavor!

# Salted Butterscotch Cookies

I cannot believe I went the first thirty years of my life thinking I didn't like butterscotch. I can't think of butterscotch without thinking about my mom's Rice Krispies treats: She'd make the traditional recipe and add a package of butterscotch morsels into the marshmallow mixture. I wasn't in love with them as a child (although I'm drooling now just thinking about them), so I guess I thought I just didn't like butterscotch. Then, a few years into blogging, I received a package of cookies from another blogger. There were a variety of flavors, but the ones I remember the most were salted butterscotch. The rich, buttery caramel flavor of the butterscotch was only enhanced by the dusting of sea salt. These cookies are my interpretation of that flavor: a brown sugar cookie filled with butterscotch chips and dusted with sea salt. You can skip the salt if you really don't want it, but I think it only enhances the flavor.

- ½ cup (113 g) unsalted butter, sliced
- 1 cup (200 g) packed brown sugar
- 1 large egg
- 1 teaspoon vanilla extract
- ½ teaspoon baking soda
- ½ teaspoon salt
- 1¼ cups (155 g) all-purpose flour
- 1¼ cups (225 g) butterscotch chips
- Sea salt, for topping

**Yield:** 18 cookies
**Prep time:** 20 minutes
**Chill time:** 1 hour
**Bake time:** 12 minutes

## INSTRUCTIONS

1 Place the butter in a small saucepan over medium-low heat. Melt, then cook, stirring often, until the butter browns, about 2 to 5 minutes, depending on the size of your pan. The butter will foam, and then little brown flecks will appear and the butter will turn a golden amber color. Don't walk away from the stove, because it can burn quickly.

2 Pour the browned butter into a large bowl. Add the brown sugar and stir or mix with an electric mixer until smooth. Stir in the egg, vanilla extract, baking soda, and salt, then stir in the flour. Stir in the butterscotch chips.

3 Scoop balls of cookie dough (each about 2 tablespoons) and place them on a parchment paper–lined cookie sheet. Chill for 1 hour.

4 Preheat the oven to 350°F (177°C). Line a second sheet with parchment paper. After they have chilled, place the cookie dough balls 2 inches (5 cm) apart on the 2 cookie sheets. Bake for 10 to 14 minutes or until the tops just lose their glossy sheen.

5 Sprinkle the hot cookies with sea salt. Let cool before removing from cookie sheets. Store in an airtight container for up to 3 days or freeze for up to 3 months.

## Tip:
These are also great with chocolate chips or toffee bits!

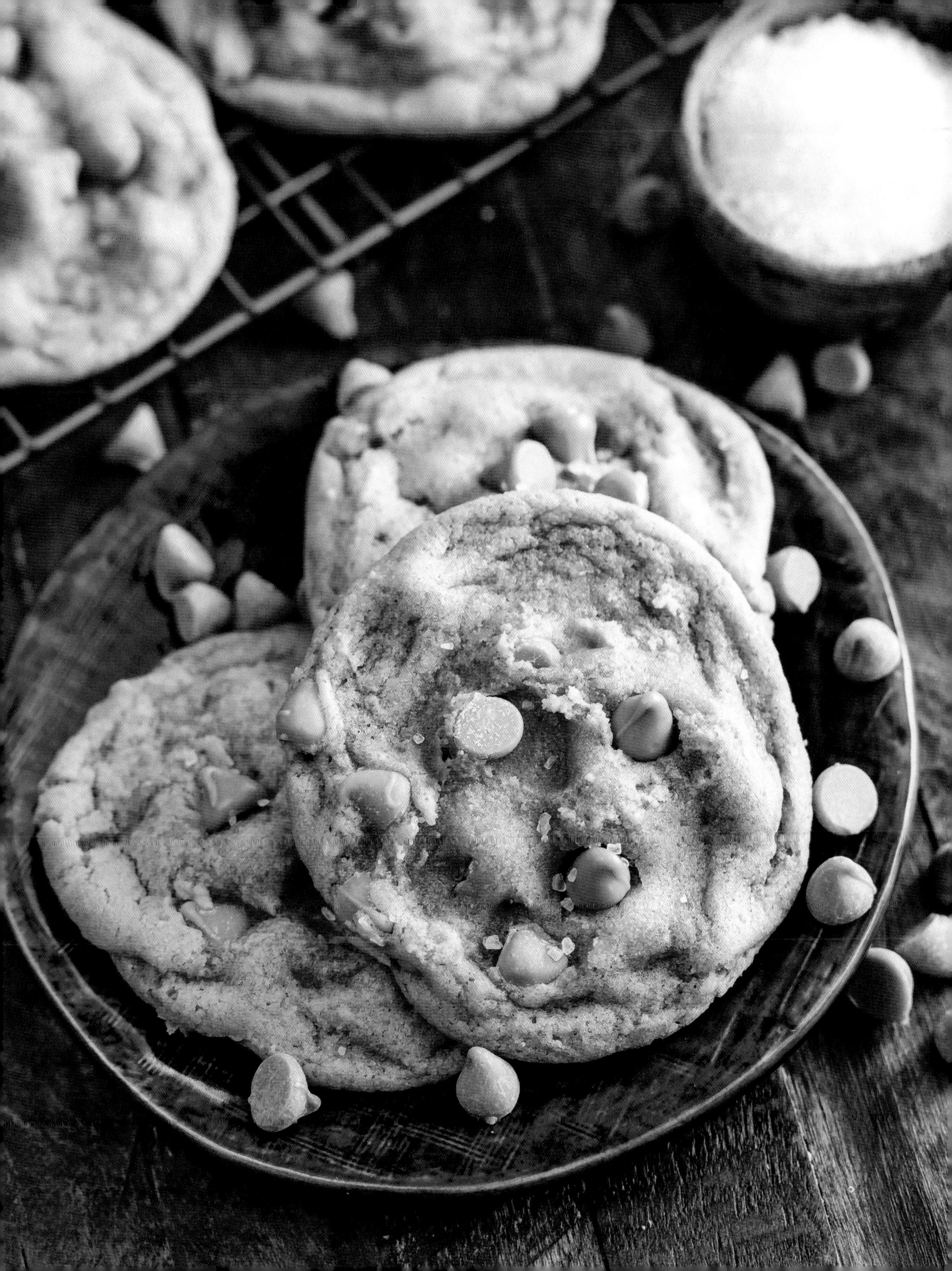

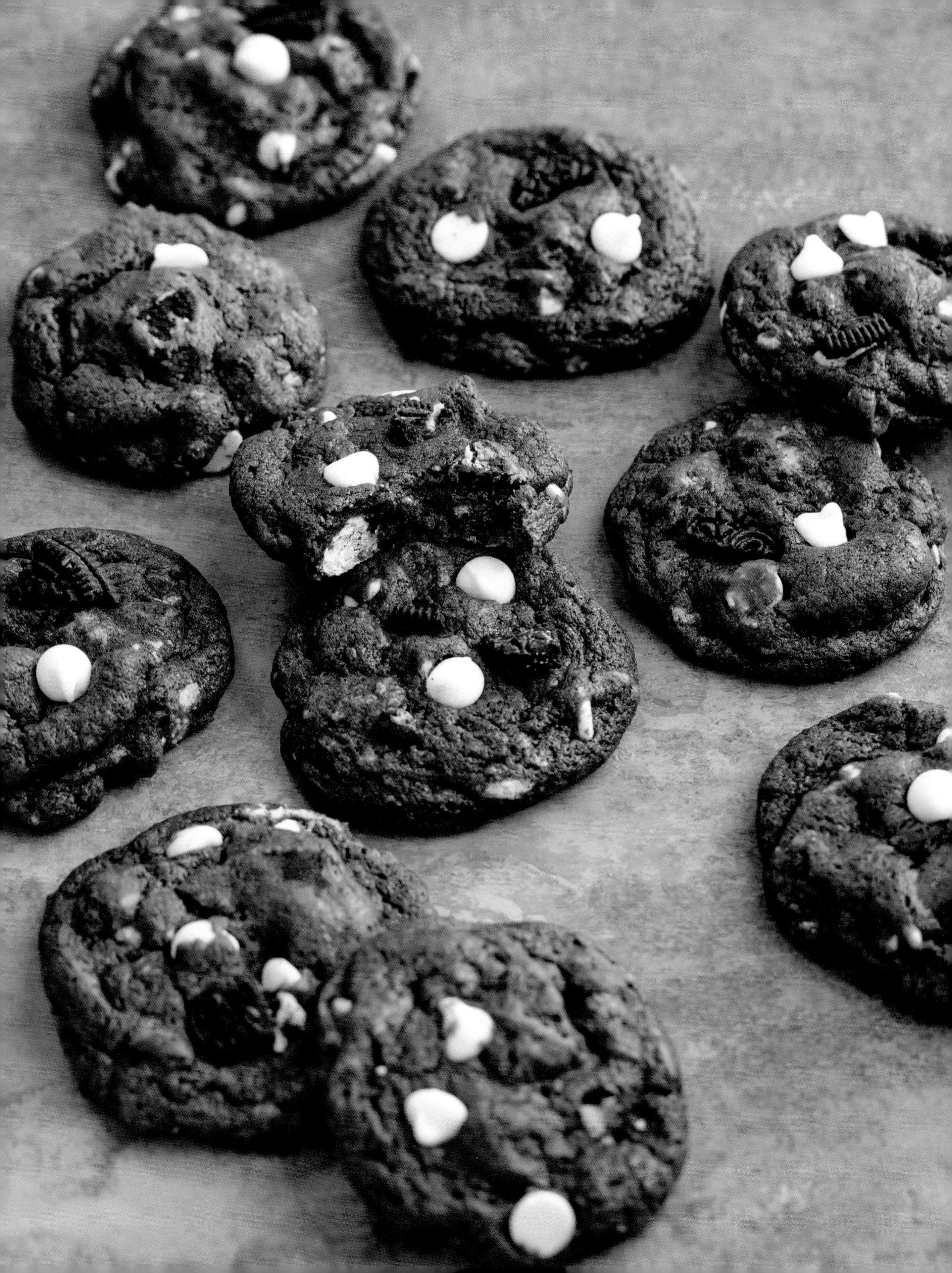

# Cookies 'n' Cream Red Velvet Cookies

On December 1, the year my daughter Jordan was five, France arrived for the first time. France is our Elf on the Shelf, a popular tradition that made someone very rich, and the first year we had him, I went all out. He showed up with a note, moved every night, made snow angels in powdered sugar, and took the Barbie car for a joyride. He even asked Jordan to be his pen pal and encouraged her to write him notes and mail them through stocking-mail (leaving them in her stocking) and promised he'd write back every day. The year Jordan was five was also the year I realized that overpromising as a parent is exhausting, and that I should have been underwhelming with our elf, so she didn't expect too much (just to save my sanity).

Similar to my parenting goals, red velvet is kind of an underwhelming flavor: What is it anyway? When coming up with a Red Velvet Cookie flavor, I wanted to channel my young parenting self and overperform, and I did it. These cookies are soft and chewy, almost fudgy in texture if they're baked properly, and the red velvet is subtle but there. It's a slightly cocoa, slightly tangy flavor that is only enhanced with all the chocolate, white chocolate, and chopped Oreos. Chocolate and red velvet are the perfect pair!

### INSTRUCTIONS

1 Whisk together the cocoa powder, salt, baking soda, and flour in a medium bowl. Set aside.

2 Stir both sugars into the melted butter in a large bowl. You can do this with a mixer or by hand with a wooden spoon or spatula. Mix in the egg, vanilla extract, milk, and vinegar.

3 Slowly stir the dry ingredients into the wet ingredients. Add the red food coloring and stir until combined. Stir in the Oreos and white chocolate chips.

4 Line a cookie sheet with a silicone baking mat or parchment paper. Scoop balls of cookie dough (each about 2 tablespoons) onto the cookie sheet. Spacing doesn't matter when chilling the dough. Chill for 30 minutes.

5 Preheat the oven to 350°F (177°C). Line an additional cookie sheet with silicone baking mats or parchment paper. Place the cookies 2 inches (5 cm) apart on cookie sheets. Bake for 11 to 14 minutes, or until they just lose their glossy sheen. Cool on the cookie sheets for at least 5 minutes before removing to a rack to cool completely.

6 Store in an airtight container for up to 3 days or freeze for up to 3 months.

- 2 tablespoons (10 g) unsweetened cocoa powder
- ½ teaspoon salt
- ½ teaspoon baking soda
- 1½ cups (186 g) all-purpose flour
- ½ cup (113 g) unsalted butter, melted
- ½ cup (100 g) packed brown sugar
- ⅓ cup (67 g) granulated sugar
- 1 large egg
- 1 teaspoon vanilla extract
- 2 teaspoons milk
- 1 teaspoon white vinegar
- 1 teaspoon red food coloring (see Tip)
- 1 cup (90 g) coarsely chopped Oreo cookies (about 8 cookies)
- ½ cup (85 g) white chocolate chips

**Yield:** 20 cookies
**Prep time:** 20 minutes
**Bake time:** 13 minutes

## Tips:

For gel food coloring, use ½ teaspoon.

Have buttermilk in your refrigerator? Omit the milk and vinegar and use 1 tablespoon (15 ml) buttermilk instead!

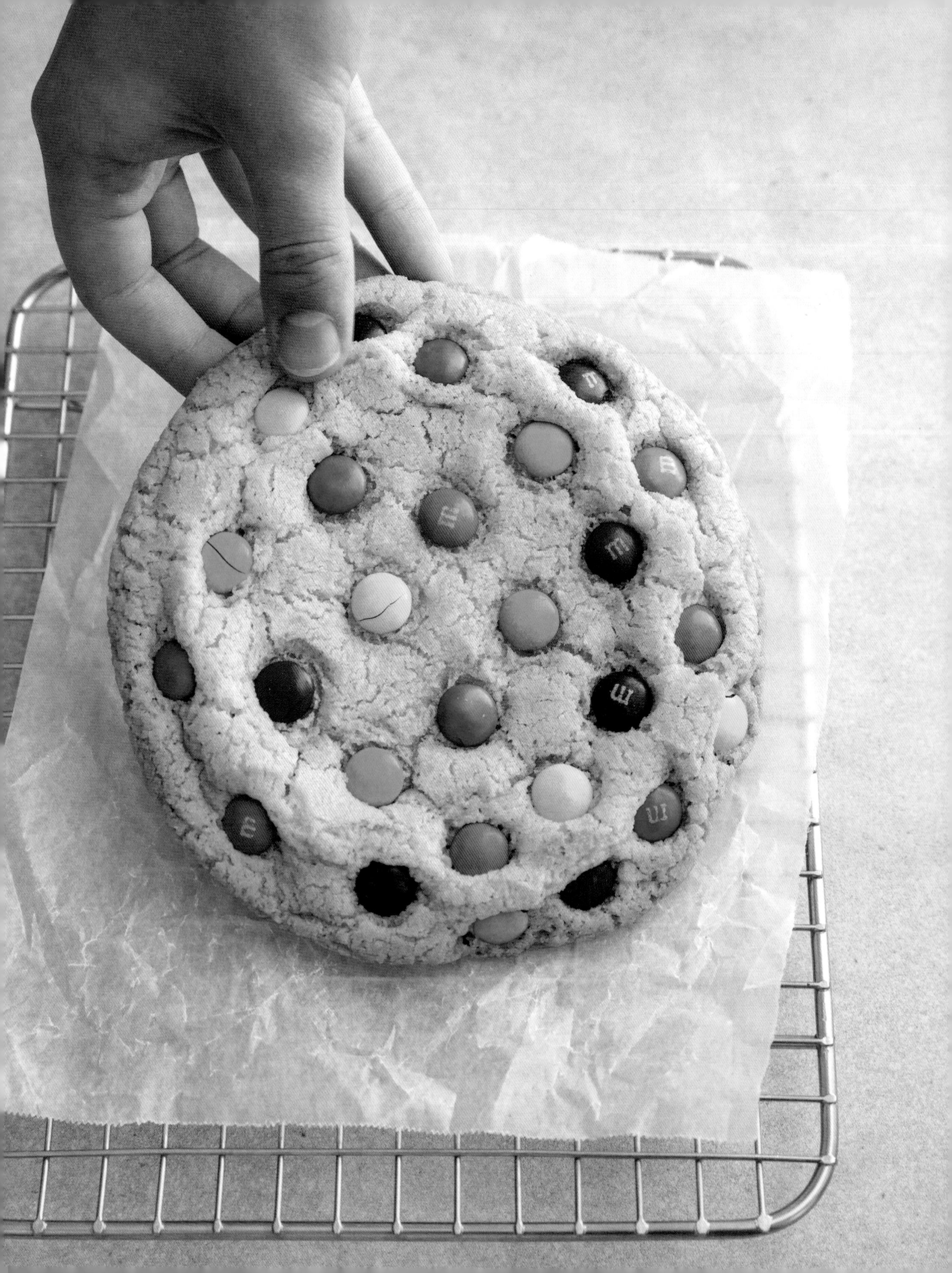

# Giant M&M Cookie

f you ever saw fourteen-year-old Dorothy cruising the Tanforan mall in her overalls and sky-high hair, you probably saw her with a Mrs. Fields M&M Cookie in her hand. I could never get enough of those cookies: crunchy on the outside and soft and chewy on the inside with the perfectly placed M&M's on top. I knew I needed to make one of those cookies in this book, for no other reason than to make the teenager inside me super excited to read it. These cookies are like those mall cookies—but better—and you can make them at home, in your pajamas, no overalls or hairspray needed.

- 3 tablespoons (42 g) unsalted butter, softened
- ¼ cup (50 g) granulated sugar
- 1 large egg yolk
- ¼ teaspoon vanilla extract
- ¼ teaspoon baking soda
- ⅛ teaspoon salt
- ½ cup (62 g) all-purpose flour
- 25 plain M&M's

**Yield:** 1 large cookie
**Prep time:** 20 minutes
**Bake time:** 18 minutes

## INSTRUCTIONS

1   Preheat the oven to 350°F (177°C). Line a cookie sheet with parchment paper or a silicone baking mat.

2   Cream the butter and sugar in a large bowl with an electric mixer until smooth. Mix in the egg yolk and vanilla extract, then mix in the baking soda and salt. Slowly mix in the flour until it forms into a cookie dough. (This may take a few minutes if using a hand mixer.)

3   Form a large ball with the dough and roll it between your palms to make it smooth. Place it in the center of the prepared cookie sheet. Press M&M's on the top close together. (They'll spread out as the cookie spreads.)

4   Bake for 17 to 20 minutes or until golden around the edges and no longer glossy in the center. Cool slightly before removing to eat.

5   Store in an airtight container for up to 3 days.

## Tip:
We love substituting Reese's Pieces in place of the M&M's!

# Lime in the Coconut Cookies

Okay, I totally named this recipe after that song. In fact, I created the recipe because I had the song stuck in my head. I don't even know any of the other words to the song, just that phrase that is in my head constantly! It's just such a great jingle that I transformed the lyrics into cookies. These are soft and crisp, with chewy coconut and a hint of lime flavor. For even more lime, you can add extract, but we like them with just a bit of zest.

## INSTRUCTIONS

1   Preheat the oven to 350°F (177°C). Line cookie sheets with parchment paper or silicone baking mats.

2   Cream the butter and both sugars in the bowl of a stand mixer fitted with the paddle attachment. (You can also use a hand mixer.) Mix in the egg and vanilla extract until smooth. Add the lime juice, zest, baking soda, and salt. Mix until combined. Mix in the flour, and then mix in the coconut.

3   Scoop balls of cookie dough (each about 2 tablespoons) and place 3 inches (8 cm) apart on the prepared cookie sheets. These do spread, so make sure to space them accordingly.

4   Bake for 12 to 15 minutes or until the cookies turn a light golden and are no longer glossy. Cool for 5 minutes on the cookie sheets before transferring to a rack to cool completely. Store in an airtight container for up to 4 days or freeze for up to a month.

- ½ cup (113 g) unsalted butter, softened
- ½ cup (100 g) packed brown sugar
- ½ cup (100 g) granulated sugar
- 1 large egg
- 1 teaspoon vanilla extract
- 1 tablespoon (15 ml) lime juice (from 1 lime)
- Zest of 2 limes
- ½ teaspoon baking soda
- ¼ teaspoon salt
- 1¼ cups (155 g) all-purpose flour
- 1½ cups (180 g) shredded sweetened coconut

**Yield:** 21 cookies
**Prep time:** 20 minutes
**Bake time:** 13 minutes

## Tip:

For even more lime flavor, add ½ teaspoon lime extract (or even lemon extract).

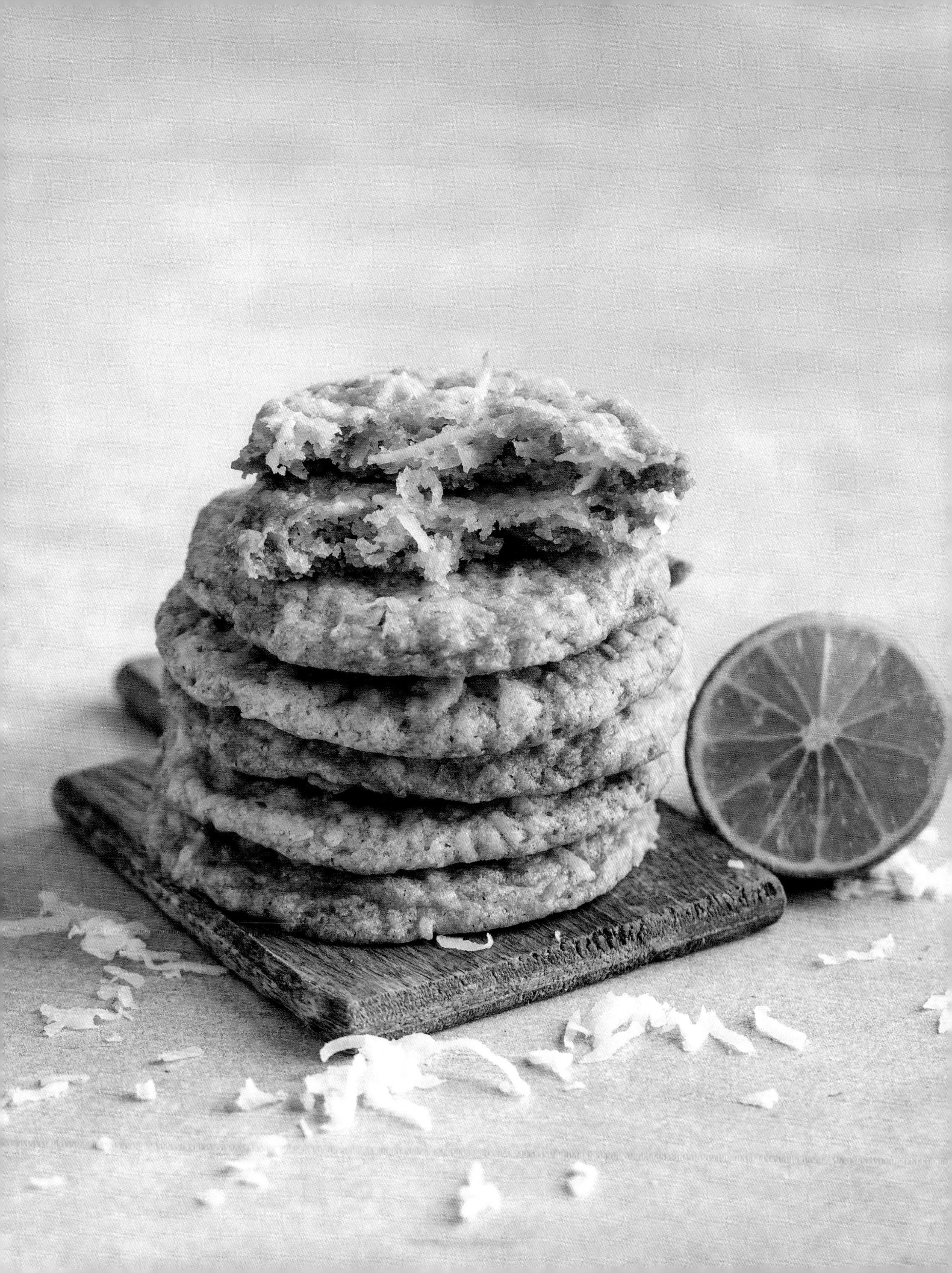

# Chocolate Candy Cane Cookies

*I* had to include a candy cane recipe in this book because I love peppermint, especially when it's mixed with chocolate. I'm not a huge fan of eating plain candy canes, but when you add them to chocolate (such as for peppermint bark), I can eat my weight in them. This is my cookie version of peppermint bark: a soft chocolate peppermint cookie dipped in chocolate and coated with crushed candy canes. You may not have peppermint extract lying around, but it's worth buying to add a little extra flavor. (Just be sure to buy peppermint and not mint extract—the plain mint tastes more like toothpaste.) And let's be honest, you probably have some candy canes left over from Christmas you can use . . . or is that just me?

## INSTRUCTIONS

1   Place the baking chocolate in a small microwave-safe bowl. Heat on 50 percent power in 30-second increments, stirring between each, until melted and smooth. Set aside to cool while mixing the cookie dough.

2   Whisk the flour, cocoa powder, baking soda, and salt in a medium bowl. Set aside.

3   Cream the butter and both sugars with an electric mixer in a large bowl until fluffy, 2 to 3 minutes. Add the vanilla extract, peppermint extract, and eggs, and mix until smooth.

4   Mix the dry ingredients into the wet ingredients until a cookie dough forms. Then mix in the chocolate chips.

5   Scoop balls of cookie dough (each about 2 tablespoons) onto a cookie sheet lined with parchment paper. There is no need to space them when chilling the dough. Chill the dough for at least 1 hour.

6   Preheat the oven to 350°F (177°C). Line 2 cookie sheets with parchment paper or silicone baking mats. Place the cookies 3 inches (8 cm) apart on the prepared cookie sheets. Bake for 11 to 15 minutes, or until they just lose their glossy sheen. Cool for at least 5 minutes on the cookie sheets before removing to a rack to cool completely before dipping.

7   Unwrap the candy canes and place them in a gallon-sized resealable bag. Seal the bag all but 1 inch (2.5 cm). Place the bag on a cutting board or cookie sheet and bang with a rolling pin to crush the candy canes. (It's important to put the bag on something because little holes will form in the bag from the broken candy canes.) Alternatively, you can crush them in a food processor. Set aside.

- 2 ounces (57 g) semi-sweet baking chocolate
- 2¼ cups (273 g) all-purpose flour
- 2 tablespoons (10 g) unsweetened cocoa powder
- 1 teaspoon baking soda
- ½ teaspoon salt
- 1 cup (226 g) unsalted butter, softened
- 1 cup (200 g) packed brown sugar
- ½ cup (100 g) granulated sugar
- 1 teaspoon vanilla extract
- ½ teaspoon peppermint extract
- 2 large eggs
- 1½ cups (255 g) semi-sweet chocolate chips
- 5 candy canes
- 12 ounces (340 g) white or chocolate candy melts

**Yield:** 30 cookies
**Prep time:** 1 hour
**Chill time:** 1 hour
**Bake time:** 13 minutes

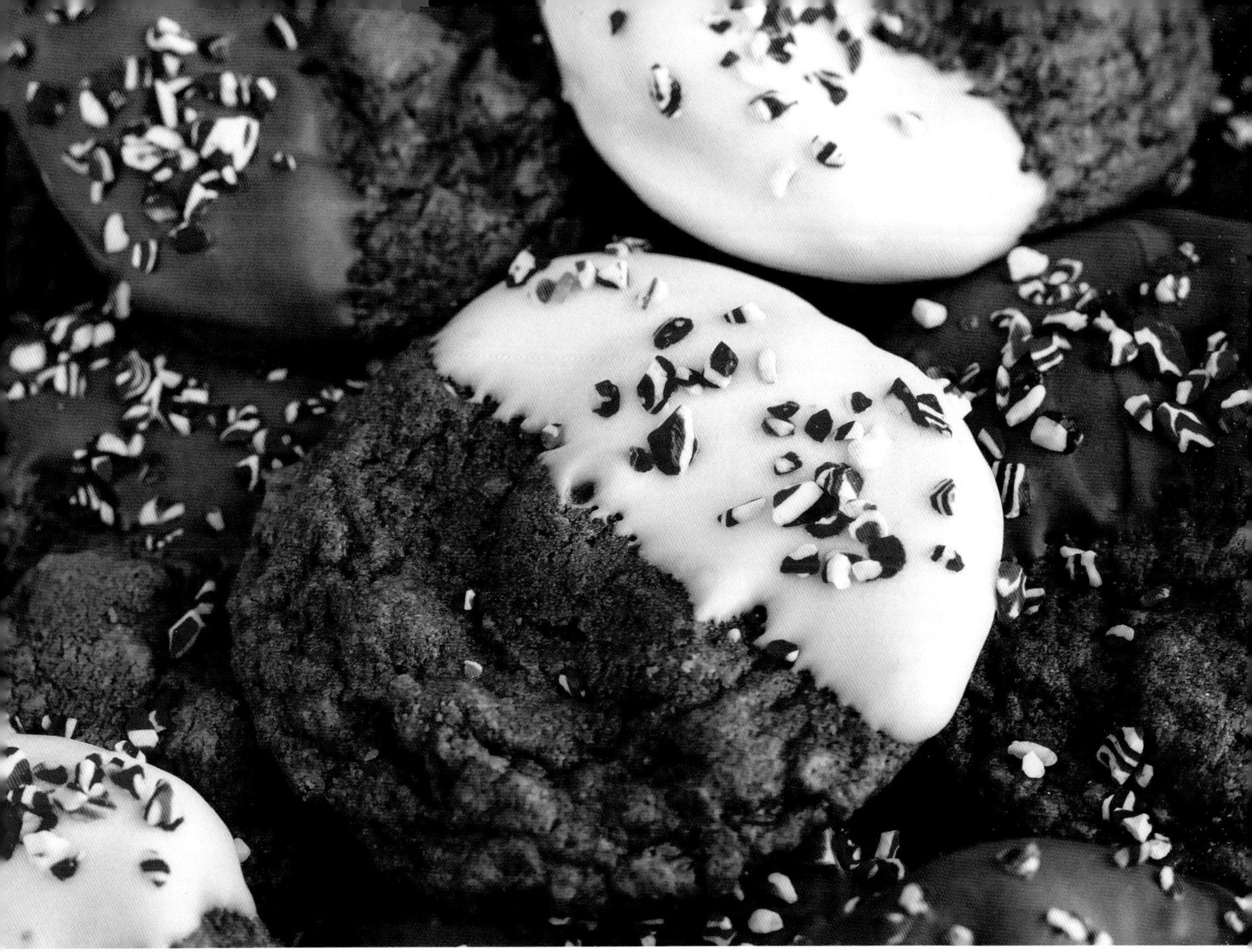

8 Heat the candy melts in a microwave-safe bowl on 50 percent power in 30-second increments, stirring between each, until they are melted and smooth (about 2 to 3 minutes). Line a cookie sheet with parchment paper.

9 Dip half of each cookie in the melted candy and lay them on the prepared cookie sheet. Sprinkle with broken candy cane pieces. Let set (or you can also chill them in the refrigerator to set the chocolate).

10 Store in an airtight container for up to 3 days or freeze for up to a month.

## Tip:

During the holidays you can often find crushed candy cane pieces sold in bags (like chocolate chips) at grocery stores with the holiday baking supplies. You'll need about ½ cup (84 g) of these pieces to sprinkle over the cookies.

# Raspberry Almond Spirals

While my normal flavor profile is that of a teenager (chips, peanut butter cups, M&M's, cookie dough), I sometimes crave more refined flavors. That's how I see these: the grown-up cookie parent to my regular go-to of Oreos stuffed in anything. There's something adult about pairing raspberry and almond together, like I'm sitting at a bistro in Paris ordering a delicate flaky croissant and espresso. These cookies are perfect in their own way with a soft but crunchy almond-flavored cookie dough filled with jam. They are perfect on holiday platters but also delicious dusted with powdered sugar, served with coffee or tea. I think the child inside you will even love them too!

## INSTRUCTIONS

1 Place the almonds in a small frying pan and cook over low heat, stirring often, never walking away from the pan, until they are lightly toasted. This will take just a few minutes. As soon as they start to get lightly golden, remove from the heat to a cutting board to cool until you can easily chop them. Finely chop the almonds and then place them in a small bowl with the 1 tablespoon (12 g) brown sugar, and stir to combine. Set aside. Take your jam out of the refrigerator to come to room temperature while you make the cookie dough.

2 Cream the butter, granulated sugar, and ¼ cup (50 g) brown sugar in a large bowl using an electric mixer. Mix until smooth and fluffy; then mix in the egg, almond extract, and salt. Slowly mix in the flour until smooth.

3 Divide the dough in half. Place a large sheet of waxed or parchment paper on your work surface. Place half the dough on the paper and flatten to about 1 inch (2.5 cm) thick with your hands. Place a second layer of wax or parchment paper on top and use a rolling pin to roll the dough into a 9- to 10-inch (23 to 25 cm) square.

4 Remove the top sheet of parchment paper. Spread half the jam over the dough, leaving a ¼-inch (6 mm) edge at the top and bottom. Sprinkle the top evenly with half the almond mixture. Roll up the dough, using the bottom sheet of paper to help you get a tight spiral.

5 Repeat with the second half of dough. Wrap each spiral in plastic wrap and chill until firm, at least 1 hour.

6 Preheat the oven to 375°F (191°C). Line 2 cookie sheets with parchment paper or silicone baking mats.

### For the Filling

- ½ cup (46 g) sliced almonds
- 1 tablespoon (12 g) packed brown sugar
- 2 tablespoons (40 g) raspberry jam

### For the Cookie Dough

- ½ cup (113 g) unsalted butter, softened
- ⅔ cup (134 g) granulated sugar
- ¼ cup (50 g) packed brown sugar
- 1 large egg
- ½ teaspoon almond extract
- ¼ teaspoon salt
- 2 cups (248 g) all-purpose flour

**Yield:** 38 cookies
**Prep time:** 45 minutes
**Chill time:** 1 hour
**Bake time:** 13 minutes

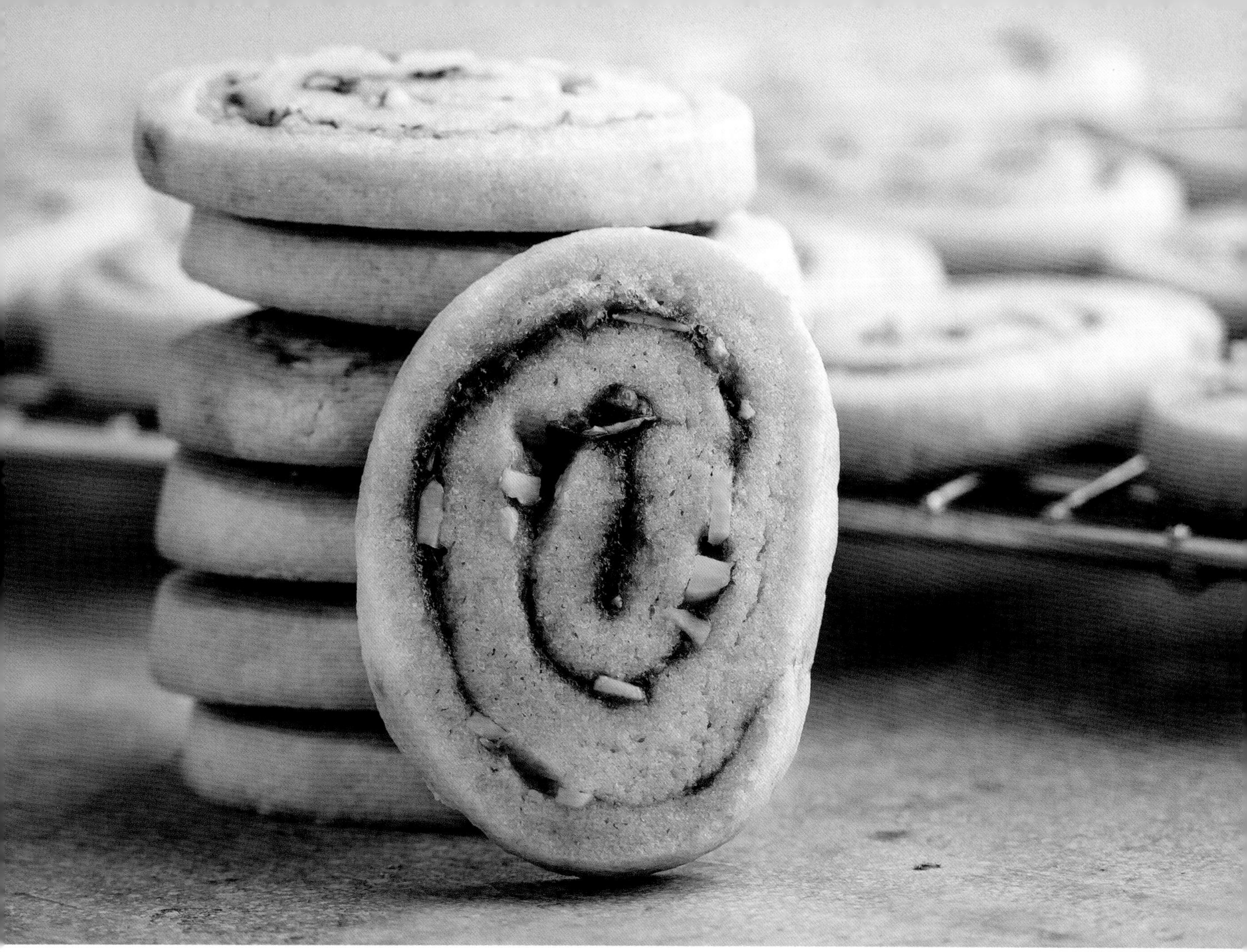

7 Slice the dough logs into ¼-inch (6 mm) thick cookies. Place the cookies 2 inches (5 cm) apart on the prepared cookie sheets. Bake for 11 to 15 minutes, until the bottoms just start to turn golden. Cool for 5 minutes on the cookie sheets before removing to a rack to cool.

8 Store in an airtight container for up to 3 days. Can be frozen for up to 2 months.

**Tip:**

If you don't have almond extract, you can substitute vanilla or even hazelnut extract.

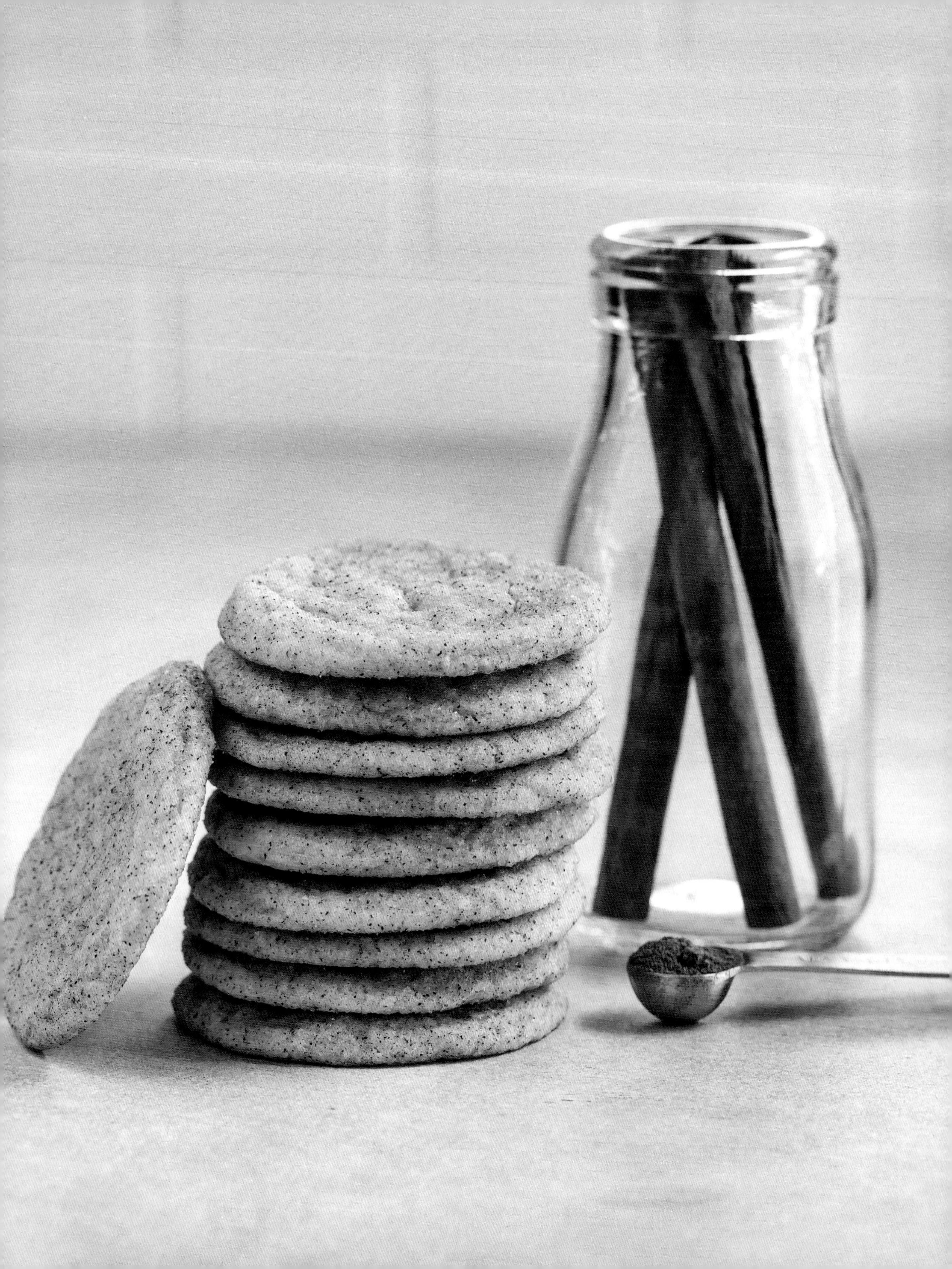

# Pumpkin Spice Snickerdoodles

**H**ow a food blogger knows it's fall: Pumpkin spice *all the things*. There are two camps of bloggers: the pumpkin-in-August ones and the not-until-October ones. Can you guess to which camp I belong? I'm team *#PumpkinInAugust* all the way! I think that's because summer where I live is so hot and miserable that pumpkin means fall, which means maybe soon I can wear jeans and closed-toe shoes again. I break out the pumpkin spice mix in July to have content ready and the second August 1 hits, I start publishing. I always start with pumpkin spice recipes first because people are looking forward to the return of the Starbucks PSL. These snickerdoodles have no pumpkin in them—just warm pumpkin spice. They're pure fall in a bite!

## INSTRUCTIONS

1   Preheat the oven to 350°F (177°C). Line 2 cookie sheets with parchment paper.

2   Cream the butter and 1 cup (200 g) granulated sugar using a stand or a hand mixer until fluffy. Mix in the egg and vanilla extract; then mix in the baking soda, cream of tartar, 1 teaspoon pumpkin pie spice, and salt. Slowly mix in the flour until the dough is combined.

3   Place ¼ cup (50 g) granulated sugar and 2 teaspoons pumpkin pie spice in a small bowl. Scoop balls of cookie dough (each about 1 tablespoon) and roll them in the spiced sugar mixture and place on the cookie sheets, 2 inches (5 cm) apart.

4   Bake for 10 to 13 minutes or until they are cracked on the tops and just lose their glossy sheen. Err on the side of underbaked for best results.

5   Store in an airtight container for up to 3 days or freeze for up to a month.

### For the Cookies

- ¾ cup (170 g) unsalted butter, softened
- 1 cup (200 g) granulated sugar
- 1 large egg
- 1 teaspoon vanilla extract
- 1 teaspoon baking soda
- 2 teaspoons cream of tartar
- 1 teaspoon pumpkin pie spice
- ½ teaspoon salt
- 2 cups (248 g) all-purpose flour

### For the Coating

- ¼ cup (50 g) granulated sugar
- 2 teaspoons ground pumpkin pie spice

**Yield:** 33 cookies
**Prep time:** 25 minutes
**Bake time:** 12 minutes

*Tip:*

Don't have the pumpkin pie spice? Make your own! Make 1 teaspoon of pumpkin pie spice by mixing ½ teaspoon cinnamon, ¼ teaspoon ground ginger, and ⅛ teaspoon each nutmeg and allspice.

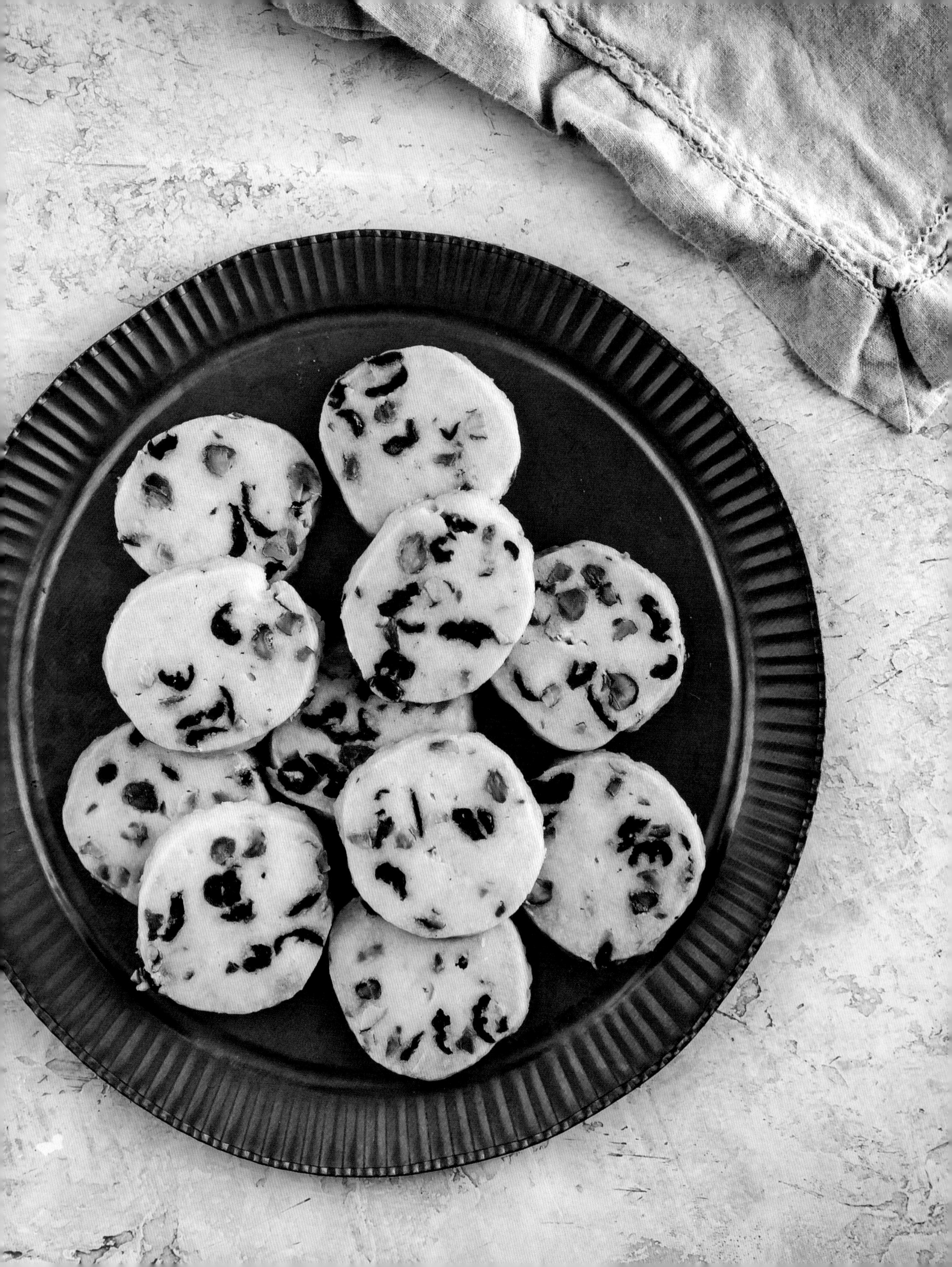

# Slice and Bake Cranberry Pistachio Shortbread

istachios are one of my favorite nuts—they're so easy for snacking. As you may have gathered from some of the other stories I've told, I grew up a pretty picky eater and, as with many other ingredients in this book, I hadn't tasted dried cranberries nor pistachios until I started blogging. Now, I love eating them together (even making my own trail mix and adding white chocolate chips). While the color combination makes these the perfect Christmas cookie, they're good any time of the year: The salty/sweet/chewy/tart combination of the pistachios and cranberries with the rich shortbread cookie are perfect just as a quick treat for a simple party. Plus, making slice and bake cookies feels like cheating because they're just so easy!

- 1 cup (226 g) unsalted butter, softened
- ⅔ cup (76 g) powdered sugar
- ½ teaspoon vanilla extract
- ⅛ teaspoon salt
- 2 cups (248 g) all-purpose flour
- ½ cup (70 g) roughly chopped roasted salted pistachios
- ½ cup (71 g) dried cranberries

**Yield:** 38 cookies
**Prep time:** 30 minutes
**Chill time:** 2 hours
**Bake time:** 16 minutes

## INSTRUCTIONS

1   In a large bowl with a hand or a stand mixer, cream the butter and powdered sugar until smooth.

2   Add the vanilla extract and salt, then mix until smooth.

3   Add the flour, 1 cup (124 g) at a time, mixing between each addition until completely incorporated. Stir in the pistachios and cranberries.

4   Divide the dough in half. Roll each half into a log 5 inches (13 cm) long and wrap them with plastic wrap. Chill for at least 2 hours or overnight.

5   Preheat the oven to 350°F (177°C). Line cookie sheets with parchment paper or silicone baking mats.

6   Slice the logs into ¼-inch (6 mm) cookies and place on the prepared cookie sheets. These don't spread, so you only need to space them about 1 inch (2.5 cm) apart.

7   Bake for 15 to 18 minutes or until the edges are lightly golden. Cool for at least 5 minutes on the cookie sheets before removing to a rack to cool completely.

8   Store in an airtight container for up to 4 days or freeze for up to a week.

## Tip:

Reduce both the pistachio and cranberry amount to ⅓ cup (47 g) and add ¼ cup (43 g) white chocolate chips for an extra flavorful cookie.

# Churro Cookies

Sandra, one of my dearest friends, helped me come up with some of the ideas for this book. I sent her my list and asked what was missing and she mentioned that her husband absolutely *loves* the Churro Cookies from a local cookie shop. Having tasted those cookies—ginormous soft and pillowy cinnamon sugar cookies topped with a cinnamon buttercream—I knew they *had* to be in the book. I set out to make a copycat version and this is it: a soft and chewy cinnamon cookie that's not a snickerdoodle but has a similar texture. The cinnamon frosting isn't required (the cookies are good plain) but, oh my goodness, they are amazing paired together. I may have eaten three in one sitting when I first made them.

## INSTRUCTIONS

1   Preheat the oven to 350°F (177°C). Line 2 cookie sheets with parchment paper or silicone baking mats.

2   Cream the butter, brown sugar, and ⅓ cup (67 g) granulated sugar in a large bowl with an electric mixer until fluffy. Mix in the egg and vanilla extract. Add the baking soda, salt, and cornstarch and mix until combined. Then slowly mix in the flour.

3   If your dough is too soft to roll, chill for 15 minutes before continuing.

4   Place ¼ cup (50 g) granulated sugar and cinnamon in a small bowl and stir to combine.

5   Scoop balls of cookie dough (each about 1 tablespoon) and roll them between your palms. Roll the balls in the cinnamon sugar and place 2 inches (5 cm) apart on your cookie sheet. These do spread, so make sure to space them accordingly.

6   Bake for 10 to 13 minutes, or until they are lightly golden and have lost their glossy sheen. Cool completely before frosting.

7   To make the frosting, beat the butter in a large bowl with an electric mixer until smooth. Slowly mix in the powdered sugar until crumbly; then mix in the salt, vanilla extract, and cinnamon. Add 1 tablespoon milk and mix until smooth, adding more milk as desired for spreadable consistency. (See Frosting Tips, page 12.)

8   You can frost the cookies any way you like, but to decorate them as shown, place the frosting in a bag fitted with an open star tip (such as Wilton No. 199). Pipe the frosting in a round swirl motion all over the top of the cookie.

### For the Cookies

- ½ cup (113 g) unsalted butter, softened
- ½ cup (100 g) packed brown sugar
- ⅓ cup (67 g) granulated sugar
- 1 large egg
- 1 teaspoon vanilla extract
- ½ teaspoon baking soda
- ¼ teaspoon salt
- 1 teaspoon cornstarch
- 1½ cups (186 g) all-purpose flour

### For the Coating

- ¼ cup (50 g) granulated sugar
- 1 teaspoon cinnamon

### For the Frosting

- ¾ cup (170 g) unsalted butter, softened
- 3 cups (340 g) powdered sugar
- ¼ teaspoon salt
- 1 teaspoon vanilla extract
- 1 tablespoon (7 g) ground cinnamon
- 1 to 3 tablespoons (15 to 45 ml) milk

**Yield:** 26 cookies
**Prep time:** 45 minutes
**Bake time:** 12 minutes

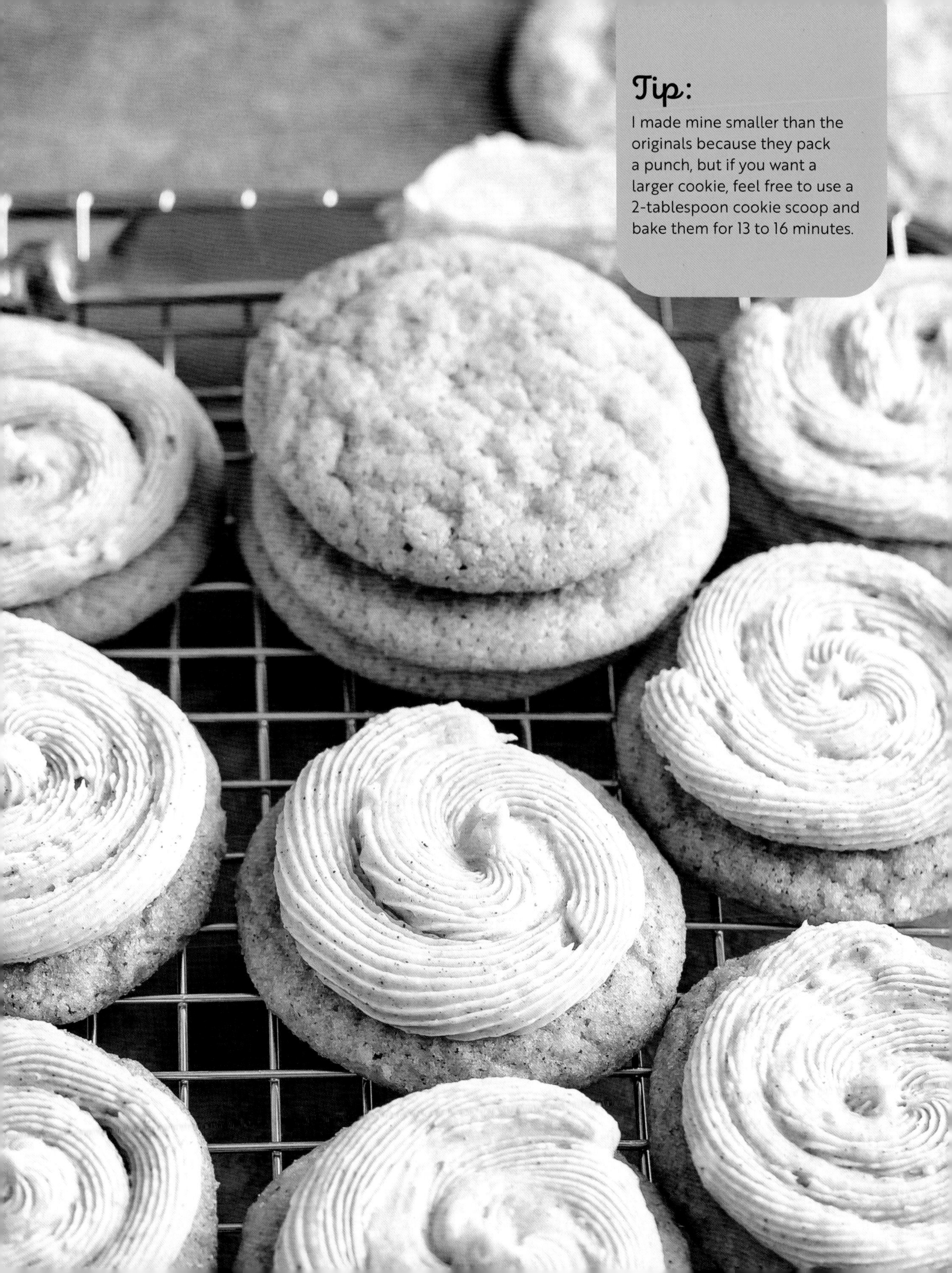

## Tip:

I made mine smaller than the originals because they pack a punch, but if you want a larger cookie, feel free to use a 2-tablespoon cookie scoop and bake them for 13 to 16 minutes.

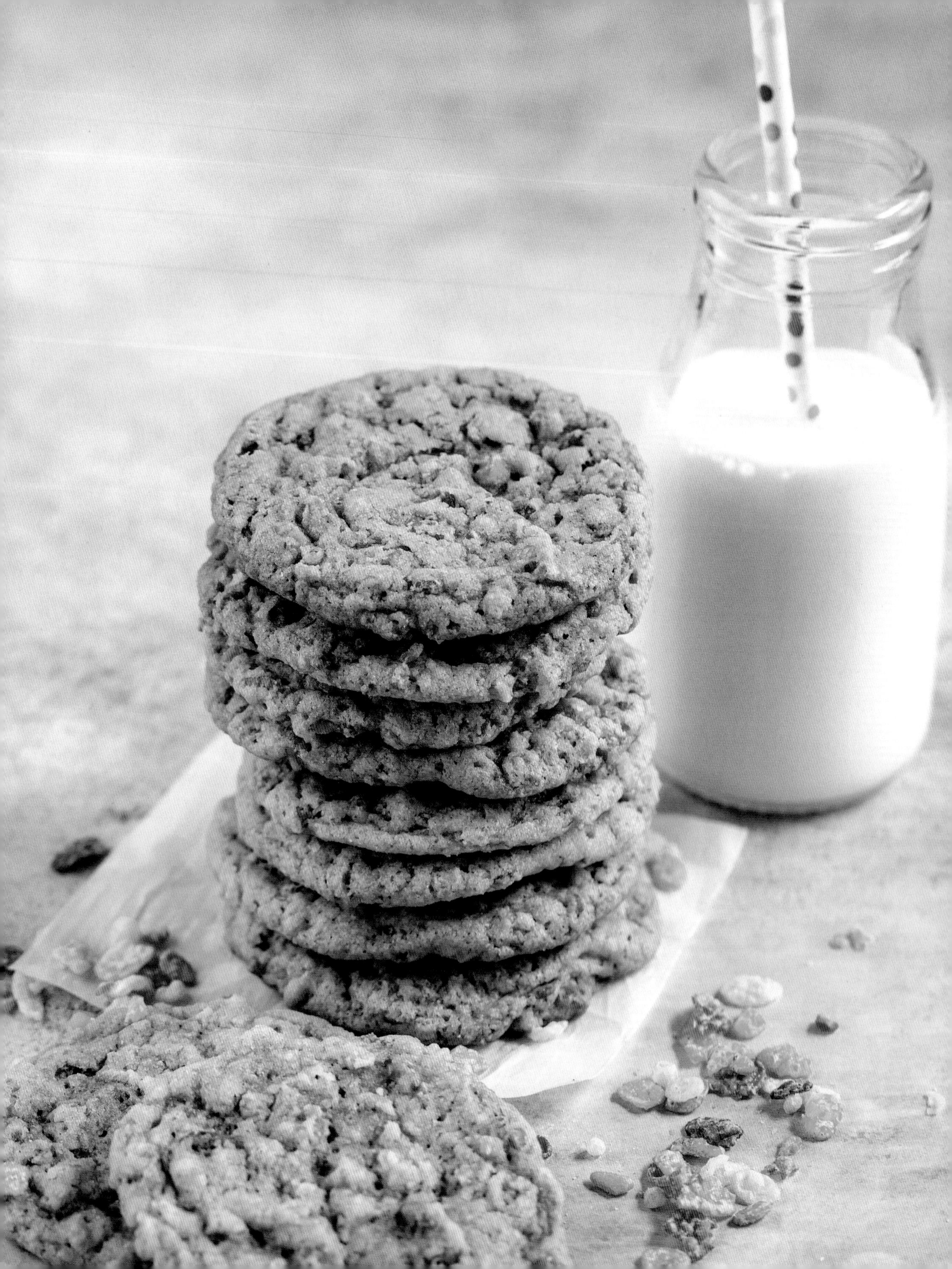

# Fruity Pebble Cookies

$\mathcal{I}$ have a cookie containing Fruity Pebbles on my blog, but I wanted something a bit different for this book. The result was exactly what I'd hoped: a flatter, crackly topped cookie with a crunchy exterior and soft interior. The Fruity Pebbles add so much flavor to these cookies; if you're looking for a way to use up that cereal without eating handfuls straight from the box, make these cookies. I promise you'll love them!

**INSTRUCTIONS**

1. Preheat the oven to 350°F (177°C). Line cookie sheets with parchment paper or silicone baking mats.

2. Cream the butter and both sugars in the bowl of a stand mixer fitted with the paddle attachment. (You can also use a hand mixer.) Mix in the egg and vanilla extract until smooth. Add the baking soda , salt, and cornstarch. Mix until combined. Mix in the flour, then mix in the Fruity Pebbles. The mixer will kind of crush some of the cereal into the dough, which is what we want.

3. Scoop balls of cookie dough (each about 2 tablespoons) and place 3 inches (8 cm) apart on the prepared cookie sheets. These do spread, so make sure to space them accordingly.

4. Bake for 12 to 15 minutes or until the cookies turn a light golden and are no longer glossy. Cool for 5 minutes on the cookie sheets before transferring to a rack to cool completely. Store in an airtight container for up to 4 days or freeze for up to a month.

- ½ cup (113 g) unsalted butter, softened
- ⅔ cup (134 g) packed brown sugar
- ⅓ cup (67 g) granulated sugar
- 1 large egg
- 1 teaspoon vanilla extract
- ½ teaspoon baking soda
- ¼ teaspoon salt
- 1 teaspoon cornstarch
- 1¼ cups (155 g) all-purpose flour
- 2 cups (89 g) Fruity Pebbles

**Yield:** 21 cookies
**Prep time:** 20 minutes
**Bake time:** 13 minutes

## Tip:

You can use any kind of cereal similar to Fruity Pebbles. We also love these with Cocoa Pebbles!

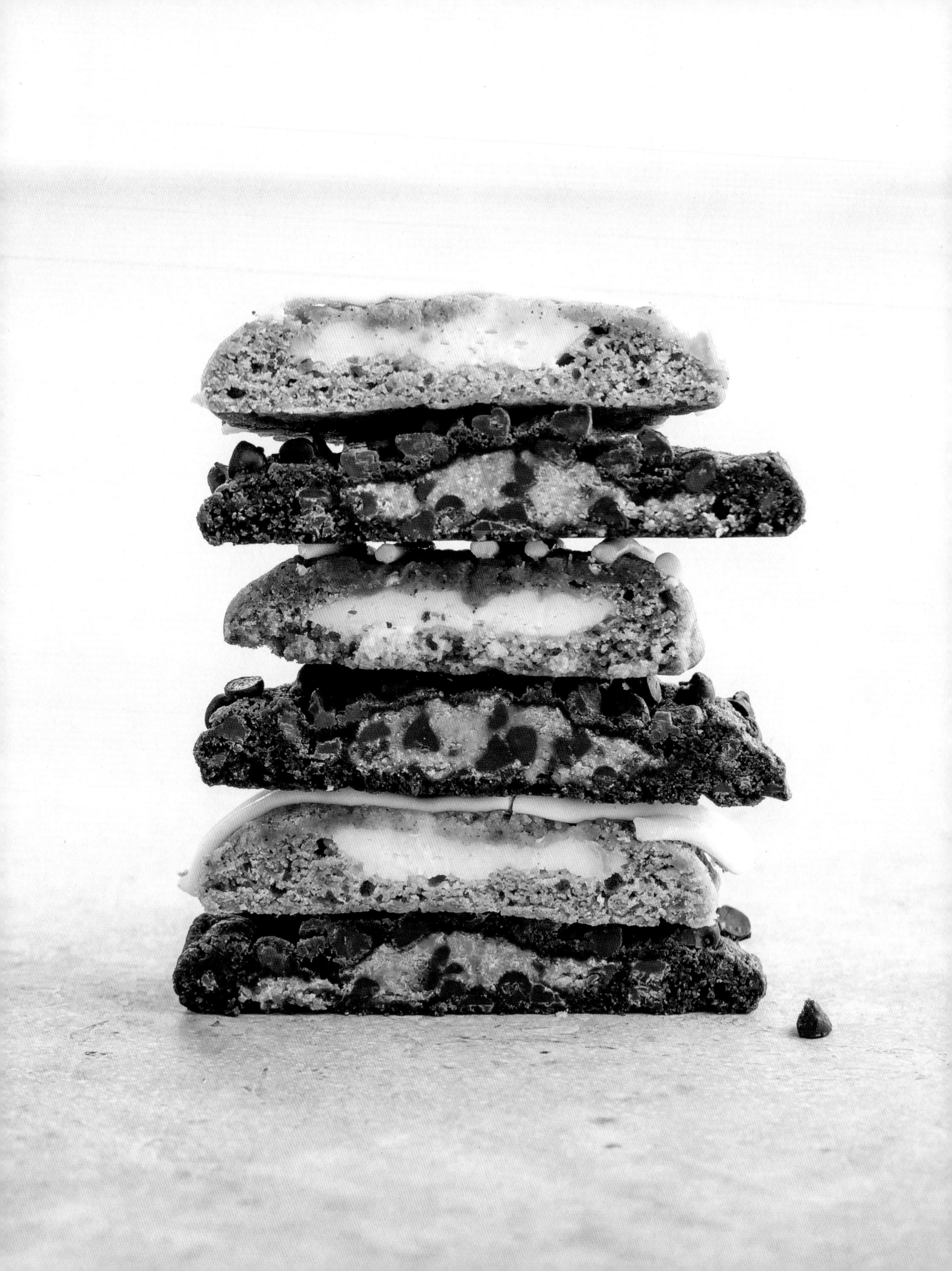

# Stuffed and Sandwiched

I can't think of any situation in which I wouldn't want an excuse to eat a stuffed or sandwiched cookie: You get *more* cookie for the price of one! With these cookies you can really play with flavor combinations: ginger and salted caramel, carrot cake and cheesecake, cookies and . . . cookies. The cookies in this chapter are big, bold, and in charge: They're not for the faint of heart!

Tips for making the cookies in this chapter:

· **Stuffing things inside cookies is a messy job, but someone has to do it.** Whether you're wrapping Nutella into the Giant Stuffed Nutella Cookie (see page 160) or rolling cheesecake into the centers of the Stuffed Carrot Cake Cookies (see page 172), expect that your hands will get a little messy. To avoid sticky hands, keep a bit of water in a small bowl nearby so you can dampen your hands as you work. This will help the dough not stick (as much).

· **Stuffed cookies are also big!** The more things you add into each one, the bigger they get, which is why some of the recipes in this chapter have a small yield.

· **When making sandwich cookies, be sure to use the 1-tablespoon cookie scoop.** After all, you'll be sandwiching two cookies together: Larger cookies equal bigger sandwiches!

· **Refer back to the Thumbprint Tips (see page 168) when making the thumbprints in this chapter.** I find a ¼ teaspoon works best for the small bite-sized cookies.

# Chocolate Marshmallow Sandwich Cookies

These cookies are my take on a homemade Oreo but with a fluffier filling. The filling is actually homemade marshmallow frosting, which is like marshmallow fluff with less stickiness. I learned how to make meringue several years ago when I visited the Duncan Hines test kitchen as one of their ambassadors. It was the first blogging trip I'd ever been on, and I thought it was so cool to see the inner workings of the kitchens. The head chef taught us to make two things: homemade meringue and pie crust from cake mix. I didn't much love the pie crust, but I have been making the meringue frosting ever since! With a candy thermometer or instant-read thermometer (whichever you have), it's so easy to do. In a pinch you can substitute marshmallow fluff for the filling of the cookies, but try making the homemade frosting—it's also fantastic toasted with a blowtorch, like a s'more!

## MAKE THE COOKIES

1   Preheat the oven to 350°F (177°C). Line cookie sheets with parchment paper or silicone baking mats.

2   In the bowl of an electric mixer fitted with the paddle attachment, cream the butter and both sugars. Mix in the egg and vanilla extract and mix until smooth.

3   In a medium bowl, whisk together the cocoa powder, baking soda, salt, and flour. Add the dry ingredients to the wet ingredients and mix until combined.

4   Scoop balls of cookie dough (each about 1 tablespoon) and place 3 inches (8 cm) apart on prepared cookie sheets. Bake for 6 to 9 minutes until they just lose their glossy sheen. Err on the side of underdone for these cookies; they taste better that way. Let cool completely before filling and making the sandwiches.

## MAKE THE FILLING

1   Fill a saucepan with about 2 to 3 inches (5 to 8 cm) of water. Bring to a boil. Find a bowl that will fit on top of the pan without touching the water. (I like to use a glass bowl over a 2-quart saucepan.)

2   Whisk the egg whites, sugar, and cream of tartar in the bowl. Place it on top of the pan holding the boiling water (over medium-high heat).

3   Whisk constantly for about 2 to 3 minutes, until the mixture reaches about 140°F (60°C).

### For the Cookies

- ½ cup (113 g) unsalted butter, softened
- ⅔ cup (134 g) packed brown sugar
- ¼ cup (50 g) granulated sugar
- 1 large egg
- 1 teaspoon vanilla extract
- ¼ cup (20 g) Hershey's Special Dark cocoa powder
- ½ teaspoon baking soda
- ¼ teaspoon salt
- 1⅓ cups (165 g) all-purpose flour

### For the Filling

- 2 large egg whites
- ⅓ cup (67 g) granulated sugar
- ⅛ teaspoon cream of tartar
- ½ teaspoon vanilla extract

**Yield:** 15 cookie sandwiches
**Prep time:** 30 minutes
**Bake time:** 7 minutes

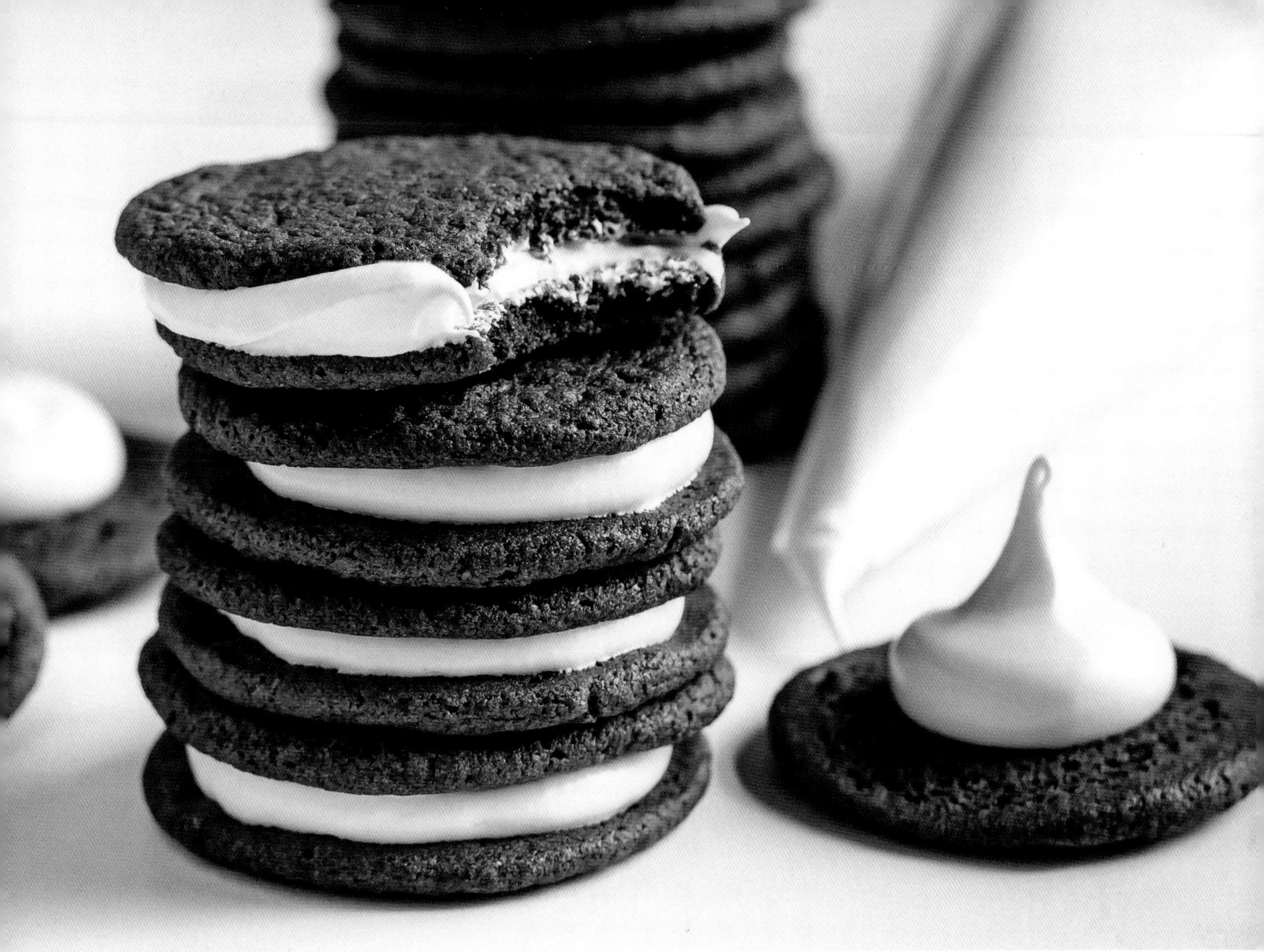

4 Immediately transfer the mixture to a stand mixer fitted with a whisk attachment. Beat at high speed until stiff peaks form, about 8 to 12 minutes depending on your mixer, adding the vanilla extract during the last minute or so of mixing.

**ASSEMBLE THE COOKIES**

1 Place the filling in a piping bag and cut off the tip. Place a dollop of filling on the bottom of a cookie and sandwich it with a second cookie.

2 Store the cookies in an airtight container for up to 3 days. The meringue filling is best eaten within 2 days. Unfilled cookies can be frozen for up to 3 months.

**Tip:**

Can't find the Special Dark cocoa powder? You can substitute regular unsweetened cocoa.

# Chocolate Caramel Pecan Cookies

I remember one Valentine's Day my dad got my mom a huge heart-shaped box of Turtles from the grocery store. Now, some women would roll their eyes at grocery store candy, but not my mom, because Turtles were her favorite. Turtles are a caramel pecan candy covered in chocolate (they look like turtles, hence the name). I don't know if she let me have one of them or not (I'm thinking not, ha!). Caramel pecan anything is her favorite, and these cookies are a take on those candies: a chocolate cookie base filled with chopped pecans and stuffed with a Rolo. If you can't find Rolo candies, you can use any brand of chocolate-covered caramels or, in a pinch, unwrapped caramel squares. Chocolate, pecan, caramel—I can see why she loved them so much!

## INSTRUCTIONS

1   Stir together the butter and both sugars until smooth and combined. You can do this by hand or use a mixer.

2   Stir in the egg, vanilla extract, salt, and baking soda; then stir in the cocoa. Add the flour and stir carefully until combined and smooth. Stir in the chopped pecans.

3   Scoop balls of cookie dough (each about 2 tablespoons) and place on a parchment paper–lined cookie sheet. Spacing doesn't matter; we are chilling the dough. Chill the dough for 30 minutes.

4   Preheat the oven to 350°F (177°C). Line 2 cookie sheets with parchment paper or silicone baking mats.

5   Press one chocolate caramel candy in the center of each cookie dough ball and roll between your palms to completely coat.

6   Place the cookies 2 inches (5 cm) apart on cookie sheets and bake for 12 to 15 minutes, or until they are no longer glossy.

7   Cool slightly on the cookie sheets before removing. Store in an airtight container for up to 3 days or freeze for up to a month.

- ½ cup (113 g) unsalted butter, melted
- ⅓ cup (67 g) granulated sugar
- ½ cup (100 g) packed brown sugar
- 1 large egg
- 1 teaspoon vanilla extract
- ½ teaspoon salt
- ½ teaspoon baking soda
- ¼ cup (20 g) unsweetened cocoa powder
- 1⅓ cups (165 g) all-purpose flour
- 1 cup (110 g) pecan halves, chopped
- 18 chocolate-covered caramel candies (such as Rolos), unwrapped

**Yield:** 18 cookies
**Prep time:** 30 minutes
**Chill time:** 30 minutes
**Bake time:** 14 minutes

## Tip:

If you can't find Rolos or a similar candy, feel free to use unwrapped caramel squares. Just know that they'll be a bit harder in the cookie (those candies are chewier than the chocolate-covered caramels).

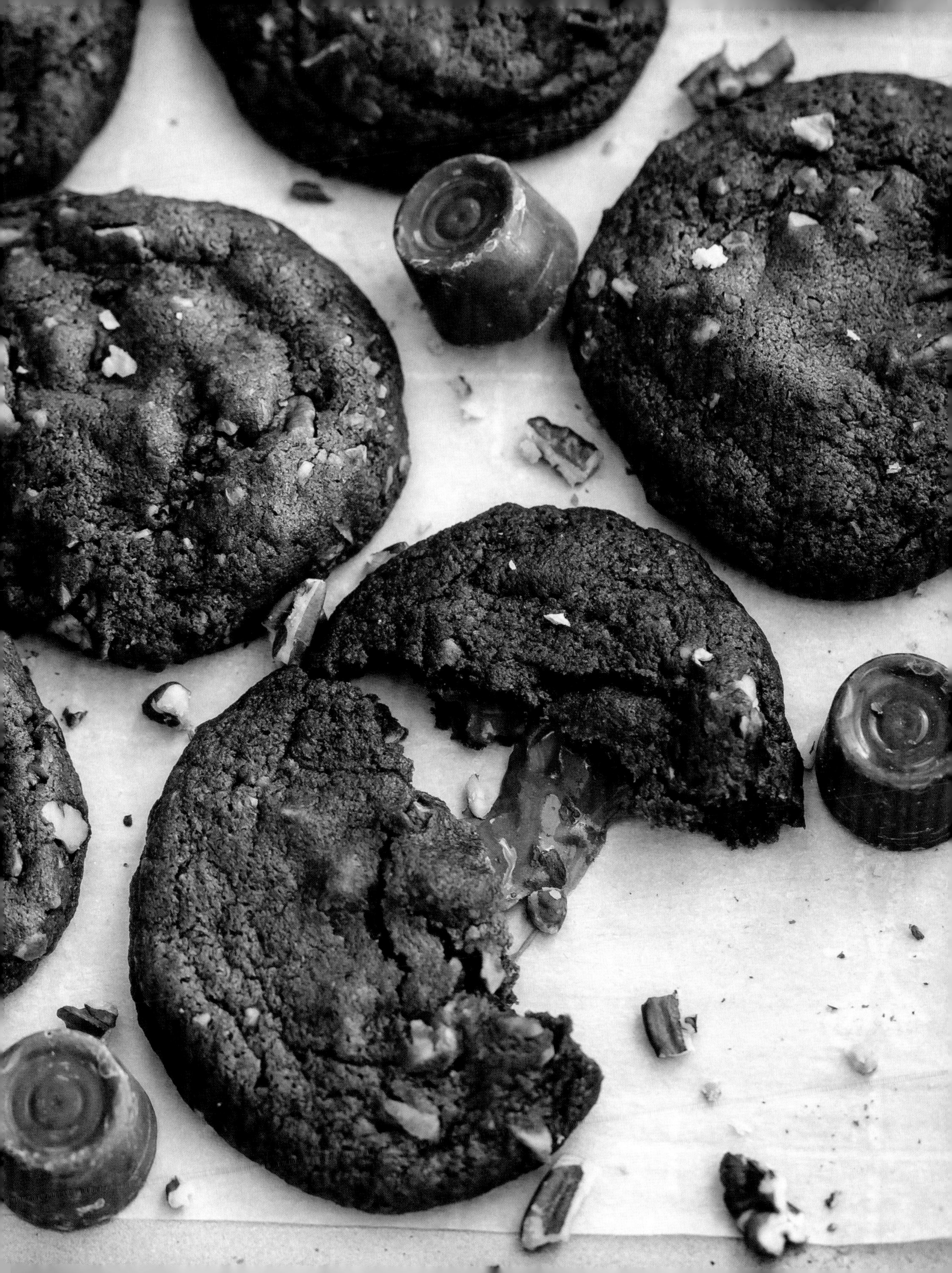

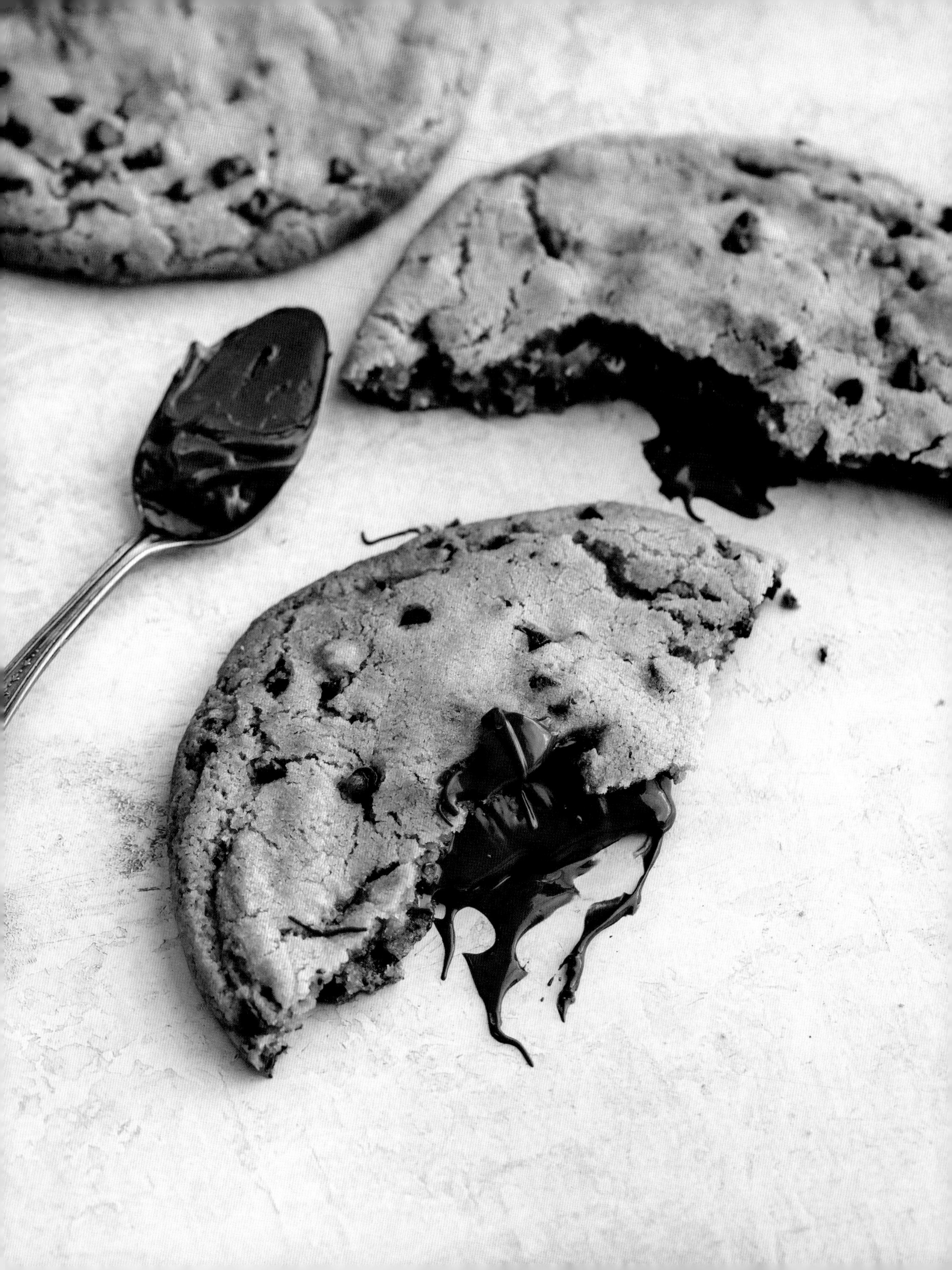

# Giant Stuffed Nutella Cookie

D o you ever have those days where you just cannot make up your mind? Getting dressed, eating breakfast, working out. All the decisions normally so easy and effortless now make you feel like a confused teenager just willing your mom to come and tell you what to do. I felt that way so much of the time when coming up with recipes for this book. I would say I had baker's block, but that wouldn't be true: I had way, way, way too many ideas. The options for stuffed cookies are endless, paired with the options for the actual cookie. Infinite possibilities? I think I went through them all. So many times, I wanted to take out the dual personality that is my baker self and give her a strong slap. "Make up your mind, baker self!" I would have yelled at her. "Make a choice!" So, I finally did (make a choice, I mean, not yell and slap myself): I decided to go old school and use Nutella—a favorite—and chocolate chip cookies—an obsession—and go from there. These are huge chocolate chip cookies full of gooey, rich Nutella. The secret to stuffing the cookies is to freeze the Nutella before wrapping it inside, so it's less messy. These cookies pack a punch, so you may want to split it with someone, and if that someone is yourself, that's a-okay.

## INSTRUCTIONS

1   Line a cookie sheet with parchment paper. Scoop two balls (2 table-spoons [42 g] each) of Nutella and place them on the cookie sheet. Freeze while preparing the cookie dough.

2   Stir together the melted butter with both sugars in a large bowl. Stir in the egg yolk, vanilla extract, baking soda, and salt. Slowly stir in the flour. Stir in the chocolate chips.

3   Divide the dough in half. Flatten slightly and add a frozen Nutella ball to each cookie dough round. Wrap the cookie dough around the Nutella and roll between your palms to seal.

4   Line a second cookie sheet with a silicone baking mat or parchment paper. Place the cookies well-spaced on the cookie sheet. Chill for 30 minutes.

5   Preheat the oven to 350°F (177°C). Lightly press the dough with your palm to flatten. Bake for 20 to 23 minutes or until just no longer glossy and lightly golden around the bottom edges. Cool before eating.

6   Store in an airtight container for up to 3 days.

- 4 tablespoons (84 g) Nutella
- 4 tablespoons (57 g) unsalted butter, melted
- ¼ cup (50 g) packed brown sugar
- 3 tablespoons (35 g) granulated sugar
- 1 large egg yolk
- ½ teaspoon vanilla extract
- ¼ teaspoon baking soda
- ¼ teaspoon salt
- ⅔ cup (82 g) all-purpose flour
- ⅓ cup (86 g) mini chocolate chips

**Yield:** 2 cookies
**Prep time:** 20 minutes
**Chill time:** 30 minutes
**Bake time:** 20 minutes

## Tip:

These are also fantastic stuffed with peanut butter! Prepare the peanut butter the same way you do the Nutella in step 1.

# Lemon Poppyseed Thumbprints

My daughter was born ten days early, which wasn't a big deal because she was fine, but she decided she wanted to be born (my water broke) and then decided to be stubborn because it was warmer inside than the raging (and atypical) storm we were having that weekend in Phoenix. The funny thing is that her birth story basically summed up her childhood personality: stubborn, impatient . . . but also wanting to just chill out under the covers. Similarly, the birth story of these Thumbprints is very similar to their personality: a little fussy but perfect nonetheless. They took me a few tries to get absolutely perfect, and I'm glad I kept trying. They're little buttery bites of shortbread that almost dissolve in your mouth, and the lemon curd gives that super punch of sweet and tart lemon flavor. This recipe is worth the extra time it takes to roll the cookie balls and fill them. I've included my favorite lemon curd recipe below, but you can also buy your favorite jar, or even use raspberry jam instead.

- ¾ cup (170 g) unsalted butter, softened
- ⅓ cup (67 g) granulated sugar
- Zest of 1 lemon
- ½ teaspoon vanilla extract
- ¼ teaspoon salt
- 1½ cups (186 g) all-purpose flour
- 1½ teaspoons poppyseeds
- 3 tablespoons (54 g) Lemon Curd (recipe on opposite page)
- Powdered sugar, for dusting

**Yield:** 28 cookies
 (¾ tablespoon size)
**Prep time:** 30 minutes
**Bake time:** 14 minutes

## INSTRUCTIONS

1   If using homemade lemon curd, make sure it's prepared and chilled overnight.

2   Preheat the oven to 350°F (177°C) and line 2 cookie sheets with parchment paper or silicone baking mats.

3   Cream the butter and sugar in a large bowl using a hand or a stand mixer. Add the zest, vanilla extract, and salt. Slowly mix in the flour until the mixture is combined. Stir in the poppyseeds.

4   Scoop balls of cookie dough that are about ¾ to 1 tablespoon in size. Roll between your palms to create a ball. Place on the cookie sheets, 2 inches (5 cm) apart.

5   Use your knuckle or thumb, or the back of a ¼ teaspoon, to press an indent in the center of each cookie. Fill each indent with ¼ teaspoon of lemon curd per cookie.

6   Bake, rotating pans throughout baking, for about 11 to 16 minutes, or until the cookie is no longer glossy and the bottoms turn light golden.

7   Cool completely before removing from cookie sheets. Store in an airtight container for up to 3 days or freeze for up to 2 months.

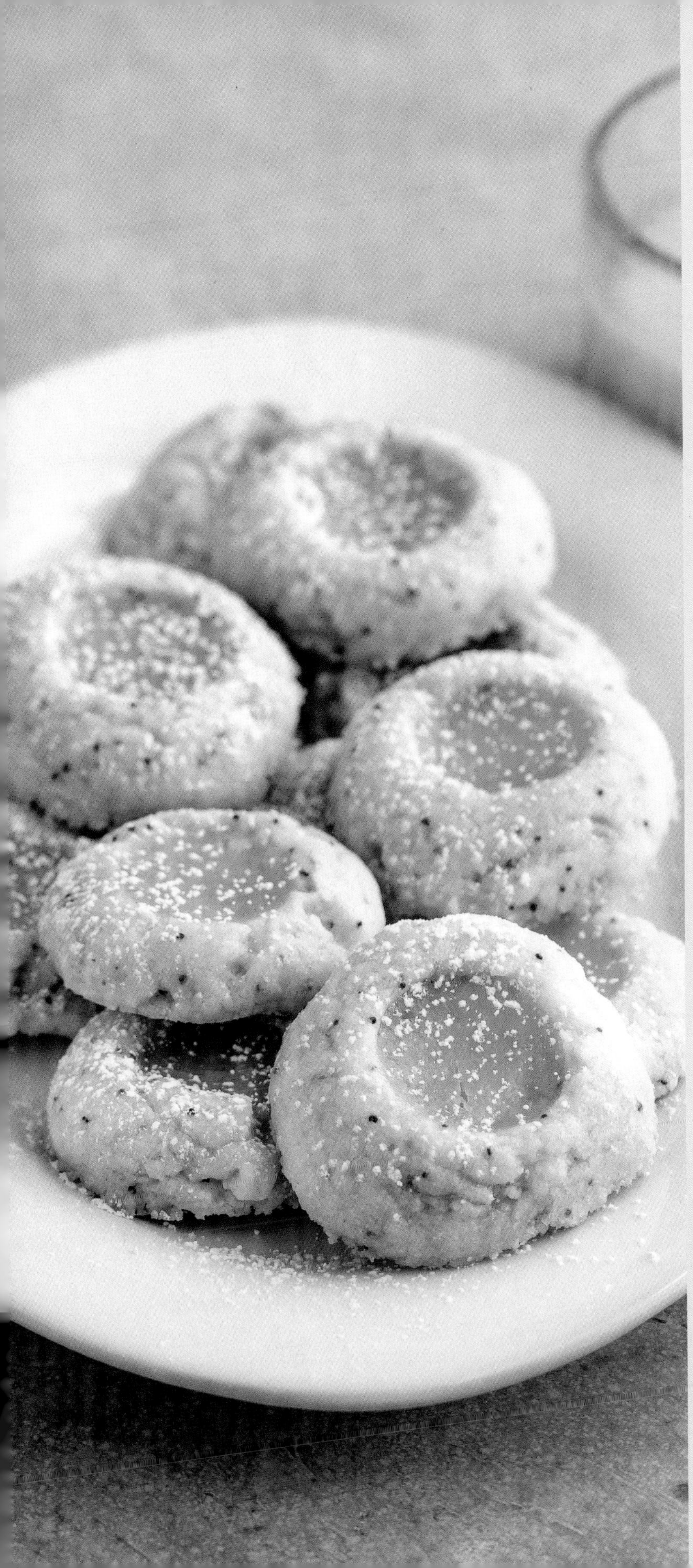

**Lemon Curd**

This recipe is rich and sweet and tart, just like lemon curd should be. You will have more curd than needed for the cookie recipe. Refrigerate leftovers in an airtight container or jar for up to a week. It's delicious on toast or scones or even just on a spoon.

- 2 large eggs, lightly beaten
- ½ cup (100 g) granulated sugar
- Pinch of salt
- ⅓ cup (80 ml) fresh lemon juice
- Zest of 1 large lemon
- 2 tablespoons (28 g) unsalted butter, diced

1 Place the eggs, sugar, salt, juice, and zest in a medium saucepan. Do not put it over the heat yet. Whisk the ingredients together until smooth.

2 Place over low heat. Stir constantly with a wooden spoon until the mixture thickens, about 4 to 5 minutes. Remove from the heat and strain into a jar or airtight container. Immediately stir in the butter until smooth and incorporated. Do not skip straining; it's important to get out any pieces of egg.

3 Cool until room temperature, and then cover and store in the refrigerator overnight before using in the cookie recipe. Makes about 1 cup (288 g) lemon curd. Store in refrigerator for up to 1 week.

# Salted Caramel Ginger Sandwiches

Of all the RV trips I went on as a kid, my favorite ones were when we got to stop in Tillamook, Oregon. Tillamook Cheese is made there, and they have a factory tour and gift shop. We would always get an ice cream cone, and jerky and cheese, and a quart of chocolate milk, which rarely made it to the end of the gift shop driveway before we drank it all. Fast-forward twenty years and I was invited to a Tillamook blogging retreat, where I got to spend a few days touring Portland and the Oregon coast with a behind-the-scenes tour of my favorite factory. (This was also the same trip I sent my husband a photo of me with a baby cow and begged for a pet and he said no.) The whole point of the trip was to highlight their ice cream, and one of our desserts was an array of cookie ice cream sandwiches. My favorite of the bunch was the salted caramel ice cream paired with ginger cookies, which I never would have guessed I'd like. The spicy ginger flavor partnered with the little bit of salty-sweet flavor from the ice cream was to die for! These cookies are my interpretation of that ice cream sandwich but without the ice cream. Instead, I made salted caramel frosting with the same caramel used in the Bacon and Caramel Brownies (see page 64). Sandwich cookies with frosting are better than ice cream because you can eat them more slowly and really savor the flavors together.

## MAKE THE COOKIES

1   Preheat the oven to 350°F (177°C). Line 2 cookie sheets with silicone baking mats or parchment paper.

2   Whisk the flour, baking soda, salt, ginger, cinnamon, and cloves in a medium bowl. Set aside.

3   Cream the butter and sugar with molasses in the bowl of an electric mixer until creamy. Add the egg and vanilla extract and mix until combined (mixture will be lumpy).

4   Add dry ingredients to wet and mix until smooth.

5   Scoop balls of cookie dough (each about 1 tablespoon) onto prepared baking sheets at least 2 inches (5 cm) apart. Bake for 9 to 11 minutes or until dark golden brown. Cool for at least 5 minutes on cookie sheets before removing to a rack to cool completely before frosting.

### For the Cookies

- 2 cups (248 g) all-purpose flour
- 1 teaspoon baking soda
- ½ teaspoon salt
- 1½ teaspoons ground ginger
- 1 teaspoon ground cinnamon
- ¼ teaspoon ground cloves
- ½ cup (113 g) unsalted butter, softened
- ¾ cup (150 g) granulated sugar, plus more for rolling
- ¼ cup (59 ml) molasses
- 1 large egg
- 1 teaspoon vanilla extract

### For the Frosting

- 1 cup (226 g) unsalted butter, softened
- ½ cup (160 g) caramel sauce (see page 64), or use store-bought caramel sauce
- 4 cups (452 g) powdered sugar
- 1 teaspoon vanilla extract
- 1 teaspoon sea salt or kosher salt, plus more to taste

**Yield:** 15 cookie sandwiches
**Prep time:** 45 minutes
**Bake time:** 10 minutes

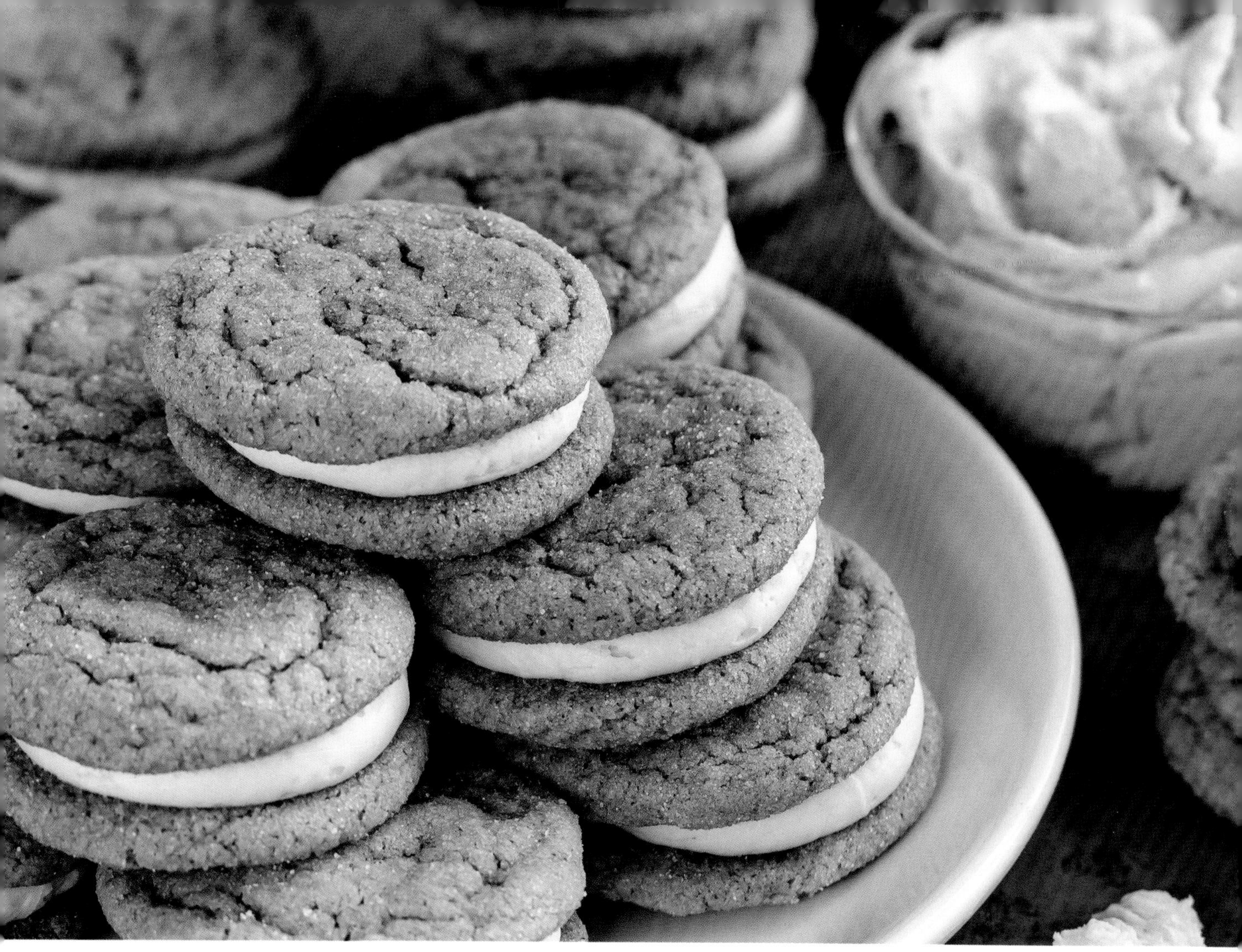

**MAKE THE FROSTING AND FILL THE COOKIES**

1 Cream the butter and caramel sauce in a large bowl with an electric mixer until smooth. Mix in the powdered sugar, vanilla extract, and salt until creamy. Add more salt to taste.

2 Place the frosting in a piping bag and pipe onto half the cookies, topping each with a second cookie.

3 Store cookies in an airtight container in the refrigerator for up to 3 days. Assembled cookies, plain cookies, and frosting can be frozen in airtight containers for up to 2 months.

**Tip:**

This frosting would also be good on cupcakes or sandwiched with almost any cookie in this book!

# Cookies²

When trying to come up with more ideas for this chapter, I asked Facebook what I should stuff inside cookies and the results were hilarious. I'd expected answers like "peanut butter" or "Nutella" and instead a few of the gems I got were "my face," "a million dollars," and "the Covid-19 vaccine." A few said "another cookie," and I took that idea and ran with it (although if I could have stuffed the vaccine inside, I wouldn't have needed the million dollars).

The math nerd in me had to name this Cookies², or Cookies Squared, because it's a cookie inside a cookie. Another name for it could be Chocolate³, because there is triple the chocolate: chocolate cookie and double the chocolate chips. This cookie got all thumbs-up from both my daughter Jordan and my mom, so that means it's worth 100 gold stars. If I were you, I'd enjoy these with a nice glass of milk.

## MAKE THE INSIDE DOUGH

1  Cream the butter and both sugars with an electric mixer in a large bowl until fluffy, about 1 to 2 minutes. Add the salt and vanilla extract and mix until smooth, then mix in the flour. Stir in the chocolate chips.

2  Scoop balls of cookie dough (each about 1 tablespoon) and place on a parchment paper–lined cookie sheet. Chill while making the outside cookie dough.

## MAKE THE OUTSIDE DOUGH

1  Wipe out the mixing bowl. Add the butter and both sugars and cream with an electric mixer, about 1 to 2 minutes.

2  Mix in the egg, vanilla extract, salt, baking soda, and cocoa. Then add the flour and stir carefully until combined and smooth. Stir in the mini chocolate chips.

3  Scoop balls of cookie dough (each about 1 tablespoon) and place on another parchment paper–lined cookie sheet. Spacing doesn't matter when chilling the dough. Chill the dough for 30 minutes, and continue chilling the inside dough until ready to assemble the cookies.

## ASSEMBLE THE COOKIES

1  Remove the chilled cookies from the refrigerator. Flatten a chocolate cookie dough ball with your hands. Place one of the chocolate chip cookie dough balls on the flattened dough. Flatten a second chocolate cookie dough ball and place it on top of the chocolate chip cookie ball. Press the edges to seal and roll between your palms to seal. Place the cookie on a cookie sheet.

### For the Inside Cookies

- ½ cup (113 g) unsalted butter, softened
- ½ cup (100 g) packed brown sugar
- ¼ cup (50 g) granulated sugar
- ¼ teaspoon salt
- 1 teaspoon vanilla extract
- ⅔ cup (83 g) all-purpose flour
- ¾ cup (126 g) mini chocolate chips

### For the Outside Cookies

- ½ cup (113 g) unsalted butter, softened
- ⅓ cup (67 g) granulated sugar
- ½ cup (100 g) packed brown sugar
- 1 large egg
- 1 teaspoon vanilla extract
- ½ teaspoon salt
- ½ teaspoon baking soda
- ¼ cup (20 g) Dutch process cocoa powder
- 1⅓ cups (165 g) all-purpose flour
- 1½ cups (255 g) mini chocolate chips
- Additional mini chocolate chips, for coating

**Yield:** 17 cookies
**Prep time:** 45 minutes
**Chill time:** 1½ to 2 hours
**Bake time:** 20 minutes

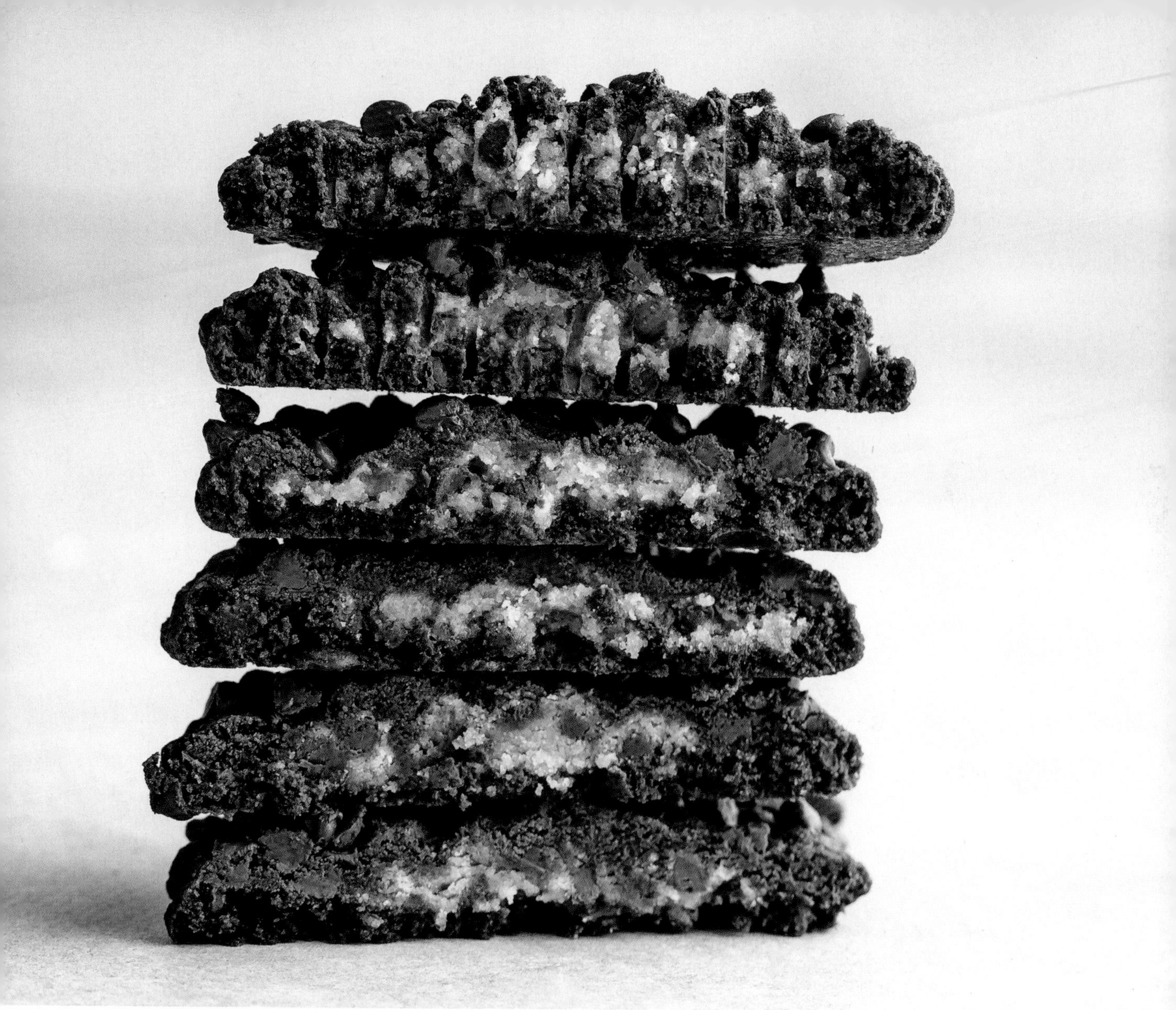

2 Repeat with the remaining cookies. No need to space them; we're chilling again.

3 Place the remaining chocolate chips in a shallow bowl. Dip one side of the large balls of dough in the chocolate chips, pressing slightly to adhere (about ½ to 1 tablespoon per ball). Place back on the cookie sheet.

4 Chill the dough balls for 1 hour.

5 You may have a couple of inside cookie dough balls left over. That's okay—they're egg-free and safe to eat raw, so enjoy.

**BAKE THE COOKIES**

1 Preheat the oven to 350°F (177°C). Line cookie sheets with parchment paper or silicone baking mats.

2 Place the chilled cookies at least 3 inches (8 cm) apart on the prepared sheets.

3 Bake for 18 to 22 minutes, or until the tops are no longer glossy. Cool for at least 10 minutes before removing from the cookie sheets.

4 Store in an airtight container for up to 3 days. Can be frozen for up to 2 months.

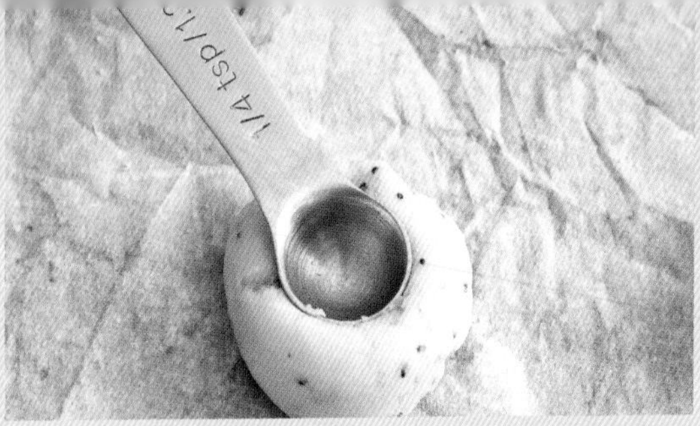
1/4 tsp

**Thumbprint Tips**

When making the cavity in a cookie cup (or a thumbprint cookie), here's an easy trick: Use the back of a ¼ or ½ teaspoon. Old-school recipes call for the handle of a wooden spoon, your thumb, or a knuckle, but I find using the rounded part of a teaspoon is so much easier!

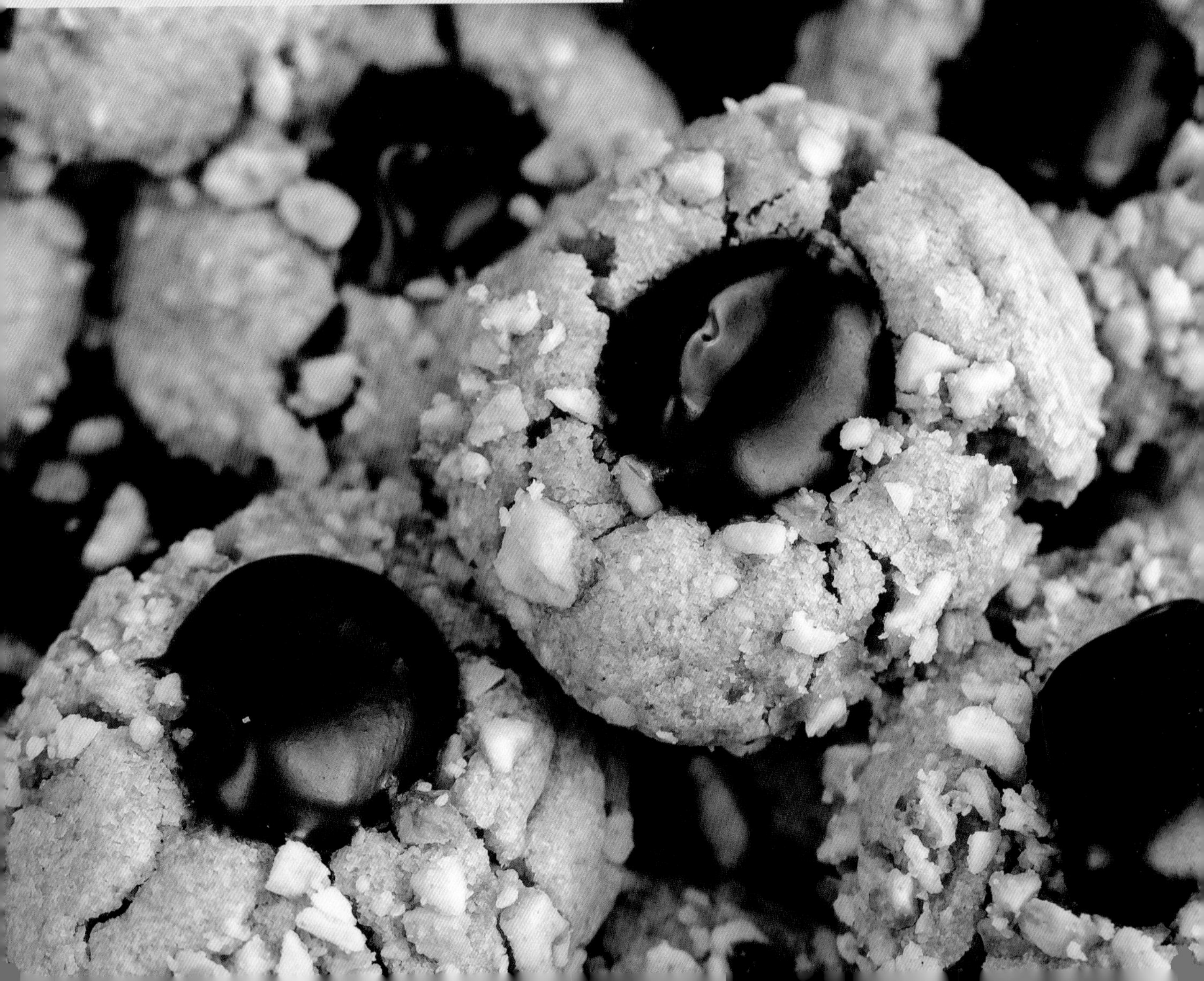

# Peanut Butter Thumbprints

℞emember those Reese's commercials from the 1980s in which someone would dip a full chocolate bar in a tub of peanut butter? I remember doing that with chocolate bars and Skippy more than once. Chocolate and peanut butter are such a classic combo—and my absolute favorite. Small and bite-sized, these peanut butter cookies are crunchy on the outside because of the chopped nuts. They'd be good as they are, but when filled with chocolate ganache they are pure heaven for people like me. And I know you like-minded people must be out there, right? I see you, hiding in the pantry with chocolate and a tub of peanut butter . . . come on out and make these cookies.

**INSTRUCTIONS**

1  Preheat the oven to 350°F (177°C). Line 2 cookie sheets with silicone baking mats or parchment paper.

2  Mix the butter and peanut butter in a large bowl with a hand mixer (or the bowl of a stand mixer fitted with the paddle attachment) until smooth. Add both sugars and cream until fluffy.

3  Add the vanilla extract, egg, baking soda, and salt and mix until smooth. Then add the flour and mix just until a cookie dough forms.

4  Place the finely chopped peanuts in a small bowl. Scoop cookie dough balls (each about 1 tablespoon) and roll them between your palms. Roll the balls in the peanuts, pressing lightly to adhere, and then place them onto the prepared cookie sheets.

5  Bake for 9 to 11 minutes, rotating pans halfway through baking, until they just lose their glossy sheen and the bottoms are slightly golden. The cookies will stay in balls during baking.

6  Immediately after removing from the oven, carefully create a thumb-print in each cookie. Use the back of a ¼ teaspoon, the handle of a wooden spoon, or your knuckle to create the indent.

7  Cool on the cookie sheets before removing and baking additional cookies.

8  While cookies are cooling, place the chocolate chips and heavy whipping cream in a microwave-safe bowl. Heat on high power for 1 minute, then whisk, heating for an additional 30 seconds or as needed to create a smooth chocolate ganache.

9  Spoon a bit of ganache into each thumbprint cavity. The ganache will harden as it cools, so wait to stack the cookies until after the ganache is completely cool.

10  Store in an airtight container for up to 3 days or freeze for up to a month.

- ½ cup (113 g) unsalted butter, softened
- ¾ cup (200 g) creamy peanut butter
- ¾ cup (150 g) packed brown sugar
- ¼ cup (50 g) granulated sugar
- 1 teaspoon vanilla extract
- 1 large egg
- ¼ teaspoon baking soda
- ¼ teaspoon salt
- 1¾ cups (217 g) all-purpose flour
- 1 cup (124 g) peanuts, finely chopped
- ⅓ cup (57 g) semi-sweet chocolate chips
- ¼ cup (59 ml) heavy whipping cream

**Yield:** 40 cookies
**Prep time:** 30 minutes
**Bake time:** 10 minutes

# PB&J Sandwich Cookies

Can I tell you something and will you promise to stay my friend? I don't really like jelly. I never have. I especially don't like jelly with peanut butter, like, in a sandwich (*shudder*). Growing up I ate plain peanut butter sandwiches. As an adult I rarely eat peanut butter sandwiches, but I still like them plain. Then, a few years ago, I was craving something: something sweet and fruity. I really wanted this sweet and fruity thing, but I didn't know what it was. I made toast for breakfast, opened the fridge to get the butter, and saw the strawberry jam. All of a sudden, I had to have that jam—the jam I'd never liked—and I had to have it on that piece of toast right then. So, I did—and I liked it. So now I eat jelly on toast, sometimes, when I'm not being boring and just using plain butter. But I still won't eat jelly on a peanut butter sandwich, no way . . . unless the peanut butter sandwich is a cookie sandwich made with peanut butter cookies, peanut butter buttercream, and strawberry jam. Even better, these cookies are gluten-free by design. I love the easiness of this recipe, and you can use any flavor jam or jelly you like.

## MAKE THE COOKIES

1  Preheat oven to 350°F (177°C). Line 2 cookie sheets with parchment paper or silicone baking mats.

2  Add the peanut butter, both sugars, egg, baking soda, and vanilla extract to a large bowl. Stir with a wooden spoon or use a hand mixer to combine. Mixture will be smooth but wet.

3  Place additional granulated sugar in a small bowl. Scoop balls of cookie dough (each about 1 tablespoon) directly into the bowl of sugar. Roll to coat and place on the cookie sheets, spacing the cookies 2 inches (5 cm) apart.

4  Use a fork to press the cookies flat with crisscross marks. If the fork sticks to the dough, dip it in sugar. Bake the cookies for 8 to 12 minutes or until light golden around the edges and slightly puffed. Cool completely before frosting.

## MAKE THE FROSTING AND ASSEMBLE THE COOKIES (SEE FROSTING TIPS, PAGE 12)

1  Beat the peanut butter and butter with a hand or a stand mixer in a large bowl until smooth, then mix in the powdered sugar 1 cup (113 g) at a time. Add the salt and vanilla extract and mix. The mixture will be crumbly. Add 2 tablespoons (30 g) heavy whipping cream (or milk) and mix until smooth, adding more cream for spreadable consistency.

### For the Cookies

- 1 cup (268 g) creamy peanut butter
- ¾ cup (150 g) packed brown sugar
- ¼ cup (50 g) granulated sugar
- 1 large egg
- ¼ teaspoon baking soda
- ½ teaspoon vanilla extract
- Additional granulated sugar, for rolling

### For the Frosting

- ½ cup (138 g) creamy peanut butter
- ¼ cup (57 g) unsalted butter, softened
- 2 cups (226 g) powdered sugar
- ⅛ teaspoon salt
- ½ teaspoon vanilla extract
- 3 to 4 tablespoons (45 to 60 ml) heavy whipping cream
- 3 tablespoons (60 g) any flavor fruit jam

**Yield:** 16 sandwiches
**Prep time:** 45 minutes
**Bake time:** 10 minutes

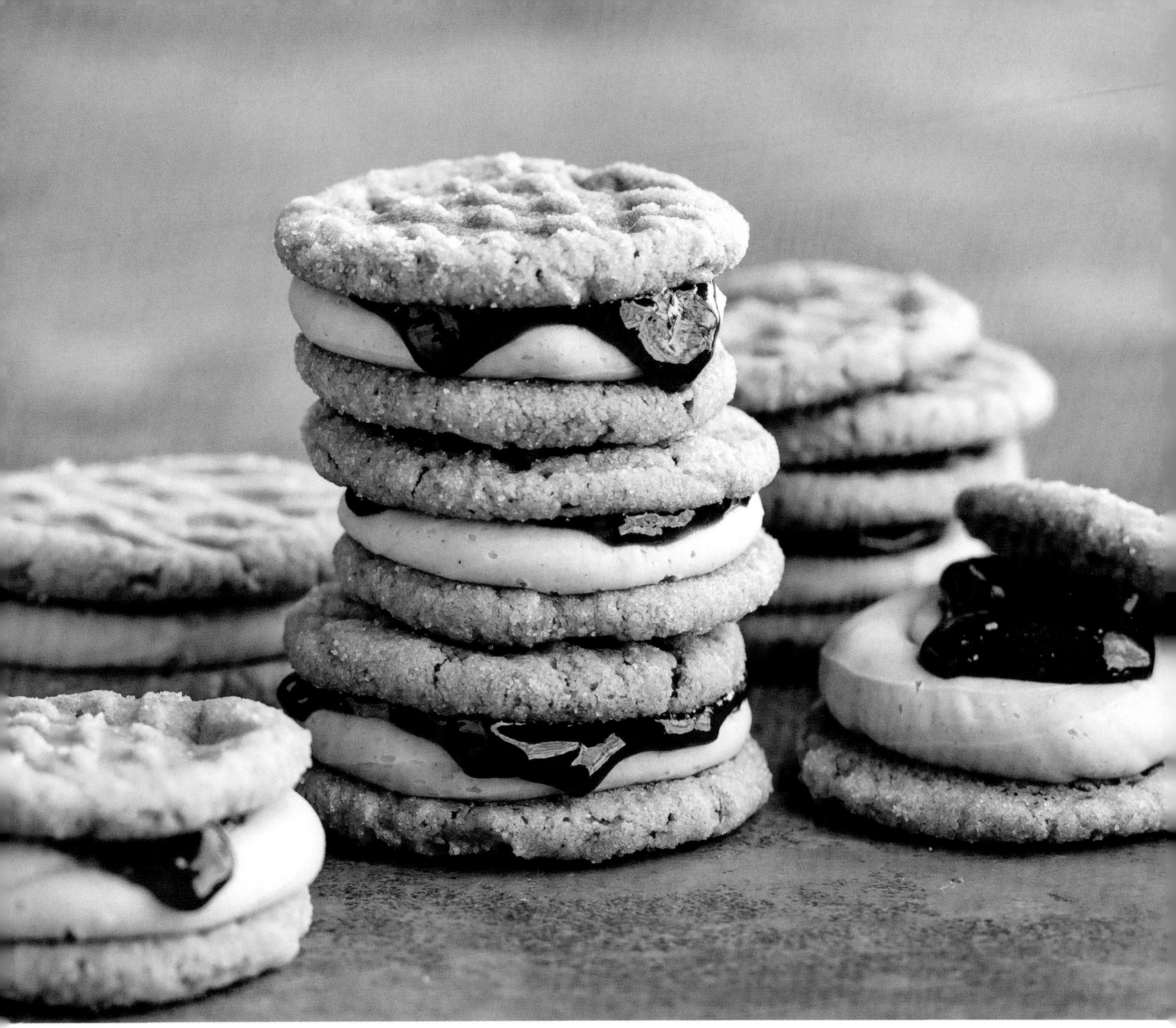

2 To assemble the cookies, place the frosting in a piping bag with the tip cut off. Turn half the cookies upside down and pipe about 1 to 1½ tablespoons frosting on top of each. These cookies are somewhat fragile because they don't have flour, so it's important to use the piping bag. Spoon about ½ teaspoon jam on top of the frosting and sandwich with a second cookie.

3 Store the cookie sandwiches in an airtight container for up to 3 days. You can make the cookies up to 24 hours ahead of time. I don't recommend freezing these as they tend to break when frozen.

# Stuffed Carrot Cake Cookies

I first married cheesecake and carrot cake back in 2011, the first time I made Carrot Cake Cheesecake Cupcakes for a friend. He'd told me those were his two favorite desserts, so I magically put them together. It's funny how the internet works: Within a year of me creating that recipe there were cheesecake-stuffed carrot cake *all the things*. This recipe is a cookie version of those cupcakes: a spiced cookie filled with carrots and stuffed with a sweet cream cheese mixture. Once baked, they are topped with white chocolate, but you could also leave them plain. These are pure heaven for carrot cake lovers, like my husband. I love making them for him to entice him into my carb-loving life, and my method often works.

## INSTRUCTIONS

1   Preheat the oven to 350°F (177°C). Line 2 cookie sheets with parchment paper or silicone baking mats. Line a third cookie sheet or large platter with parchment paper.

2   Beat the cream cheese, granulated sugar, and vanilla extract in a large bowl using a hand mixer until smooth. Scoop even-sized (each about 1 tablespoon) balls of the cheesecake mixture onto the third prepared cookie sheet or platter. Freeze while preparing the cookie dough.

3   In a small bowl, whisk the flour with baking soda, cinnamon, ginger, and salt. Set aside.

4   Cream the butter and brown sugar in a large bowl with an electric mixer 1 to 2 minutes. Mix in the egg and vanilla extract until smooth.

5   Add the dry ingredients to the wet ingredients and mix until smooth. Stir in the carrots.

6   Scoop balls of cookie dough (each about 1 tablespoon) onto a prepared cookie sheet. Spacing isn't necessary when chilling the dough. Chill for 30 minutes.

7   After chilling, remove the cookie dough from the refrigerator and the frozen cheesecake filling balls from the freezer. The assembling step is a bit messy, so place a small bowl of water next to your work surface.

**For the Filling**
- 8 ounces (224 g) cream cheese
- ¼ cup (50 g) granulated sugar
- 1 teaspoon vanilla extract

**For the Cookies**
- 1¾ cups (217 g) all-purpose flour
- ½ teaspoon baking soda
- 1 teaspoon cinnamon
- ¼ teaspoon ground ginger
- ¼ teaspoon salt
- ½ cup (113 g) unsalted butter, softened
- ¾ cup (150 g) packed brown sugar
- 1 large egg
- 1 teaspoon vanilla extract
- 1 cup (90 g) shredded carrots (see tip)
- ½ cup (85 g) white chocolate chips, for topping

**Yield:** 15 to 16 cookies
**Prep time:** 1 hour
**Chill time:** 30 minutes
**Bake time:** 19 minutes

*Tip:*

Be sure to shred the carrots yourself instead of buying them pre-shredded, which tend to be thicker and won't perform as well in the recipe.

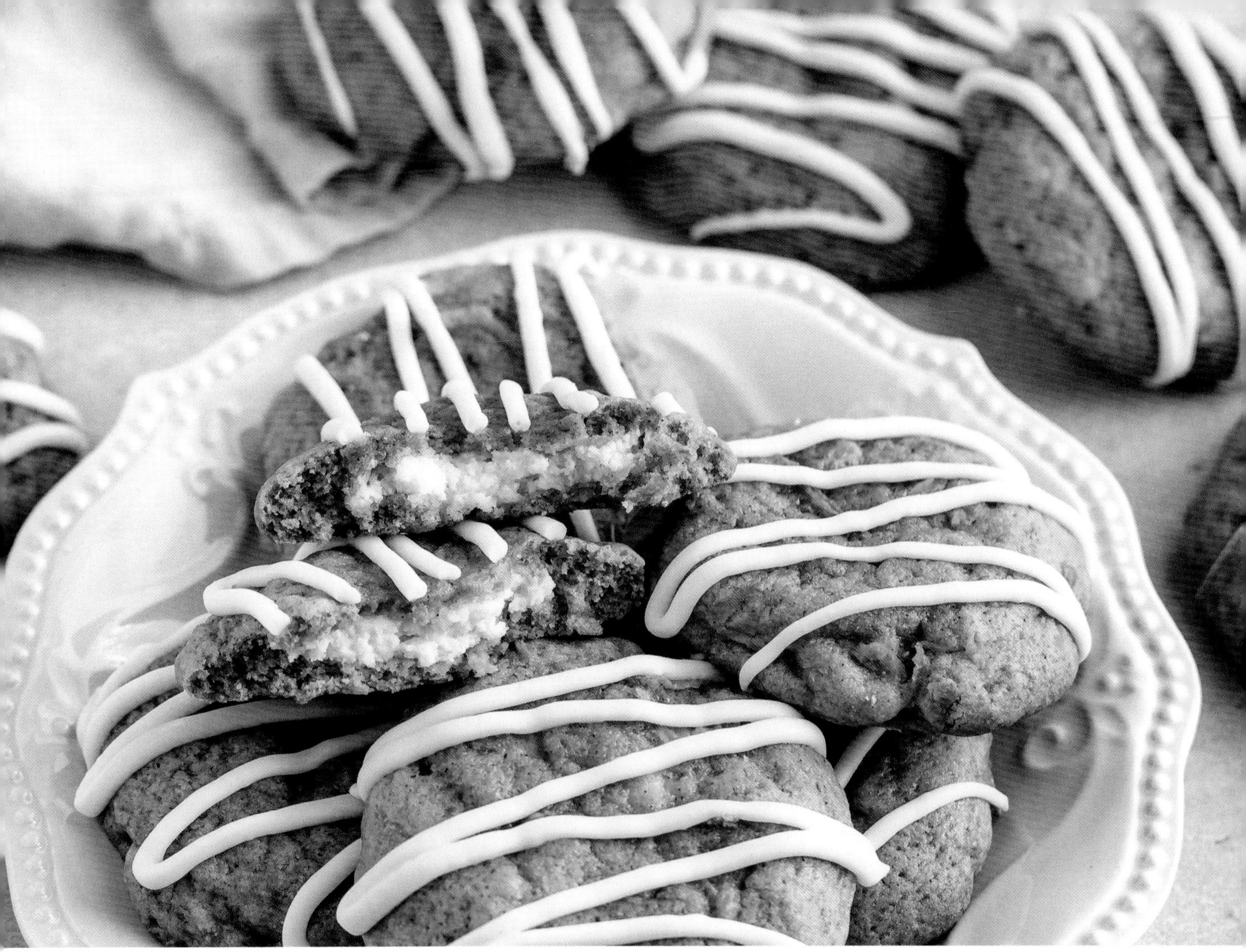

8 Assemble the cookies by flattening a cookie dough ball, placing a cheesecake ball on top, and then topping with a second piece of flattened cookie dough. Pinch to seal edges (you don't want any of the cheesecake mixture showing, if possible) and roll between your palms to form a cohesive ball. The dough is sticky, so lightly wet your hands as needed so it doesn't stick too much. Place at least 4 inches (10 cm) apart on the prepared cookie sheets. Flatten slightly with the palm of your hand.

9 Bake the cookies for 17 to 21 minutes or until they lose their glossy sheen. Cool completely before removing from the cookie sheets.

10 To top cookies, place white chocolate chips in a small bowl. Heat in the microwave at 50 percent power for 1 minute. Stir, then heat on 50 percent power in 30-second increments, stirring between each, until melted and smooth. Place the chocolate in a sandwich bag and cut off one tip. Pipe drizzles on cookies as desired. Let sit to dry, at least 30 minutes (or chill to set).

11 Store in an airtight container for up to 3 days or freeze (frosted or unfrosted) for up to 2 months.

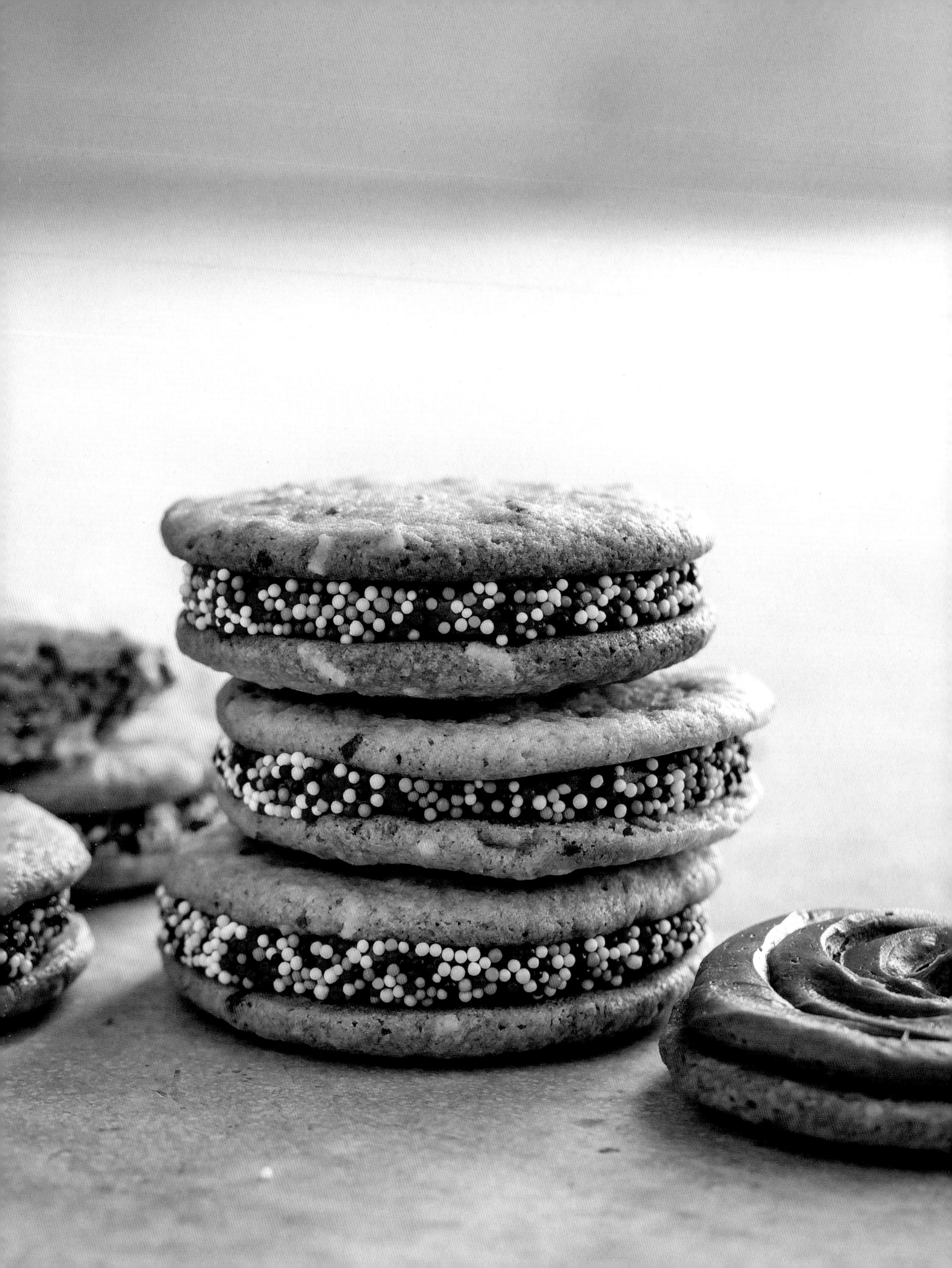

# Birthday Cake Sandwich Cookies

My daughter doesn't like cake, so her birthday treats are usually some sort of cookie. Next year I'm totally making these sandwich cookies for her: They're an easy vanilla cookie with sprinkles filled with my favorite chocolate frosting. If you love yellow cake with chocolate frosting, this is the cookie version! The best part about them is that you can use any color sprinkles, so I can see making these for a birthday or any holiday, or even a graduation party.

## MAKE THE COOKIES

1  Preheat the oven to 350°F (177°C). Line 2 cookie sheets with parchment paper or silicone baking mats.

2  Whisk the flour, baking soda, and salt in a medium bowl. Set aside.

3  Cream the butter, granulated sugar, and brown sugar in a large bowl using an electric mixer until smooth. Then mix in the vanilla extract and egg.

4  Add the dry ingredients to the wet ingredients and mix until smooth. Stir in the sprinkles.

5  Scoop balls of cookie dough (each about 1 tablespoon) onto the prepared cookie sheets, 2 inches (5 cm) apart. Bake for 10 to 13 minutes, or until golden around the edges. Cool completely before filling.

## MAKE THE FILLING AND ASSEMBLE

1  Beat the butter with an electric mixer until smooth, and then slowly mix in the powdered sugar, 1 cup (113 g) at a time. Mix in the cocoa (the mixture will be crumbly). Add the vanilla extract and salt, and then add 1 tablespoon (15 ml) milk and mix until smooth. Add an additional tablespoon milk and mix until combined, adding more milk as needed for spreadable consistency.

2  To assemble the cookie sandwiches, spread or pipe about 1 to 2 tablespoons filling on each cookie, using half the cookies and sandwiching with the remaining cookies. Place additional sprinkles in a shallow bowl and roll the edges to coat.

3  Store the cookies in an airtight container for up to 3 days. Cookies can be made up to 24 hours in advance, or frozen for up to 2 months. Freeze the cookie sandwiches in a single layer for up to 2 months as well.

### For the Cookies

- 1½ cups (186 g) all-purpose flour
- ½ teaspoon baking soda
- ¼ teaspoon salt
- ½ cup (113 g) unsalted butter, softened
- ¼ cup (50 g) granulated sugar
- ⅔ cup (134 g) packed brown sugar
- 1 teaspoon vanilla extract
- 1 large egg
- ½ cup (90 g) rainbow sprinkles

### For the Filling

- ¾ cup (170 g) unsalted butter, softened
- 3 cups (339 g) powdered sugar
- 3 tablespoons (15 g) cocoa powder
- 1 teaspoon vanilla extract
- ¼ teaspoon salt
- 2 to 3 tablespoons (30 to 45 ml) milk
- Additional rainbow sprinkles (nonpareils)

**Yield:** 16 cookie sandwiches
**Prep time:** 45 minutes
**Bake time:** 12 minutes

## Tip:

You can also fill these with the vanilla buttercream I use for my Three-Layer Cookie Cake (see page 106).

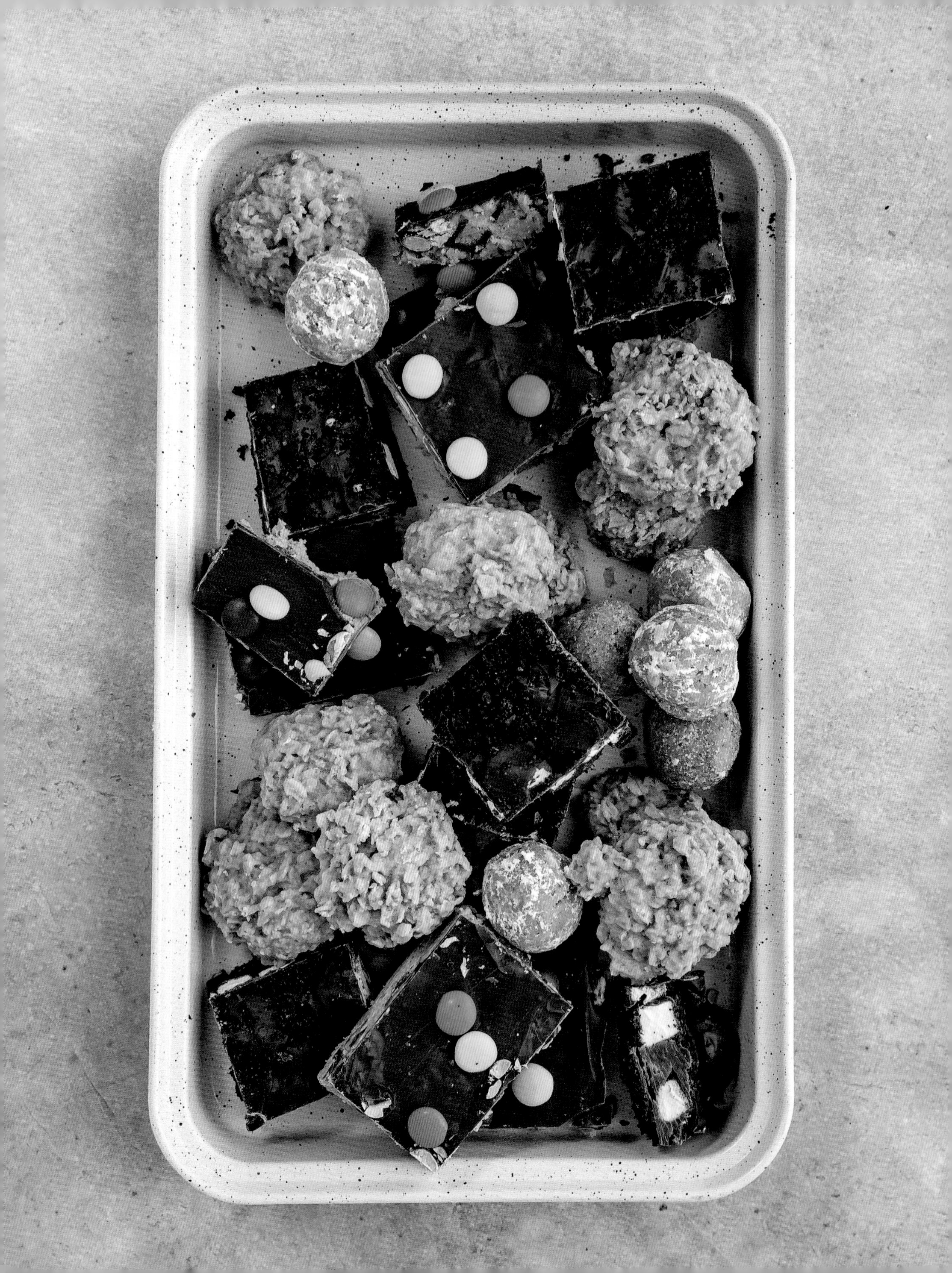

# No Oven, No Problem: No-Bake Cookies and Bars

There are months of the year I don't want to turn on my oven because it's over 100°F (38°C) outside and my A/C is already running at top speed. Those are the days I reach for no-bake recipes, and those bars and cookies are my favorite. These are often the easiest cookies to make and often last longer (and are more stable) than a traditional cookie, which also makes them great for holiday shipping and gifting. From peanut butter to cookie butter, chocolate to cookie dough, you're going to decide you don't even need an oven anymore to enjoy cookies!

Many no-bake recipes involve melting chocolate chips. Here are some chocolate melting tips:

- When melting chocolate chips in the microwave, be sure to use 50 percent power, especially if you're using white chocolate.

- Be sure to stir it often during melting. I like to start with one minute on 50 percent power, then stir, then continue heating in 30-second increments, stirring well between each, until the chocolate is melted and smooth. Stirring between each heating will allow the heat to evenly distribute and reduce burning.

- Sometimes, if you notice the chocolate doesn't seem to be melting, add 1 teaspoon of vegetable oil or shortening to the bowl. The extra fat helps it get started melting.

- Remember that all microwaves heat differently, so get to know yours and how it heats, if it needs more or less time, and so on.

- You can also melt chocolate on the stove. To do this, I recommend placing a heat-proof bowl over a pot with water in it (make sure the water does not touch the bowl). Bring the water to a boil and heat the chocolate in the bowl, stirring almost constantly, until it's melted and smooth.

**Happy no-baking!**

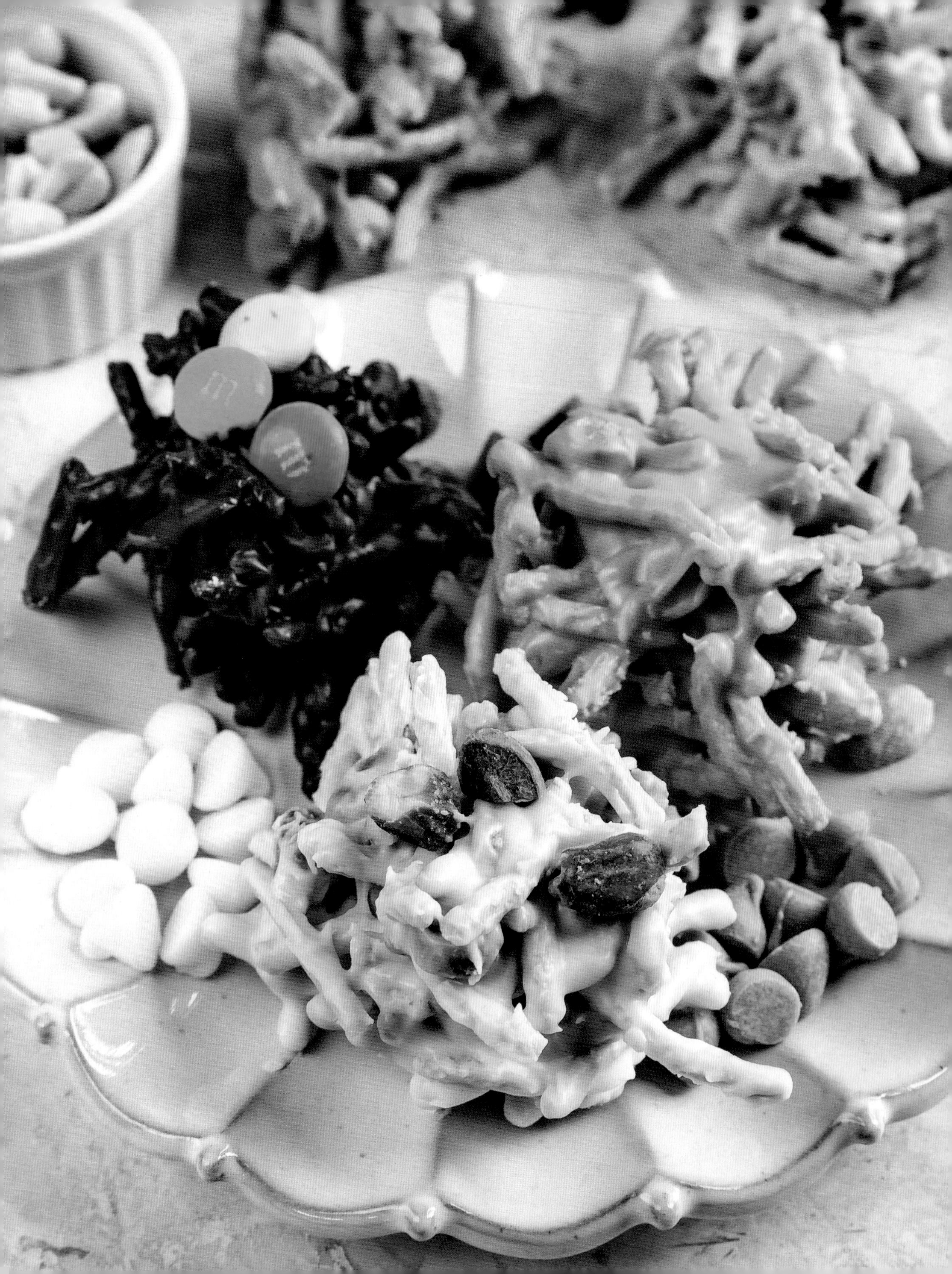

# Haystack Cookies

While these are often seen on holiday cookie platters, Haystack Cookies are fun to make all year long—especially in summer when you're craving something crunchy and sweet but don't want to turn on the oven. I love how versatile this recipe is: Just a few base ingredients can be easily jazzed up to make tons of new flavor combinations. I'm listing three of my favorites, but the different cookies you can make are endless!

## INSTRUCTIONS

1   Line a large, rimmed cookie sheet with parchment paper.

2   Place the chocolate chips (using the chips specified in one of the variation lists at right) and oil or shortening in a large microwave-safe bowl. Heat on 50 percent power in 30-second increments, stirring between each, until the chocolate is melted and smooth, about 3 minutes total, depending on your microwave.

3   Once the chocolate is melted and smooth, stir in the chow mein noodles and nuts, if using. Stir to coat all the chow mein pieces with chocolate.

4   Using 2 spoons, scoop and drop piles of haystacks onto the cookie sheet. Press the mixture together as you drop it so the pieces adhere to themselves as the chocolate hardens. Sprinkle with sprinkles, candies, or other desired toppings. Chill to set.

5   These will last in an airtight container for up to 2 weeks if kept in the refrigerator.

### For the Base Recipe

- 2 cups (340 g) chocolate chips (white chocolate, chocolate, or butterscotch, or a combination)
- 1 teaspoon vegetable oil or shortening
- 3 cups (172 g) crunchy chow mein noodles
- 1 cup (weight varies) mix-ins (see variations)
- Sprinkles or candy for topping, optional

### For Variation 1 (White Chocolate Pistachio Haystack Cookies)

- 2 cups (340 g) white chocolate chips
- 1 cup (135 g) salted pistachios

### For Variation 2 (Butterscotch Peanut Haystack Cookies)

- 1 cup (191 g) butterscotch chips
- 1 cup (170 g) white chocolate chips
- 1 cup (149 g) peanuts

### For Variation 3 (Plain with Sprinkles or Candy)

- 2 cups (340 g) semi-sweet chocolate chips
- Sprinkles or small candies (such as M&M's) for decoration

**Yield:** 16 to 20 cookies, depending on size
**Prep time:** 10 minutes

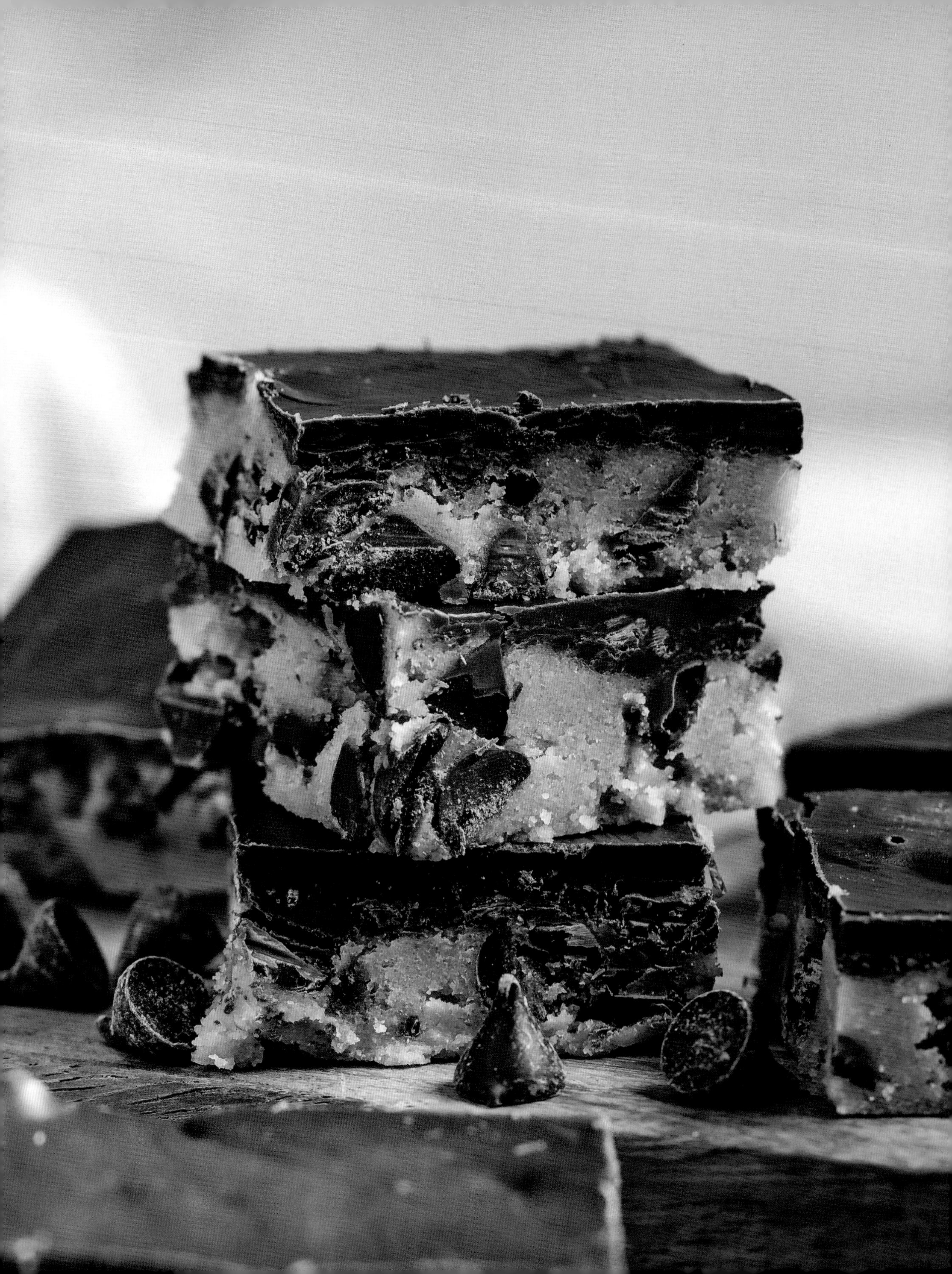

# Chocolate Chip Cookie Dough Bars

**W**hen I was young, I had a kids' cookbook that contained a really yummy chocolate chip cookie recipe. The recipe was called "Forget the Cookies and Give Me the Batter Chocolate Chip Cookies," and that was the truth—every time I made it, I found myself sneaking at least a cookie (or two) worth of the raw dough. Over the past few years cookie dough shops and treats have appeared all over the place, and it's finally acceptable to eat raw cookie dough—as long as it's eggless, that is! This recipe makes my favorite cookie dough safe to eat and turns it into a no-bake bar similar to fudge, which, in my opinion, is way better than any fudge ever!

## INSTRUCTIONS

1 Line an 8 × 8–inch (20 × 20 cm) pan with foil for easy removal. Set aside.

2 Cream the butter and both sugars on low speed until light and fluffy, 1 to 2 minutes. Mix in the salt, vanilla extract, and milk and beat until smooth.

3 Add the flour and mix until smooth. Then stir in 1 cup (170 g) chocolate chips.

4 Press the mixture into an even layer in the prepared pan.

5 Place the remaining 1 cup (170 g) chocolate chips in a microwave-safe bowl. Add the oil and heat on high power in 30-second increments, stirring between each, until melted and smooth. Pour the chocolate over the cookie dough in the pan and spread until smooth.

6 Chill to set, at least 1 hour. Remove entire square from the pan using the foil, remove the foil, and slice into squares.

7 Store in an airtight container in the refrigerator for up to 4 days.

- ½ cup (113 g) unsalted butter, softened
- ½ cup (100 g) packed brown sugar
- ¼ cup (50 g) granulated sugar
- ½ teaspoon salt
- 1 teaspoon vanilla extract
- 2 tablespoons (30 ml) milk
- 1 cup (124 g) all-purpose flour
- 2 cups (340 g) chocolate chips, divided
- 2 tablespoons (30 ml) vegetable oil or shortening

**Yield:** 24 bars
**Prep time:** 25 minutes
**Chill time:** 1 hour

---

### Using Cooked Flour

If you are concerned about eating raw flour, you can toast your flour to make it safer to eat. To toast flour, spread it in a single layer on a baking sheet and bake for 5 minutes at 350°F (177°C).

# Ultimate Peanut Butter Bars

**M**y love of peanut butter cups knows no bounds; I've spent my entire life craving them pretty much daily. These bars are a re-creation of my favorite candy in no-bake dessert form: a textured peanut butter filling with a chocolate coating, and I add lots of extra peanut butter candy for good measure. If you're a peanut butter cup–aholic like me, you will absolutely *love* these bars.

## INSTRUCTIONS

1  Line a 9 × 13–inch (23 × 33 cm) pan with foil and spray with nonstick cooking spray.

2  Stir the melted butter, cracker crumbs, powdered sugar, and ¾ cup (200 g) peanut butter in a large bowl until smooth. The mixture will be thick. Stir in the chopped peanut butter cups and Reese's Pieces. Press into the prepared pan.

3  Melt the chocolate chips with 2 tablespoons (34 g) peanut butter. Heat on high in 30-second increments, stirring between each, until melted and smooth. Spread over the top of the bars. If desired, sprinkle with additional peanut butter cups and/or Reese's Pieces.

4  Chill the bars for 2 hours to let them set, then slice into squares.

5  Store in an airtight container in the refrigerator for up to 4 days.

### For the Filling

• ½ cup (113 g) unsalted butter, melted

• 2 cups (148 g) Ritz Cracker crumbs (about 55 crackers)

• 1¼ cups (143 g) powdered sugar

• ¾ cup (200 g) creamy peanut butter

• 1 cup (139 g) peanut butter cups, unwrapped and coarsely chopped

• 1 cup (206 g) Reese's Pieces

### For the Coating

• 1 cup (170 g) chocolate chips

• 2 tablespoons (34 g) peanut butter

**Yield:** 24 bars
**Prep time:** 25 minutes
**Chill time:** 2 hours

*Tip:*
You can use any kind of cracker crumbs (saltine or butter crackers) in this recipe, or substitute graham cracker crumbs. We also love using M&M's in place of the Reese's Pieces.

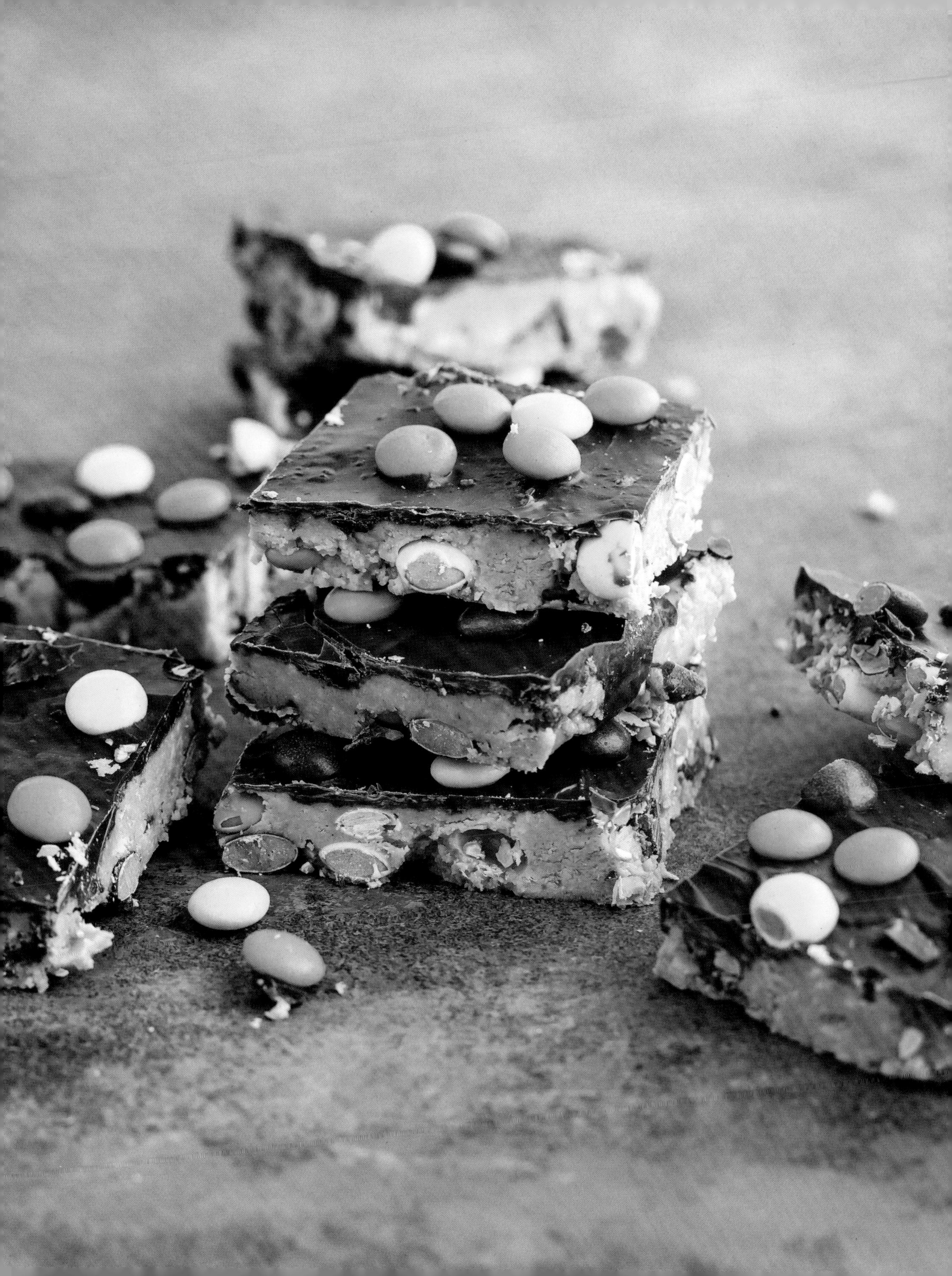

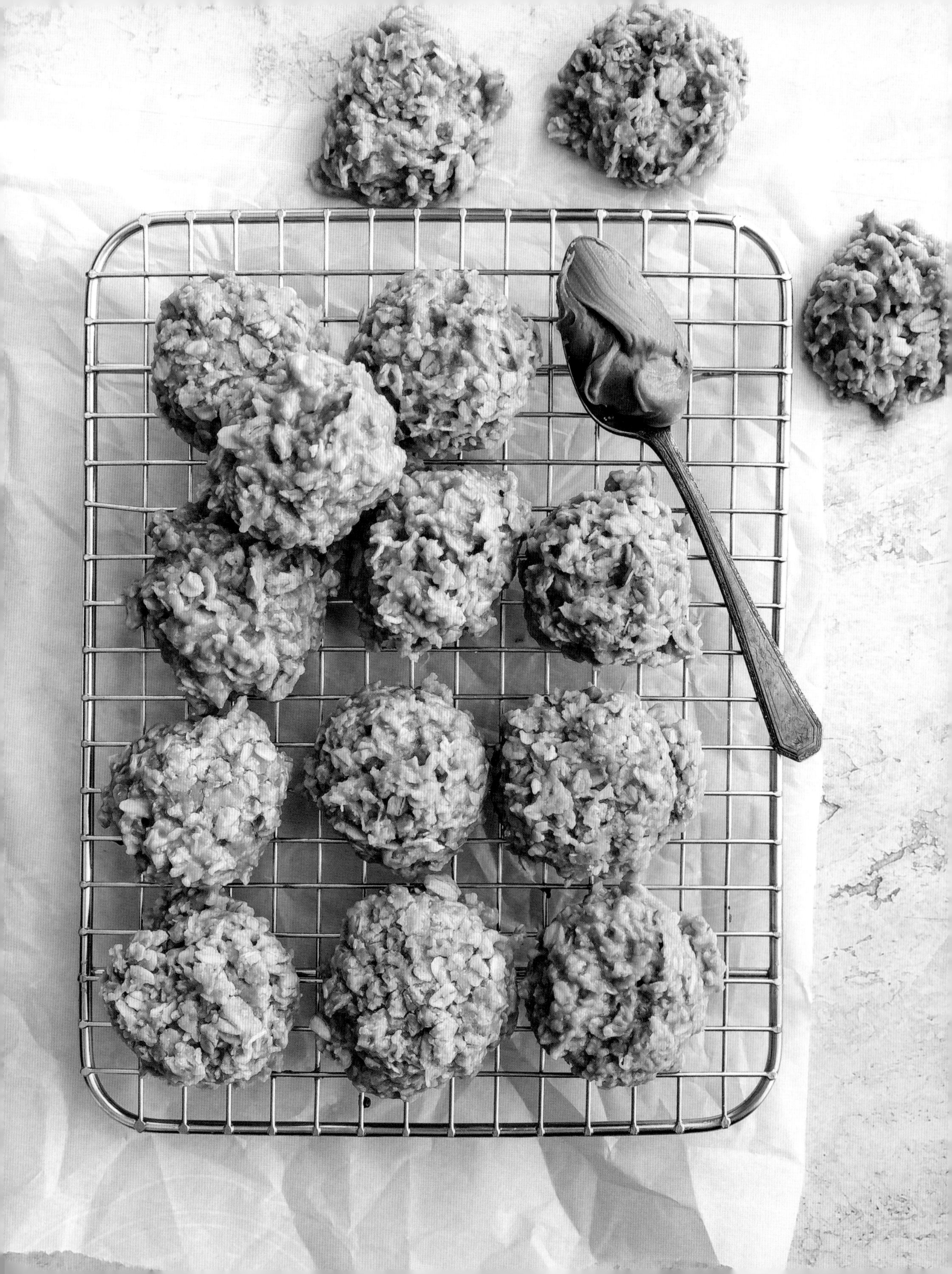

# Biscoff Oatmeal No-Bakes

If you've never had Biscoff, then you need to run to the store to get some. Biscoff is the original name brand, but you can also find it at Trader Joe's, where it's called Cookie Butter. Cookie Butter describes it perfectly: It's a spread with the same texture as peanut butter, but it's made of Speculoos cookies. The flavor is reminiscent of a spiced caramel cookie, and it's fabulous in all forms. I love it on a spoon, on toast, or baked into cookies. These are a classic no-bake cookie, the kind you grew up with, made by boiling milk with butter and sugar and stirring in oats. But instead of using peanut butter, I used Biscoff, and the result is so good. I put these in the freezer to avoid my temptation but can't stop going back for more.

- ½ cup (113 g) unsalted butter, diced
- 1¾ cups (350 g) granulated sugar
- ½ cup (119 ml) nonfat milk
- ½ cup (120 g) Biscoff or Cookie Butter Spread
- 1 teaspoon vanilla extract
- ¼ teaspoon salt
- 3 cups (255 g) quick-cooking oats

**Yield:** 24 cookies
**Prep time:** 30 minutes

## INSTRUCTIONS

1  Line 2 cookie sheets with parchment paper.

2  It's very important that all your ingredients are measured and ready to go before you start. Make sure you've read the directions before making these cookies. The process goes quickly!

3  Melt the butter in a 3-quart (2.8 L) saucepan over medium heat. Stir in the sugar and milk. Whisk until smooth and then bring to a boil and cook for about 2 to 3 minutes, stirring occasionally. Note: You *must* boil it long enough or it will not set. To be sure of this, boil the mixture until it reaches 230°F (110°C) on a candy or instant-read thermometer. Time will vary depending on the size of your pan and heat of your stove.

4  Remove from the heat and stir in the Biscoff, vanilla, salt, and oats.

5  Use a cookie scoop to drop balls of the cookie mixture (each about 2 tablespoons) onto the prepared cookie sheets. Let sit to set or chill to harden more quickly.

6  Store in an airtight container in the refrigerator for up to 4 days. Can be frozen for up to 2 months.

## Tip:

It's really important to cook the mixture long enough, so I recommend using an instant-read or candy thermometer. While it's annoying to have yet another kitchen tool, an instant-read thermometer, which is my favorite, can be purchased inexpensively on Amazon and is useful for so many things when baking and cooking.

# Caramel Crunch Bars

My daughter Jordan has been a super tester for this book: She tasted almost every single recipe! If you didn't think you could get tired of cookies, try writing a cookbook about them. Jordan's first words after tasting these bars was "Yum!", followed quickly by, "Mom, they're really, really good, but they're so much better because they're not cookies." Don't let that deter you, though: If you're looking for a can't-be-easier treat, this is it. Five ingredients, quick and easy steps, no oven needed. These will be a hit all summer long—and at the holidays too!

- 22 graham cracker squares, divided
- 11 ounces (311 g) caramel bits or caramel squares, unwrapped
- 2 tablespoons (30 ml) heavy whipping cream
- 1 cup (170 g) chocolate chips
- 1 tablespoon (15 ml) vegetable oil

**Yield:** 36 bars
**Prep time:** 25 minutes
**Chill time:** 2 hours

## INSTRUCTIONS

1   Line an 8 × 8–inch (20 × 20 cm) pan with foil and spray with non-stick cooking spray. It's important to line your pan so you can easily remove the bars once the caramel hardens.

2   Place a single layer of graham cracker squares (about 10) in the pre-pared pan, breaking some to fit.

3   Place the caramel bits or squares and heavy whipping cream in a medium microwave-safe bowl. Heat for 1 minute, then stir. Heat in additional 30-second increments, stirring well between each, until caramel is melted and smooth. Pour and spread caramel evenly over the graham crackers.

4   Immediately layer with more graham cracker squares, about 10, breaking to fit.

5   Place the chocolate chips and oil in a small microwave-safe bowl. Heat at 50 percent power for 1 minute, then stir. Heat in additional 30-second increments at 50 percent power, stirring well between each, until the chocolate is melted and smooth. Spread the chocolate evenly over the top layer of graham crackers.

6   Crush remaining graham crackers between your fingers and sprinkle the crumbs over the chocolate. Chill to set, at least 2 hours.

7   Remove the entire slab of bars from the pan using the foil overhang. Carefully remove the foil and slice into squares with a sharp knife.

8   Store in an airtight container in the refrigerator for up to a week. Serve at room temperature.

## Tip:

Don't have graham crackers? You can use saltine crackers or matzo crackers instead!

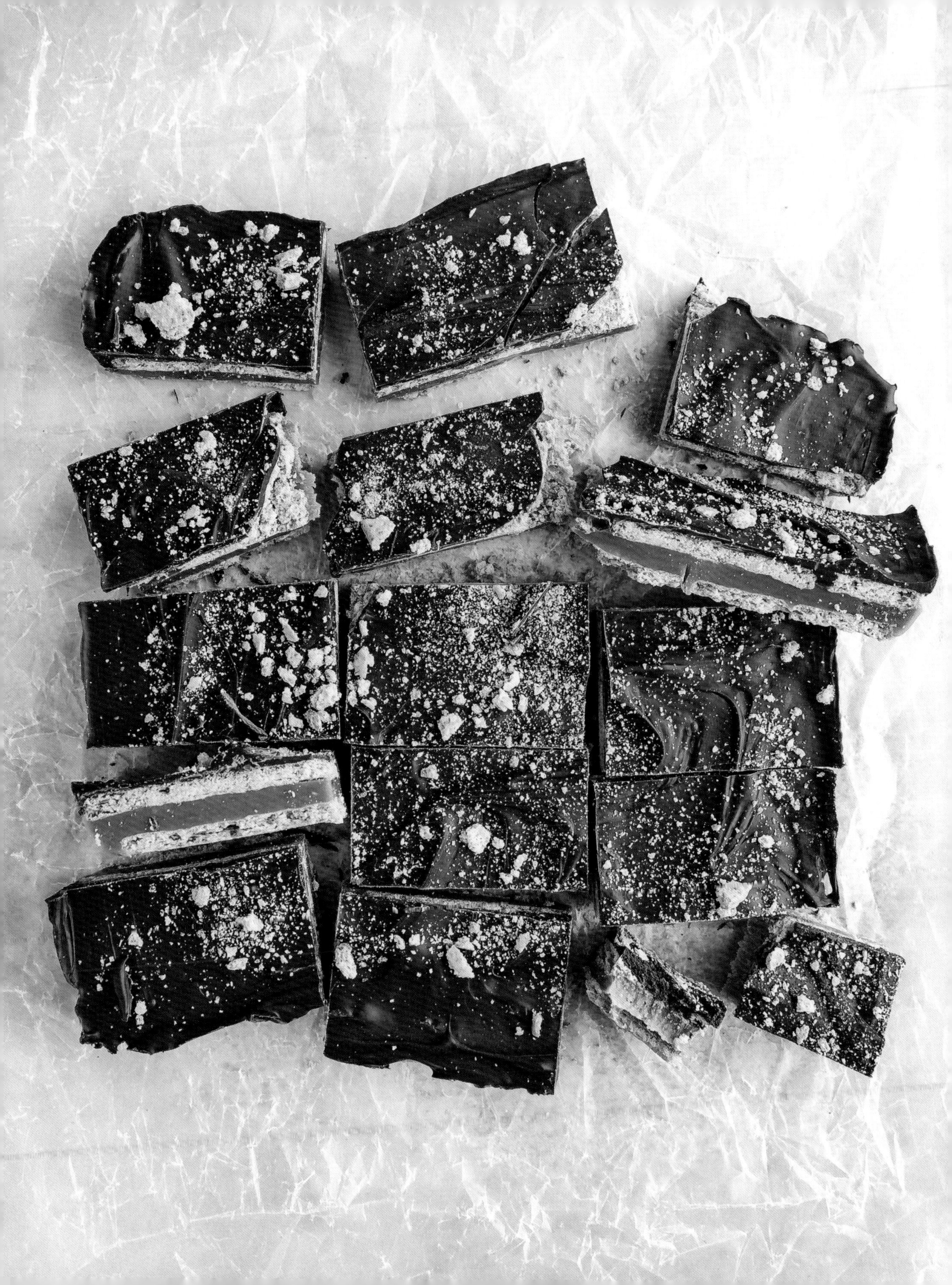

# Sugar Cookie Bites

My definition of being a wild teenager: eating raw cookie dough. Raw sugar cookie dough was a guilty pleasure of mine for many years, even into adulthood. I wouldn't even make it myself: I'd buy a tube from the grocery store to make cookies and eat the dough instead, even though the package always warned me not to. Now that my wild days are behind me, I like to make my own raw cookie dough—without the eggs. One batch of these will satisfy any craving, plus they're fun to make for a dessert table or even holiday cookie platters. You can change up the sprinkle colors as desired or coat them in chocolate to turn them into truffles!

## INSTRUCTIONS

1   Line a cookie sheet with parchment paper.

2   Cream the butter and sugar in a large bowl with an electric mixer. Mix in both extracts and milk, then slowly mix in the flour until smooth and combined.

3   Scoop balls of cookie dough (each about 1 tablespoon) and roll between your palms to form a ball.

4   Place nonpareils or sprinkles in a bowl and roll the balls in it, pressing lightly to adhere.

5   Place on the cookie sheet. Chill to set. Store in an airtight container in the refrigerator for up to 1 week.

- ½ cup (113 g) unsalted butter, softened
- 1 cup (200 g) granulated sugar
- 1 teaspoon vanilla extract
- ¼ teaspoon almond extract
- 2 tablespoons (30 ml) milk
- 1 cup (124 g) all-purpose flour (see Using Cooked Flour, page 181)
- ⅓ cup (67 g) nonpareils or ⅓ cup (65 g) sprinkles, for coating

**Yield:** 24 bites
**Prep time:** 30 minutes

## Tip:

You can also make these into dipped truffles by melting 16 ounces (453 g) of candy melts (any flavor) and dipping the truffles, then chilling to set.

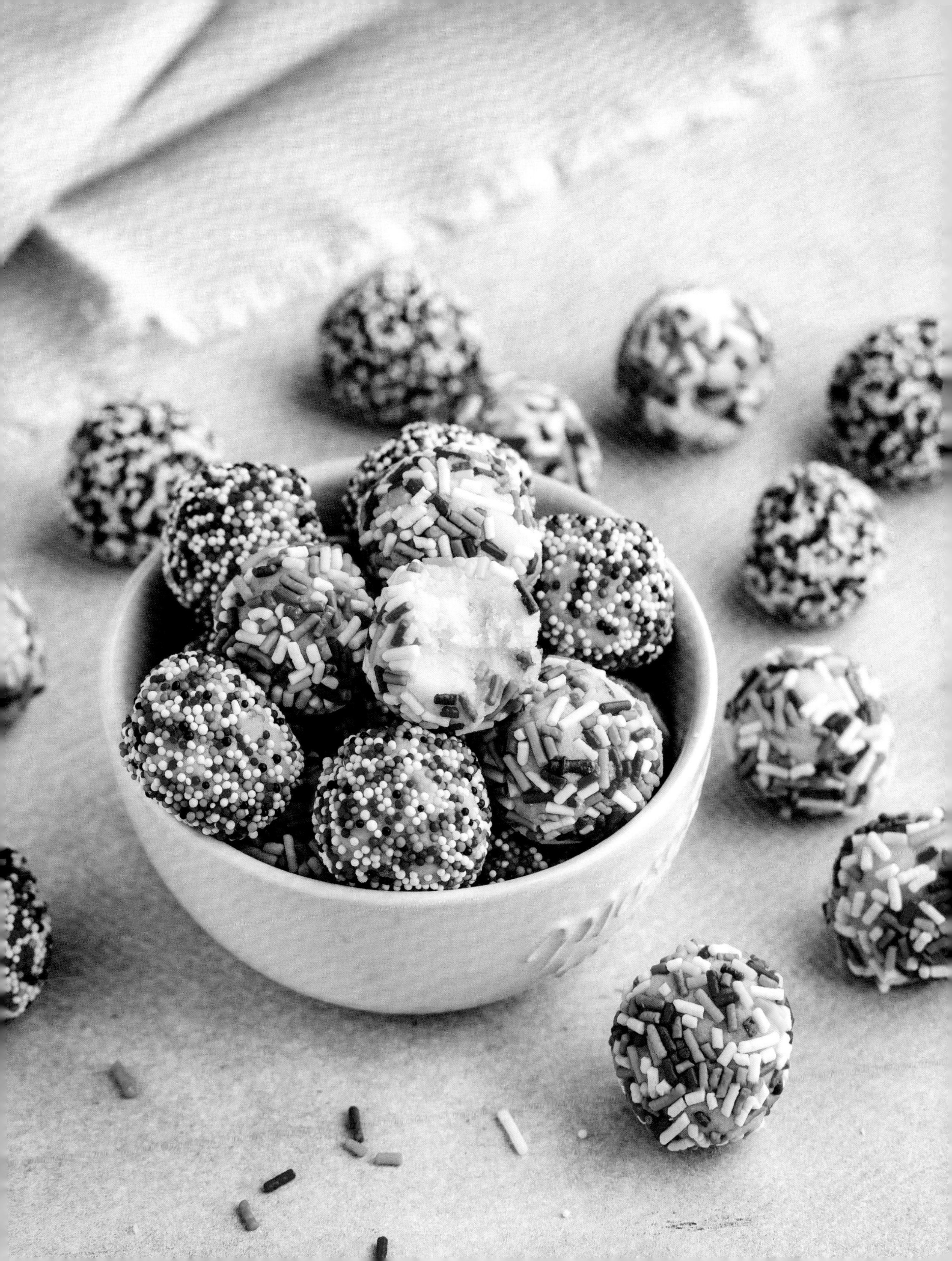

# Cookies 'n' Cream Mud Bars

Whenever you see no-bake recipes online, they either are creamy and layered or include peanut butter, or both. While I love peanut butter more than most things, I wanted to vary some of the recipes in this chapter because not everyone likes peanut butter (and so many are allergic). That's how this recipe was born: I wanted a non-peanut-butter bar recipe that was easy and didn't have a ton of ingredients. Most of the time recipes like this are made in the summer or at the holidays, and those are the times we want an easy and fast recipe without a ton of guesswork, right? These bars fit the bill: just five ingredients and they take less than twenty-five minutes to assemble. I called them Mud Bars because they are an homage to one of my favorites: Mississippi Mud Brownies. And believe me, you won't miss all the work that goes into that traditional recipe!

- 26 Oreo cookies
- 5 tablespoons (71 g) unsalted butter, melted
- 2 cups (340 g) semi-sweet or milk chocolate chips
- 1 tablespoon (15 ml) vegetable oil
- 2 cups (102 g) mini marshmallows

**Yield:** 16 bars
**Prep time:** 25 minutes
**Chill time:** 1 hour

## INSTRUCTIONS

1 Line an 8 × 8–inch (20 × 20 cm) pan with foil and spray with nonstick cooking spray.

2 Place the cookies in a food processor and pulse until they are fine crumbs. If you don't have a food processor, first roughly chop the cookies and then add them to a large gallon-sized resealable bag. Seal all but 1 inch (2.5 cm) of the bag and roll with a rolling pin.

3 Reserve 1 tablespoon (7 g) cookie crumbs for the topping.

4 Place the remaining cookie crumbs in a large bowl and top with the melted butter. Stir with a fork until thoroughly combined. Press firmly into the prepared pan.

5 Place the chocolate chips and oil in a medium microwave-safe bowl. Heat at 50 percent power for 1 minute, then stir. Continue heating at 50 percent power, in 30-second increments, stirring well between each, until melted and smooth.

6 Spread about 2 to 3 tablespoons of the chocolate in a very thin layer over the crust and immediately sprinkle mini marshmallows over the top. Press lightly to adhere.

7 Spread the remaining chocolate evenly over the marshmallows. Use a spatula to spread the chocolate, keeping the marshmallows in a single layer and making sure the marshmallows are completely coated. Sprinkle with the reserved cookie crumbs. Chill to set, at least 1 hour.

8 Cut into bars and serve. Store in an airtight container in the refrigerator for up to 1 week.

*Tip:*
Use *any* flavor Oreos or even use other brands of sandwich cookie!

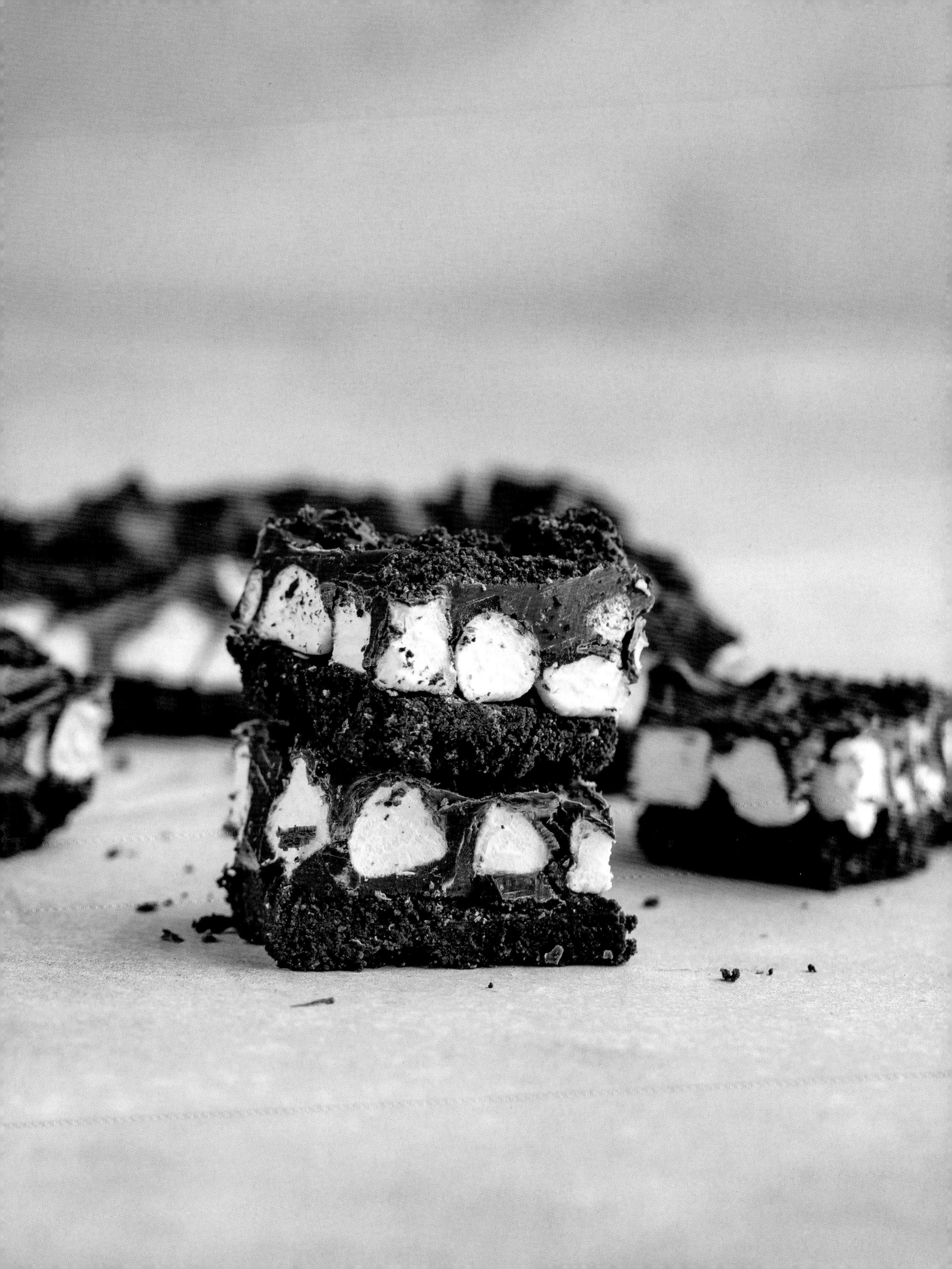

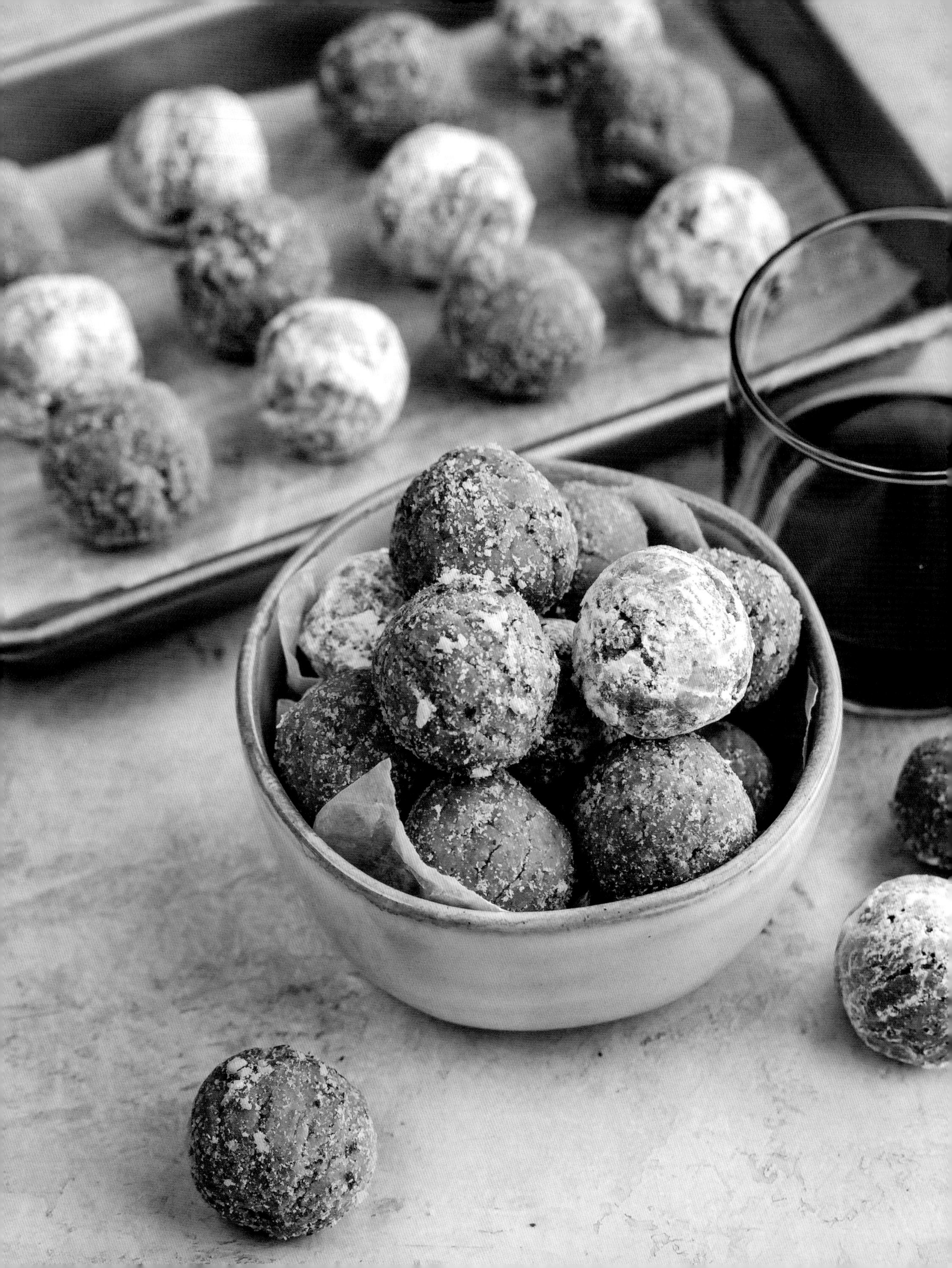

# Amaretto Bites

oes anyone remember the popularity of The Body Shop in the 1990s? I remember after one opened at our mall, we'd go in there and play with all the scents. I don't even know if they still have all the little beakers holding scents with which you could mix your own perfume, but I'd often walk out of there smelling like a botanical garden–stuffed cookie. Today, if I had a chance to mix any scents into a perfume, a major player would be almond. Almond extract, amaretto, almond paste: All of them are absolutely intoxicating to me. It's not just the smell; I love the flavor of almond too, which is why I always have amaretto on hand to make cocktails or fudge or little bites like this. These are reminiscent of holiday rum balls but with amaretto instead. If you love that flavor profile, these will be as intoxicating to you as The Body Shop was to me!

### INSTRUCTIONS

1  Line a cookie sheet with parchment paper. Set aside.

2  Place the wafers in the bowl of a large food processor and pulse until they are fine crumbs, pulsing as needed to get big chunks broken up. Add the almonds and pulse until the almonds are also fine crumbs, being careful not to pulse so much that it turns to a paste.

3  Add the powdered sugar and pulse a few times to combine, and then add the corn syrup, amaretto, and vanilla extract. Run the food processor until the mixture comes together, stopping and scraping the sides as needed. If the dough is too dry, you can add another teaspoon of corn syrup.

4  Scoop balls (each about 1 tablespoon) and roll between your palms. Roll in the desired coating and place on the cookie sheet.

5  Enjoy at room temperature or store in an airtight container for up to a week in the refrigerator.

- 11 ounces (approximately 311 g) vanilla wafers
- ½ cup (52 g) sliced almonds
- 1 cup (113 g) powdered sugar
- 2 tablespoons (30 ml) corn syrup
- 6 tablespoons (3 ounces or 89 ml) amaretto liqueur
- ½ teaspoon vanilla extract

**Coating Options**
- Powdered sugar
- Finely crushed almonds
- Finely crushed vanilla wafers
- Cocoa powder

**Yield:** 28 cookies
**Prep time:** 30 minutes

## Tip:
You can substitute rum, whiskey, Baileys, or any liquor you want in place of the amaretto.

# Nutty Slice and No-Bake Cookies

There have been lots of food trends over the years that I've been blogging: Pop Tarts stuffed in cookies, hot chocolate bombs, cake pops, and baked doughnuts are just a few of the ones I've tried. But my absolute favorite trend of all time: making charcuterie mainstream and cool. I mean, over my forty-some years of being alive, I've served salami, cheese, and crackers for dinner more times than I can count, but now it has a cool name and a fancy serving plate. And now dessert charcuterie is even a trend (formerly called a dessert table, where everything is just served on its own platters). But I'm down for it: I love serving charcuterie at parties or for dinner, and I always include something sweet. If I'm being lazy, I throw on some chocolate-covered almonds or a broken-up semi-sweet chocolate bar, but if I'm being more intentional with my charcuterie-ing, I make cookies like these. These are like fudge but filled with extra pieces of crunchy mix-ins, then rolled and sliced like slice-and-bake cookies. I used vanilla wafer cookies and pecans in this, but you can use any sort of mix-ins you like (see the options in the Tip below). They're perfect on your holiday platter, but they go fantastic on a cheese board too.

- 3 cups (510 g) semi-sweet chocolate chips
- 1 (14-ounce or 396 g) can sweetened condensed milk
- 1 teaspoon vanilla extract
- Pinch salt
- 1½ cups (150 g) chopped pecans (walnuts, almonds, pistachios, or peanuts may be used)
- 1½ cups (103 g) chopped vanilla wafer cookies (about 28 cookies)

**Yield:** 36 cookies
**Prep time:** 30 minutes
**Chill time:** 3 hours

## INSTRUCTIONS

1   Prepare all ingredients before starting: Chop the nuts and cookies; measure the vanilla extract and salt. Lay 2 sheets of parchment paper on your work surface.

2   Place the chocolate chips and sweetened condensed milk in a 3-quart (2.8 L) saucepan. Heat over medium-low heat, stirring often, until the chocolate chips are melted and smooth. The mixture will be thick.

3   Remove from the heat and immediately stir in the vanilla extract and salt. Add the chopped nuts and cookies and stir until combined. Again, the mixture will be thick.

4   Divide the chocolate mixture between each sheet of parchment paper. Use your hands to form the mixture into logs. Wrap in plastic wrap and chill until firm, at least 3 hours.

5   To form the cookies, slice each log in ¼-inch to ½-inch (6 to 12 mm) slices, as desired. These are hard to slice straight from the refrigerator but will be easier if you let them sit at room temperature for about 15 to 20 minutes before slicing.

6   Serve or store between layers of parchment paper. Store the sliced cookies in an airtight container in the refrigerator for up to 3 days, or wrap each log well with plastic wrap and seal in an airtight container for up to 2 weeks (in the refrigerator).

## Tips:

You can use any chopped cookies you want. Graham crackers, chocolate chip, Oreos—anything you like will work.

Use any kind of nuts.

You can also reduce the amount of nuts and/or cookies and add chopped candy, like peanut butter cups or Snickers bars.

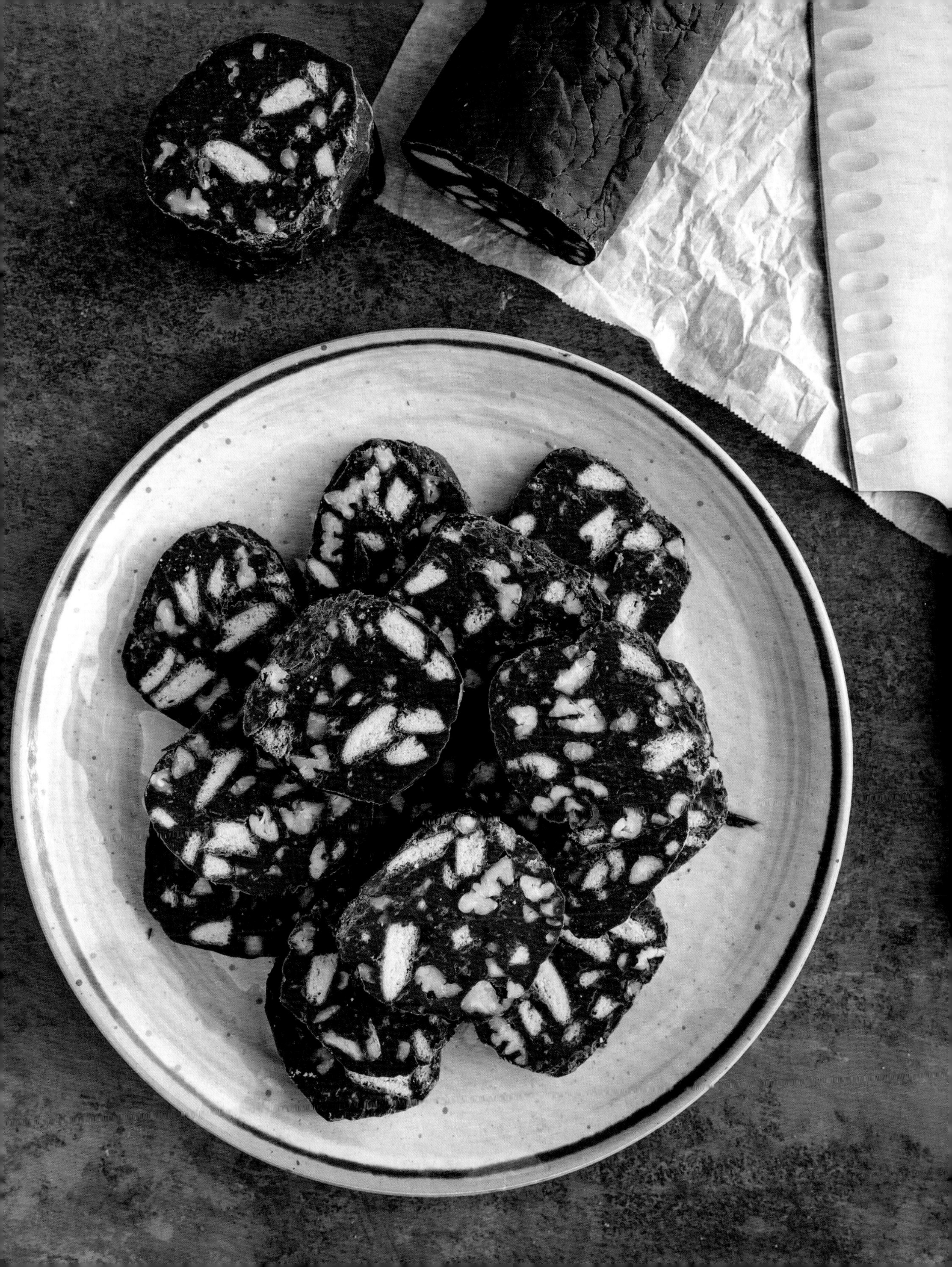

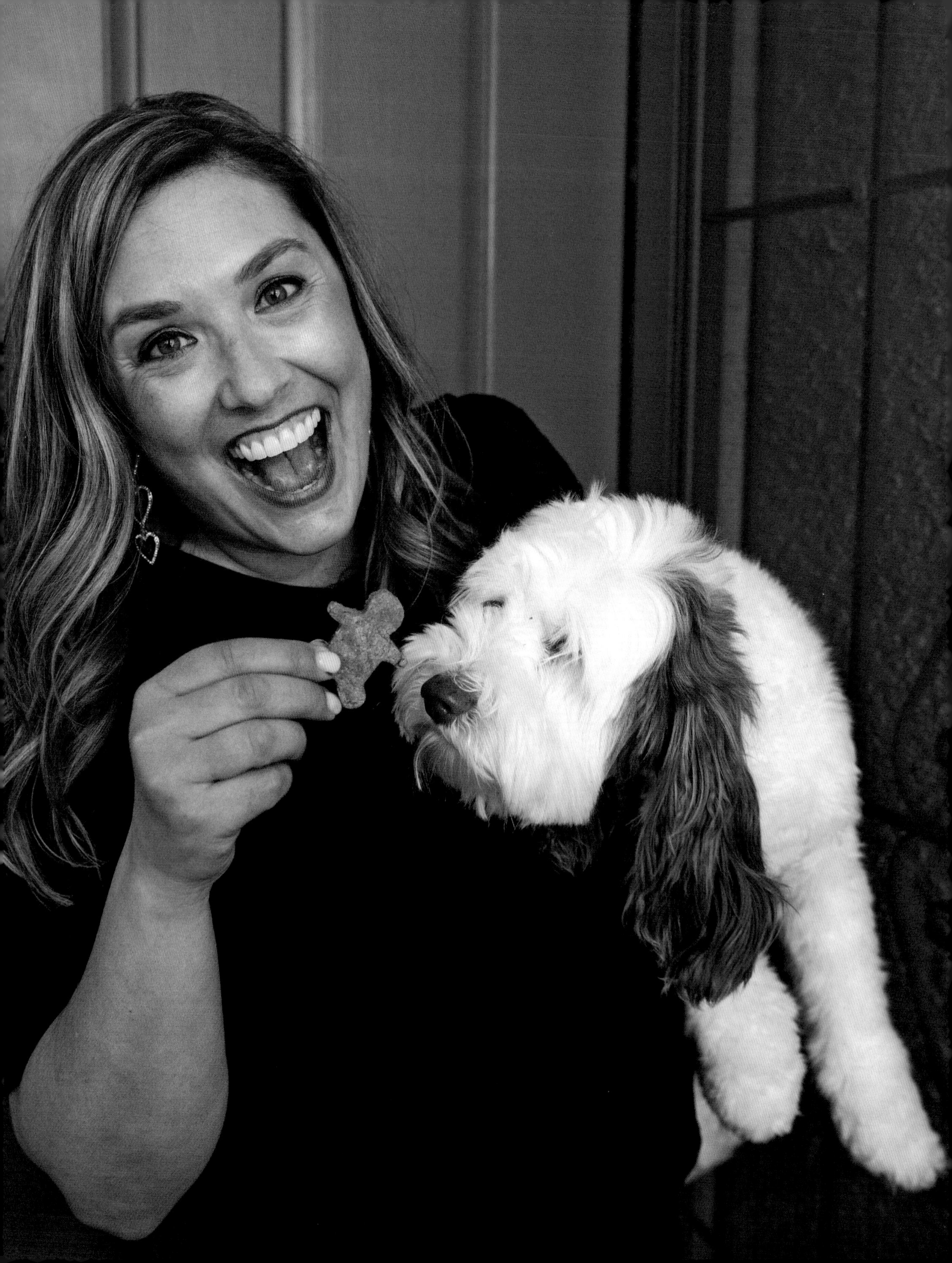

# For Man's Best Friend: Dog Cookies for Your BFF

# CHAPTER 8

I couldn't write this book without a little nod to my labradoodle, Abby. We got her as a puppy and the only way to really describe my relationship with her is to say that she and I are imprinted on each other. She is obsessed with me: always at my feet, always wherever I am. I think she's almost more popular with my readers than I am, as she makes cameo appearances in all of my videos and most of my Instagram stories. Abby takes after her mother: She loves sweets. I mean, sure, she likes when I roast chicken too, but sweet-flavored cookies are her favorite. She is a whopping 15 pounds (7 kg) of fur and bones because she doesn't love meals—but she does love treats. To keep her from wasting away, I constantly make her homemade dog cookies, and I thought I'd share a few of my favorites here. These recipes are for those people who love their dogs as much as they do the people in their lives—and their furry BFFs.

Some notes before you get started:

· You can use any cookie cutters (find some fun ones on Amazon). Or, just use a biscuit cutter or glass to make round cookies.

· Sizing matters: Different shapes and sizes of cookie cutters will produce bigger or smaller cookies, taking more or less time to bake.

· These recipes have been tested with both whole wheat flour and all-purpose. I recommend using whole wheat flour, as it's better for your pup, but you can use either.

· As always, make sure you know what your dog can and can't eat, or consult your vet before feeding them human food or homemade cookies.

# Ginger's Gingerbread Cookies

J first made these cookies for our golden retriever, Ginger. She was obsessed with molasses; she would follow me around the kitchen whenever she saw me get the jar from the pantry. These cookies can be made in any shape and are really easy to make without tons of work. Our current pup, Abby, may have never known Ginger, but they sure do have their love of molasses in common! Once she had a taste of these cookies, she stalked me until I packaged them up for gifts and got them away from her little nose.

## INSTRUCTIONS

1   Preheat the oven to 350°F (177°C). Line 2 cookie sheets with parchment paper or silicone baking mats.

2   Mix together the molasses, honey, water, and vegetable oil in a large bowl using a hand mixer. Mix in the baking soda and ginger, then mix in 1 cup (124 g) of flour at a time. Mix until a stiff dough forms.

3   Once you can't mix anymore, turn the mixture out onto a lightly floured surface and knead with your hands to form a cohesive ball. Roll the dough to ¼-inch (6 mm) thick. Cut out desired shapes using small cookie cutters, re-rolling the dough as needed. (Be sure the sizes are appropriate shapes for dogs, so they are not eating a cookie that is too big for them.)

4   Place the cutouts 1 inch (2.5 cm) apart on the prepared pans. Bake for 10 to 15 minutes, rotating the pans halfway through baking. Baking time will be dependent on how big your cutouts are.

5   Cool completely before giving a cookie to your dog. Store leftovers in an airtight container for up to 3 days or freeze for up to a month.

- ⅓ cup (79 ml) molasses
- 2 tablespoons (40 g) honey
- ½ cup (118 ml) water
- ¼ cup (55 g) vegetable oil
- 1 teaspoon baking soda
- 1 teaspoon ground ginger
- 3 cups (372 g) all-purpose flour

**Yield:** 50 to 60 cookies
**Prep time:** 30 minutes
**Bake time:** 12 minutes

## Tip:

These make great gifts! Simply package in airtight containers and give to your pup's doggy friends as holiday treats.

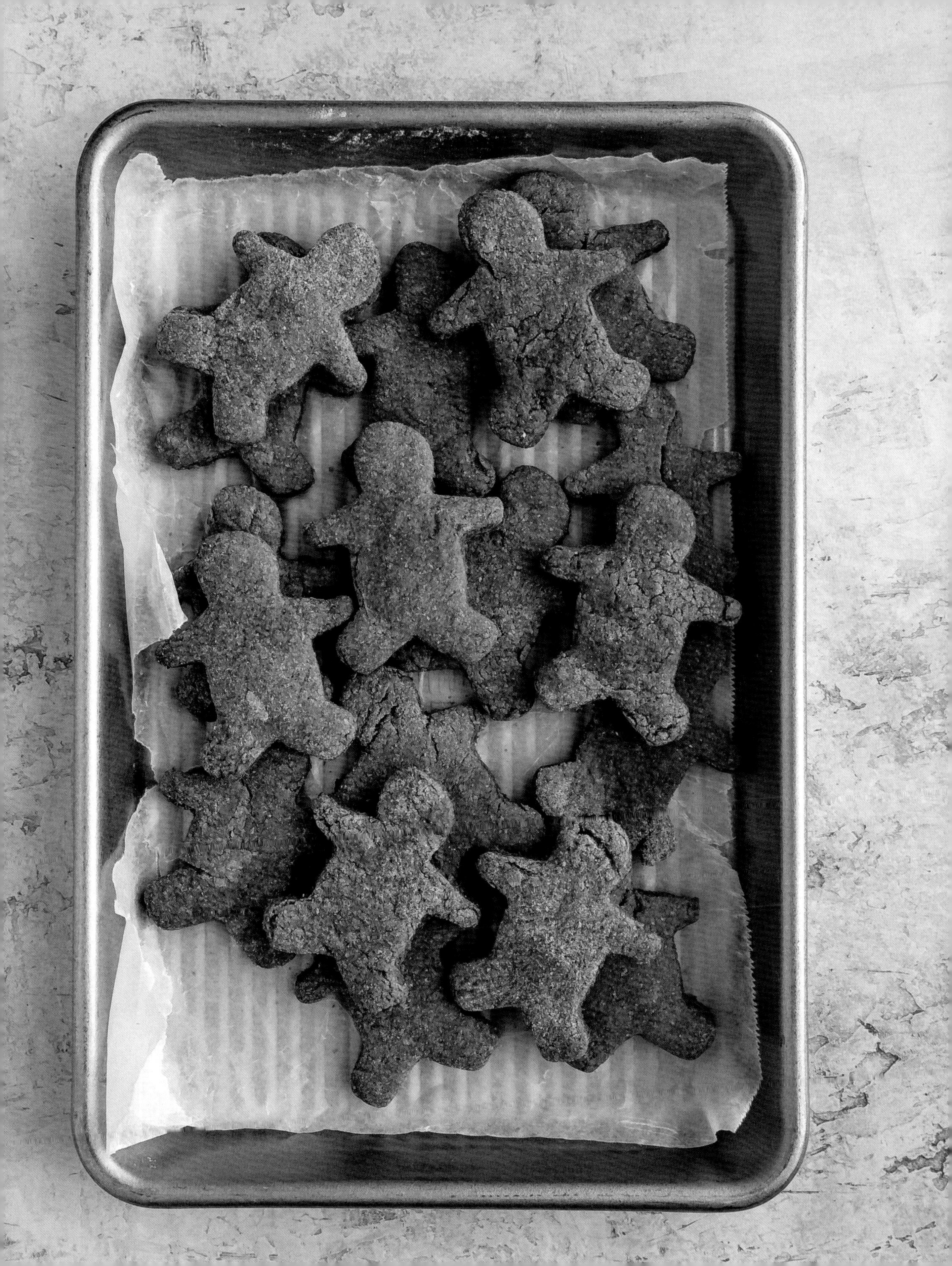

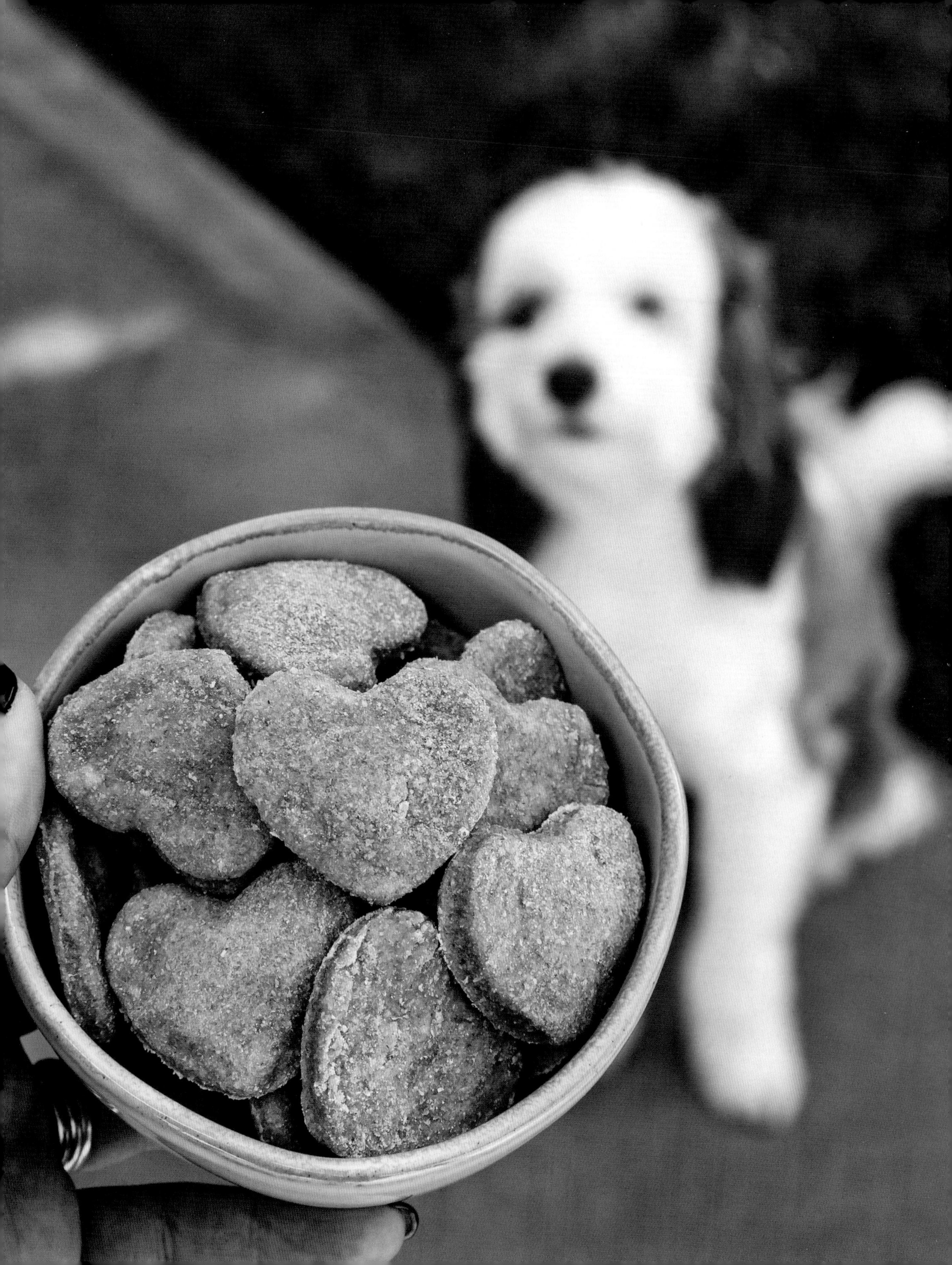

# Abby's Favorite Vanilla Cookies

**W**e are avid Starbucks drinkers and so, of course, we bring Abby all the time. When she was a puppy, we started getting her puppuccinos, which are little cups of whipped cream. Somehow, we created a monster because she not only has a major sweet tooth but goes absolutely nuts anytime we go to Starbucks and don't bring her one. It's gotten to the point I even buy cans of ready-made whipped cream to give her as a treat. These cookies are simple and a little sweet with some vanilla extract thrown in because she is definitely *#teamvanilla*.

## INSTRUCTIONS

1 Preheat the oven to 350°F (177°C). Line 2 cookie sheets with parchment paper or silicone baking mats.

2 Stir together the flour, salt, vanilla extract, honey, water, and egg. Stir until dough is shaggy and cannot be stirred by hand anymore.

3 Turn the dough out onto a floured surface and knead until it comes together, adding more flour to the board and/or dough so it doesn't stick.

4 Roll the dough into a large rectangle, about ¼-inch (6 mm) thick. Use a 1-inch or 2-inch (2.5 or 5 cm) cookie cutter to cut out cookies, re-rolling the dough as needed. Place the cookies on the prepared cookie sheets.

5 Bake small cookies for 12 to 17 minutes or until the bottoms are lightly golden. Cool completely before feeding to your dog or storing the cookies. Cookies will dry out as they cool (they will be soft but firm).

6 Store in an airtight container for up to 3 days or freeze for up to a month.

- 2 cups (248 g) whole wheat flour
- ½ teaspoon salt
- 1 teaspoon vanilla extract
- 2 tablespoons (40 g) honey
- ½ cup (118 ml) water
- 1 large egg

**Yield:** 36 1-inch (2.5 cm) size cookies
**Prep time:** 30 minutes
**Bake time:** 15 minutes

## Tip:
You can substitute molasses for the honey, if desired. The number of cookies and bake time will depend on the size of the cookie cutter.

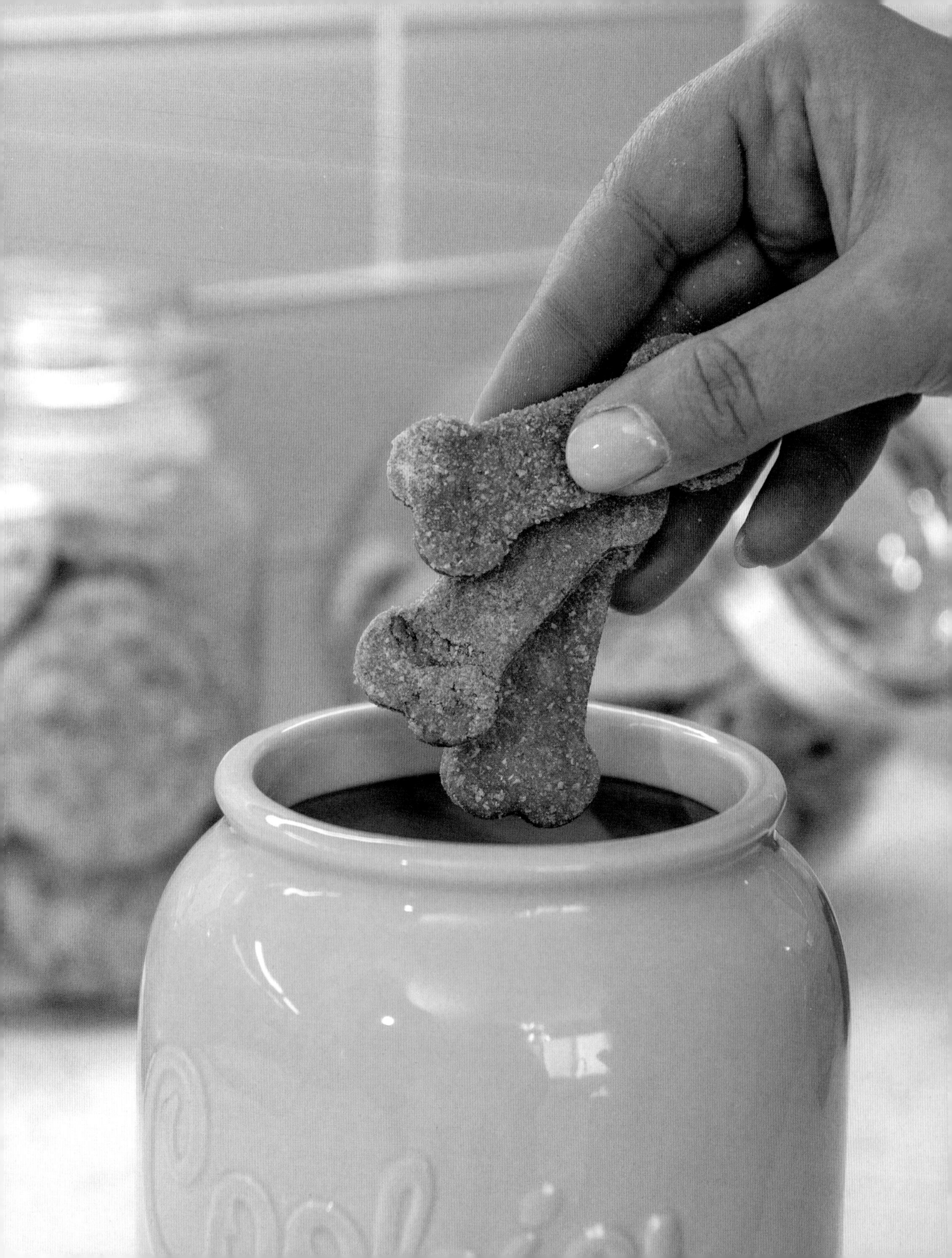

# Pumpkin Dog Cookies

These were another cookie that Ginger absolutely loved. I really wish Ginger and Abby had met because Abby could have learned a thing or two from her big sister! One of those things: how to be a dog. Abby 100 percent thinks she's human, and along with that comes childish behaviors. She often stays with a friend, Lauri, who is her second mom. Lauri adds pumpkin to Abby's food and she gobbles it right up, so I tried that at home but she turned her nose up and made me throw it all away and wash her bowl before she'd eat again. The only way I am able to get Abby to eat pumpkin is when I make it into cookies—then she loves them. And I'm pretty sure it's the molasses and honey she really wants and getting her to eat the pumpkin is just a happy by-product of the whole situation.

- ½ cup (122 g) pumpkin puree
- 1 tablespoon (20 g) honey
- 1 tablespoon (15 ml) molasses
- 1 large egg
- 1½ cups (186 g) whole wheat flour

**Yield:** 36 2-inch (5 cm) size cookies
**Prep time:** 30 minutes
**Bake time:** 18 minutes

## INSTRUCTIONS

1   Preheat the oven to 350°F (177°C). Line 2 cookie sheets with parchment paper or silicone baking mats.

2   Stir together the pumpkin puree, honey, molasses, and egg until smooth. Stir in the flour until you get a shaggy dough and can't stir anymore.

3   Turn the dough out onto a floured surface and knead until it comes together, adding more flour to the board and/or dough so it doesn't stick.

4   Roll the dough into a large rectangle, about ¼-inch (6 mm) thick. Use a 1-inch or 2-inch (2.5 or 5 cm) cookie cutter to cut out cookies, re-rolling the dough as needed. Place the cookies on the prepared cookie sheet.

5   Bake small cookies for 15 to 18 minutes or until the bottoms are lightly golden. Cool completely before feeding to your dog or storing the cookies. Cookies will dry out as they cool (they will be soft but firm).

6   Store in an airtight container for up to 3 days or freeze for up to a month.

**Tip:**

If you prefer, use 2 tablespoons (40 g) either honey or molasses instead of a combination. The amount of cookies and bake time will depend on the size of the cookie cutter.

# Acknowledgments

It seems strange to say that writing a cookbook is difficult and all-encompassing when you write recipes on a blog for a living, but it's so true. The mental time it takes to think up ideas, the physical time it takes to write and test—it's a true labor of love, and it takes a village to get it done. My village was large, and I am so thankful for every person in it!

First, I have to thank my editor Dan, and the entire team at The Quarto Group, for having the faith in me to write this book. The day I saw his email in my inbox, I knew that Dan would have a hand in changing my life, helping me to do this next thing I longed to do, and for that I'll be forever grateful.

Of course, I have to thank the most prominent people in my village: my husband, Mel, and my daughter, Jordan. Mel, without your love and unwavering support I would not have gotten to the place where I could write this book. You have always believed in me even when I didn't believe in myself. Oh, and dishes—I can't not mention how thankful I am that you did all the dishes!

Jordan, every time I see you, I think of the world of possibility, both that you have inside you and that you have given me. Through you I've opened my eyes to the world and can really see it, and I can see inside myself the qualities I see in you that I've never allowed to surface. Thank you for being you, for being such an inspiration, and for always tasting even if you were *so over cookies*.

I also want to give a shout-out to my parents, Bill and Betty, for their unwavering support, always commenting and reading, supporting me, testing and tasting, and for giving me the love of food (and the work ethic) that would inspire me to start this whole thing in the first place.

There are a countless number of women I could mention here, boss ladies who lift me up, show me the way, and inspire me every single day. For every one of you I've come to know on this crazy blogging journey, I want to thank you. Sandra, thank you for inspiring me to always do better, be better, and love hard. Lisa, thank you for always giving me your ear when I needed it. Holly, thank you for being an endless cheerleader, always, and Cathy, thank you for helping me find the woman that was always inside of me.

Of course, to the testers! All of you blog readers who signed up and those of you who painstakingly tested and tried and reported on the recipes in this book. Thank you for your time and your excitement! And to my blog readers as a whole: This book would not exist if it wasn't for all of you.

This book was completely conceived and written during the 2020 COVID-19 pandemic. I note this only to serve as a lesson, for myself and others, that even in times of stress and hopelessness, never stop believing in yourself and your ability to *do*, that someday, somewhere, there is always a light, a rainbow, a reason to keep going . . . and in my case a whole lot of cookies.

# About the Author

**D**orothy Kern is the founder, writer, and photographer of the popular food blog, *Crazy for Crust*, where she shares all things sweet (and sometimes savory), always with a slice of life. She sees baking and the creating of food as warmth and love and strives to share recipes that will inspire others to get in the kitchen and create their own happiness and memories through baking.

Having wanted to be a teacher since she was young, Dorothy started her career as a high school algebra and geometry teacher, trading in her compass for diapers after her daughter was born, then returning to her love of teaching through blogging back in 2010. Since then, she's reached hundreds of millions of people through her love of pie, cookies, and all things dessert. She's been featured on or in *Rachael Ray Magazine, Woman's World Magazine, Buzzfeed, Good Housekeeping, Redbook*, and many more.

When she's not working, you can find Dorothy reading a book or binge-watching Bravo, often while online searching for sparkly shoes or earrings, or planning her next trip to anywhere. She's 100 percent a California girl with dreams of living at the beach with her husband, teenage daughter, and precocious labradoodle-turned-second-child, Abby.

Find Dorothy online at CrazyforCrust.com or @crazyforcrust on all social media. Share your love of cookies by tagging her and using *#crazyforcookiescookbook*.

# Index

## R



## S



## T



## U



## V



## W



## Z

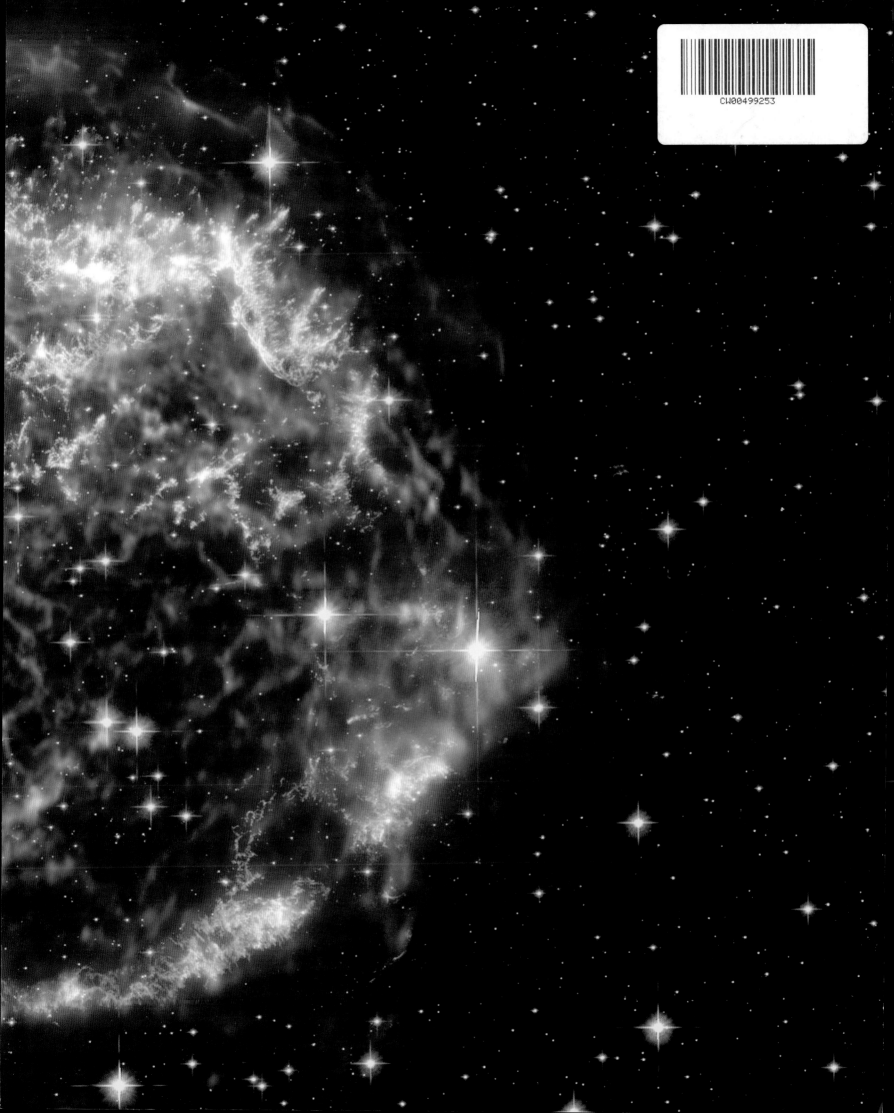

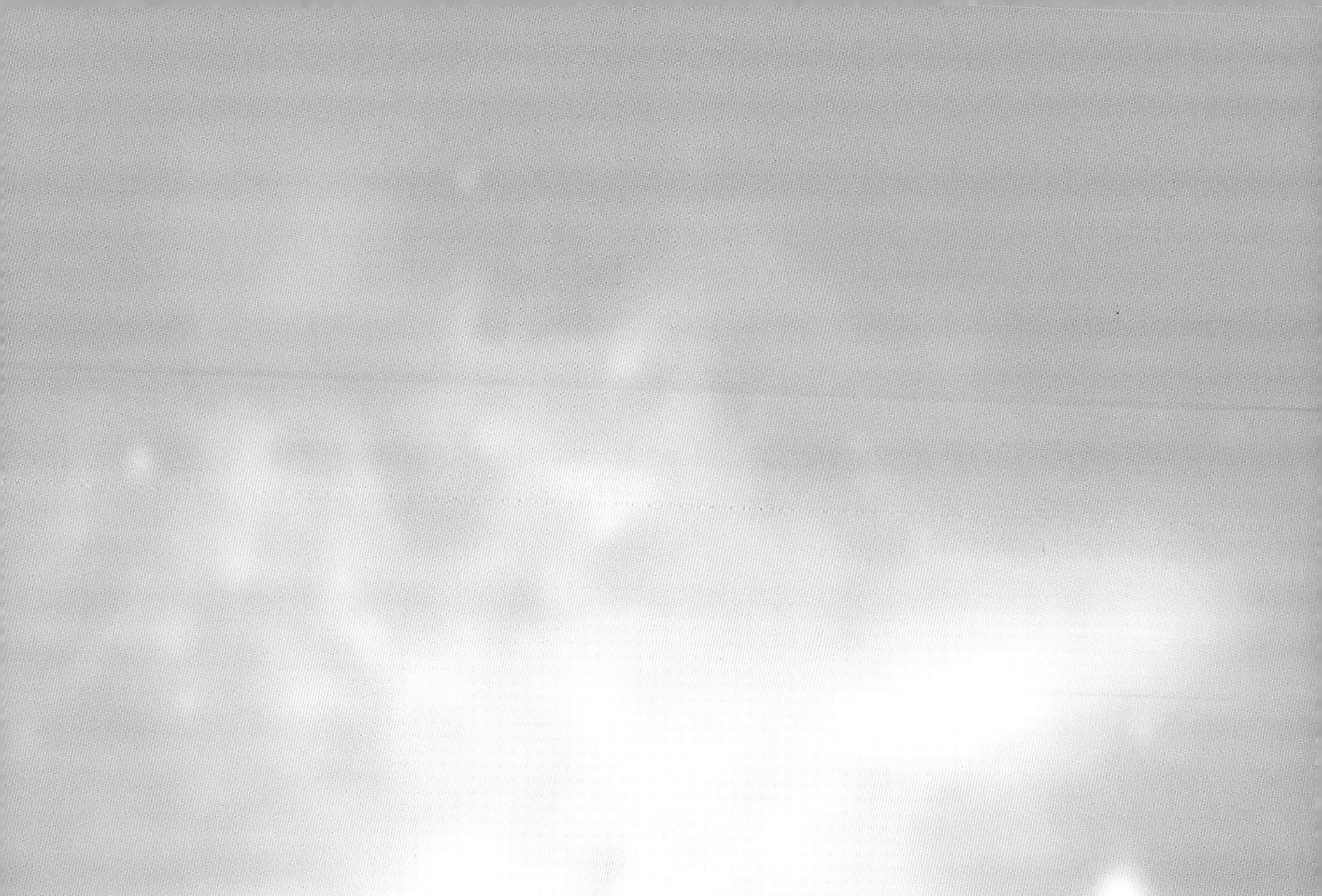

# HIDDEN UNIVERSE

Lars Lindberg Christensen, Robert Fosbury, Robert Hurt

WILEY-VCH

# HIDDEN UNIVERSE

## The Authors

Lars Lindberg Christensen
Robert Fosbury
ESA/Hubble
ESO/ESA/ST-ECF
Garching, Germany

Robert Hurt
Spitzer Science Center
Pasadena
USA

## Layout & Illustrations

Nuno Marques &
Martin Kornmesser
ESA/Hubble
ESO/ESA/ST-ECF
Garching, Germany

COVER: MULTI-WAVELENGTH VIEW OF MESSIER 82

The cover shows a composite of images of the active galaxy Messier 82 from the Hubble Space Telescope, Chandra X-ray Observatory, and Spitzer Space Telescope. X-ray observations from Chandra appear here in blue, infrared light from Spitzer appears in red, Hubble's observation of hydrogen-alpha emission appears in orange and Hubble's bluest observation appears in blue-green.

FIGURE 1: MULTI-WAVELENGTH VIEW OF CASSIOPEIA A
(INSIDE FRONT COVER)

This stunningly colourful picture shows the rich structure of the supernova remnant Cassiopeia A. It is composed of images using three different wavebands of light. Infrared data from the Spitzer Space Telescope are coloured red; visible data from the Hubble Space Telescope are yellow; and X-ray data from the Chandra X-ray Observatory are green and blue. Located 10 000 light-years away in the constellation of Cassiopeia, Cassiopeia A is the remnant of a once massive star that died in a violent supernova explosion that would have been seen from Earth some 325 years ago had it not been behind clouds of obscuring dust. It consists of a dead star, called a neutron star, and a surrounding shell of material that was blasted off as the star imploded.

All books published by Wiley-VCH are carefully produced. Nevertheless, authors, editors, and publisher do not warrant the information contained in these books, including this book, to be free of errors. Readers are advised to keep in mind that statements, data, illustrations, procedural details or other items may inadvertently be inaccurate.

**Library of Congress Card No.:**
applied for

**British Library Cataloguing-in-Publication Data**
A catalogue record for this book is available from the British Library.
Bibliographic information published by
the Deutsche Nationalbibliothek

The Deutsche Nationalbibliothek lists this publication in the Deutsche Nationalbibliografie; detailed bibliographic data are available on the Internet at <http://dnb.d-nb.de>.

© 2009 WILEY-VCH Verlag GmbH & Co. KGaA, Weinheim

Printed in the Federal Republic of Germany
Printed on acid-free paper

**Composition:** Hagedorn Kommunikation GmbH, Viernheim
**Printing:** betz-druck GmbH, Darmstadt
**Bookbinding:** Litges & Dopf GmbH, Heppenheim

**ISBN**: 978-3-527-40866-5

**FIGURE 2: MESSIER 81**

This image of Messier 81 combines data from the Hubble Space Telescope, the Spitzer Space Telescope and the Galaxy Evolution Explorer (GALEX) missions. The GALEX ultraviolet data were from the far-ultraviolet portion of the spectrum. The Spitzer infrared data were taken in the mid-infrared. The Hubble data were taken at the blue portion of the visible part of the spectrum. Compare with the purely infrared and ultraviolet images of this object in Figure 38 and Figure 47.

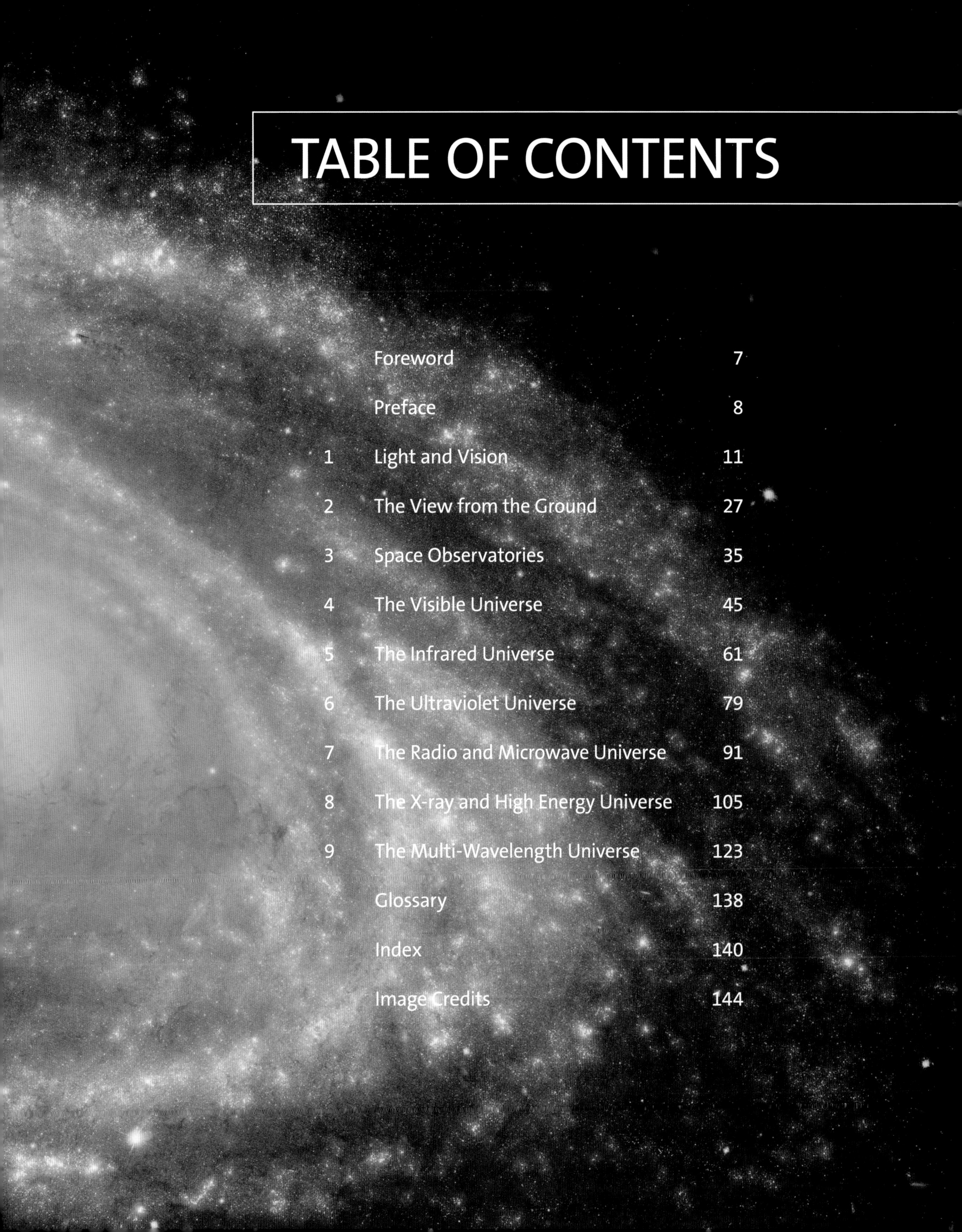

# TABLE OF CONTENTS

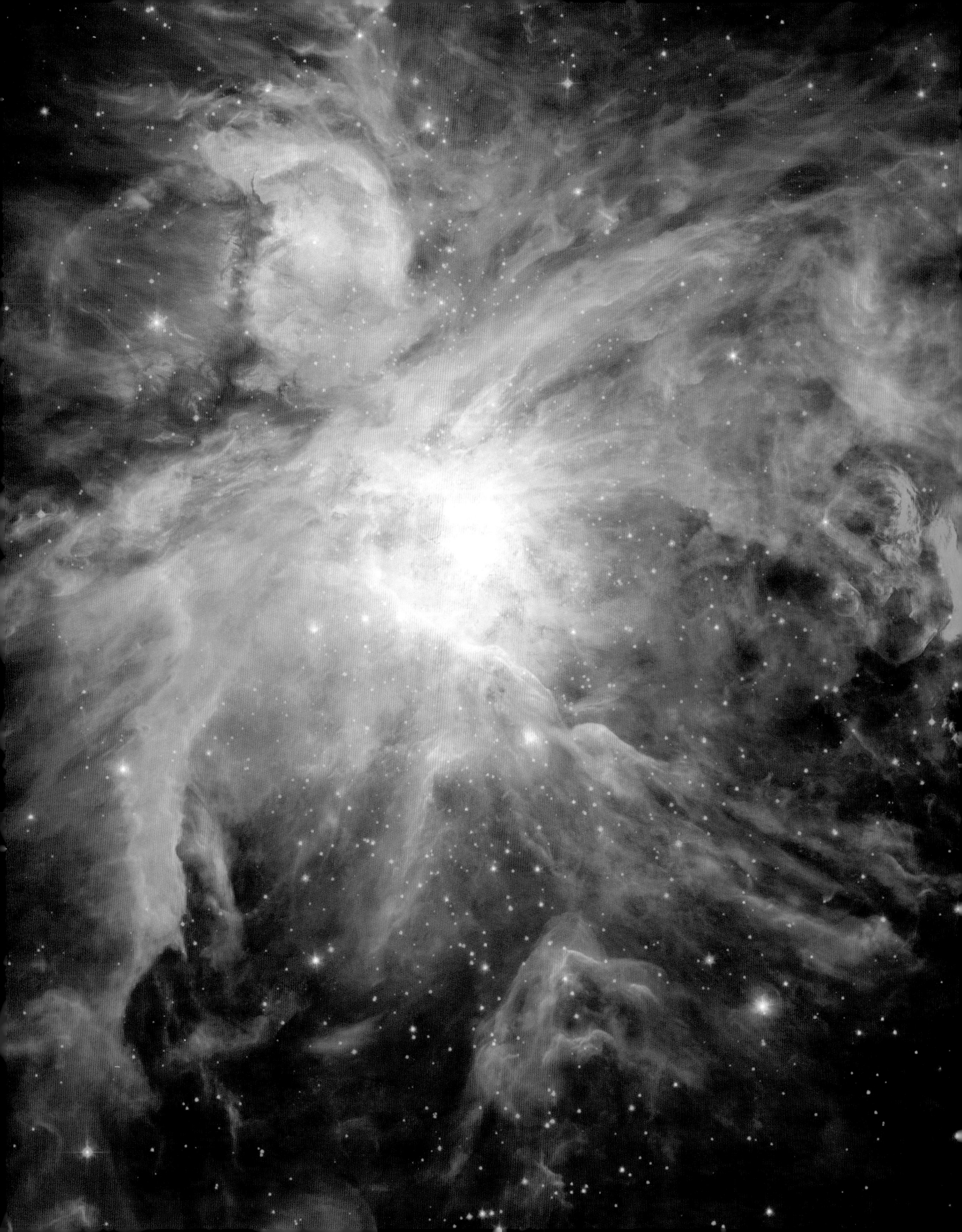

# FOREWORD

**FIGURE 3: THE ORION NEBULA IN INFRARED AND VISIBLE LIGHT**

Images from the Spitzer and Hubble Space Telescopes have been combined to form a striking infrared and visible-light composite. Swirls of green in Hubble's ultraviolet and visible-light view reveal radiation emitted by a gas formed predominantly of hydrogen and sulphur atoms that have been heated and ionised by intense ultraviolet radiation. Spitzer's infrared view exposes carbon-rich organic molecules in the cloud (wisps of red and orange).

The last fifty years have been a glorious period for astronomical research. For the first time in our history, we have been able to study the Universe at all the different wavelengths emitted by celestial objects without the absorption and blurring produced by the Earth's atmosphere.

The opening up of space and the development of large telescopes with exquisite angular resolution permits the study of celestial objects in unprecedented detail. The parallel development of physics and astrophysical theory used in interpreting these data has provided the answer to some of the larger questions that mankind has asked for millennia. We can now explain the birth and death of the stars, the formation of planets, the structure of galaxies along with their formation and evolution, the age of the Universe and its beginning and the formation of the chemical elements. However, the recent discoveries of dark matter and dark energy ensure that we remain properly humble. All but a few percent of the mass-energy of the Universe is in forms we do not yet know or understand. This clearly demonstrates how far we have yet to go in trying to understand our cosmos and our place in it.

Together with these amazing discoveries, there has been a great change in how astronomy is done and communicated. Astronomers now have access to the latest and best data from nearly all the observational facilities in space and on the ground, without regard to nationality or institutional affiliation. This leads to a very effective scientific use and re-use of the existing data. A great effort has also been made to share the results with students, teachers and the general public. This book is a splendid example of the results.

The reader is taken on a tour of the Universe as we know it. Explanatory text guides us through it, but the greatest impact comes from the pictures themselves. It is extraordinary that in most cases the perception created by the images corresponds closely to our understanding of what is actually happening. Thus I think this book is much more than a coffee-table curiosity, but rather a true window on the Universe.

Washington DC, 15 August 2008

**Riccardo Giacconi**

Recipient of the Nobel Prize in Physics, 2002

# PREFACE

Until 400 years ago, when Galileo first turned his telescope towards the heavens, our perception of the Universe was limited by our eyes and the thoughts and ideas arising from what we saw. The huge leap in capability that even such a simple instrument could realise set us on the path of creating ever more powerful instruments to satisfy our voracious appetite for knowledge.

Nonetheless, until the mid-20th century our view of the Universe was limited almost entirely to the narrow band of light that could penetrate the Earth's atmosphere and was visible either to our eyes or to sensitive photographic plates loaded at the focus of increasingly large telescopes. With these resources alone, the discoveries were still stupendous: the mapping of our Solar System, the identification of the mechanism that makes stars shine and determines how long they live, the realisation that there are a multitude of galaxies like our own Milky Way and that they constitute an expanding Universe. The profound revolution in physics during the first half of the century brought with it the understanding of how light is emitted and how to read the subtle messages it carries concerning the physical state and chemical composition of stars and nebulae.

Stimulated by the development of radar for military use, the first major expansion of our view was the result of the development of radio astronomy, leading to the realisation that the Universe could look very different to us when seen through new "eyes" tuned to a different type of radiation.

The launch of Sputnik in 1957 paved the way for astronomy's escape from the absorbing and distorting effects of the Earth's atmosphere. With truly clear skies, generations of exploratory spacecraft and orbiting observatories have produced a wondrous and often breathtakingly beautiful view of a Universe whose richness could not have been imagined. A string of new discoveries has come from this fleet of new space-based instruments and observatories, and each new insight has been firmly placed within the existing framework of understanding by astronomers. Meanwhile the impressive arsenal of today's ground-based facilities bears witness to the continuing success of the modern large and highly evolved versions of the traditional telescope.

This book will enable you to peer through these exotic new telescopes and see some of the more spectacular images that have become the icons of modern astronomy. By expanding your vision beyond the visible into an array of "colours" that span the full spectrum of light, you will be able to gain a more complete picture of the Universe than has ever been possible before. These images are truly a legacy to be appreciated by everyone. Obtained using facilities built by governments and public institutions across the globe, they allow us all to better understand our place in a spectacular Universe, once hidden, but now revealed.

**About the Book**

This book is divided into nine chapters dealing with various aspects of the unseen Universe. The first three discuss the way we perceive the Universe, using our eyes and with telescopes on the ground and in space. The next five chapters each discuss a wavelength band, starting with the most familiar, visible light, and then moving outwards on each side of the spectrum into the less familiar: infrared, ultraviolet, radio/microwaves and X-rays/gamma rays. In the final chapter we attempt to gather the individual threads of the story into one, somewhat coherent, view of the totality of the multi-wavelength Universe.

When we took up the task of writing this book we knew that we were stepping into unknown territory. It is no easy task to communicate unseen phenomena, especially those caused by often unfamiliar physics far from our everyday experience. We have had to use an arsenal of important physical terms such as "spectrum" and "blackbody radiation", but we have kept the use of jargon to a minimum and have provided explanations of the most unfamiliar terms in the glossary at the end of the book. The first occurrence of each of these glossary words in each chapter is marked in bold.

**Acknowledgements**

We offer thanks to many of our colleagues working hard in observatories and in science communication machine rooms around the world. Many of the stunning images in this book were developed using all the talents of these astronomers and graphics experts. We would like to extend an extra thank-you to the Chandra team led by Megan Watzke and Kimberly Kowal Arcand and the Spitzer team led by Gordon Squires for their frequent efforts to compare their X-ray and infrared images with other wavelengths and thereby contribute to the unveiling of the hidden Universe. Thanks also go to Anne Rhodes, Laura Simurda and Chris Lawton for excellent editorial help in preparing this book.

Munich 9 July 2008

**Lars Lindberg Christensen**
**Robert Fosbury**
**Robert Hurt**

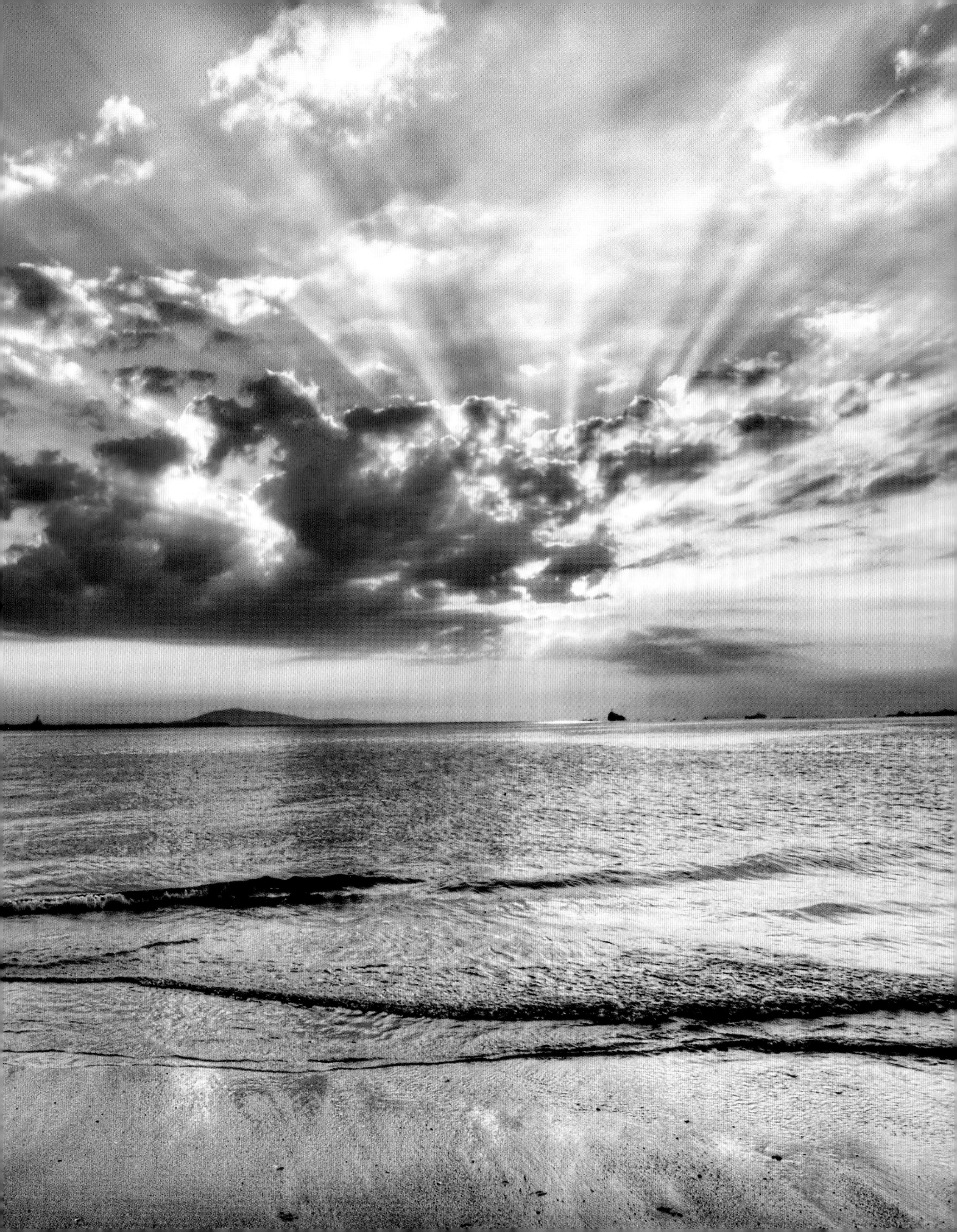

# 1 LIGHT AND VISION

**FIGURE 4: LIGHT AND COLOUR**

A sunset with crepuscular rays. The sunbeams radiating from our local star, the Sun, give us the feeling that our world is flooded with light.

Ours is a Universe of light...

The light we see defines the way we understand the world around us. What is solid and what is insubstantial, what is bright and what is dark, what is beautiful and what is ugly. All of these concepts derive from visual cues. But since our vision is inextricably linked to the nature of the Sun, in a real sense even our aesthetics are deeply rooted in astronomy. Perhaps it is no wonder that images of the Universe can trigger such a sense of awe. But the light from the Universe contains so much more than the light we can see for ourselves...

*" Every newborn baby is the result of 3 billion years of evolution and a demonstration of the physical connection between the human organism and the Universe "*

When a baby opens its eyes for the first time it finds itself bathed in light. Every newborn baby is the result of 3 billion years of evolution and a demonstration of the physical connection between the human organism and the Universe. Our eyes are biological detectors shaped by evolutionary advantage to utilise best the flood of light from our nearest star, the Sun. It is no coincidence at all that our eyes see exactly the spread of colours over which our Sun radiates most brightly. It exemplifies the beauty of biological efficiency, and reminds us that if we lived near a star that shone differently, we would have formed a different concept of what constitutes "visible" light.

## Human Colour Theory

How does our eye see colour and what makes the **spectrum** of colour? Our eyes are biological light detectors, allowing our brains to construct images from the signals passing down the optic nerve. Human eyes have three different types of colour-sensitive cells that allow us to differentiate three fundamental, or **primary**, **colours** of light: red, green, and blue. Combinations of these three primary hues produce the entire spectrum of colours that we can see, from pale pastels to bold, vivid tones.

How do the other colours relate to the primary hues of red, green and blue? It is all in the combinations and proportions. Equal pairs of primary colours produce the **secondary colours** of light. Red and green combine to form yellow. Green and blue yield cyan, while blue and red make magenta. Other shades, like teal, orange or purple, emerge by varying the proportions of the three primaries slightly. If red, green and blue are all present in equal amounts, then the result is white, while black is just the complete absence of all of them. Such colour combinations are known as **additive** as they reflect the operation of the human eye as light of different colours is added.

*"Any image we see can be broken down into three greyscale components representing red, green and blue light"*

The simplicity in this arrangement of colours makes it easy for us to record and present full colour images using digital technology. Any image we see can be broken down into three greyscale components representing red, green and blue light. A television or computer monitor uses separate red, green and blue elements (LEDs, backlit LCDs, or glowing phosphors) to present these images together so that we see the full colour result. Likewise in print, choosing the right combination of inks can recreate an image that will reflect the right combinations of red, green and blue into our eyes to represent the full colour image (See Box: Subtractive colours).

GREEN
lime
amber
orange
RED
Magenta
purple
BLUE
Cyan
teal

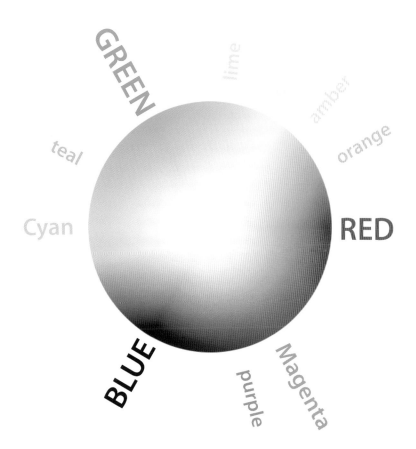

**FIGURE 5: COLOUR WHEEL**

The three fundamental colours of light, as seen by our eyes, are red, green and blue. Combinations of these three primary hues produce the entire spectrum of colours that we perceive, seen here organised in a so-called colour wheel. The secondary colours, cyan, magenta and yellow, fall exactly between the primaries, and other hues fall at other locations. Note that our eyes are most sensitive to slight shifts between red and green, with more recognisable colours falling between them than any other two primaries.

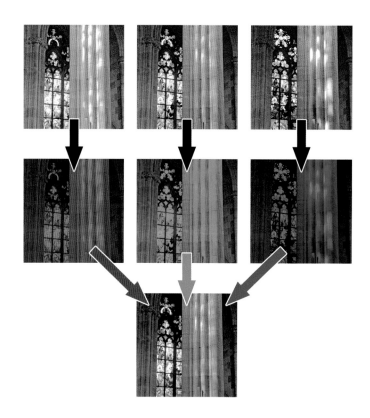

**FIGURE 6: FROM GREYSCALE TO COLOUR**

Any colour image can be represented as three greyscale images capturing the red, green and blue components separately. By assigning the correct primary colour to each one and combining them additively, the full range of colours our eye can see will emerge.

It is important to note that these interpretations of colour should really be thought of as the nature of human colours. Our three-colour system is a result of evolutionary processes, but it is far from the only possible way that our eyes could have turned out. Other animals have no colour vision or can see a little way into other parts of the spectrum. If we had one additional colour receptor then we would perceive a significantly more complex, four-dimensional array of colours, which would be much harder to describe on the printed page.

## Subtractive Colours

There is often confusion in understanding the primary colours of light (red, green and blue) and how they relate to the so-called primary colours schoolchildren are taught for painting (typically, blue, red and yellow). The process our eye uses to see colour is an additive one. Light from each colour either enters the eye or it does not. If all the colours are present equally, then we see them all combine to give white.

Paints work in an opposite way, in a **subtractive** manner. A blank piece of paper is white, and reflects all the light that falls on it. Coloured paint subtracts out some of the colours from the light and we see only the colours that are not absorbed by the paint. For instance, a paint that absorbs only red light will have a cyan (an additive mixture of blue and green) colour, while one that absorbs only blue light will be yellow. When you mix paints together, you combine their subtractive properties. So, mixing cyan and yellow paint will subtract both red and blue from the white light leaving only green to be reflected.

Note that the true primary colours of the subtractive process, which is used in printing, are cyan, magenta and yellow. The primary subtractive colours are just the secondary additive colours, and vice versa.

**FIGURE 7: LIGHT AS ELECTROMAGNETIC WAVES**

The alternating oscillating electric (red) and magnetic (blue) fields are perpendicular to each other in space. They travel as a wave of light in the direction of the arrow, with each set of oscillating fields generating the next crest in the wave.

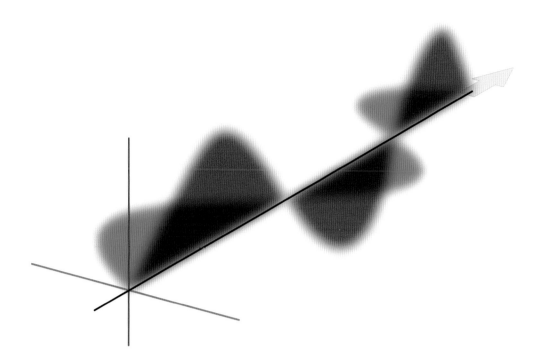

# What is Light?

Understanding how we see colour helps us interpret our human perception of light better, but a more fundamental question remains. What is light itself?

The nature of light was a hotly debated topic throughout the early history of science. In the late 17th century Christiaan Huygens argued that light had a wave-like nature. However by the early 18th century, Isaac Newton's competing theory that light was composed of particles had become the dominant view.

At the beginning of the 19th century, experiments by Thomas Young and Augustin-Jean Fresnel demonstrated that light clearly showed wave like properties, producing effects similar to those seen in waves on the surface of water. It seemed that the answer was near.

But what kind of wave was light? By the late 19th century James Clerk Maxwell had formulated his revolutionary equations showing electric and magnetic fields to be two aspects of the same phenomenon. Light, it seemed, was a wave composed of alternating electric and magnetic fields.

**FIGURE 8: THE WAVELENGTHS OF VISIBLE LIGHT**

The visible part of the spectrum is a tiny sliver of the full spectrum between 380 and 740 nanometres (nm), or billionths of a metre. Yellow light, for instance, has a wavelength of about 570 nm.

400
450
500
550
600
650
700
750


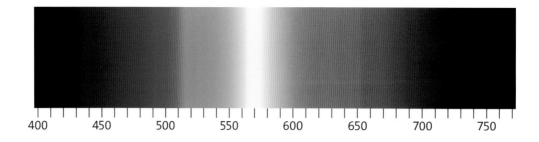

So light is understood to be an **electromagnetic wave**. The spacing between the successive peaks of the electric (or magnetic) field is known as its **wavelength**, and the wavelength determines the colour of the light. Shorter wavelengths correspond to bluer colours, while longer wavelengths are redder.

That light was an electromagnetic wave seemed irrefutable, but its particle nature was soon to reappear. In the early 20th century Albert Einstein was able to explain some confusing experimental results known as the **photoelectric effect** (this effect is used today as the underlying principle behind solar power cells) by showing that light could posses both wave and particle properties. This bizarre notion, known as **wave-particle duality**, would become one of the fundamentals of the emerging science of quantum mechanics and earned Einstein the 1921 Nobel Prize in Physics. When we study light, we will often refer to its particle and wave properties independently, but it is important to remember that both are fundamentally a part of its nature.

The modern view is that electromagnetic waves are parcelled up into particle-like packets. Known as **photons**, these packets define the amount of energy carried within the light. A photon's wavelength and energy are completely interrelated — shorter, redder wavelengths correspond to higher energies, while the longer, bluer wavelengths have lower energies. Scientists often use energy and wavelength interchangeably as they are inversely proportional.

Another fundamental result concerning the nature of light is that it moves at the same speed through space, regardless of its wavelength. It is quite fast, moving at nearly 300 000 kilometres per second. In fact, the speed of light is the ultimate "speed limit"; nothing in the Universe can travel faster.

Even so, the size of the Universe is so large that this speed limit can become quite significant. Light from our Sun still takes eight minutes to reach us, and light from the nearest star has been travelling for four years before arriving at the Earth. The **light-year** becomes a handy way for astronomers to measure distance, defined as how far light travels in one year.

> *"Scientists usually divide the electromagnetic spectrum up into seven bands: radio, microwave, infrared, visible, ultraviolet, X-ray and gamma ray"*

## The Electromagnetic Spectrum

When we think of the spectrum, usually we picture a swathe of colour running from violet to red. But the colours visible to our eyes are only a tiny slice of the entire **electromagnetic spectrum** of light. The full spectrum spans a variety of spectral **bands** that we do not necessarily think of as light, but really are just light with a different wavelength. Scientists usually divide the electromagnetic spectrum up into seven bands: radio, microwave, infrared, visible, ultraviolet, X-ray and gamma ray. These divisions are for human convenience and are not precisely defined by physics, though they do correlate roughly with the different technologies used in each band. Nature provides an electromagnetic spectrum that is continuous and without bounds, but humans usually prefer to divide things into pieces and name them.

Gamma Ray
X-ray
Ultraviolet
Visible
Infrared
Microwave
Radio
0.1 pm
1 pm
10 pm
100 pm
1 nm
10 nm
100 nm
1 µm
10 µm
100 µm
1 mm
1 cm
10 cm
1 m


**FIGURE 9: THE FULL ELECTROMAGNETIC SPECTRUM**

The range of the spectrum of light spans the seven bands shown in this figure. Of them, visible light falls near the centre of the figure, and is defined by the limits of human vision. The corresponding wavelengths are indicated along the bottom (on a logarithmic scale). The boundaries between the other bands are fairly arbitrary , but have been divided up for convenience in studying different parts of the spectrum. Note that the spectrum is open-ended, as there is neither a shortest nor a longest wavelength of light.

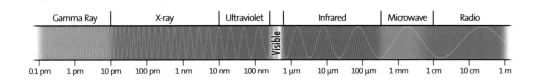

The wavelength of a photon of light determines its energy and where it falls in the spectrum. The spectrum spans an incredible range of wavelengths — in principle it is infinite and continuous — but typically observations are made from hundreds of metres in the radio to less than one thousandth of one billionth of a metre for gamma rays (1 pm). It is usually convenient to use different units of length for waves in the different parts of the spectrum. In this book we will use the following units:

- Centimetre (cm), hundredth of a metre: radio
- Millimetre (mm), thousandth of a metre: microwave
- Micrometre (µm, sometimes called a micron), millionth of a metre: infrared
- Nanometre (nm), billionth of a metre: X-rays, ultraviolet, visible
- Picometre (pm), trillionth of a metre: X-rays, gamma rays

Radio waves are at the lowest energy end of the spectrum and have the longest wavelengths. There is no defined longest wavelength for radio, though it becomes technologically impractical to detect anything far past the kilometre range. Radio waves are used extensively for broadcast communications, and our radio-loud civilisation does make it challenging to detect faint astronomical sources against the broadcast chatter.

Microwaves are also used for communications, including mobile phones. Microwaves are commonly divided into the millimetre and sub-millimetre bands, which in part denote differences in the detector technologies used in astronomy. They are also familiar from their use in microwave ovens. These exploit the fact that microwave radiation is strongly absorbed by water: a property that is important if we want to observe microwaves from space on the ground.

Infrared light spans the gap between visible and microwave light. Infrared light is often thought of as "heat radiation" since warm objects radiate infrared radiation that we can feel.

Visible light constitutes the spectrum that can be seen by human eyes, and it is by far the narrowest band of the spectrum, even though it is naturally the most familiar to us.

Ultraviolet light begins beyond the blue end of the spectrum. On Earth it is perhaps best known for its sun-tanning effects.

X-rays are at such high energies beyond the ultraviolet that each photon has enough energy to penetrate many materials. This makes X-ray exposures a useful way of probing the internal structures of people and animals.

Gamma rays fall at the far end of the spectrum and have the very shortest wavelengths. The energy in each photon is so high that it can have very destructive effects. Gamma rays can disrupt electronics and damage DNA, and in sufficient quantities they can be lethal. Only the highest energy events in the Universe generate gamma rays.

## *" How can we present images from invisible bands of light? "*

## Seeing Invisible Light

When we browse a book of photographs, the colours we see are a reliable constant. A clear sky will always seem blue and the leaves of a tree will always seem green. The combinations of red, green and blue seen by our eyes match the way we represent them in print or on a screen. This process can be described as showing the **natural colours** as our eye sees them.

But, as we have learned, the Universe of light extends well beyond the tiny slice of the visible. Colour can take on an entirely new meaning, referring to parts of the spectrum unseen by our eyes, but accessible to our technology. How can we present images from invisible bands of light?

Since our eyes can only see red, green and blue, these are the only choices available when rendering pictures from outside our range of vision. It is a simple process to take images made from any part of the spectrum and then display them in red, green and blue. The result is a colour image that vividly displays a way of seeing something our eyes alone could not perceive.

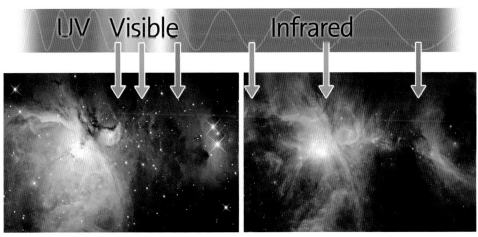

"Natural" Colours     "Representative" Colours

**FIGURE 10: MAPPING THE INVISIBLE TO THE VISIBLE**

Our eyes can only perceive the primary colours red, green, and blue. Here two different colour mappings are shown for the Orion Nebula. To the left is the "natural colour" in which we are presented with the colours much as our eye would see them (though greatly amplified in brightness). To the right we have three infrared exposures mapped into red, green and blue. This is called a "representative colour" mapping.

*" In a multi-wavelength Universe, colour becomes an unimaginably broad palette for the astronomer "*

In these images, what we see as red, green and blue no longer shows us the natural colours our eyes would see, but instead presents **representative colours** of the broader spectrum of light. Historically the term "false colour" has been used to describe such processing of images, but that term is misleading. "False" implies that the colours are somehow "fake" or "colourised", as when an artist paints colours onto a black and white photograph. Representative colour images show real variations in colour from across the spectrum that have been shifted into a representation that works with our — relatively — limited eyes.

In a multi-wavelength Universe, colour becomes an unimaginably broad palette for the astronomer. Red, green and blue can now mean radically different things in different pictures as they bring the entire spectrum into view for us, and that alone provides an exotic beauty to be enjoyed.

There is even more to appreciate if we pause to consider what the colours actually represent in each case. How colour is used provides a kind of map legend, helping us to interpret the different things we see in each image. In this book, many images are presented, along with colour keys that show which parts of the spectrum are represented by the various colours. Knowing this mapping allows colour to become a guide, not just to our aesthetic reaction, but to our scientific understanding as well. We can transcend the limits of our biological evolution and experience the full spectrum from a Universe that would otherwise be hidden!

> *" Electromagnetic radiation is produced by a surprisingly small number of phenomena that, when blended together, produce the fantastically varied Universe we see "*

## Producing Light

Our Universe is filled with light, but where does it come from? Electromagnetic radiation is produced by a surprisingly small number of phenomena that, when blended together, produce the fantastically varied Universe we see.

In the most basic sense, light is a series of oscillating electric and magnetic fields. So it should come as no surprise that light is generated from the motions and transitions of particles charged with electricity. If you take an electron or proton and shake it back and forth, you will inevitably produce light. This classical view is complicated a bit by the processes of quantum mechanics, but together they lead to a set of basic processes that help us interpret what we see anywhere across the Universe.

### Blackbody Radiation

Most of the light in the world around us originates in a process curiously named **blackbody radiation**. This is a spectrum of light that only depends on the temperature of the object, whether it be a rock, a person, a star or even the entire Universe itself!

The basic idea is simple. Imagine an object that perfectly absorbs every photon of light that falls on it — this object would be perfectly black as no light would be reflected from it. Since photons carry energy, the object would heat up as it absorbed more and more photons. The only way such an object could be in equilibrium with its environment is if it radiated an amount of energy equal to what it received. Such radiation is called blackbody radiation and is exclusively a function of an object's temperature.

The physics governing blackbody radiation is known as **Planck's Law**. Blackbody radiation has a consistent shape, shifting in brightness and wavelength as the temperature of the radiating blackbody object changes. If one increases the temperature of a blackbody, the peak of the brightness moves to shorter or bluer wavelengths. This effect is called **Wien's Displacement Law**.

**FIGURE 11: BLACKBODY RADIATION FROM DIFFERENT OBJECTS**

The emission of light from different objects as a function of temperature repeats the important blackbody shape. However the peak of the brightness shifts dramatically in wavelength with increasing temperature. For instance, our Sun has a temperature of nearly 6000 K (yellow line, 5500 °C or 5778 K to be precise) and is brightest in the visible part of the spectrum around the colour yellow. If the Sun were half as hot (3000 K, orange line), it would be about 100 times fainter at the colour yellow, and its peak brightness would shift to the infrared. Note that both axes of this plot are logarithmic; each tick mark is a factor of 10 larger than its predecessor.

Ultraviolet
Visible
Infrared
Microwave
Radio
24 000 K
12 000 K
6000 K
3000 K
1500 K
750 K
300 K
100 K
30 K
10 K
2.7 K
Bellatrix
Rigel
Sun
Mira
Brown Dwarf
Warm Dust
Cold Dust
Cosmic Background
Brightness (factors of 10)
10 nm
100 nm
1 µm
10 µm
100 µm
1 mm
1 cm
10 cm
Wavelength

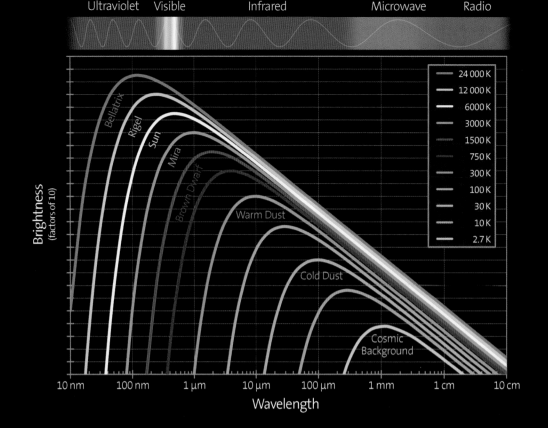

*“ Even people emit blackbody radiation ”*

Our Sun, with a temperature of about 5500 °C (about 5800 **Kelvin**), is brightest in the yellow part of the spectrum. Hotter stars will be brightest in the ultraviolet. Even people emit blackbody radiation; with a body temperature of about 37 °C (roughly 310 K), we emit most brightly at infrared wavelengths of around 10 micrometres, but are far too cool to shine in visible colours.

Blackbody radiation is truly ubiquitous and will be mentioned often below. It is the glow of the Sun, of incandescent light bulbs. It is emitted by people, planets and cold, dark clouds of interstellar dust. It is often described as **thermal radiation**, and it is the cosmic thermometer that astronomers use. Measuring an object’s blackbody spectrum allows us to measure its temperature effectively, even from billions of light-years away!

> *" Spectral lines in distant stars and galaxies allows us to measure their chemical composition and determine physical properties from afar "*

## Spectral Line Radiation

The revolution of quantum mechanics at the start of the 20th century changed our understanding of the Universe forever, and gave us amazing tools to probe the structure of matter even from great distances. **Spectral lines** are specific wavelengths of light that are emitted and absorbed by every kind of atom and molecule and act as a unique fingerprint. Identifying known spectral lines in distant stars and galaxies allows us to measure their chemical composition and determine physical properties like their temperature, density and motions from afar.

A fundamental principle of quantum mechanics is that when we start looking at the smallest scales in the Universe, we find that energy comes only in discrete packets, or quanta. Within an atom, the electric forces that bind the negatively charged electrons whirling around the positively charged nucleus only permit certain orbits at specific levels of energy. These levels vary, depending on the element (how many protons and neutrons are in the nucleus) and how many electrons are bound to it.

Nothing comes for free, however, and the tally of energy must always balance. An electron in a lower energy level can be bumped up to a higher level if it gobbles up a passing photon that has just the right amount of energy. Conversely, if an electron in a higher energy level drops to a lower one, it must emit a photon of an exactly matching amount of energy.

Since the energy of a photon is directly related to its wavelength, each energy transition in the atom (or molecule) corresponds to a precise wavelength of light. This light is known as a spectral "line" because of how exact the wavelength has to be. The term comes from the line's appearance in an instrument, called a spectrograph, that is used to measure the composition of light entering it through a narrow slit.

Spectral lines can be seen as an **emission line** if the electron drops from a high level to a low level and emits a photon, or as an **absorption line** if the electron absorbs a passing photon of the right wavelength from a background source.

**Fluorescence**, or **re-emission**, is a common term used to describe a process where a high energy photon is absorbed by a body — which need not be hot — and is transformed into one or more lower energy (redder) photons. This is familiar in fluorescent — or cold — lights where ultraviolet emission (from an electrically-excited gas, like mercury) excites a material on the inside of the glass envelope to produce visible light. This can be a very passive process, like the use of fluorescent paints to capture blue light and radiate it as a vivid green, yellow or red. Even white writing paper contains a fluorescent dye that responds to blue/ultraviolet light and makes it glow "whiter-than-white".

Astronomers use their knowledge of the various chemical fingerprints of known atoms and molecules to identify the composition of distant stars and nebulae. The beautiful colours of the nebulae shown in this book arise largely because of fluorescence driven by the fiercely hot, embedded stars.

**FIGURE 12: EXAMPLES OF FLUORESCENCE**

This image shows different minerals emitting visible light when exposed to ("invisible") ultraviolet radiation. The same thing happens across the Universe as clouds of dust and gas re-emit longer wavelength light when exposed to higher energy radiation from nearby stars.

*" There are a number of other processes in the Universe that create light in more exotic ways "*

## Non-thermal Radiation

There are a number of other processes in the Universe that create light in more exotic ways, at least when compared with our day to day experience. For instance, charged electrons and protons that are passing through magnetic fields will move along oscillating spiral paths that produce electromagnetic waves (**synchrotron radiation**). Fast-moving charged particles that deflect one another from their electric field interactions can also generate light (**bremsstrahlung radiation**). Such processes are particularly evident in the radio part of the spectrum and will be discussed at greater length in Chapter 7.

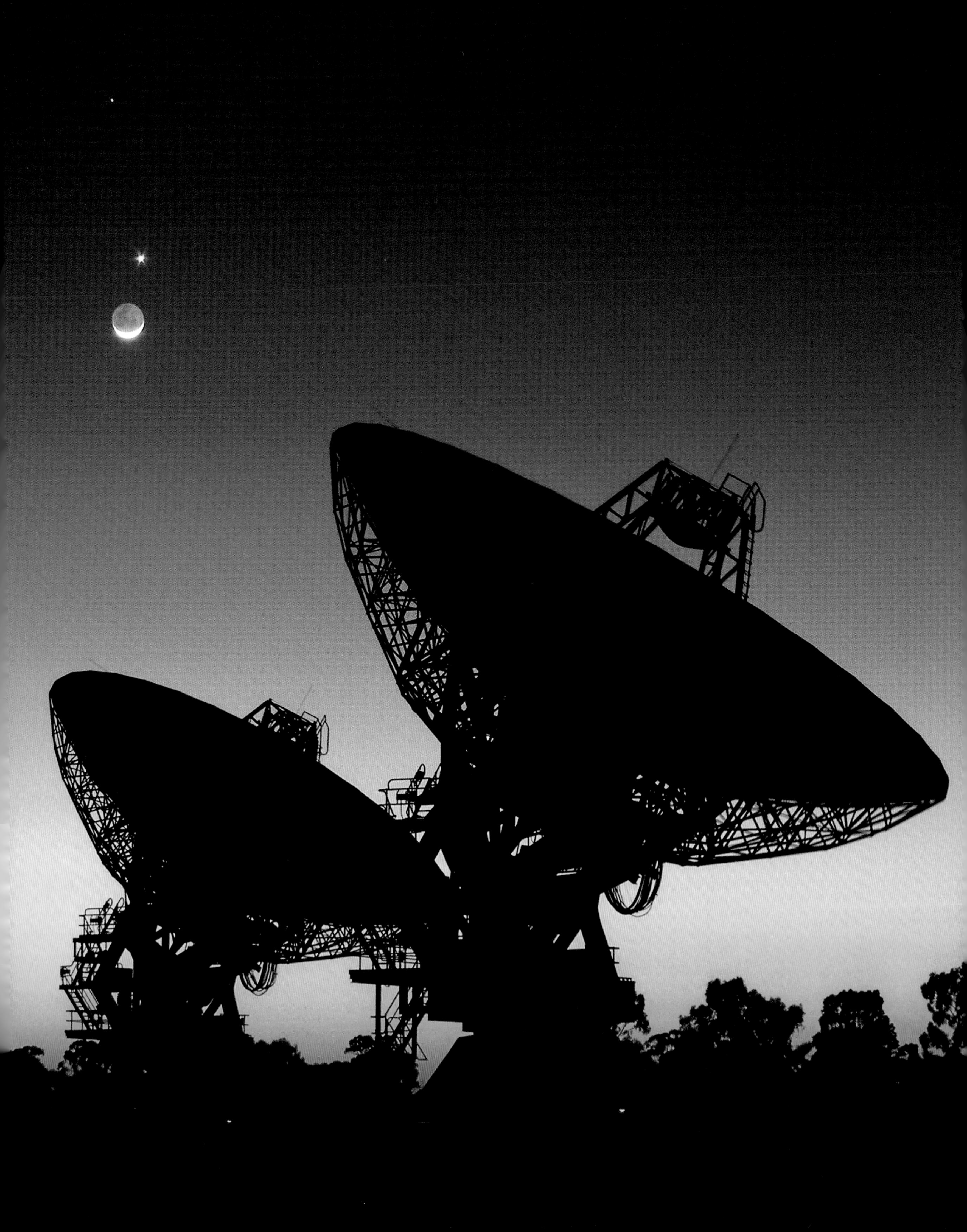

# 2 THE VIEW FROM THE GROUND

**FIGURE 13: THE AUSTRALIAN RADIO TELESCOPE ARRAY**

This beautiful image shows parts of the Australia Telescope Compact Array (ATCA) near the town of Narrabri in rural New South Wales. It was taken just before sunrise with Mercury, Venus and the Moon all appearing close together in the sky behind the array. Mercury is the highest of the three bright celestial beacons. The ATCA consists of six radio telescopes, each one larger than a house. Sometimes combined with more distant telescopes — like the 64-metre Parkes dish — they can form one of the highest resolution measurement devices in the world.

Astronomy is an observational science. Apart from the use of space probes in the Solar System, it is not possible to carry out experiments *in situ*, and information must be gleaned from light signals collected by telescopes and measured with instruments such as cameras and spectrometers, which spread out the light into its constituent wavelengths and allow a closer study. Most of the telescopes in existence observe the heavens from the ground — often from remote mountain tops to get above as much of the Earth's disturbing atmosphere as possible. But ground-based telescopes are much more than the well known visible-light telescopes that collect light from remote stars and galaxies with gigantic mirrors...

*" Galileo pioneered the scientific method by thoroughly documenting all the new astronomical bodies and phenomena he saw with the telescope "*

The telescope was invented in the early 17th century by Dutch spectacle makers and used for astronomical research for the first time by the Italian Galileo Galilei in 1609. Galileo pioneered the scientific method by thoroughly documenting all the new astronomical bodies and phenomena he saw with the telescope: craters on the Moon, Jupiter's moons and spots on the Sun.

Since Galileo, thousands of observatories have been built around the world, and, since the 1960s, also in space. There are many advantages to be gained by observing from space (see Chapter 3), but it is expensive to launch telescopes and, with the notable exception of the Hubble Space Telescope, it is not possible to repair and upgrade them once they are there. Consequently, good sites on the ground are very attractive places to build large and powerful telescopes. These can then be continuously upgraded as new technology becomes available. Ground-based telescopes, working at visible, infrared and radio wavelengths, are forefront devices that usually work to complement the expensive, and usually smaller, space telescopes.

## Atmospheric Obstacles

Telescopes located on the ground must cope with the distorting and **absorbing/scattering** effects of the atmosphere. Even at the most carefully chosen locations, the atmosphere is completely or partially opaque over large tracts of the **electromagnetic spectrum** (see Figure 14).

From the highest energy gamma rays, right through the X-ray band to the near-ultraviolet, at a wavelength of around 300 nm, the atmosphere completely absorbs radiation and astronomers are blind from the ground. The visible-light band is relatively transparent, especially from high-altitude sites, and there are a number of useable windows in the infrared extending up to wavelengths of about 20 micrometres. Then comes a long stretch of the spectrum, covering the far-infrared, up to wavelengths just short of 1 mm,

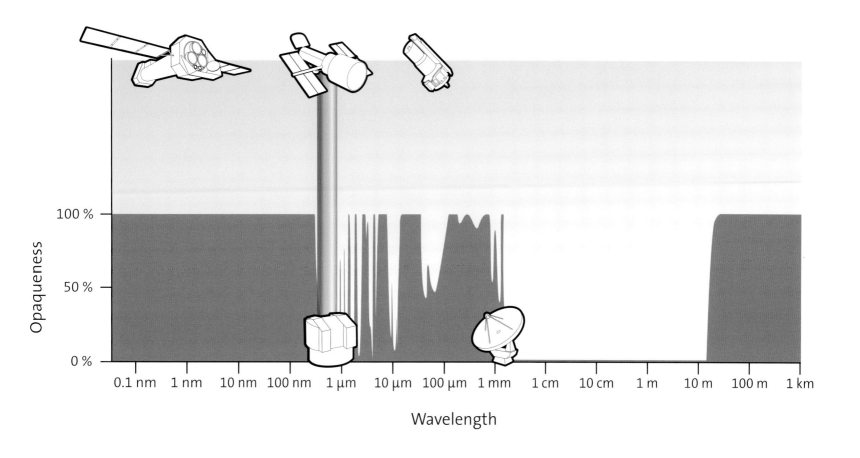

Opaqueness

100 %

50 %

0 %

0.1 nm   1 nm   10 nm   100 nm   1 µm   10 µm   100 µm   1 mm   1 cm   10 cm   1 m   10 m   100 m   1 km

Wavelength

where all radiation is again absorbed except in a few "holes" where the atmosphere is fairly transparent. In the so-called millimetre and sub-millimetre part of the spectrum, the principal absorber of light is water, and in this region observations can only be carried out effectively at very high, dry sites like the 5000-metre high Chajnantor plain on the Northern Chilean altiplano, the site of ALMA. For longer radio wavelengths, from around 1 centimetre upwards, the atmosphere is very transparent, although it is still capable of distorting radio "images" when conditions are not optimal. The Earth's ionosphere finally cuts in at wavelengths of around 20 metres. As well as absorbing and scattering light, the atmosphere will radiate light during the night when it is not illuminated by the Sun. In the near-infrared, certain gas molecules, notably the combination of a single oxygen and a hydrogen atom (the so-called OH radical), emit strongly, making the sky appear quite bright. At longer infrared wavelengths, the atmosphere is bright simply because it emits heat radiation.

Not only does atmospheric transmission reduce or block the radiation coming from astronomical objects, but the turbulence, all too familiar to any airline passenger, bends the incoming light through small angles that change continuously with time and position on the sky. Astronomers call this atmospheric phenomenon "seeing". The quality of the seeing usually seriously limits the amount of fine detail that can be observed by ground-based telescopes in stars and galaxies (also known as the **resolution**). To com-

**FIGURE 14: THE OPAQUENESS OF THE ATMOSPHERE**

The opaqueness of the atmosphere measured on a scale from 0% to 100% (completely opaque) with some major astronomical telescopes. Three space observatories are seen at the top (from left): the XMM-Newton telescope, the Hubble Space Telescope and the Spitzer Space Telescope. At the bottom two ground-based telescopes (VLT and ALMA) are seen in two of the "windows" in the atmosphere where light can reach the Earth's surface.

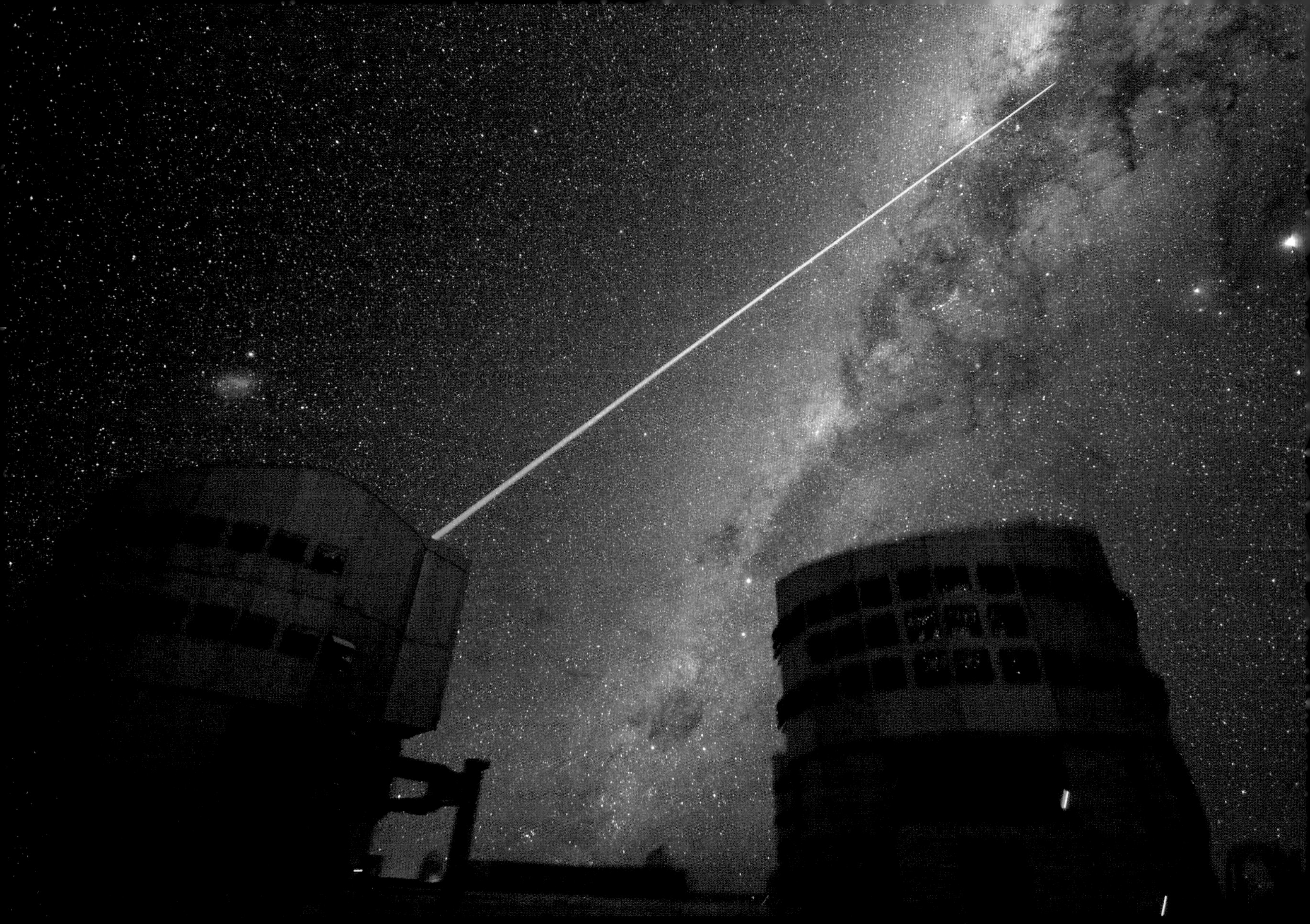

**FIGURE 15: ADAPTIVE OPTICS AT WORK AT THE VLT**

The Very Large Telescope in Chile with a laser used to create an artificial star in the sky to help with adaptive optics corrections.

pensate for some of this atmospheric distortion, modern telescopes and instruments often incorporate high-speed devices that can measure and correct for some of these distorting effects. Called “Adaptive Optics” (AO) these techniques are rapidly increasing in sophistication and can, under suitable conditions, exploit much of the intrinsic capability of large ground-based telescopes to make very sharp images (the larger a telescope is, the better resolution it has).

To measure the changes in the atmosphere in order to calculate the right correction to make, AO systems need to use a reasonably bright star close to the object or field being observed. If a sufficiently bright star does not exist nearby, the telescope can project a laser beam into the sky to make an artificial star within the field of view (Figure 15). This “star” is the result of light being reflected from a layer of sodium atoms that is always present 90 kilometres up in the upper atmosphere.

# Types of Ground-based Telescopes

The technological development of telescopes has accelerated tremendously since the development of computers and advanced electronics. The ingenuity needed to overcome the seeing problem and to exploit the isolated gaps in the atmospheric absorption (see Figure 14) is truly outstanding. Telescopes today are often a far cry from the simple tube with lenses that Galileo so successfully pointed at the night sky. At the risk of oversimplifying, the many different ground-based telescopes fall roughly into seven different categories: classic visible-light reflecting telescopes (some with quite good near-infrared observing abilities), solar telescopes, sub-millimetre telescopes, radio telescopes (often linking together in giant arrays called interferometers), cosmic-ray observatories, neutrino telescopes and gravitational-wave telescopes. For some of these instruments, the label "telescope" seems to be a real misnomer. Examples of all these types of telescopes are seen in Figure 16.

# Future Ground-based Observatories

Several new ground-based observatories are being planned and/or built at the moment. In the visible-light band the focus is on size. Three extremely large telescopes are in different phases of construction and development at the moment. The European Extremely Large Telescope (E-ELT), with a mirror diameter of 42 metres, is planned for 2017. It has a revolutionary design that includes five mirrors and advanced adaptive optics to correct for the turbulent atmosphere. The E-ELT will likely be built somewhere in northern Chile or in the Canary Islands.

Two large projects are also under way in the US. The Giant Magellan Telescope is planned for completion in 2016 and consists of seven 8.4-metre primary mirrors. Together they will catch as much light as a 21.5-metre mirror and provide the same resolving power as a virtual 24.5-metre giant. This huge instrument will be built at the Las Campanas Observatory in Chile, which is already home to the twin 6.5-metre Magellan Telescopes. The Californian Thirty Meter Telescope is also due to be completed in 2016 and is more like a giant version of the Keck Telescope. Almost 500 individual segments will make up one enormous 30-metre mirror. This will be able to collect ten times more light than the Keck Telescope and to see three times more detail.

The Atacama Large Millimeter/submillimeter Array (ALMA) consists of 66 high precision antennas and is currently under construction at Llano de Chajnantor in Chile, 5000 metres above sea level. The individual telescopes can be relocated in a variety of configurations by giant trucks to produce unsurpassed observations of millimetre-wave emissions from remote galaxies or relatively nearby star-forming regions.

The international Square Kilometer Array (SKA) will be a gigantic network of dish antennas and flat receivers with a total collecting area of approximately one square kilometre that will provide astronomers with an unsurpassed view of the radio Universe. The SKA will be constructed either in Australia or in southern Africa and will be 50 times more sensitive than any other radio instrument.

**FIGURE 16: EXAMPLES OF GROUND-BASED TELESCOPES**

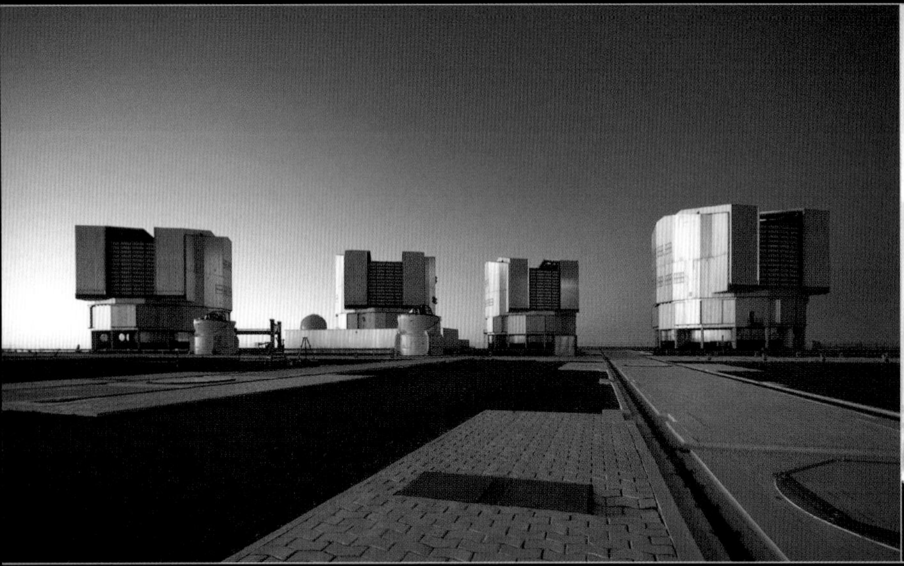

**The Very Large Telescope:** A system of four separate visible/infrared telescopes each with an 8.2-metre main mirror. The VLT was built and is operated by the European Southern Observatory. It is located at the Paranal Observatory on Cerro Paranal, a 2635-metre high mountain in the Atacama desert in northern Chile. The individual telescopes can form an **interferometer**, supplemented by four smaller 1.8-metre auxiliary telescopes.

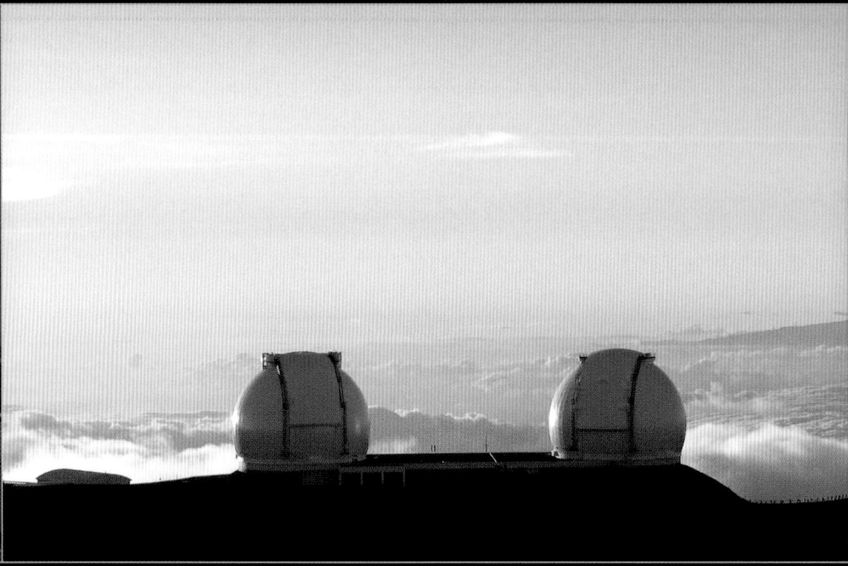

**The Keck Telescopes:** Keck is a two-telescope astronomical observatory at the 4145-metre summit of Mauna Kea in Hawaii. The primary mirrors of each of the two telescopes are composed of 36 hexagonal mirror segments and are 10 metres in diameter. The telescopes can also operate together to form a single interferometer.

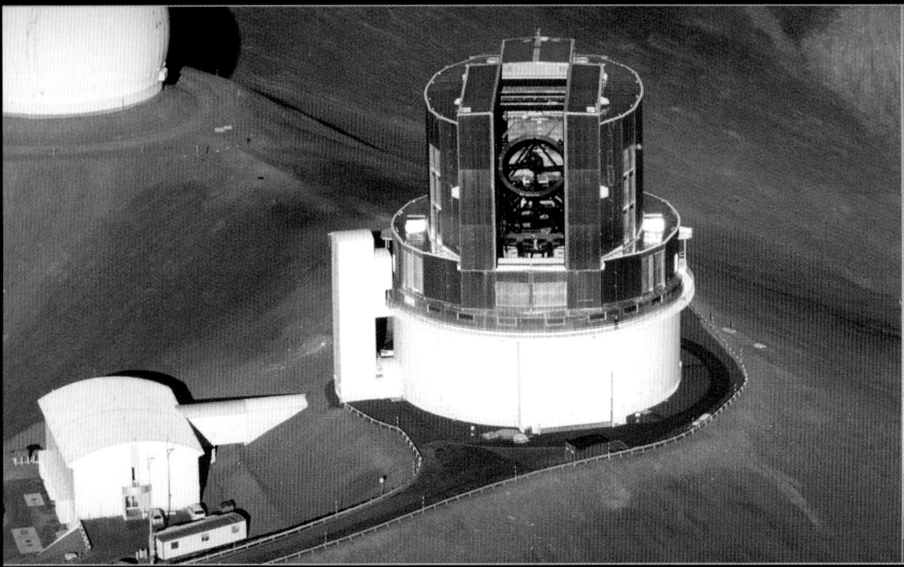

**The Subaru Telescope:** Subaru is the 8.2-metre telescope built by the National Astronomical Observatory of Japan and is located on Mauna Kea. It is named after the open star cluster known in English as the Pleiades.

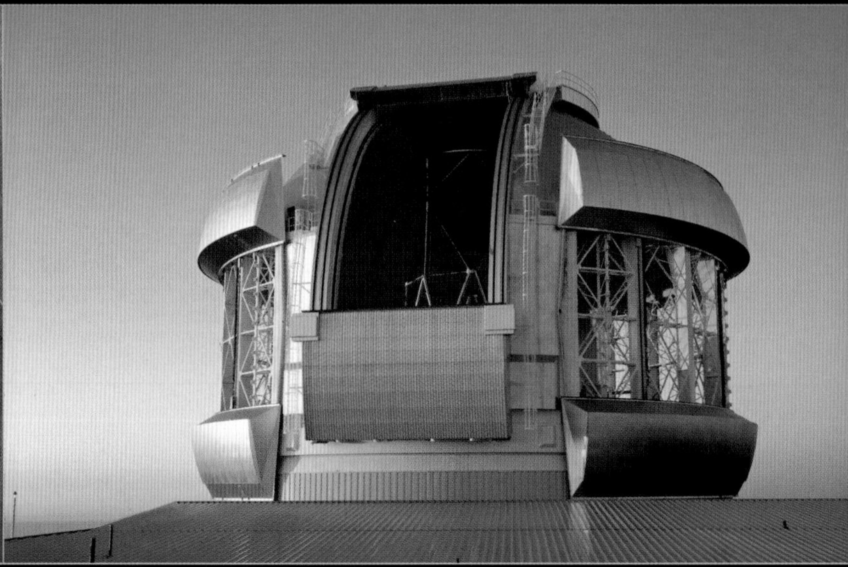

**The Gemini Observatory:** Gemini consists of two 8.1-metre telescopes, one on Mauna Kea and one on Cerro Pachón in Chile.

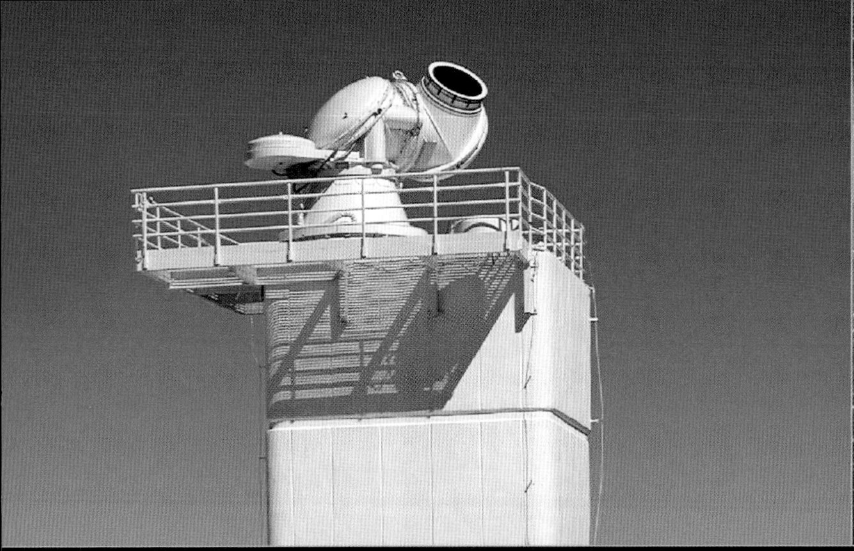

**The Swedish Solar Telescope:** The Swedish Solar Telescope is a 1-metre telescope at Roque de los Muchachos Observatory, on La Palma in the Canary Islands. It is the second largest refracting telescope in the world and uses a vacuum tube to create the sharpest images of the Sun with adaptive optics.

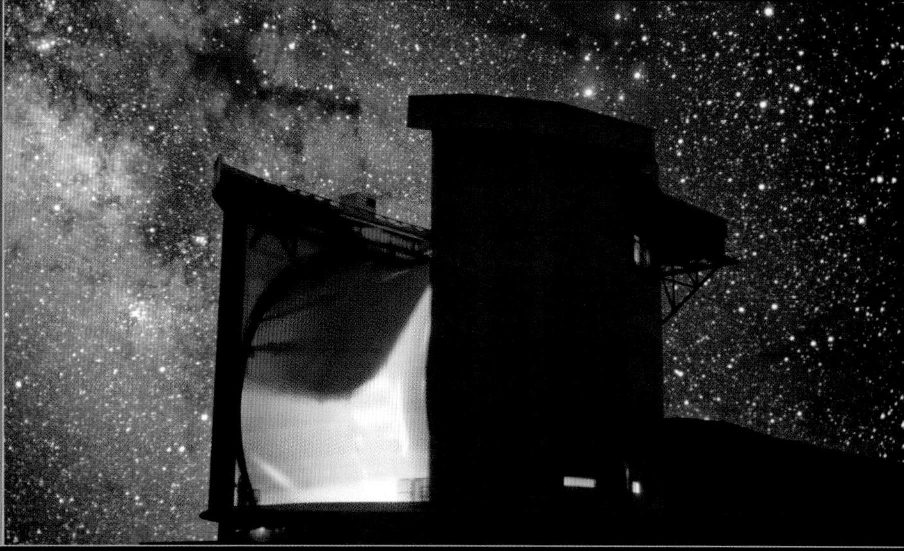

**The James Clerk Maxwell Telescope:** JCMT is a 15-metre sub-millimetre telescope at Mauna Kea Observatory in Hawaii. It is the largest sub-millimetre telescope in the world and is used to study the Solar System, interstellar dust and gas and distant galaxies.

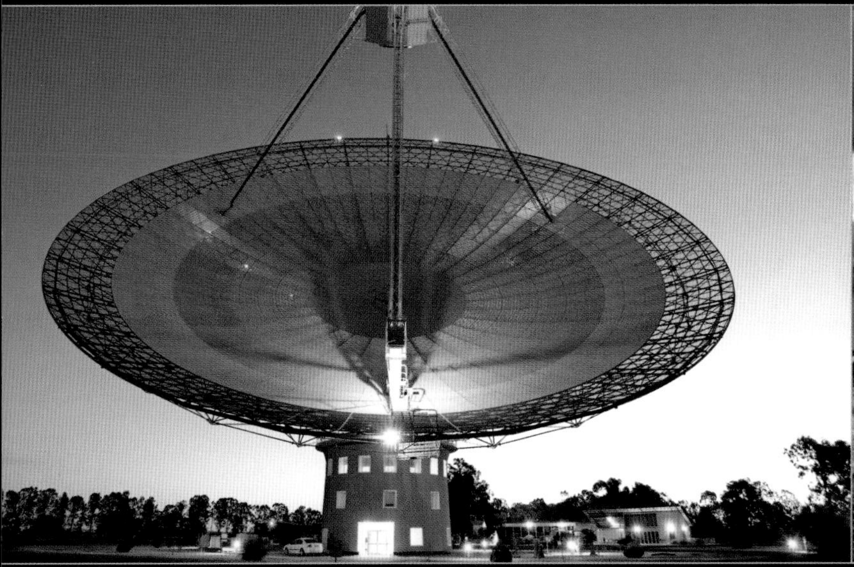

**The Parkes Observatory:** Parkes is a 64-metre steerable radio telescope near the town of Parkes, New South Wales, Australia. This telescope relayed parts of the television footage of the Apollo 11 Moon landing to the world. It also pinpointed the first quasar in 1963.

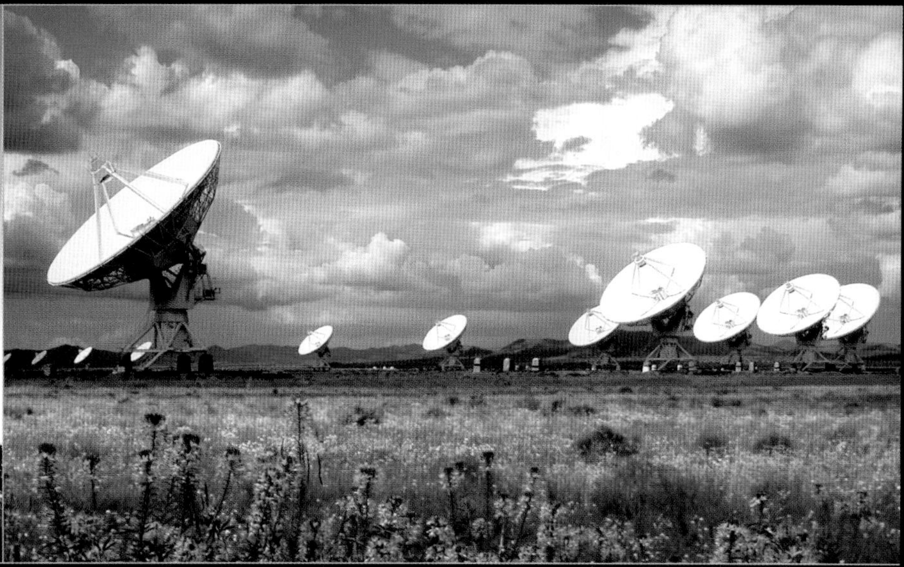

**The Very Large Array:** VLA consists of 27 independent antennas, each of which has a dish diameter of 25 metres. The antennas are positioned along the three arms of a Y-shape, each of which measures 21 km and can be used for very precise interferometry.

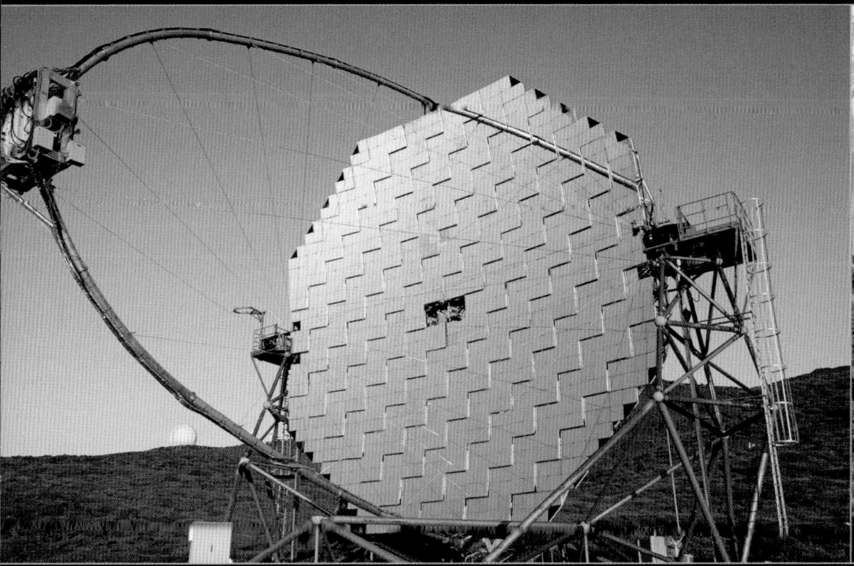

**The Major Atmospheric Gamma-ray Imaging Cherenkov Telescope:** MAGIC is a 17-metre gamma-ray telescope situated at the Roque de los Muchachos Observatory on La Palma, one of the Canary Islands, at about 2200 m above sea level. It detects particle showers released by cosmic gamma rays using Cherenkov radiation, i.e., the faint light radiated by the charged particles in the showers.

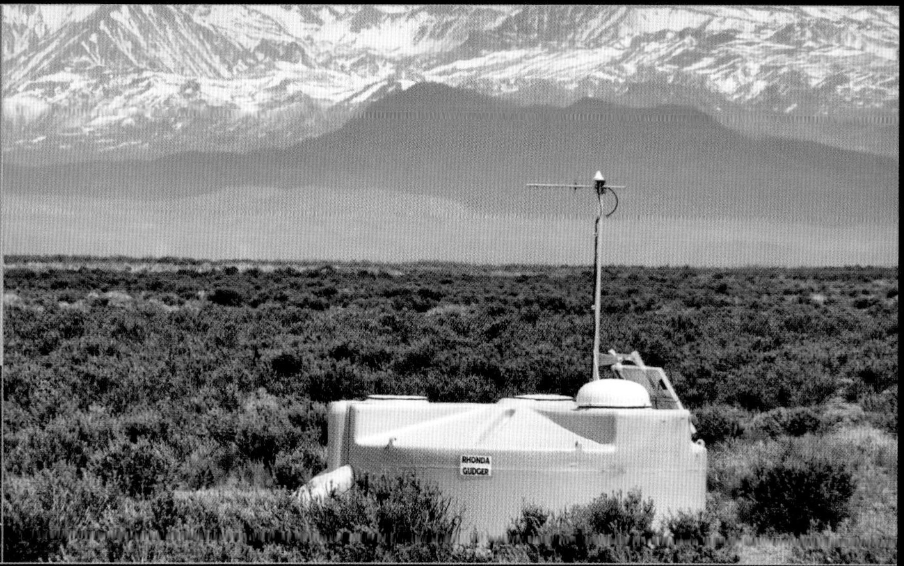
RHONDA
GUDGER

**The Pierre Auger Observatory:** Sixteen hundred water tanks, spread out over an area of 3000 square kilometres, make up the Pierre Auger Observatory at Pampa Amarilla in Argentina. The water tanks detect the high energy particles created when cosmic rays penetrate the Earth's atmosphere. They are supplemented by optical detectors that can measure the fluorescence of nitrogen in the atmosphere as it is traversed by the high energy particles. The observatory was officially inaugurated in mid-November 2008.

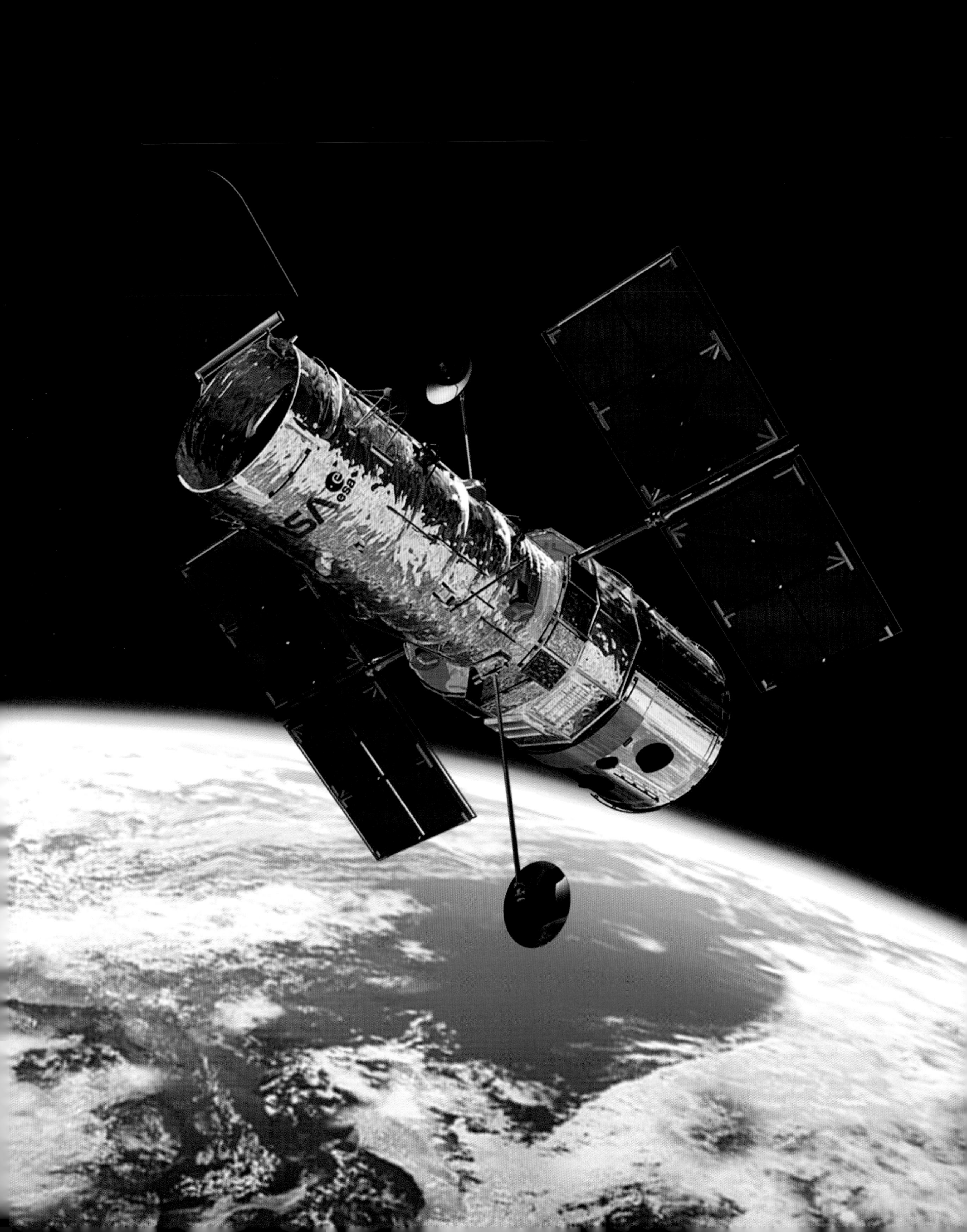
esa

# 3 SPACE OBSERVATORIES

**FIGURE 17: HUBBLE, THE BEST-KNOWN SPACE OBSERVATORY**

This illustration shows the NASA/ESA Hubble Space Telescope in its high orbit, 600 kilometres above Earth.

Astronomical observatories in space have revolutionised our knowledge of the Universe. They are one amongst the many types of satellites launched since the beginning of the space age, devoted to a great variety of applications including Earth observation, communication and broadcasting, navigation and military, right up to fully habitable space stations. Space observatories give access to light that is not visible from the ground and provide an undisturbed view of the star- and galaxy-studded sky. Expensive yes, but unbeatable in the search for the elusive photons from the hidden Universe.

**FIGURE 18: TEN EXAMPLES OF PAST AND CURRENT SPACE OBSERVATORIES**

Some of the most important astronomical observatories in space and the part of the electromagnetic spectrum where they function. Short wavelengths (X-ray, ultraviolet etc.) are on the left, long wavelengths are on the right.

WMAP
Spitzer
Hubble
Hipparcos
SOHO
IUE
GALEX
Chandra
XMM-Newton
Integral
Gamma Ray
X-ray
Ultraviolet
Visible
Infrared
Microwave
Radio
0.1 pm
1 pm
10 pm
100 pm
1 nm
10 nm
100 nm
1 µm
10 µm
100 µm
1 mm
1 cm
10 cm
1 m


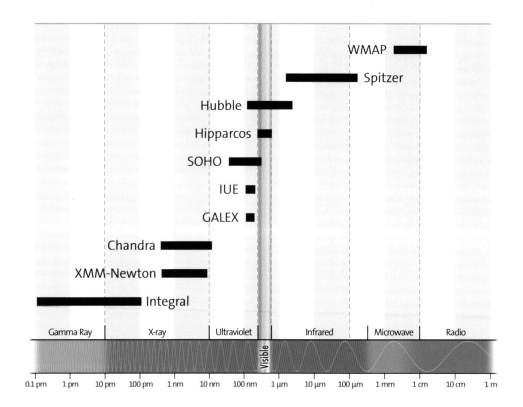

The space age began with the launch of Sputnik by the Soviet Union in 1957. Only five years later, in 1962, NASA launched the first true astronomical research satellite, OSO-1. Since those first steps, more than 100 different astronomical observatories have been launched — some better known than others. They have contributed a wealth of information in many new fields of astronomy.

Most astronomical satellites orbit the Earth but, for some purposes, there are advantages to choosing other locations and orbits. Some instruments are affected by the radiation belts associated with the Earth's magnetic field, which can affect sensitive detectors and electronic circuits, while other spacecraft need to keep well away from the heat radiated into space by our home planet.

A sort of "half-way-house" between the ground and space can be provided by high altitude balloons such as BOOMERanG, which is a cosmic microwave background observatory, or SOFIA, an infrared telescope flown in a converted Boeing 747 aircraft. Such experiments avoid many of the disadvantages of being on the ground while being considerably less expensive than spacecraft.

> *" More than 100 different astronomical observatories have been launched into space "*

As mentioned in Chapter 2 there are several compelling reasons for launching telescopes into space, the most important being the escape from the absorption, emission and turbulence associated with the atmosphere. The elevated vantage point gives access to light that is not visible from the ground and provides an undisturbed view of the star- and galaxy-studded sky. What hinders our exploitation of the ideal space environment? High (often referred to as "astronomical") cost is one factor, but the long lead times associated with the development of these complex and remotely controlled devices and the risk that is taken when they are blasted into space atop a rocket are also significant considerations.

These are some of the reasons why observatories are still being built on the ground. On Earth it is easier to upgrade to the latest technology and to build larger telescopes that gather more light. In general space and ground-based telescopes are complementary, but with important synergies between them. For that reason, research teams frequently make use of both space and ground-based instruments to investigate a particular phenomenon.

## Reliability

When launching an observatory into space on a mission that may last years or even decades, the reliability of its component parts looms large in the thoughts of the designers. With the notable exception of Hubble, which is serviced by teams of astronauts flown on the Space Shuttle, most spacecraft become inaccessible after launch.

> *" Almost like a small autonomous city in space, a research satellite consists of a wide range of basic components "*

All the mechanics and electronics have to be thoroughly tested to ensure they can endure the harsh conditions they will experience during and after launch. Severe vibration, large temperature changes and a hostile radiation environment are all factors to be taken into account. As well as using well-tested and high quality components, it is usual to build in as much redundancy between systems as is reasonably possible. It usually takes years to go through this intensive space qualification. Meanwhile, technological advances continue and it becomes a race to get the best possible hardware on board before the design is "frozen" preceding launch.

In addition to these considerations, some spacecraft rely on the continuing use of fuel or other consumables such as liquid or solid gas coolants that will ultimately limit their useable life.

## What is Inside?

Some research satellites are quite similar to the telescopes in observatories on the ground, but others are fundamentally different. Almost like a small autonomous city in space, a research satellite consists of a wide range of basic components: the main mirror, telescope tube, detectors, energy supply (batteries and solar panels), communications equipment, computer, navigation equipment and hundreds or even thousands of sensors. The different parts are shown in Figure 19.

### Main Mirror

A common feature for most space observatories is the main mirror. It is not the magnification that is the major criterion here, but the light-collecting area. The larger the mirror, the more light it can receive and the fainter the objects it can observe. The further away from visible wavelengths that a space observatory observes, the more specialised the mirror and the structures around it have to be.

Spitzer

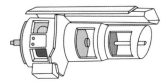

**FIGURE 19: INSIDE SPACE OBSERVATORIES**

Sketches of three famous space observatories and their most important components: Spitzer, Hubble and XMM-Newton.

Hubble

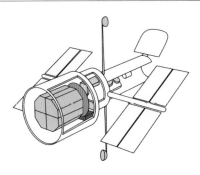

XMM-Newton

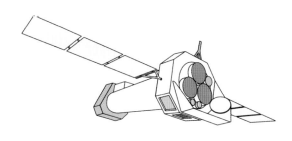

Key

| | | | |
|---|---|---|---|
| ▪ Batteries | ▪ Computer | ▪ Mirror | ▫ Solar Panels |
| ▪ Communications antenna | ▪ Navigation / Pointing System | ▪ Scientific instruments | ▫ Telescope |

When observing visible light, normal mirrors are used and the light arrives almost perpendicular to the mirror (90°). In contrast, X-rays have such enormous energies that the photons — light particles — would simply pass through the mirror if they hit it head on. Instead, a series of nested cylindrical mirrors is used so that the light grazes the mirror surface at an angle of only half a degree or so and therefore is only slightly deflected by each mirror in the series. It eventually arrives in focus at the detectors further down the tube (which needs to be quite long).

A gamma-ray satellite cannot use mirrors at all and the light, or radiation, must fall directly onto the detector, sometimes through a cleverly designed shadow mask (called a coded-mask) that enables the construction of proper images.

*" All parts have to be measured and weighed — just as you would carefully select equipment and food for a week-long backpacking trip "*

### Telescope Tube

The main purpose of the tube is to shield the mirror and detectors from unwanted light and to stabilise the observatory. The violently changing temperatures in space make the telescope "breathe" — contracting when it is cold and expanding when it is warm. For very precise instruments, often positioned with nanometre accuracy, this can give rise to problems. It is necessary to focus a space telescope from time to time because of these small changes. The more solid a telescope tube, the smaller the "breaths" — but at the price of increased weight and cost. A satellite engineer must be a ruthless packer and the master of travelling light. It is murderously expensive to construct and launch satellites (about 100 000 € per kilogramme of satellite). Thus, all parts have to be measured and weighed — just as you would carefully select equipment and food for a week-long backpacking trip.

### Detectors

Detectors are components that receive a great deal of attention from the astronomers. It is here that the light is registered and translated into electrical signals. They are the eyes of the telescope. The physics of the detector depends on the wavelength it needs to see and there are many kinds in operation. For visible-light telescopes, the trusty standard is the CCD (Charge Coupled Device) which is similar to those found in countless digital cameras (though the astronomical variety are usually cooled to way below 0° C to reduce the background "noise"). The technological advances in detectors have been immense over the past 25 years.

### Solar Cells and Batteries

The energy supply for a space observatory usually comes from the Sun via large solar cell panels that convert light to electricity, which is stored in batteries for use when the satellite is in the Earth's shadow.

### Communications Equipment

Parabolic antennas are usually used to communicate back and forth with the ground. At times, and always in the case of Hubble, special relay satellites are used to pass communications back to Earth.

*" A wide range of groundbreaking astronomical satellites will soon be launched by NASA and the European Space Agency "*

### Computer

Onboard computers are used to organise and process the data and to store and carry out the instructions needed to make observations. As with other high-tech components in space, the computers are always slightly out of date. For instance, the Hubble Space Telescope uses an 80486 processor that was developed in the late 80s.

### Navigation and Pointing Control

Both the orientation and the position of a research satellite must be precisely known at all times. In many cases a hierarchy of systems is used to control the satellite's orientation. In the case of Hubble, where the whole spacecraft is stabilised to a few thousandths of an arcsecond, the systems include a sun-sensor, magnetometers, star trackers, gyroscopes and special optical interferometers that lock onto guide stars close to the source or field being observed.

### Sensors

Hundreds or even thousands of sensors continuously update engineers about the conditions onboard measuring temperature, currents, pressure etc.

## Future Space Observatories

A wide range of groundbreaking astronomical satellites will soon be launched by NASA and the European Space Agency (ESA). By the time this book is printed ESA's Planck and Herschel telescopes will have been launched as a double-pack. Planck will observe the microwave radiation from the Big Bang with unprecedented precision. Herschel will observe light from cold objects and distant **redshifted** galaxies in the infrared and sub-millimetre wavelength bands using the largest single mirror yet launched into space for astronomy.

ESA's GAIA will be launched in 2011 to map the precise positions of a billion of the Milky Way's stars.

The NASA/ESA/Canada Space Agency's successor to Hubble will be the James Webb Space Telescope, JWST, to be launched in roughly 2014. JWST will have a 6.5-metre main mirror and is designed to observe the light from the first stars and galaxies formed in the Universe, which will be seen redshifted into the infrared.

**FIGURE 20: EXAMPLES OF SPACE OBSERVATORIES**

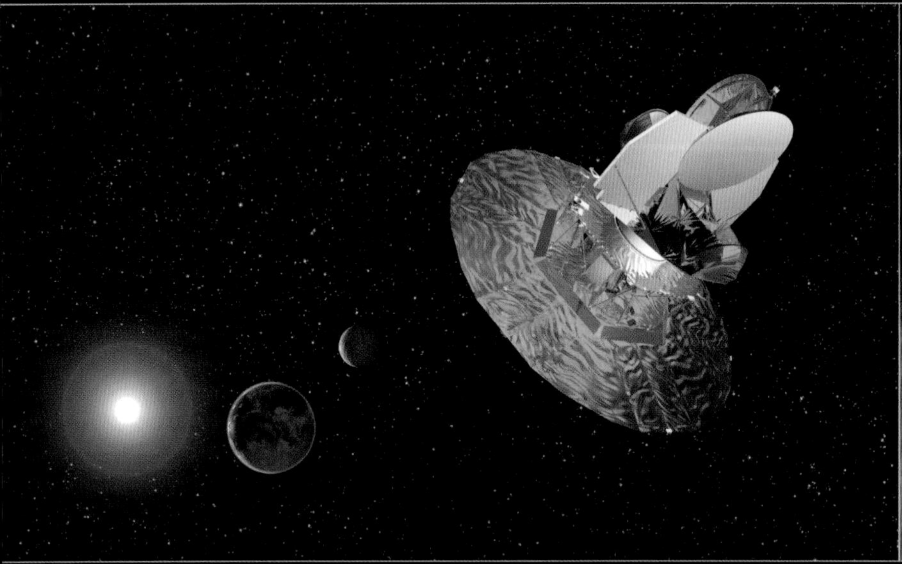

**WMAP:** In 2003 the Wilkinson Microwave Anisotropy Probe (WMAP) measured the cosmic microwave background so well that many of the different cosmological parameters could be nailed down, such as the age of the Universe (13.7 billion years), the expansion velocity of the Universe (71 km/s/Mpc), and the general composition of the Universe (23% dark matter, 72% dark energy and 5% normal matter). WMAP builds on the COsmic Background Explorer that measured the first tiny temperature differences in the microwave radiation.

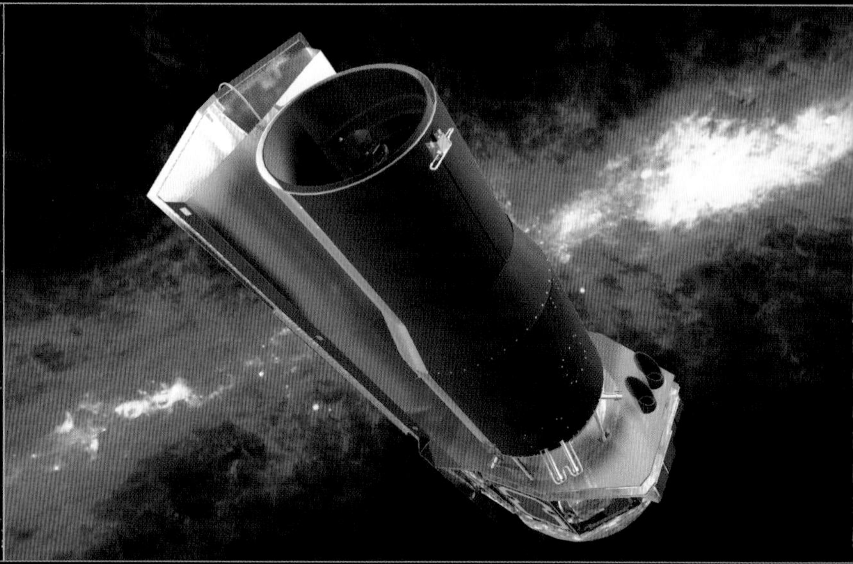

**Spitzer Space Telescope:** Spitzer is an infrared telescope with a 0.85-metre mirror that is embedded in a sort of large thermos flask of liquid helium. It has made its mark on astronomy by being extremely sensitive and by having the highest resolution (sharpest vision) among the infrared space telescopes. Spitzer builds on the legendary work of the Infrared Astronomical Satellite (IRAS) and the Infrared Space Observatory (ISO).

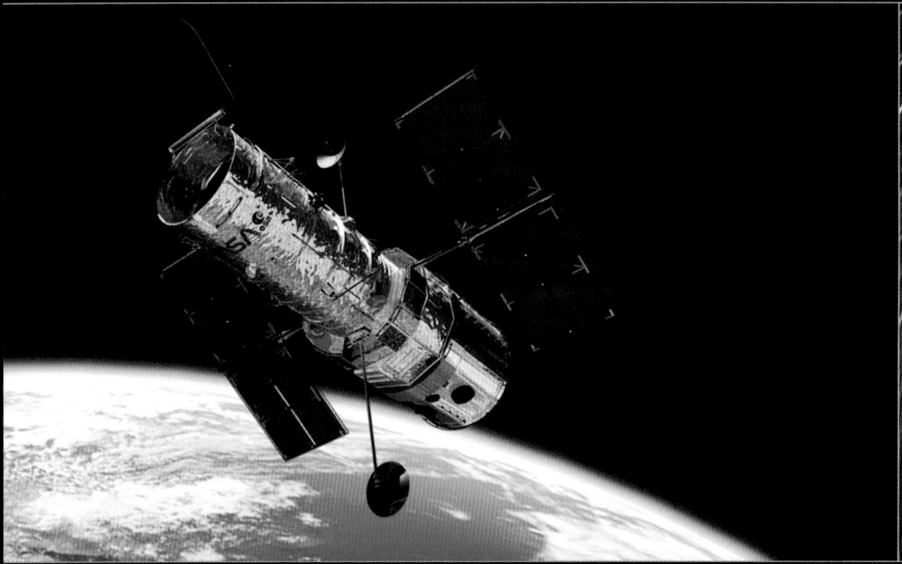

**Hubble:** The Hubble Space Telescope is perhaps the best-known telescope in the world. It functions as a super-sharp digital camera, delivering the clearest images so far of the objects it observes. Hubble has improved our knowledge about many areas in astronomy and has, for instance, shown that there are black holes in the centres of most galaxies.

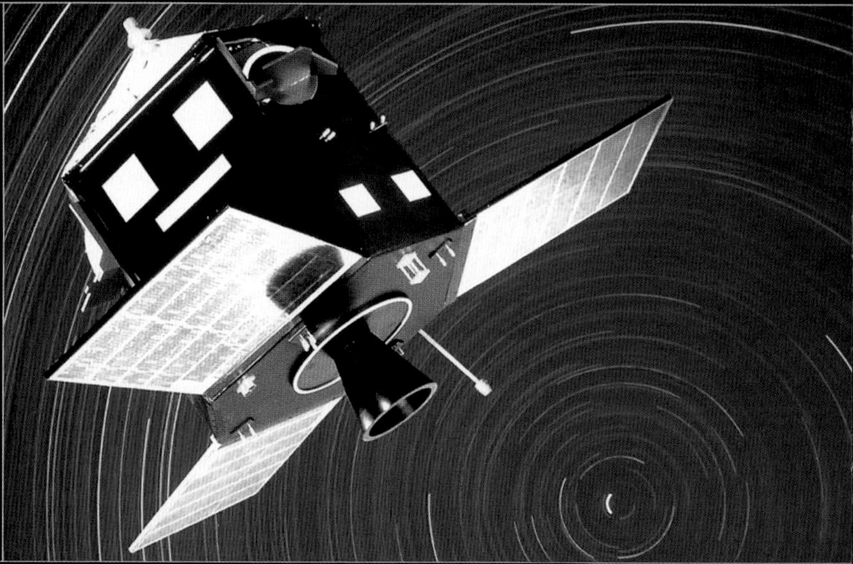

**Hipparcos:** Hipparcos was launched in 1989 by ESA and was the first research satellite dedicated to the measurement of the positions of the stars. Hipparcos mapped millions of stars very precisely and laid an indispensable foundation for most other branches of astronomy. Apart from establishing the general network of star positions, Hipparcos also identified stars that will pass through the solar neighbourhood in the future.

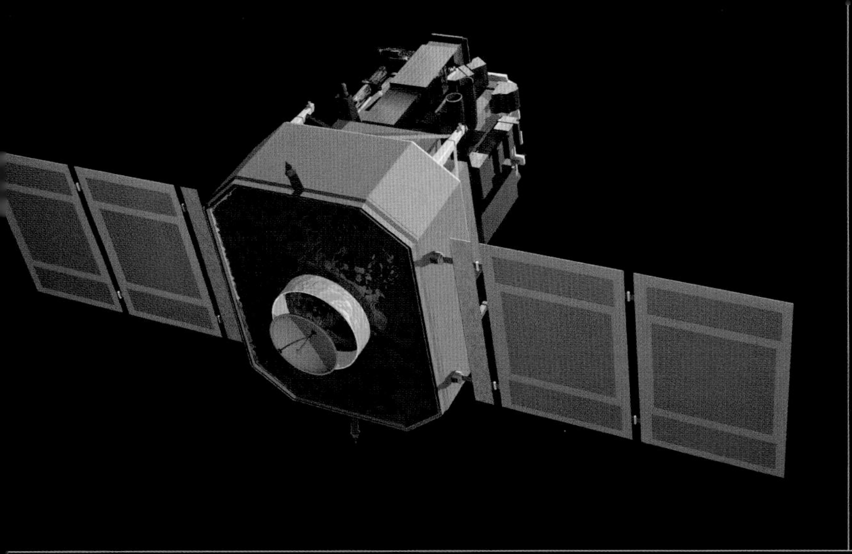

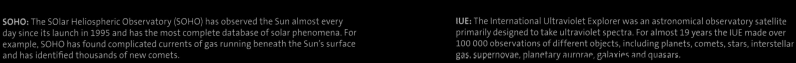

**SOHO:** The SOlar Heliospheric Observatory (SOHO) has observed the Sun almost every day since its launch in 1995 and has the most complete database of solar phenomena. For example, SOHO has found complicated currents of gas running beneath the Sun's surface and has identified thousands of new comets.

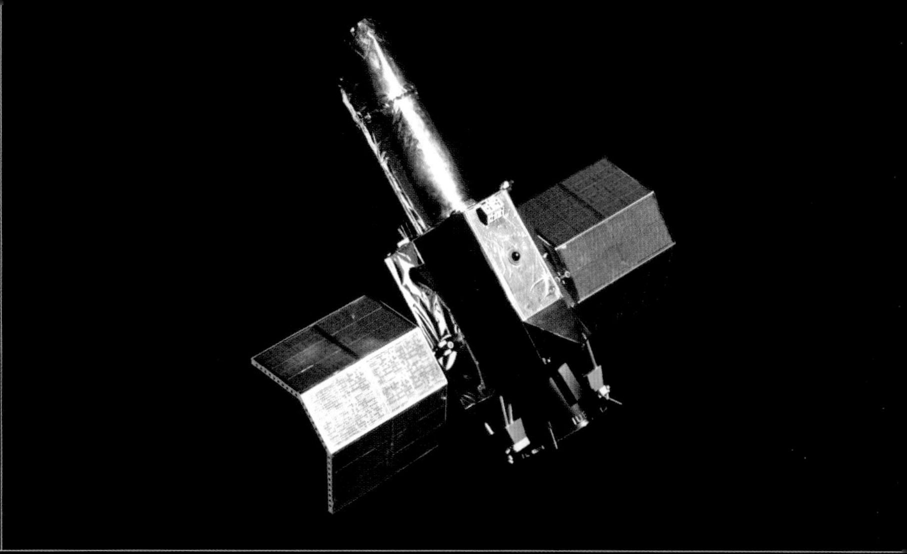

**IUE:** The International Ultraviolet Explorer was an astronomical observatory satellite primarily designed to take ultraviolet spectra. For almost 19 years the IUE made over 100 000 observations of different objects, including planets, comets, stars, interstellar gas, supernovae, planetary aurorae, galaxies and quasars.

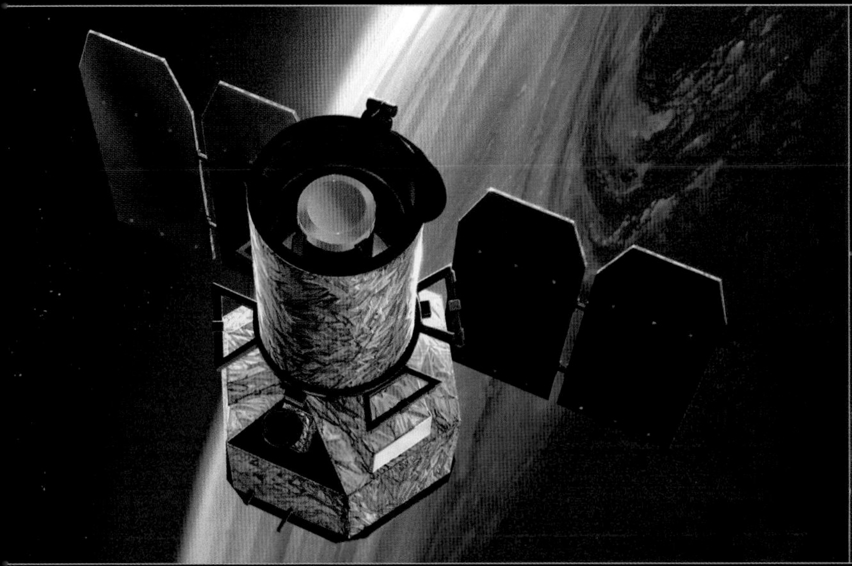

**GALEX:** The Galaxy Evolution Explorer is an orbiting space telescope observing galaxies in ultraviolet light. GALEX's observations are telling scientists how galaxies, the basic structures of our Universe, evolve and change.

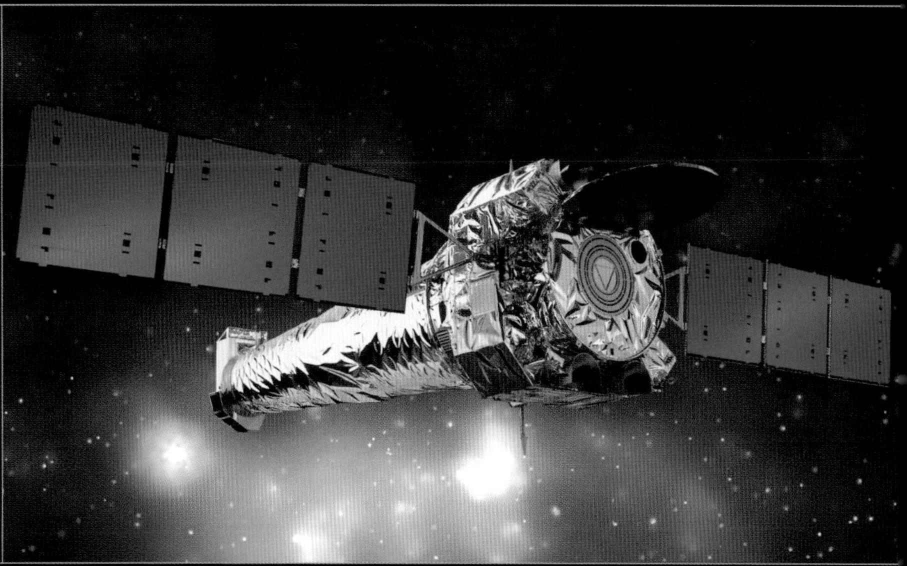

**Chandra:** The NASA Chandra X-ray Observatory has the sharpest vision of all X-ray telescopes. Among the highlights from Chandra have been the best images of supernova remnants and the best views into the lives of neutron stars and black holes.

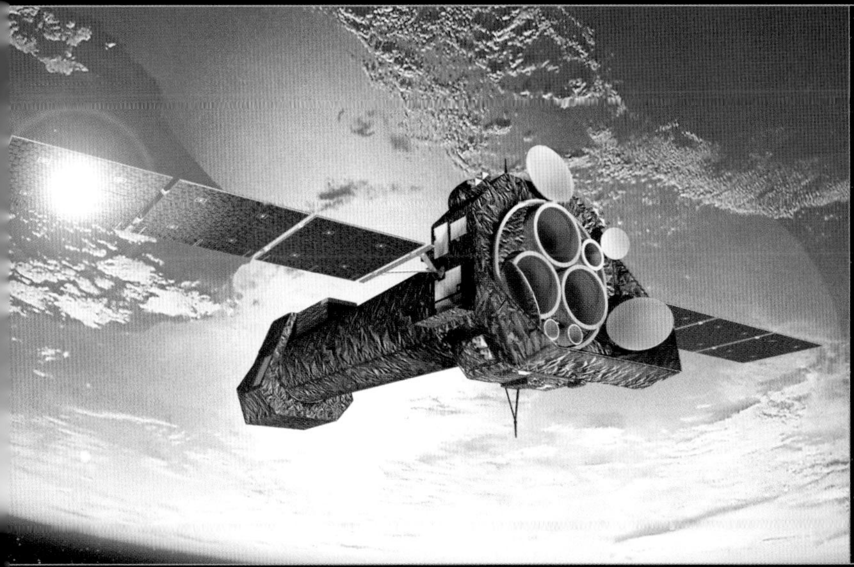

**XMM-Newton:** The XMM-Newton telescope was launched by ESA in 1999 and is currently the world's largest X-ray telescope. Its 58 nested mirrors collect X-ray light very effectively and make it possible to measure the compositions of stars and galaxies better than any other X-ray telescope. It has helped to trace the history of a wide range of galaxy clusters by measuring X-ray radiation from their otherwise invisible 10-100 million degree hot gas.

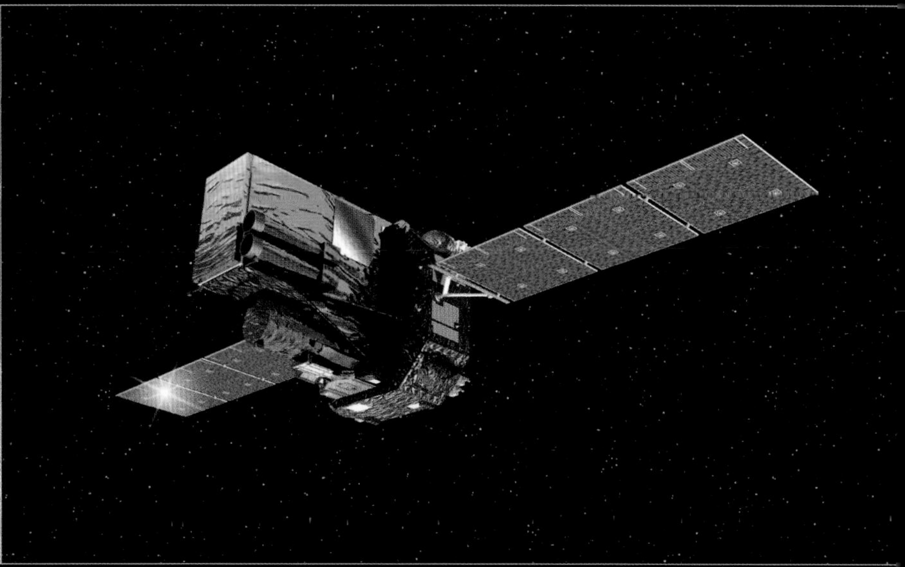

**Integral:** Integral is the first space observatory that can simultaneously observe phenomena in gamma rays, X-rays and visible light. It keeps a watchful eye on black holes, neutron stars and the so-called gamma-ray bursts.

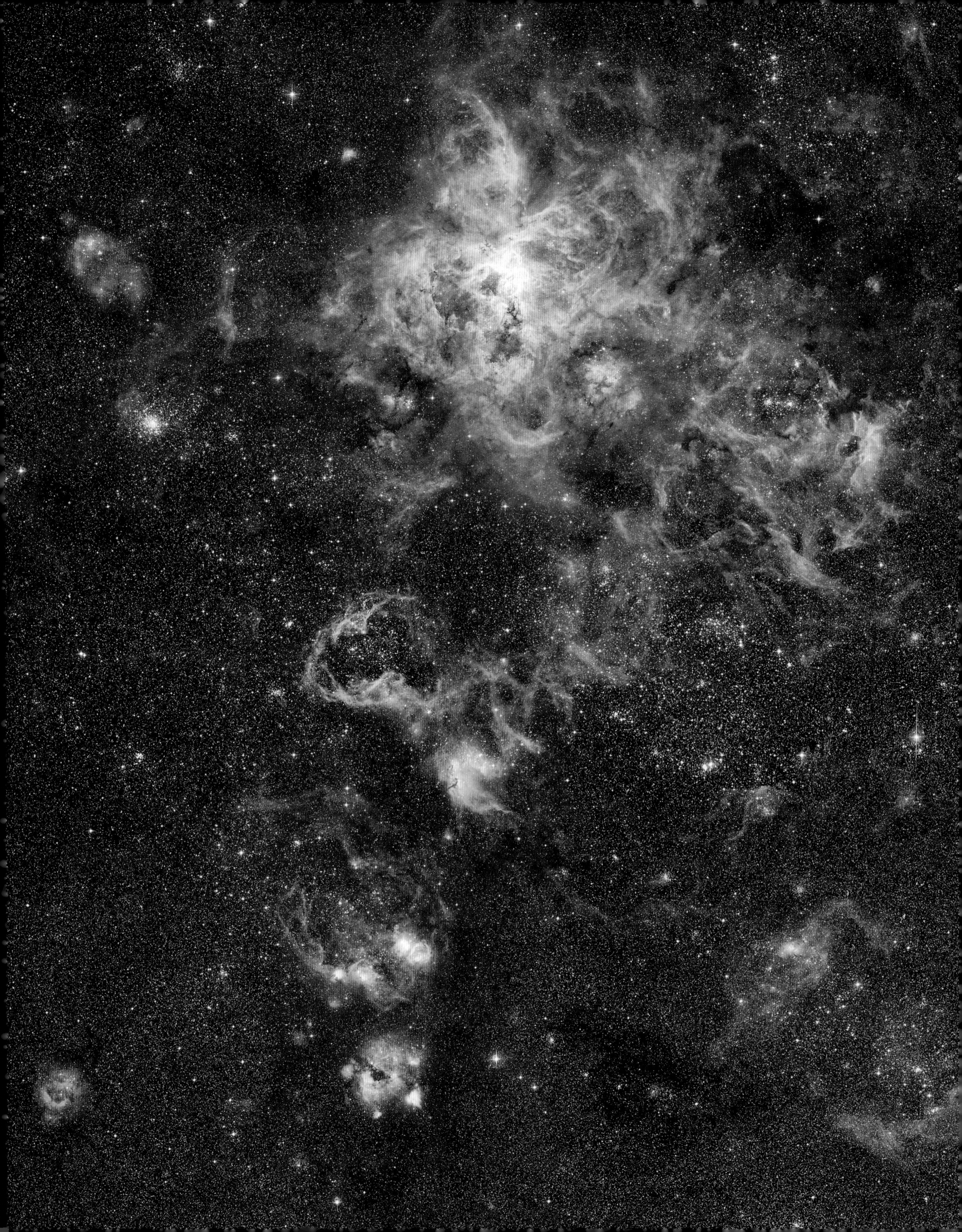

# THE VISIBLE UNIVERSE

**FIGURE 21: TARANTULA NEBULA**

This beautiful one degree square mosaic of the Tarantula nebula region of the Large Magellanic Cloud was taken through four different colour filters (blue, green/yellow, ionised oxygen in green and ionised hydrogen in red) with the ESO/MPG 2.2-metre telescope on La Silla in Chile. The Tarantula nebula is the youngest, most active star-forming region in our local group of galaxies and is hot enough to excite oxygen atoms to glow green. The red parts of the nebula emit light from excited hydrogen atoms, glowing with the light of somewhat older, cooler stars. The blue star clusters sprinkled over the field are even older and no longer have a surrounding nebula. The scattered remnants of the huge, dusty molecular cloud that mothered all of this activity can still be seen obscuring the background stars.

The visible part of the electromagnetic spectrum is the astronomical base camp. This is where people first started to look at the sky with the naked eye many thousands of years ago and it remains the reference point for research taking place in all other wavelength bands. The visible band is home to the majority of the starlight and, although many scientists and engineers are finding ingenious ways to exploit the non-visible bands, there are still many secrets left to explore in the visible...

Before the first radio observations were made in the 1930s (see Chapter 7), all that was known about the Universe came from observations in the visible part of the **spectrum**. Scientists were not even aware of the "hidden Universe" beyond the boundaries of the visible. For many years a kind of narrow-sightedness existed amongst astronomers that could perhaps be called "visible-light chauvinism" — an exaggerated focus on the processes that are visible to our eyes. For all that the visible part of the spectrum is very important and information-rich, it is just a tiny part of the full story. Although this book is about the cosmic radiation that we cannot see for ourselves, a chapter on the visible Universe is necessary to set the scene.

The visible wavelengths are called "visible" because they are the wavelengths that we can see naturally. Natural selection has forged a connection between our eyes and the Sun's light, most of which emerges in the visible range. Our eyes are biologically tuned to be sensitive where the Sun is brightest. Coincidentally, like the Sun — which is a perfectly ordinary G dwarf star — many other stars emit a large part, or even the majority, of their light in the visible range.

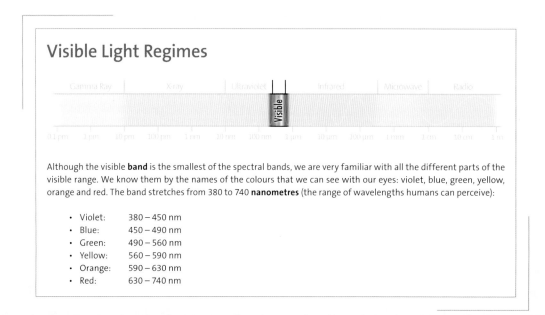

## Visible Light Regimes

Gamma Ray
X-ray
Ultraviolet
Visible
Infrared
Microwave
Radio
0.1 pm
1 pm
10 pm
100 pm
1 nm
10 nm
100 nm
1 μm
10 μm
100 μm
1 mm
1 cm
10 cm
1 m

Although the visible **band** is the smallest of the spectral bands, we are very familiar with all the different parts of the visible range. We know them by the names of the colours that we can see with our eyes: violet, blue, green, yellow, orange and red. The band stretches from 380 to 740 **nanometres** (the range of wavelengths humans can perceive):

- Violet: 380 – 450 nm
- Blue: 450 – 490 nm
- Green: 490 – 560 nm
- Yellow: 560 – 590 nm
- Orange: 590 – 630 nm
- Red: 630 – 740 nm

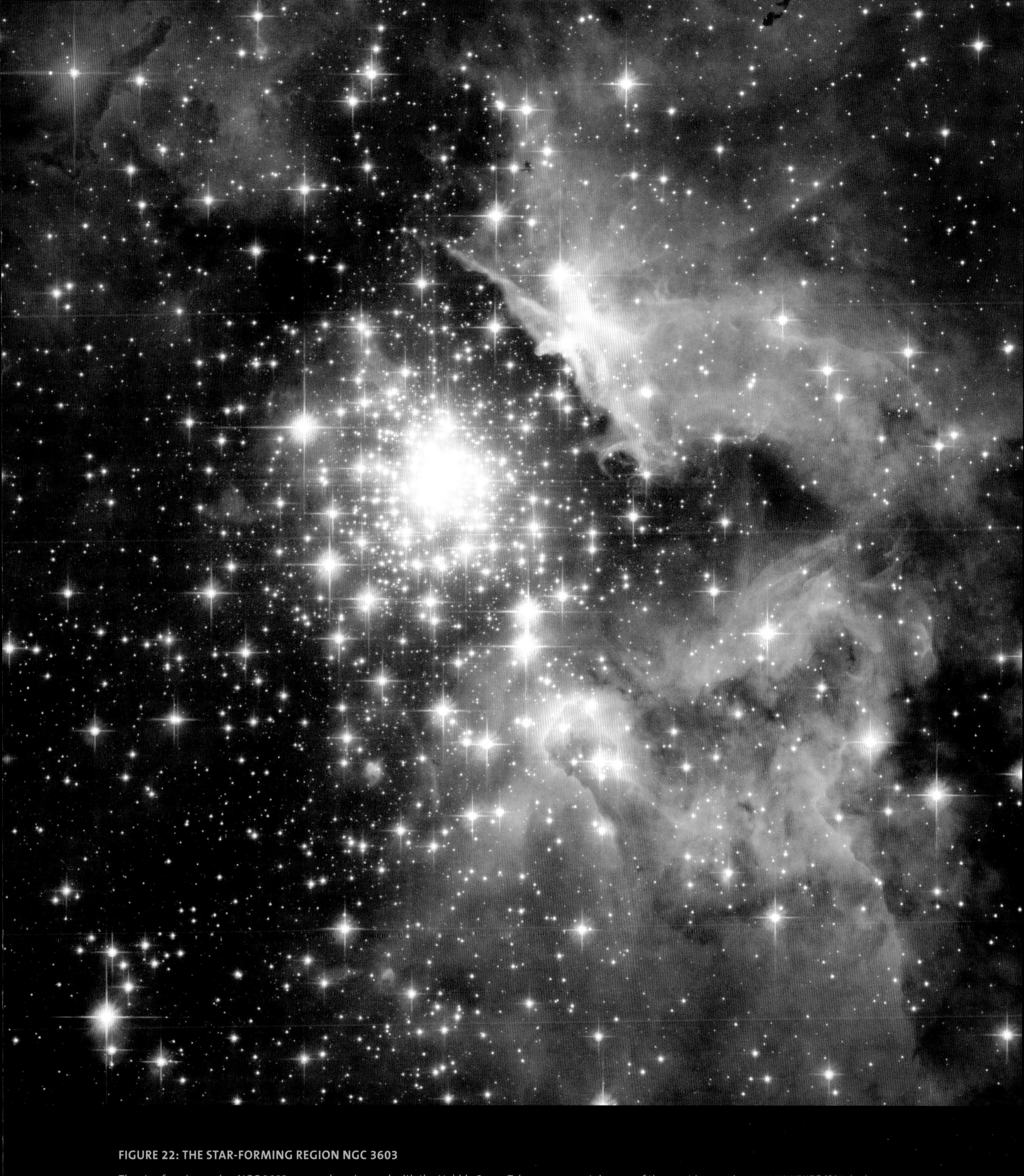

**FIGURE 22: THE STAR-FORMING REGION NGC 3603**

The star-forming region NGC 3603 — seen here imaged with the Hubble Space Telescope contains one of the most impressive massive young star clusters in the Milky Way. Bathed in gas and dust, the cluster generated in a huge surge of star formation thought to have occurred around a million years ago. The hot blue stars at the core are responsible for carving out a huge cavity in the gas seen to the right of the star cluster, in NGC 3603's centre. The red colour in the upper left may either be a colder star or a star partly obscured by dust.

FIGURE 23: OUR SUN

Venus in transit across the Sun as seen in hydrogen-alpha light.

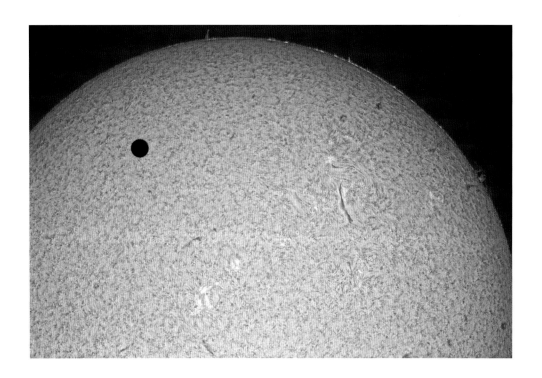

# The Colours of the Stars

When looking at the night sky it is possible, but not necessarily easy, to distinguish the different colours in the stars. Aldebaran, the eye of the Bull in Taurus, is reddish, and Rigel in Orion's right foot is bluish, but, as seen in Figure 24, the colours are subtle.

FIGURE 24: THE COLOURS OF THE STARS

The seven standard stellar types O to M are seen with colours from bluish to reddish. Note that the colours are pastels and not very saturated.

O B A F G K M
Rigel (B)
Aldebaran (K)

Stars are gaseous spheres that radiate in a way that is characteristic of the temperature near their surface. This is the important **blackbody radiation** described in Chapter 1. The Sun has a surface temperature of about 5500 °C and its colour is rather similar to that of a 5500 °C blackbody. Small differences arise because of a variety of processes stemming from the specific chemical composition of the Sun; few things in the Universe radiate like an ideal blackbody.

Sun
Brightness
300
400
500
600
700
800
Wavelength (nm)

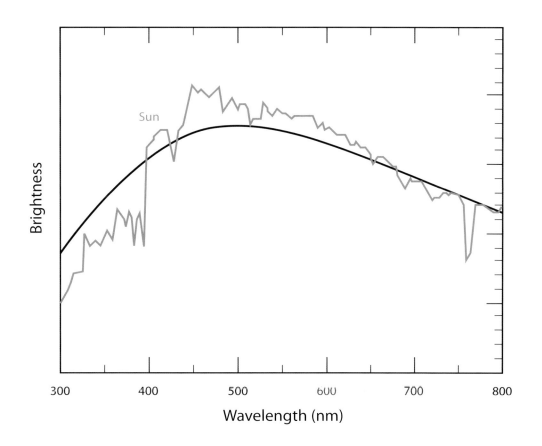

**FIGURE 25: OUR SUN, NEARLY A BLACKBODY**

The actual spectrum of the Sun (as seen outside the atmosphere) compared with the spectrum of a blackbody with the Sun's surface temperature of 5500 °C. The general similarity is clear and the differences can be attributed to the effects of absorption by the atoms of particular chemical elements in the Sun.

If the Sun's blackbody temperature is approximated to a printed colour (although this is somewhat dependent on print-technical issues and the white point that is chosen), it looks peachy-pink, not the white or yellow that we would see if we were foolish enough to look directly at it. Seen directly, the Sun's light is simply too bright and saturates the colour-sensitive cones in our eyes. The small differences between the Sun's spectrum and a precise blackbody spectrum are due to spectral lines (described below).

**FIGURE 26: THE REAL COLOUR OF OUR SUN**

The Sun's colour would look slightly peachy-pink (as in the rectangle to the left), if our eyes were not blinded by its bright light. (NB: Never look directly at the Sun with your eyes or a telescope.)

## " The visible colour of a star depends on its temperature "

The visible colour of a star depends on its temperature, which determines the wavelength of the peak of its spectrum, according to **Wien's Displacement Law** (illustrated in Figure 11). Depending on where the peak falls, a different colour results. Only a few star types have blackbody temperatures that peak in the visible range, but much of the light from all stars is visible to our eyes.

The fact that the typical star's spectrum peaks in the visible means that visible-light observations are very effective in distinguishing stars of different temperatures and other properties, such as size and chemical composition. Measuring both sides of the blackbody brightness peak gives the best "leverage" in determining colour.

### Why are there no Green Stars?

Figure 11 also answers a fascinating question: Why don't we see green stars in the sky or in photographs? Because the blackbody curves are relatively wide, the emission falls across a range of different colours that blend with the peak colour of the curve and dilute it. A hot star will, for instance, have a blackbody spectrum that peaks in the blue, and it will look bluish. A relatively cool star will have a blackbody spectrum that peaks in the red, and it will look reddish. Green lies in a narrow band squeezed between blue and red, so a star with an intermediate temperature will have its peak in the green, but it won't appear green. Its emission will extend out to include both blue and red colours that will blend in and make the star appear whitish.

## Spectral Lines — Atomic Fingerprints

As was described in Chapter 1, the spectral lines that are imprinted on the light arriving from distant stars and galaxies are a veritable gold mine of information for astronomers. Many of the most important spectral lines for atoms and molecules are found in the visible-light range and they have become effective tools for astronomers, who use these lines as their principal tool for understanding the physics of distant stars and galaxies.

> *" The energy that eventually results in the emission of light from the outer layers of stars originates from nuclear fusion processes occurring deep in the ultra-hot stellar core "*

The energy that eventually results in the emission of light from the outer layers of stars originates from nuclear fusion processes occurring deep in the ultra-hot stellar core. As in a hydrogen bomb, it is here that mass is converted into energy according to Einstein's famous equation, $E = mc^2$, as hydrogen and helium are gradually processed to heavier elements. The energy released in the deep interior does not escape from the surface very quickly — it takes some ten million years for any change in the core of the Sun to be apparent at the surface.

It is only close to the surface that the different chemical elements imprint their signatures on the escaping light, allowing distant astronomers to map the stellar structure and composition — an amazing capability that was undreamt of even as late as the mid-19th century.

## The Colour of the Universe

What is the colour of the Universe? This seemingly simple question has only recently been addressed by astronomers Karl Glazebrook and Ivan Baldry. It is difficult to take an accurate and complete census of all the light in the Universe. However, using the 2dF Galaxy Redshift Survey — a survey of more than 200 000 galaxies that measured the light from a large volume of the Universe — the question has finally been tackled. A "cosmic spectrum", which represents the sum of all the energy in the local volume of the Universe emitted at different visible wavelengths of light, was constructed:

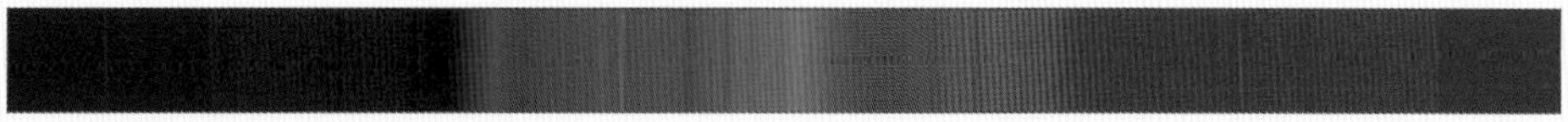

Which average colour would this give? The result actually appears almost white, perhaps with a slight pinkish tint (and again depending somewhat on printing technology). This is the colour seen in the background of this box.

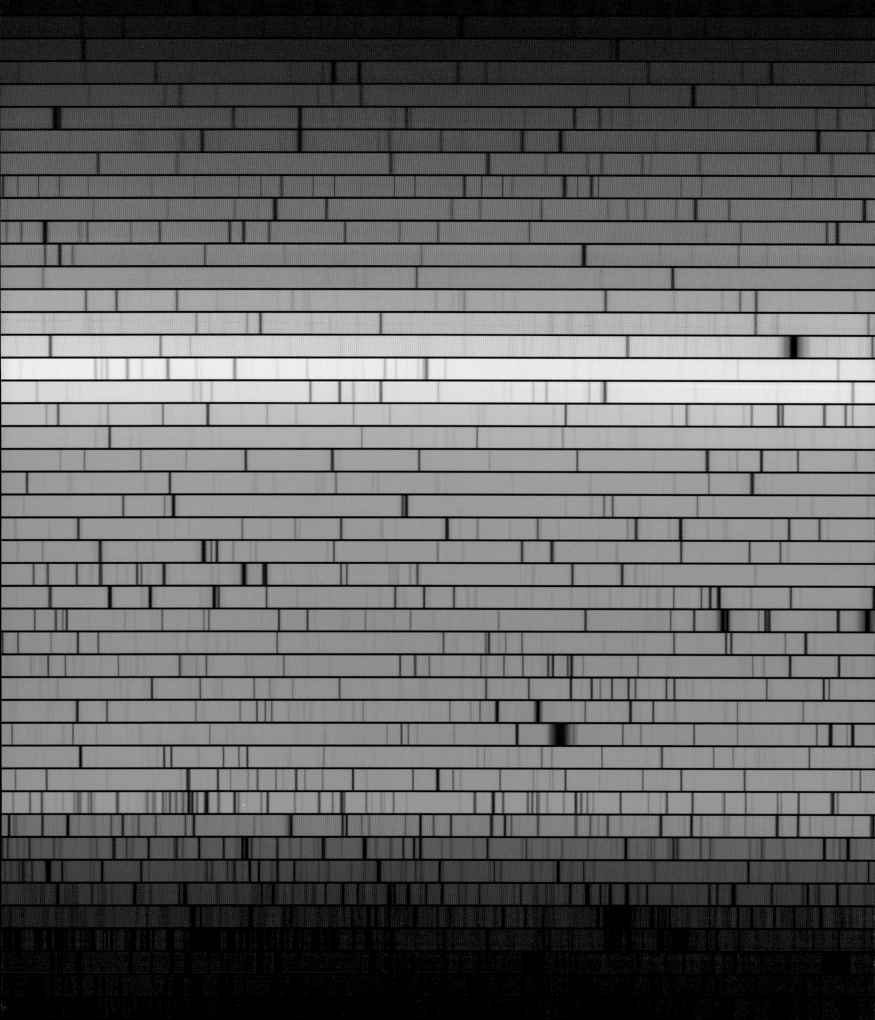

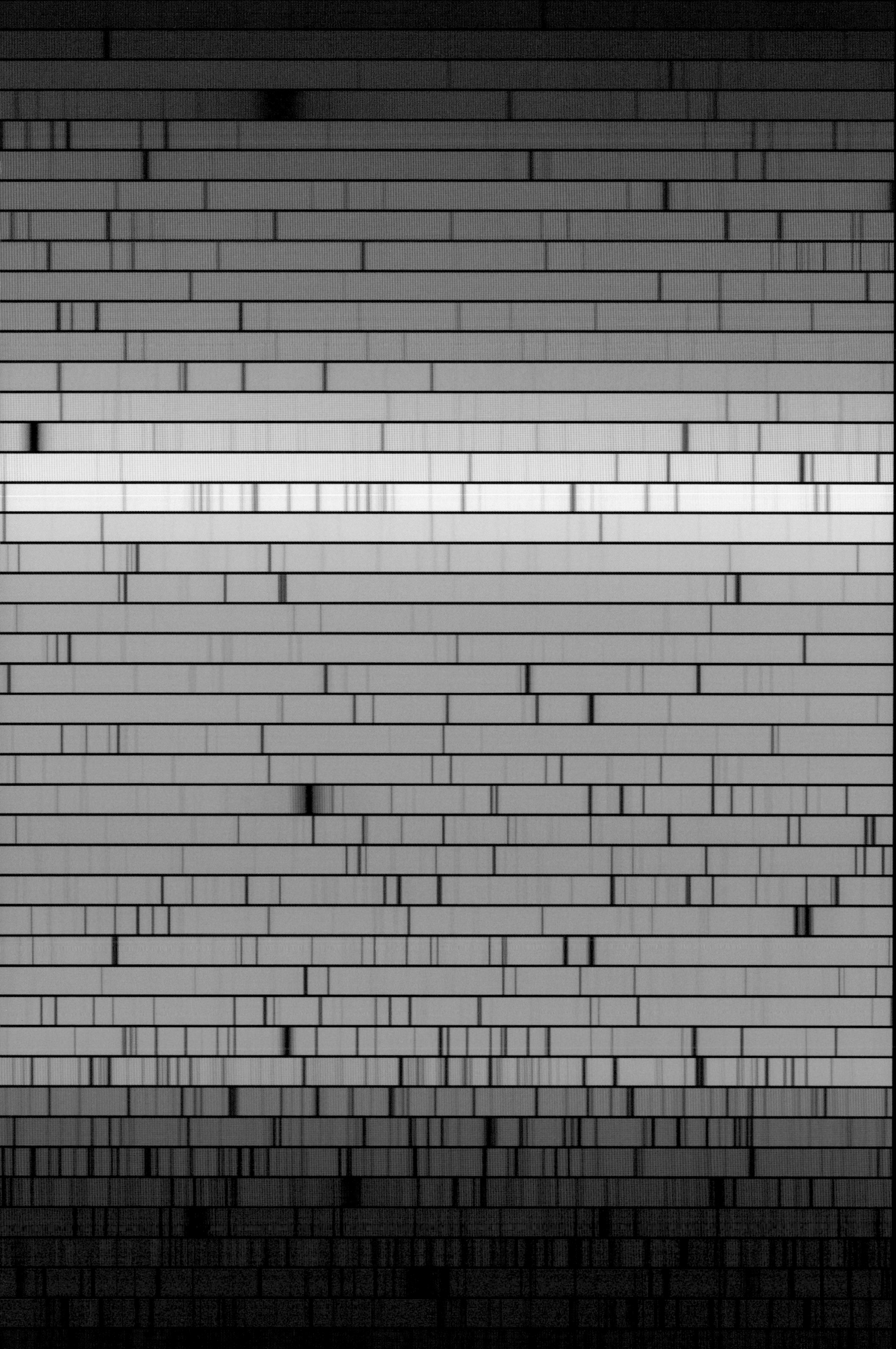

**FIGURE 27: SOLAR SPECTRUM**

This amazing image shows a high resolution spectrum of the light from our Sun littered with absorption lines, each a fingerprint of a particular atomic or molecular process. The spectrum was made from digital data obtained at a solar telescope at Kitt Peak National Observatory and covers the range of visible light from 400 nm in blue to 700 nm in red. Because of the way it was obtained, the spectrum has been divided into many separate strips that are stacked one on top of the other in this image. The rather broad, dark feature at the top right, red part, is due to hydrogen while the pair of strong yellow lines is produced by sodium.

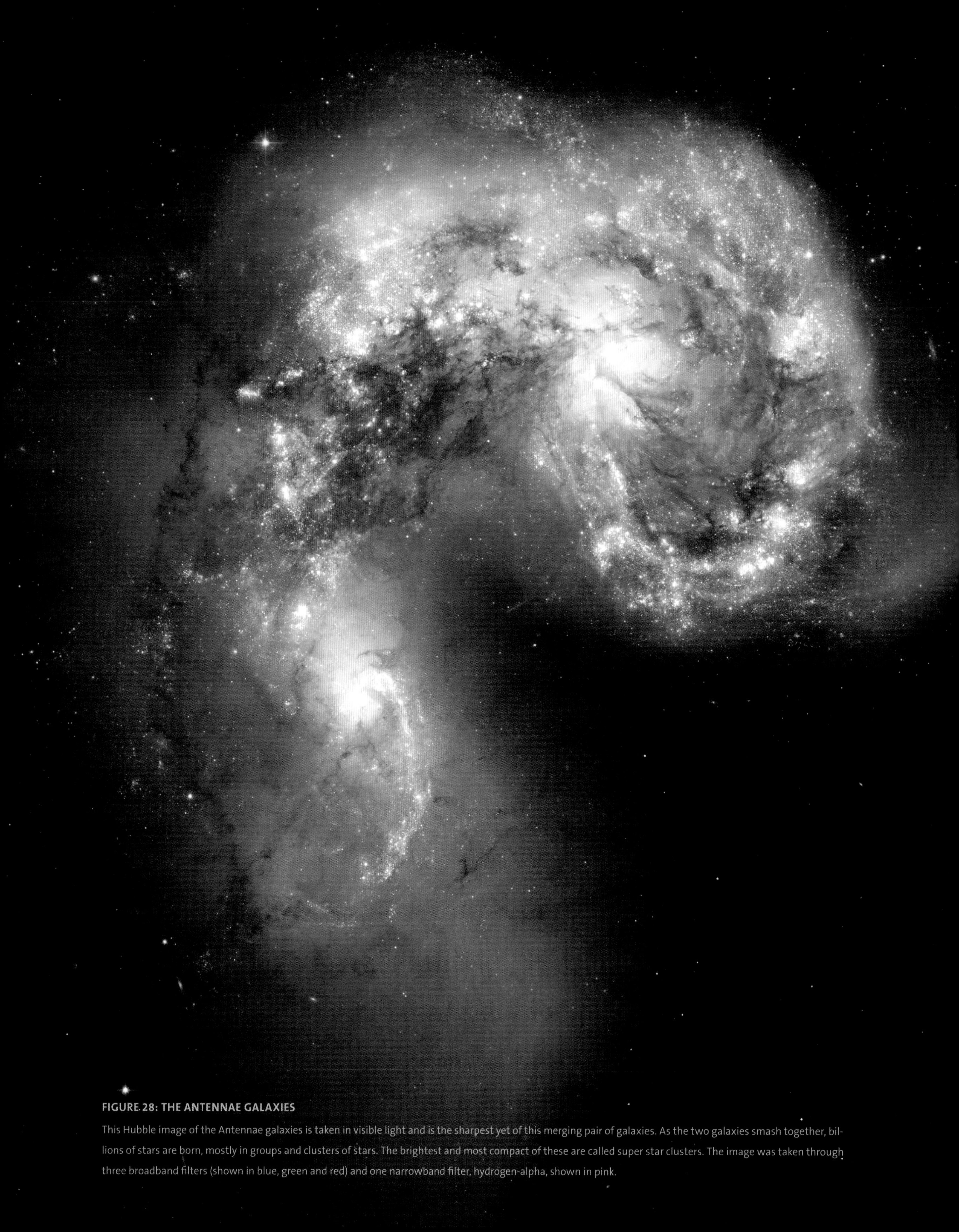

**FIGURE 28: THE ANTENNAE GALAXIES**

This Hubble image of the Antennae galaxies is taken in visible light and is the sharpest yet of this merging pair of galaxies. As the two galaxies smash together, billions of stars are born, mostly in groups and clusters of stars. The brightest and most compact of these are called super star clusters. The image was taken through three broadband filters (shown in blue, green and red) and one narrowband filter, hydrogen-alpha, shown in pink.

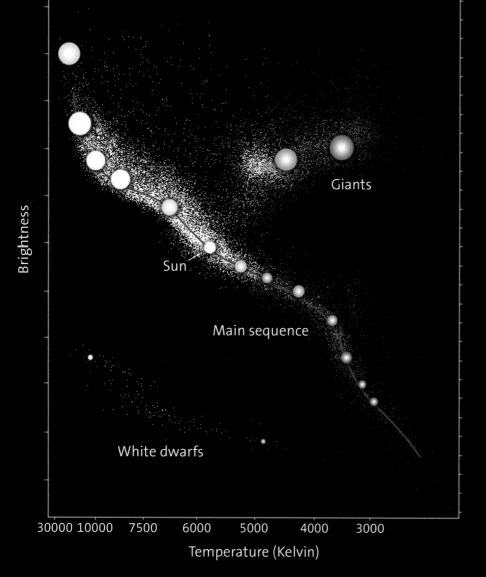

Giants
Sun
Main sequence
White dwarfs
Brightness
30000 10000 7500 6000 5000 4000 3000
Temperature (Kelvin)

**FIGURE 29: HERTZPRUNG-RUSSELL DIAGRAM**

In the Hertzprung-Russell diagram the temperatures of stars are plotted against their brightness. The position of a star in the diagram provides information about its present evolutionary stage and its mass. Stars that fuse hydrogen into helium lie on the diagonal branch, the so-called main sequence. When a star's fusion processes cannot continue any longer, it finally evolves into a white dwarf (bottom-left corner) or it explodes as a supernova. Its final fate depends on its mass and whether it exists in a double-star system. The seven standard stellar types O to M are indicated at the top.

# Stellar Evolution

From a curious astronomer's perspective, one of the interesting things about stars is that they change colour and brightness throughout their lives. Typical life-spans range from about a million years for very massive stars to tens or hundreds of billions of years for smaller stars like our Sun. The more massive a star is, the brighter it shines and the shorter its lifespan.

Around 1910, the Dane Ejnar Hertzsprung, and the American Henry Norris Russell, made a huge leap forward in our understanding of stellar evolution, or the "lives of stars", when they plotted stellar colour against intrinsic brightness (which astronomers call **luminosity**). The resulting diagram, now called the Hertzprung-Russell diagram in their honour,

> " *Many of the objects in this book would be too faint to really see very clearly even if we visited them in some fantastic future spaceship* "

**FIGURE 30: THE DOUBLE CLUSTER IN PERSEUS**

This remarkable visible-light photo of the Double Cluster in Perseus was taken by amateur astrophotograher Robert Gendler. The pair of open clusters resides some 7500 light-years from our Sun in the Perseus arm of the Milky Way. The clusters are among the brightest, densest, and closest of the open clusters containing moderately massive stars. Many of the stars in the two clusters are blue, hot O and B type giants, some shining 60 000 times brighter than our Sun.

is an invaluable tool for stellar astronomy. Stars of the same mass (and, strictly speaking, chemical composition) trace out the same course, called an evolutionary track, through the diagram. Stars with different masses will have different evolutionary tracks, meaning astronomers can extract considerable information about the mass and evolutionary status of stars from just their colour and brightness.

## Are the Colours Real?

As Chapter 1 showed, the concept of colour is very subjective and depends both on the eyes that do the seeing and the process used to make the pictures. Many of the objects in this book would be too faint to really see very clearly even if we visited them in some fantastic future spaceship. A nebula that appears faint to the naked eye from Earth would look just as faint if you were much closer; but it would appear larger. And certainly the colours would be barely discernable or invisible, since the colour-sensitive cones in our eyes work poorly under low light conditions.

Another complication is that most of the images in this book were made using light from "invisible" parts of the spectrum. For images made in X-rays, ultraviolet, infrared etc., the familiar colours are often assigned so that the "reddest" light is red and the "bluest" light is blue. With these **representative colour** images it is possible to map the invisible light to make images that we can see and appreciate.

On top of all this, some images are taken through special narrowband filters that only allow a specific wavelength to pass. These are designed to target individual atomic or molecular processes and thus have very different "vision" than our broader red-, green- and blue-sensitive eyes. These **enhanced colour** images are often colour-coded in a way that may not represent the proper colour, but provides the maximum amount of information. These are often beautiful demonstrations of how the science of modern astronomy mimics artistic choices.

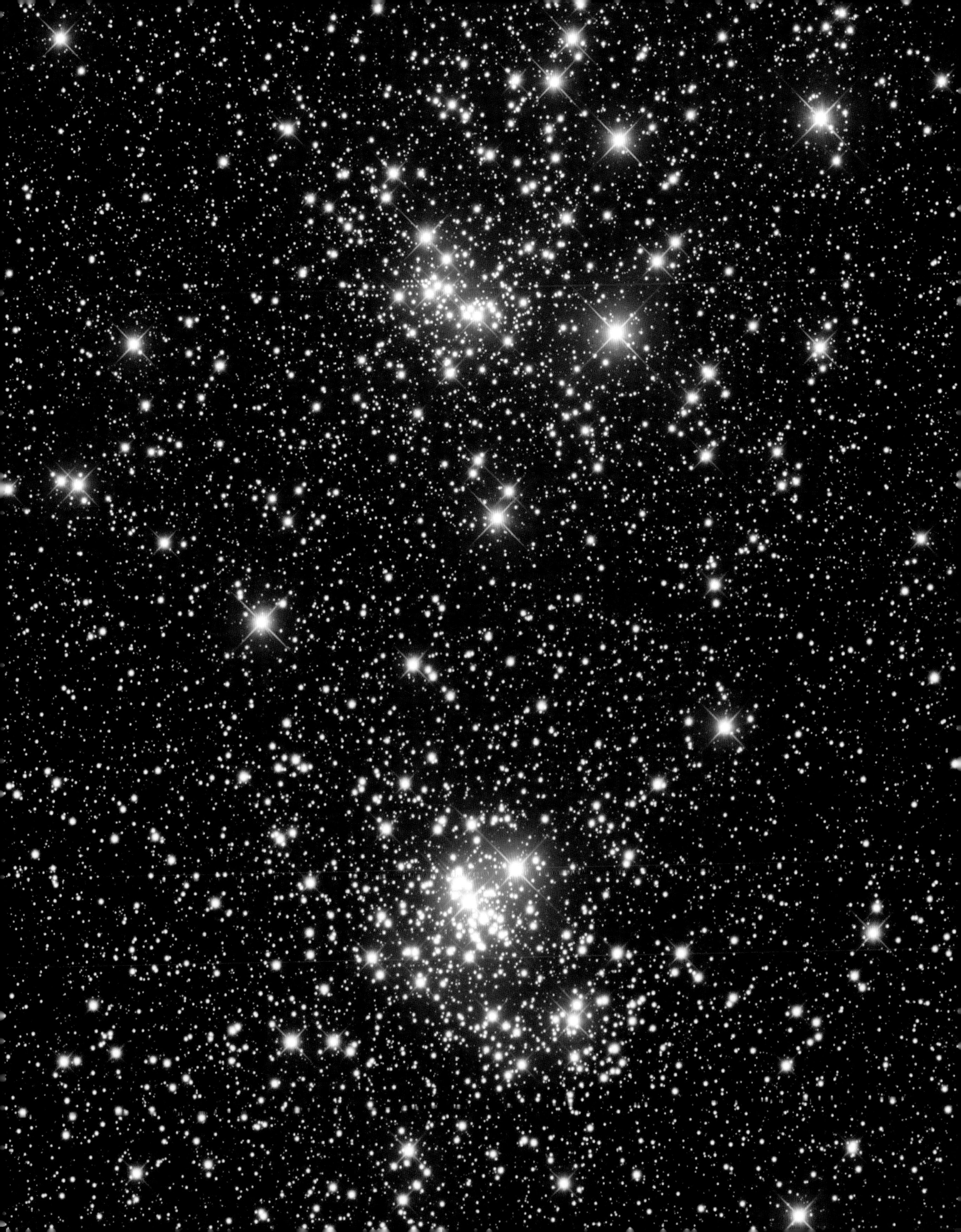

*"The visible become invisible, but, in so doing, reveals much about the Universe"*

**FIGURE 31: THE HUBBLE ULTRA DEEP FIELD**

This view of nearly 10 000 galaxies is the deepest image of the cosmos so far. Called the Hubble Ultra Deep Field, this galaxy-studded view represents a deep core sample of the Universe, cutting across billions of light-years. The snapshot includes galaxies of various ages, sizes, shapes and colours. The smallest, reddest, or most redshifted galaxies may be among the most distant known — existing when the Universe was just 800 million years old. The nearest galaxies — the larger, brighter, well-defined spirals and ellipticals — thrived about 1 billion years ago when the cosmos was 13 billion years old. In this image, blue and green correspond to colours that can be seen by the human eye, such as hot, young, blue stars and the glow of Sun-like stars in the discs of galaxies. Red represents near-infrared light. The image required 800 exposures lasting 11.3 days.

## Invisible Becomes Visible & Visible Invisible

There is a special case where some of the "invisible" radiation from the Universe can become visible to our eyes, or at least to our visible-light cameras: ultraviolet light from very distant objects is sometimes **redshifted** into the visible range. The Universe is expanding and, as a result, the more distant an object is from us, the more its light is "stretched" to longer, redder wavelengths.

But the Universe gives and takes. The redshift also shifts the redder parts of the visible part of a distant galaxy's light into the "invisible" infrared, so we don't really gain anything in terms of the amount of light we can see. And for the farthest galaxies that we know of today, which are seen from a time when the Universe was nearly 13 billion years younger, the redshift is so extreme that the blue slope of the blackbody-like spectrum of even the hottest stars is shifted into the infrared, making them practically invisible to our eyes and to visible-light telescopes. This is one of the reasons astronomers so sorely need sensitive infrared telescopes like NASA's Spitzer Space Telescope and, in the future, the much larger and more sensitive NASA/ESA/CSA James Webb Space Telescope — to chase the elusive redshifted visible starlight into the infrared as we observe objects from an era closer and closer to the Big Bang.

A special technique, using the substantial redshifts of the most distant objects, has allowed astronomers to begin to map out the star formation history of the Universe from its very early stages until the present. As we observe objects that are farther and farther away and the redshift moves their light through the visible spectrum, it turns out that at very large distances — 12-13 billion light-years — the objects suddenly disappear, or drop out, first from the bluer and then the redder filter images. This is because hydrogen gas in the distant Universe absorbs most or all of the far-ultraviolet light from the most distant objects. Finding these "drop-out galaxies" is a common and very successful method of sifting out the faint and elusive, truly distant objects from the intrinsically fainter numerous, but closer ones. The visible become invisible, but, in so doing, reveals much about the Universe.

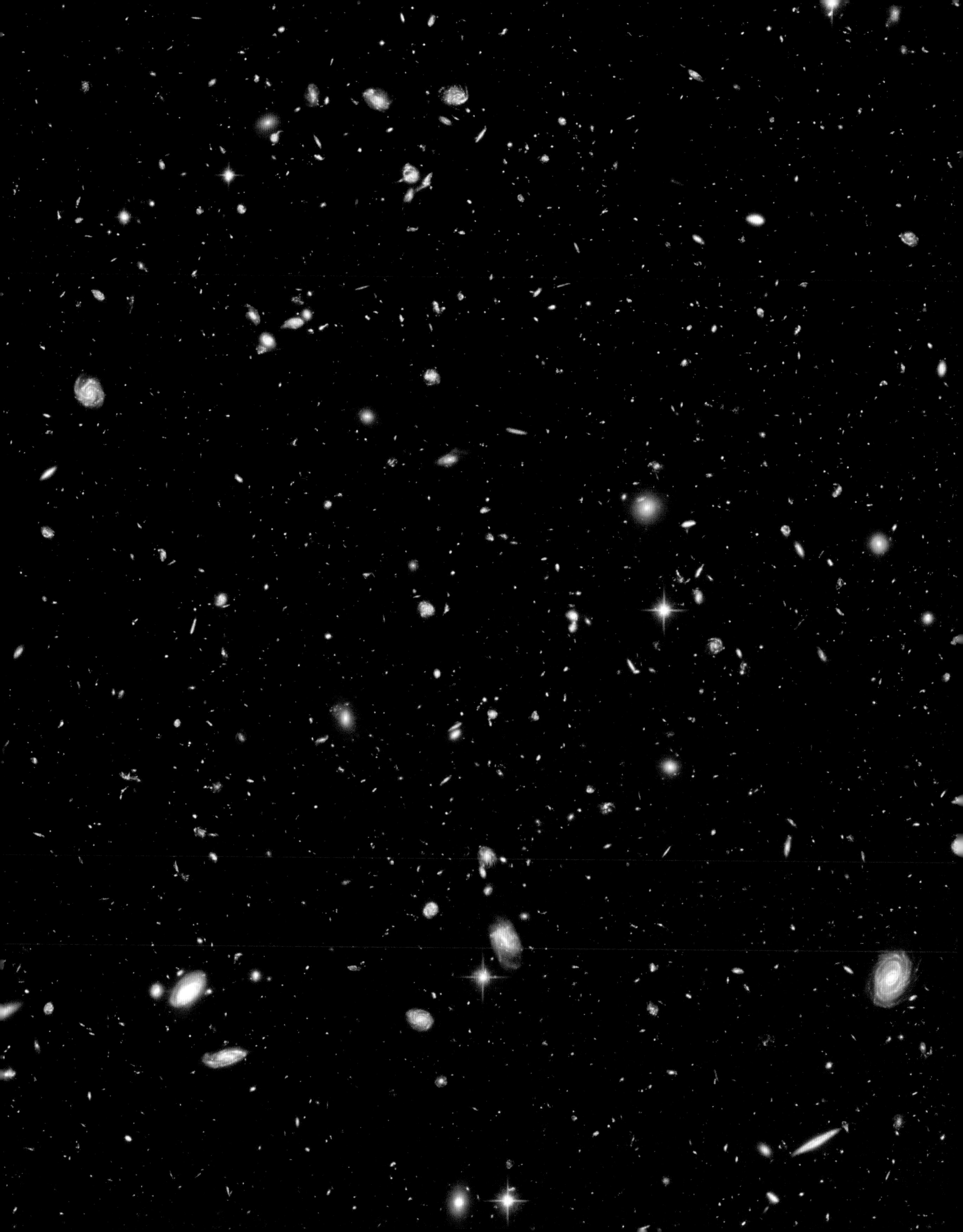

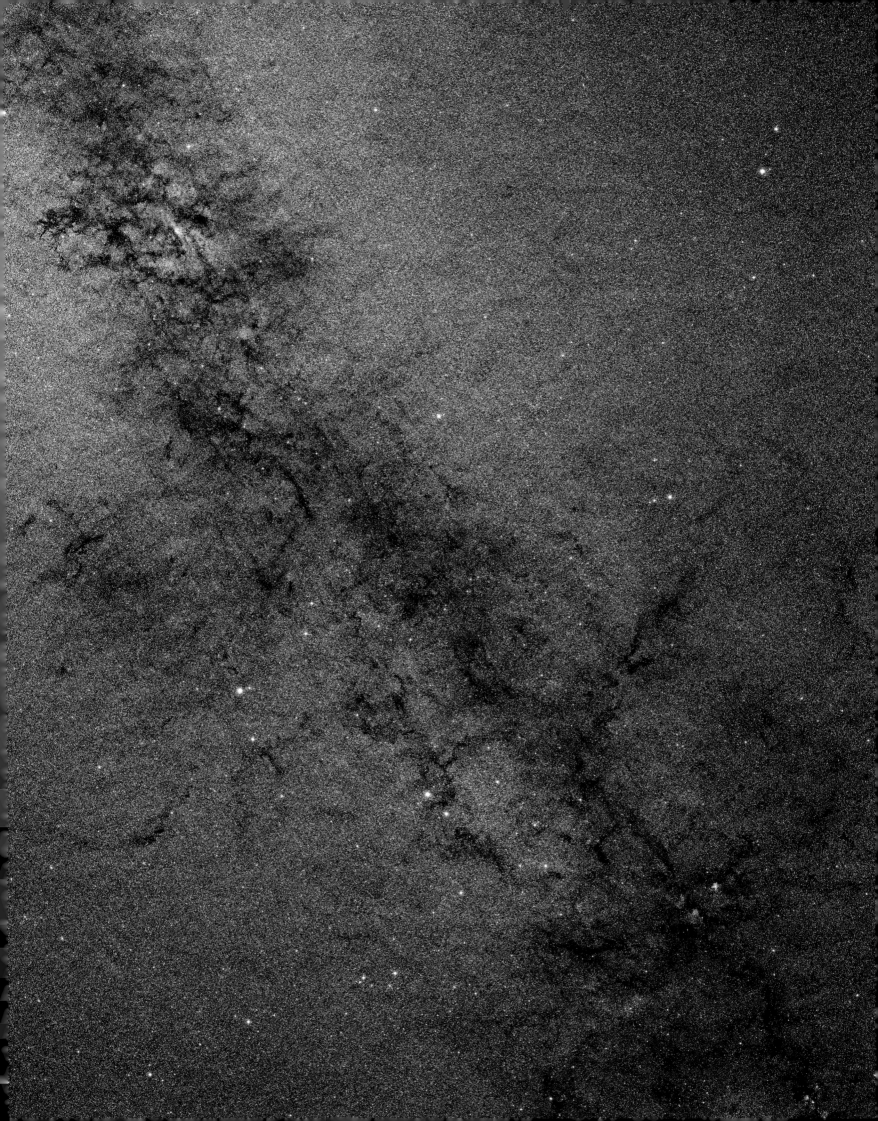

#  THE INFRARED UNIVERSE

**FIGURE 32: THE MILKY WAY CENTRE**

The centre of our Milky Way galaxy is located in the constellation of Sagittarius. When viewed in the visible part of the spectrum, most of the stars are hidden behind thick clouds of dust. This

The infrared band lies just beyond the deepest red we can see.

This band of the electromagnetic spectrum is a window onto

a cool, dust-filled Universe. By allowing us to peer through the

obscuring dust, strewn between the stars like an interstellar fog,

## *“Infrared radiation reveals the hidden, the cold and the dusty”*

Infrared radiation reveals the hidden, the cold and the dusty. While the term “infrared” is often synonymous with the idea of heat, in astronomy it is actually more valuable for studying objects that are cool by Earthly standards. It gives astronomers a very different view of the Universe that complements the familiar visible perspective.

The infrared **spectrum** starts just beyond the reddest light visible to our eyes and ranges out to **wavelengths** up to a hundred times longer than visible light. While the visible spectrum is confined to a narrow **band** between 380 and 740 **nanometres** (0.38 to 0.74 **micrometres**), the infrared spectrum extends out from the upper end of the visible to around 400 micrometres.

### Infrared Regimes

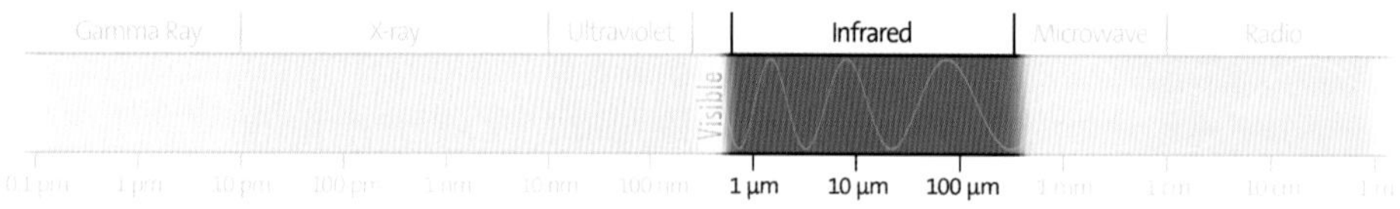
Gamma Ray
X-ray
Ultraviolet
Infrared
Microwave
Radio
Visible
1 µm
10 µm
100 µm

The infrared spectrum is generally divided into three **regimes**, the near-, mid- and far-infrared. These divisions are observational definitions and not precisely bounded, but do provide useful guidelines.

Near-infrared: 0.8–5.0 micrometres

The near-infrared regime begins just beyond the extreme limits of the reddest light visible to the human eye and extends out to wavelengths about ten times longer than the eye can see. The properties of near-infrared radiation are similar to those of light, and the same technologies will usually work in the near-infrared. The atmosphere is largely transparent in the near-infrared, although there are some absorption bands caused by various molecules (primarily water).

Mid-infrared: 5.0–40 micrometres

The mid-infrared regime spans wavelengths that are roughly 10 to 100 times longer than those visible to humans. Thermal emission from objects close to room temperature, including people, peaks in this band; industrial thermal-imaging cameras typically operate at around 10 microns. The Earth’s atmosphere has a few windows of reasonable transparency, but becomes essentially opaque beyond 14 microns.

Far-infrared: 40–400 micrometres

Far-infrared radiation wavelengths range from about 100 to 1000 times longer than visible light. This band primarily covers thermal emission from cold objects at temperatures that can be as low as 10 degrees above **absolute zero**. The Earth’s atmosphere is completely opaque at these wavelengths; far-infrared telescopes must be in space — or very close to it — and cryogenically cooled to below -263 °C to operate effectively.

# History

Sir William Herschel could be considered the father of infrared astronomy. Following his discovery of the planet Uranus in 1787, his investigations led him to discover the existence of infrared radiation in 1800.

Wondering how much heat came with different colours in the Sun's spectrum, Herschel placed a series of blackened thermometers into a spectrum of sunlight refracted through a glass prism. He noted that the measured temperatures increased towards the red part of the spectrum, and when he placed a thermometer just beyond the red it showed the highest temperature of all.

**FIGURE 33: THE RHO OPHIUCHI CLOUD**

The impressive Rho Ophiuchi cloud is one of the heavenly meeting points for astronomers in search of young stars. Located 540 **light-years** away in the constellation of Ophiucus, near the celestial equator, this dusty region is the nest of more than one hundred newborn stars. This image was made with ESA's Infrared Space Observatory (ISO), from a 7.7-micrometre infrared exposure (shown as blue), and a 14.5-micrometre infrared exposure (shown as red).

The launch of the Infrared Astronomical Satellite (IRAS) in 1983 opened up a new era in infrared astronomy. From its orbital vantage point beyond an atmosphere largely opaque to infrared light, IRAS gave us our first view of the sky at far-infrared wavelengths. Among

**FIGURE 35: THE INFRARED SKY SEEN WITH 2MASS**

As the previous image this is also a panoramic view of the entire sky, as seen by the Two Micron All-Sky Survey. The measured brightnesses of half a billion stars have been combined into colours representing three distinct wavelengths of infrared light: blue at 1.2 micrometres, green at 1.6 micrometres and red at 2.2 micrometres. This map is not a combination of actual digital images, but has been reconstructed from a catalogue of stars that were measured from images collected over three years. This image is centred on the core of our own Milky Way galaxy, toward the constellation of Sagittarius. The reddish stars seemingly hovering in the middle of the Milky Way's disc — many of them never observed before — are partly obscured at the shortest wavelengths by the densest dust clouds in our galaxy. The two faint smudges seen in the lower right quadrant are our neighbouring galaxies, the Small and Large Magellanic Clouds.

its most amazing discoveries was the "infrared cirrus", the telltale glow of the diffuse dust clouds that are strewn throughout our galaxy.

Space-based successors to IRAS include the European Space Agency's Infrared Space Observatory (ISO), launched in 1995, and NASA's Spitzer Space Telescope, launched in 2003. Each advancement in technology has brought increased sensitivity and improved resolution.

The most ambitious ground-based survey of the infrared sky to date is the Two Micron All-Sky Survey (2MASS). Observations collected between 1997 and 2001 have produced a digital map of the entire sky at near-infrared wavelengths.

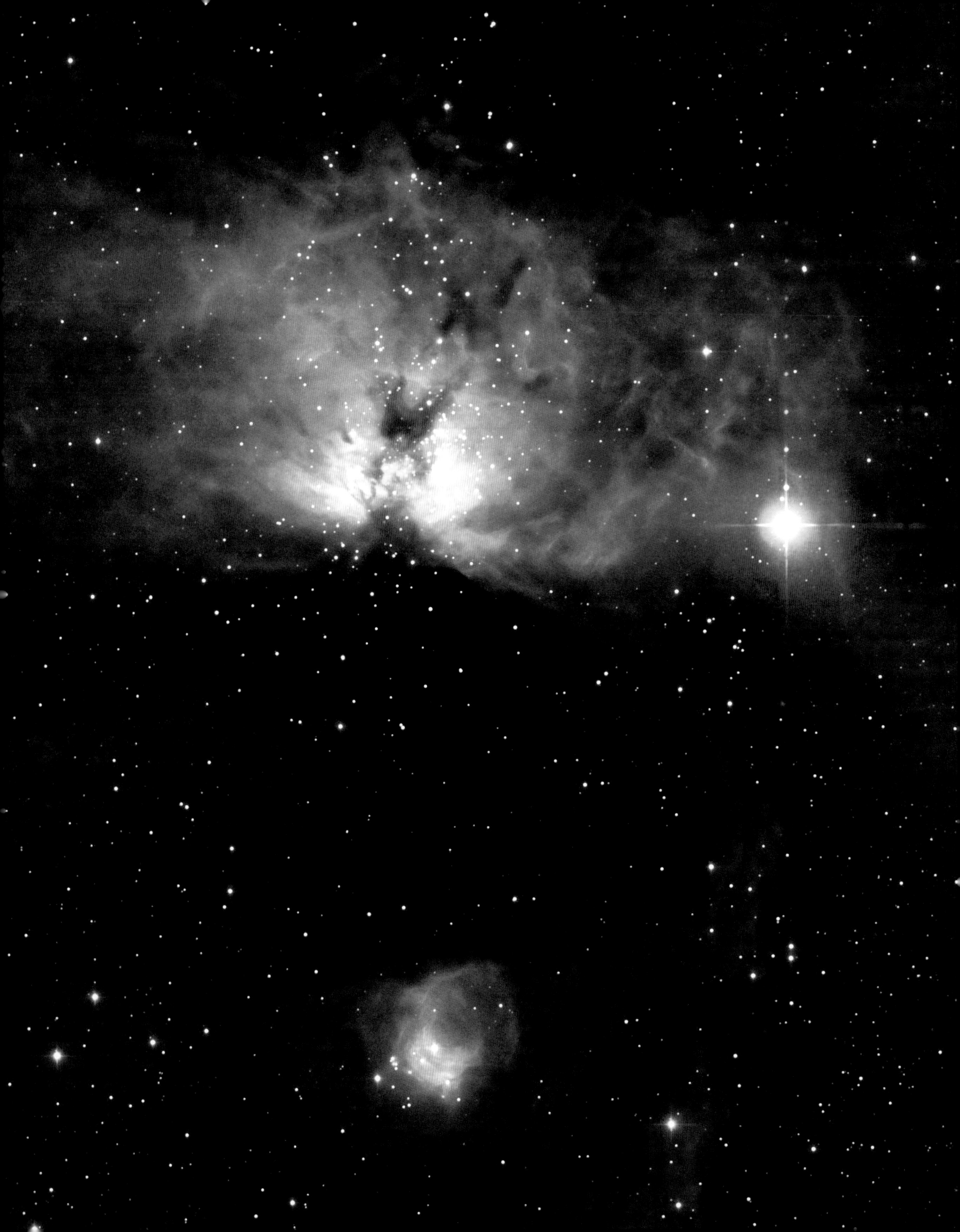

*“ At a casual glance it may be difficult to tell the difference between a visible and an infrared telescope ”*

**FIGURE 36: THE FLAME NEBULA**

NGC 2024, also known as the Flame Nebula, is located at a distance of about 1000 light-years and is part of the Orion Molecular Cloud Complex (Orion B). At near-infrared wavelengths, seen here with 2MASS, the dust in the dark lane separating the two halves of the nebula becomes more transparent, revealing a dense stellar cluster. The cluster is thought to be less than one million years old. To the south of the Flame Nebula lies the famous Horsehead Nebula, a cloud of dust seen in visible light as a silhouette against a field of glowing gas. In the near-infrared the glowing gas is gone and only a faint trace of the Horsehead can be seen in the reflected light near the bottom right of the image (see Chapter 7).

## Visible-light Technologies for Infrared Light

Infrared astronomy employs much the same technology that is used for visible-light measurements. At a casual glance it may be difficult to tell the difference between a visible and an infrared telescope. Light reaching a polished mirror is reflected and focussed onto an instrument chamber. The detectors look much like the digital arrays found in consumer digital cameras, though the actual semiconductor technologies are different and optimised for infrared wavelengths.

Many visible-light telescopes, when equipped with suitable detectors, also function equally well in the near-infrared. While the Earth's atmosphere is opaque at many infrared wavelengths, a few windows exist in the near- and mid-infrared bands. Even so, placing a telescope in space can be very advantageous and is essential in the far-infrared where the atmosphere is completely opaque. In the mid- and far-infrared, it is also often necessary to adjust the component materials since the optical properties (transparency, reflectivity) of materials can depend strongly on wavelength.

Cryogenic cooling is a critical component of infrared telescopes. Objects at room temperature generate quite a lot infrared radiation and would flood the detectors. It would be like shining a torch onto a visible-light detector while trying to image a faint object. Near-Infrared telescopes are typically cooled with liquid nitrogen at (about -195 °C) while mid- and far-infrared telescopes require liquid helium to reach much lower operating temperatures (-267 °C or below).

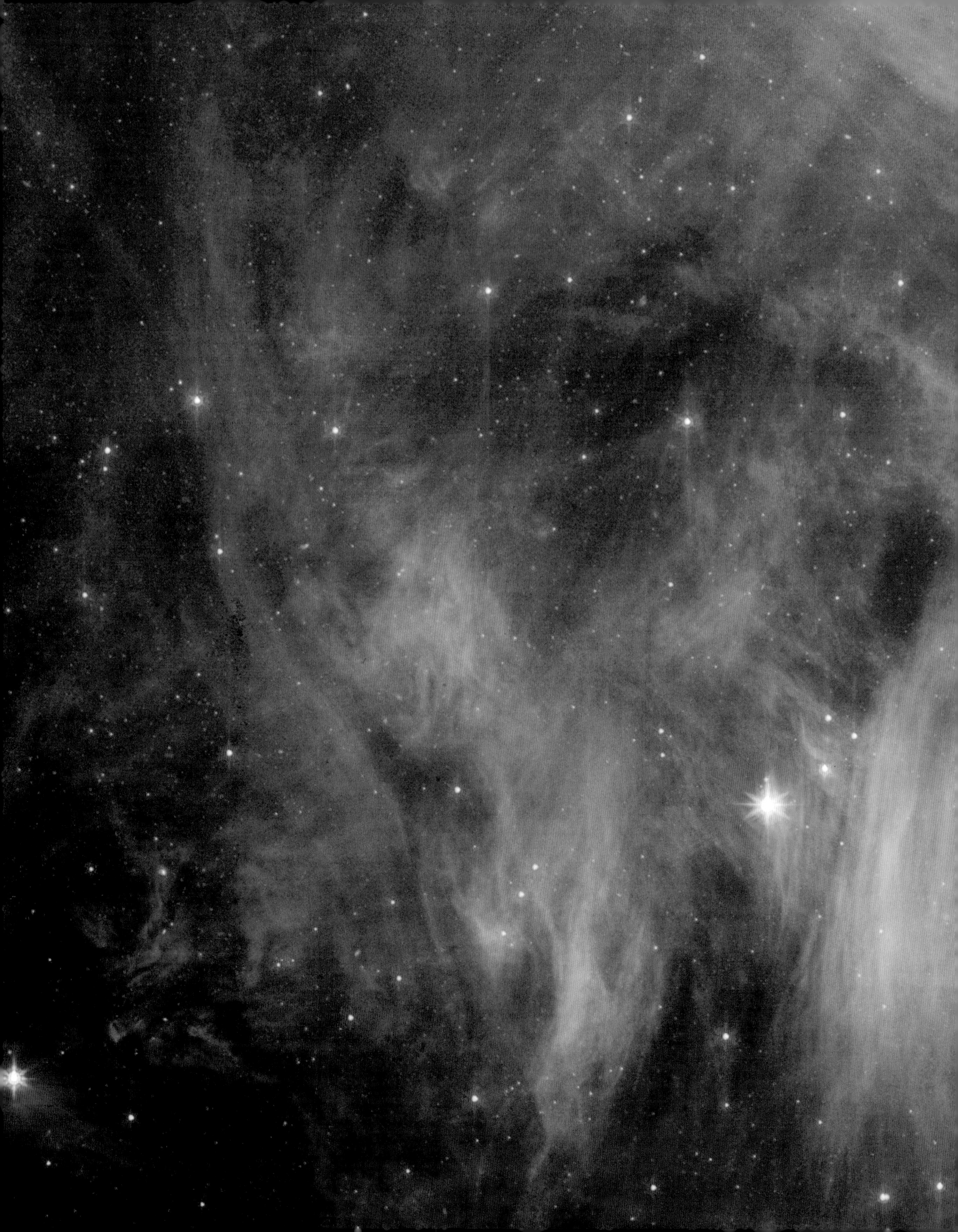

**FIGURE 37: THE PLEIADES STAR CLUSTER**

The Seven Sisters, also known as the Pleiades star cluster, seem to float on a bed of feathers in this infrared image. Clouds of dust sweep around the stars, swaddling them in a gauzy veil. The Pleiades are located more than 400 light-years away in the constellation of Taurus. This infrared image from Spitzer highlights a spider's web of dust filaments associated with the cloud through which the cluster is travelling, coloured yellow, green and red in this view. The densest portion of the cloud appears in yellow and red, and the more diffuse outskirts are shown in green. One of the parent stars, Atlas, can be seen at the bottom, while six of the sisters are visible at top. Additional stars in the cluster are sprinkled throughout the picture in blue.

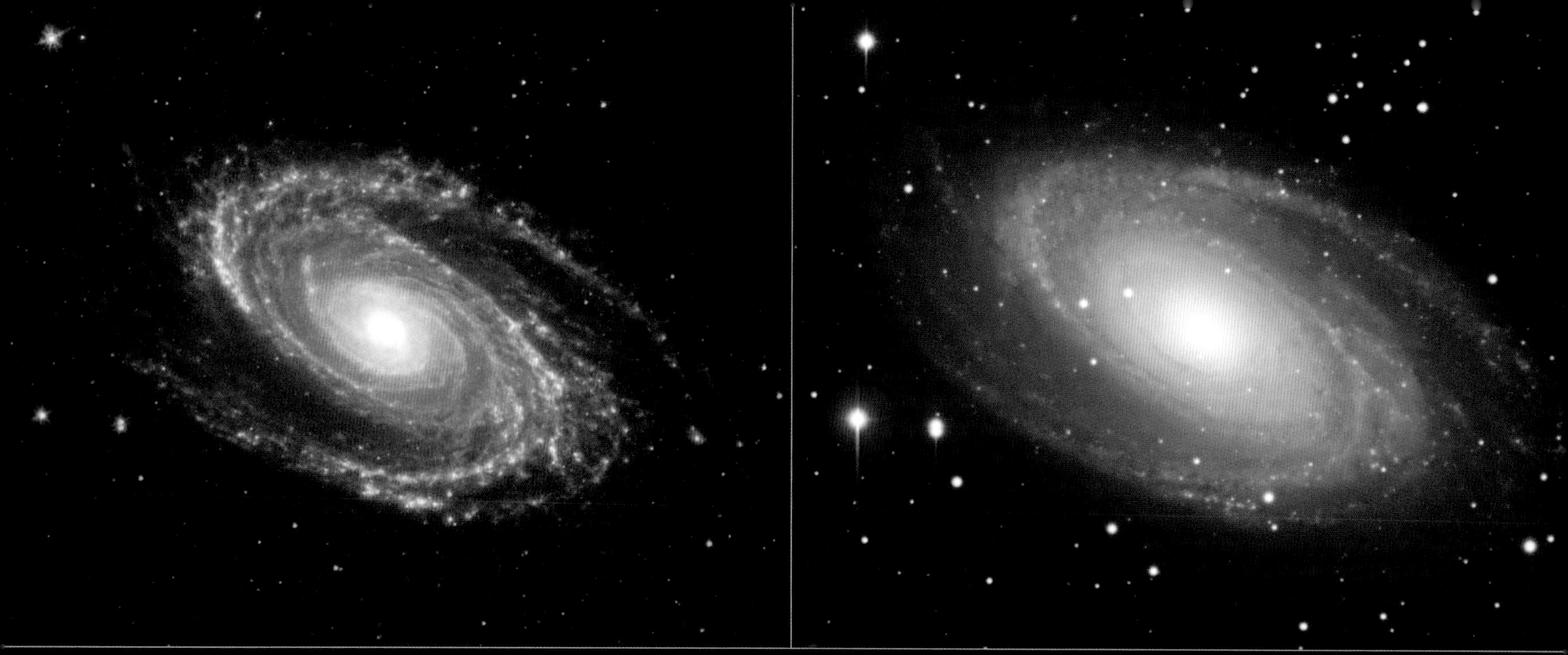

**FIGURE 38: INFRARED AND VISIBLE-LIGHT MESSIER 81**

The magnificent spiral arms of the nearby galaxy Messier 81 are highlighted in the image to the left from NASA's Spitzer Space Telescope. The image is a composite mosaic of infrared emission at 24 micrometres (red) combined with eight micrometres (green) and 3.6 micrometres (blue). A visible-light image of Messier 81, obtained with the ground-based Isaac Newton Telescope on La Palma, is shown to the right. Dust lanes that absorb the visible light and appear dark in the image to the right radiate strongly in the infrared (left, especially in 8 and 24 micrometres). Upon absorbing ultraviolet or visible light from newly born stars, a dust grain is heated and re-emits the energy in the infrared.

# Sources of Infrared Light

Even though infrared **blackbody radiation** is similar to visible light, the longer wavelengths involved present a very different Universe to the astronomer. Only the hotter stars emit the bulk of their blackbody radiation in the visible spectrum, while the blackbody emission from the far more numerous cooler stars peaks in the infrared.

As a result, our view of the visible Universe is very strongly biased towards the hottest stars, which can appear to be thousands of times brighter than their cooler counterparts. This gives us a skewed view if we are interested in the overall distribution of stars. Stars less massive than our Sun are far more numerous in the galaxy, but account for a disproportionately small amount of the visible light.

## Blackbody Radiation (Dust)

Starlight is of decreasing importance in the infrared spectrum as the wavelengths lengthen. Towards the mid- and far-infrared, dust clouds become the major player.

While the dust floating in interstellar space can be very cold, even matter that is at temperatures as low as -250 °C (20 K) will still emit blackbody radiation strongly in the far-infrared. Dust that is warmed by nearby stars to -170 °C (100 K) will be brightest in the mid-infrared. What dust lacks in brightness it makes up for in surface area. The fine particles are spread out through space, akin to the way a small piece of chalk can be ground up to cover a large area of blackboard.

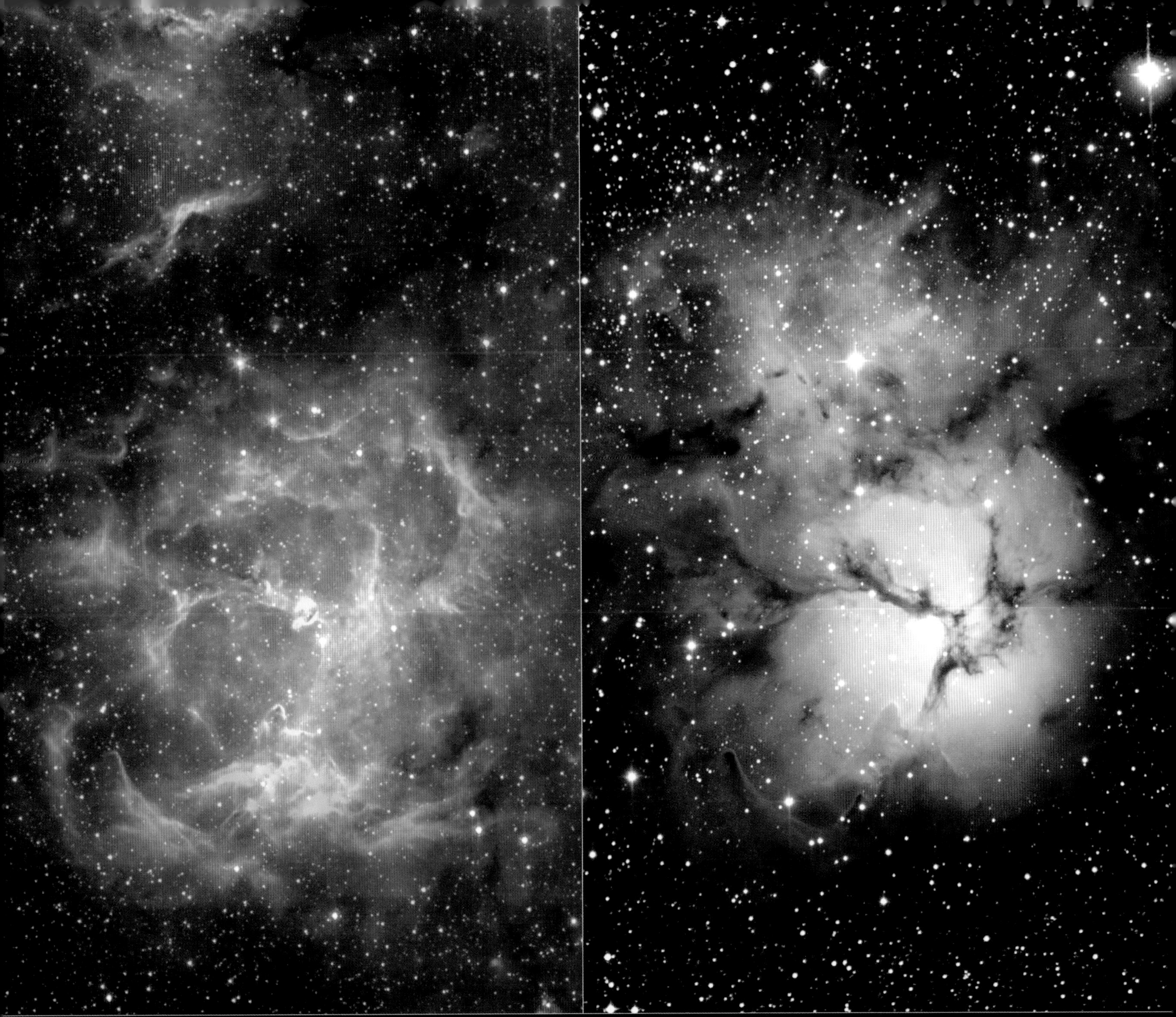

**FIGURE 39: THE TRIFID NEBULA IN INFRARED AND VISIBLE LIGHT**

The Trifid Nebula is a giant star-forming cloud of gas and dust located 5400 light-years away in the constellation of Sagittarius. This representative colour Spitzer Space Telescope image (left) reveals a different side of the Trifid as compared to the well-known visible-light Trifid (right). Where dark lanes of dust are visible tri-secting the nebula in visible light, this dust glows brightly in the Spitzer picture. Spitzer has uncovered 30 massive embryonic stars and 120 smaller newborn stars throughout the Trifid Nebula, in both its dark lanes and in the luminous clouds. These stars are visible as yellow or red spots. The red colours in the image come from the thermal glow of warm dust, while the greens are from carbon-based dust glowing under in the illumination of the nearby stars.

*Where this dust is warmed by starlight, often at the sites of current star formation, it can glow very brightly"*

Looking at the sky in mid- to far-infrared wavelengths reveals a rich Universe of dusty filaments and clouds that appear as inky black blotches in the near-infrared and the visible. Where this dust is warmed by starlight, often at the sites of current star formation, it can glow very brightly. This spectacular transformation of dust into a luminous cloud exemplifies the idea that "dark is light" in the infrared.

## Why do Infrared Stars Look Blue in these Images?

When viewed in visible light, stars have a broad range of colours ranging from red to white to blue (see the figure below). However, in images spanning the near- and mid-infrared regimes, like many shown here from the Spitzer Space Telescope, the stars all appear to be the same colour — pale blue in the colour representation usually used in these images.

In the visible, a cool star will appear red because its emission is brightest at the low energy, red end of the spectrum and drops off towards the blue. Conversely, a very hot star will be brightest in the blue or even ultraviolet and will be fainter in red light.

In an infrared image (where the shorter, higher energy wavelengths are mapped to blue and longer, lower energy wavelengths to red), almost all stars are hot enough to peak in the near-infrared or visible and will therefore appear brightest in the wavelengths rendered as blue. Moreover, pretty much every star, whether hot or cold, has the same fall-off towards the mid-infrared, so they will all have the same colour! Aficionados speak of the "Rayleigh-Jeans" tail of the blackbody spectrum after two famous English physicists.

The figure shows the blackbody curves of some prominent stars and of infrared emitters such as warm and cold dust as well as the cosmic microwave background for comparison (see Chapter 7).

Ultraviolet
Visible
Infrared
Bellatrix
Rigel
Sun
Mira
Brown dwarf
24,000 K
12,000 K
6,000 K
3,000 K
1,500 K
Brightness (factors of 10)
10 nm
100 nm
1 µm
10 µm
100 µm
1mm
Wavelength

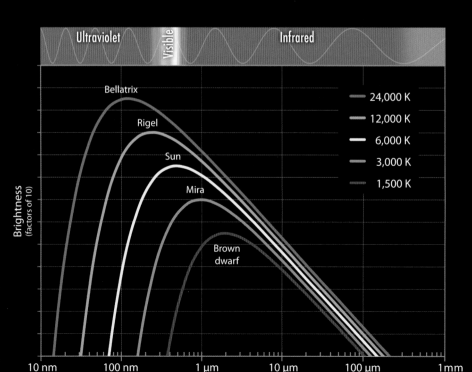

## " *Dark is light in the infrared* "

### Spectral Lines

In the visible spectrum nebulae can glow with the light of hot gases emitting spectral lines characteristic of each element. These processes continue into the infrared. Since infrared light contains less energy than visible wavelengths, it typically takes less energy to stimulate the emission of infrared spectral lines. This can produce a wide variety of signatures from elements and molecules at cooler temperatures that are not hot enough to emit in the visible part of the spectrum.

Of particular interest in the infrared is a broad band of emission from organic dust molecules. These carbon-based compounds can glow brilliantly in the mid-infrared when stimulated to fluoresce by nearby stars.

**FIGURE 40: THE CENTRE OF THE MILKY WAY**

This dazzling infrared image from Spitzer shows hundreds of thousands of stars crowded into the swirling core of our spiral Milky Way galaxy. In visible-light pictures, this region cannot be seen at all because dust lying between Earth and the Milky Way centre blocks our view.

> *" The infrared shows us a completely different picture. The dark, patchy obscuration is all but gone and we can see our own galaxy with clarity "*

## Dust Becomes Transparent

In a dark, clear sky we can see a band of light stretching from horizon to horizon. Commonly known as the Milky Way, it is the only way we can see our own galaxy directly from our location inside its disc. The dark patches we see scattered across this band of light are the result of obscuring dust clouds filling the galaxy and greatly impeding our view of distant stars and nebulae. So many stars are lost to our view that even our galaxy's centre is deeply obscured when viewed in visible light.

The infrared shows us a completely different picture. The dark, patchy obscuration is all but gone and we can see our own galaxy with clarity. Even the location of the centre of the Milky Way was a mystery for many years. In the 1920s Harlow Shapley used clever, indirect methods to determine that the centre lay towards the constellation of Sagittarius, but today a simple infrared map of the sky painlessly reveals the galactic bulge and central star cluster. In the near- to mid-infrared bands only the very densest, darkest clouds remain opaque (see Box: Dust transparency in the infrared).

This transparency in the infrared also allows astronomers to witness the process of star birth. Stars form at the cores of gravitationally collapsing clouds of gas and dust. These dusty cocoons prevent visible light from escaping, but can be penetrated by sufficiently long wavelengths of infrared light. Filaments of dust that are so dense that they remain opaque in the infrared, stand out like markers advertising the star formation within.

Infrared dust transparency can be a boon for those studying other galaxies as well. By using infrared radiation to look through the obscuring dust lanes, the underlying population of stars becomes obvious. Structural features like spiral arms, bulges and bars become easy to discern. At longer wavelengths the dust itself becomes luminous, enabling a complete picture of the dense regions that give rise to new populations of stars.

**FIGURE 41: THE CONSTELLATION OF ORION IN THE INFRARED**

The familiar winter sky constellation of Orion takes on a spectacular guise in the infrared, as seen in this representative colour image constructed from data collected by IRAS. This picture covers an area equivalent to a magazine held at arm's length (24 x 30 degrees). The warmest features are stars that are brightest at 12 micrometres (blue). The interstellar dust is cooler and shines more brightly at 60 micrometres (green) and 100 micrometres (red). The brightest features here are nebulae that can also be studied in visible light. The brightest yellow region is the Sword of Orion, containing the Great Orion Nebula (M42 and M43, also see Figure 3). Above it to the left is the nebulosity around the belt star Zeta Orionis, which contains the Flame Nebula (bright spot, also see Figure 36) and the Horsehead Nebula (not visible at this scale, also see Figure 56). Few of the familiar bright stars in Orion are obvious in the infrared, although Betelgeuse is obvious in the upper centre of the picture as a blue-white dot. The large ring to the right of Betelgeuse is the remnant of a supernova explosion, centred on the star Lambda Orionis (just beyond the top of the image).

## Dust Transparency in the Iinfrared

When you watch a sunset the normally white light of the Sun yellows and reddens as it sinks lower and passes through more and more layers of the atmosphere. Very small particles, such as dust grains and even gas molecules in the air, scatter blue light more than red. The same thing happens when starlight passes through interstellar dust clouds and this transparency increases even more dramatically when moving from red to infrared light.

Dust is composed of tiny particles of carbon- and silicon-derived materials. These microscopic particles can scatter and absorb photons of light. In sufficient quantities, dust clouds can render vast regions of space opaque to the transmission of light.

However, dust plays favourites when it comes to light. The bluest colours with the shortest wavelengths are blocked much more efficiently than the reddest colours. Essentially, as the wavelength of light increases beyond the size of the dust particles, the particles are less of an obstacle. The effect becomes even more pronounced in the infrared as the wavelengths grow by an order of magnitude or more. Only the very densest of dust clouds will block near- and mid-infrared light. This allows astronomers to peer into regions obscured in visible light by looking at these longer wavelengths.

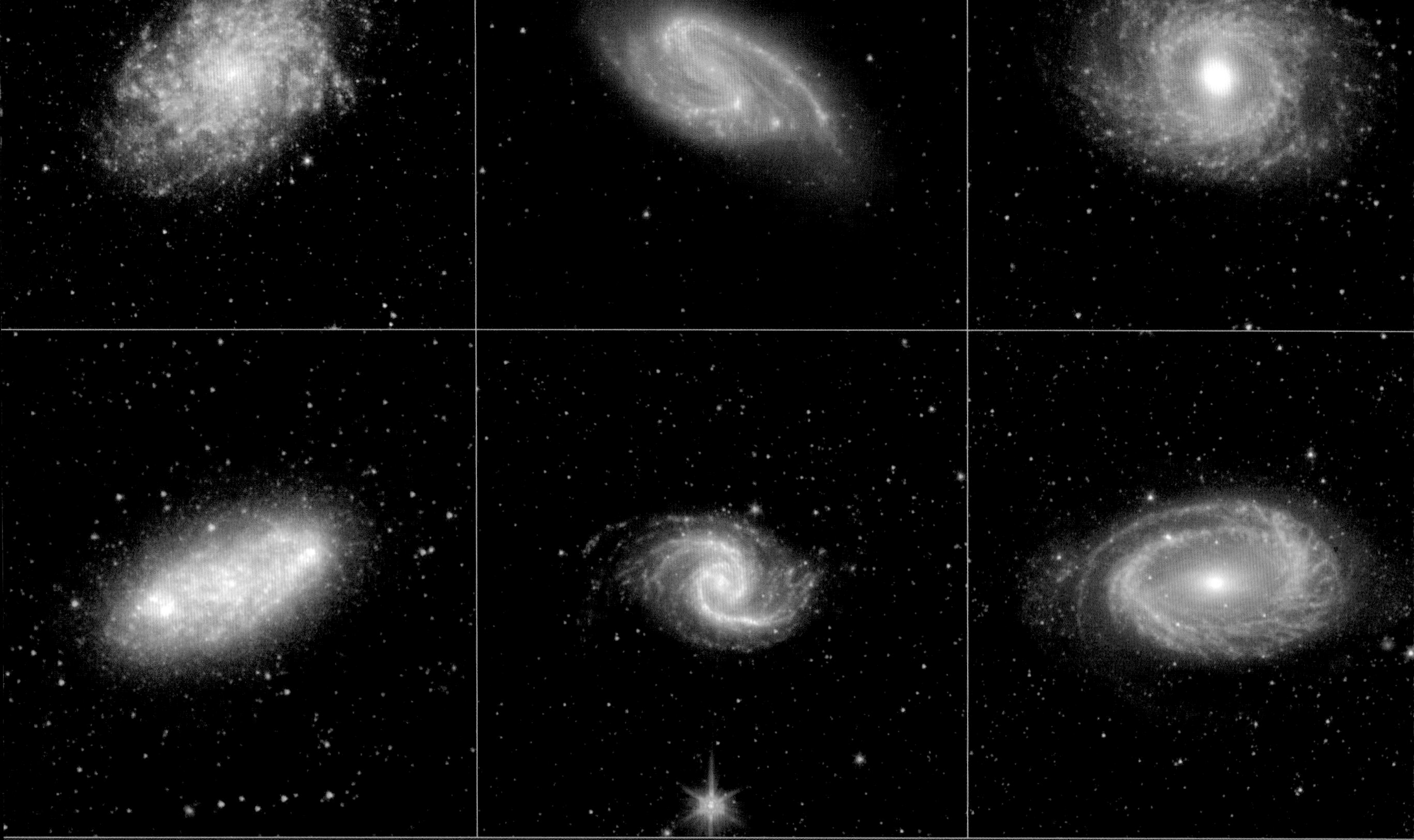

**FIGURE 42: ASSORTED GALAXIES SEEN WITH SPITZER**

These images were captured by the Spitzer Space Telescope as part of the Spitzer Infrared Nearby Galaxy Survey (SINGS) Legacy Project. The SINGS images are four-channel representative colour composites, where blue indicates emission at 3.6 micrometres, green corresponds to 4.5 micrometres, and red to 5.8 and 8.0 micrometres. The contribution from starlight at 3.6 micrometres has been subtracted from the 5.8- and 8-micrometre images to enhance the visibility of the dust features. The faint blue light is coming from mature stars, while the "glowing" pink spiral arms indicate active star formation and dust emission. Starting from upper left the galaxies are NGC 7793, Messier 66, Messier 95, NGC 2976, NGC 1566 and NGC 4725.

**FIGURE 43: AN UNTRADITIONAL VIEW OF THE LARGE MAGELLANIC CLOUD**

This vibrant image from NASA's Spitzer Space Telescope shows the Large Magellanic Cloud, a satellite galaxy of our own Milky Way. The infrared image, a mosaic of 300 000 individual tiles, offers astronomers a unique chance to study the lifecycle of stars and dust in a single galaxy. The blue colour in the picture, seen most prominently in the central bar, represents starlight from older stars. The chaotic, bright regions outside this bar are filled with hot, massive stars buried in thick blankets of dust. The red colour around these bright regions is from dust heated by stars, while the red dots scattered throughout the picture are either dusty, old stars or more distant galaxies. The greenish clouds contain cooler interstellar gas and molecular-sized dust grains illuminated by ambient starlight.

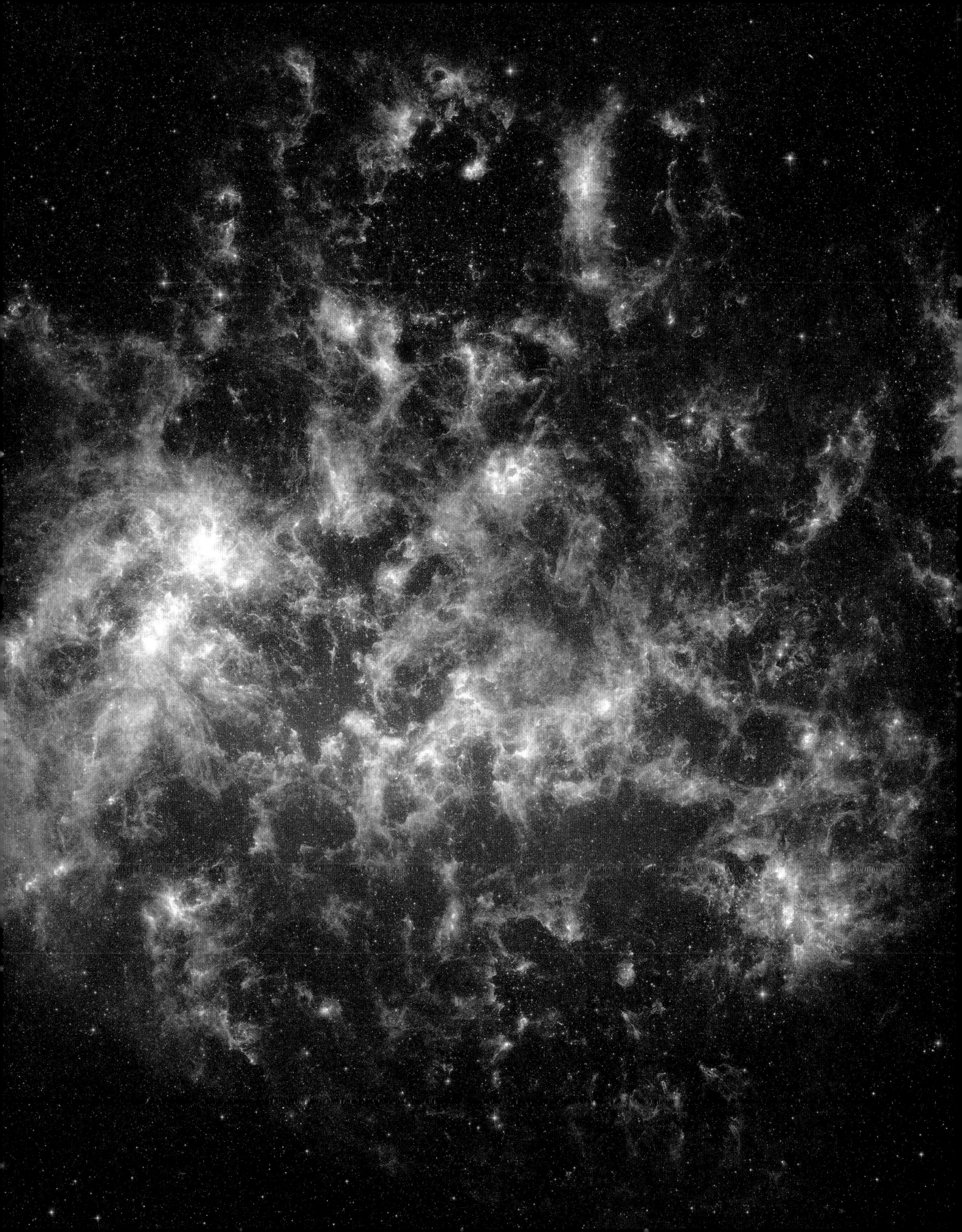

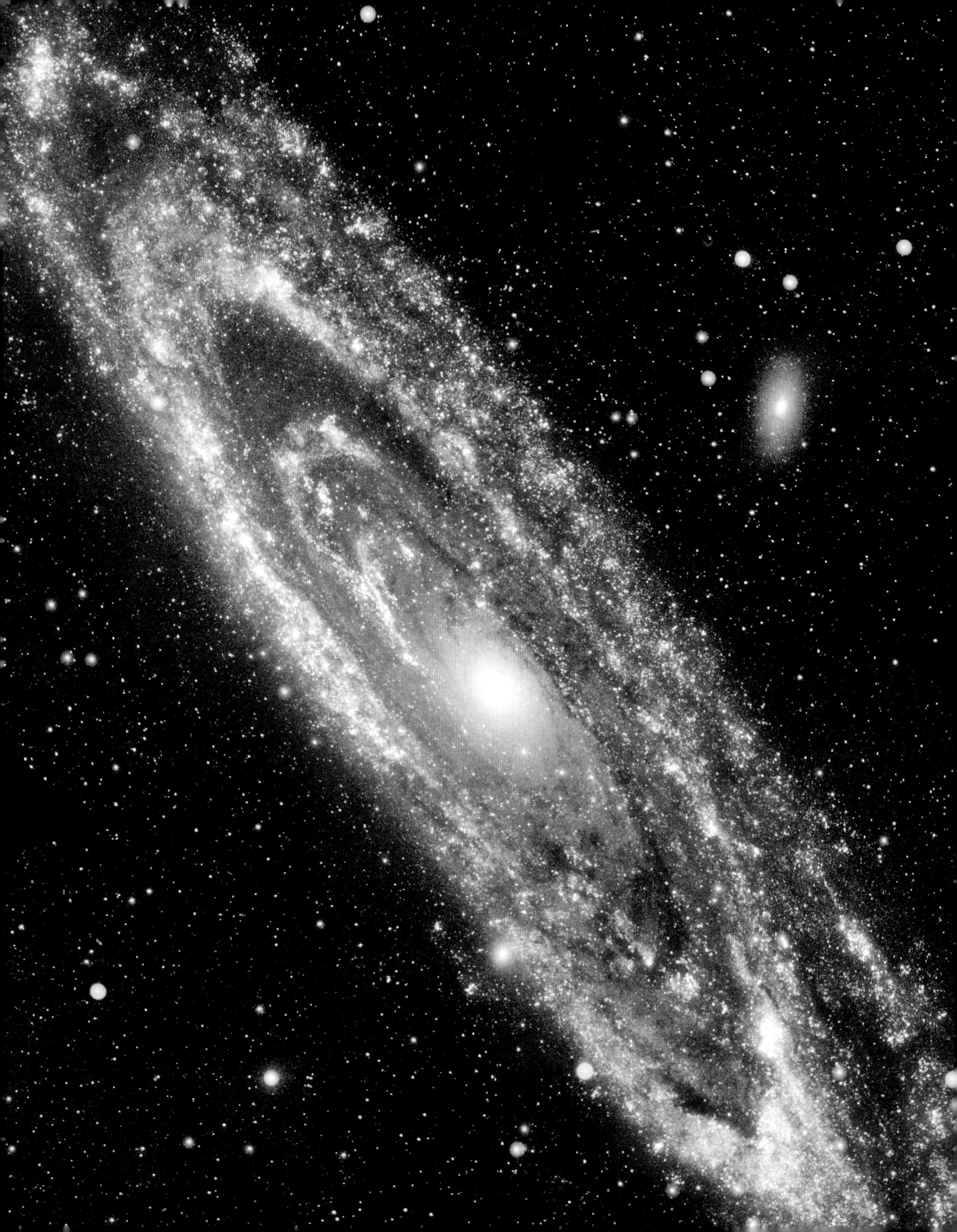

# THE ULTRAVIOLET UNIVERSE

**FIGURE 44: ANDROMEDA IN THE ULTRAVIOLET**

Approximately 2.5 million light-years away, the Andromeda Galaxy, or M31, is the Milky Way's largest galactic neighbour. The entire galaxy spans some 260 000 light-years— a distance so large that 10 images from the Galaxy Evolution Explorer stitched together were needed to produce this view of the galaxy next door. The wisps of blue making up the galaxy's spiral arms are neighbourhoods that harbour hot, young, massive stars. The central orange-white ball reveals a congregation of cooler, old stars that formed long ago. Andromeda is so bright and so close that it is one of only three galaxies that can be spotted from Earth with the naked eye. This view is a two-colour composite, where blue represents far-ultraviolet light, and yellow is near-ultraviolet light.

Ultraviolet light falls beyond the limits of what we can see at the blue end of the spectrum. In human terms the word ultraviolet calls to mind images of sore skin resulting from overexposure to the Sun, an indication of the high energy of this form of light.

The hottest stars in the Universe are brightest in ultraviolet light. The dusty clouds that give birth to these massive, luminous objects are in turn sculpted and shaped under the onslaught of the high energy photons they emit. Ultraviolet light shows us where the action is in star formation — amongst the young, the massive and the hot stars.

*“ Paradoxically, ultraviolet light drives the very processes in our atmosphere that keep much of it from reaching the ground ”*

Ultraviolet light largely originates in the glow of stars. The hottest and most massive stars glow brightest in the ultraviolet, but even our cooler Sun still produces a fair amount of light in this part of the **spectrum**. The ultraviolet spectrum starts just beyond blue-violet at a **wavelength** of 400 **nanometres** and includes wavelengths down to 10 nanometres at the extreme end. Remember the rule: the shorter the wavelength, the higher the energy. A single ultraviolet **photon** can carry as much energy as 50 or more photons of red light!

## Ultraviolet Regimes

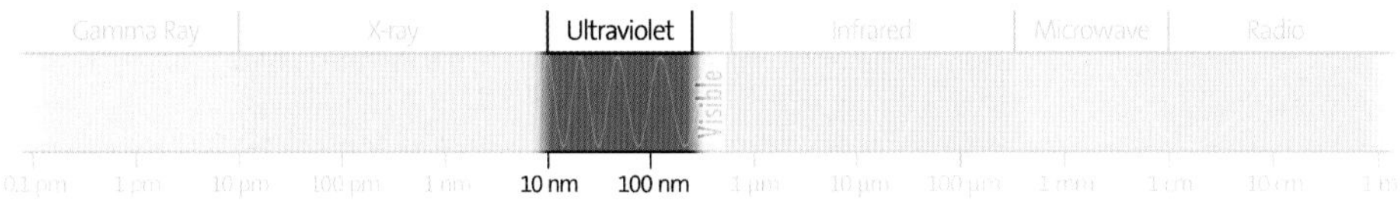
Gamma Ray
X-ray
Ultraviolet
Infrared
Microwave
Radio
Visible
10 nm
100 nm

The ultraviolet spectrum can be broken down into four **regimes** of increasing energy.

Near-ultraviolet: 400–300 nm

These wavelengths lie just beyond the limit of human vision and encompass the “black light” often used at parties to illuminate a variety of **fluorescent** materials such as white paper, paints, inks and even teeth and nails. Near-ultraviolet radiation from the Sun reaches the Earth most readily and can be observed from the ground.

Mid-ultraviolet: 300–200 nm

Increasingly filtered out by atmospheric ozone, mid-ultraviolet radiation from the Sun still reaches the ground in sufficient doses to cause sunburns and damage that can lead to skin cancer.

Far-ultraviolet: 200-122 nm

The atmosphere is essentially opaque to far-ultraviolet radiation, so space telescopes or high-flying rockets must be used to observe in this regime. This light is sufficiently destructive to kill bacteria easily and so can be used to sterilise objects. It also poses the greatest threat to the spread of life by panspermia — the transport of organisms through space on and near the surface of rocks that may eventually land on a planet as a meteorite.

Extreme-ultraviolet: 122–10 nm

This most energetic band of ultraviolet extends to the border of the X-ray spectrum. Extreme-ultraviolet emission is usually associated with the very hottest stars in the Universe.

On Earth we are sheltered from much of the Sun's ultraviolet as the ozone in our upper atmosphere filters out a great deal of the Sun's shorter wavelength ultraviolet. Significant absorption begins beyond around 300 nm, making ground-based observations very difficult at anything other than near-ultraviolet wavelengths. While a bane to astronomers, this makes exposure to sunlight much safer for us. Ultraviolet photons carry much more energy than visible photons, enough to do damage to our skin and even the DNA in our cells.

Paradoxically, ultraviolet light drives the very processes in our atmosphere that keep much of it from reaching the ground. Ozone, which is the primary filter against the more harmful forms of ultraviolet, is actually produced in the upper atmosphere when incoming ultraviolet photons interact with oxygen molecules.

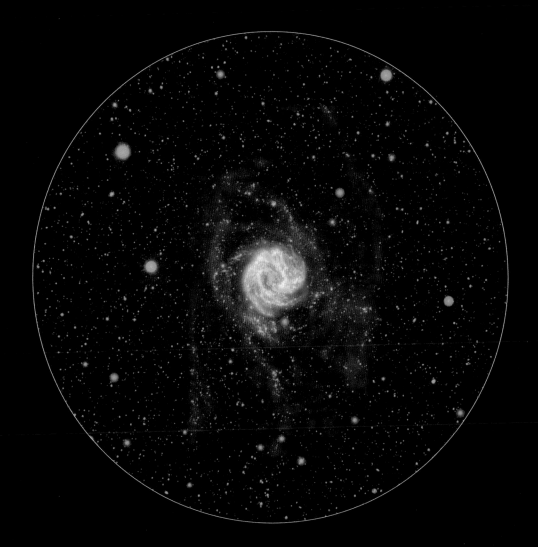

**FIGURE 45: WHAT LIES BEYOND THE EDGE OF A GALAXY?**

This deep ultraviolet view of the Southern Pinwheel Galaxy M83 has revealed an unexpected surprise. Beyond the well-known visible disc of this classic spiral are faint but clear ultraviolet arms (rendered here in blue and green) far out beyond any that had been seen before. But these loosely wound arms of hot young stars are not alone in the outer reaches. Radio imaging of the hydrogen gas (shown in red: see Chapter 7) in this galaxy shows extended gas arms that line up perfectly with the ultraviolet arms. There is an entire cycle of star formation going on far beyond what was once considered to be the disc of the galaxy!

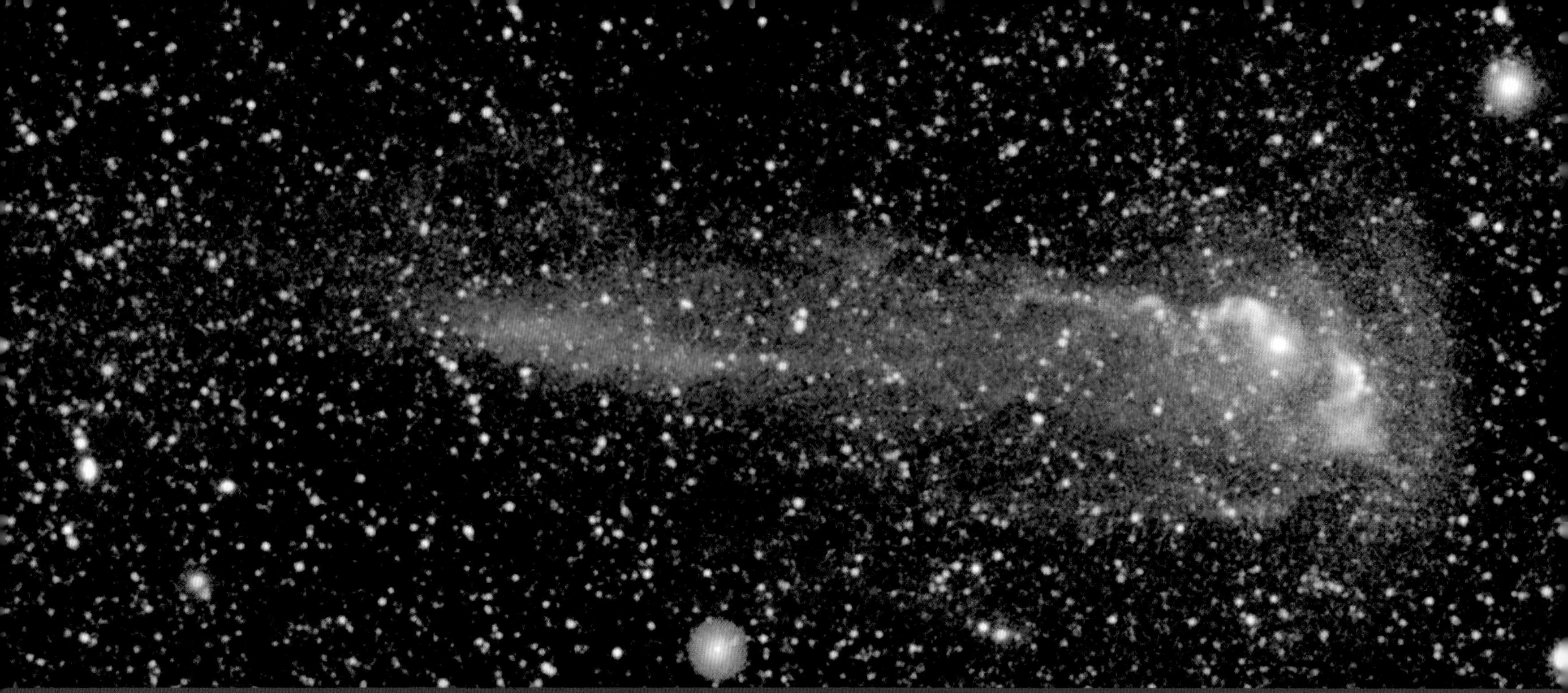

**FIGURE 46: SURPRISING MIRA**

Mira is a well-known variable star that has been studied thoroughly for about 400 years, so how is it that until recently nobody realised that it had a vast comet-like tail? The answer is that the tail appears only in the glow of ultraviolet light (left) and until NASA's Galaxy Evolution Explorer caught it unexpectedly, nobody even thought to look for it! In visible light (right) the star is bright, but there is no hint of the tail. The tail is composed of the outflow of material from Mira as it rapidly ploughs through interstellar space. The shock of this passage stimulates the trailing hydrogen molecules to glow.

# History

The German physicist Johann Ritter first discovered the existence of ultraviolet light in 1801, only one year after William Herschel had discovered infrared light. Inspired by Herschel's explorations of what lay beyond the red, Ritter wanted to know if an invisible form of light extended beyond the blue as well.

Ritter's "detector" was chemical silver chloride (commonly used in black and white photographic paper), which turns black when exposed to light. Passing sunlight through a glass prism, he placed samples of silver chloride along the different colours of the spectrum. While it showed little reaction in red light, it became ever darker towards the bluer colours. Most significantly, the strongest reaction lay beyond the visible blue-violet end of the spectrum. There was indeed another kind of light hiding beyond violet!

Ritter's discovery of these so-called "chemical" rays established the idea that the visible spectrum is embedded within a wider spectrum of light, the rest of which is invisible to our eyes. We have subsequently learnt that not all creatures are as insensitive to ultraviolet light as humans are. A number of birds, bees and other insects are known to see into the ultraviolet — an ability tapped into by some flowering plants that have ultraviolet guide-marks for pollinating insects that are invisible to us.

# Sources of Ultraviolet

### Blackbody

Most of the ultraviolet light we see in the Universe comes from the hotter stars. Ultraviolet light comes from the short wavelength/high energy side of **thermal blackbody radiation** and is emitted at high temperatures. Stars with temperatures greater than 7500 °C are actually brightest in the ultraviolet. The most massive stars in the Universe can be hotter than 40 000 °C and their blackbody radiation peaks in the extreme ultraviolet. The first stars to form in the Universe may have been ultra-massive and may have reached temperatures above 100 000 °C while, even now, the exposed cores of stars that have blown off gas to form planetary nebulae can be even hotter. Nonetheless, even a star as cool as the Sun, at a mere 5500 °C, will still generate a significant amount of ultraviolet light.

### Spectral Lines

In addition to thermal blackbody radiation, there are a number of **spectral lines** that are found throughout the ultraviolet part of the spectrum. Many common elements including the most abundant — hydrogen and helium — have important transitions in this part of the spectrum and these are frequently used by astronomers to study gas that can both absorb and emit these characteristic ultraviolet photons. Even the most common molecule in the Universe, molecular hydrogen, consisting of two hydrogen atoms bound to one another, has its primary emission in the ultraviolet.

*" While near-ultraviolet light can be observed from the ground, the advantages of space grow rapidly at mid-ultraviolet and beyond "*

**FIGURE 47: THE ULTRAVIOLET MESSIER 81**

The magnificent Messier 81 spiral galaxy appears in the glow of ultraviolet light in this two-colour composite. The orbiting observatory spies the galaxy's "sizzling young starlets" as wisps of bluish-white swirling around a central golden glow. The tints of gold at M81's centre come from a "senior citizen" population of smouldering stars. Far-ultraviolet light is rendered as blue, and near-ultraviolet as yellow.

## Ultraviolet Telescopes

As with the infrared, ultraviolet telescopes can employ many of the same optical technologies used in visible-light telescopes, particularly in the near-ultraviolet band. Mirrors designed to reflect and focus ultraviolet light, however, need to be machined to greater precision due to the shorter wavelengths. Contamination of mirrors and lenses by stray organic deposits are particularly damaging in the ultraviolet and optics and instruments have to be kept scrupulously clean at all times.

While near-ultraviolet light can be observed from the ground, the advantages of space grow rapidly at mid-ultraviolet and beyond. The Hubble Space Telescope, as well as working in the visible, has ultraviolet instruments — both cameras and spectrometers — that are sensitive down to far-ultraviolet wavelengths.

Detectors optimised for visible light do lose efficiency at shorter ultraviolet wavelengths, so the most sensitive ultraviolet telescopes have technologies designed especially for this part of the light spectrum. For instance, the Galaxy Evolution Explorer, or GALEX, uses an innovative detector that tabulates the position and arrival time of each incoming ultraviolet photon. Computer programs can use this tabular data to build up images later, rather than generating a complete image by directly reading out from the detector array, as is common with other telescopes.

While GALEX has been designed for sensitivity to see the distant and faint ultraviolet sources in the Universe, other telescopes like the Solar and Heliospheric Observatory (SOHO) trade sensitivity for rugged design — this is necessary when studying the brightest ultraviolet source in our sky: the Sun.

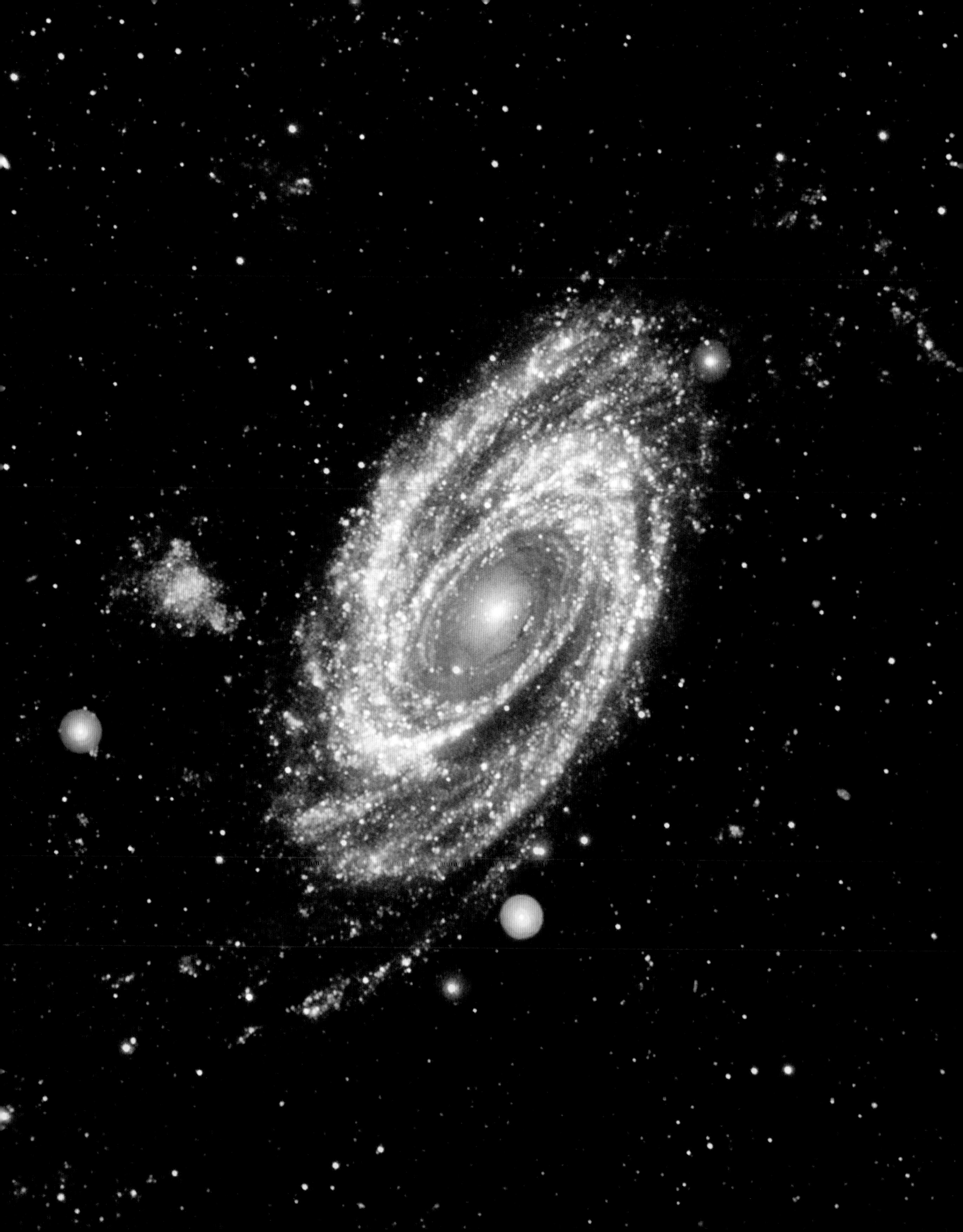

**FIGURE 48: AURORAE ON JUPITER AND SATURN**

The Hubble Space Telescope has captured Jupiter's northern and southern aurorae (left) as well as the dynamic nature of Saturn's southern aurorae (right). Images taken in ultraviolet light show the aurorae, seen as bright ovals overlaid on top of visible-light photos. If seen only in ultraviolet, Jupiter and Saturn are mostly dark and dominated by the glow of the aurorae. The images of Saturn were taken over four days from 24 January 2004.

# Ultraviolet Science

### Sun and Planets

The Sun is a rich laboratory for ultraviolet study since this **band** of the spectrum highlights the hottest gases in the solar chromosphere and corona. The temperature of the Sun actually increases above its visible surface through the extended corona. Hot charged gas clings to the otherwise invisible magnetic fields, tracing its activity.

Looking at ultraviolet spectral line emission from trace amounts of iron in the outer solar atmosphere, the corona, it is possible to observe how the Sun's violently active magnetic fields can actually heat this region. Temperatures here can range from tens of thousands to millions of degrees centigrade, far in excess of its surface temperature of 5500 °C.

*“ Ultraviolet light also allows us to probe the magnetic fields of other planets in the Solar System ”*

Ultraviolet light also allows us to probe the magnetic fields of other planets in the Solar System. Charged particles ejected from the solar corona can become trapped in these fields. Spiralling down towards the poles, they can produce glowing discharges in the atmosphere, or aurorae. These aurorae can be especially bright in the ultraviolet, making them easy to pick out in the upper atmospheres of Jupiter and Saturn where the solar ultraviolet illumination is, by contrast, quite faint.

**FIGURE 49: THE SOLAR CYCLE**

The image on the left shows a composite ultraviolet view of the Sun where three different ultraviolet wavelengths of light (17 nm, 19 nm and 28 nm) have been rendered as red, yellow and blue. The montage on the right shows a sequence of ultraviolet images taken over the course of 11 years. During this time the Sun progressed through an entire cycle of its activity. The enhanced flare and sunspot activity at the solar maximum stand out particularly vividly in the ultraviolet, which traces the structure of the hottest gases in the outer layers of the Sun.

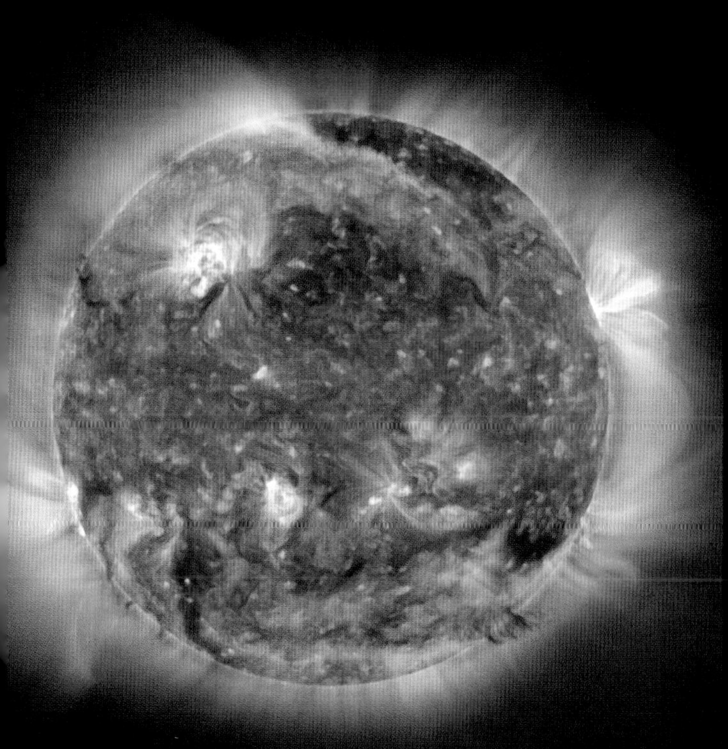

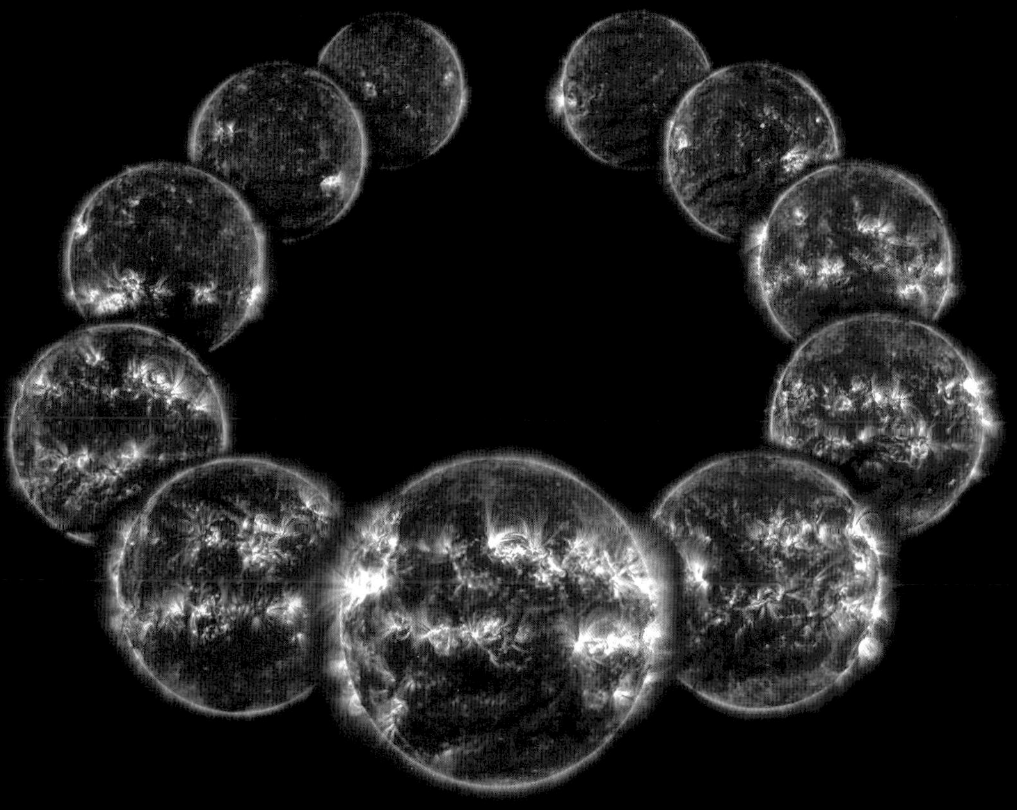

*“ A star 20 times as massive as the Sun is over 20 000 times as bright, and most of that light is emitted in the extreme-ultraviolet ”*

**FIGURE 50: TRACES OF AN ANCIENT EXPLOSION**

Looking deeply around the double star system Z Camelopardalis astronomers were surprised to find hints of a shell, seen only in ultraviolet light, in this observation from NASA's Galaxy Evolution Explorer. The shell appears to be the expanding remnant of a nova explosion from a few thousand years ago. Such an explosion would have burnt off the outer layers of a white dwarf star known to be orbiting a companion in the Z Camelopardalis system. The yellow-white traces are the only surviving evidence of this earlier explosion.

### Star Formation

Beyond the limits of the Solar System, the dominant source of ultraviolet is from hotter stars. Stars similar to the Sun can contribute significantly in the near-ultraviolet band, but in the far-ultraviolet the most massive stars dominate our view.

These huge stars are relatively few in number, but they make up for their lack of numbers by their brightness. A star 20 times as massive as the Sun is over 20 000 times as bright, and most of that light is emitted in the extreme-ultraviolet. The most massive stars do not live long — just a few million years — the blink of an eye in comparison to the 10 billion-year life expectancy of the Sun. So massive stars do not wander far from their birthplaces and their ultraviolet light identifies current regions of active star formation. In some galaxies this has led to the discovery of extended spiral structures far beyond the visible-light disc (see for instance Figure 47).

## Sculpting the Pillars

Massive stars have a strong influence on the star-forming regions that produced them. As soon as a massive star ignites the nuclear fusion in its core, the high temperature stimulates a torrent of ultraviolet radiation. The energy in far- and extreme-ultraviolet photons is so great that it can actually break down the surrounding dust molecules and evaporate the dust in the regions that gave birth to these stars in the first place.

Wherever these young, brilliant stars are found, there are usually massive dust clouds in the process of being destroyed by the intense light from the infant stars. The denser regions of the cloud erode more slowly under the onslaught, leaving behind impressive pillars of dust and gas. Since these regions are the densest clouds in the area, they will often harbour more baby stars in the process of formation.

Whenever massive pillars of dust are seen in visible or infrared light, they point the way to a precursor generation of newly formed stars that are still nearby.

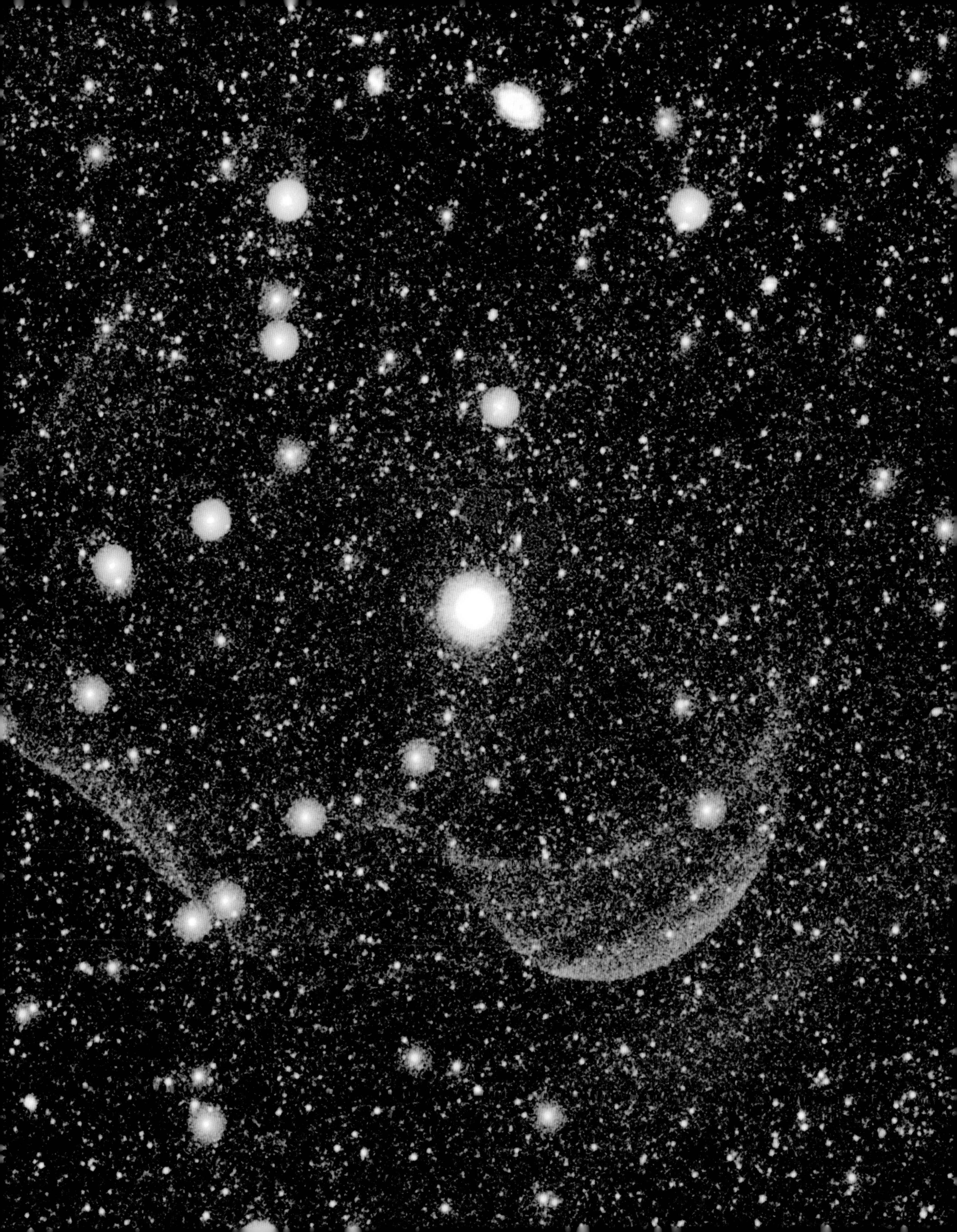

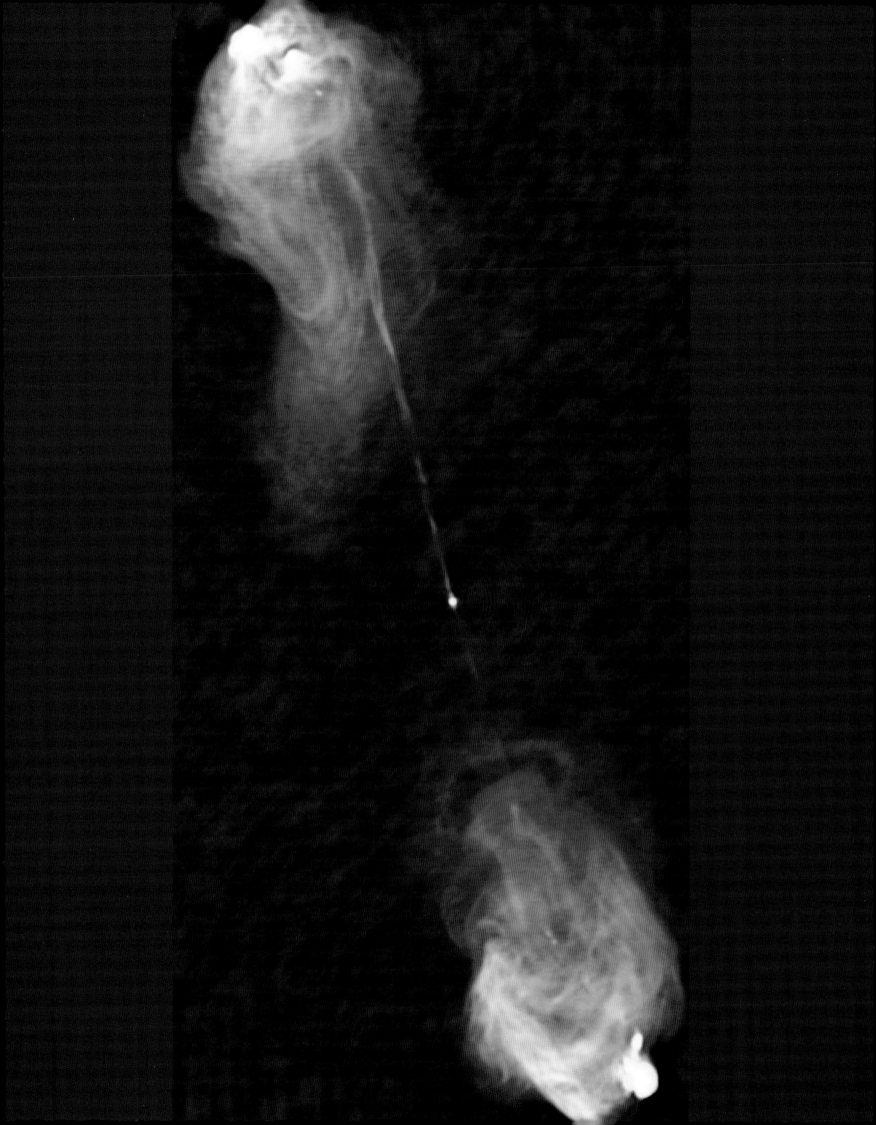

# THE RADIO AND MICROWAVE UNIVERSE

**FIGURE 51: RADIO IMAGE OF CYGNUS A**

Cygnus A was one of the first sources of cosmic radio radiation to be identified with a visible-light object in the sky. Seen in visible light it is a nondescript elliptical galaxy, a faint smudge like multitudes of others that provides no hint that it is by far the most powerful radio source in our reasonably local neighbourhood (if you can call a distance of 800 million light-years local). This radio image was made with the Very Large Array (see Chapter 2) in New Mexico and it shows the double-lobed structure that is so characteristic of the powerful radio sources associated with some galaxies and quasars. The energy that supplies the radiation from these lobes is channelled from the nucleus of the associated galaxy along narrow jets that are clearly seen in this image. The source of all this energy is the collapse of material onto a rapidly spinning supermassive black hole in the core of the galaxy. With a mass of around a billion times the mass of the Sun (or 300 times more massive than the black hole at the centre of our own Milky Way galaxy), this Active Galactic Nucleus (AGN, see Box: Black holes, quasars and Active Galactic Nuclei below) will appear as a quasar when seen from some directions.

Seen with radio telescopes, the sky is unrecognisable to a visible-light astronomer. In place of the stars in the Milky Way there are objects sprinkled throughout the entire Universe. Radio sources are rare but often intrinsically very powerful, making them detectable at very large distances. The emissions from these radio galaxies, quasars and titanic stellar explosions are the result of immensely energetic sub-atomic particles speeding through regions of twisted magnetic fields. This process is quite different from that producing the heat radiation from the surfaces of stars and it leads us to the sites of some of the most violently energetic action in the Universe.

> *"The first radio observations led to the realisation that the Universe could look very different to us when seen through new 'eyes' tuned to a different radiation"*

Beyond the far limits of infrared light, we move into the radio **spectrum**. At the shortest **wavelengths** (on the order of a millimetre or so) we have the band dubbed microwaves, which are commonly used in wireless phones. At longer wavelengths the radio spectrum spans centimetres, metres and upwards. The radio spectrum is open and unbounded in the sense that there is no "longest" radio wavelength. However, in practical terms, low energies and extreme wavelengths beyond a kilometre or so become very difficult to generate or detect.

Initially astronomers were not very optimistic about the possibility of even seeing the objects they already knew at radio wavelengths. They could calculate the amount of radio radiation expected from stars — and it was puny. Even so, starting in 1932 and subsequently stimulated by the development of radar for military use during the Second World War, radio astronomy was mankind's first major excursion into the hidden Universe. The first radio observations led to the realisation that the Universe could look very different to us when seen through new "eyes" tuned to a different radiation.

## Radio Regimes

Microwave
Radio
1 mm
1 cm
10 cm
1 m

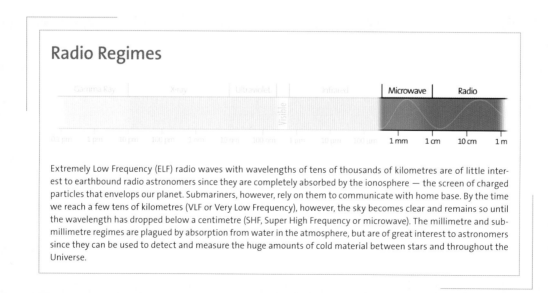

Extremely Low Frequency (ELF) radio waves with wavelengths of tens of thousands of kilometres are of little interest to earthbound radio astronomers since they are completely absorbed by the ionosphere — the screen of charged particles that envelops our planet. Submariners, however, rely on them to communicate with home base. By the time we reach a few tens of kilometres (VLF or Very Low Frequency), however, the sky becomes clear and remains so until the wavelength has dropped below a centimetre (SHF, Super High Frequency or microwave). The millimetre and submillimetre regimes are plagued by absorption from water in the atmosphere, but are of great interest to astronomers since they can be used to detect and measure the huge amounts of cold material between stars and throughout the Universe.

> *"The first interferometers enabled the identification of sources that were mysteriously inconspicuous to visible-light telescopes"*

Although the Sun, because it is so close, was soon identified as a discrete source of radio waves, it was found that the few other bright radio sources in the sky were seen in regions lacking very prominent stars.

The race was on to match these sources of radio radiation to objects that were already familiar to astronomers in visible light. The problem here was that early radio telescopes, despite their significant size, could not precisely locate the positions of the radio sources in the sky (see Box: Resolution of a telescope).

Since it would be hard — and costly — to build a single radio telescope that would be large enough to achieve the needed resolution, telescope builders had to do some lateral thinking and figure out how to connect widely spaced antennas in a way that would allow them to act as a single, larger telescope. The resulting technique of interferometry (see Box: Interferometry) is now widely used, especially at radio wavelengths, to enable high resolution imaging using arrays of many telescopes. By mounting some telescopes on satellites, telescopes in these arrays can even be separated by distances greater than the diameter of the Earth.

The first interferometers enabled the identification of sources that were mysteriously inconspicuous to visible-light telescopes — peculiar-looking galaxies and the apparent remnants of stellar explosions called supernovae. Why do these emit such copious amounts of radio radiation and so little visible light?

## Resolution of a Telescope

The ability of a telescope to distinguish fine details, known as its spatial resolving power, depends in a relatively simple way on both the telescope size and the wavelength of the radiation it is imaging: the greater the number of wavelengths of light that fit across a telescope mirror or lens, the higher the resolution of the telescope. Since radio waves are typically 100 000 times longer than visible waves, a radio telescope would have to be about 240 km in diameter to achieve the same resolving power as Hubble, which has a mirror that is only 2.4 metres across.

# Interferometry

The largest single-dish radio telescope at Arecibo in Puerto Rico is an impressive 305 metres across, yet achieves nothing like the resolution achieved by even the smallest visible-light telescope. Moreover, the dish cannot be steered and is restricted to observing a narrow band of the sky. However, following the first successful experiments in 1946 in Australia, astronomers have used the technique of interferometry to build arrays of telescopes that combine the signals in a way that achieves the resolution (but not the collecting area) of an instrument the size of the largest antenna separation. Using interferometry astronomers can combine the light waves from two telescopes by aligning the wave crests and troughs precisely. The largest interferometric arrays combine signals from telescopes scattered across the globe, acting together as a single instrument nearly the size of the Earth, and able to ascertain the positions of sources with an extraordinary accuracy that is beyond even the largest visible-light telescopes. The earliest and most notable developments of this technique took place in Cambridge, England with Martin Ryle and Antony Hewish winning the Nobel Prize for Physics in 1974, the first time the Prize was given for astronomy.

## Synchrotron Radiation

The glow of the radio sky stems from processes that are very different from those seen at visible, infrared and ultraviolet wavelengths. **Thermal blackbody** processes (see Chapter 1) are not strong in this part of the spectrum. Most bright radio sources are the sites of violently energetic events, such as black holes, where electrically charged sub-atomic particles are accelerated to very nearly the speed of light. It is the motions of these fast-moving charged particles that most commonly generate radio light.

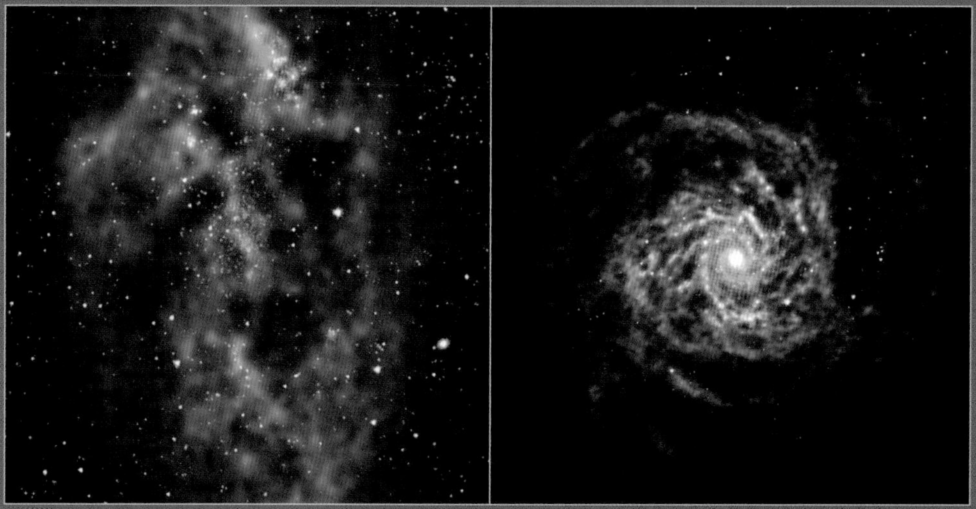

**FIGURE 52: THINGS IMAGES OF IC 2574 AND MESSIER 74**

In these images we see the dwarf galaxy IC 2574, left, and spiral galaxy Messier 74, right. The images were constructed from data taken with the Very Large Array (VLA, seen in blue), from Spitzer (seen in red) and from GALEX combined with Spitzer (seen in purple) as part of the THINGS survey. The VLA radio emission comes from atomic hydrogen gas. Because atomic hydrogen emits radio waves at a specific frequency, astronomers can measure the motions of the gas by noting the **Doppler shift** in frequency caused by those motions.

As the term **electromagnetic radiation** hints, the effects of electric and magnetic fields are tightly interrelated. When a charged particle like an electron or proton moves through a magnetic field it is deflected and sent on a spiralling course along the magnetic field lines. This oscillating charge will give up some of its energy to the emission of radiation, particularly at radio wavelengths.

Some of the earliest particle accelerator devices built by physicists were known as "synchrotrons". The radio waves emitted by the accelerated particles, and the associated energy loss as the particles spiralled through the devices' magnetic field, led to the name **synchrotron radiation**. Amazingly, the Universe is filled with many cosmic synchrotrons on all scales, and the well-studied process on Earth lets us understand similar processes occurring across the Universe.

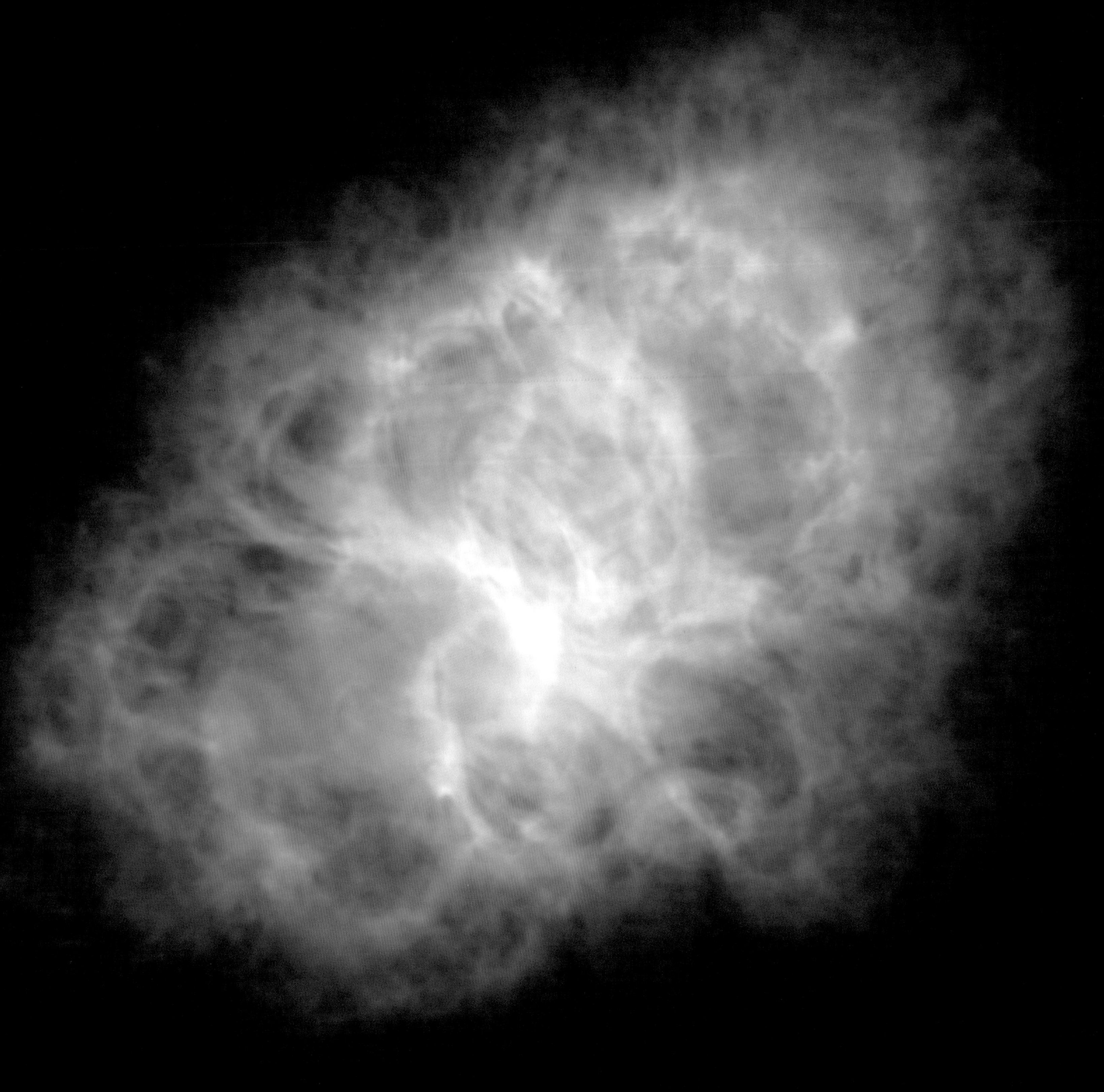

**FIGURE 53: THE CRAB NEBULA IN RADIO**

The famous Crab nebula (object number one in Messier's catalogue) is the remnant of a star that was seen to explode in the year 1054 by Chinese observers — an event that we now call a supernova. The extended structure that we see now, almost a thousand years later, is surprisingly similar when imaged with radio, infrared, visible-light and X-ray telescopes. This is because the radiation we see in all of these different wavelengths comes from the same mechanism: very high speed electrons (and probably also antimatter electrons, called positrons) spiralling around a tangled magnetic field. This kind of radiation is called **synchrotron** radiation. The most energetic electrons and positrons radiate X-rays while the less energetic ones can radiate radio waves. Those with energies in between radiate in the visible and infrared. The origin of these energetic particles is thought to be a spinning neutron star or pulsar left behind after the star exploded.

At the most energetic sites in the Universe, synchrotron radiation may be emitted across the entire electromagnetic spectrum and can also be seen with telescopes in the infra-red, visible, ultraviolet and X-ray range. The synchrotron mechanism in and around black holes generally accounts for the most powerful radio sources in the sky, such as Cygnus A (see Figure 51). These are not, however, the only targets for radio telescopes to examine.

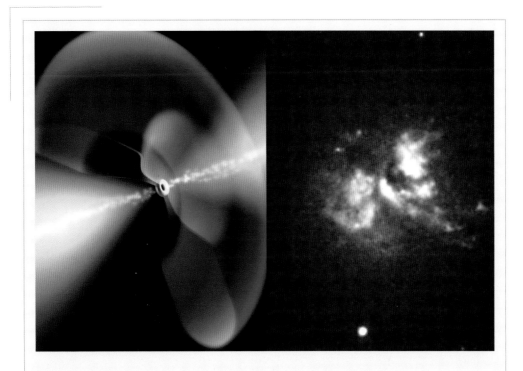

## Black Holes, Qquasars and Active Galactic Nuclei

An Active Galactic Nucleus, or AGN, consists of a spinning supermassive black hole at a galaxy's core that is being fed by gas or disrupted stars coming from the surrounding galaxy. As the material falls inwards it will usually form itself into a spinning disc orbiting the black hole. A small portion of the infalling material never reaches the black hole but is spun up by surrounding magnetic fields and ejected at nearly the speed of light as oppositely directed jets perpendicular to the disc, often radiating copious amounts of radio radiation. If one of the jets points roughly towards us, we will get a relatively clear view of the regions very close to the black hole where much of the light is emitted and we see a quasar. On the other hand, if we see the disc edge-on, our view of the AGN may be obscured by the material in the disc. It is only in the last couple of decades that astronomers have begun to appreciate how the many differing types of AGN can be understood simply in terms of how their appearance varies depending on which direction we view them from.

# Bremsstrahlung

Another radio-generating process involves direct interactions between fast-moving charged particles. The regions of glowing gas excited by hot stars, namely star-forming regions and planetary nebulae, are suffused with energetic electrons and protons that buzz around at high speed. Sometimes they come close enough to one another to be deflected by the interaction of their electrical charges. The process of deflection causes the emission of radiation that is often seen most clearly at radio and X-ray wavelengths (though it can be seen in other parts of the spectrum as well). Observations of such radiation from star-forming regions enable astronomers to learn about properties such as the temperature of the gas. This radiation from interacting particles is known as **bremsstrahlung** or "braking radiation". It is closely related to the process used to make X-rays for medical diagnoses, where high speed electrons are stopped by a metal target, the sudden deceleration (braking), causing the emission of X-rays.

# Radio Gas

One of the most important realisations, and subsequent discoveries, in radio astronomy was that hydrogen, by far the most common gas in the Universe, could emit and absorb radio radiation with a wavelength of 21 cm (see Box: 21-cm radiation). Measuring this radiation with radio telescopes opened up rich opportunities for studying the motions of the gas both within and beyond the Milky Way by exploiting the **Doppler effect**. Astronomical "speed cameras" can measure the gas even in regions that are completely obscured from view in the visible spectrum. One of the principal applications of this study has been in the measurement of the masses of spiral galaxies. This fundamental property can be derived from the rotational speed of gas orbiting the galaxy at a given radius.

## 21-cm Radiation

Hydrogen is the simplest of all atoms and is by far the most abundant element in the Universe. The atom consists of just a single proton and a single electron, each of which has what physicists call a spin. When the atom is isolated and undisturbed — as can be the case in interstellar space — it will have a proton and an electron whose spin axes point in opposite directions (anti-parallel). Even a mild disturbance to an atom can cause the electron spin to flip to a parallel state, a tiny change in energy. The transition back to the first, or antiparallel, state would happen after some ten million years for a completely isolated atom and result in the emission of a single photon of 21-cm wavelength radio radiation. In practice, interactions with other particles can dramatically reduce this long wait, and of course there are a lot of hydrogen atoms in the Universe. So this characteristic radiation is easily seen with radio telescopes. Stimulated by Jan Oort in the Netherlands, Hendrik van de Hulst in 1944 predicted that hydrogen gas could emit this radiation and, in 1951, Ewen and Purcell at Harvard University in the USA first observed the 21-cm spectral line from space. It has since become a fundamental tool for radio astronomy.

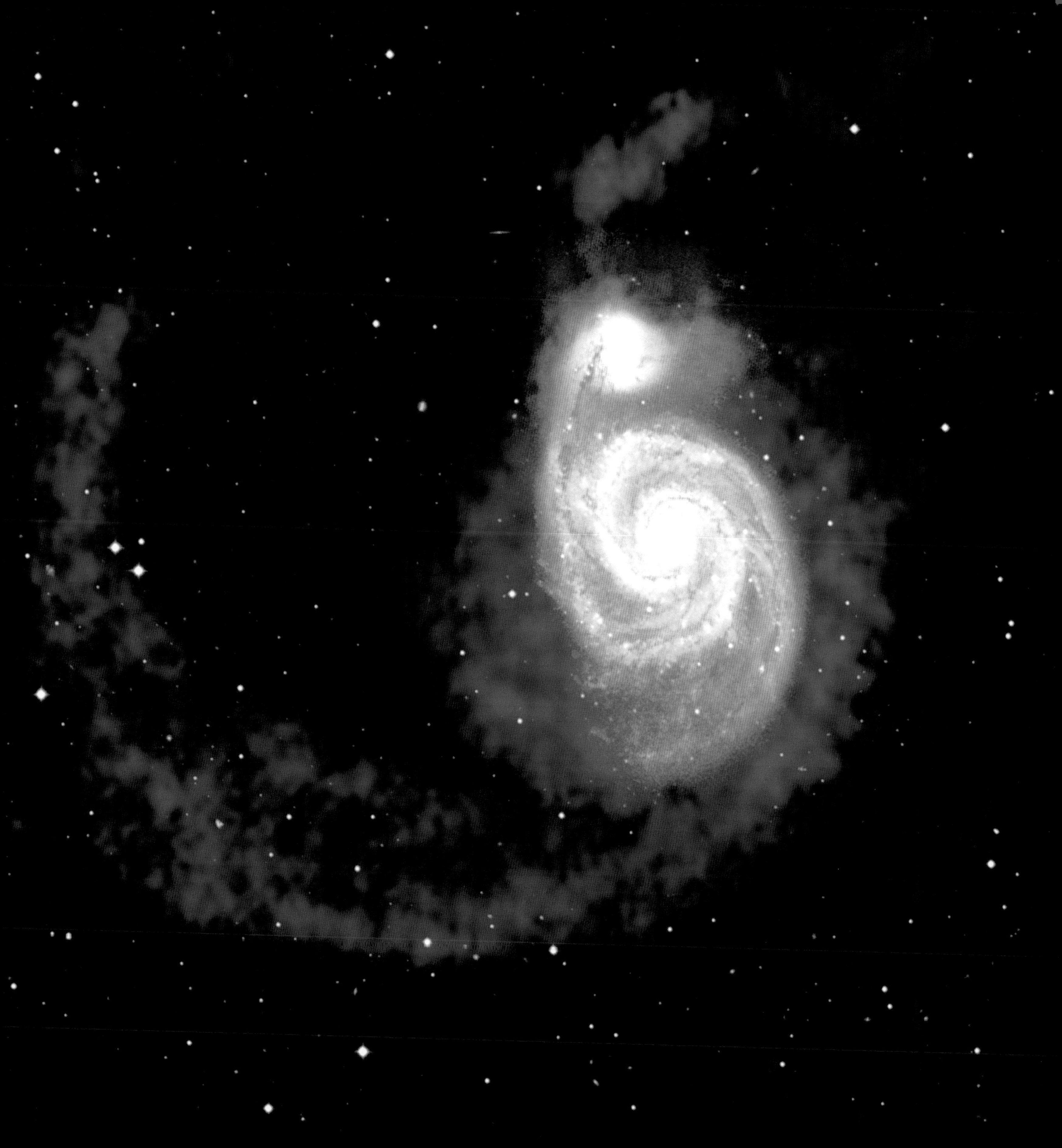

**FIGURE 54: THE WHIRLPOOL GALAXY IN RADIO**

This image of the spiral galaxy M51, also known as the Whirlpool Galaxy, and its companion NGC 5195 (top) combines observations of neutral hydrogen emission (in blue) obtained with the Very Large Array with visible-light images from the Digitized Sky Survey. The visible-light data show the emission of stars in these galaxies as well as the dust; the latter can be seen as dust lanes in the spiral arms of M51 itself and in obscuring the eastern (left hand) part of the companion. They also show foreground stars in our own Milky Way galaxy as well as some background galaxies. The long tidal tail of neutral hydrogen (left) was shaken loose by the gravitational interaction of these two galaxies.

*dust and a brew of molecules that broadcast their identification signatures at very specific radio wavelengths"*

## Cool Stuff

Although radio astronomy was built on the study of synchrotron radiation from energetic particles, there is increasing interest in the emission of radio waves from large but very cool regions in the Universe. Sometimes called molecular clouds, these clumps of gas are cool enough to contain dust (see Chapter 5) and a brew of molecules that broadcast their identification signatures at very specific radio wavelengths as they ready themselves to give birth to new generations of stars.

Much of the heat radiation from these cool regions falls in parts of the radio spectrum — wavelengths of a few tenths of a millimetre — that are difficult or impossible to see from the ground because of absorption by the atmosphere (see Box: Heat from cold objects). ESA's Herschel spacecraft (see Chapter 3) is designed to make observations of these wavelengths possible.

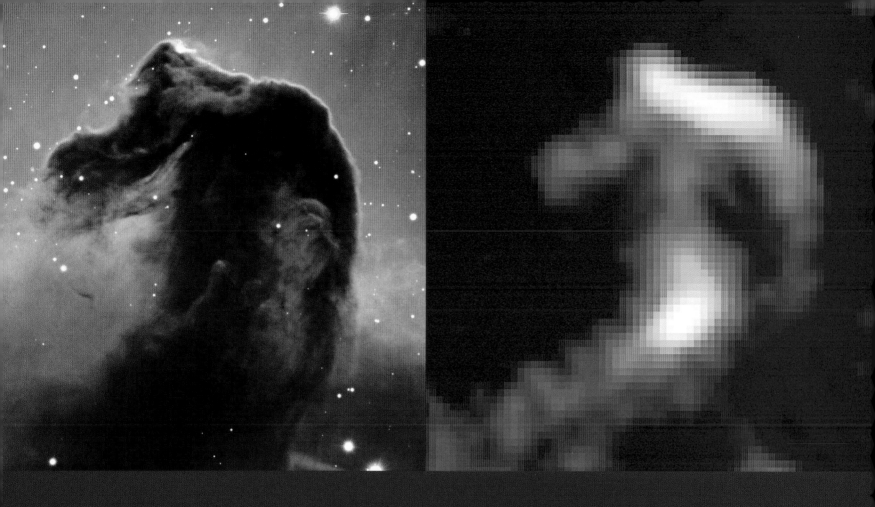

## Heat from Cold Objects

Detecting heat radiation from cool objects does sound a bit strange. But it is a perfectly legitimate occupation for an astronomer. Blackbodies emit radiation with an intensity and a spectrum that is determined uniquely by the temperature and the area of the emitting surface (see Chapter 1). A gas cloud that is really cool, say -240 °C, will radiate a blackbody spectrum peaking at a wavelength of about one tenth of a millimetre. The empty sky around the cloud will appear cooler than this and so our far-infrared telescope will see a bright patch against a darker background. In the distant Universe, at a redshift above 3 or so, the emission will become accessible to sub-millimetre telescopes like ALMA (see Chapter 2).

**FIGURE 56: THE HORSEHEAD NEBULA IN VISIBLE LIGHT AND SUB-MILLIMETRE RADIATION**

An image of the famous Horsehead Nebula in Orion made with the single-dish sub-millimetre telescope APEX at a wavelength close to 1 millimetre (870 micrometres). At this wavelength, the cool dust glows rather than absorbs. The new and much larger ALMA telescope (see Chapter 2) will allow objects like this to be seen in as much detail as we can now see in the more familiar visible wavelength pictures.

Usually in astronomy it is easier to detect and study objects in our neighbourhood rather than strain to see faint ones in the furthest reaches of the Universe. When trying to do this kind of astronomy from the ground, however, the **redshift** of very distant objects can help us by moving the cool heat radiation into a part of the radio spectrum where, at least from very dry observatory sites, the atmosphere is transparent. This convenient shift allows for the use of much larger microwave telescope collecting areas than can currently be launched into space and it is one of the primary justifications for building the Atacama Large Millimeter Array (ALMA, see Chapter 2).

> **"** *The biggest of all bodies is the Universe itself, and, stunningly, we can see the faint remnant of the glowing fireball of the Big Bang all around us* **"**

## Cosmic Microwave Background

Objects simply glowing as blackbodies, like stars, are rarely prominent targets for radio telescopes. The emitted energy falls off dramatically from the infrared into microwaves and radio. If the source has a tremendous surface area, the total cumulative output of radio waves can be substantial. The biggest of all bodies is the Universe itself, and, stunningly, we can see the faint remnant of the glowing fireball of the Big Bang all around us. This afterglow was discovered in 1965 and is known as the cosmic microwave background radiation.

This radiation was emitted from a "surface" at about 3000 °C when the Universe was 375 000 years old and the fireball was becoming transparent. The radiation from this epoch now pervades all of space and, due to the expansion of the Universe over the last 13.7 billion years or so, has now cooled to a temperature of -270 °C (2.7 K). At this temperature the emission peaks at a wavelength of around 2 mm in the microwave part of the radio spectrum.

How do we see this radiation now and what does it tell us about the Universe? Observations at this wavelength are difficult from the ground but can be, and have been, done. High-flying balloons and spacecraft are better platforms and have been used to produce some of the most profound and remarkably precise measurements in the history of science.

When this ancient signal was discovered by Arno Penzias and Robert Wilson (who received the 1978 Nobel Prize in Physics for their discovery), they recognised — after eliminating all other possible sources of radiation, including a goodly amount of pigeon droppings in the receiver — that the excess signal they were seeing in their microwave telescope was the echo of the Big Bang: the cosmic microwave background.

**FIGURE 57: THE COSMIC MICROWAVE BACKGROUND**

The most distant "object" we can see when we point our telescopes towards the sky is the fireball resulting from the Big Bang: the event at the origin of our Universe. About 375 000 years after the Big Bang itself, the fireball had cooled from unimaginably high temperatures to around 3000 °C (roughly half of the temperature of the surface of the Sun). The surface of the fireball was radiating like a blackbody (see Chapter 1) as the continuing expansion made it transparent. This all-pervading radiation has remained one of the constituents of the Universe as it has continued to expand up until the present time, some 13.7 billion years later. So what does the fireball look like? As a result of the expansion, the radiation has cooled by more than a factor of a thousand from the 3000 K when it was emitted, to 2.7 K (-270 °C) today. This is seen as microwave radio radiation coming very uniformly from the entire sky. This all-sky map from NASA's Wilkinson Microwave Anisotropy Probe spacecraft shows the measurements of the temperature of the cosmic microwave background resulting from five years of measurements. The colour codes show the very small — about one part in 100 000 — temperature variations whose precise measurement reveals an astonishingly accurate picture of the geometry, age and content of the Universe. An earlier NASA satellite experiment called COBE, designed to characterise the cosmic microwave background, resulted in the 2007 Noble Prize for Physics being awarded to John Mather and George Smoot.

The radiation is seen with microwave instruments as an extremely uniform "surface" over the entire sky. The deviations from the uniformity of the radiation temperature over the sky amount to only about one part in 100 000, but the information in these tiny temperature variations contains the "crown jewels" of modern cosmology. The data provide a wealth of fundamental information about the size, age, content and ultimate fate of the Universe.

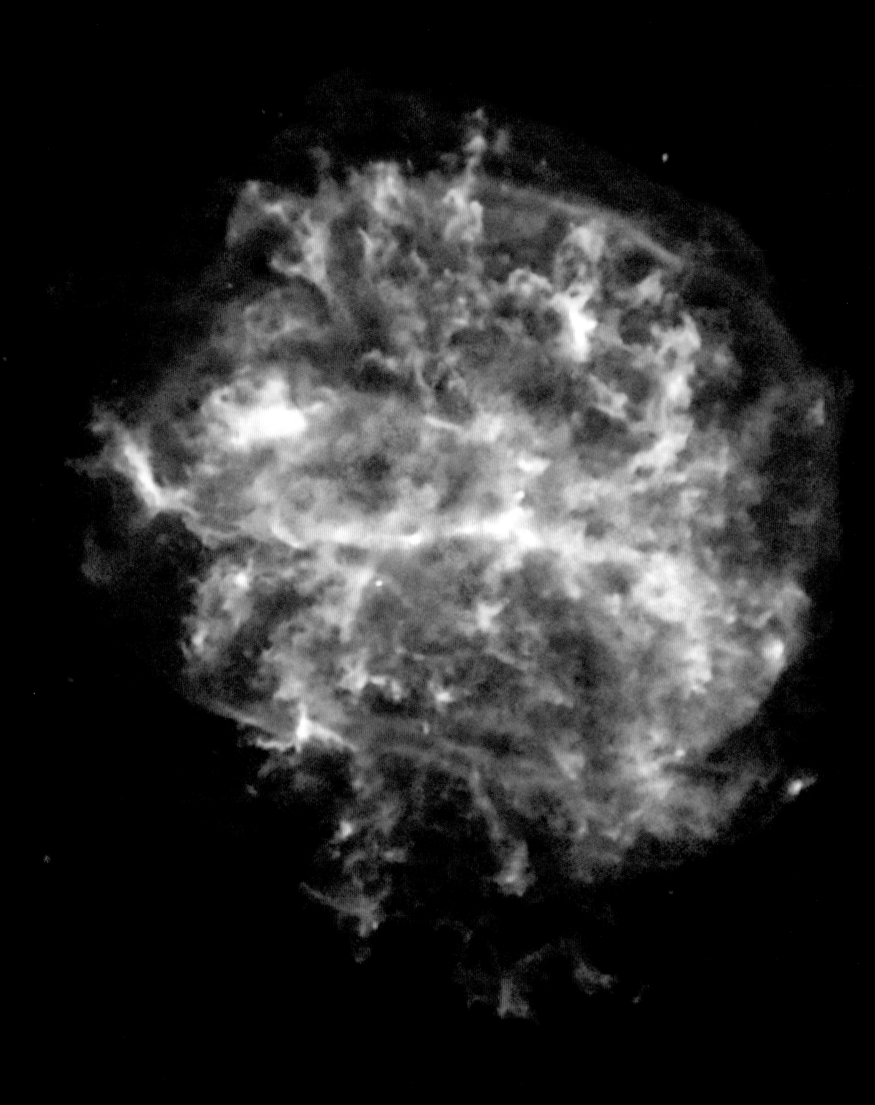

# THE X-RAY AND HIGH ENERGY UNIVERSE

**FIGURE 58: SUPERNOVA REMNANT G292.0+1.8 IN X-RAYS**

This beautiful Chandra X-ray Observatory image shows the supernova remnant G292.0+1.8. This is the aftermath of the death of a massive star. Ejected material from the supernova races outwards and slams into the surrounding gas creating intense shock waves that heat the material and make it emit X-rays. By mapping the distribution of X-rays in different energy bands, the Chandra image traces the state of the material ejected by the supernova. The results imply that the explosion was not symmetrical. For example, blue (silicon and sulphur) and green (magnesium) are seen strongly in the upper right, while yellow and orange (oxygen) dominate the lower left. These elements light up at different temperatures, indicating that the temperature is higher in the upper right portion of G292.0+1.8.

Beyond the ultraviolet we reach the highest energies of the electromagnetic spectrum. From X-rays to the even more energetic gamma rays, the increasingly rare photons have to be counted one by one. Only the most dramatic phenomena will generate light at this far end of the spectrum. This means that X-rays and gamma rays are our window into the study of cataclysmic processes such as the explosions of massive stars and the neutron stars and black holes they leave behind, as well as hot plasmas in galaxy clusters and in nearby stars.

X-ray and gamma-ray **photons** have **wavelengths** so tiny that they must be measured in billionths (**nanometres**) and trillionths (**picometres**) of metres. There is no "smallest" wavelength at the gamma-ray end of the **spectrum** beyond the practical limits of just how much energy can be crammed into a single photon by the processes that generate them. Astronomers detect these photons on a case-by-case basis, making it challenging to build up images in the X-ray band, and even more impractical in the gamma-ray band. In fact, very few gamma-ray "images" have been constructed to date, so the focus in this chapter will largely be on X-rays.

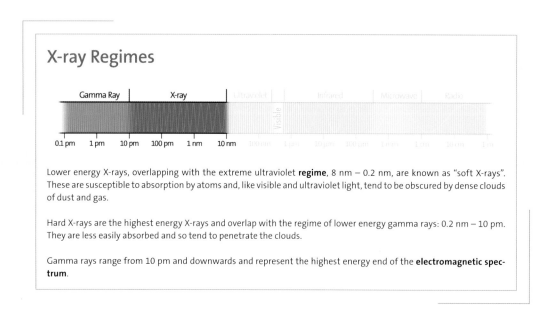

## X-ray Regimes

Gamma Ray
X-ray
Ultraviolet
Visible
Infrared
Microwave
Radio
0.1 pm
1 pm
10 pm
100 pm
1 nm
10 nm

Lower energy X-rays, overlapping with the extreme ultraviolet **regime**, 8 nm – 0.2 nm, are known as "soft X-rays". These are susceptible to absorption by atoms and, like visible and ultraviolet light, tend to be obscured by dense clouds of dust and gas.

Hard X-rays are the highest energy X-rays and overlap with the regime of lower energy gamma rays: 0.2 nm – 10 pm. They are less easily absorbed and so tend to penetrate the clouds.

Gamma rays range from 10 pm and downwards and represent the highest energy end of the **electromagnetic spectrum**.

# Sources of X-rays

### Thermal X-rays

X-ray photons have energies that are thousands of times larger than the visible-light photons detected by our eyes. If these photons were purely the result of **thermal**, or **blackbody**, processes, there would have to be many objects with temperatures between about a million and a hundred million °C (see Figure 59). The discovery of some sources at these temperatures came as a surprise since even the most massive stars are not nearly this hot.

But while the stars themselves may not reach temperatures of millions of degrees, the explosion of massive stars can. As the hot debris blasted out by the explosion slams into the surrounding interstellar medium, the resulting shock waves can heat it even more. It is a kind of cosmic sonic boom, but instead of hearing the boom, we see the photons generated from the shock. These supernova remnants can make spectacular targets for X-ray telescopes.

However, it does not take a supernova to heat up at least some of the gas around a star. Even our Sun has an outer "atmosphere", or corona, that can reach millions of degrees. Falling outside of what we think of as its visible surface, this sparse gas is heated by processes that puzzled the astronomers who discovered its X-ray emission. Violent phenomena on the surface — often around the darker, slightly cooler sunspots on the Sun's surface — create sound and magnetic waves that propagate upwards into the increasingly tenuous outer atmosphere, the chromosphere and the corona. As the density decreases, the waves become more and more extreme, rather like water waves breaking on a shelving beach. Eventually they become shock waves that superheat the gas.

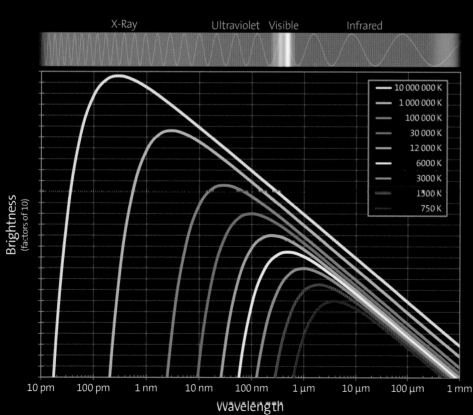

| | |
|---|---|
| —— | 10 000 000 K |
| —— | 1 000 000 K |
| —— | 100 000 K |
| —— | 30 000 K |
| —— | 12 000 K |
| —— | 6000 K |
| —— | 3000 K |
| ·········· | 1300 K |
| ········· | 750 K |

**FIGURE 59: HOT BLACKBODIES**

Here blackbody radiation from 1 million degree warm objects is compared with the blackbody radiation from different stars.

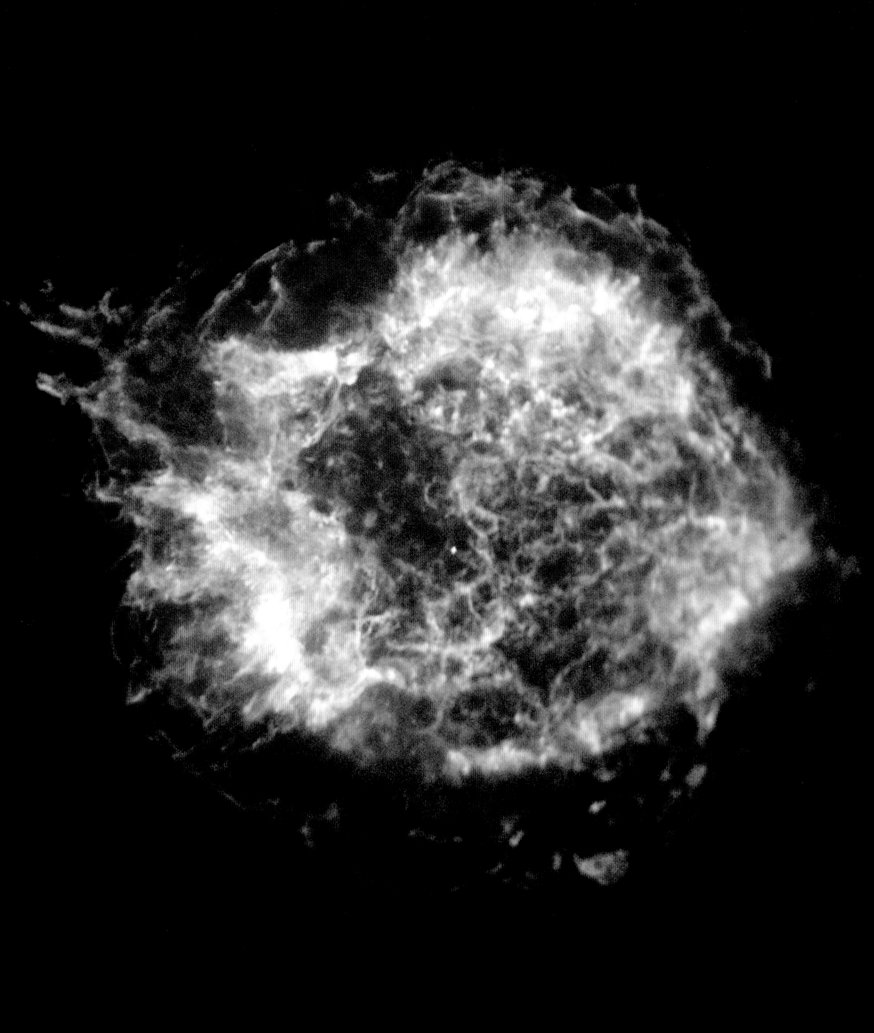

*" Although a few experiments have been done from high-flying balloons, X-ray astronomy can only really be done from space "*

### Spectral Line X-rays

We have seen that in other parts of the spectrum, changes in the electron energy state in atoms can generate **spectral line** emissions at specific wavelengths. For light elements like hydrogen and helium, such lines tend to appear in ultraviolet, visible and infrared light. However, more massive elements with larger clouds of electrons can have "inner electron" transitions of such high energies that they create X-ray spectral lines.

The temperatures required to generate X-ray spectral lines are quite high, since you never get energy out without putting it in. However, the exploding material from supernovae can easily stimulate these lines. This provides a powerful tool that astronomers can use to study the composition of material thrown out in such blasts.

### Non-thermal Processes

However, X-rays also come from sources that are not necessarily hot enough to generate them as thermal blackbody radiation. Such process are dubbed **non-thermal**. For instance, in some regions charged particles like electrons and protons are boosted to nearly the speed of light (sometimes slung along whirling magnetic fields, like beads on a string). When such particles are forced to change direction as they pass along these magnetic fields, they emit **synchrotron** radiation (see chapter 7) and can be seen throughout the **electromagnetic spectrum**, including as X-rays.

## Observing X-rays

Although a few experiments have been done from high-flying balloons, X-ray astronomy can only really be done from space. X-rays are known to penetrate objects like human bodies in hospitals and hand-baggage at airports, but they are completely absorbed by the Earth's atmosphere. X-ray astronomy was born with the space age. Riccardo Giacconi and his collaborators detected X-rays of non-terrestrial origin during the first part of the 1960s by flying experiments in sounding rockets. The ability to construct and launch X-ray satellite observatories has since created a vibrant branch of astronomy that deals with high energy and high temperature phenomena in the Universe. In 2002, Giacconi was awarded the Nobel Prize for Physics for this work.

**FIGURE 60: CASSIOPEIA A IN X-RAYS**

This X-ray image, taken with the Chandra satellite (see Chapter 3) shows the youngest supernova remnant in the Milky Way galaxy. Called Cassiopeia A, it is at a distance of some 11 000 light-years and — were it not for the fact that it was shrouded in a dense cocoon of dust when the massive star exploded — would have easily been seen by observers just over three centuries ago. As well as being a bright source of X-rays, Cassiopeia A is the most brilliant radio source in the sky apart from the Sun. The material blasted from the star in the explosion (seen as red and green in this image) is heated to around ten million °C. The expansion shell (blue) is moving outwards at sixteen million km/hr and is at the even higher temperature of thirty million degrees. As this shell bumps into the surrounding interstellar gas, it creates a shock wave that heats the gas to these high values. These shock regions are thought to be one of the sites where cosmic ray particles are accelerated to speeds very close to light speed. A multi-wavelength view of Cassiopeia A is seen in Figure 1.

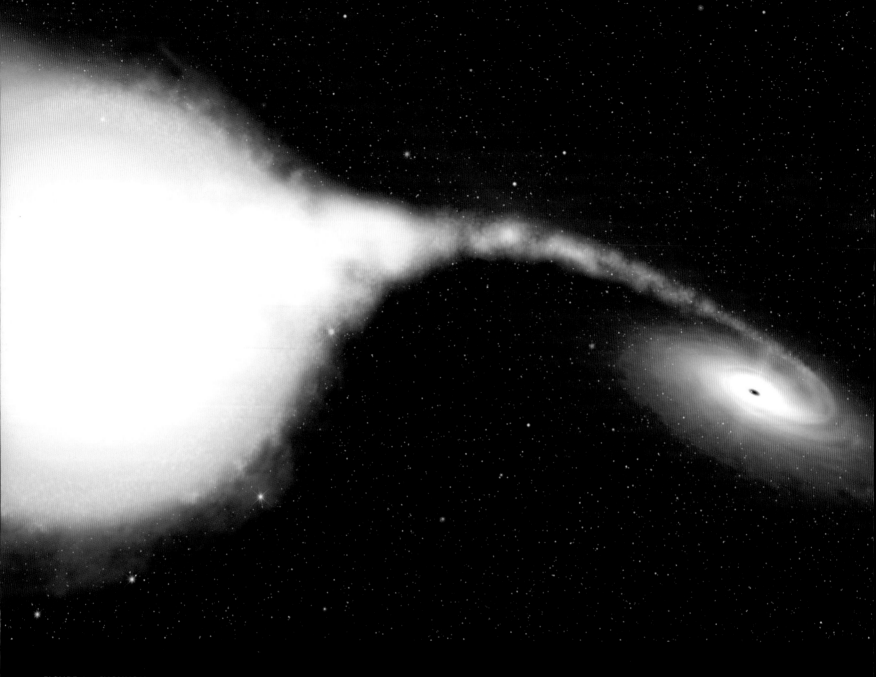

## FIGURE 61: CYGNUS X-1 (ARTIST'S IMPRESSION)

Cygnus X-1 is located about 10 000 light-years from Earth. It is one of the more violent places in our Galaxy. The black hole, Cygnus X-1, contains about five times the mass of the Sun, squeezed into a tiny sphere a few kilometres in diameter. Because of its density, it possesses an enormous gravitational field, which is pulling matter away from its companion star, HDE 226868. The companion is a massive star, known as a blue supergiant. It has an extremely hot surface temperature of 30 000 °C. As the gas spirals towards the black hole, it is heated even further and emits X-rays and gamma rays.

# X-ray Sources

### White Dwarfs, Neutron Stars and Black Holes

Compact sources of X-rays include white dwarf and neutron stars as well as black holes. Gas that streams into the intense gravitational attraction of these objects is heated by friction to millions of degrees during its fall. Certain types of binary stars that contain one of these ultra-compact objects and a much larger companion that can supply material to fall onto it are often bright X-ray sources. The radiation emitted by such a hot body is extremely intense so that X-rays can be seen from very small regions. Often cooler objects have to be very large to show up in telescopes as they radiate at longer and less energetic wavelengths. This ability to delve into the innermost zones of some of the most bizarre and energetic objects in the Universe is a powerful incentive to build ever larger and more sensitive X-ray telescopes.

## Active Galaxies

Strangely enough, an X-ray image of the Moon led astronomers to understand the nature of galaxies across the Universe better. A remarkable image taken in 1990 by the ROSAT satellite clearly shows the disc of the Moon, one side illuminated by reflected X-rays from the Sun, the other seen in darkened silhouette against what appears to be a background sky bright with X-rays. For many years it was unclear what exactly could be producing this cosmic X-ray background. Is it a uniform glow like the cosmic microwave background seen in the radio, or does it come from multitudes of faint individual sources? This background was detected by the first rocket experiments in the early 1960s and the mystery persisted for decades.

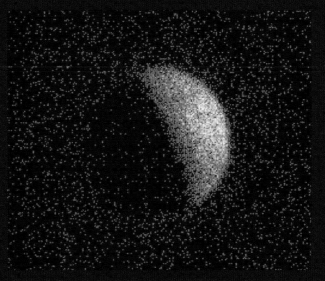

As the resolving power of X-ray telescopes improved it became apparent that, unlike the truly diffuse cosmic microwave background (see Chapter 7), the X-ray background appears to be largely composed of individual sources very uniformly distributed across the sky. If the radiation originated in our Milky Way, such uniformity would be difficult to understand and so it was assumed that the sources were at large (also called "cosmological") distances. It has now become clear that most of the radiation originates in active galaxies that emitted the X-rays when the Universe was middle-aged.

Some relatively nearby galaxies also emit large amounts of X-ray radiation. In many of them, this radiation seems to be associated with the energy release from material surrounding supermassive black holes that may reside at the centres of all galaxies. When this black hole is radiating, it is called an active galactic nucleus or AGN. Only a small fraction of nearby galaxies have active black holes at any one time. However, this fraction seems to have been larger in the cosmic middle ages, as seen in the XMM-Newton Deep Field image in Figure 63. This seems to have been a special time in the history of the Universe, late enough for the central black holes to have become big, yet early enough that the galaxies were still very gas-rich with fuel to power the activity. Today, the gas in galaxies is more settled and more rarely gets close enough to feed the black hole and create an AGN.

**FIGURE 62: THE X-RAY SHADOW OF THE MOON**

This remarkable X-ray image of the Moon was taken in 1990 by the ROSAT satellite and shows individual X-ray detections in the camera as dots. At first glance one sees the bright part of the Moon reflecting X-rays from the Sun, but if one looks closer the dark side of the Moon can be seen to shadow a background of X-ray emitting objects (the fainter signal "in front" of the dark part of the lunar disc is thought to arise in the very outer parts of the Earth's atmosphere). This is a stunning view of the so-called X-ray background radiation that has puzzled astronomers since the very earliest days of X-ray astronomy in the 1960s. It is now realised that almost all of the X-ray background is coming from a tapestry of active galaxies radiating in the Universe's "middle-age".

**FIGURE 63: THE SUBARU/XMM-NEWTON DEEP FIELD**

A current very deep view, with over one hundred hours of exposure and nearly three Moon-diameters across, of part of the X-ray sky seen by ESA's XMM-Newton satellite. This shows how the X-ray background breaks up into discrete sources that differ from one another in "colour". In this image, blue codes the sources that contain a high proportion of high energy (called "hard") X-rays while red represents those dominated by the lower energy ("soft") X-rays.

**FIGURE 64: HOT GAS IN THE GALAXY CLUSTER MS0735.6+7421**

An image of the galaxy cluster MS0735.6+742, about 2.6 billion light-years away in the constellation of Camelopardus. The visible-light view taken with Hubble in 2006 shows the cluster of galaxies (in white) together with some background galaxies and foreground stars. The Chandra Observatory image (blue) shows the distribution of fifty million degree gas that pervades the cluster except for the huge cavities — nearly seven times the diameter of the Milky Way — at the top and bottom of the picture, which are filled with very high speed charged particles and a magnetic field: a combination that efficiently emits radio waves. The radio image (red) is from the VLA in New Mexico (see Chapter 2). The process that powers the radio emission — jets from the central supermassive black hole — has pushed aside gas weighing some trillion times the mass of the Sun.

# Clusters of Galaxies

Galaxies are not solitary, but tend to come in clusters, sometimes containing hundreds, or even thousands, of members. Through cosmic history they grow by gravitationally attracting individual galaxies and smaller groups of galaxies. Such clusters are also significant sources of X-ray light. In fact, the bigger the cluster, the brighter the diffuse glow of X-rays generally appears.

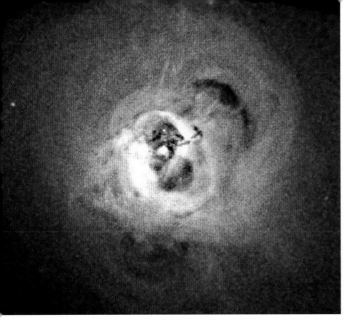

**FIGURE 65: CENTRE OF THE PERSEUS GALAXY CLUSTER**

Traditionally X-ray images of clusters of galaxies have shown relatively smooth distributions of very hot (ten to a hundred million degrees) gas. This image of the Perseus Galaxy Cluster, taken with the sharp-eyed Chandra X-ray Observatory, tells a different story. Enormous bright loops, ripples and jet-like streaks are apparent in the image. The dark blue filaments in the centre are likely due to a galaxy that has been torn apart and is falling into the central giant galaxy NGC 1275. The hot gas pressure is assumed to be low in certain areas of the cluster because unseen bubbles of high energy particles have displaced the gas. The plumes are due to explosive venting from the vicinity of the supermassive black hole. The venting produces sound waves that heat the gas throughout the inner regions of the cluster and prevent it from cooling and making stars at a high rate. This process has slowed the growth of one of the largest galaxies in the Universe. It provides a dramatic example of how a relatively tiny, but massive, black hole at the centre of a galaxy can control the heating and cooling behaviour of gas far beyond the confines of the galaxy.

## X-rays Shine Light on Dark Matter

Sometimes it takes something you can see to help you understand something else you can't. Such is the case with the so-called dark matter in galaxies and clusters. Astronomers measuring the motions of stars in galaxies, and of galaxies in clusters, calculate that there must be a lot more mass around than the matter we can see, even when using the whole electromagnetic spectrum. Thus it has been given the name "dark" — partly as we can't see it, but perhaps more as a sign of our ignorance about its nature.

A dramatic X-ray result published in 2006, however, helped confirm the reality of dark matter and give us more insights into its properties. Astronomers assembled the composite image of the "Bullet Cluster" above. This is actually composed of two colliding clusters, many members of which can be seen in the background visible-light image. Overlaid on this are the X-ray gas emission (red) and a map of the majority of the mass of the cluster (blue). The concentration of mass is determined using the effect of **gravitational lensing** to indicate where light from the background galaxies behind the Bullet Cluster is distorted most by the mass of the cluster. Where the distortion is greatest, the Bullet Cluster must have the most mass.

The offset between the red X-ray gas and the blue mass measurement shows an amazing difference between the normal and the dark matter in the two clusters. The red bullet-shaped clump on the right is the hot gas from one cluster, which passed through the hot gas from the other larger cluster during the collision. Both gas clouds were slowed by a drag force, similar to air resistance, during the collision. In contrast, the dark matter was not slowed by the impact because it — apparently — does not interact directly with itself or the gas except through gravity. Therefore, during the collision the dark matter clumps from the two clusters moved ahead of the hot gas, producing the separation of the dark and normal matter seen in the image. This result is dramatic direct evidence that most of the matter in the clusters is dark, and very different from normal matter!

Astronomers have concluded that this X-ray glow comes from vast, sparse clouds of gas that fill the apparent voids between the galaxies within a cluster. This gas, likely ejected at various times from member galaxies in the clusters, appears to be heated as it collides with the pre-existing material. It can reach temperatures between ten and a hundred million degrees, with larger clusters heating the gas more. Diffuse gas at these temperatures cools very slowly, so these clusters retain their hot halos for billions of years.

Studies of these huge X-ray halos show that they contain a significant fraction of the total observable mass in the Universe. The fact that the gas is rich in elements such as iron tells us that this hot material must have been processed by the earlier generations of stars that are the main source of heavier elements. A recent study of X-ray halos has also helped astronomers study the nature of an even more massive "dark-matter" component to clusters that cannot be seen directly (see Box: X-rays shine light on dark matter).

## The Solar System

Although the 5500 °C surface of the Sun radiates the light that illuminates and warms the Earth, the extended — but very tenuous — outer regions of its atmosphere can reach temperatures of two million degrees or so. This solar corona is heated

**FIGURE 66: MILLION-DEGREE-HOT GAS ON THE SUN**

An image of a solar flare taken with NASA's TRACE satellite. TRACE was pointed at the edge of the Sun and took the image in light just on the border between X-ray and ultraviolet (extreme ultraviolet light).

by waves that are generated in the turbulent upper layers of the Sun and propagate outwards to deposit their energy well above the visible surface. As we go farther outwards, the corona expands to become the solar wind that pervades the Solar System and, guided by magnetic fields, affects all the planets and their satellites. Astronomers can normally only study these energetic phenomena in the outer solar atmosphere clearly in ultraviolet or X-rays, although during total solar eclipses, some phenomena can be seen in visible and infrared light. Such activity can include occasional super-energetic events called solar flares that can even affect us on Earth, disrupting communications and producing stunning auroral displays near the poles.

As noted previously, X-ray observations of the Moon have arguably helped us more in understanding active galaxies than in advancing our knowledge of Earth's closest neighbour. In fact, the Moon was the target for one of the very first searches for X-rays beyond the Earth and the Sun by Giacconi and his collaborators in 1962. Although this rocket-launched experiment failed to find the Moon, it did find the brightest X-ray source outside the Solar System, Scorpius X-1!

However, other planets in the Solar System have been detected in X-rays. On Jupiter, auroral displays can be seen vividly near the poles. Conversely on Saturn, the fainter X-ray glow is brightest along the planet's equator. The interactions between energetic solar radiation and atoms near the surfaces of many other objects in the Solar System, including Mars, Venus and comets, have been seen in X-ray emission as well.

**FIGURE 67: SATURN IN X-RAYS**

Unlike Jupiter, Saturn is brightest near its equator in the light of X-rays. In fact the energy profile of this faint X-ray glow is very similar to that of the Sun, indicating that these X-rays are primarily just reflected sunlight. Effectively, it means the process lighting up Saturn in X-rays is much the same as in visible light.

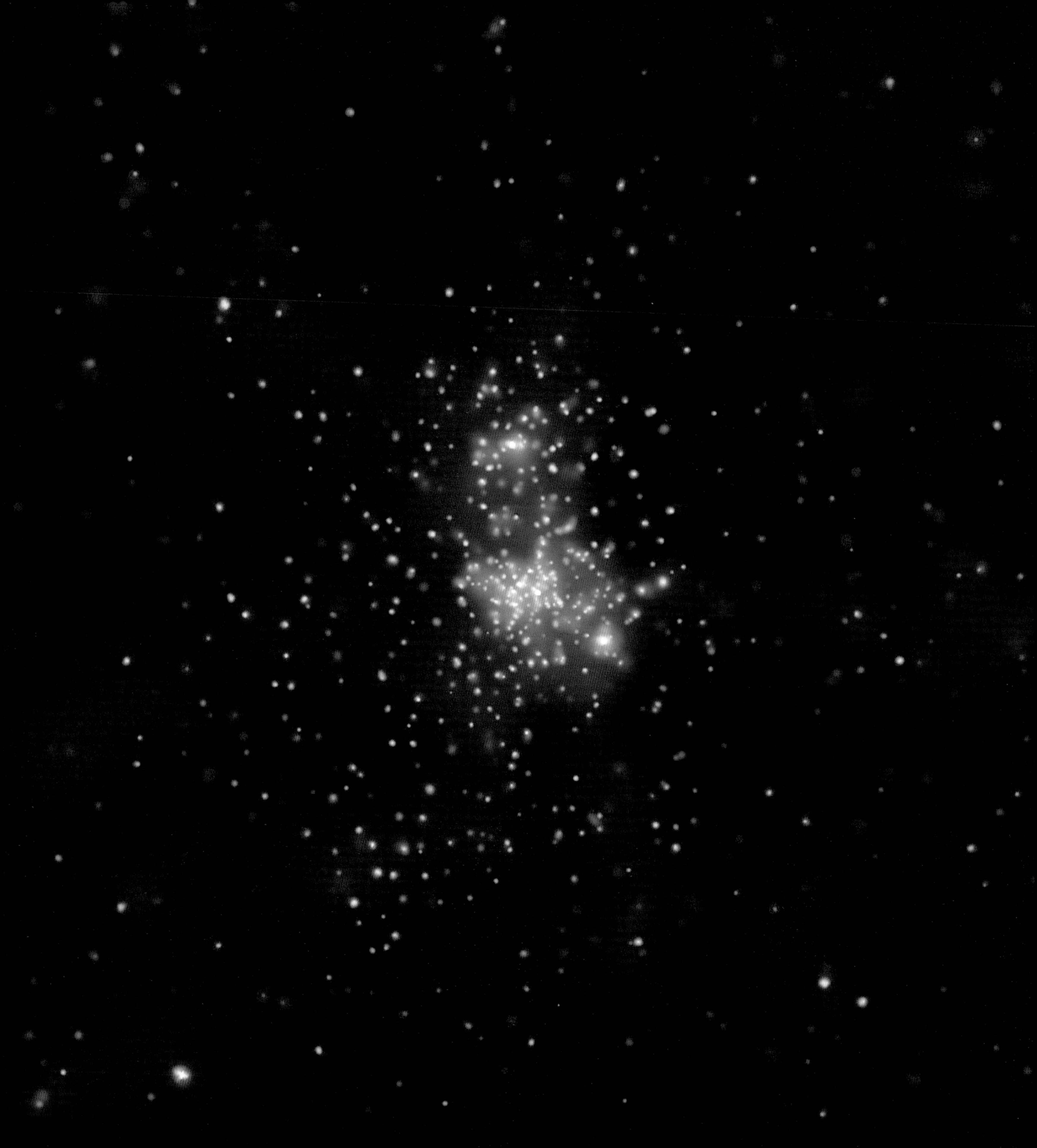

**FIGURE 68: WESTERLUND 2 SEEN IN X-RAYS**

This Chandra X-ray Observatory image shows Westerlund 2, a young star cluster with an estimated age of about one or two million years. Until recently little was known about this cluster because it is heavily obscured by dust and gas. However, using infrared and X-ray observations to overcome this obscuration, Westerlund 2 has become regarded as one of the most interesting star clusters in the Milky Way galaxy. It contains some of the hottest, brightest and most massive stars known. The bluer colours correspond to higher energies.

**FIGURE 69: THE X-RAY MILKY WAY**

The mosaic from the Chandra X-ray Observatory gives a new perspective on how the turbulent central region of the Milky Way affects the evolution of our galaxy as a whole. Hot gas appears to be escaping from the centre into the rest of the Milky Way. The outflow of gas, chemically enriched from the frequent destruction of stars, will distribute these elements into the galactic suburbs. The bluer hues indicate X-rays at the highest energies, red at the lowest. Because it is "only" about 26 000 light-years from Earth, the centre of our Milky Way provides an excellent laboratory to learn about the wondrous phenomena taking place in the cores of galaxies.

# Pushing the Limits: Gamma Rays

Gamma rays fall at the highest energy end of the electromagnetic spectrum, and overlap with high energy hard X-rays. While X-rays are emitted in processes where electrons make transitions from one energy level to another, gamma rays are typically emitted by transitions that take place within the atomic nucleus itself or by particles that are accelerated to very high energies. Gamma-ray astronomy takes us directly to the edgiest, most violent physics in the Universe. But gamma rays, like X-rays, are largely absorbed by the atmosphere. The first data came from the Explorer 11 satellite in 1961, which detected fewer than 100 gamma-ray photons — just enough to suggest the existence of a low-level gamma-ray background that scientists attributed to the interaction of high energy charged particles (cosmic rays) with interstellar gas. Individual gamma-ray sources were first seen in the 1970s, although matching them to objects seen in other wavelengths is very difficult because the resolution of the gamma-ray detectors is very poor. Even today roughly half the gamma-ray sources known remain unclassified and a mystery, despite the sterling work of veteran observatories like the Compton Gamma Ray Observatory, which logged the gamma-ray sky for almost ten years from 1991-2000.

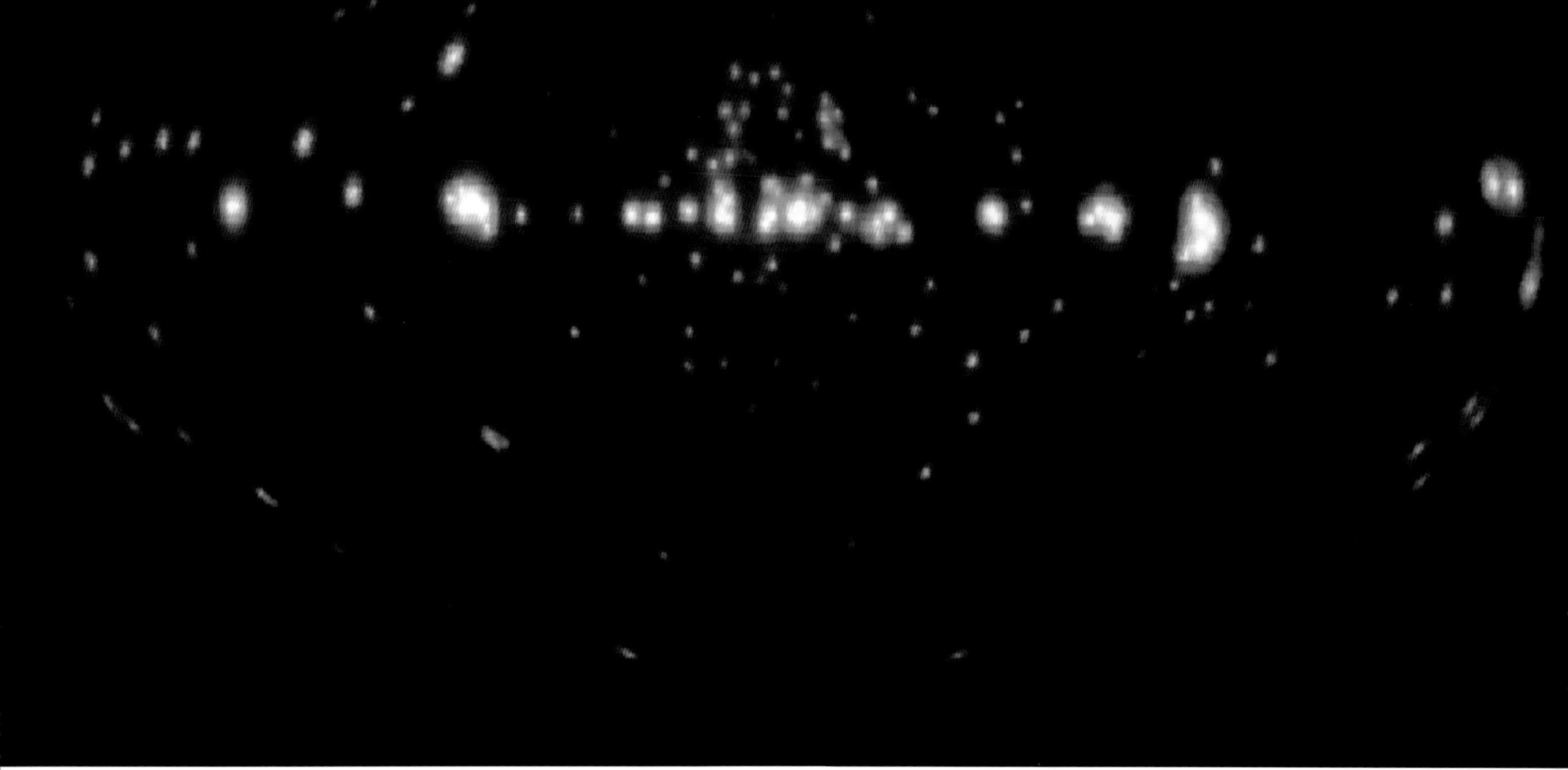

**FIGURE 70: GAMMA-RAY SOURCE MYSTERY**

This all-sky map was constructed from a list of 271 sources of gamma-ray emission detected by the Compton Gamma Ray Observatory during its mission. It contains a mix of sources within the Milky Way (the horizontal line of sources at the middle of the diagram) and throughout the extragalactic sky. However, the identity and nature of these sources is largely still a mystery. In large part it is due to the difficulty in identifying the location of each source precisely. Newer generations of gamma-ray telescopes, such as the Gamma Ray Large Area Space Telescope (GLAST), launched in 2008, have a much higher resolving capability and can help identify these mystery objects, and doubtless uncover more mysteries as well.

## Gamma-ray Bursts

Brief intense bursts of gamma rays, now known to be burning more brightly than a million trillion Suns, were discovered in the late 1960s by defence satellites looking for gamma rays produced in nuclear tests. These gamma-ray bursts are surprisingly common, with events detected two or three times a week, and have been the subject of intense study. The bursts can last from milliseconds to as long as a minute, and many of the longer bursts are now thought to be linked to very high energy supernovae — sometimes known as hypernovae — and the collapse of bright, fast-burning, short-lived stars to form black holes. The BeppoSAX satellite was successful in identifying the "afterglow" of some of these gamma-ray bursts — traces of lower energy radiation, either X-ray or even visible light that persists after the original bursts, that allowed astronomers to establish that the sources of these bursts were located far beyond our local group of galaxies, at

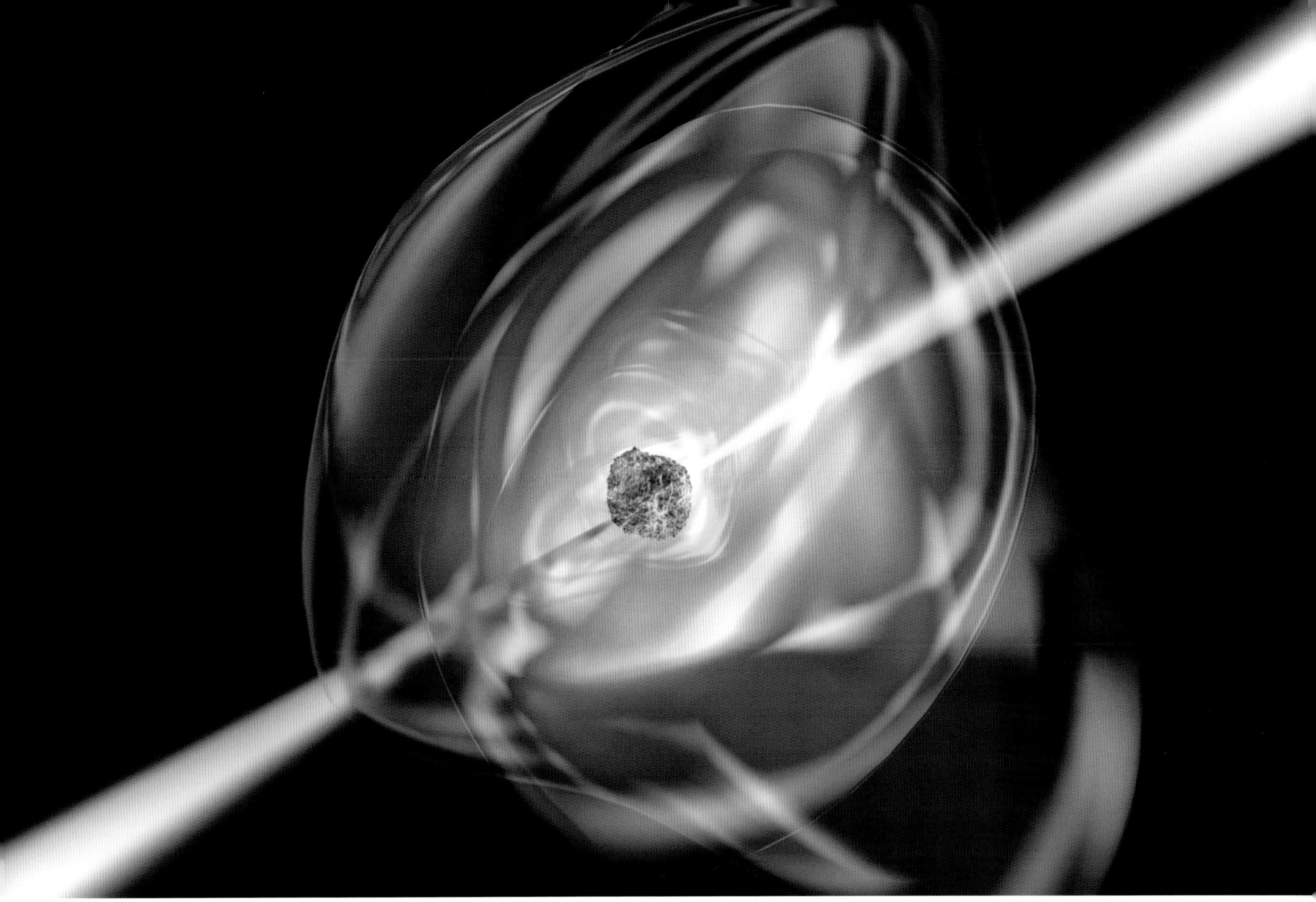

**FIGURE 71: HIGH-ENERGY PULSAR**

Artist's impression of an anomalous X-ray pulsar — a type of neutron star first spotted pulsing low-energy X-rays into space during the 1970s by the Uhuru X-ray satellite. AXPs are extremely rare with only seven known to exist. Initially, AXPs were thought to be members of an X-ray binary system, with the X-ray emission produced by matter falling from a companion star onto the AXP.

distances of eight billion light-years and more. Further advances in understanding, and perhaps some hints for the mechanism behind the very shortest — and ultra-mysterious — gamma-ray bursts have come from from NASA's Swift satellite, launched in 2004. SWIFT is able to train X-ray and visible-light telescopes on a new burst within a minute — and so has been able to catch a star as it explodes.

Other instruments like INTEGRAL and the newly-launched GLAST space telescopes, as well as the MAGIC telescopes in the Canary Islands, are ushering in a revolution in gamma-ray astronomy as their improved resolution and sensitivity will allow astronomers to probe the secrets of black holes, neutron stars and other sources of gamma rays.

*" X-ray and gamma-ray photons may be fewer in number, but their ability to illuminate the most exotic and bizarre objects in the Universe makes them an invaluable tool for astronomers "*

# The X-ray/High Energy Revolution

Without a doubt, our view of the Universe has changed drastically since the first observations of extraterrestrial X-rays. Thousands of X-ray sources and numerous other objects that are characterised by high energy processes have been discovered. These processes are often associated with "extreme physics" — extremely strong gravitational and magnetic fields that accelerate particles to relativistic energies, gas heated to temperatures of hundreds of millions of degrees and exotic objects such as neutron stars and black holes. Time scales are often short, indicating very compact objects. The associated high energies and short wavelengths make X-ray observations the tool of choice to probe the physics of neutron stars, the neighbourhood of black holes and the hot gas between galaxies. X-rays have allowed us to explore active stellar coronae and to pick out the very hot stars associated with the enormous regions of hot gas known as "superbubbles" that have presumably been heated by intensive stellar winds. In the hunt for black holes, an enormous exotic zoo of X-ray binary stars has been discovered and explored. X-ray astronomy still provides the most promising means of studying the existence, the properties and the effects of black holes in the Universe. By looking at supernova remnants, galaxies and, not least, at the active cores of galaxies in considerable detail, evidence has accumulated that these active galaxies are driven by supermassive black holes. Other enigmas are also being tackled — X-ray studies of clusters of galaxies have found new evidence concerning the existence of dark matter and its properties.

At the highest energy end of the electromagnetic spectrum, new space telescopes like GLAST have given gamma-ray astronomy new impetus in the quest for understanding gamma-ray bursts and pinpointing elusive gamma-ray objects across the Universe.

X-ray and gamma-ray photons may be fewer in number than other, lower energy wavelengths, but their ability to illuminate the most exotic and bizarre objects in the Universe makes them an invaluable tool for astronomers.

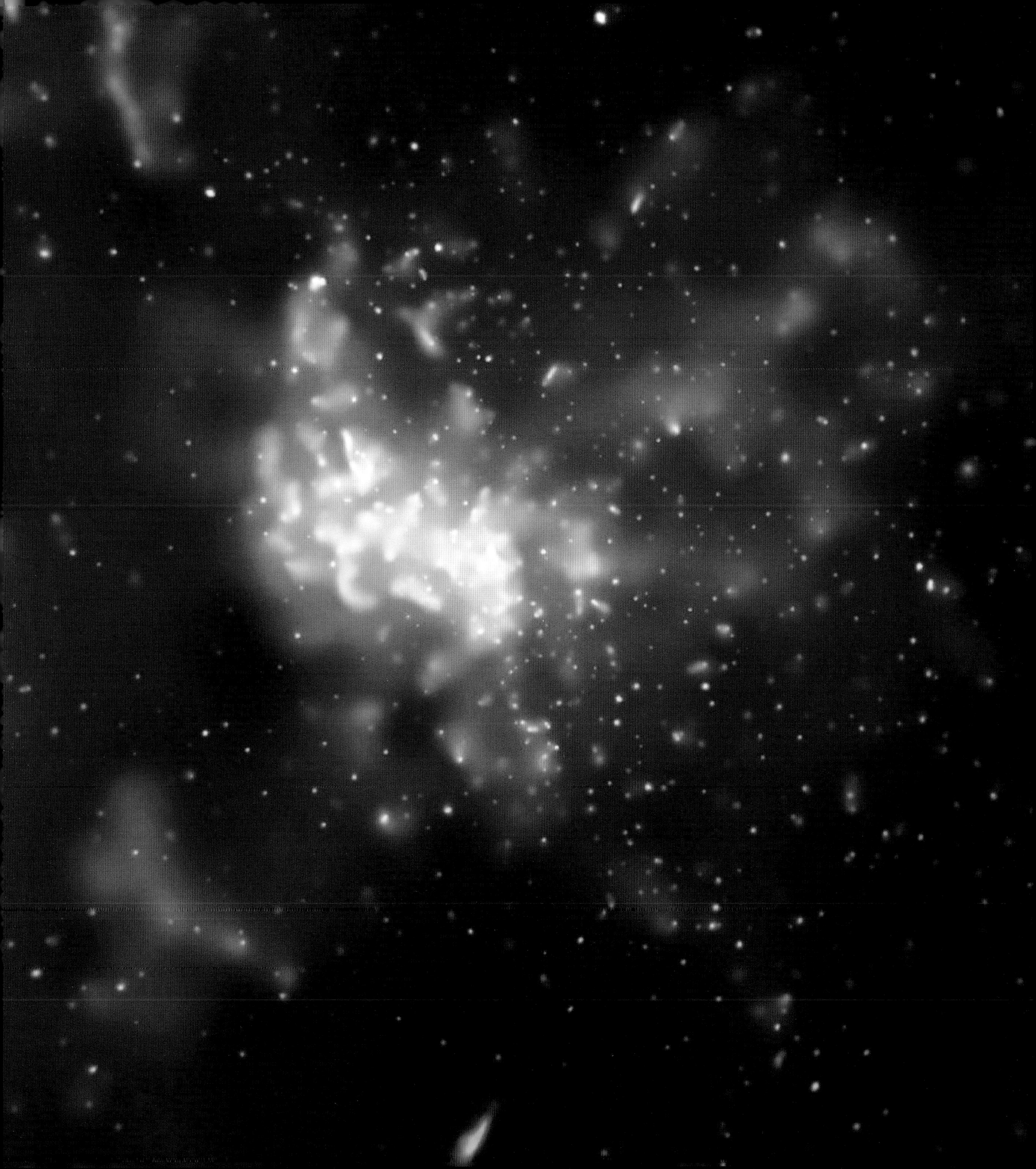

**FIGURE 72: SAGITTARIUS A*, OUR LOCAL SUPERMASSIVE BLACK HOLE**

This Chandra image of the supermassive black hole at our Galaxy's centre, a.k.a. Sagittarius A*, was made from the longest X-ray exposure of that region to date. In addition to Sagittarius A* more than two thousand other X-ray sources were detected in the region, making this one of the richest fields ever observed.

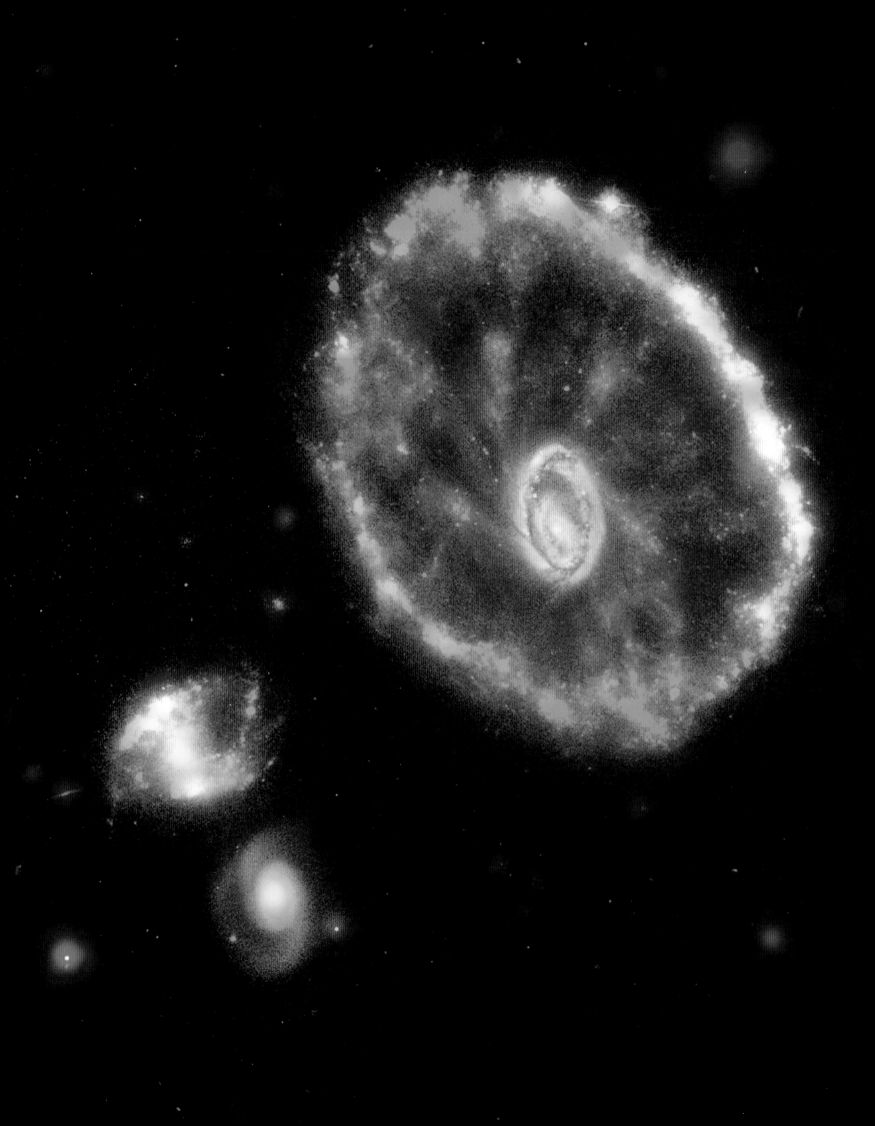

# THE MULTI-WAVE-LENGTH UNIVERSE

**FIGURE 73: A MULTI-WAVELENGTH VIEW OF THE CARTWHEEL GALAXY**

This amazing image shows a truly panchromatic view of the Cartwheel galaxy. In purple we see the X-rays (Chandra X-ray Observatory); ultraviolet light (Galaxy Evolution Explorer) in blue; in green we show the visible light (Hubble Space Telescope) and red is infrared light (Spitzer Space Telescope). A few hundred million years ago, a smaller galaxy plunged through the heart of a large spiral galaxy, creating expanding ripples of star formation. In this image, the first ripple appears as an ultraviolet-bright blue outer ring where associations of stars tens of times as massive as the Sun are forming. The clumps of pink along the outer blue ring are regions where both X-rays and ultraviolet radiation are superimposed, likely to be collections of binary star systems containing a black hole. The yellow-orange inner ring and nucleus at the centre of the galaxy result from the enhanced combination of visible and infrared light here. This region of the galaxy represents the second ripple, or ring wave, created in the collision, but has much less star formation activity than the first (outer) ring. The faint wisps of red spread throughout the interior of the galaxy are from dust. Based on its position, velocity and apparent lack of gas, the green galaxy at the bottom left of the picture, seen principally in the visible-light glow of less massive stars, is thought to be source of the "splash"

Astronomy began as a visual science. For thousands of years, humans used little more than their eyes to observe and record the light from the stars. All this changed 400 years ago when Galileo first turned his telescope towards the heavens, dramatically expanding our ability to see and understand the Universe. Yet, for the next 350 years, the potential of this magnificent device was limited to that tiny sliver of the spectrum visible to human eyes. As we have seen in this book, a series of technological advances over the past 50 years or so has given us access to the hidden Universe: the cosmic domains of radio waves, infrared light, ultraviolet light, X-rays and gamma rays. Layer by layer, the cosmic onion has been peeled away to reveal a richness and complexity that was unimaginable from our long-held visible perspective. We show the fundamental change in worldview brought about by expanding our perception to include the full spectrum of light.

*" By pulling all the individual wavelength bands together — radio through gamma rays — we can try to paint a much more holistic picture of the vastness of space "*

This book is about our recently *expanded* multi-wavelength view of the Universe. This new perspective has made us realise that the Universe "out there" is much richer and more complex than our visual experience suggested. The profound change of viewpoint brought about by the development of quantum mechanics in the early 20th century launched a deep and mind-wrenching adventure into those aspects of the physical world that are not so open to our direct perception. Like nothing else at the time, quantum mechanics expanded our concept of physical reality and inspired philosophers and scientists alike. The discovery of radio waves from the cosmos in 1932 was the first of many steps in the revelation of the full **electromagnetic spectrum** emitted by objects beyond the Earth. Steps that slowly moved astronomy from a visual science to one governed by phenomena that stretch our imagination. Going hand in hand with the physical understanding enabled by the quantum revolution, our new view of the Universe would have been unimaginable to a scientist even a century ago.

This chapter presents the full view of the hidden Universe. By pulling all the individual **wavelength bands** together — radio through gamma rays — we can try to paint a much more holistic picture of the vastness of space and its contents. This is a field of research that is rapidly developing as new pieces of the jigsaw are shaped and put into place. It employs the full breadth of our scientific knowledge.

The active galaxy Centaurus A serves as an example of this holistic view, taking us on a journey through the entire electromagnetic spectrum following the same order as the chapters in this book. It is the nearest active galaxy (see Box: Black holes, quasars and Active Galactic Nuclei in Chapter 7) to Earth, at a distance of 10 million light-years, and is well-observed over a very wide range of wavelengths. We will examine how each slice of the spectrum illuminates different aspects of this galaxy, and how they all combine to provide a more complete overall view.

**FIGURE 74: CENTAURUS A IN VISIBLE LIGHT**

The active radio galaxy Centaurus A seen in visible light with ESO's 2.2-metre telescope (left) and the Hubble Space Telescope (right). An older population of stars is seen as the soft glow of yellowish-white light. A dramatic dark lane of dust girdles the galaxy. Clusters of newborn stars are seen in blue and silhouettes of dust filaments are interspersed with blazing orange-glowing gas.

# Centaurus A in Visible Light

The Centaurus A galaxy, also known as NGC 5128, is one of the most studied objects in the southern sky. The British astronomer James Dunlop noticed the unique appearance of this galaxy as early as 1826, although he was unaware that its beautiful and spectacular appearance is due to an opaque dust lane that covers the central part of the galaxy (see Figure 74). This dust is likely to be the debris remaining from a cosmic merger that took place some 100 million years ago between a giant elliptical galaxy and a smaller, dust-rich spiral galaxy.

In visible light it is easy to see the soft, hazy elliptical glow of Centaurus A's old population of red giant and red dwarf stars. Brilliant blue clusters of young hot stars lie along the edge of the dark dust lane, and the silhouettes of the dust filaments are interspersed with blazing glowing gas (seen in yellow/red).

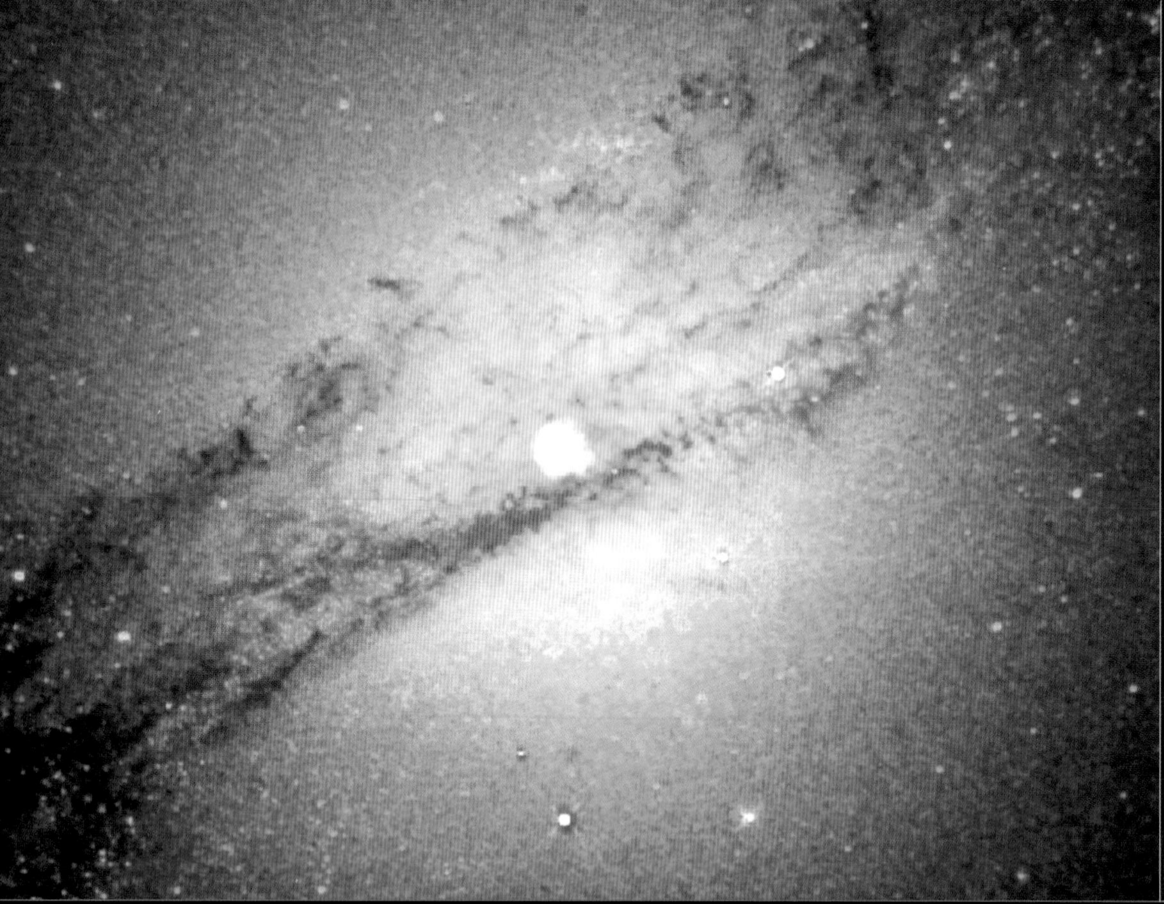

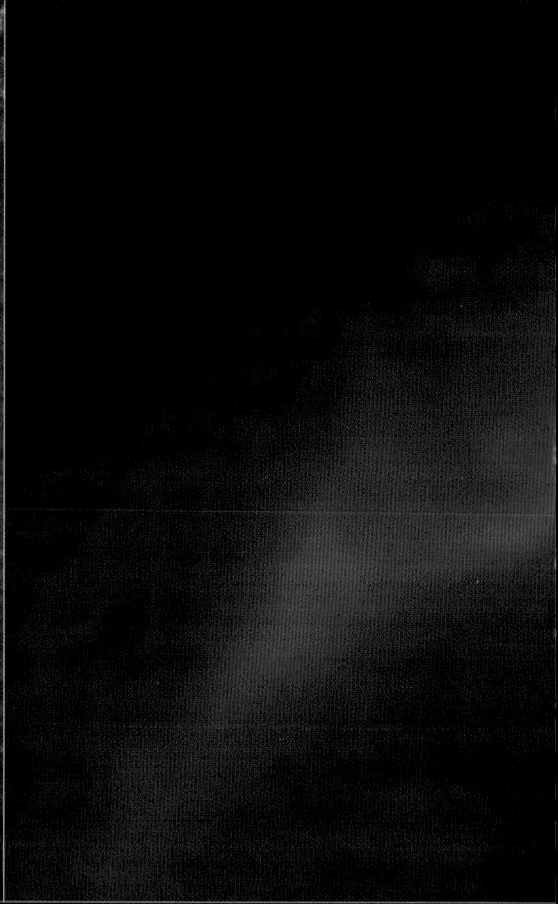

**FIGURE 75: CENTAURUS A IN THE INFRARED**

To the left a near-infrared, ground-based image of Centaurus A taken with ESO's New Technology Telescope at La Silla. Moving further into the infrared, the dust lane becomes more transparent and starts to glow (shown in red in the ISO image in the middle). Finally the Spitzer image to the right shows, in unprecedented detail, the centre of Centaurus A, which is seemingly twisted into a parallelogram-shaped structure of dust. ISO's and Spitzer's abilities both to see through the dust and also to see it glowing allowed the telescopes to peer into the centre of Centaurus A.

## Centaurus A in the Infrared

Until quite recently, the details of the centre of Centaurus A remained largely unknown, hidden by the dense dust lane that completely obscures the central parts of the galaxy in visible light. To peer into the centre, observations must be carried out at infrared wavelengths where the dust becomes much more transparent. (See Box: Dust transparency in the infrared in Chapter 5).

Observations of the dust emission in the mid-infrared spectral **regime** were carried out in the 90s with the ISOCAM camera carried by ESA's Infrared Space Observatory (ISO). They revealed a 15 000 light-year long, parallelogram-shaped structure of dust. This bar may serve to funnel gas towards the nucleus of the galaxy.

Peering even closer into the centre in 1997, the near-infrared camera on the Hubble Space Telescope revealed a thin gaseous disc of material close to the centre. This looked very much like an accretion disc that was feeding material into a central black hole.

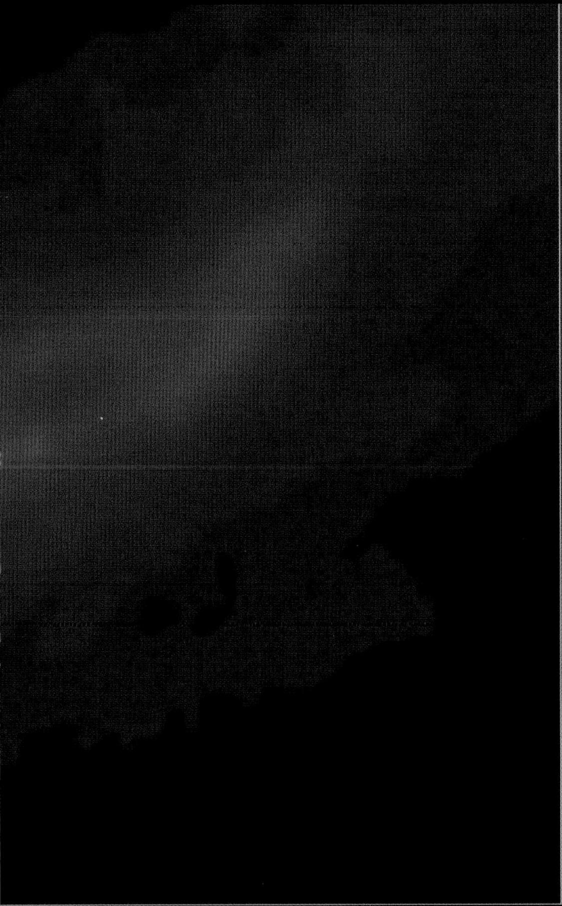

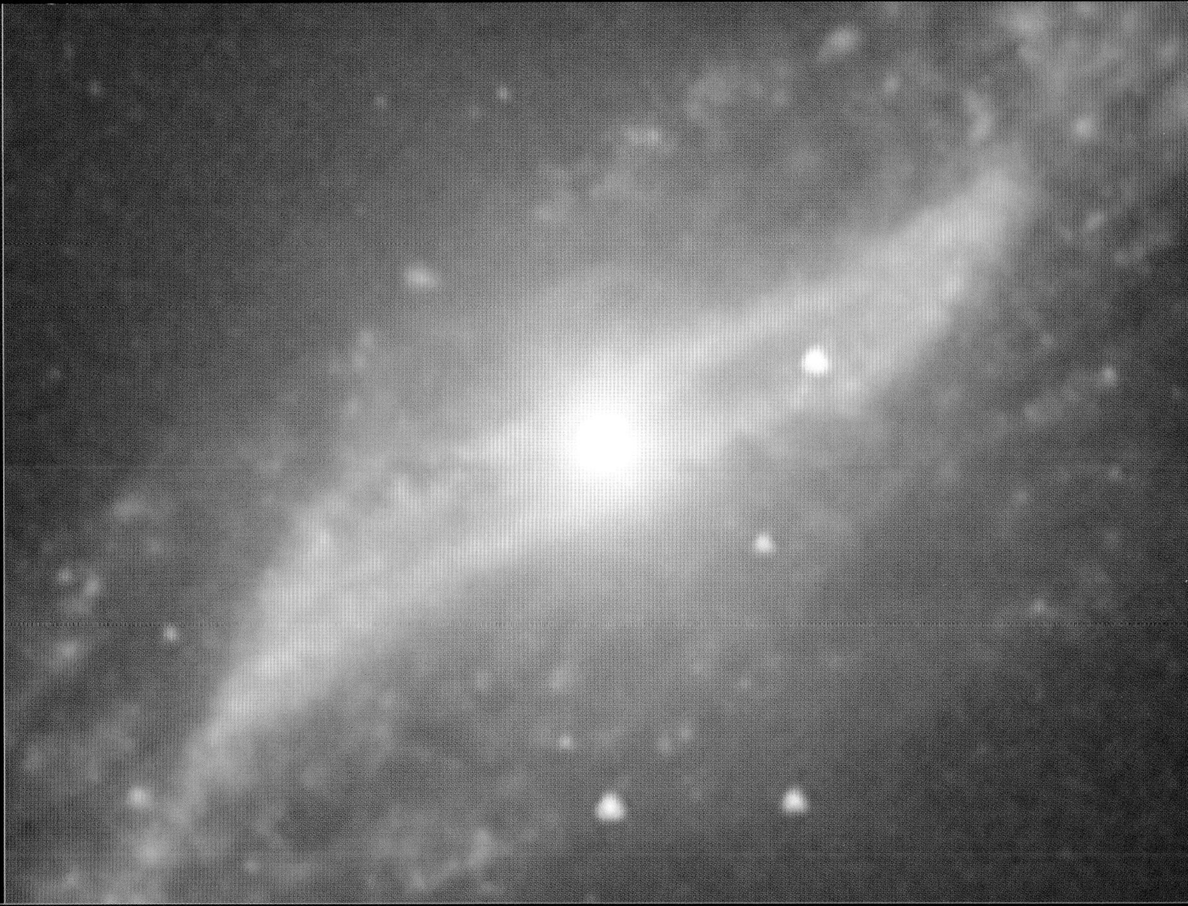

By measuring the rapid stellar motions in the centre using near-infrared **spectroscopy** with ESO's Very Large Telescope, astronomers concluded that the enormous mass within the central region could not be caused by normal stars, as it would then have been much more luminous, but had to be caused by a supermassive black hole. This had already been suspected from previous radio observations (see below).

Remarkably sharp observations made in 2004 with the Spitzer Space Telescope showed the inner parallelogram-shaped structure of dust in high detail. Astronomers made a computer model that explains how such a strange geometric structure could arise. In this model, a spiral galaxy falls into an elliptical galaxy, becoming warped and twisted in the process. The folds in the warped disc, when viewed nearly edge-on, take on the appearance of a parallelogram. The model predicts that the leftover parts of the intruding galaxy will ultimately flatten into a plane before being entirely devoured by Centaurus A. Warped discs like this are the "smoking guns" of galactic cannibalism, providing proof that one galaxy once made a meal of another.

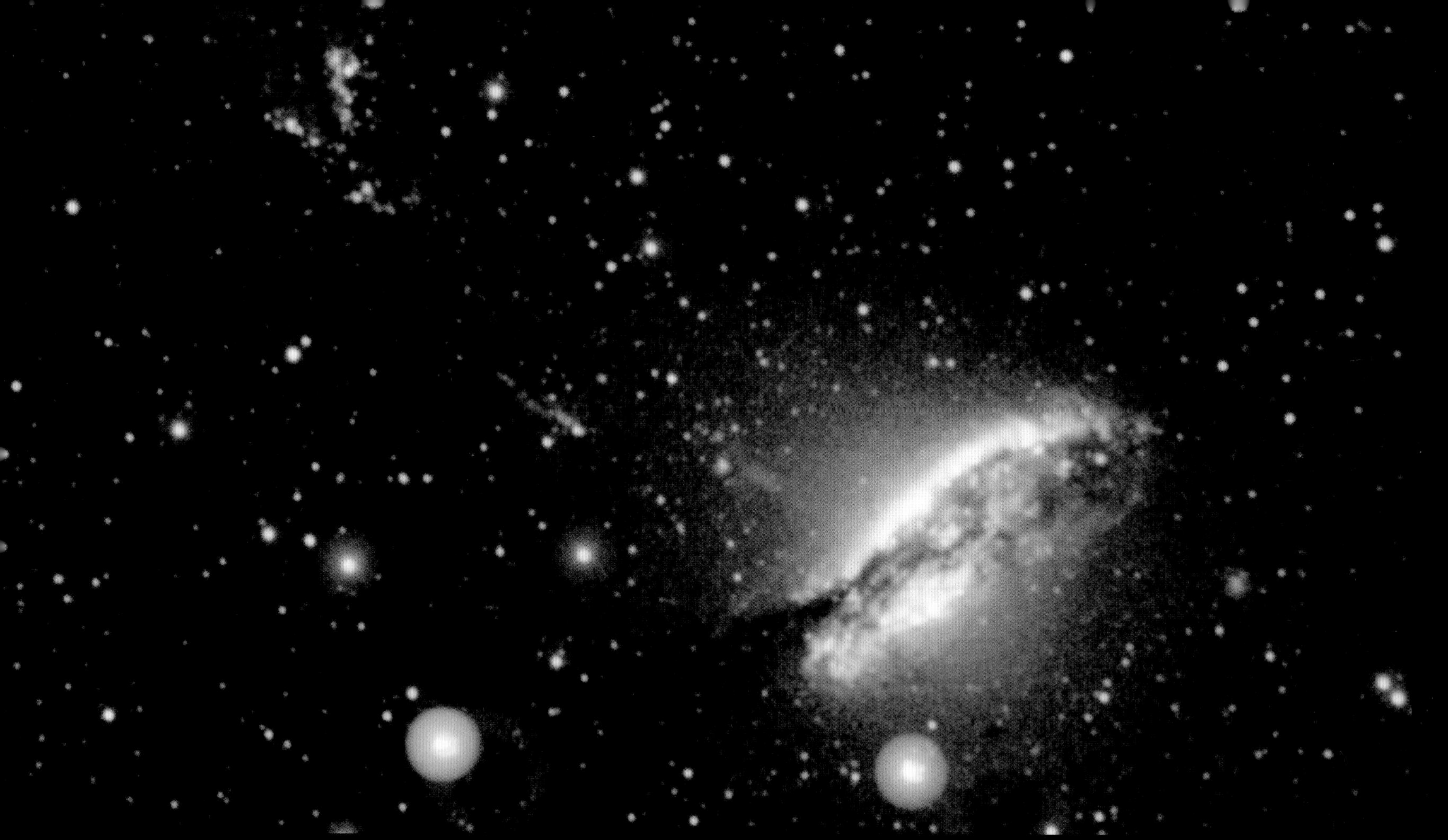

**FIGURE 76: CENTAURUS A IN THE ULTRAVIOLET**

This image was taken by GALEX in the ultraviolet and shows regions of hectic star formation associated with the dust lane. The strings of blue knots extending to the top left of the galaxy are thought to be regions influenced by the powerful jets (see Figure 77) originating from the central black hole.

## Centaurus A in the Ultraviolet

Ultraviolet observations made with GALEX show extensive ultraviolet emission in the centre from young super-star-clusters (seen in blue in the visible-light image), especially along the edge and on the upper surface of the dust lane. Most of the ultraviolet emission in the galaxy appears to result from intense star formation in the disc. None appears to be associated with the old stellar population in the main body of the galaxy and no ultraviolet emission from the central black hole has been detected, as it is presumably obscured by the dust lane.

Strings of ultraviolet light associated with the radio and X-ray jets (see Figure 77 and Figure 78) are seen extending some 130 000 **light-years** from the centre to the top-left. These are thought to be either gas illuminated directly by the jets or indirectly by young stars whose birth has been induced by the passage of the jets through this part of the galaxy.

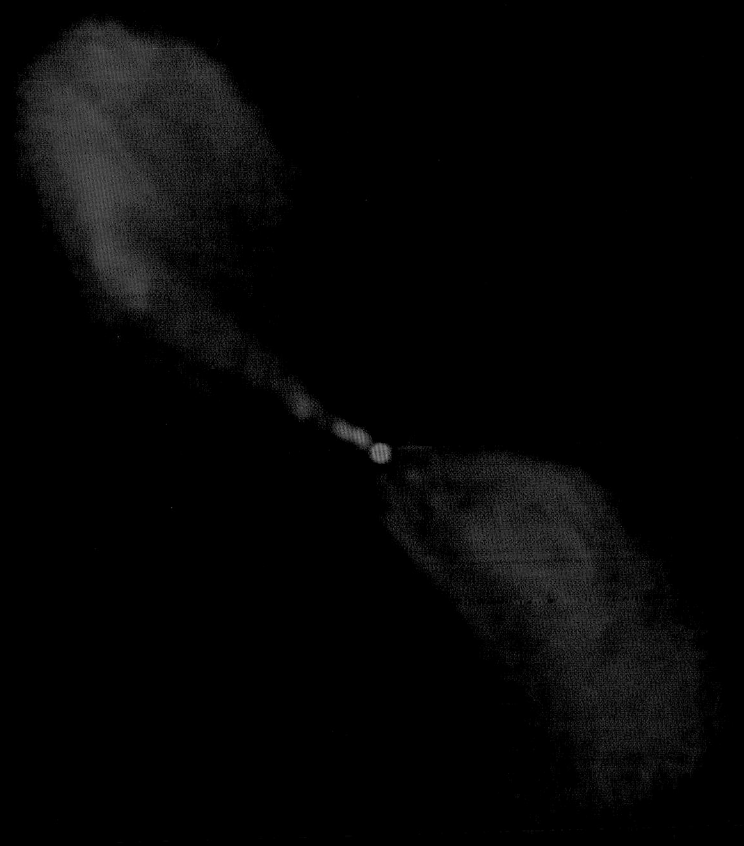

**FIGURE 77: CENTAURUS A IN RADIO**

Centaurus A is one of the brightest radio sources in the sky, here seen with the Very Large Array. Most of the radio emission does not come directly from the narrow, straight supersonic jets, but from the broader "lobes" where strong shocks form near the ends of the jets. The material in the lobes is believed to have been supplied by the jets over millions of years. This image was created from observations made with the Very Large Array. Other radio observations with a single dish telescope (the Parkes 64-metre telescope in Australia: featured in the movie "The Dish") show a much larger pair of lobes from an earlier outburst of activity extending over nine degrees on the sky (eighteen times the size of the Moon).

# Centaurus A in Radio

Centaurus A is one of the brightest radio sources in the sky (its name indicates that it is the strongest radio source in the Centaurus constellation). At a distance of 10 million light-years, it is also the nearest radio galaxy. The radio emission from the very compact centre exhibits strong activity (see Box: Black holes, quasars and Active Galactic Nuclei in Chapter 7). It has been suspected for some time that this powerful energy release is due to accretion of material onto a supermassive black hole. The most likely mass of this "central beast" is about 50 million times the mass of the Sun.

Two impressive straight and narrow jets — beams of high energy particles — shoot many millions of light-years from the supermassive black hole in the centre of the galaxy into intergalactic space in opposite directions. These particles emit radio waves, which we can use to trace the jets and determine how much energy is being transported.

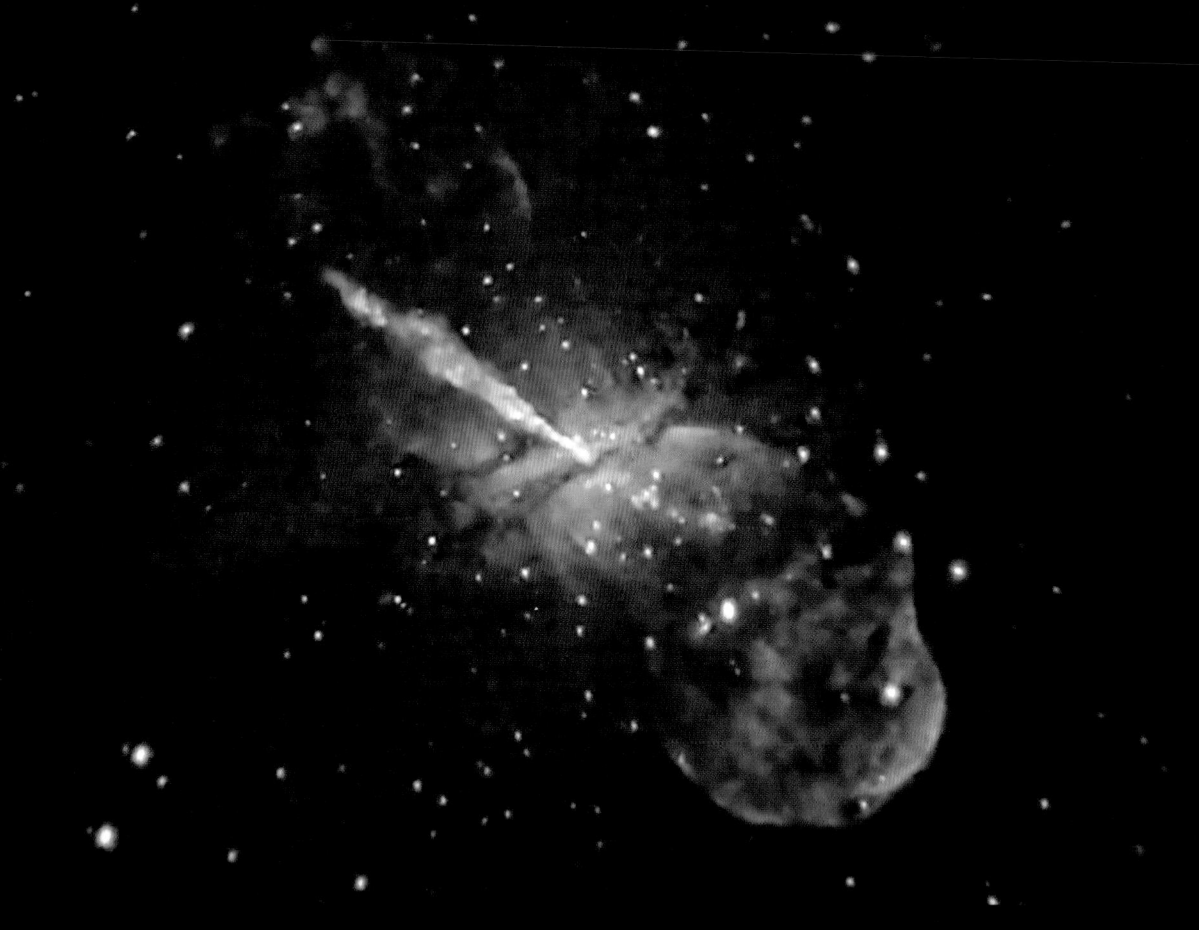

**FIGURE 78: CENTAURUS A IN X-RAYS**

This X-ray image of Centaurus A is the result of a long exposure from the Chandra Observatory that lasted over seven days. It shows high energy X-rays in blue, intermediate energy in green and lower energy in red. The jet — pointing towards the top left — and the fainter counter-jet, are driven directly by the central black hole and are also seen clearly at radio wavelengths (see Figure 77). The bubbles of high-energy particles inflated by the jets are seen in green, especially in the lower part of the image. The dark green and blue bands running almost perpendicular to the jet are dust lanes that partly absorb X-rays.

## Centaurus A in X-rays

The spectacular X-ray view of Centaurus A reveals the dramatic galaxy-wide effects of the supermassive black hole at its very centre. Opposing jets of high energy particles can be seen extending to the outer reaches of the galaxy. These jets, which are also seen at radio wavelengths (see Figure 77), protrude dramatically from the central region. Both are driven directly by the central black hole and are thought to be important vehicles for transporting and distributing energy from the black hole across the much larger distance associated with a galaxy, possibly affecting the rate at which stars form there.

High energy electrons spiralling around magnetic field lines produce the X-ray emission from the jet and counterjet. This emission quickly saps the energy from the electrons, so they must be continually reaccelerated or the X-rays would fade out. Knot-like features in the jets detected in the Chandra image show where the acceleration of particles to high energies is currently occurring, and provides important clues to understanding the process that accelerates the electrons to near-light speeds.

The inner part of the X-ray jet close to the black hole is dominated by these knots of X-ray emission, which probably come from shock waves — akin to sonic booms — caused by the jet. Farther from the black hole, there is more diffuse X-ray emission in the jet. The cause of particle acceleration in this part of the jet is unknown.

Hundreds of point-like sources are also seen in the Chandra image. Many of these are X-ray binaries that contain a stellar-mass black hole and a companion star in orbit around one another.

**FIGURE 79: COMBINED MULTI-WAVELENGTH IMAGE OF CENTAURUS A**

This multi-wavelength view shows Centaurus A with X-ray, visible and radio images combined: the Chandra image, the ESO 2.2-metre visible-light image and the VLA radio image. Although this image represents a much larger part of the electromagnetic spectrum, it is still only one selected representation of the underlying physical reality.

## A Multi-wavelength View of Centaurus A

Each band of light reveals something unique about Centaurus A, but how can we get a global picture? It is possible to pick and choose from different portions of the spectrum to produce a composite image that spans a wider range of light. Figure 79 is one such representation of the full reality that shows three of the six wavelength bands discussed in this book. However, the basic limitation of our eyes' ability to see only three colours makes it difficult to display the full range of variations across the spectrum in a single image.

Images are powerful tools for seeing how the proportions of light vary from one part of an object to another, but they are limited to our coarse ability to distinguish only a few possible colours. Another powerful tool of the astronomer is to create a graph showing exactly how the total emitted light changes as a function of colour/wavelength. By sacrificing the ability to look at different parts of the object you gain the opportunity to see the variations in light across the spectrum very precisely and thus obtain a more complete picture of the global physical processes at work in the object.

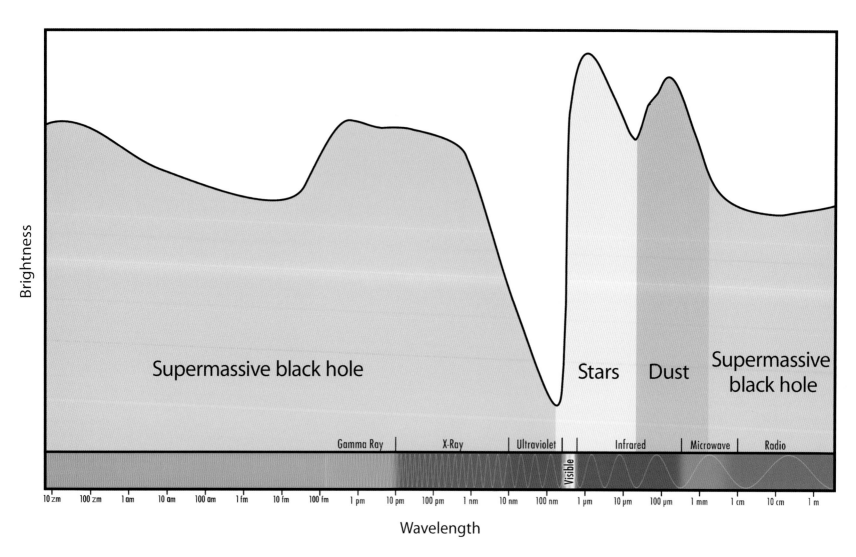

**Brightness**

Supermassive black hole

Stars Dust Supermassive black hole

| Gamma Ray | X-Ray | Ultraviolet | Visible | Infrared | Microwave | Radio |

10 zm  100 zm  1 am  10 am  100 am  1 fm  10 fm  100 fm  1 pm  10 pm  100 pm  1 nm  10 nm  100 nm  1 µm  10 µm  100 µm  1 mm  1 cm  10 cm  1 m

**Wavelength**

**FIGURE 80: FULL SPECTRUM OF CENTAURUS A**

This complete spectrum of Centaurus A spans everything from the highest energy gamma rays to the longest wavelength radio waves. It shows the totality of light coming from the entire galaxy as a function of wavelength. This type of curve is known to connoisseurs as a Spectral Energy Distribution (or SED for short) and comprises data from many different types of telescopes and detectors. The origin of the different types of radiation is indicated. Starlight dominates only in the rather narrow region around the visible band (the shape of the curve resembles closely the blackbody, see Figure 11). A bump in the infrared comes from dust that is warmed by both absorbed starlight and some of the radiation from the supermassive black hole, re-emitting the energy as cooler, longer wavelength thermal radiation. Most of the other emission is ultimately driven by the infall of matter onto the supermassive black hole at the core of the galaxy which is not seen directly in visible light because of obscuration by the central dust band.

Until now it has been rare for objects to be investigated over the full range from radio to gamma rays, but it is becoming more practical to do this. Centaurus A's almost complete multi-wavelength **spectrum** is seen in Figure 80. Data in this form need special care in interpretation. It is important to know where the radiation is coming from within the object: most of the radio emission is coming from the extended lobes while the X-ray emission is coming from the active nucleus and the associated jets and the visible light is coming from the extended, elliptical distribution of stars.

In the most general terms, a plot like this tells us something very profound about the global energy processes within a galaxy. The starlight in a galaxy comes from the nuclear

*" Astronomers increasingly rely on multi-wavelength studies of all types of objects including stars, nebulae and galaxies to help piece together the science of the Universe "*

reactions taking place deep within the cores of its stars. The energy released by the nuclear fusion occurring at the immense temperatures and pressures at the heart of a star slowly diffuses to the surface where it is radiated away, mostly as visible, ultraviolet and near-infrared light. This energy comes from the conversion of matter to energy according to Einstein's famous equation, $E = mc^2$, and it results in the conversion of light chemical elements, e.g. hydrogen and helium, to heavier ones: carbon, nitrogen, oxygen etc. This is ultimately the process that changes the chemical composition of the Universe over time, forging the heavy elements necessary for planets and life.

The energy coming from the supermassive black hole in the galaxy core comes, however, from a very different physical process. Material falling into the phenomenally strong gravity well of a black hole accelerates to high velocities as it is constricted to a confined space. Even an asteroid dropped into the Earth's gravity will generate copious light and heat when it impacts the ground, but far greater energies are released from materials spiralling into unimaginably more massive black holes! In the spectrum of Centaurus A in Figure 80, the energy may be emitted in many different ways in the different spectral bands, but ultimately much of it comes from this process of dropping matter into a black hole.

Of course Centaurus A is only one example of a galaxy we have examined across the entire spectrum. Astronomers increasingly rely on multi-wavelength studies of all types of objects including stars, nebulae and galaxies to help piece together the science of the Universe. Each type of phenomenon has its own unique spectral footprint, and not every kind of object is seen in every part of the spectrum. By synthesising studies from all wavelengths of light, astronomers gain access to the underlying interplay of the many, and often complex, phenomena.

Using spectra like this it can be deduced that the amount of energy arising from the starlight is roughly comparable to that coming from gravitational collapse onto the supermassive black hole. These are very different processes and it is not obvious why they should produce even remotely similar amounts of energy. There must be an intriguing link between them and astronomers are just beginning to understand what it might be. It seems as if the black hole can act as a kind of "thermostat" that controls how the star-filled galaxy can grow and evolve. If the galaxy tries to grow too vigorously, the central black hole is fed such a rich diet that it becomes over-excited and so bright that it blows the gas and dust out of the galaxy and effectively stops the formation of new stars. This "feedback" between the central black hole and the stars in galaxies is becoming one of the core ideas in current astrophysics, with profound implications for how the Universe looks and behaves.

## Post Script

We have come a long way in our attempt to reveal the hidden Universe. Along the way we have discussed the individual mechanisms that give rise to the various flavours of light or electromagnetic radiation, such as **thermal emission** from **blackbodies** or the more exotic forms arising from fast-moving charged particles. As we cross the finishing line we show an example (Figure 80) of the comprehensive multi-wavelength spectrum that represents our state-of-the-art view of one of the most exotic of objects in the Universe. Needless to say, we have only covered part of the full story.

In March 2008 Science magazine published some of the first results from the Pierre Auger Observatory in Argentina that observes cosmic rays. Following observations between January 2004 and August 2007, the Pierre Auger Collaboration announced the detection of 21 amazing particles from space with "wavelengths" below $2 \times 10^{-26}$ m (above $5.7 \times 10^{19}$ electron volts). At least two of these cosmic rays are likely to have come from Centaurus A — which would make it the first time high energy cosmic rays have been traced back to an individual galaxy. This result has triggered a surge in theoretical papers explaining why Centaurus A's black hole has to be a source of high energy cosmic rays. In Figure 80 this result would have to be plotted roughly 5 cm outside the figure on the left! The highest energy cosmic ray yet detected had about the same energy as a tennis ball moving at 150 kilometres per hour.

So, the electromagnetic radiation that we have focused on in this book is not the sole window we have on the visible and the hidden Universe — there are other messengers reaching us from space and we are scrambling to decode the story they have to tell. What are these messengers and what kind of telescopes do we need to catch them?

High energy cosmic rays, mostly consisting of protons (hydrogen nuclei), but also helium nuclei (alpha particles), electrons and the occasional nucleus of a heavier element, interact with particles in the Earth's atmosphere creating flashes of blue light and showers of other particles that can be seen by detectors on the ground. Cosmic ray telescopes can have devices to image both the light flashes from the upper atmosphere and the showers of secondary particles triggered by the original particle.

Other cosmic particle messengers include the elusive neutrino that is so shy of detection that it can travel through a block of lead the size of the Solar System without noticeable hindrance. Neutrinos coming from the hot core of the Sun are so numerous that some 50 trillion of them pass through your body every second — and you don't feel a thing! Needless to say, it is very difficult to build a "neutrino telescope". But it can be done and astronomers have detected neutrinos from the Sun and also from Supernova 1987A in the Large Magellanic Cloud that was seen to explode on the 23 February 1987.

Spacetime itself can be made to oscillate and such disturbances could be seen as yet another kind of messenger from space — gravitational waves. Although none have been detected directly, there is powerful indirect evidence for the phenomenon. Russell Alan Hulse and Joseph Hooton Taylor, Jr. from Princeton University observed radio pulses from pulsar PSR B1913+16 that arrived at Earth sometimes a little earlier and other times a little later than expected. These irregularities were traced to a companion star whose orbit was evolving in a way that was precisely predicted by the application of Einstein's General Theory of Relativity, and which can be used to calculate the emission of gravitational radiation from the system. Hulse and Taylor were awarded the 1993 Nobel Prize for Physics for their work. A number of gravitational wave telescopes are now operating, under construction or in planning.

The development of this range of "non-light" telescopes is already having a major impact on astrophysics and will spawn very exciting areas of research in the future. One of the consequences is that high energy physicists and astronomers are learning one another's languages and jargon, stimulating a cooperation that will bring new perspectives to our quest to understand the world we inhabit.

New windows are being opened on hidden parts of the Universe. As has happened repeatedly through history, our perception of the physical reality, and with it our world view, is changing. One can only wonder how much more is hiding out there...

# THE AUTHORS

**Lars Lindberg Christensen**

Lars is a science communication specialist heading ESO-Hubble outreach group in Munich, Germany, where he is responsible for public outreach and education for VLT, La Silla, ALMA (the largest and most expensive ground-based astronomical project currently under construction), ELT (the largest visible light/near-infrared telescope in planning), and ESA's part of the Hubble Space Telescope.

He obtained his Master's Degree in physics and astronomy from the University of Copenhagen, Denmark. Before assuming his current position, he spent a decade working as a science communicator and technical specialist for the Tycho Brahe Planetarium in Copenhagen.

Lars has more than 100 publications to his credit, most of them in popular science communication and its theory. His other productive interests cover several major areas of communication, including graphical, written, technical and scientific communication. He has written a number of books, notably *Eyes on the Skies* (Wiley, 2009) *The Hands-On Guide for Science Communicators* (Springer, 2007) and *Hubble — 15 Years of Discovery* (Springer, 2006). His books have been translated into Finnish, Portuguese, Danish, German and Chinese.

He has produced material for a multitude of different media from star shows, laser shows and slide shows, to web, print, television and radio. His methodology is focussed on devising and implementing innovative strategies for the production of efficient science communication and educational material. This work involves collaborations with highly skilled graphics professionals and technicians. Some of the products of these collaborations are visible at: www.eso.org and www.spacetelescope.org.

Lars is Press Officer for the International Astronomical Union (IAU), initiator of the ESA/ESO/NASA Photoshop FITS Liberator project, executive editor of the peer-reviewed *Communicating Astronomy with the Public* journal, director of the *Hubblecast* video podcast, manager of the IAU International Year of Astronomy 2009 Secretariat and the Executive producer and director of the science documentary *Hubble — 15 Years of Discovery*. In 2005 he received the Tycho Brahe Medal for his achievements in science communication.

### Robert (Bob) Fosbury

Bob works for the European Space Agency as part of ESA's collaboration with NASA on the Hubble project. Carried out in collaboration with the European Southern Observatory (ESO) near Munich in Germany, this work benefits greatly from the unique scientific environment that ESO provides. He started doing this in 1985, five years before launch. During the latter part of this period, Bob served on NASA's Ad Hoc Science Working Group and ESA's Study Science Team as they developed the instrument concepts for the James Webb Space Telescope, the next generation of space observatory.

Bob has published over two hundred scientific papers on topics ranging from the outer atmospheres of stars, the nature of quasars and active galaxies to the physics of forming galaxies in the most distant reaches of the Universe. He started his career at the Royal Greenwich Observatory (RGO) in Herstmonceux, England in 1969 and was awarded his DPhil by the nearby University of Sussex in 1973. He then became one of the first Research Fellows at the newly constructed Anglo Australian Observatory 4-metre telescope in New South Wales, Australia before going on to ESO, then based at CERN in Geneva, Switzerland. This was followed by a spell of seven years as a staff member at the RGO, working on instruments for the new observatory on La Palma in the Canary Islands and on the pioneering Starlink astronomical computer network.

Bob was interim Head of the ESO Public Affairs Department in 2008. He maintains a lifelong interest in the study of natural phenomena of all kinds and is particularly interested in atmospheric optics and the origin of natural colour. He is an enthusiastic photographer and likes to develop innovative techniques for infrared, ultraviolet and stereo imaging.

### Robert Hurt

Robert Hurt is the visualisation scientist for the Spitzer Space Telescope, the infrared component of NASA's Great Observatory programme. Receiving his Ph.D. from UCLA for radio studies of starburst galaxies, his research has combined radio and infrared studies of star formation in the Milky Way and beyond.

His backgrounds in astronomy, photography and digital art all contribute to his role as visualisation scientist for Spitzer. In addition to rendering astronomical datasets and illustrating science topics, he also produces the popular *Hidden Universe* video podcast. His other current projects include the ESA/ESO/NASA FITS Liberator (a free tool for importing and processing astronomy data in Adobe© Photoshop©) and metadata standards for the Virtual Astronomy Multimedia Project (www.virtualastronomy.org). Robert lives in Los Angeles, California, USA, near Venice Beach.

# GLOSSARY

**Absorption**: Light can be absorbed by gases, liquids or solids. The energy associated with the light **photon** is transformed into a different form, either as heat or by a change in state of the absorber.

**Absorption bands**: This term usually refers to a range of **wavelengths** absorbed by a molecule when light causes a change in its electronic, vibrational or rotational state. The term "band" refers to its appearance in a **spectrum** where a series of **absorption lines** closely spaced in wavelength can look like a single broader band.

**Absorption line**: An absorption line appears in a spectrum when **photons** of a particular **wavelength** cause electrons in atoms or molecules to jump to a higher energy state. Lines are specific to particular atoms and molecules and are used to identify chemical elements and the physical state (temperature, pressure) of a gas in astronomical sources. See also **emission line**.

**Additive colours**: Colour model in which colours are produced by combining various percentages of red, green and blue light. White is produced by mixing 100% of each primary, whereas black is produced by the complete absence (i.e. 0%) of each primary. The additive colour model is used by computer monitors to produce their display. See also **subtractive colours**.

**Band**, see **wavelength band**.

**Blackbody radiation**: Also known as cavity radiation, **blackbody radiation** is the characteristic spectrum of light emitted by a perfectly absorbing body heated to a particular temperature. The radiation depends only on the temperature and not on the composition of the emitter. A cavity with a small hole through which the emitted radiation can be observed is used to simulate a blackbody. See also **Planck's Law** and **Displacement Law**.

**Bremsstrahlung**: German for "braking radiation", **bremsstrahlung** is emitted when a speeding charged particle, such as an electron, decelerates as it approaches and is deflected by another charged particle. The kinetic energy of motion is transformed into **electromagnetic radiation**.

**Doppler effect:** The change in frequency (or **wavelength**) of a **photon** emitted by one body when observed from another body moving relative to the first. The apparent wavelength of an identified **spectral line** from a known atom can be used to infer the speed along the line of sight of a distant emitter or absorber.

**Dust re-emission**: Clouds of dust surrounding a luminous object, such as a star, a cluster of stars or a radiating black hole, will become heated by radiation from the object and will re-radiate the absorbed energy at a longer (lower energy) wavelength. Often ultraviolet energy from a region of star formation is transformed into far-infrared radiation by dust heated to a temperature of around -230 °C.

**Electromagnetic radiation**: Electric and magnetic field components that oscillate perpendicular to one another and to the direction of propagation. The words light and radiation are often used interchangeably for electromagnetic radiation.

**Electromagnetic spectrum**: The ensemble of **electromagnetic radiation** spanning the entire range of **wavelength**s (or frequencies).

**Emission line**: The radiation of a particular **wavelength** (or frequency) emitted by an atom (or molecule) when one of its electrons jumps from a higher to a lower energy state. See also **absorption line**.

**Enhanced colours**: Astronomical exposures are sometimes obtained through special filters that isolate a narrow range of **wavelengths** — usually to capture the emission from a particular type of excited atom such as hydrogen, oxygen, sulphur etc. When such exposures are combined to form a colour picture, the result is called **enhanced colour**. See also **representative colour** and **natural colour**.

**Fluorescence**: Arises when short **wavelength** radiation, for example ultraviolet (sometimes called "black light"), excites an object (gas, solid or liquid) to emit light of a longer wavelength.

**Frequency**: See **wavelength**.

**Gravitational lensing**: Occurs when the presence of a very massive object in space, such as a cluster of galaxies causing a local distortion of spacetime that acts like a lens by bending the path of light rays that travel past or through the region.

**Kelvin**: A temperature scale with the same unit increment as degrees Celsius, but with a zero-point at absolute zero (rather than the freezing point of water). 0 Kelvin = -273.15 °C.

**Light-year**: The distance travelled by light in empty space during one year. It is equal to 9 460 730 472 581 km.

**Luminosity**: The amount of energy radiated by an astronomical body per unit time. It is related to the apparent brightness by the distance from the source to the observer.

**Micrometre**: A millionth of a metre.

**Nanometre**: A billionth of a metre.

**Natural colour**: When a picture is constructed using exposures taken through red, green and blue filters that approximately match the colour sensitivity of the cells in our eyes, the result is called **natural colour**. See also **representative colour** and **enhanced colour**.

**Non-thermal radiation**: Radiation from processes in the Universe that are not related to **blackbody emission**, e.g. **synchrotron radiation** or **bremsstrahlung**.

**Picometre**: A trillionth of a metre.

**Photoelectric effect**: Some surfaces will emit electrons when illuminated with light below a given wavelength. The fact that changes in the intensity of the light affect the number of emitted electrons, but not their energy, caused Einstein to realise that this was proof that **electromagnetic radiation** came in discrete "packets", now called **photons**. For this and other contributions to physics, he received the Nobel Prize in 1921.

**Photometry**: Technique used by astronomers to measure the intensity of light from objects. See also **spectroscopy**.

**Photon**: Light particle. The photon possesses both particle and wave properties. See **wave-particle duality**.

**Planck's Law**: Describes the radiation from a **blackbody** with a given temperature. It predicts that a blackbody will radiate energy at all **wavelengths**, and that the radiation will peak at a given wavelength related to the temperature of the blackbody. See also **blackbody radiation** and **Wien's Displacement Law**.

**Primary colours**: Usually defined as red, green and blue corresponding to the colour sensitivity of the different receptor cells in the human eye.

**Radiation**: See **electromagnetic radiation**.

**Redshift**: The reddening, or "stretching", of the light emitted from an object as it moves away from the observer. The typical redshift is seen in light emitted from a distant galaxy and is caused by the Universe's expansion. The redshift is proportional to the distance of the object and is often used as a distance estimator.

**Re-emission**: Re-radiation of absorbed energy at a longer **wavelength** than that received.

**Regime**: See **wavelength regime**.

**Representative colour**: When a picture is constructed using exposures taken in "invisible" spectral bands, the result is called representative colour. See also **enhanced colour** and **natural colour**.

**Resolution**: The ability to distinguish details. Often used to describe the precision with which a telescope measures and records.

**Scattering**: Light can be deflected by — or bounce off — small particles including electrons, atoms, molecules or dust grains. This process is known as **scattering** and is related to reflection from solid bodies.

**Secondary colours**: A colour made by mixing two **primary colours**.

**Spectral line**: A dark or bright line in a **spectrum**, resulting from an excess or deficiency of **photons** in a narrow wavelength range.

**Spectral line radiation**: Radiation from **spectral lines**.

**Spectroscopy**: Technique used by astronomers to measure the intensity of light from objects as a function of the **wavelength** of the light. See also **photometry**.

**Spectrum**: The distribution of light intensity as a function of wavelength. See also **absorption line** and **emission line**.

**Subtractive colours**: Colour model in which colours are produced by combining various percentages of the subtractive primaries, cyan, magenta, and yellow. Used in printing and in mixing paints. See also **additive colour**.

**Synchrotron radiation**: Emission occurring when relativistic electrons spiral (and hence change velocity) when passing through magnetic fields. See also **non-thermal radiation**.

**Thermal radiation**: See **blackbody radiation**.

**Wavelength**: The distance between two wave peaks. Wavelength is inversely proportional to frequency. Often the three terms wavelength, frequency and energy are used interchangeably (the higher wavelength, the lower the energy and the lower the frequency).

**Wavelength bands**: The seven sections of the full **electromagnetic spectrum** (in order of decreasing wavelength): radio, microwave, infrared, visible, ultraviolet, X-ray and gamma ray.

**Wavelength regimes**: The sub-divisions of each **wavelength band** in the **electromagnetic spectrum**, e.g. near-infrared, mid-infrared and far-infrared.

**Wave-particle duality**: The concept that all known forms of matter and energy exhibit both wave-like and particle-like properties. This is a central concept of quantum mechanics.

**Wien's Displacement Law**: The inverse relationship between the **wavelength** of the peak of the emission of a **blackbody** and its temperature (the higher temperature, the lower the wavelength). See **blackbody radiation** and **Planck's Law**.

# INDEX

# IMAGE CREDITS

**p0-1**
NASA /JPL-Caltec /Steward Observatory (O. Krause)

**p4-5**
NASA/ESA/Harvard-Smithsonian Centre for Astrophysics (A. Zezas); GALEX data NASA/JPL-Caltech/GALEX Team/Harvard-Smithsonian Centre for Astrophysics (J. Huchra et al.); Spitzer data
NASA/JPL/Caltech/Harvard-Smithsonian Centre for Astrophysics.

**p6**
NASA/JPL-Caltech/ University of Toledo (T. Megeath)/STScI (M. Robberto)

**p10**
iStockphoto.com/espion

**p13**
Robert Hurt

**p14**
Robert Hurt

**p15**
Robert Hurt

**p16**
ESA/Hubble

**p17**
Robert Hurt

**p19**
Robert Hurt

**p22**
Robert Hurt

**p24**
Hannes Grobe; Creative Commons 2.5 Generic License

**p26**
James Cook University (Graeme L. White, Glen Cozens)

**p29**
ESA/Hubble (Francesca Granato/Nuno Marques)

**p30**
ESO (Yuri Beletsky)

**p32-33**
ESO; W. M. Keck Observatory; David Seal; Polar Fine Arts/Gemini Observatory/National Science Foundation (Neelon Crawford); Göran Scharmer; Nik Szymanek; Shaun Amy; NRAO/AUI (Kelly Gatlin, Patricia Smiley); Max-Planck-Institut für Physik, Munich (Robert Wagner); Observatorio Astronómico de La Plata (Guillermo E. Sierra);

**p34**
ESA/Hubble

**p36**
ESA/Hubble

**p39**
ESA/Hubble (Francesca Granato)

**p42-43**
NASA/JPL-Caltech; WMAP/NASA; Hubble/NASA/ESA; Hipparcos/ESA; SOHO/ESA; XMM-Newton/ESA; Chandra X-ray Observatory/NASA; INTEGRAL/ESA/D. Ducros; IUE/ESA; NASA/JPL-Caltech

**p44**
ESO

**p46**
Robert Hurt

**p47**
NASA/ESA/Hubble Heritage (STScI/AURA)-ESA/Hubble Collaboration

**p48**
The VT-2004 programme/Stephan Seip; ESA/Hubble

**p49**
R. L. Kurucz, I. Furenlid, J. Brault & L. Testerman & ESA/Hubble (Nuno Marques)

**p51**
Karl Glazebrook and Ivan Baldry (http://www.pha.jhu.edu/~kgb/cosspec)

**p52-53**
Kitt Peak FTS/AURA/N.A.Sharp/NOAO/NSO/NSF

**p54**
Hubble (James Long)/NASA/ESA/the Hubble Heritage Team (STScI/AURA) – ESA/ Hubble Collaboration/Space Telescope Science Institute (B. Whitmore)

**p55**
Richard Powell; Creative Commons Attribution ShareAlike 2.5

**p57**
Rob Gendler (www.robgendlerastropics.com)

**p59**
NASA/ESA/the HUDF Team/STScI (S. Beckwith)

**p60**
2MASS/G. Kopan/R. Hurt/Atlas Image [or Atlas Image mosaic] obtained as part of the Two Micron All-Sky Survey (2MASS), a joint project of the University of Massachusetts and the Infrared Processing and Analysis Center/California Institute of Technology, funded by the National Aeronautics and Space Administration and the National Science Foundation

**p62**
Robert Hurt

**p63**
ISOCAM/ESA ISO (Alain Abergel)

**p64**
IRAS/NASA/JPL-Caltech

**p65**
IRAS/2MASS/NASA/JPL-Caltech (J. Carpenter, T. H. Jarrett, & R. Hurt)

**p66**
IRAS/2MASS/NASA/JPL-Caltech (G. Kopan, R. Hurt)

**p68-69**
NASA/JPL-Caltech/SSC/Caltech (J. Stauffer)

**p70**
NASA/JPL-Caltech/University of Arizona (K. Gordon)/Harvard-Smithsonian Center for Astrophysics (S. Willner) & the Isaac Newton Telescope on La Palma (Jonathan Irwin)

**p71**
NASA/JPL-Caltech/SSC/Caltech (J. Rho)

**p72**
Robert Hurt

**p73**
NASA/JPL-Caltech/Spitzer Science Center/Caltech (S. Stolovy)

**p75**
IRAS/NASA/JPL-Caltech

**p76**
NASA/JPL-Caltech/University of Arizona (R. Kennicutt)/the SINGS Team

**p77**
NASA/JPL-Caltech/STScI (M. Meixner)/the SAGE Legacy Team

**p78**
NASA/JPL-Caltech

**p80**
Robert Hurt

**p81**
VLA/MPIA/NASA/JPL-Caltech

**p82**
POSS-II/DSS/NASA/JPL-Caltech/Caltech (C. Martin)/OCIW (M. Seibert)

**p83**
POSS-II/DSS/NASA/JPL-Caltech/Caltech (C. Martin)/OCIW (M. Seibert)

**p85**
NASA/JPL-Caltech/Harvard-Smithsonian CfA (J. Huchra)

**p86**
NASA/ESA/University of Michigan (John Clarke)/Boston University (J. Clarke)/STScI (Z. Levay)

**p87**
SOHO/ESA/NASA

**p89**
NASA/JPL-Caltech/OCIW (M. Seibert)/SSC (T. Pyle)/ SSC (R. Hurt)

**p90**
NRAO/AUI

**p92**
Robert Hurt

**p94**
NAIC Arecibo Observatory, a facility of the NSF

**p95**
NRAO/AUI/NSF (Walter et al.)

**p96**
VLA/NRAO

**p97**
ESA/NASA/the AVO project (Paolo Padovani)

**p97**
Robert Fosbury

**p99**
A. H. Rots/A. Bosma/J. M. van der Hulst/E. Athanassoula/P. C. Crane/J. M. Uson.

**p100**
Tom Dame/ Dap. Hartmann/ P. Thaddeus

**p101**
APEX/MPIfR/ESO/OSO (Axel Weiss and the LABOCA commissioning team)

**p103**
WMAP/NASA

**p104**
**X-ray**
NASA/CXC/Penn State (S. Park et al.)

**p106**
Robert Hurt

**p107**
Robert Hurt

**p108**
NASA/CXC/MIT/U Mass Amherst (M. D. Stage et al.)

**p110**
ESA/Hubble

**p111**
ROSAT (J. Schmitt et al.)

**p112**
XMM-Newton/ESA/Leicester University/XMM-Newton Survey Science Centre (Ian Stewart and Mike Watson)

**p112**
X-ray: NASA/CXC/Univ. Waterloo (B. McNamara);
Visible: NASA/ESA/STScI/Univ. Waterloo (B. McNamara);
Radio: NRAO/Ohio Univ. (L. Birzan et al.)

**p113**
X-ray: NASA/CXC/CfA (M. Markevitch et al.);
visible light: Magellan/NASA/STScI/ U. Arizona (D. Clowe et al.);
Lensing Map: ESO WFI/Magellan/NASA/STScI/ U. Arizona (D. Clowe et al.)

**p113**
NASA/CXC/IoA (A.Fabian et al.)

**p114**
TRACE/NASA/Lockheed Martin

**p115**
X-ray: NASA/U. Hamburg (J.Ness et al);
Optical: NASA/STScI

**p116**
NASA/CXC/ Univ. de Liège (Y. Naze et al.)

**p117**
ESA

**p118-119**
NASA/Univ. Mass (D.Wang et al.)

**p121**
NASA/CXC/MIT (F.K.Baganoff et al.)

**p122**
NASA/JPL-Caltech/SSC/Caltech (P. N. Appleton)

**p125**
ESO/NASA/ESA/STScI (C.J. Schneier)

**p126-127**
NASA/JPL-Caltech/SSC/Caltech (J. Keene)

**p128**
SSC/NASA/JPL-Caltech

**p129**
VLA/NSF/Univ. Hertfordshire(M.Hardcastle)

**p130**
CXC/CfA/NASA (R.Kraft et al.)

**p131**
X-ray:CXC/CfA/NASA (R. Kraft et al);
Radio: NSF/VLA/Univ. Hertfordshire (M.Hardcastle);
Optical: VLT/ISAAC/ESO (M.Rejkuba et al.)

**FIGURE 82: THE WHIRLPOOL GALAXY'S MANY GUISES (INSIDE BACK COVER)**

The Whirlpool Galaxy, or Messier 51, is one of the closest spiral galaxies in the sky. It is an example of a large spiral merging with a smaller galaxy (top). Starting from left, the Chandra image of Messier 51 shows the X-ray emission from hot gas and point sources like black holes. The GALEX image shows ultraviolet emission from star formation (note the absence of star formation in the companion galaxy). The Hubble visible-light image shows the old stars in yellow, new in blue and star-forming regions in pink. The infrared image from Spitzer reveals stars and the glow from clouds of interstellar dust. Finally the false colour radio image (right) shows synchrotron radiation emitted by accelerated particles in magnetic fields.

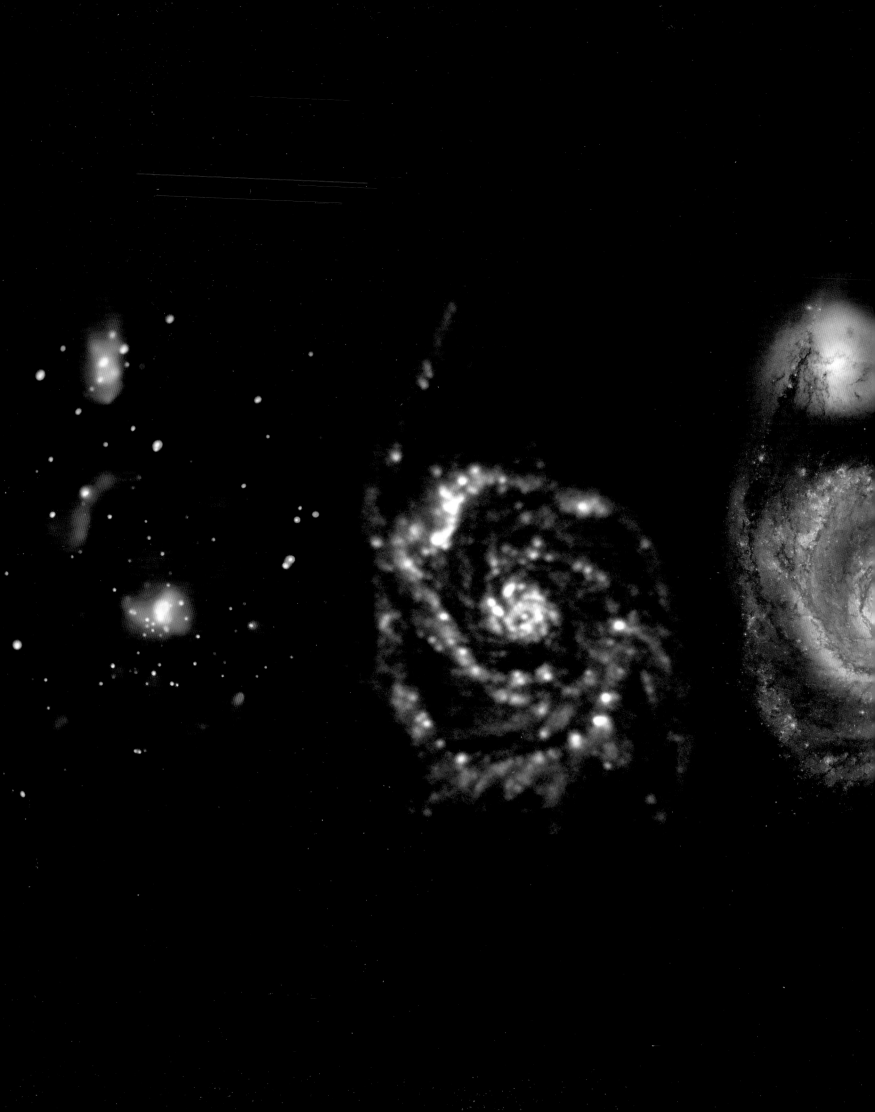